D1666351

European Yearbook of International Economic Law

EYIEL Monographs - Studies in European and International Economic Law

Volume 26

Series Editors

Marc Bungenberg, Saarbrücken, Germany
Christoph Herrmann, Passau, Germany
Markus Krajewski, Erlangen, Germany
Jörg Philipp Terhechte, Lüneburg, Germany
Andreas R. Ziegler, Lausanne, Switzerland

EYIEL Monographs is a subseries of the European Yearbook of International Economic Law (EYIEL). It contains scholarly works in the fields of European and international economic law, in particular WTO law, international investment law, international monetary law, law of regional economic integration, external trade law of the EU and EU internal market law. The series does not include edited volumes. EYIEL Monographs are peer-reviewed by the series editors and external reviewers.

Jens Velten

Screening Foreign Direct Investment in the EU

Political Rationale, Legal Limitations, Legislative Options

 Springer

Jens Velten
Hamburg, Germany

ISSN 2364-8392 ISSN 2364-8406 (electronic)
European Yearbook of International Economic Law
ISSN 2524-6658 ISSN 2524-6666 (electronic)
EYIEL Monographs - Studies in European and International Economic Law
ISBN 978-3-031-05602-4 ISBN 978-3-031-05603-1 (eBook)
https://doi.org/10.1007/978-3-031-05603-1

Doctoral thesis, Leuphana University Lüneburg, 2021

This Springer imprint is published by the registered company Springer Nature Switzerland AG
The registered company address is: Gewerbestrasse 11, 6330 Cham, Switzerland

Acknowledgements

Writing this book was an exciting journey and enriching experience, and it is now my great pleasure to thank all those who made this possible.

I would, first of all, like to thank my supervisor Professor Jörg-Philipp Terhechte for his outstanding support throughout my entire research project. Further, I would like to thank Professor Jelena Bäumler and Professor Christian Tams for their detailed reviews and helpful feedback on this book.

In addition, I am deeply thankful for the inspiring visiting research stays at Columbia Law School, New York, and the Centre for Trade and Economic Integration ('CTEI') of the Graduate Institute, Geneva. In particular, I would like to thank Professor Petros Mavroidis and Professor Karl Sauvant, my sponsors at Columbia Law School, for their excellent and thought-provoking classes on WTO law and the economics of FDI as well as many enriching discussions on my research. A special thank you also goes to Professor Joost Pauwelyn as the supervisor of my research stay at the CTEI for his valuable feedback and for giving me the opportunity to present my research at one of the CTEI's Geneva International Economic Law Sessions. Further, I would like to thank all those at Columbia Law School, the CTEI, and the WTO for the inspiring, motivating discussions on my research and beyond.

I am also very grateful for the generous scholarship of the German Academic Scholarship Foundation (*Studienstiftung des Deutschen Volkes*) which allowed me to make my research a truly independent project.

Last but not least, I would like to thank my family and friends for their endless support throughout this project. Dieser Dank gilt natürlich ganz besonders meinen Eltern, ohne die nicht nur die Promotion, sondern auch der gesamte Weg dorthin unmöglich gewesen wären.

Hamburg, Germany   Jens Velten
February 2022

Contents

List of Abbreviations

AG	Advocate General at the ECJ
BIT	Bilateral Investment Treaty
CFIUS	Committee on Foreign Investment in the United States
Commission	European Commission
Council	Council of the European Union
CPC	UN Provisional Central Product Classification of 1990 (for more details, see Bibliography)
DSB	WTO Dispute Settlement Body
ECJ	European Court of Justice
EU	European Union
EU Schedule	Schedule of Specific Commitments in the GATS of the EU, GATS/SC/157
FATF	Financial Action Task Force
FDI	Foreign direct investment
FTA	Free trade agreement
Global Forum	Global Forum on Transparency and Exchange of Information for Tax Purposes
IEC	International Electrotechnical Commission
IMF	International Monetary Fund
IPA	Investment Protection Agreement
IPL	International Private Law
ISO	International Organization for Standardization
M&A	Merger and acquisition
MNE	Multinational enterprise
MFN	Most-favoured-nation treatment
NT	National treatment
OECD	Organisation for Economic Co-operation and Development
Parliament	European parliament
R&D	Research and Development
RTA	Regional trade agreement

Scheduling Guidelines	Guidelines for the Scheduling of Specific Commitments under the General Agreement on Trade in Services (see for more details List of WTO Documents)
Sectoral Classification List	Services Sectoral Classification List by WTO Group of Negotiations on Services (see for more details List of WTO Documents)
SOE	State-owned enterprise
UN	United Nations
UNCTAD	United Nations Conference on Trade and Development
WTO	World Trade Organization

Chapter 1
Introduction

Foreign Direct Investment ('FDI') from third countries—a desired investment form to boost the EU's economy or a threat to important EU and Member States interests that is to be defeated? The answer obviously depends on the concrete FDI at issue, but also differs on a more general level among the actors in the EU and Members States. While some tend to emphasize the economic advantages of FDI, others rather stress the risks FDI poses to certain societal interests. In any case, however, concerns vis-à-vis FDI in the EU have been rising and the screening of FDI has been identified as a key policy response.

To begin with, the EU and Member States concerns vis-à-vis foreign investors derive from a variety of major policy challenges. The most discussed challenge is the current shift in international relations towards a multipolar geoeconomic world order.[1] The power of countries like the United States and some European countries, which shaped the world order after World War II, is challenged by other countries—most importantly: China. Conflicts in this new multipolar world are increasingly permeating the economic field.[2] National interests and geopolitical goals are pursued by economic, rather than military instruments, and economic transactions are evaluated based on their effect on national interest.[3] In line with this development, the EU is now seeking 'strategic autonomy',[4] and is regarding China as a 'strategic

---

[1] For the notion 'multipolar world order' see e.g. Commission, 'Reflection Paper on Harnessing Globalisation' COM (2017) 240 final, p. 12. See also Lippert et al. (2019), pp. 27–33. This book was written before Russia's invasion of Ukraine in February 2022. It does therefore not specifically discuss this event and its implications.

[2] Commission, COM (2017) 240 final (n. 1) p. 16, ('economic diplomacy'). Wigell (2016), pp. 135–136; Roberts et al. (2019), p. 657. With an analysis of China's emergence and its role in geoeconomics, Blackwill and Harris (2016), ch 4.

[3] For this definition of 'geoeconomic' see Blackwill and Harris (2016), p. 20.

[4] The notion 'strategic autonomy' is alia used in EU, 'Shared Vision, Common Action: A Stronger Europe: A Global Strategy for the EU's Foreign and Security Policy' (28 June 2016), pp. 9, 19, 46;

J. Velten, *Screening Foreign Direct Investment in the EU*, EYIEL Monographs - Studies in European and International Economic Law 26, https://doi.org/10.1007/978-3-031-05603-1_1

competitor' and 'systemic rival'.[5] As another result, foreign investors are increasingly perceived as agents of rivalling third-country governments.[6] Again, this is particularly prevalent in the case of China, since its government is closely cooperating with Chinese companies[7] to achieve ambitious industrial policy goals.[8]

Another important policy challenge to which FDI screening in the EU responds is digitalization. Digitalization is contributing to redistributing global technological and economic leadership. Economies that shaped the industrial era are challenged by emerging economies that embrace, foster, and promote new, fast changing digital solutions and services. In addition, the protection of private information, especially personal data, is gaining paramount importance.[9] It is also against this background that EU actors promote technological and digital sovereignty.[10]

A very recent policy challenge is the Covid-19 crisis, which caused major disruptions in inter alia international relations. Exporters seized large parts of medical products, countries were supporting research activities of 'their' companies in search of a vaccine, and the amount of international trade generally dropped. As a result, many actors in the EU questioned the reliability of global value networks, in particular for the supply of vital medical products such as pharmaceuticals and hospital equipment.[11]

Many trading partners of the EU responded to these three challenges—a shift in international relations, digitalization, and the Covid-19 crisis—by increasing

---

Council, 'Council Conclusions on Security and Defence in the context of the EU Global Strategy' 9178/17, pp. 5, 18; Commission and High Representative of the Union for Foreign Affairs and Security Policy, 'EU-China - A Strategic outlook' (Joint Communication) JOIN (2015), pp. 5, 8; Commission, 'A New Industrial Strategy for Europe' (Communication) COM (2020) 102 final, pp. 3, 13. Strategic autonomy may be defined as the 'ability to set one's own priorities and make one's own decisions in matters of foreign policy and security' as well as to be a rule-giver, rather than a rule-taker at the international level, see Lippert et al. (2019), p. 5.

[5] Commission and High Representative of the Union for Foreign Affairs and Security Policy, 'EU-China - A Strategic outlook' (Joint Communication) JOIN (2015), p. 5, reaffirmed by European Council, 'Conclusions of European Council Meeting (1 and 2 October 2020)' EUCO 13/20, para. 26.

[6] Accordingly, foreign ownership of domestic firms is under scrutiny, see Commission, 'Foreign Direct Investment in the EU: Following up on the Commission Communication "Welcoming Foreign Direct Investment while Protecting Essential Interests" of 13 September 2017' (Commission Staff Working Document) SWD (2019) 108 final, pp. 7–15.

[7] Wu (2016); Buckley et al. (2018), p. 14.

[8] Wübbeke et al. (2016). See in particular the Belt and Road Initiative; on this e.g. van der Putten et al. (2016); Chaisse and Matsushita (2018).

[9] See Cavelty (2019), who discusses this under the concept of 'cyber-security'.

[10] See e.g. Commission, 'A Union that Strives for More. My Agenda for Europe: Political Guidelines for the Next European Commission 2019-2024' (16 July 2019), p. 13; Commission, 'A European Strategy for Data' (Communication) COM (2020) 66 final, 5, p. 16; European Parliamentary Research Service (2020).

[11] Commission, 'Guidance to the Member States concerning Foreign Direct Investment and Free Movement of Capital from Third Countries, and the Protection of Europe's Strategic Assets, ahead of the Application of Regulation (EU) 2019/452 (FDI Screening Regulation)' (Communication) COM (2020) 1981 final.

barriers to trade and investment.[12] This in turn gives rise to a fourth policy challenge for the EU. The success of many EU businesses depends on open markets abroad to export their products. The EU thus has a strong interest to keep foreign markets open and to further liberalize them. This is even more so, since the EU itself is relatively open to foreign investors, and hence demands a similar degree of openness from its trading partners. The importance of this policy goal for the EU is well illustrated by the recent compromise on a Comprehensive Agreement on Investment with China ('EU-China CAI'), which was reached despite major political differences.[13] The EU-China CAI therefore remains significant even though its ratification is currently on hold in particular due to differences between EU and China over China's treatment of the Uyghur population.[14]

Finally, the EU is confronted with a crisis of multilateralism—a system to regulate globalization that the EU by nature cherishes and promotes,[15] and of which it is benefitting largely. For example, multilateral responses to the above outlined policy challenges are often lacking. Instead, bi- and plurilateral agreements are surging,[16] and trade policy is increasingly 'geopoliticized',[17] inter alia by invoking security exceptions to exert national interests despite conflicting obligations of international law.[18]

In light of these major policy challenges, it is possible to identify four main concerns that the EU and Member States have vis-à-vis investors from third-countries (together 'EU and Member States concerns vis-à-vis foreign investors')—and which of course differ among the different actors in the EU. The concerns are related sometimes to the investors themselves, sometimes to their perceived role as representatives or even instruments of their home-country governments.[19]

---

[12] UNCTAD (2019), pp. 3–4; OECD (2020a), pp. 6–7; OECD (2020b), pp. 3–5.

[13] So far, the EU and China have agreed on the most important aspects, but the concrete scope of commitments remains uncertain, see Commission, 'EU-China Comprehensive Agreement on Investment: The Agreement in Principle' (30 December 2020) <https://trade.ec.europa.eu/doclib/cfm/doclib_section.cfm?sec=120> accessed 2 February 2022.

[14] See e.g. Ni (2021).

[15] Art 21(1) subpara. 2, (2)(h) TEU.

[16] WTO, 'Regional Trade Agreements: Database: "RTAs Currently in Force"' <https://rtais.wto.org/UI/charts.aspx> accessed 2 February 2022, which is based on Art XXIV GATT 1994 and Art V GATS, and shows an increase from 213 Regional Trade Agreements ('RTAs') in force in 2010 to 305 in 2020.

[17] Meunier and Nicolaidis (2019), pp. 105–109, with a critical review of literature on the 'politicization of trade'.

[18] See e.g. current WTO panel proceedings *US—Steel and Aluminium Products*, in which seven WTO members filed complaint against the US. The seven WTO members are Turkey (DS564), China (DS 544), the EU (DS 548), Norway (DS 552), Russia (DS 554), India (DS 547), and Switzerland (DS 556). Mexico (DS 551) and Canada (DS 550) found a mutual solution with the US, and thus dropped their complaint. Describing this development Prazeres (2020), pp. 142–144.

[19] For a different categorization of concerns see Moberg and Hindelang (2020), pp. 1430–1431, who omit a reference to competition and private information, but add general 'market economy

First, the EU and Member States are concerned that foreign investors may distort competition in the internal market. Namely, foreign investors might be subject to less stringent competition and state aid rules in their home countries than the EU imposes. Part of this concern is also that foreign governments might use state aid to facilitate investments in sectors that are of strategic importance in the current geoeconomic shift.

Second, the EU and Member States are increasingly reluctant to accord foreign investors a treatment that the investors' home countries do not reciprocate to EU investors.

Third, there is concern that the investor or her home-country government pursues an objective that may harm specific EU interests, which are crucial to defend given the above-outlined policy challenges. These EU interests seek to protect assets deemed particularly sensitive. They reach from narrow defence, to 'critical',[20] and most broadly 'strategic'[21] assets.

Fourth, the foreign investor's investment may generally undermine the protection of EU citizens' private information, inter alia by information transfer to the investor's home country where the EU's data protection standards do not apply.

To meet the EU and Member States concerns vis-à-vis foreign investors, the EU has identified FDI screening mechanisms as a key policy response.[22] In 2019 the EU adopted Regulation 2019/452 'establishing a framework for the screening of foreign direct investments into the Union' ('Screening Regulation').[23] In particular, the Screening Regulation provides a framework for mechanisms to screen investment on the grounds of 'security or public order' at Member State level. It entered into full effect on 11 October 2020. In addition, a new screening mechanism may already be underway: On 5 May 2021, the European Commission ('Commission') has submitted the 'Proposal for a Regulation of the European Parliament and of the Council on foreign subsidies distorting the internal market' ('Foreign Subsidies Regulation Proposal'), a mechanism specifically addressing investment in EU companies that

---

concerns' due to SOEs and the concern to render existing Member State screening mechanisms ineffective. See also Zwartkruis and de Jong (2020), pp. 450–453, based on different concepts of security.

[20] The term 'critical' was first used in the EU to designate 'critical infrastructures' that needed particular protection vis-à-vis terroristic threats, see Council Directive 2008/114/EC of 8 December 2008 on the identification and designation of European critical infrastructures and the assessment of the need to improve their protection (Critical Infrastructure Directive) [2008] OJ L 345/75.

[21] The notion 'strategic' stems from the EU's Foreign and security policy—namely, the concept of 'strategic autonomy'. 'Strategic' is e.g. used in Arts 22(1) subpara. 1, 26(1) subpara. 1 TEU. For the concept of 'strategic autonomy' see n. 4.

[22] Other policy responses that focus on foreign investment are inter alia generally prohibiting investment in certain sectors, maintaining state monopolies or specific state rights in sensitive sectors, and ongoing risk assessment, see OECD (2020a), pp. 18–19; Zwartkruis and de Jong (2020), pp. 453–454.

[23] Art 1(1) Regulation (EU) 2019/452 of the European Parliament and of the Council of 19 March 2019 establishing a framework for the screening of foreign direct investments into the Union (Screening Regulation) [2019] OJ L 79/I/1.

is facilitated by foreign subsidies.[24] Both mechanisms provide one main common and one different cornerstone.

Both screening mechanisms focus on Foreign *Direct* Investment ('FDI') through mergers and acquisitions ('M&A'). This focus derives from the EU and Member States concerns vis-à-vis foreign investors. All four concerns focus on investors who obtain a certain level of influence on an EU company. This level of influence is well-described by the concept of FDI. Foreign *Direct* Investment offers effective partic-ipation in the management and control of the target, whereas the other main investment form, portfolio investment, only seeks short-term financial gain.[25] *M&A* FDI, as opposed to greenfield investment, is an investment into an *existing* domestic asset, and thus addresses the concerns' focus on existing EU companies.

Both mechanisms, however, differ on the grounds on which they screen M&A FDI. The Foreign Subsidies Regulation Proposal specifically targets M&A FDI that is facilitated by foreign subsidies. The Screening Regulation, on the other hand, proposes to screen FDI on the rather imprecise, seemingly broad screening ground of 'security or public order'.

Indeed, while the Foreign Subsidies Regulation Proposal may be a prelude to more interest-specific FDI screening mechanisms, the current landscape of invest-ment screening in the EU after the Screening Regulation is still circling around the notions of security and public order. The Screening Regulation leaves essentially two legislative options to the Member States in order to meet their concerns vis-à-vis foreign investors through FDI screening: an FDI screening mechanism based on the Screening Regulation and its screening ground 'security or public order', or on the ground of exception to the freedom of capital movement 'public policy or public security' within the meaning of Art 65(1)(b) TFEU.[26]

This gives rise to the question: If Member States choose to meet their concerns vis-à-vis foreign investors by screening FDI, are the available legislative options, FDI screening mechanisms on the grounds of 'security or public order' and 'public policy or public security', consistent with this political rationale? In other words, can EU and Member States in fact meet their concerns vis-à-vis foreign investors with screening mechanisms on these grounds? It will be argued that this is not the case, since these screening grounds come with major legal limitations pursuant to EU and International economic law.

As a result, the EU and Member States may be inclined to adopt alternative legislative options for FDI screening mechanisms that go beyond the screening grounds circling around the notions of security and public order. Yet, do the EU and Member States have the flexibility to adopt such broader FDI screening mech-anisms? The legal limitations for broader legislative options are mainly determined

---

[24] Commission, 'Proposal for a Regulation of the European Parliament and of the Council on foreign subsidies distorting the internal market' COM (2021) 223 final.

[25] Art 2(1) Screening Regulation.

[26] Overall, there are four options, which will be discussed below. For a brief analysis see Velten (2020b).

by the EU's and Member States' obligations vis-à-vis third countries and foreign investors pursuant to EU primary law—namely, the freedoms of capital movement and establishment in Arts 63(1) and 49 TFEU—as well as International economic law, in particular the GATS.

This book will address both questions on current and alternative legislative options for FDI screening mechanisms based on a doctrinal analysis of the relevant laws, case law, and scholar contributions. Where necessary and appropriate to provide a conclusive answer, the following will submit new definitions and tests. This includes inter alia a definition of 'essential security interests' and 'public order' pursuant to Arts XIV*bis* and XIV(a) GATS, a test on the delimitation of the freedoms of capital movement and establishment, the interpretation of Art 64(2) and (3) TFEU, as well as the definition of several GATS notions in light of FDI as trade in services. As the questions suggest, the EU and Member States concerns vis-à-vis foreign investors will not be questioned, but become the theoretical framework through which the EU's and Member States' flexibility to screen FDI is assessed.

This book differs in mainly three ways from other scholar contributions on FDI screening and the related legal questions.[27]

First, the book is written against the background of the recent Screening Regulation. The regulation not only adds another legislative option for FDI screening mechanisms, but also has significant implications on the EU's and Member States' flexibility to adopt broader FDI screening mechanisms pursuant to EU primary law.[28] Second, the book will answer both questions in light of not only EU law, but also International economic law, in particular WTO law. An in-depth analysis of International economic law in the context of FDI screening has, as far as known not been done so far.[29] The analysis will not only address the recent WTO panel reports on the WTO security exceptions—namely *Saudi Arabia—IPR Protection*[30] and *Russia—Traffic in Transit*,[31] but also provide an overview of the consequences of the recent EU-UK Trade and Cooperation Agreement and a possible EU-China CAI. Third, the book is more policy-oriented than other legal scholar contributions. It will

---

[27] On the Screening Regulation see in particular Herrmann (2019), de Kok (2019), Korte (2019), Schill (2019), Bourgeois and Malathouni (2020), Cremona (2020), Fassion and Natens (2020), Moberg and Hindelang (2020), Hindelang and Moberg (2021).

[28] The above-cited contributions focus on analyzing the Screening Regulation, but mostly without looking at the Member States' implementation of the Screening Regulation or future mechanisms at EU level.

[29] Only Geiger (2013) provides a rather detailed analysis, but omits a discussion of WTO case law and of most available literature. With a brief WTO law analysis in the Screening Regulation's context, see Fassion and Natens (2020).

[30] *Saudi Arabia—Measures concerning the Protection of Intellectual Property Rights*, Panel Report (16 June 2020) WT/DS567/R, WTO Online Database doc no 20-4200, on Art 73(b)(iii) TRIPS, the adoption of the report has been suspended by agreement of both parties, see communications from Saudi Arabia (WT/DS567/9) and Qatar (WT/DS567/9) both of 7 January 2022.

[31] *Russia—Measures Concerning Traffic in Transit*, Panel Report (5 April 2019) WT/DS512/R, WTO Online Database doc no 19-2105, on Art XXI(b)(iii) GATT.

analyze the potential of FDI screening mechanisms as an appropriate policy means to meet the EU and Member States concerns vis-à-vis foreign investors. Accordingly, the book will determine the legal limitations of current options for FDI screening mechanisms and define alternative legislative options that comply with the limitations set by EU law and International economic law.

In concreto, this book will proceed in three parts.

Chapter 2 will set out the background of FDI screening in the EU from a political, economic, and legislative perspective. Section 2.1 will identify and further explain the four EU and Member States concerns vis-à-vis foreign investors. Section 2.2 will examine the economic background of FDI generally and, more concretely, of the FDI at focus of the EU and Member States concerns. This provides context to the political and legislative background, and already lays the basis for subsequent legal arguments, especially in the realm of the freedom of capital movement. Section 2.3 will map the legislative landscape of FDI screening in the EU. It will identify essentially two current options for screening grounds in FDI screening mechanisms at Member State level: either 'security or public order' within the meaning of the Screening Regulation, or 'public policy or public security' pursuant to Art 65(1)(b) TFEU. Finally, Sect. 2.4 translates the different perspectives into definitions of FDI, Foreign investor, and FDI Screening mechanism that will be the basis for the following analysis.

Chapters 3 and 4 of the book will deal with the two above-posed questions in turn: Can FDI screening mechanisms based on the currently available screening grounds meet the EU and Member States concerns vis-à-vis foreign investors? And if not, do the EU and Member States have the flexibility to adopt broader FDI screening mechanisms?

Accordingly, Chap. 3 will assess the Member States' flexibility to screen FDI pursuant to the available screening grounds 'security or public order' and 'public policy or public security'. Section 3.1 will interpret the Screening Regulation to argue that its screening ground 'security or public order' must be interpreted in accordance with Arts XIV*bis* and XIV(a) GATS. It will then conclude that a so interpreted screening ground fails to considerably meet the EU and Member States concerns vis-à-vis foreign investors.[32] Section 3.2 will find that the second option for Member States, FDI screening on the grounds of 'public policy or public security' pursuant to Art 65(1)(b) TFEU, is even narrower than the Screening Regulation option. Hence, both current FDI screening options for Member States fail to significantly meet the EU and Member States concerns.

Chapter 4 will therefore assess whether the EU and Member States have the flexibility to adopt FDI screening mechanisms on broader grounds than 'security or public order'. The assessment will be based on FDI Screening mechanisms as defined in Sect. 2.4 against the political, economic, and legal background of FDI screening in the EU.

---

[32] Section 2.1 was in parts pre-published as Velten (2020a).

Section 4.1 will determine the competence for FDI Screening mechanisms on broader grounds than 'security or public order'. Section 4.2 will then analyze the limits to such FDI Screening mechanisms pursuant to EU law—namely, the freedoms of capital movement and establishment, and Art 64 TFEU as a ground of exception. The limits deriving from International economic law will be assessed by Sect. 4.3. An overview of possible obligations will analyze a variety of different legal sources, including EU Free Trade Agreements ('FTAs'), the EU-UK Trade and Cooperation Agreement, and a possible EU-China CAI. Nevertheless, the most relevant agreement for the theses submitted in this book remains the WTO's GATS: Sect. 4.3 will therefore focus on the GATS's scope, its obligations, and grounds of exception beyond Arts XIV*bis* and XIV(a) GATS. Both Sects. 4.2 and 4.3 will show that the EU's flexibility to adopt FDI Screening mechanisms depends on their personal and substantial scope. Section 4.4 will therefore summarize the legislative options for FDI Screening mechanisms that ensure maximum flexibility to define a broader screening ground than 'security or public order'.

Finally, Chap. 5 will summarize the main findings and recapitulate how these reflect the political and legislative background of FDI screening in the EU as well as the rationale of the uni-, bi-, pluri- , and multilateral obligations of EU and Member States to grant FDI and Foreign investors access to the internal market. On this basis, the book will also point to alternative policy means that may complement FDI Screening mechanisms to more effectively meet EU and Member States concerns vis-à-vis foreign investors.

References

Blackwill RD, Harris JM (2016) War by other means: geoeconomics and statecraft. A council on foreign relations book. Harvard University Press, Cambridge

Bourgeois JHJ, Malathouni E (2020) The EU regulation on screening foreign direct investment: another piece of the puzzle. In: Bourgeois JHJ (ed) EU framework for foreign direct investment control. Kluwer Law International, Alphen aan den Rijn, pp 169–191

Buckley PJ, Clegg LJ, Voss H, Cross AR, Liu X, Zheng P (2018) A retrospective and agenda for future research on Chinese outward foreign direct investment. J Int Bus Stud 49:4–23. https://doi.org/10.1057/s41267-017-0129-1

Cavelty MD (2019) Cyber-security. In: Collins A (ed) Contemporary security studies, 5th edn. Oxford University Press, Oxford, pp 410–426

Chaisse J, Matsushita M (2018) China's 'Belt And Road' Initiative: mapping the world trade normative and strategic implications. J World Trade 52:163–185

Cremona M (2020) Regulating FDI in the EU legal framework. In: Bourgeois JHJ (ed) EU framework for foreign direct investment control. Kluwer Law International, Alphen aan den Rijn, pp 31–55

de Kok J (2019) Towards a European framework for foreign investment reviews. Eur Law Rev 44: 24–48

European Parliamentary Research Service (2020) Digital sovereignty for Europe. EPRS Ideas Paper. https://www.europarl.europa.eu/thinktank/en/document.html?reference=EPRS_BRI (2020)651992. Accessed 2 Feb 2022

Fassion J, Natens B (2020) The EU proposal for FDI control: the WTO on the sidelines? In: Bourgeois JHJ (ed) EU framework for foreign direct investment control. Kluwer Law International, Alphen aan den Rijn, pp 121–134

Geiger F (2013) Beschränkungen von Direktinvestitionen aus Drittstaaten. Nomos, Baden-Baden

Herrmann C (2019) Europarechtliche Fragen der deutschen Investitionskontrolle. Zeitschrift für europarechtliche Studien 22:429–476. https://doi.org/10.5771/1435-439X-2019-3-429

Hindelang S, Moberg A (eds) (2021) YSEC yearbook of socio-economic constitutions 2020: A Common European Law on Investment Screening (CELIS). YSEC Yearbook of Socio-Economic Constitutions. Springer, Cham

Korte S (2019) Regelungsoptionen zum Schutz vor Fremdabhängigkeiten aufgrund von Investitionen in versorgungsrelevante Unternehmen. WiVerw (GewA):79–141

Lippert B, von Ondarza N, Perthes V (2019) European strategic autonomy: actors, issues, conflicts of interests. SWP research paper 4. https://www.swp-berlin.org/fileadmin/contents/products/research_papers/2019RP04_lpt_orz_prt_web.pdf. Accessed 2 Feb 2022

Meunier S, Nicolaidis K (2019) The geopoliticization of European trade and investment policy. J Common Mark Stud 57:103–113. https://doi.org/10.1111/jcms.12932

Moberg A, Hindelang S (2020) The art of casting political dissent in law: the EU's framework for the screening of foreign direct investment. Common Mark Law Rev 57:1427–1460

Ni V (2021) EU parliament 'freezes' China trade deal over sanction. The Guardian. https://www.theguardian.com/world/2021/may/20/eu-parliament-freezes-china-trade-deal-over-sanctions. Accessed 2 Feb 2022

OECD (2020a) Acquisition- and ownership-related policies to safeguard essential security interests: current and emerging trends, observed designs, and policy practice in 62 economies'. OECD Secretariat, Paris

OECD (2020b) Investment screening in times of COVID-19 – and beyond. OECD Secretariat, Paris

Prazeres TL (2020) Trade and national security: rising risks for the WTO. World Trade Rev 19:137–148. https://doi.org/10.1017/S1474745619000417

Roberts A, Choer Moraes H, Ferguson V (2019) Toward a geoeconomic order in international trade and investment. J Int Econ Law 22:655–676. https://doi.org/10.1093/jiel/jgz036

Schill SW (2019) The European Union's foreign direct investment screening paradox: tightening inward investment control to further external investment liberalization. Leg Issues Econ Integr 46:105–128

UNCTAD (2019) National security-related screening mechanisms for foreign investment: an analysis of recent policy development. Investment Policy Monitor 22. https://investmentpolicy.unctad.org/publications/1213/investment-policy-monitor-special-issue%2D%2D-national-security-related-screening-mechanisms-for-foreign-investment-an-analysis-of-recent-policy-developments. Accessed 2 Feb 2022

van der Putten F-P et al (2016) Europe and China's New Silk Roads: a report by the European Think-tank Network on China (ETNC). https://merics.org/de/studie/europe-and-chinas-new-silk-roads. Accessed 2 Feb 2022

Velten J (2020a) The investment screening regulation and its screening ground 'security or public order'. CTEI Working Paper Series. https://repository.graduateinstitute.ch/record/298429. Accessed 2 Feb 2022

Velten J (2020b) FDI screening regulation and the recent EU guidance: what options do Member States have?. Columbia FDI Perspective 284. http://ccsi.columbia.edu/publications/columbia-fdi-perspectives/. Accessed 2 Feb 2022

Wigell M (2016) Conceptualizing regional powers' geoeconomic strategies: neo-imperialism, neo-mercantilism, hegemony, and liberal institutionalism. Asia Europe J 14:135–151. https://doi.org/10.1007/s10308-015-0442-x

Wu M (2016) The 'China, Inc.' challenge to global trade governance. Harv Int Law J 57:261–324

Wübbeke J et al (2016) Made in China 2025: the making of a high-tech superpower and the consequences for industrial countries. MERICS Papers on China 2. https://merics.org/de/studie/made-china-2025-0. Accessed 2 Feb 2022

Zwartkruis W, de Jong B (2020) The EU regulation on screening of foreign direct investment: a game changer? Eur Bus Law Rev 31:447–474

Chapter 2
Setting Out the Background of FDI Screening in the EU

Assessing the EU's and Member States' flexibility to screen FDI from a legal perspective requires to understand the broader background of FDI screening in the EU. Therefore, this chapter will start by setting out the political, economic, and legislative background of FDI screening in the EU (Sects. 2.1–2.3), before defining its key notions FDI and FDI Screening mechanism (Sect. 2.4).

Section 2.1 maps out the political background by identifying and further explaining the EU and Member States concerns vis-à-vis foreign investors. These concerns are the reasons for the recent shift in the EU towards a stricter stance on incoming FDI. Therefore, they serve as the theoretical framework through which this book assesses the EU's and Member States' flexibility to screen FDI.

To better understand the forms of FDI that are at the centre of the EU and Member States concerns vis-à-vis foreign investors, Sect. 2.2 will lay out the economics of FDI. In addition, the economic analysis will question an important argument that is often invoked when interpreting legal provisions, namely Fundamental freedoms: FDI generally contributes to economic growth and development, and thus deserves protection by any legal provisions that is intended to further economic growth and development. Based on this argument, some want to grant as much legal protection to FDI as possible.

Against the political and economic background, Sect. 2.3 will lay out the legislative background of FDI screening in the EU. It will present and explain the actions that the EU has taken so far in order to meet the concerns vis-à-vis foreign investors. This includes first and foremost the Screening Regulation that has become an important option for a legal basis for Member State FDI screening mechanisms. Section 2.3 will conclude that the currently available options for FDI screening

J. Velten, *Screening Foreign Direct Investment in the EU*, EYIEL Monographs - Studies in European and International Economic Law 26, https://doi.org/10.1007/978-3-031-05603-1_2

mechanisms in the EU all circle around the notions of security and public order as screening grounds.

Last, anticipating the shortcomings of such FDI screening mechanisms to meet the EU and Member States concerns vis-à-vis foreign investors that Chap. 3 will reveal, Sect. 2.4 will look beyond the Screening Regulation. It will therefore explore alternatives to central notions of FDI screening, deduced from the EU and Member States concerns vis-à-vis foreign investors. The accordingly defined notions of FDI, Foreign investor, and FDI Screening mechanisms will be used in Chap. 4 to assess the EU's and Member States' flexibility to screen FDI pursuant to EU and International economic law.

2.1 Political Background

The political rationale behind FDI screening in the EU is manifold and differs widely among the relevant actors; Commission, European Parliament ('Parliament'), and Council of the European Union ('Council'); as well as among and within Member States. For example, some put more emphasis on the economic advantages and are afraid that FDI screening may deter FDI they so urgently need. This is particularly true for capital scarce Member States.[1] Others rather stress the risks FDI poses to certain societal interests. The EU and Member States concerns as such are nevertheless, at least to some extent, shared among the relevant actors as was shown during the process to adopt the Screening Regulation. The discussions around the Screening Regulation allow to identify four main concerns vis-à-vis foreign investors. One may therefore conclude that, if the EU or Member States choose to screen FDI, it is to meet these concerns.

On this premise, the two central questions arise that this book seeks to answer: Do current FDI screening mechanisms, namely the Screening Regulation, allow the EU and Member States to meet the concerns vis-à-vis foreign investors? And if not, do the EU and Member States have the flexibility to adopt new FDI screening mechanisms that do meet these concerns? The EU and Member States concerns vis-à-vis foreign investors therefore become the benchmark for the legal assessment of the Screening Regulation and the EU's and Member States' flexibility to screen FDI generally.

Hence, Sect. 2.1 lays out the point of departure for this book. To identify the EU and Member States concerns vis-à-vis foreign investors, the following sections will analyze the political discussions around FDI screening. By linking the concerns vis-à-vis foreign investors to FDI screening, the EU and Member States themselves set these concerns as a benchmark for the effectiveness of FDI screening—at least to some extent. The following thus omits to question the concerns' validity, but will

---

[1]Bismuth (2020), p. 106, lists Ireland, Spain, Portugal, Greece, and the 'Nordic countries'. For the mixed picture of FDI effects on host countries see Sect. 2.2.2.

only categorize the concerns in order to provide the political rationale behind the legislative and facilitate the legal assessment of the above two questions.[2]

The section will be divided according to the four main concerns vis-à-vis foreign investors: (1) foreign investors distorting competition in the EU (competition concern), (2) the foreign investors' home countries failing to accord EU investors a treatment similar to that the EU accords to 'their' investors (reciprocity concern), (3) foreign investors operating the FDI in a way that harms the EU and Member States interests (harmful investor concern), and (4) harm to EU citizens' private information (private information concern).[3]

2.1.1 Competition Concern

The first main concern of the EU and Member States that led to a stricter stance on FDI inflows is about foreign investors who may distort competition in the internal market. Generally, EU and Member States are concerned that foreign investors may not be subject to the same competition rules, especially regarding state aid, in the form of either direct subsidies, or indirect financial or non-financial support.[4] Accordingly, the foreign investor may have an advantage vis-à-vis EU competitors who must respect the strict competition rules in the EU, namely the competition rules for public undertakings in Art 106 TFEU as well as the general prohibition of competition-distorting state aid in Art 107 TFEU. Naturally, this concern mostly relates to State-Owned Enterprises ('SOEs'), even though private firms may receive similar state support.[5]

More concretely, the competition concern may play out in two phases of FDI. The first phase is the undertaking of the FDI as such. With access to public funding an investor may have a competitive advantage over other investors. In particular, a subsidized foreign investor, whether an SOE or not, will be able and willing to pay a much higher prize for the FDI target than EU investors who are bound by EU competition rules. As a result, FDI deals are undertaken that would otherwise not have been possible. This does not only deprive other potential investors of FDI targets, but also risks to distort the efficient allocation of resources.[6]

---

[2]For the former see Sect. 2.3; for the latter see Chaps. 3 and 4.

[3]The following is in part based on Velten (2020a). Some authors suggest another categorization of concerns, see Chap. 1, n. 19.

[4]Parliament, 'Report on the Proposal for a Regulation of the European Parliament and of the Council establishing a framework for screening of foreign direct investments into the European Union (COM (2017) 487)' A8-0198/2018, amendment 44; Commission, 'Welcoming Foreign Direct Investment while Protecting Essential Interests' (Communication) COM (2017) 494 final, p. 5.

[5]Miroudot and Ragoussis (2013), p. 60; Martini (2008), p. 316; Weller (2008), p. 858.

[6]Commission, 'White Paper on Levelling the Playing Field as regards Foreign Subsidies' COM (2020) 253 final, p. 7.

Similar risks occur in the phase after the FDI has taken place. A foreign investor who is not subject to rules similar to Arts 106 and 107 TFEU may provide the FDI target with means that would not be available under normal competitive conditions. Hence, the FDI target may use these additional means to the detriment of its competitors. In other words, EU firms and sectors that had been privatized or at least submitted to strict competition rules now risk to be re-nationalized or (re-) monopolized.[7] Economic gains that privatization and strict competition rules were supposed to bring might thus get lost.

To address the competition concern, the EU and Member States may be inclined to screen FDI specifically from investors who are more likely to have received state support that would violate EU competition rules. An alternative may be to compare competition rules of the EU to those of other states. Investors from states that are found to provide less competition protection, namely regarding state aid, may be (more strictly) screened.

Both scenarios explain why the competition concern often focuses on investors from China and Russia, as well as the United Arab Emirates, Qatar, and Kuwait.[8] The economies of all these states are characterized by governments that take a much more interventionist approach towards private business decisions than the EU or Member States, without having competition rules in place that are comparable to Arts 106, 107 TFEU.

Often this consideration is boiled down to focusing on foreign SOE investors.[9] This reduction, however, neglects two aspects. First, in the EU SOEs also play a prominent role; the actual concern is about the lack of competition laws that prevent market distortions. Second, public ownership is the clearest and most obvious, but by far not the only form of government intervention on a company's business decisions. Informal networks of private businesses and the government can have the same competition distorting effect.[10] These informal networks are particularly important in China where public-private relations are not necessarily a matter of ownership, but informal *lishu* relationships.[11]

---

[7] Martini (2008), p. 322; Weller (2008), p. 858; Geiger (2013), p. 70.

[8] Commission, 'Foreign Direct Investment in the EU: Following up on the Commission Communication "Welcoming Foreign Direct Investment while Protecting Essential Interests" of 13 September 2017' (Commission Staff Working Document) SWD (2019) 108 final, pp. 56–57.

[9] Commission, 'Reflection Paper on Harnessing Globalisation' COM (2017) 240 final, p. 15; Commission, COM (2017) 494 final (n. 4), pp. 5, 6.

[10] See Commission, SWD (2019) 108 final (n. 8), p. 61, which first focuses on FDI of SOEs, before adding a paragraph on state influence generally, arguing that the influence could take place in state-owned and private companies.

[11] Buckley et al. (2018), p. 14.

2.1.2 Reciprocity Concern

The second main concern vis-à-vis foreign investors that led the EU and Member
States to take a stricter stance on FDI inflows is the reciprocity concern. The EU and
Member States are increasingly reluctant to accord favourable treatment to investors
from home countries that in turn do not accord similarly favourable treatment to EU
investors. Favourable treatment in this sense means, on the one hand, market access
to foreign investors, for example for FDI, and, on the other hand, investor treatment
and protection after market access. These concerns are particularly strong vis-à-vis
countries from which FDI inflows have increased, and thus inter alia Brazil, China,
India, and Russia.[12]

This concern relates to FDI screening in the EU in two ways. First, the EU and
Member States could screen FDI of investors from those home countries more
strictly that the EU and Member States perceive as providing particularly
unfavourable treatment to EU investors. Second, a generally stricter stance on FDI
inflows may provide the EU and Member States with more leverage to motivate
other states to improve EU investor treatment. (Stricter) FDI screening may be one
part of such stricter stance.

2.1.3 Harmful Investor Concern

The third EU and Member State concern vis-à-vis foreign investors is about investors who pursue an objective that, if realized, harms the EU's and Member States'
interests in existing domestic assets.

Point of departure for the harmful investor concern is that the investment gives
the foreign investor influence over a domestic target. The investor can thus impose or
at least significantly shape the FDI target's business decisions according to his own
interests. The investor's interest in such business decisions may either be a genuine
investor interest following commercial or other considerations, or stem from another
actor behind the investor, in particular the home country government. Examples of
potentially harmful business decisions are a significant decrease in quality or quantity of a certain good or service or even the disruption of its supply.

Spinning this concern a little further, EU and Member States are also concerned
that the FDI target, influenced by the foreign investor, transfers certain important
assets to the investor's home country, such as technology, know-how, and business
secrets. Insofar, the concern can therefore play out in mainly two ways. First, the EU
and Member States may be deprived of an asset, good, or service. Second, this asset,
good, or service may be turned against them. According to the second scenario of
concern, the investor may either instrumentalize the asset to assert own or third-party

---

[12]Commission, COM (2017) 494 final (n. 4), p. 3; Commission, SWD (2019) 108 final (n. 8), p. 13;
Martin-Prat (2020), p. 96.

interests to the detriment of EU and Member States—for instance, by disrupting supply with electricity through the FDI target.[13] Or, the investor may make the asset available to a competing actor, in particular a third country, who may then use the asset to the detriment of EU and Member States interests.

These two scenarios of concern allow to limit the harmful investor concern to situations along mainly four cornerstones. First, EU and Member States are concerned about investments that give the investor a certain level of control over the investment target. As a result of the obtained level of control, the investor can influence the target's decisions in accordance with his interests. This concept of control is well described by the notion of FDI as opposed to portfolio investment, which will be described in more detail in Sect. 2.2.

Second, the EU and Member States are concerned that their interest in an *existing* domestic asset may be harmed. Therefore, the concern focuses on M&A investments.[14]

Third, the harmful investor concern, as the competition and reciprocity concerns, also explains the EU's and Member States' focus on state-owned or -controlled, as well as subsidized or otherwise state-influenced investors. Investors from certain countries are found to be more likely influenced by non-commercial objectives that differ from EU and Member States interests and therefore more likely to be harmful in the sense described above.[15] The countries of concern are namely China as well as Russia, the United Arab Emirates, Qatar, and Kuwait.[16]

The fourth and last cornerstone for FDI screening to meet the harmful investor concern is about the cases in which EU and Member States consider the risk of harmful investor interests high enough to screen and eventually prohibit the FDI. Part of a liberalized, mainly private economy is that market actor interests are not completely aligned with, sometimes even opposed to public interests. A stable and free economy will usually tolerate such incongruence, and mainly focus on providing a guiding framework. However, in some cases the EU and Member States find the investor interest to have such a high potential to harm public interest that they indeed consider to intervene in private business decisions—for instance, by screening and eventually prohibiting the investment. Such exceptional cases are FDIs in assets in which harmful investor objectives have potentially severe consequences ('sensitive assets').

---

[13] See e.g. in the WTO dispute *European Union and its Member States—Certain Measures Relating to the Energy Sector*, Panel Report (10 August 2018) WT/DS476/R, WTO Online Database doc no 18-5025, para. 7.1172, the EU argued for a threat of its energy security posed by FDI from third countries. The EU claimed that a foreign government could incentivize companies that are controlled by its citizens to act in accordance with own political interests.

[14] For a more detailed definition of FDI and portfolio investment, as well as FDI in the form of M&A or greenfield investment, see Sects. 2.2.1 and 2.4.1.

[15] See Commission, COM (2017) 240 final (n. 9), p. 15. It is more appropriate to consider state influence generally, rather than focusing on SOEs only, see Sect. 2.1.1.

[16] See Chap. 1, n. 8.

There is disagreement as to which assets make the incongruency of investor and public interests so important that FDI screening seems justified. In fact, defining these sensitive assets is one of the settings in which the major trade-off in the realm of FDI screening takes place: welcoming FDI to contribute to the EU's economic growth on the one and pursuing other public interests on the other hand, namely security, public order, or economic or geopolitical policies. The question is: What assets are sensitive enough to politically justify the screening of FDI, which is generally welcome, yet risks to be deterred by too strict screening mechanisms? Mainly three sensitive asset concepts are discussed. They partly overlap.

2.1.3.1 Defence Sector

The narrowest discussed concept of sensitive assets is generally referred to as the defence sector. On the one hand, a functioning defence sector is supposed to enable a state to defend itself, primarily against external threats. On the other hand, another state may use its defence capacities against the EU and its Member States. The defence sector therefore encompasses all assets that supply the military with the necessary means to fulfil these functions, in particular arms, munitions, and war material.[17] Such assets include goods, services, and intellectual property rights with both a civilian and military use, including 'all items which can be used for both non-explosive uses and assisting in any way in the manufacture of nuclear weapons or other nuclear explosive devices' ('dual-use products').[18] This broader understanding of the defence sector is also underlined by the increased use of notions such as 'civil-military'[19] and 'generic services'.[20]

---

[17] Art 346(1)(b) TFEU provides this description to further substantiate the notion 'essential security interests'.

[18] For a definition see Council Regulation (EC) No 428/2009 of 5 May 2009 setting up a Community regime for the control of exports, transfer, brokering and transit of dual-use items (Dual-use Regulation) [2009] OJ L 134/1, art 2 point 1. This notion is e.g. used in Council, 'EU Cyber Defence Policy Framework' 14413/18, pp. 17–18.

[19] EU, 'Shared Vision, Common Action: A Stronger Europe: A Global Strategy for the EU's Foreign and Security Policy' (28 June 2016) <https://op.europa.eu/en/publication-detail/-/publication/3eaae2cf-9ac5-11e6-868c-01aa75ed71a1> accessed 2 February 2022, p. 45; see also Council, 'Council Conclusions on Security and Defence' 8910/20, paras. 8, 10, 11.

[20] See EU, 'EU Funding for Dual Use: A pratical guide to accessing EU funds for European Regional Authorities and SMEs' (October 2014) <https://s3platform.jrc.ec.europa.eu/-/eu-funding-for-dual-use-guide-for-regions-and-smes?inheritRedirect=true> accessed 2 February 2022, pp. 7, 8; task description of European Defence Agency on its own website; <https://www.eda.europa.eu/what-we-do/activities/activities-search/dual-use-research> accessed 2 February 2022.

2.1.3.2   Critical Infrastructure, Technology, Inputs

Another rather narrow concept of sensitive assets consists of firms that own, operate, or produce critical infrastructure, technology, and inputs. In the Directive 2008/114/EC on critical infrastructure, the EU defines critical infrastructure as:

> an asset, system or part thereof . . . which is essential for the maintenance of vital societal functions, health, safety, security, economic or social well-being of people, and the disruption or destruction of which would have a significant impact in a Member State as a result of the failure to maintain those functions.[21]

Accordingly, for the purposes of this book critical infrastructure, technology, and inputs are defined as comprising assets, systems, technologies, or inputs essential for the maintenance of vital societal functions, health, safety, security, or economic or social well-being of people. The focus of critical infrastructure, technology, and inputs is thus on protecting vital, existing societal functions. Typical sectors in which critical assets can be found are information technology, telecommunication, health, water, electricity, food, finance, and insurance.[22]

2.1.3.3   Strategic Infrastructure, Technology, Inputs

The broadest concept of sensitive assets that are considered to justify FDI screening are strategic infrastructure, technology, and inputs—a shiny, but imprecise term. Strategic assets are sometimes also referred to as assets possessing 'key enabling technologies'.[23] The term 'strategic' is closely related to the prominent concept of the EU's 'strategic autonomy'.[24] This describes the EU's ability to set its own priorities, make its own decisions, and give, rather than take rules in international relations.[25] The concept of strategic thus originally stems from fields of external policies, namely the Common Security and Defence Policy, but is now increasingly used in other policy fields. In its New Industrial Strategy the Commission stated, for instance:

---

[21] Council Directive 2008/114/EC of 8 December 2008 on the identification and designation of European critical infrastructures and the assessment of the need to improve their protection (Critical Infrastructure Directive) [2008] OJ L 345/75, art 2(a).

[22] See German Act on the German Federal Office for Information Security (Gesetz über das Bundesamt für Sicherheit in der Informationstechnik) s 2(10).

[23] France, Germany, and Italy (2017b), pp. 3–4; Parliament, 'Building an Ambitious EU Industrial Strategy as a Strategic Priority for Growth, Employment and Innovation in Europe' (Resolution) 2017/2732 (RSP), para. 20; Commission, COM (2017) 494 final (n. 4), pp. 7, 11 (which the European Council welcomed in the context of enhancing reciprocity in the fields of public procurement and investment, European Council, 'Conclusions of European Council Meeting (22 and 23 June 2017)' EUCO 8/17, para. 17).

[24] See Chap. 1, n. 4, 21.

[25] For this definition see Chap. 1, n. 4.

Europe's strategic autonomy is about reducing dependence on others for things we need the most: critical materials and technologies, food, infrastructure, security and other strategic areas. They also provide Europe's industry with an opportunity to develop its own markets, products and services which boost competitiveness.[26]

While the Commission listed energy, telecommunication, digital, transport, and space as strategic sectors,[27] France, Germany, and Italy adopted a broader understanding. They defined enabling technologies as including 'technical knowledge that represents a significant advance over the status quo and has a major potential for innovation'.[28] Both understandings go far beyond the defence sector, and, at least the three Member States' proposal also significantly exceeds the concept of critical infrastructure, technology, and inputs. Accordingly, the focus of the strategic asset concept is not so much on protecting vital, existing societal functions. Protecting strategic assets rather serves long-term geopolitical, industrial, and economic goals with the end to preserve or enhance the EU's strategic autonomy.[29]

To be sure, one must not confuse the term strategic assets with the notion of 'strategic FDI', which is also often used in the context of FDI screening.[30] By this notion, EU actors express their concern that the investor takes his decisions not on commercial, profit-driven, but political, state-induced grounds.[31] Hence, the label of strategic FDI does not refer to a specific interest that the FDI may harm. Instead, it describes an increased risk that a harm to a specific interest may be realized. For example, an FDI into a target that produces ammunition is first and foremost of concern because it takes place in the defence sector. Such FDI may harm the EU and Member States interests, for example, through know-how transfer to the investor's home country. The home country might then benefit from the transferred know-how to produce ammunition, which in turn might be used against the EU and Member

---

[26] Commission, 'A New Industrial Strategy for Europe' (Communication) COM (2020) 102 final, p. 13. On the New Industrial Strategy and the notion 'strategic autonomy' and 'strategic assets' see also Pohl (2020), pp. 151–153.

[27] Commission, SWD (2019) 108 final (n. 8), pp. 7, 11; Commission, COM (2020) 102 final (n. 26), pp. 13, 14. See also the misleading Commission, 'Guidance to the Member States concerning Foreign Direct Investment and Free Movement of Capital from Third Countries, and the Protection of Europe's Strategic Assets, ahead of the Application of Regulation (EU) 2019/452 (FDI Screening Regulation)' (Communication) COM (2020) 1981 final, 1, Annex, pp. 1, 3, in which, even in the title, the terms critical and strategic assets are being used as synonyms. See Velten (2020b).

[28] France, Germany, and Italy (2017b), p. 2.

[29] See for a more detailed description of this consideration Lippert et al. (2019), pp. 23–25.

[30] France, Germany, and Italy (2017a), p. 1; France, Germany, and Italy (2017b), pp. 3–4; Commission, COM (2017) 494 final (n. 4), p. 2; Commission, 'Proposal for a Regulation of the European Parliament and of the Council establishing a framework for screening of foreign direct investments into the European Union' COM (2017) 487 final, pp. 2–3.

[31] See e.g. Wübbeke et al. (2016) on the example of China and its 'Made in China 2025' strategy according to which the Chinese government supports investments in specific sectors and technologies that it considers crucial for its economic development—e.g. manufacturing, robotics, cloud computing, and big data.

States in a military confrontation. The risk of know-how transfer and of such use increases if the FDI is driven by political, state-induced motivations. In this sense, the FDI may be strategic for the home country.[32]

Putting this second meaning of 'strategic FDI' aside, the term of strategic infrastructure, technology, and inputs describes not so much protecting vital societal functions, but long-term geopolitical, industrial, and economic goals. Hence, the notion of strategic infrastructure, technology, and inputs includes technologies such as artificial intelligence, robotics, and big data processing, as long as they are not necessary for the defence sector or critical assets.[33] It also entails considerations to strengthen competitive advantages in order to facilitate building globally competitive domestic firms, as well as certain assets of specific geopolitical importance.[34] Interestingly, the European Parliament's proposal to add strategic infrastructure, technology, and EU autonomy as an FDI screening factor in the Screening Regulation was rejected.[35]

2.1.4   Private Information Concern

The EU's and Member States' fourth and last concern vis-à-vis foreign investors is that the investor gains access to private information, especially personal data that the FDI target possesses. According to the scenario of concern, the private information may get processed by IT systems of the foreign investor, and thus reach the investor's home country. Therefore, EU and Member States are concerned that if the investor's home country does not guarantee the same level of private information protection, unauthorized third parties could gain access to private information of EU citizens, and exploit them to their detriment.

This concern particularly addresses business secrets and personal data. In both cases, those to whom the information belongs may suffer significant harm. The harm may be particularly severe if sensitive personal data are concerned. For a definition of sensitive personal data, one may refer to Art 9(1) of the GDPR.[36] This provision, as a principle, prohibits the processing of inter alia 'genetic data, biometric data for

---

[32] Commission, COM (2020) 253 final (n. 6), p. 7.

[33] This defence dimension of the EU's 'strategic autonomy' is included in the above-defined defence sector. For the defence dimension of 'strategic autonomy' see Council, 'Council Conclusions on Security and Defence in the context of the EU Global Strategy' 9178/17; Council, 14413/18 (n. 18).

[34] For a recent discussion of new, broader national security concepts in light of the current changes of geopolitical order, see e.g. Roberts et al. (2019), pp. 664–669.

[35] Parliament, A8-0198/2018 (n. 4), amendments 39–41.

[36] Regulation (EU) 2016/679 of the European Parliament and of the Council of 27 April 2016 on the protection of natural persons with regard to the processing of personal data and on the free movement of such data, and repealing Directive 95/46/EC (GDPR) [2016] OJ L 119/1.

the purpose of uniquely identifying a natural person, data concerning health or data concerning a natural person's sex life or sexual orientation'.[37]

Though this concern is in part overlapping with the harmful investor concern, it deserves its own category. According to the harmful investor concern, the foreign investor has a concrete interest in exploiting certain private information data to the detriment of its owners. This is particularly relevant in critical sectors such as telecommunication or health services, where suppliers process many, often sensitive data. However, the mere fact that an FDI leads, without intention, to a transfer of private information in an investor's home country already causes concern. The private information may be less protected if the home country's private information protection laws fall short of the EU's protection standards. This private information concern constitutes the fourth category of EU and Member States concern vis-à-vis foreign investors.

2.1.5 Conclusion

The EU and Member States have four main concerns vis-à-vis foreign investors on competition, reciprocity, harmful investor interests, and private information. The concerns are particularly serious vis-à-vis investors from China, but investors from other countries like Russia, United Arab Emirates, Brazil, and India are also in focus. Though some actors in the EU emphasize the economic advantages of FDI instead, the EU and Member States have, based on these concerns, adopted a stricter stance on FDI, in particular by FDI screening. Accordingly, the four EU and Member States concerns vis-à-vis foreign investors become the benchmark for the effectiveness of FDI screening mechanisms. From this perspective, FDI screening mechanisms are only effective if they allow EU and Member States to significantly meet these concerns.[38]

Before turning to the legislative background in Sects. 2.2 and 2.3 will provide the economic background of FDI screening in the EU. For the reasons illustrated above, the political discussion focuses on FDI as the form of foreign investment, not the main alternative investment form, portfolio investment. The following section will explain the notion of FDI from an economic perspective. This will also help to better understand the EU and Member States concerns vis-à-vis foreign investors and their legislative reactions.

---

[37] Other sensitive personal data pursuant to GDPR (n. 36) art 9(1) are 'personal data revealing racial or ethnic origin, political opinions, religious or philosophical beliefs, or trade union membership'.

[38] Section 2.3 will further explain how the EU and Member States concerns vis-à-vis foreign investors explain the legislative steps towards FDI screening mechanisms at EU level; Chap. 3 will analyze to what extent the legislative steps can meet the EU and Member States concerns.

2.2   Economic Background

The economics of FDI are critical for the theses this book submits. On the one hand, they further explain the political rationale of and sometimes reluctance to screen FDI. On the other hand, a comprehensive legal analysis of FDI protection has to consider its economics and be transparent about it.[39] The (purported) economic effects of FDI impinge on a scholar's legal analysis, namely when interpreting a provision on the basis of its object and purpose. This is particularly relevant in the realm of the Fundamental freedoms. As will be shown in Sect. 4.2.3.3, some scholars argue that the freedom of capital movement should always protect FDI and its foreign investor, even if this may undermine the personal scope of the freedom of establishment that excludes foreign investors that are not seated in the EU (Art 54 (1) TFEU). These scholars claim that FDI is generally positive for economic development. Accordingly, as the Fundamental freedoms intend to enhance economic development in the EU, they argue that FDI must be protected by the Fundamental freedoms to the greatest extent possible. This rationale, however, is erroneous if FDI is in fact not outright positive for economic development.

The following paragraphs will briefly introduce the economic concept of FDI. A particular focus will lie on clarifying its role as an activity of multinational enterprises, in addition to FDI as a mere capital movement (Sect. 2.2.1). This will allow for an assessment of the effects of incoming FDI on the host country (Sect. 2.2.2).

2.2.1   What Is FDI from an Economic Perspective?

As mentioned, the concept of FDI has two layers that explain the different motivations behind and the effects of FDI: FDI as Multinational Enterprise ('MNE') activity and as capital movement.[40] Based on these different layers, FDI can be categorized according to several criteria. These categories will later help to assess which categories of FDI are at the centre of EU and Member States concerns vis-à-vis foreign investors, and thus of FDI screening mechanisms.

---

[39] See van Aaken (2011), p. 31; who rightly criticizes the missing consideration of economic arguments in legal literature. Otherwise, economic and social sciences considerations would not be transparent, which in turn impedes critical scientific scrutiny.

[40] Heiduk and Kerlen-Prinz (1999), pp. 23–54; Lipsey (2004), pp. 334–335 ('capital flow story' and 'entrepreneurship story'); Brakman and Garretsen (2008), p. 1.

2.2.1.1 FDI as MNE Activity and as Capital Movement

First, FDI is closely linked to the concept of MNE, 'an enterprise that owns or, in some way, controls value-added activities in more than one country'.[41] In this sense, FDI is the activity that allows the investor to exercise ownership or control and therefore to become an MNE. It is 'the transfer of a package of assets or intermediate products';[42] an 'entrepreneurship story'.[43] FDI as an MNE activity includes all forms of tangible assets, as well as managerial, organizational expertise, technology, and aspects of entrepreneurship.[44] Financial capital is typically, but not necessarily transferred.[45] MNE activity can even take non-equity forms—for example, contracting, franchising, or licensing.[46] Moreover, an MNE can technically, though unlikely in practice, undertake FDI by raising capital on rather than transferring it to the host country market.[47]

The second layer of FDI is FDI as an investment, and hence a capital movement. Taking this perspective, the Organization for Economic Co-operation and Development ('OECD') defines FDI as follows:

> Foreign direct investment reflects the objective of establishing a lasting interest by a resident enterprise in one economy (direct investor) in an enterprise (direct investment enterprise) that is resident in an economy other than that of the direct investor. The lasting interest implies the existence of a *long-term relationship* between the direct investor and the direct investment enterprise and a *significant degree of influence* on the management of the enterprise.[48]

---

[41] Dunning and Lundan (2008), p. 201. Others even seem to use MNE and FDI as synonyms Kindleberger (1970), p. 1; Hofmann (2013), p. 23. For alternative definitions of MNE see Perlmutter (1969), p. 9.

[42] Dunning and Lundan (2008), p. 7.

[43] Lipsey (2004), p. 335.

[44] Dunning and Lundan (2008), p. 7. Cantwell (1994), pp. 303–304; explicitly differentiates between FDI and MNE, describing the former as a means of financing MNE activity, and thus as a mere proxy of MNE activity. This, however, limits the concept of FDI too much to the second layer of FDI, FDI as a capital movement.

[45] This book does not discuss the different definitions of capital. For such a discussion in a legal context see e.g. Lübke (2006), pp. 112–113; Hindelang (2009), pp. 45–46. Both argue for a modern understanding of capital including financial capital.

[46] UNCTAD, 'World Investment Report 2011: Non-equity Modes of International Production and Development' (New York, 2011), p. xi.

[47] MNE statistics measure MNE activity mostly by FDI inflow and stock as a proxy for all MNE activities focusing on equity forms of FDI. This neglects non-equity forms of international production and FDI that is financed on the host market (cf. Cantwell (1994), pp. 303–304). MNE activities statistics are therefore often inaccurate, UNCTAD, 'World Investment Report 2011' (n. 46), p. 11.

[48] OECD, 'Benchmark Definition of Foreign Direct Investment' (Paris, 2008), para. 117 (emphasis added). The IMF follows this definition, IMF, 'Balance of Payments and International Investment Position Manual' (Washington, DC, 2009), paras. 1.29, 6.8.

Characteristic elements of the definition are 'long-term relationship' and 'significant degree of influence on the management'. For statistical purposes, these conditions are presumed fulfilled if the investor holds 10% or more of the voting power.[49] Investment that gives the investors less influence qualifies as portfolio investment.[50] The latter is thus seen as an investment without the interest to participate in the target's management, and thus for short-term capital interests only.

Both perspectives, FDI as an MNE activity and as a capital movement, show that FDI requires control of a domestic asset. Such control can be exercised through minority ownership.[51] From the perspective of capital movement, this is made clear by the OECD definition based on a 10% threshold, though only as a proxy for statistically determining the investors' lasting interest.[52] FDI as an MNE activity, on the other hand, describes a situation in which the extraterritorial element is strong enough to consider the business activity foreign.[53] Minority ownership can fulfil this strong foreign element, too.[54]

2.2.1.2   Different FDI Categories

Having stated the definition of MNE activity and FDI, the discussion can now turn to categorizing FDI. Many categorizations start with the patterns and motives of firms that engage in international production.[55] This is where many categorizations of FDI, which are necessary to later assess FDI effects on host countries, become relevant.

First, an MNE may directly invest in a host country in two forms. On the one hand, the firm can set up a new facility. This form is often referred to as greenfield investment.[56] On the other hand, the MNE can merge with or acquire (shares of) an existing asset.[57] This is sometimes also described as brownfield investment.[58]

The second form of FDI includes sequential forms of FDI that is, the acquisition of additional shares, capital increase, or an investment for restructuring of an existing

---

[49] OECD, 'Benchmark Definition of Foreign Direct Investment' (n. 48), para. 117.

[50] ibid.; IMF, 'BPM6' (n. 78), para. 6.54.

[51] For a detailed discussion of control as a defining element of FDI see Sect. 4.2.3.2.4.

[52] OECD, 'Benchmark Definition of Foreign Direct Investment' (n. 48), paras. 11, 117. See also Lübke (2006), p. 106; Hofmann (2013), p. 22.

[53] Collins (2017), p. 3.

[54] Dunning and Lundan (2008), p. 7; Kerner (2014), p. 806.

[55] The most prominent result of this approach is the 'OLI paradigm', according to which a firm decides on the internationalization of its production based on advantages of *O*wnership, *L*ocation and *I*nternalization; developed by Dunning (1977).

[56] OECD, 'Benchmark Definition of Foreign Direct Investment' (n. 48), para. 598, also describing such investment illustratively as *ex nihilo*, from nothing.

[57] UNCTAD, 'World Investment Report 2000: Cross-border Mergers and Acquisitions and Development' (New York, 2000), pp. 140–144, which specifies the different firm motives for both forms.

[58] Krugman et al. (2017), p. 225.

asset.[59] These sequential forms of FDI also form part of a third categorization of FDI that is based on whether the investment is new, builds upon a prior investment (sequential), or will serve as a platform for multiple other investments.[60]

A third categorization considers whether the internalization of production is vertical or horizontal in the value-added chain, or goes beyond the value-added chain of one product to form a conglomerate.[61]

Fourth, FDI can be categorized by sectors.

Fifth and finally, FDI differs according to the investor's, often overlapping, motives: An investor may inter alia seek natural resources, efficiency, markets, or strategic assets.[62] Natural resources are either physical resources, such as mineral fuels and agricultural, products; labour; or knowledge, including technological, managerial, marketing, and organizational skills.[63] An efficiency seeking investor will try to achieve economies of scale or scope, or diversify its business risks through FDI. Market seeking FDI aims at sustaining or protecting existing markets, or exploit or promote new markets.[64] Finally, an investor may undertake FDI to acquire assets for its long-term strategy to achieve global competitiveness. This form of FDI is usually undertaken through M&A.[65] The strategic asset seeking motive is dominant with new market players who seek to catch up with market leaders ('latecomers').[66] Moreover, the strategic asset seeking motive plays an important role because nowadays competition is global. Latecomers therefore have to quickly acquire global competitive advantages to stay in the market.[67] Necessary managerial and organizational knowledge is bought on the market through FDI.[68] Accordingly, these firms aim not to exploit own but acquire others' advantages.[69]

---

[59] OECD, 'Benchmark Definition of Foreign Direct Investment' (n. 48), p. 598.

[60] Eden (2003), p. 292.

[61] UNCTAD, 'World Investment Report 2000' (n. 57), p. 101. See also Cantwell (1994), p. 307.

[62] Dunning and Lundan (2008), pp. 67–77; and with a slightly different categorization combining natural resource and asset-seeking FDI, UNCTAD, 'World Investment Report 1998: Developments and Determinants' (New York, 1998), p. 91.

[63] Dunning and Lundan (2008), pp. 68–69. See also Lipsey (2004), p. 355.

[64] Dunning and Lundan (2008), p. 70.

[65] Dunning and Lundan (2008), pp. 72–74.

[66] Globerman and Shapiro (2009), p. 23.

[67] Aharoni (2010), p. 42, who argues that domestic firms only have the choice between 'acquire or being acquired'. For the fact of early internationalization by skipping traditional phases, see Broadman (2010), pp. 326–327.

[68] Aharoni (2010), pp. 43–44.

[69] Globerman and Shapiro (2009), p. 25.

2.2.1.3 Categorizing the EU and Member States Concerns Vis-à-Vis Foreign Investors

Both the two layers of FDI as MNE activity and capital movement, as well as the five categories of FDI show that the EU and Member States concerns vis-à-vis foreign investors are in fact only about a small group of investment categories.

The EU and Member States concerns depart from the fact that a foreign investor owns and controls an existing domestic asset that is worthy of protection. The concerns are hence focused on FDI in the form of M&A, not on other non-equity forms of international production. Additionally, the concerns are not (only) about FDI as a mere capital movement, but about the investor as exercising entrepreneurial activities in the acquired domestic asset.

Moreover, the concerns mainly concentrate on developing economies. This does not only stem from the political will to safeguard technological advantages from home countries and investors with no or at least less knowledge than the acquired asset. Developing countries also happen to be at the centre of security concerns regarding political influence; for example, from regimes in China and Iran. Another country of concern, Russia, is considered a 'transition economy'.[70] Both statuses typically mean a lower level of knowledge, particularly technological knowledge, which is crucial for assessing FDI effects.[71]

Last but not least, the EU and Member States concern to safeguard technological advantages addresses knowledge-intensive sectors and investors who seek technology and knowledge (natural resources and strategic assets). This corresponds with current SOE and developing country FDI that often seeks technology and knowledge in developed markets following a long-term political strategy to upgrade its own economy and global competitiveness.[72] The security concern, however, relates to all sectors in which disruptions have wide societal effects. Therefore, other sectors and motives are also relevant.

The categorization of EU and Member States concerns vis-à-vis foreign investors countries allows two conclusions. First, the concerns focus on a small part of MNE activities and forms of FDI: equity MNE activities in the form of M&A FDI from developing countries or economies in transition (together referred to as developing

---

[70] UNCTADStad classifies no Member State as developing country, see UNCTAD, 'Development Status Groups and Composition' UNCTADSTAT <https://unctadstat.unctad.org/EN/Classifica tions/DimCountries_DevelopmentStatus_Hierarchy.pdf> accessed 2 February 2022. In the WTO developing country status is warranted by self-designation.

[71] For limitations to this assumption see Sect. 2.2.2.2.

[72] For SOEs in general UNCTAD, 'World Investment Report 2013: Global Value Chains: Investment and Trade for Development' (New York, 2013), p. 13. Perea and Stephenson (2017), pp. 114–115, emphasize China as an example, citing other studies. See also Globerman and Shapiro (2009), pp. 36–38. The Chinese government's strategy is part of the 'Made in China 2025' plan, cf. Wübbeke et al. (2016), pp. 7–8. Another motive of Chinese FDI is to outbalance a positive balance of payment and to exploit new foreign markets to compensate for overcapacities at home, Perea and Stephenson (2017), p. 106; for the renewable energies sector see Lv and Spigarelli (2015), p. 14.

countries). Accordingly, if the EU or the Member States wanted to adopt screening mechanisms to meet their concerns vis-à-vis foreign investors, the larger parts of MNE activities remain, at least in theory, unaffected.[73] Second, the following assessment of FDI effects on the host countries can be limited to M&A FDI from developing countries with a particular focus on technology- and knowledge-seeking FDI in technology- and knowledge-intensive sectors.

2.2.2 Host Country Effects of M&A FDI

Against the background provided in the previous section, the discussion can now turn to the effects of FDI in the host country. Given the above categorization, this assessment may be limited to M&A FDI from developing to developed countries, with a particular focus on technology- and knowledge-seeking motives in technology- and knowledge-intensive sectors.

For a long time FDI was regarded as generally positive for the host country ('Washington Consensus'). Accordingly, countries, in particular developing countries, were encouraged to liberalize incoming FDI to enhance economic growth, hence development.[74] Since then scholars added more nuances to this picture, and now agree that the realization of positive FDI effects in fact depends on the individual circumstances of each investment.[75] Positive FDI effects in the host country may be attenuated or even reversed, in particular where the investor possesses inferior levels of technology and knowledge. In addition, FDI may have negative effects.

The following will analyze the positive and negative FDI effects in the host country. The analysis will be limited to M&A FDI from developing countries, with a particular focus on technology- and knowledge-seeking FDI. This form of FDI typically comes with various factors that attenuate or even reverse positive effects of FDI in the host country. The probability that this form of FDI is overall beneficial to the host country's economic growth and development is thus considerably attenuated.

---

[73] Obviously, this conclusion relies on the assumption that a policy can address these categories specifically without affecting other FDI categories.

[74] Moran et al. (2005), p. 2. For a critical discussion on the emergence of the term 'Washington Consensus' see Williamson (2004-2005), p. 195. Williamson is perceived as the term's inventor after having written the article Williamson (1990). In the context of international investment law, van Aaken (2011), pp. 34–36, challenges the generally positive perception of investment effects on host countries.

[75] Lipsey (2004), p. 369; Javorcik (2008), p. 140; Sornarajah (2017), p. 72. See also Sasse (2011), p. 15, who shows surprise about the positive perception of FDI in both developing and developed countries despite the unclear evidence. Rodrik (1999), p. 24, opposed the positive view of FDI early with the strong—controversial—statement: 'In general, there is little reason to believe that . . . one dollar of DFI [Direct Foreign Investment] will contribute to more than a dollar of any other kind of investment'. Moran et al. (2005), p. 2; dismiss the Washington Consensus as a misleading conventional wisdom.

2.2.2.1   FDI as Source of Capital

FDI is first and foremost a source of capital. In this sense, the term capital also contains tangible assets, in which financial capital and other, especially human, resources materialize. In case of M&A FDI, however, the transfer of capital is less evident. The investor may choose to operate the existing assets without transferring own assets.[76] Only the inflow of financial capital as a result of FDI seems generally established.[77] From this, two effects of FDI derive—positive or negative, depending on the host country.

First, the inflow of capital through FDI influences a country's balance of payments.[78] Countries with a positive balance of payments will welcome the negative effect of incoming capital, whereas those with a negative balance may be less welcoming. In the EU Member States' balances of payment differ greatly, causing a different perception of balance of payment effects of FDI.[79] Moreover, the positive balance effect will turn negative if it is outbalanced by outflows of capital from the FDI target to the foreign investor, in particular capital stemming from FDI income and intra-firm trade between the target and investor.[80]

Generally positive and more important though is that capital inflows enhance the host country's potential for production. An increase in production is likely to result in growth and higher income.[81]

There are, however, two situations in which these effects will not materialize. First, the investor may, at least partially, raise capital for the FDI investment in the host country itself.[82] Accordingly, the value of capital inflow is lower than expected or publicly announced. Second, the asset's former owner may transfer the capital to

---

[76]Lipsey (2004), p. 335.

[77]See e.g. UNCTAD, 'World Investment Report 2000' (n. 57), p. 164; OECD, 'Benchmark Definition of Foreign Direct Investment' (n. 48), para. 2.

[78]Kerner (2014), p. 804; Collins (2017), p. 24.

[79]According to the OECD's Balance of Payments BPM6 for the fourth quarter of 2019, the EU has a positive balance of payment of ca US$87.0 billion. Among Member States the picture differs greatly. On the one hand, countries like Germany (US$69.5 billion), Italy (US$17.5 billion), and the Netherlands (US$23.2 billion) have highly positive balances, others have a deficit—e.g. Ireland (US$19.7 billion), France (US$4.5 billion), and Czech Republic (US$0.8 billion). For these seasonally adjusted USD quarterly current account values, see OECD, 'Balance of Payments BPM 6' (Paris) <https://stats.oecd.org/Index.aspx?DataSetCode=MEI_BOP6> accessed 2 February 2022. The values of 2019 are more representative given the developments following the Covid-19 crisis.

[80]UNCTAD, 'World Investment Report 2000' (n. 57), p. 165.

[81]Generally emphasizing this advantage of FDI, Rodrik (1999), p. 29, who emphasizes this positive effect for developing countries, which are by definition scarce in capital; Lipsey (2004), p. 334, who links this effect to the entrepreneurship story, rather than to the capital flow story; Javorcik (2008), p. 139; Hofmann (2013), p. 26; Matthes (2017), pp. 4–5. See also Buckley et al. (2018), p. 13.

[82]Kindleberger (1970), p. 11; UNCTAD, 'World Investment Report 2000' (n. 57), p. 164; Barba Navaretti and Venables (2004), p. 40. See also Alfaro (2017), p. S7, who stresses that capital raising on the local market may crowd out domestic firms.

another country.[83] To the extent he does so, the inflowing capital leaves the country immediately after the FDI. It can thus not enhance the host country's potential for production.

Second, the enhancement of the host country's production potential is considerably reduced if investors are not subject to efficiency constraints when allocating their resources. Normally, foreign investors are expected to choose their M&A FDI target by its competitiveness. For some investors, however, other criteria are more important. Namely, SOEs and investors who are significantly funded by their home country are more likely to choose their targets for other reasons than competitiveness—for example, for gaining access to technology and knowledge. This may lead to the negative FDI effect of financing uncompetitive firms.[84] In case of FDI by state-owned enterprises into privatized former state-enterprises, this negative effect is—at least politically—even more harmful, since ending public ownership was the host country's intent of the privatization in the first place.[85]

Consequently, FDI is an important source of capital to host countries enhancing their potential productivity—as any capital transferring investment, such as portfolio investment. Nevertheless, even this most obvious positive effect of FDI in host countries may turn negative according to certain factors.

2.2.2.2 Technology and Knowledge Transfer

Technology and knowledge transfer to the acquired firm and spill-over effects beyond this firm are seen as the most important advantages of FDI for the host economy.[86] An increase in technology and knowledge enhances the host country's productivity and competitiveness.[87] These effects are exclusive to FDI because, in contrast to other investment forms, FDI includes the investor's control of and entrepreneurial activity in the FDI target.

---

[83] For the mechanisms of capital flow to shareholders and beyond see Lipsey (2004), p. 353.

[84] Globerman and Shapiro (2009), pp. 34 and 40, who also stress that empirical evidence on the inferior efficiency of Chinese SOEs is 'not conclusive'. Chinese private companies might be similarly inefficient.

[85] Describing this as political concerns in Germany about Sovereign wealth fund investments, Martini (2008), p. 316; Weller (2008), p. 858.

[86] OECD, 'Benchmark Definition of Foreign Direct Investment' (n. 48), para. 2; Javorcik (2008), pp. 139–140; van Aaken (2011), p. 35; Hofmann (2013), p. 120. For a detailed discussion on the process of spill-overs from the acquired firm to its employees, competitors in the same sector, and ultimately to the economy of the host country in general, see Dunning and Lundan (2008), ch 11; for productivity and knowledge specifically, Lipsey (2004), pp. 358–365. The differentiation of technology and knowledge is based on a personal aspect. Technology, on the one hand, is an intangible asset independent from a person, but inherent in a certain MNE activity. Knowledge, on the other hand, is a broad concept that covers human expertise and skills on technology, management, marketing, and organization (distinction implied by Dunning and Lundan (2008), p. 112). Hence, only a specific person or a group of people can be knowledgeable.

[87] Alfaro (2017), pp. S11–S12; Collins (2017), p. 23.

The transfer of technology and knowledge is explained through FDI as an MNE activity. When an MNE engages in production on a foreign market, it uses its technology and its employees' knowledge. Depending on the acquired firm's competitiveness[88] as well as the category of FDI, in particular sectors and motives, different technology and knowledge will be transferred to a varying extent.[89] An MNE may, for example, seek a specific foreign market for selling its products and therefore acquire a domestic firm with production facilities and a distribution network (horizontal FDI). In this scenario, the investor will usually implement its own processes to the extent they guarantee a competitive advantage vis-à-vis the acquired firm and host market competitors. To this end, the MNE will transfer technology and knowledge to the FDI target.[90]

In any case, however, such transfer can only have a positive effect in the host country if the investor has technology and knowledge that is superior to the technology and knowledge of the FDI target and the host country in general.[91] In case of FDI from developing countries, this condition will often not be met.[92] Indeed, even developing countries are home to leading firms in some technology sectors, especially China. Moreover, firms from developing countries tend to have better knowledge in managing and organizing production in volatile, diverse business environments.[93] Yet, other skills are often inferior to what the FDI target and the host country as a whole possess.[94] If the investor's motive is precisely to acquire a technological or knowledge advantage, the investor will by definition have a lower level of technology and knowledge. The potential positive effect of FDI may even be reversed into a negative effect if the investor seeks technology and knowledge only to transfer it to its home country.

As a result, the most important positive effect of FDI is often attenuated in case of FDI from developing countries; for technology- and knowledge-seeking FDI it might even be reversed into a negative effect. Put differently, the mere fact that an

---

[88] For this argument regarding the acquisition of already competitive firms, UNCTAD, 'World Investment Report 2000' (n. 57), p. 163.

[89] This is contrary to greenfield investments where the investor must transfer technology and knowledge, irrespective of its quality, to the host country to provide for its production facilities, see also ibid., p. 170.

[90] In case of M&A FDI, the transfer of technology and knowledge may take longer than with greenfield investment because the asset has already production facilities available. These production facilities serve as a basis on which the investor can build without necessarily having to transfer cutting-edge technology. See ibid., pp. 174–175. In addition, the MNE will consider numerous factors to decide if and, if yes, to what extent to transfer technology and knowledge to the host country. If the host country only accepts the FDI under the condition of a joint venture with a domestic firm, or even of specific technology transfer requirements, the investor may transfer older technology, Moran (2006), pp. 7–8.

[91] This fact is often taken for granted when assessing FDI effects, see Lipsey (2004), p. 358.

[92] Trebilcock (2015), p. 130; Matthes (2017), pp. 5–6. For knowledge on management and organization Rugman (2010), p. 85.

[93] Buckley et al. (2018), pp. 16–17.

[94] Globerman and Shapiro (2009), pp. 28–29; Aharoni (2010), p. 44; Rugman (2010), p. 85.

investment is coming from another country does not make it a better investment; it must come along with more advanced technology or knowledge than already accessible for the asset or the host country generally.[95]

2.2.2.3 Enhancing Production and R&D Capacities, Employment, Competition

A third advantage generally associated with FDI is its positive effect on the host country's production, and Research and Development ('R&D') capacities, employment, and competition.[96] This, again, is subject to reservations: one for short term effects of M&A FDI specifically and another for FDI in general.

At least in the short term, M&A FDI, in contrast to greenfield investment, fails to create new production capacities at the moment of investment. Without new production or R&D capacities, no additional employment and competition to market incumbents is created. Even negative effects may occur if the investor restructures the asset and, for efficiency and rationalization purposes, reduces production and R&D capacity, as well as employment. This rationale fails for FDI that saved production and R&D capacity and employment by taking over a target in distress.[97]

In the long run, both M&A and greenfield FDI have similar effects on production or R&D capacities, employment, and competition—positively, but also negatively.[98] One determining factor for the FDI effects in this regard is the investor's motive; for instance, in case of technology- and knowledge-seeking FDI.[99] If the technology and knowledge is transferable,[100] the investor may not enhance host country capacities. Instead, the investor may focus on transferring the technology and knowledge to other production facilities in their home country or elsewhere. As a result, the investor may even neglect the supply in the host market, causing less competition and ultimately leading to disinvestment.

---

[95] In the same vein, Barba Navaretti and Venables (2004), p. 182, who emphasizes that the methodological problem is 'to single out the strict causal effect of foreign ownership on performance'.

[96] Rodrik (1999), p. 24; UNCTAD, 'World Investment Report 2000' (n. 57), pp. 172–192; Collins (2017), p. 24.

[97] UNCTAD, 'World Investment Report 2000' (n. 57), p. 160. The report also highlights another case in which greenfield investment is not an option: A host country decides to privatize a public domestic company. For this second case see also Kalotay and Hunya (2000), pp. 40–41.

[98] UNCTAD, 'World Investment Report 2000' (n. 57), pp. xxiv–xxv; Globerman and Shapiro (2009), pp. 30–31; Sauvant et al. (2010), p. 367.

[99] Also emphasizing the importance of the investor motives, UNCTAD, 'World Investment Report 2000' (n. 57), p. 163. In case of a mere financial motivation, however, the investment would rather constitute portfolio investment.

[100] Technology and knowledge may also be non-transferable—e.g. because they are intrinsically linked to domestic employees who are reluctant to move to another country. See ibid., p. 180. However, the report refers to this non-transferable technology and knowledge to argue that the investor will avoid laying off employees with technology specific knowledge.

Another factor that leads to negative effects of FDI on production and R&D capacities, employment, and competition is the asymmetric market power of the investor. An investor with excessive market power compared to domestic competitors may reduce their market share or push them completely out of the market. Asymmetric market power may stem from general efficiency advantages,[101] as well as a monopoly or oligopoly position in the home market, often the case for SOEs and other state-funded firms.[102]

Consequently, M&A FDI is generally less advantageous for production and R&D capacity, employment, and competition compared to greenfield investment in the short term. This comparison does not apply if M&A is the only available investment option because an existing asset needs to be taken over. More importantly, however, in the long term, the effects of FDI on production and R&D capacity, employment, and competition are mixed. They depend on the investment, the investor's motives, and the firm's performance on the market.

2.2.2.4 Access to Foreign Markets and Integration in Global Production Networks

Last but not least, a purely positive effect of M&A FDI is the host country asset's access to new markets and a global production network. Of course, even after (partial) acquisition by a foreign investor, the target, its employees and suppliers, as well as the investor, depending on its motives, still want to strengthen the asset's performance and competitiveness. To this end, it may be crucial to gain access to specific foreign markets[103] and integrate in global production networks.[104] Usually, firms in developed countries will be well-positioned in the latter; but to get access to the former is more difficult, especially in closed or complex markets. The foreign investor may facilitate the target's access to these markets.

This positive effect of M&A FDI becomes particularly relevant to technology- and knowledge-seeking FDI from developing countries. Developing country markets are often closed or complex. Moreover, for technology- and knowledge-seeking FDI access to new markets is usually particularly important. Such FDI is typically undertaken in high technology sectors in which the targets have competitive advantages due to their technology and knowledge. These advantages can be exploited on foreign markets.[105] This effect becomes more important the more the acquired firm relies on exports, and the more attractive the foreign market is. Especially big and

---

[101] ibid., p. 170.

[102] ibid., p. xxiii.

[103] Sauvant et al. (2010), p. 20; Hofmann (2013), p. 120; Matthes (2017), p. 5. See on this EU policy goal generally, Commission, COM (2017) 494 final (n. 4), p. 6.

[104] Matthes (2017), p. 5. Beyond the economic effect, the global economic integration also has a pacifying geopolitical effect, see e.g. Preisser (2013), p. 50.

[105] Indeed, exploiting new markets may even be necessary to finance costly R&D efforts.

growing markets like China and India offer immense business opportunities for developed country firms.

This positive effect of FDI is therefore particularly important for firms from developed countries with global competitive advantages deriving from technology and knowledge.

2.2.2.5 Mixed Effects of M&A FDI from Developing Countries

The above shows mixed economic effects for host countries of FDI that is at the centre of EU and Member States concerns vis-à-vis foreign investors: M&A FDI from developing countries with a particular focus on technology- and knowledge-seeking FDI.

Insofar, positive effects that are associated with FDI do often not apply. Foreign-ness does not by itself lead to positive effects of investment in a country.[106] The key advantage of FDI, technology and knowledge transfer, does often not occur, except for some specific managerial and organizational knowledge. In case of technology- and knowledge-seeking FDI this aspired positive effect even turns negative if the acquired assets are transferred to and used for production in other countries. Positive FDI effects on production and R&D capacity, employment, and competition also depend on each investment. Again, such effect will not occur as often if the investor is only seeking technology and knowledge.

At the same time, two generally positive effects remain: inflow of capital and access for the FDI target to foreign markets. The inflow of financial capital is attenuated to the extent the capital is raised on the host country market or if the seller transfers it out of the host country.

To be sure, this section does not argue that FDI, even technology- and knowledge-seeking M&A FDI from developing countries into developed countries, in principle fails to contribute to economic growth and development. Instead, the above analysis showed that these positive effects of FDI are not automatically achieved, but depend on each specific investment, in particular in case of technol-ogy- and knowledge-seeking M&A FDI from developing countries into developed countries.

---

[106] Barba Navaretti and Venables (2004), p. 43, on MNEs in comparison to domestic companies. In a similar direction Buckley et al. (2018), p. 14; who suggest that FDI is less beneficial to host countries if induced by home country factors.

2.2.3   Consequences of Mixed Host Country Effects for Legal Analysis

The conclusion on the mixed economic effects on host countries of M&A FDI from developing countries with a particular focus on technology- and knowledge-seeking FDI will become crucial for the legal analysis of FDI protection.

When assessing the protection of FDI by a specific legal provision, namely the Fundamental freedoms in the TFEU, it is a common argument that the provision must protect FDI to the largest extent possible, since the provision intended to, and FDI in fact did, foster economic growth and development. Given the above conclusions, however, this argument is flawed. One cannot generally argue that every M&A FDI from developing countries, especially technology- and knowledge-seeking FDI, fosters economic growth and development. It would therefore be wrong to argue that the provision must protect any FDI to the largest extent possible. This is especially so if such an interpretation would undermine other valid arguments that weigh in favour of protecting FDI less.

The economic background of FDI also puts the political background of FDI screening into perspective. It sheds further light on the trade-off between encouraging FDI to foster economic growth and development on the one, and pursuing other public interests on the other hand, namely security, public order, or economic or geopolitical policy. If a certain FDI is less likely to contribute to economic growth and development, the EU and Member States may be more inclined to screen, and eventually prohibit, this FDI for other public interests.

With this consideration linking the political and economic background of FDI, the discussion can now turn to the legislative steps the EU and Member States took to meet their concerns vis-à-vis foreign investors.

2.3   Legislative Background

Sections 2.1 and 2.2 showed in which political and economic context the EU and Member States act when adopting FDI screening mechanisms. Traditionally, the legislative landscape of FDI screening in the EU has been shaped by Member States. Nearly half of the Member States already had FDI screening mechanisms in place at national level before the EU adopted the Screening Regulation. However, the mechanisms differed greatly, especially in their scope regarding investors, investments, and sectors. The screening grounds were typically limited to security and public order interests.[107]

Following rising concerns vis-à-vis foreign investors and uncertainty about Member States competences for broader FDI screening mechanisms, calls for an

---

[107] See for this summary of investment screening mechanisms at Member State level, Commission, COM (2017) 494 final (n. 4), p. 7.

EU-wide approach grew louder. Nevertheless, the EU was still hesitant to take a harmonized, stricter stance on FDI inflows. Among its reasons were not only the economic advantages of FDI inflows and the EU's traditionally open investment policy, but also the often vague concerns vis-à-vis foreign investors and diverging positions among EU actors and Member States.

Ultimately, a group of Member States gave the last push towards an EU-wide approach on FDI screening. After two letters from France, Germany, and Italy,[108] followed by discussions among EU stakeholders, consensus was reached that the EU should take steps to address the concerns vis-à-vis foreign investors. FDI screening was perceived as one appropriate means to this end. At the same time, different positions among Commission, Parliament, and Council members remained. Not every actor shared the concerns vis-à-vis foreign investors, at least not to the same extent. In addition, some Member States rather emphasized the potential positive economic effects of FDI, and were concerned that FDI screening and similar measures may deter FDI that they so urgently needed.[109]

Against this complex background, the Commission proposed the Screening Regulation,[110] and later the Foreign Subsidies Regulation Proposal.[111] While the latter proposes an FDI screening mechanism at EU-level, the Screening Regulation is much more deferential towards Member States. It only provides an additional, non-mandatory option for Member State FDI screening mechanisms based on the new screening ground 'security or public order'.

2.3.1 Screening Regulation

The first major step towards a stricter, harmonized stance on FDI inflows was the Screening Regulation.[112] Adopted on 19 March 2019, after a relatively speedy process and some amendments to take Parliament and Council positions into account,[113] the Screening Regulation applies since 11 October 2020.[114] Due to diverging stakeholder positions,[115] the Screening Regulation struck a compromise that remains highly deferential towards Member States, and leaves significant room

---

[108] France, Germany, and Italy (2017a, b).

[109] Bismuth (2020), p. 106, lists Ireland, Spain, Portugal, Greece, and the 'Nordic countries'. For the mixed picture of FDI effects on host countries see Sect. 2.2.2.

[110] Commission, COM (2017) 487 final (n. 30).

[111] Commission, 'Proposal for a Regulation of the European Parliament and of the Council on foreign subsidies distorting the internal market' COM (2021) 223 final.

[112] Art 1(1) Regulation (EU) 2019/452 of the European Parliament and of the Council of 19 March 2019 establishing a framework for the screening of foreign direct investments into the Union (Screening Regulation) [2019] OJ L 79/I/1.

[113] Parliament, A8-0198/2018 (n. 4).

[114] Art 17 Screening Regulation.

[115] Moberg and Hindelang (2020), p. 1428.

for every Member State to adopt its own stance on FDI inflows. More concretely, instead of creating a general, mandatory EU-wide FDI screening mechanism, the Screening Regulation provides two elements that should contribute to harmonizing FDI screening in the EU.

First, the Screening Regulation introduces a compulsory cooperation mechanism between Member States and Commission for FDI screening at Member State level. In light of a missing EU-wide FDI screening mechanism, this element seeks a minimum level of EU-wide cooperation on screening individual FDI. The mechanism intends to ensure that a Member State in which an FDI occurs at least takes into account the interests of other Member States and the Commission. Nevertheless, the cooperation mechanism is first and foremost an information sharing mechanism; actual cooperation relies on the Member States' willingness to take other stakeholders' interests into account.[116] Hence, the Screening Regulation's first element can only be regarded as a minor step towards FDI screening harmonization.

Second and more importantly, the Screening Regulation provides a new, harmonized option for Member State FDI screening based on the new screening ground 'security or public order'. This option adds to the two already existing options for FDI screening mechanisms at Member State level. Nevertheless, it is still left to Member States to decide whether to adopt an FDI screening mechanism at all, and, if so, which option to adopt.[117] As a consequence, the Screening Regulation now offers the Member States four options.

As a first option, Member States may decide not to adopt any FDI screening mechanism. The second and third option for Member States are explicitly mentioned in Recital (4) and Art 1(2) Screening Regulation. Accordingly, the Member States remain free to adopt FDI screening mechanisms on the grounds of 'public policy or public security' within the meaning of Art 65(1)(b) TFEU,[118] or on the grounds of 'essential security interests' pursuant to Art 346(1)(b) TFEU.[119] Member States FDI

---

[116] Most importantly, the Member State in which the FDI takes place must only 'give due consideration' to other Member States' comments and the Commission's opinion (Arts 6(9), 7(7) Screening Regulation). For more details see e.g. Bourgeois and Malathouni (2020), pp. 182–185; Neergaard (2020), pp. 157–159; Zwartkruis and de Jong (2020), pp. 467–472.

[117] Recital (8) of the Screening Regulation explicitly states: 'The decision on whether to set up a screening mechanism or to screen a particular foreign direct investment remains the sole responsibility of the Member State concerned.'

[118] Recital (4) Screening Regulation.

[119] Art 1(2) Screening Regulation, which provides further: 'This Regulation is without prejudice to each Member State having sole responsibility for its national security, as provided for in Article 4(2) TEU'. The screening ground 'national security' may therefore constitute a fourth option for Member State FDI screening mechanisms. However, Art 4(2) TEU first and foremost clarifies that Member States keep their national identity and any essential state functions that follow from this identity. National security is one of these functions. The Member States' right to protect security and public order interests, however, is more concretely preserved by the provisions in Arts 346(1)(b) TFEU and 65(1)(b) TFEU (in conjunction with all other similar Fundamental freedom exceptions). See generally on Art 4(2) TEU and its context, e.g. Puttler (2016), paras. 13–21; Schill and Krenn (2020), paras. 14, 39–41.

screening mechanisms on these grounds are therefore not affected by the Screening Regulation's framework.[120]

The newly created fourth option now allows Member States to adopt a screening mechanism based on the requirement that an FDI is 'likely to affect security or public order'. As will be further argued in Chap. 3, this screening ground goes beyond the scope of FDI screening mechanisms on the grounds of 'public policy or public security' and 'essential security interests' within the meaning of Arts 65(1)(b) and 346(1)(b) TFEU respectively.[121]

To the extent Member States adopt the fourth option, an FDI screening mechanism on the grounds of 'security or public order', the Screening Regulation's framework provides some additional formal and substantial cornerstones. Art 3 Screening Regulation provides minimum formal requirements for transparent, reliable screening procedures. For instance, the Member State screening mechanism shall not discriminate between third countries, they must apply transparent time frames, and screening decisions must be subject to judicial recourse.[122] While the Screening Regulation omits an explicit, general definition of the requirement 'likely to affect security or public order', Art 4 Screening Regulation provides some further substantiations.[123]

In Art 4(1), the Screening Regulation provides a non-exhaustive list of interests that qualify as interests of 'security or public order': critical infrastructure, technology, and inputs; as well as sensitive information, and the freedom and pluralism of media. The Screening Regulation lists as examples of critical infrastructure, inter alia, energy, water, health, data processing and storage, and defence. The Parliament's proposal to also include strategic assets was rejected.[124] Art 4(2) Screening Regulation, on the other hand, provides factors that may be taken into account when assessing whether an FDI is *likely to affect* security or public order'. Given the risk scenario of foreign government influence behind an investor, the most relevant factor is 'whether the foreign investor is directly or indirectly controlled by the

---

[120] See also Velten (2020b) in which the author identifies four different policy options for Member States: no FDI screening mechanism, a Fundamental freedom option based on Art 65(1)(b) TFEU, a Screening Regulation option strictly based on the restrictive notion of critical infrastructure, technology, and inputs (see Sect. 2.1.3.2), and a Strategic Asset option, which seeks to interpret the Screening Regulation's screening ground 'security or public order' as also encompassing strategic assets (see Sect. 2.1.3.3).

[121] Moreover, the Member States lack competence to adopt an FDI screening mechanism on broader grounds than those defined in Arts 65(1)(b) and 346(1)(b) TFEU, see Sect. 4.1.

[122] Art 3(2), (3), (5) Screening Regulation.

[123] One may read Commission, COM (2020) 1981 final (n. 27) 1, Annex, pp. 1 and 3, as seeking to establish an interpretation of 'security or public order' that encompasses the broad notion of strategic assets. This, however, would ignore the Screening Regulation's adoption process, in which the Parliament's proposal to include the notion of 'strategic assets' in Art 4(1) Screening Regulation was rejected (Parliament, A8-0198/2018 (n. 4), amendments 39, 40). See also Velten (2020b).

[124] See Parliament, A8-0198/2018 (n. 4), amendments 39, 40.

government . . . of a third country, including through ownership structure or significant funding'.[125]

One year after the adoption of the Screening Regulation, the Commission found the number of Member States with FDI screening mechanisms in place to have increased from eleven to eighteen Member States, omitting, however, any details whether these mechanisms are based on the Screening Regulation's screening ground 'security or public order' or another ground.[126] At the same time, the numbers reveal that there are still nine Member States opting for the first option not to adopt a screening mechanism at all. The Commission tries to convince these Member States, but has no enforceable means at hand.[127]

Germany is an example of Member States that did implement the Screening Regulation by amending its FDI screening regime as provided in its Foreign Trade and Payments Act[128] and Foreign Trade and Payments Ordinance.[129] As the prior FDI screening regime was already based on the screening ground 'public order or security' (but had to be interpreted in accordance with 'public security or public order' within the meaning of Arts 36, 52(1) and 65(1)(b) TFEU[130]), Germany focused on complementing it with the newly introduced prefix 'likely to affect'.[131,132]

Overall, despite the Screening Regulation's new screening ground 'security or public order', the general approach to FDI screening in the EU remains largely the same. On the one hand, FDI screening remains largely in the responsibility of Member States. On the other hand, the available grounds of FDI screening continue to circle around the notions of security and public order. Chapter 3 will examine whether FDI screening on these grounds allows Member States to significantly meet their concerns vis-à-vis foreign investors.

---

[125] Art 4(2)(c) Screening Regulation.

[126] Commission, 'First Annual Report on the screening of foreign direct investments into the Union' (Report) COM (2021) 714 final, p. 6.

[127] ibid., p. 7.

[128] German Foreign Trade and Payments Act (Außenwirtschaftsgesetz), as amended as of 25 August 2021.

[129] German Foreign Trade and Payments Ordinance (Außenwirtschaftsverordnung), as amended as of 25 August 2021.

[130] See Foreign Trade and Payments Act, s 4(1), subparas. 4 as adopted before its amendment on 17 July 2020.

[131] See Foreign Trade and Payments Act, ss 4(1), subparas. 4 and 4a, and 5(2), as well as Foreign Trade and Payments Ordinance, s 55(1) and (1b). While before FDI could be screened if there was a threat to public order or security ('Gefährdung der öffentlichen Ordnung oder Sicherheit'), screening is now allowed if an FDI is 'likely to affect public order or security' ('voraussichtliche Beeinträchtigung der öffentlichen Ordnung oder Sicherheit').

[132] For the Regulation's implementation in other Member States see Commission, 'List of Screening Mechanisms Notified by Member States: (pursuant to Art 3(7) and (8) Screening Regulation, updated on an ongoing basis)' (3 December 2021) <https://trade.ec.europa.eu/doclib/docs/2019/june/tradoc_157946.pdf> accessed 2 February 2022.

2.3.2 Foreign Subsidies Regulation Proposal

Only a little more than a year after the adoption of the Screening Regulation, the Commission proposed an additional instrument to meet the EU and Member States concerns vis-à-vis foreign investors. On 17 June 2020 the Commission issued its 'White paper on levelling the playing field as regards foreign subsidies' ('White Paper'),[133] which led to the Foreign Subsidies Regulation Proposal. With the proposal, the Commission specifically addresses foreign subsidies. The Commission proposes three policy modules at EU-level, including an FDI screening mechanism on a competition-related screening ground that is much more targeted than the Screening Regulation's screening ground 'security or public order'.

The Foreign Subsidies Regulation Proposal departs from the notion of foreign subsidies, defined as:

> a financial contribution which confers a benefit to an undertaking engaging in an economic activity in the internal market and which is limited, in law or in fact, to an individual undertaking or industry or to several undertakings or industries.[134]

Accordingly, foreign subsidies may be paid to undertakings established in the EU within the meaning of Art 54(1) TFEU, or undertakings that are in other ways active in the EU, in particular by seeking to acquire an EU-established undertaking or participating in EU bidding processes.[135]

The Foreign Subsidies Regulation Proposal goes on to focus on the main competition concern: foreign subsidies that distort the internal market.[136] At the same time, the proposal allows distortive effects to be outbalanced by positive effects on the development of the relevant economic activity.[137] The White Paper illustratively described this balancing as the 'EU Interest test'. Based on this test, positive effects 'such as creating jobs, achieving climate neutrality and protecting the environment, digital transformation, security, public order and public safety and resilience' can be taken into account when deciding whether to adopt redressive measures.[138]

More concretely, the Foreign Subsidies Regulation Proposal consists of three modules to address possible market distortions by foreign subsidies.

The first module constitutes the core of the proposal. It generally allows the Commission to impose a variety of different redressive measures if in any market situation a foreign subsidy causes internal market distortions.[139] These measures may take various forms, including dissolving the concentration that was facilitated

---

[133] Commission, COM (2020) 253 final (n. 6).

[134] Commission, Foreign Subsidies Regulation Proposal (n. 111) art 2(1).

[135] ibid., art 1(2), sentence 2.

[136] For a definition of distortive foreign subsidies, see ibid., arts 3 and 4.

[137] ibid., art 5(1).

[138] Commission, COM (2020) 253 final (n. 6), p. 17.

[139] Commission, Foreign Subsidies Regulation Proposal (n. 111), art 6.

by the foreign subsidies (for example, the merger) or repaying the received subsidies.[140]

The second and third modules are based on this general provision but address particularly relevant market situations: 'concentrations' and public procurement processes. The second module is the most important in this book's context because it proposes a new FDI screening mechanism at EU level for (partial) acquisitions of EU targets that are facilitated by foreign subsidies.[141] In this regard, the Foreign Subsidies Regulation Proposal incorporates well-known notions from the Merger Regulation, in particular 'concentrations'.[142] Accordingly, it does not apply to FDI generally but only to FDI that gives 'decisive influence' over the target.[143] Such concentrations, if above certain thresholds of turnover or subsidy amounts, must be notified to the Commission,[144] who may then conduct an *ex ante* investigation, and either clear the FDI, possibly in conjunction with additional commitments, or prohibit it.[145]

The third and last module concerns public procurement. The authority procuring the contract at issue may exclude a bidder from the procurement process if it received a foreign subsidy that distorts the bidding process.[146]

In sum, the Foreign Subsidies Regulation Proposal proposes a bouquet of different policy measures beyond FDI screening to specifically meet the EU and Member States competition concern. At the same time, the proposal may also attenuate the reciprocity concern. Modules one to three may generally raise barriers for FDI, thereby increasing the EU's leverage in international negotiations for achieving better conditions for EU investors abroad.

Consequently, the Commission's proposal provides a promising alternative to the Screening Regulation's approach: legislative measures at EU level that more specifically address the concern at issue, including an FDI screening mechanism on a different, more specific screening ground than security, public order, or public policy.

Nevertheless, the Foreign Subsidies Regulation Proposal's adoption and its exact scope are still uncertain. Moreover, the Commission's proposal does not address the harmful investor and private information concern. Indeed, regarding these two concerns, it is much less likely that Member States will agree on the proposals' more harmonized approach. Due to the EU's long-existing exclusive competences in

---

[140]ibid., art 6(3)(g) and (h).

[141]ibid., pp. 22, 29.

[142]Council Regulation (EC) No 139/2004 of 20 January 2004 on the control of concentrations between undertakings (Merger Regulation) [2004] OJ L 24/1.

[143]For the definition of control and FDI in this context, see in particular Sect. 4.2.3.2.2 and Chap. 4, n. 147.

[144]Commission, Foreign Subsidies Regulation Proposal (n. 111) arts 19(1), 18(3). Thresholds are based on turnover or the financial contribution received from third countries.

[145]ibid., arts 23, 24(3).

[146]ibid., arts 26–32.

the realm of competition, Member States may be more inclined to accept a more harmonized approach on foreign subsidies than on the harmful investor and private information concerns.[147]

As a result, FDI screening mechanisms at Member State level circling around the notions of security or public order remain the standard approach to meet EU and Member States concerns vis-à-vis foreign investors.[148]

2.3.3 Fragmented FDI Screening Landscape in the EU with an Additional Security-Based Screening Ground: 'Security or Public Order'

The analysis of the Screening Regulation and the Foreign Subsidies Regulation Proposal thus allows three main conclusions for the legislative background of FDI screening in the EU. First, the Foreign Subsidies Regulation Proposal shows that FDI screening in the EU is still evolving, at least regarding the EU and Member States competition concern vis-à-vis foreign investors. Second, despite Commission efforts for harmonization, FDI screening in the EU largely remains the responsibility of the Member States, resulting in a fragmented FDI screening landscape. Third, the Screening Regulation added a new screening ground of 'security or public order' as a Member State legislative option for FDI screening mechanisms. This screening ground, however, seems similar to those already previously available: 'public policy or public security' within the meaning of Art 65(1)(b) TFEU, and 'essential security interests' pursuant to Art 346(1)(b) TFEU.

2.4 Defining FDI and FDI Screening Mechanism in Light of the Concerns Vis-à-Vis Foreign Investors

Before analyzing the EU's and Member States' flexibility to screen FDI on these screening grounds circling around the notions of security and public order in Chap. 3, Sect. 2.4 will define the key notions on which the legal analysis will be built: FDI and FDI screening mechanism. The definitions will go beyond those provided by the Screening Regulation. Accordingly, they seek to adopt the EU and Member States concerns vis-à-vis foreign investors to the largest extent possible. This lays the ground for Chap. 4, which will look beyond the Screening Regulation to assess the EU's and Member States' flexibility to adopt FDI Screening

---

[147] See Arts 101–109 TFEU, as well as e.g. Council Regulation (EC) No 139/2004 of 20 January 2004 on the control of concentrations between undertakings (Merger Regulation) [2004] OJ L 24/1.

[148] For a brief early analysis of the Commission's White paper on foreign subsidies and its implications for EU FDI screening and merger control, see Svetlicinii (2021).

mechanisms on broader than the already available screening grounds, such as 'security or public order'.

The first key notion of FDI screening in the EU is FDI itself. According to the harmful investor and private information concern, the EU and Member States are concerned that (1) a foreign investor gains (2) influence over a domestic target that allows her to shape the investment target's business decisions according to her harmful interests. These two aspects of concern are addressed by different elements in the notion of FDI. The first aspect, foreign investor, is incorporated in the element of 'foreign'. The element of 'direct', on the other hand, relates to the aspect of gaining influence over domestic assets. Accordingly, Sects. 2.4.1 and 2.4.2 will define these two different elements of FDI separately.

Section 2.4.3 will then identify six cornerstones to define an FDI Screening mechanism that adopts the EU and Member States concerns vis-à-vis foreign investors to the largest extent possible. Chapter 4 will then assess to what extent the EU and Member States have the flexibility to adopt a so designed FDI Screening mechanism pursuant to EU and International economic law.

2.4.1   *Foreign* **Direct** *Investment*

The first important notion of FDI screening in the EU is the notion of *direct* investment as in Foreign direct investment. This element of FDI refers to the level of control that the investor gains over the domestic asset.

Art 2(1) Screening Regulation defines FDI as:

> investment of any kind by a foreign investor *aiming to establish or to maintain lasting and direct links* between the foreign investor and the entrepreneur to whom or the undertaking to which the capital is made available in order to carry on an economic activity in a Member State, *including investments which enable effective participation in the management or control* of a company carrying out an economic activity.[149]

The last subordinate clause 'including ... effective participation in the management or control of a company' specifically addresses M&A FDI, the Screening Regulation's focus due to the EU and Member States harmful investor and private information concerns.

The Screening Regulation's definition reiterates well-established definitions of FDI that are relevant in the realm of FDI screening. First, in EU law the Capital Movement Directive provides the same definitory elements of 'lasting and direct links' and 'effective participation' in 'management or control'.[150] The Capital

---

[149] Emphasis added.

[150] Council Directive 88/361/EEC of 24 June 1988 for the implementation of Article 67 of the Treaty [on the former European Communities Treaty] (Capital Movement Directive) [1988] OJ L 178/5, Annex I, Explanatory notes: 'Investments of all kinds by natural persons or commercial, industrial or financial undertakings, and which serve to establish or to maintain lasting and direct

Movement Directive's definition is also valid for FDI as a capital movement within the meaning of the freedom of capital movement in Art 63(1) TFEU,[151] as well as for FDI as one area of the EU's exclusive competence on the Common commercial policy.[152] Second, some treaties in the realm of investment to which the EU is party provide similar definitions—namely, the OECD Code of Capital Movements.[153] FTAs concluded by the EU, however, often use the notion 'establishment' instead of FDI.[154] Third, the OECD and International Monetary Fund's ('IMF') definition of FDI is also very similar, except for the statistical threshold of 10% voting rights to establish an effective participation.[155]

Hence, many relevant sources of law and economics apply a definition that is similar to the Screening Regulation. The following will therefore adopt the Screening Regulation's definition of M&A Foreign *direct investment* as follows:

> Investment of any kind by an investor aiming to establish or to maintain lasting and direct links between the investor and the entrepreneur to whom or the undertaking to which the capital is made available (FDI target) by enabling effective participation in the management or control of the FDI target.

---

links between the person providing the capital and the entrepreneur to whom or the undertaking to which the capital is made available in order to carry on an economic activity.'

[151] The status of Capital Movement Directive (n. 150) as guidance for defining capital movement is settled case law, see Case C-446/04 *Test Claimants in the FII Group Litigation* [2006] EU:C:2006: 774, para. 179; Case C-560/13 *Wagner-Raith* [2015] EU:C:2015:347, para. 23. In literature see e.g. Smit (2012), pp. 61–62. Critical Herz (2014), pp. 281–287.

[152] Opinion 2/15 *EU-Singapore Free Trade Agreement* [2017] EU:C:2017:376, para. 80, in which the ECJ refers to judgments on the freedom of capital movement, which in turn cite the definition of FDI pursuant to the Capital Movement Directive (n. 150) Annex I. Most authors are in favour of such a consistent notion of FDI in the TFEU; see e.g. Puig (2013), p. 140; Hahn (2016), paras. 24–25; Nettesheim (2018), para. 21. Müller-Ibold (2013), para. 17, suggests an own FDI definition, which comes very close to the definition in the Capital Movement Directive. Cottier and Trinberg (2015), paras. 54–58, are referring to the Capital Movement Directive, while also demanding the investor to obtain ‚definite influence' on the FDI target. The notion 'definite influence' stems from ECJ case law to define the notion of establishment through investments within the meaning of Art 49 TFEU (see Sect. 4.2.3.2.2). Cottier's and Trinberg's proposal thus confuses the definition of FDI and establishment. Some authors question to define FDI in Art 207 TFEU as under the freedom of capital movement, see e.g. Herrmann (2010), p. 209; Weiß (2020), paras. 45–46. In another contribution Weiß even calls the definition of FDI under Art 207 TFEU particularly controversial, Weiß (2016), p. 537.

[153] OECD Code of Capital Movements, Annex A, List A sec I: 'Investment for the purpose of establishing lasting economic relations with an undertaking such as, in particular, investments which give the possibility of exercising an effective influence on the management thereof'.

[154] See e.g. Art 8.2.1(f) EU-Vietnam FTA ('with a view to establishing or maintaining lasting economic links'). In CETA the parties also refer to establishment, but omit a definition, see Arts 8.4–8.8 CETA.

[155] See Sect. 2.2.1.1.

2.4.2   Foreign *Direct Investment and* Foreign *Investor*

Having defined the element of direct in foreign direct investment, the discussion now turns to defining the other crucial FDI element: 'foreign'.

Defining when a Direct investment is foreign depends on the purpose of the definition. When seen from the perspective of an economy's balance of payments, the emphasis lies on the inflow of capital from another national economy. Accordingly, the OECD definition, for instance, refers to an investment 'by a resident enterprise in one economy ... in an enterprise ... that is resident in an[other] economy'.[156]

FDI screening and the EU and Member States concerns, however, focus on the foreignness of the investor, not the capital. At least the harmful investor and private information concern are about foreign investors who gain influence on a domestic asset. From this perspective, a Direct investment becomes foreign if it is undertaken by a foreign investor.[157] But what exactly makes an investor foreign? As FDI is rarely undertaken by individual natural persons, the following will focus on defining the foreignness of undertakings, whether they form a juridical person or are otherwise legally organized.[158]

The Screening Regulation chooses a formal, legalistic definition: the investor's place of legal organization. Art 2(1) Screening Regulation first defines FDI as Direct investment by a foreign investor.[159] Art 2(2) Screening Regulation then defines foreign investor as 'a natural person of a third country or an undertaking of a third country, intending to make or having made a foreign direct investment'. Art 2 (7) Screening Regulation adds that '"undertaking of a third country" means an undertaking constituted or otherwise organised [*sic*] under the laws of a third country'. Hence, the Screening Regulation defines the foreignness of an investor according to the place of his legal organization (legal organization option).[160]

---

[156]OECD, 'Benchmark Definition of Foreign Direct Investment' (n. 48), para. 117.

[157]Accordingly, the definition of FDI in the Capital Movement Directive (n. 150), Annex I, Explanatory notes, and in the OECD Code of Capital Movements omit any references to the foreignness of FDI, see full definitions in n. 150, 153.

[158]Accordingly, the Screening Regulation omitted a definition of a foreign investor who is a natural person. The foreignness of a natural person is usually defined by the fact that the person does not possess a citizenship of the country at issue, here of a Member State.

[159]Art 2(1) Screening Regulation: '"foreign direct investment" means an investment of any kind *by a foreign investor* aiming to establish or to maintain lasting and direct links *between the foreign investor* and the entrepreneur to whom or the undertaking to which the capital is made available'.

[160]The German FDI screening mechanism pursuant to German Foreign Trade and Payments Ordinance (n. 129), ss 55–59, still applies a different, but not less formal definition. It defines a foreign investor as an investor who is 'foreign to the Union' ('*Unionsfremder*'). German Foreign Trade and Payments Act (n. 128) s 2(19), (18), defines a juridical person who is foreign to the Union as a non-EU established juridical person, meaning a person with neither a registered office, nor central administration in the EU.

However, there are alternatives to define the foreignness of an investor. On the one hand, the investor may be defined as foreign depending on its place of registered office, central administration, or principal place of business (together establishment option).[161] On the other hand, the investor's foreignness may be determined by the citizenship of those who (ultimately) control him (control option). Every option addresses a specific risk scenario that is in different ways relevant to the EU and Member States concerns vis-à-vis foreign investors.

The establishment option addresses the risk scenario that the foreign investor may be influenced by her home country government. The state in which a company has its registered office, central administration, or principal place of business has the possibility to impose laws or regulations, as well as to provide public funding. The same is valid for the legal organization option applied by the Screening Regulation. If a company is organized under the laws of a third country, the company is subject to this country's laws, and thus influence. Both options therefore address three concerns. First, state funding may result in distortions of competition (competition concern). Second, the company's home country can use policy measures such as laws and funding to try to align the company's business decisions with its interests when undertaking and operating an FDI. These interests may be contrary to commercial considerations and the EU and Member States interests (harmful investor concern). Third, as a result of the FDI, private information of EU citizens may get processed by the investor's IT systems, and therefore become subject to weaker private information protection laws of the country in which the investor is 'established' (private information concern).

In addition, the establishment option of principal place of business further addresses the risk scenario of know-how transfer. Only if the investor has another place of business outside of the EU, will she be able to transfer know-how outside of the EU's and into another country's reach.

The control option addresses company constructions that consist of multiple layers of subsidiaries. The option may be applied in two ways. A simpler control option is to look only at the next layer behind the investor.[162] If the investor is controlled by an undertaking, not a natural person, the undertaking's foreignness must be defined in accordance with one of the above-analyzed options. A more complex control option moves further up the control chain, if necessary, until the ultimate controlling individual. Generally, the second, more complex option is only rarely used.[163] Nevertheless, this complex control option addresses the risk scenario

---

[161] These three alternative criteria also define an EU company within the meaning of the freedom of establishment (Arts 49(1), 54(1) TFEU).

[162] See second element of the definition of 'juridical person of another Member' in Art XXVIII(m)(ii), (n) GATS; similarly, Art 8.1 CETA.

[163] See e.g. Regulation (EC) No 1008/2008 of the European Parliament and of the Council of 24 September 2008 on common rules for the operation of air services in the Community (Recast) [2008] OJ L 293/3, arts 4(f), 2(9); Directive 2009/73/EC of the European Parliament and of the Council of 13 July 2009 concerning common rules for the internal market in natural gas and repealing Directive 2003/55/EC [2009] OJ L 211/94, arts 11(1)–(3), 2(36).

that the investor disguises foreign and foreign public ownership. Foreign State influence through public ownership can only be reliably unveiled by assessing the ultimate controlling actor behind an investor.

Consequently, the legal organization, establishment, and control options for defining the foreignness of an investor for FDI screening address different risk scenarios that are all relevant to the EU and Member States concerns vis-à-vis foreign investors. For analyzing the EU and Member States concerns vis-à-vis foreign investors, it is therefore best to define foreign investors in the realm of FDI screening by an alternative combination of all options. Accordingly, Foreign direct investment is defined as follows:

> *Foreign* direct investment is a direct investment by an investor who:
>
> (i)   is constituted or otherwise organized under the laws of a third country;
> (ii) has its registered office, central administration, or principal place of business in a third country; or
> (iii) is ultimately controlled by at least one person of a third country.[164]

For defining the notion control in subparagraph (iii), indicative value may be drawn from Directive 2009/73/EC, Art 2(36). In order to prevent the EU's energy security from any potential harm due to the investor's interest, the directive sets out an authorization requirement for gas transmission system operators who are 'controlled' by a person or persons from third countries. This rationale may well be transposed to the FDI screening context. Therefore:

> '[C]ontrol' means any rights, contracts or any other means which, either separately or in combination and having regard to the considerations of fact or law involved, confer the possibility of exercising decisive influence on an undertaking, in particular by
>
> (a) ownership or the right to use all or part of the assets of an undertaking; or
> (b) rights or contracts which confer decisive influence on the composition, voting or decisions of the organs of an undertaking.

This definition of foreign investors, based on the three options legal organization, establishment, and control, takes the EU and Member States concerns vis-à-vis foreign investors fully into account.

Moreover, the definition includes the two scenarios of how FDI is typically legally organized. In the first scenario the FDI is undertaken by an entity that was formed in accordance with the law of a third country, has its registered seat and central administration in a third country, and has no substantial business activities in the EU (Scenario 1). Accordingly, the investor qualifies as foreign by applying the legal organization or establishment option. In the second scenario, the FDI is undertaken by a company that was founded with the single purpose to undertake one specific FDI, without any prior business activity in the EU (special purpose vehicle, in the following 'SPV'). To facilitate the FDI as much as possible, the SPV

---

[164] It is another question whether from a lawmaker's perspective such a multi-layered, complex definition of the element of foreign in Foreign direct investment is appropriate when taking into account the costs of administering FDI screening mechanisms.

will usually be formed in accordance with the law of a Member State and its registered seat and central administration in the EU ('EU SPV'). However, it will be controlled by a person of a third country. This second scenario is thus (only) included by the definition based on the control option (Scenario 2). In both scenarios, a foreign State may itself be the investor or stand behind the investor.

It is important to note that the so defined notion of foreignness differs from other definitions in EU primary law and International economic law. This will become crucial when assessing the EU's and Member States' flexibility to adopt FDI screening mechanisms pursuant to EU primary law in Sect. 4.2.

2.4.3   FDI Screening Mechanism

The last key notion is FDI screening mechanism. Slightly amending the definition of 'screening mechanism' in Art 2(4) Screening Regulation one may generally define FDI screening mechanism as:

> an instrument of general application, such as a law or regulation, and accompanying administrative requirements, implementing rules or guidelines, setting out the terms, conditions and procedures to assess, investigate, authorise, condition, prohibit, or unwind foreign direct investments on certain screening grounds and criteria.[165]

This definition shows that an FDI screening mechanism consists of different cornerstones: personal and substantial scope, screening ground and criteria, and procedural design. These cornerstones determine whether an FDI screening mechanism may meet the EU and Member States concerns vis-à-vis foreign investors.

The following will define these cornerstones in light of the EU and Member States concerns vis-à-vis foreign investors. As a point of departure, these definitions ignore political, administrative, and legal limits. Accordingly, the definitions reach beyond the Screening Regulation. These definitions thus show namely how the EU and Member States may design FDI screening mechanisms beyond security-related screening grounds. This will set the basis for analyzing the EU's and Member States' flexibility to adopt such broader mechanisms in Chap. 4 pursuant to EU primary law and International economic law.

The first and second cornerstones of FDI screening mechanisms is their personal and substantial scope. As shown in Sect. 2.4.2, both are deeply intertwined as the notion *Foreign* direct investment depends on the definition of foreign investor. The EU and Member States concerns show that an FDI screening mechanism will only apply to foreign investors. An FDI screening mechanism will thus apply to FDI as defined in Sects. 2.4.1 and 2.4.2. In accordance with the EU and Member States

---

[165] Art 2(4) Screening Regulation: 'an instrument of general application, such as a law or regulation, and accompanying administrative requirements, implementing rules or guidelines, setting out the terms, conditions and procedures to assess, investigate, authorise, condition, prohibit or unwind foreign direct investments on grounds of security or public order'.

concerns vis-à-vis foreign investors, the notion of foreign investors should be very broad, inter alia encompassing foreign-controlled investors. Indeed, such a definition will cause higher administrative costs due to investigations into the persons that ultimately control the investor.

The substantial scope may further be narrowed in light of the EU and Member States concerns. They focus on M&A FDI. In particular, the harmful investor and private information concerns are about protecting existing domestic assets, and thus about these assets becoming influenced by foreign investors. Such restriction to FDI seems even reasonable for the competition concerns that in theory also arises following greenfield investments. The Foreign Subsidies Regulation Proposal, which specifically addresses the competition concern, also limits the proposed screening mechanism to M&A investments.

From a practical perspective, it may seem appropriate to further refine the general FDI definition by determining a numerical threshold for the notion of 'effective participation in the management or control of the FDI target'. Such level of control, however, depends on many circumstances of the case, such as statutory or contractual veto or board member nomination rights. Therefore, a numerical threshold would miss its purpose as a reliable proxy for the abstract notion 'effective participation'.

The third cornerstone is the screening ground. FDI screening mechanisms will intend to meet the EU and Member States concerns vis-à-vis foreign investors: competition, reciprocity, harmful investor, and private information concern. They will therefore design the FDI screening ground accordingly.

The fourth cornerstone describes more concrete screening criteria. An FDI screening mechanism will take the possible influence of foreign governments into account when assessing whether an FDI raises concern. This rationale explains two differentiations that FDI screening mechanisms may be making. On the one hand, the FDI screening mechanism may assume that an FDI poses a higher risk if the investor is a publicly owned or controlled company, often approximated with the— narrower—notion of SOEs. These publicly influenced companies are evidently more susceptible to the influence of their government. On the other hand, FDI screening mechanisms may focus on countries whose governments are perceived to exert more influence on business decisions, or to generally have low levels of private information or intellectual property rights protection. Thus, countries like China, Russia, and the United Arab Emirates come into focus.[166] This differentiation may manifest itself in more screening of FDI from these countries than FDI from other countries— for example, authorities could more often open an in-depth investigation, or more often prohibit investments from these countries.[167] In order to avoid *de jure* third

---

[166] See Sects. 2.1.1, 2.1.3 and 2.1.4.

[167] For the typical stages of FDI Screening mechanisms, see sixth cornerstone below.

country discrimination, it is unlikely that the personal scope of FDI screening mechanisms will be limited to these countries.[168]

The last cornerstones five and six describe the procedural design of the screening mechanisms.

The fifth cornerstone of FDI screening mechanisms in the EU describes the consequence of an FDI ban as a rule or an exception. On the one hand, the mechanism may generally ban incoming FDI with the possibility to authorize a specific FDI in an individual administrative decision (*Erlaubnisvorbehalt*) ('Case 1'). On the other hand, the mechanism may generally authorize incoming FDI with the possibility for the government to prohibit an individual investment (*Verbotsvorbehalt*) ('Case 2'). In Case 2, the government may open a screening process at any time within a certain period after the investment or its—mandatory or voluntary—notification. Legally, this uncertainty will manifest in a statutory condition precedent to the contract between investor and asset.[169] Otherwise, it is too difficult to unwind the investment. Disinvestment is highly complex, requires an alternative investor that acquires the foreign investor's shares, and may thus also severely harm the domestic FDI asset. Both Cases 1 and 2 seem reasonable alternatives to design FDI screening mechanisms in accordance with the EU and Member States concerns vis-à-vis foreign investors. The Screening Regulation omits to address this issue.[170] The following will define FDI screening mechanisms as comprising both Cases 1 and 2.

The sixth and second procedural cornerstone is the procedure of screening itself. While every mechanism will differ in details, four common steps can be identified: a preliminary assessment of the investment, a second in-depth investigation, possible negotiations and conditions to remedy risks, and, finally, the decision of prohibition or clearance. The process may end after any of these steps.[171]

FDI screening mechanisms based on these six cornerstones capture the EU and Member States concerns vis-à-vis foreign investors. When the following refers to 'FDI Screening mechanisms', reference is made to FDI screening mechanisms that incorporate these six characteristics. Chapter 3 will focus on the third cornerstone, the screening ground, and assess whether the EU and Member States may meet their concerns vis-à-vis foreign investors with an FDI Screening mechanism on the screening grounds of 'security or public order' and 'public policy or public security'. Chapter 4 will then assess the EU's and Member States' flexibility to adopt FDI Screening mechanisms on broader grounds than 'security or public order'. To this

---

[168] See Art 3(2) Screening Regulation, which requires Member States not to discriminate between third countries.

[169] See for example in German Foreign Trade and Payments Act (n. 128) s 15(2). The Screening Regulation is silent on this procedural aspect of FDI screening.

[170] In the Foreign Subsidies Regulation Proposal, the Commission proposes a Case 2 FDI screening mechanism with a compulsory notification requirement in case the received subsidies exceed a certain threshold, see Sect. 2.3.2.

[171] For a similar procedure see Commission, Foreign Subsidies Regulation Proposal (n. 111), art 24(3).

end, Chap. 4 will take into account all of the above FDI Screening mechanism cornerstones. Different personal and substantial scopes come with different flexibility to define the screening ground.

2.5 FDI Screening Mechanisms as a Reflection of the Political, Economic, and Legislative Background

In sum, the political, economic, and legislative background paint a fragmented, complex picture of FDI screening in the EU. The EU and many Member States have chosen FDI screening as one means to meet the increasing concerns vis-à-vis foreign investors. These concerns may be categorized in four groups: competition, reciprocity, harmful investor, and private information concerns. The four concerns are not limited to, but often particularly strong vis-à-vis investors from certain countries, especially China, but also Russia, United Arab Emirates, Brazil, and India. Inter alia, competition and private information laws accord less protection compared to EU laws, and governments in these countries are found to exert more influence on business decisions, thereby amplifying the competition, harmful investor, and private information concern.

Economically, the EU and Member States concerns vis-à-vis foreign investors are limited to M&A FDI with a particular focus on technology- and knowledge-seeking FDI from developing countries. This excludes other forms of FDI—namely, portfolio investments, greenfield FDI, and other forms of M&A FDI that potentially are also or even more beneficial to the EU's economy. For the specific categories of M&A FDI in focus the effects on economic effects in the EU are mixed. One can thus not argue that they are always beneficial to the EU's economy. This argument will gain importance when assessing the protection of FDI by the freedoms of capital movement and establishment.

Against the political and economic background, the EU and Member States finally decided to take a stricter stance on FDI—at EU level. Adopting the Screening Regulation was one legislative step in this direction, the Commission's Foreign Subsidies Regulation Proposal may pave the way for a second step. Nevertheless, even with the Screening Regulation FDI screening in the EU largely remains the responsibility of the Member States, thereby perpetuating a fragmented FDI screening landscape. The Screening Regulation proposes an FDI screening mechanism at Member State level on the screening grounds of 'security or public order' in accordance with some formal and substantial cornerstones. However, Member States are still free not to adopt any FDI Screening mechanism, and there remains a considerable number of Member States that takes this approach. One reason may be that they consider the potential economic advantages of FDI more important than their concerns vis-à-vis foreign investors. The two other options are an FDI Screening mechanism on the grounds of 'public policy or public security' within the meaning of Art 65(1)(b) TFEU, or based on 'essential security interests' pursuant to Art 346(1)(b) TFEU.

As a result, if the Member States want to meet their concerns vis-à-vis foreign investors by adopting and operating FDI Screening mechanisms, they are limited to screening grounds circling around the notions of security and public order.

Hence, the political, economic, and legislative background of FDI screening in the EU lets emerge two fundamental questions. First, do FDI Screening mechanisms on screening grounds circling around the notions of security and public order allow the EU and Member States to meet their concerns vis-à-vis foreign investors? Second, if not, do EU and Member States have the flexibility to adopt FDI Screening mechanisms on broader grounds that would (better) allow them to meet their concerns vis-à-vis foreign investors?

In particular, to answer the second question, the key notions of FDI and FDI Screening mechanism must be defined in a way that reflects the outlined political, economic, and legislative background.

FDI is:

1. an investment of any kind by an investor aiming to establish or to maintain lasting and direct links between the investor and the entrepreneur to whom or the undertaking to which the capital is made available (FDI target) by enabling effective participation in the management or control of the FDI target; and
2. an investment by an investor who:

   (a) is constituted or otherwise organized under the laws of a third country;
   (b) has its registered office, central administration, or principal place of business in a third country; or
   (c) is ultimately controlled by at least one citizen of a third country.[172]

FDI Screening mechanism consists of six cornerstones. First and second, FDI Screening mechanisms only apply to M&A FDI of foreign investors as defined above. Second, they intend to meet the EU and Member States concerns vis-à-vis foreign investors, and thus define their screening ground accordingly. Fourth, FDI Screening mechanisms will take the possible influence of foreign governments into account when assessing whether an FDI raises concern. This may result in a non-explicit focus on certain third countries. Fifth, FDI Screening mechanisms may operate with either a general ban for incoming FDI with the possibility to exceptionally authorize a specific FDI, or a general authorization of incoming FDI with the possibility to exceptionally prohibit the FDI. Sixth, FDI Screening mechanisms operate on four common steps: a preliminary assessment of the investment, a

---

[172] "'[C]ontrol" means any rights, contracts or any other means which, either separately or in combination and having regard to the considerations of fact or law involved, confer the possibility of exercising decisive influence on an undertaking, in particular by (a) ownership or the right to use all or part of the assets of an undertaking; or (b) rights or contracts which confer decisive influence on the composition, voting or decisions of the organs of an undertaking.'

second in-depth investigation, possible negotiations and conditions to remedy risks, and, finally, the decision of prohibition or clearance.

With these definitions of FDI and FDI Screening mechanism in mind, the discussion can now turn to answering the two fundamental questions of FDI screening in the EU on the reach of FDI Screening mechanisms on screening grounds circling around the notions of security and public order, and the EU's and Member States' flexibility to adopt FDI Screening mechanisms on broader grounds.

References

Aharoni Y (2010) Reflections on multinationals in a globally interdependent world economy. In: Sauvant KP, McAllister G, Maschek WA (eds) Foreign direct investments from emerging markets: the challenges ahead. Palgrave Macmillan, New York, pp 37–60

Alfaro L (2017) Gains from Foreign Direct Investment: macro and micro approaches: World Bank's ABCDE conference. World Bank Econ Rev 30(Suppl 1):S2–S15. https://doi.org/10.1093/wber/lhw007

Barba Navaretti G, Venables A (2004) Multinational firms in the world economy. Princeton University Press, Princeton

Bismuth R (2020) Reading between the lines of the EU regulation establishing a framework for screening FDI into the Union. In: Bourgeois JHJ (ed) EU framework for foreign direct investment control. Kluwer Law International, Alphen aan den Rijn, pp 103–114

Bourgeois JHJ, Malathouni E (2020) The EU regulation on screening foreign direct investment: another piece of the puzzle. In: Bourgeois JHJ (ed) EU framework for foreign direct investment control. Kluwer Law International, Alphen aan den Rijn, pp 169–191

Brakman S, Garretsen H (2008) Foreign direct investment and the multinational enterprise: an introduction. In: Brakman S, Garretsen H (eds) Foreign direct investment and the multinational enterprise. MIT Press, Cambridge, pp 1–9

Broadman HG (2010) Multinational enterprises from emerging markets: implications for the north and the south. In: Sauvant KP, McAllister G, Maschek WA (eds) Foreign direct investments from emerging markets: the challenges ahead. Palgrave Macmillan, New York, pp 325–331

Buckley PJ, Clegg LJ, Voss H, Cross AR, Liu X, Zheng P (2018) A retrospective and agenda for future research on Chinese outward foreign direct investment. J Int Bus Stud 49:4–23. https://doi.org/10.1057/s41267-017-0129-1

Cantwell J (1994) The relationship between international trade and international production. In: Greenaway D, Winters LA (eds) Surveys in international trade. Wiley-Blackwell, Oxford, pp 303–328

Collins D (2017) An introduction to international investment law. Cambridge University Press, Cambridge

Cottier T, Trinberg L (2015) Art 207 AEUV. In: von der Groeben H, Schwarze J, Hatje A (eds) Europäisches Unionsrecht: Vertrag über die Europäische Union - Vertrag über die Arbeitsweise der Europäischen Union - Charta der Grundrechte der Europäischen Union, 7th edn. Nomos, Baden-Baden

Dunning JH (1977) Trade, location of economic activity and the MNE: a search for an eclectic approach. In: Ohlin BG, Hesselborn P-O, Wijkman PM (eds) The international allocation of economic activity: proceedings of a Nobel symposium held at Stockholm. Macmillan, London, pp 395–418

Dunning JH, Lundan SM (2008) Multinational enterprises and the global economy, 2nd edn. Elgar, Cheltenham

Eden L (2003) A critical reflection and some conclusions on OLI. In: Cantwell J, Narula R (eds) International business and the eclectic paradigm: developing the OLI framework. Routledge, London, pp 277–297

France, Germany, Italy (2017a) Proposals for ensuring an improved level playing field in trade and investment. Paris, Berlin, Rome

France, Germany, Italy (2017b) European investment policy: a common approach to investment control. Paris, Berlin, Rome

Geiger F (2013) Beschränkungen von Direktinvestitionen aus Drittstaaten. Nomos, Baden-Baden

Globerman S, Shapiro DM (2009) Modes of entry by Chinese firms in the United States: economic and political issues. In: Sauvant KP (ed) Investing in the United States: is the US ready for FDI from China? Elgar, Cheltenham, pp 22–44

Hahn M (2016) Art 207 AEUV. In: Calliess C, Ruffert M (eds) EUV/AEUV: Das Verfassungsrecht der Europäischen Union mit Europäischer Grundrechtecharta, 5th edn. CH Beck, Munich

Heiduk G, Kerlen-Prinz J (1999) Direktinvestitionen in der Außenwirtschaftstheorie. In: Döhrn R, Heiduk G (eds) Theorie und Empirie der Direktinvestitionen. Duncker & Humblot, Berlin, pp 23–54

Herrmann C (2010) Die Zukunft der mitgliedstaatlichen Investitionspolitik nach dem Vertrag von Lissabon. EuZW:207–212

Herz B (2014) Unternehmenstransaktionen zwischen Niederlassungs- und Kapitalverkehrsfreiheit: Grundlegung einer Abgrenzungslehre. Nomos, Baden-Baden

Hindelang S (2009) The free movement of capital and foreign direct investment: the scope of protection in EU law. Oxford University Press, Oxford

Hofmann P (2013) The impact of international trade and FDI on economic growth and technological change. Springer, Berlin

Javorcik BS (2008) Can survey evidence shed light on spillovers from foreign direct investment? World Bank Res Obs 23:139–159. https://doi.org/10.1093/wbro/lkn006

Kalotay K, Hunya G (2000) Privatization and FDI in Central and Eastern Europe. Transl Corp 9: 39–66

Kerner A (2014) What we talk about when we talk about foreign direct investment. Int Stud Q 58: 804–815. https://doi.org/10.1111/isqu.12147

Kindleberger CP (1970) American business abroad: six lectures on direct investment, 2nd edn. Yale University Press, New Haven

Krugman PR, Obstfeld M, Melitz MJ (2017) International economics: theory & policy. Pearson, Harlow

Lippert B, von Ondarza N, Perthes V (2019) European strategic autonomy: actors, issues, conflicts of interests. SWP research paper 4. https://www.swp-berlin.org/fileadmin/contents/products/research_papers/2019RP04_lpt_orz_prt_web.pdf. Accessed 2 Feb 2022

Lipsey RE (2004) Home- and host-country effects of foreign direct investment. In: Baldwin RE, Winters LA (eds) Challenges to globalization: analyzing the economics. University of Chicago Press, Chicago, pp 333–382

Lübke J (2006) Der Erwerb von Gesellschaftsanteilen zwischen Kapitalverkehrs- und Niederlassungsfreiheit. Nomos, Baden-Baden

Lv P, Spigarelli F (2015) The integration of Chinese and European renewable energy markets: the role of Chinese foreign direct investments. Energy Policy 81:14–26. https://doi.org/10.1016/j.enpol.2015.01.042

Martini M (2008) Zu Gast bei Freunden?: Staatsfonds als Herausforderung an das europäische und internationale Recht. DÖV:314–322

Martin-Prat M (2020) The European Commission proposal on FDI screening. In: Bourgeois JHJ (ed) EU framework for foreign direct investment control. Kluwer Law International, Alphen aan den Rijn, pp 95–98

Matthes J (2017) Unternehmensübernahmen durch chinesische Firmen in Deutschland und Europa: Unter welchen Bedingungen besteht Handlungsbedarf?. IW-Report 30/2016. Institut der deutschen Wirtschaft, Köln

Miroudot S, Ragoussis A (2013) Actors in the international investment scenario: objectives, performance and advantages of affiliates of state-owned enterprises and sovereign wealth funds. In: Echandi R, Sauvé P (eds) Prospects in International Investment Law and Policy: World Trade Forum. Cambridge University Press, Cambridge, pp 51–72

Moberg A, Hindelang S (2020) The art of casting political dissent in law: the EU's framework for the screening of foreign direct investment. Common Mark Law Rev 57:1427–1460

Moran TH (2006) Harnessing foreign direct investment for development: policies for developed and developing countries. Center for Global Development, Washington, DC

Moran TH, Graham EM, Blomström M (2005) Introduction and overview. In: Moran TH, Graham EM, Blomström M (eds) Does foreign direct investment promote development? Institute for International Economics, Washington, DC, pp 1–19

Müller-Ibold T (2013) Vorb Art 206–208 AEUV. In: Lenz CO, Borchardt K-D (eds) EU-Verträge Kommentar: EUV – AEUV – GRCh, 6th edn. Bundesanzeiger Verlag, Cologne

Neergaard A (2020) The adoption of the regulation establishing a framework for screening of foreign direct investments into the European Union. In: Bourgeois JHJ (ed) EU framework for foreign direct investment control. Kluwer Law International, Alphen aan den Rijn, pp 151–167

Nettesheim M (2018) Art 207 AEUV. In: Streinz R (ed) EUV/AEUV: Vertrag über die Europäische Union und Vertrag über die Arbeitsweise der Europäischen Union, 3rd edn. CH Beck, Munich

Perea JR, Stephenson M (2017) Outward FDI from developing countries. In: World Bank Group (ed) Global Investment Competitiveness Report 2017/2018: foreign investor perspectives and policy implications. World Bank Group, Washington, DC, pp 101–134

Perlmutter HV (1969) The tortuous evolution of the multinational corporation. Columbia J World Bus 4:9–18

Pohl J (2020) Emergency, security and strategic autonomy in EU economic regulation. ERA Forum 21:143–154

Preisser MM (2013) Sovereign wealth funds: Entwicklung eines umfassenden Konzepts für die Regulierung von Staatsfonds. Mohr Siebeck, Tübingen

Puig RV (2013) The scope of the new exclusive competence of the European Union with regard to 'Foreign Direct Investment'. Leg Issues Econ Integr 40:133–162

Puttler A (2016) Art 4 EUV. In: Calliess C, Ruffert M (eds) EUV/AEUV: Das Verfassungsrecht der Europäischen Union mit Europäischer Grundrechtecharta, 5th edn. CH Beck, Munich

Roberts A, Choer Moraes H, Ferguson V (2019) Toward a geoeconomic order in international trade and investment. J Int Econ Law 22:655–676. https://doi.org/10.1093/jiel/jgz036

Rodrik D (1999) The new global economy and developing countries: making openness work. Johns Hopkins University Press, Baltimore

Rugman AM (2010) The theory and regulation of emerging market multinational enterprises. In: Sauvant KP, McAllister G, Maschek WA (eds) Foreign direct investments from emerging markets: the challenges ahead. Palgrave Macmillan, New York, pp 75–87

Sasse JP (2011) An economic analysis of bilateral investment treaties. Gabler Verlag, Wiesbaden

Sauvant KP, Maschek WA, McAllister G (2010) Foreign direct investment by emerging market multinational enterprises, the impact of the financial crisis and recession, and challenges abroad. In: Sauvant KP, McAllister G, Maschek WA (eds) Foreign direct investments from emerging markets: the challenges ahead. Palgrave Macmillan, New York, pp 3–29

Schill SW, Krenn C (2020) Art 4 EUV. In: Grabitz E, Hilf M, Nettesheim M (eds) Das Recht der Europäischen Union: EUV/AEUV, 71st edn. CH Beck, Munich

Smit D (2012) EU Freedoms. Non-EU countries and company taxation, Kluwer Law International, Alphen aan den Rijn

Sornarajah M (2017) The international law on foreign investment, 4th edn. Cambridge University Press, Cambridge

Svetlicinii A (2021) Chinese state owned enterprises and EU merger control. Routledge, Milton

Trebilcock MJ (2015) Advanced introduction to international trade law. Elgar, Cheltenham

van Aaken A (2011) Opportunities for and limits to an economic analysis of international law. Transl Corp Rev 3:27–46. https://doi.org/10.1080/19186444.2011.11658271

Velten J (2020a) The investment screening regulation and its screening ground 'Security or Public Order'. CTEI Working Paper Series. https://repository.graduateinstitute.ch/record/298429. Accessed 2 Feb 2022

Velten J (2020b) FDI screening regulation and the recent EU guidance: what options do Member States have? Columbia FDI Perspective 284. http://ccsi.columbia.edu/publications/columbia-fdi-perspectives/. Accessed 2 Feb 2022

Weiß W (2016) Kompetenzverteilung bei gemischten Abkommen am Beispiel des TTIP. DÖV:537–548

Weiß W (2020) Art 207 AEUV. In: Grabitz E, Hilf M, Nettesheim M (eds) Das Recht der Europäischen Union: EUV/AEUV, 71st edn. CH Beck, Munich

Weller M-P (2008) Ausländische Staatsfonds zwischen Fusionskontrolle, Außenwirtschaftsrecht und Grundfreiheiten. ZIP:857–865

Williamson J (1990) What Washington means by policy reform. In: Williamson J (ed) Latin American adjustment: how much has happened? Institute for International Economics, Washington, DC, p 5

Williamson J (2004–2005) The strange history of the Washington Consensus. J Post Keynesian Econ 27:195–206

Wübbeke J et al (2016) Made in China 2025: the making of a high-tech superpower and the consequences for industrial countries. MERICS Papers on China 2. https://merics.org/de/studie/made-china-2025-0. Accessed 2 Feb 2022

Zwartkruis W, de Jong B (2020) The EU regulation on screening of foreign direct investment: a game changer? Eur Bus Law Rev 31:447–474

Chapter 3
FDI Screening Mechanisms on the Grounds of 'Security or Public Order' and 'Public Policy or Public Security'

EU and Member States concerns vis-à-vis foreign investors are manifold: competition, reciprocity, harmful investors, private information. FDI screening has been identified as one means to meet these concerns. However, FDI screening in the EU still circles around the notions of security and public order.

The Screening Regulation made clear that Member States have three options if they want to adopt an FDI Screening mechanism. First, they may, and according to the Commission should,[1] adopt FDI Screening mechanisms on the grounds of 'security or public order' in accordance with the formal and substantial cornerstones provided by the Screening Regulation. Second, the Member States may base their FDI Screening mechanism on the ground of exception 'public policy or public security' that the freedom of capital movement provides to Member States in Art 65(1)(b) TFEU. Third, Member States may revert to the general exception to their EU Treaties obligations, 'essential security interests' pursuant to Art 346(1)(b) TFEU.

Hence, the EU's and Member States' current legislative options to meet their concerns vis-à-vis foreign investors through FDI Screening mechanisms are limited to these three screening grounds. Do FDI Screening mechanisms on these grounds allow Member States to meet the EU and Member States concerns vis-à-vis foreign investors?

An FDI Screening mechanism on the grounds of 'essential security interests' pursuant to Art 346(1)(b) TFEU can clearly only meet these concerns to a very small

---

[1] Commission, 'Guidance to the Member States concerning Foreign Direct Investment and Free Movement of Capital from Third Countries, and the Protection of Europe's Strategic Assets, ahead of the Application of Regulation (EU) 2019/452 (FDI Screening Regulation)' (Communication) COM (2020) 1981 final, 2, Annex, p. 1.

© The Author(s), under exclusive license to Springer Nature Switzerland AG 2022   57
J. Velten, *Screening Foreign Direct Investment in the EU*, EYIEL Monographs -
Studies in European and International Economic Law 26,
https://doi.org/10.1007/978-3-031-05603-1_3

extent. Art 346(1)(b) TFEU is a narrow exception that allows Member States to pursue military interests.[2] Accordingly, FDI Screening mechanisms on the grounds of 'essential security interests' may only allow Member States to meet their harmful investor concern to the extent it plays in the defence sector. Such FDI Screening mechanisms can therefore not meet EU and Member States other concerns vis-à-vis foreign investors.

Therefore, the following focuses on analyzing the scope of the first and second option: FDI Screening mechanisms on the screening grounds 'security or public order' and 'public policy or public security'. Each section will generally define both notions. Next, the abstract definition will be applied to the EU and Member States concerns vis-à-vis foreign investors to assess whether both screening grounds allow the EU and Member States to meet these concerns.

3.1 FDI Screening Mechanisms Based on the Screening Regulation's Notion 'Security or Public Order': An Interpretation in Accordance with the GATS

The Screening Regulation creates a new screening ground: 'security or public order'. In order to assess the scope of the screening ground regarding the EU and Member States concerns vis-à-vis foreign investors, this section will define both of its elements: security and public order.

Section 3.1.1 will interpret the Screening Regulation to argue that this notion is neither a distinct notion of secondary law, nor a mere variation of the TFEU exception 'public policy or public security'. Instead, it references and thus is defined by the notions of 'essential security interests' and 'public order' within the meaning of Arts XIV*bis*(1)(b) and XIV(a) GATS. After some general remarks in Sect. 3.1.2 on interpreting the GATS generally, and the notions of 'essential security interests' and 'public order' more specifically, Sects. 3.1.3 and 3.1.4 will define these screening grounds. They will then apply the definitions to the EU and Member States concerns vis-à-vis foreign investors to determine to what extent the concerns are covered by an FDI Screening mechanism on the screening ground 'security or public order'.[3] Section 3.1.5 will summarize the results.

---

[2]Wegener (2016b), para. 2; Korte (2019), p. 88; Jaeckel (2020), para. 3.

[3]Section 3.1 was in parts pre-published as Velten (2020).

3.1.1 Interpreting 'Security or Public Order' in Accordance with the GATS

The EU can define a legal notion as it deems appropriate for the pursued legislative purpose. As a rule, a notion's meaning in one legal source must not be identical to the notion's meaning in other legal sources; even if identically or similarly drafted, and even if provided in closely related legal contexts. Literal meaning of 'security or public order', the Screening Regulation's recitals, and its context nevertheless show that the notion 'security or public order' must be interpreted in accordance with Arts XIV(a) and XIV*bis*(1)(b) GATS.

The Screening Regulation's recitals strongly weigh against 'security or public order' as a distinct notion of secondary law. In Recital (3) the Screening Regulation mentions the screening ground 'security or public order' for the first time, and for its definition refers to International economic law:

> Pursuant to the international commitments undertaken in the World Trade Organization (WTO), in the Organisation for Economic Cooperation and Development, and in the trade and investment agreements concluded with third countries, it is possible for the Union and the Members States to adopt restrictive measures relating to foreign direct investment *on the grounds of security or public order*, subject to certain requirements.[4]

Recital (35) more concretely states that the screening ground 'security or public order' shall first and foremost comply with the relevant requirements of Arts XIV (a) and XIV*bis* GATS:

> The implementation of this Regulation by the Union and the Member States should comply with the relevant requirements for the imposition of restrictive measures on grounds of security and public order in the WTO agreements, including, in particular, Article XIV (a) and Article XIV bis of the General Agreement on Trade in Services (12) (GATS). It should also comply with Union law and be consistent with commitments made under other trade and investment agreements.

In both recitals the notion 'security or public order' is directly linked to International economic law and the GATS, even though the term 'security' is usually referred to as 'essential security interests' (see inter alia Art XIV*bis*(1)(a) and (b) GATS).

At the same time, the Screening Regulation omits a distinct wording as well as an own definition of 'security or public order'. Art 4 Screening Regulation only provides a non-exhaustive list of factors that *may* be taken into account when assessing whether an FDI is 'likely to affect security or public order'. Art 4 Screening Regulation thus substantiates, but not constitutively defines 'security or public order'.

An argument for the screening ground 'security or public order' to be interpreted as a distinct notion of secondary law would be that only this approach allowed an interpretation in accordance with the object and purpose of the Screening Regulation, namely to meet the EU and Member States concerns vis-à-vis foreign investors.

---

[4]Emphasis added.

Yet, this object and purpose is not as clear as it may seem. Indeed, the EU and Member States concerns have been incorporated to some extent into the Screening Regulation—but so have the reference to the GATS notions and with it the intention to ensure compliance with WTO law at all times. In addition, it has been shown that the concerns vis-à-vis foreign investors are generally but not in all aspects shared among the different actors in the EU and Member States.[5] This is illustrated by the different sensitive asset concepts as part of the harmful investor concern, and the fact that the Parliament's proposal to include the broadest concept 'strategic assets' into the Screening Regulation was rejected.[6] Last but not least, certain Member States were reluctant to agree to the Screening Regulation or a broader version of it to avoid deterring FDI inflows. Against this background, the incorporation of the GATS notions may rather be understood as a compromise that ensures a harmonized, somewhat restricted interpretation of the screening ground based on the GATS to which the EU and all Member States are a party and could therefore agree.

Taking up this argument of a harmonized interpretation, one may also be inclined to argue that it would be more obvious and appropriate to interpret the term 'security or public order' instead in accordance with an EU law notion, and thus the TFEU notion 'public policy or public security' in, for example, Art 65(1)(b) TFEU, the ground of exception to the freedom of capital movement.[7] However, four arguments weigh against this interpretation.

First, the above cited Recitals (3) and (35) primarily refer to 'security or public order' pursuant to International economic law and the GATS respectively. The reference to 'Union law' comes second, without referring to any concrete provision. Rather, Recital (4) of the Screening Regulation explicitly states that the Screening Regulation 'is without prejudice to' the Member States' right to adopt an FDI Screening mechanism in accordance with Art 65(1)(b) TFEU, and thus with the screening ground 'public policy or public security'.[8] Hence, Recital (4) assumes that the screening ground of FDI Screening mechanisms in accordance with the Screening Regulation is different than mechanisms based on Art 65(1)(b) TFEU. In other words, the Screening Regulation seeks to provide Member States with an additional option of screening grounds for FDI Screening mechanisms. Interpreting 'security or public order' in accordance with Art 65(1)(b) TFEU would contradict this purpose.

---

[5] See Sects. 2.1 and 2.3.1.

[6] Parliament, 'Report on the Proposal for a Regulation of the European Parliament and of the Council establishing a framework for screening of foreign direct investments into the European Union (COM (2017) 487)' A8-0198/2018, amendments 39–41.

[7] Also highlighting this literal convergence, Moberg and Hindelang (2020), p. 1427, fn. 99. Reading the screening ground 'security or public order' as referencing and substantiating 'public policy or public security' within the meaning of Art 65(1)(b) TFEU, Herrmann (2019), p. 465; Bismuth (2020), p. 107.

[8] Also against the Screening Regulation harmonizing 'public policy or public security' within the meaning of Art 65(1)(b) TFEU, Moberg and Hindelang (2020), p. 1452. For this interpretation of the Screening Regulation see also Sect. 2.3.1.

Second, if the legislator had wanted to reference the TFEU notion 'public policy or public security', it could have easily avoided confusion by replicating this notion in the Screening Regulation rather than opting for the term 'security or public order'. Admittedly, the GATS notion 'essential security interests' is also not replicated word by word. However, using this term would have caused confusion with the notion of 'essential interests of security' in Art 346(1)(b) TFEU ('essential interests of its [the Member State's] security'). Accordingly, the Screening Regulation had to choose the more neutral term 'security' as second element of its screening ground.

Third, the Screening Regulation was adopted based on the EU's exclusive competence on Common commercial policy pursuant to Art 207(2) TFEU. Arts XIV(a) and XIV*bis* GATS belong to International economic law—the core policy field of the EU's Common commercial policy. If the Screening Regulation had wanted to harmonize 'public policy or public security' within the meaning of Art 65(1)(b) TFEU in the realm of FDI screening, the Screening Regulation would have been based on the shared internal market competence of Art 64(2) and (3) TFEU.[9]

Fourth, it is erroneous to argue that an interpretation of 'security or public order' in accordance with Art 65(1)(b) TFEU is necessary to ensure compliance with the freedom of capital movement.[10] This argument neglects other grounds on which the EU may restrict the freedom of capital movement. Art 64(2) and (3) TFEU even allow the EU to restrict FDI inflows without any substantial condition.[11] An interpretation of 'security or public order' in accordance with the GATS may therefore still guarantee the Screening Regulation's compliance with the freedom of capital movement. At the same time, it even, at least in part, ensures compliance with other EU and Member States obligations from International economic law deriving from other bi- and plurilateral agreements, for exception grounds of the latter are often drafted similarly to the WTO exceptions.[12]

---

[9]Cremona (2020), pp. 53–54. *Contra* Herrmann (2019), pp. 465–466, without specifically addressing the conflict between harmonization and internal market competences on the one, and trade facilitation and Common commercial policy on the other hand. In more detail on the competence for regulating incoming FDI, see Sect. 4.1.

[10]Presenting this Commission argument Cremona (2020), p. 34. On the Regulation's compliance with the freedom of capital movement see, e.g. de Kok (2019), pp. 27–30.

[11]Discussing the scope of Art 64(2) and (3) TFEU, Korte (2019), pp. 125–127 and 130. Korte stresses that the EU must always respect the principle of proportionality pursuant to Art 5(4) TFEU. Another ground of exception would be the unwritten ground 'overriding reasons in the public interest' as developed by the ECJ in Case C-8/74 *Dassonville* [1974] EU:C:1974:82; Case C-120/78 *Rewe v Bundesmonopolverwaltung für Branntwein* [1979] EU:C:1979:42 (hereafter *Cassis de Dijon*). For more detail see n. 178.

[12]Many of the grounds of exception in International economic law are drafted similarly or even identically to Arts XIV(a) and/or XIV*bis* GATS—e.g. Arts 28.3(2)(a), 28.6(b) CETA and Arts 32.1.1 and 2, 32.2 of the US-Mexico-Canada Agreement. To be sure, the different wording, context, and purpose of these International economic law provisions will usually prevent an identical interpretation. However, a justification under the GATS may still indicate that the FDI screening will also be justified under the International economic law source at issue.

Consequently, the screening ground 'security or public order' must be interpreted in accordance with the GATS notions 'essential security interests' and 'public order'. The GATS reference goes beyond simply ensuring that the Screening Regulation, Member State screening mechanisms, and individual FDI screening comply with WTO law, or that they will prevail in WTO dispute settlement. EU and Member States may reach compliance with WTO law by many more parameters, in particular a lack of sector-specific commitments, other available grounds of exception, or a lenient burden of proof in dispute settlement. Instead, the Regulation incorporates the definition of 'essential security interests' and 'public order' pursuant to Arts XIV(a) and XIV*bis*(1)(b) GATS, isolated from other GATS parameters. As a result, if foreign investors proceed against screening of their FDI, the definition of the GATS notions will be subject to review by EU and Member State courts.

Before defining 'security or public order' accordingly, one last aspect requires attention: the prefix before the screening ground 'security or public order'.

The Regulation allows the screening of FDI that is '*likely to affect* security or public order'.[13] This prefix requires a probability for a screened FDI to harm a Member State's 'security or public order'. Again, as a point of departure, the EU can define this probability nexus as it deems appropriate for the legislative purpose. However, the prefix's distinct interpretation collides with the Screening Regulation's reference to Arts XIV(a) and XIV*bis*(1)(b) GATS. As will be shown in Sects. 3.1.3 and 3.1.4, a probability nexus between the covered interests and, in case of FDI screening, the actual investment is also inherent in the GATS notions 'essential security interests' and 'public order'. For instance, Footnote 5 to the GATS defines 'public order' as a '*genuine* and sufficiently serious threat to a fundamental interest of society'.[14] The question thus arises: In what relation are the inherent probability nexus of the GATS notions and the Regulation's prefix?

One may read the Screening Regulation's reference to the GATS notions of 'essential security interests' and 'public order' as carving out their inherent probability nexus and only referencing the interests they cover. The probability nexus would then solely be defined by the prefix 'likely to affect'. Accordingly, in the example of Art XIV(a) GATS, only the element 'sufficiently serious threat to fundamental interests of society' not 'genuine threat' would apply.

Two reasons weigh against this reading. The Recitals (3) and (35) of the Screening Regulation do not indicate that the probability nexus should be carved out from their reference to the GATS notions. In addition and more importantly, both notions 'essential security interests' and 'public order' are inseparable from the probability nexus they provide. This will be further shown in Sects. 3.1.3 and 3.1.4. Due to the difficulties of universally defining important state interests, the definition of the protected interests greatly relies on the WTO members themselves. Against this background, the probability nexus constitutes a crucial constraining element to

---

[13] Art 1(1) Screening Regulation (emphasis added).

[14] Emphasis added. An alternative probability nexus may be 'immediate threat' or merely a 'risk'.

rebalance an otherwise too deferential definition. If this nexus were substituted by the possibly less stringent probability nexus of the Screening Regulation, the entire reference to the GATS notions would be undermined. In other words, the definition of 'essential security interests' and 'public order' is impossible without the related probability nexus.[15]

Consequently, the potential collision between the prefix 'likely to affect' and the threat nexus provided by the GATS notions 'essential security interests' and 'public order' must be resolved in favour of the latter. One must therefore interpret 'likely to affect' as expressing the GATS inherent threat nexus. This is also in line with the above explained purpose of the screening ground, namely to ensure that the Member States' FDI Screening mechanisms comply with the GATS.

Therefore, after some general remarks on the interpretation of the GATS as well as Arts XIV(a) and XIV*bis*(1)(b) GATS, the following will define the GATS notions of 'essential security interests' and 'public order'. This includes the threat nexus that both provisions require. It will be shown that both legal concepts cover the EU and Member States concerns vis-à-vis foreign investors only in a few, high-profile cases of FDI.

3.1.2 General Remarks on Interpreting the GATS Exceptions 'Essential Security Interests' and 'Public Order'

As initially stated, the Screening Regulation's screening ground 'security or public order' must be defined in accordance with the grounds of exception of 'essential security interests' (Art XIV*bis* GATS) and 'public order' (Art XIV(a) GATS). On this basis it will be assessed whether the screening ground 'security or public order' covers the EU and Member States concerns vis-à-vis foreign investors. The interpretation of Arts XIV*bis* and XIV(a) GATS is based on the framework of interpretative means set by Arts 31 and 32 VCLT, which will be outlined in Sect. 3.1.2.1. Against this background, Sect. 3.1.2.2 will set the point of departure for the following analysis.

3.1.2.1 Interpretative Means in WTO Law

The means to interpret WTO law derive, pursuant to Art 3.2 DSU, from 'customary rules of interpretation of public international law'. This refers to Arts 31 and 32 VCLT.[16] Art 31(1) VCLT provides:

---

[15] For a more detailed discussion see Sects. 3.1.3.2 and 3.1.4.2.

[16] *United States—Standards for Reformulated and Conventional Gasoline*, Appellate Body Report (29 April 1996) WT/DS2/AB/R, WTO Online Database doc no 96-1597, p. 17. Howse (2016),

A treaty shall be interpreted in good faith in accordance with the *ordinary meaning* to be given to the terms of the treaty in *their context* and in the light of *its object and purpose*.[17]

Hence, Art 31(1) VCLT allows three means of interpretation: the ordinary meaning of the term, its context, and the treaty's object and purpose. Art 32 VCLT lists supplementary means of interpretation.

Every interpretation starts with and is limited by the ordinary meaning of the term.[18] For its assessment, the panels and Appellate Body usually consult the (*New*) *Shorter Oxford English Dictionary*[19] or other dictionaries.[20] Originally, the adjudicating bodes relied heavily on the ordinary meaning of the term.[21] Today, however, the WTO adjudicating bodies increasingly turn to other interpretative means.[22]

One of the other interpretative means is a term's context. It refers to the 'entire text of the treaty . . ., including title, preamble and annexes . . . and any protocol to it, and the systematic position of the phrase in question within that ensemble'.[23] Pursuant to Art 31(2) and (3) VCLT, the context also goes beyond the treaty itself, comprising subsequent treaties and agreements, as well as other relevant rules of international law concluded between the parties. Finally, it includes other agreements that the parties refer to.

The object and purpose of the treaty is another crucial means of interpretation, in particular if the literal meaning and context fail to offer any conclusive

---

p. 44, points out that the Appellate Body is, if not in the past, at least today taking into account all interpretative means of Arts 31, 32 VCLT, in particular the context, and the objective and purpose.

[17] Emphasis added.

[18] Dörr (2018a), para. 57.

[19] See e.g. *United States—Measures Affecting the Cross-Border Supply of Gambling and Betting Services*, Appellate Body Report (7 April 2005) WT/DS285/AB/R, WTO Online Database doc no 05-1426, n. 193, pp. 266–268; *Argentina—Measures Relating to Trade in Goods and Services*, Appellate Body Report (14 April 2016) WT/DS453/AB/R, WTO Online Database doc no 16-2077, n. 606. For panel reports see e.g. *United States—Measures Affecting the Cross-Border Supply of Gambling and Betting Services*, Panel Report (10 November 2004) WT/DS285/R, as modified by Appellate Body Report WT/DS285/AB/R, WTO Online Database doc no 04-2687, paras. 6.20–6.21; *European Union and its Member States—Certain Measures Relating to the Energy Sector*, Panel Report (10 August 2018) WT/DS476/R, WTO Online Database doc no 18-5025, para. 7.302, n. 655–657.

[20] *US—Gambling*, Panel Report (n. 19), para. 6.57, cites e.g. the *Penguin Pocket English Dictionary* (1988) and the *New Oxford Thesaurus of English*. *China—Measures Affecting Trading Rights and Distribution Services for Certain Publications and Audiovisual Entertainment Products*, Appellate Body Report (21 December 2009) WT/DS363/AB/R, WTO Online Database doc no 09-6642, para. 354, refers to *The American Heritage Dictionary of the English Language*.

[21] One may speculate on the reasons. It may have been considered more appropriate or intended to avoid criticism of judicial activism (with this possible explanation Hudec (1998), p. 633). The latter criticism came from some WTO members, especially the US, Bhala and Witmer (2020), pp. 64–65. Hudec (1998), p. 633, finds it impossible to belief that, despite earlier 'literalism', adjudicating bodies were not influenced by evident purposes. In the same vein, representing many, Hilf and Goettsche (2003), pp. 11–17.

[22] See for example *US—Gambling*, Appellate Body Report (n. 19), para. 236; *China—Publications and Audiovisual Products* (n. 20), para. 348.

[23] Dörr (2018a), para. 44.

interpretation. Both terms, object and purpose, are generally understood as one element, often referred to as *telos*.[24] Despite Art 31(1) VCLT's wording, it also includes the *telos* of not only the treaty as a whole, but also of each term and provision in the treaty.[25]

An important aspect of the object and purpose is a term's or provision's effectiveness—its *effet utile*.[26] However, this must not lead to the focus on one purpose blind to other purposes of the same treaty. Accordingly, the Appellate Body seems to understand the effectiveness narrowly, using the effectiveness as an argument to assign every term and provision a meaning.[27]

The object and purpose of the GATS generally is multifaceted. The Appellate Body has derived several GATS purposes from its preamble: transparency, security and predictability of obligations,[28] progressive liberalization,[29] and pursuing national policy objectives,[30] meaning the right to regulate 'provided that they respect the rights of other Members under the GATS'.[31] Pursuant to the preamble, WTO members desire an 'overall balance of rights and obligations, while giving due respect to national policy objectives'.[32] Hence, none of these purposes is absolute. Instead, these purposes complement and balance each other.

This is especially true for the divergent purposes of progressive liberalization and the right to regulate.[33] Striking an appropriate balance between these two purposes is one of the most controversial issues in WTO law. It must be sought when interpreting the term 'measures affecting trade in services', as well as of all other GATS provisions. How is that balance achieved?

---

[24] Dörr (2018a), paras. 53–54.

[25] See for example on the purpose of Art III(1), (2) GATT *Japan—Taxes on Alcoholic Beverages*, Appellate Body Report (4 October 1996) WT/DS8/AB/R, WT/DS10/AB/R, and WT/DS11/AB/R, WTO Online Database doc no 96-3951, p. 12.

[26] Dörr (2018a), para. 56.

[27] *Japan—Alcoholic Beverages II* (n. 25), para. 18; see also *US—Gambling*, Panel Report (n. 19), paras. 6.49–6.50, which deducts the principle of *effet utile* from the interpretation method of good faith.

[28] *US—Gambling*, Appellate Body Report (n. 19), paras. 188–189.

[29] *China—Publications and Audiovisual Products* (n. 20), para. 394.

[30] *Argentina—Financial Services*, Appellate Body Report (n. 19), paras. 6.117, 6.260. However, the Appellate Body did not follow the panel in applying this purpose in a way that limits a competitive notion of 'less favourable treatment'. On the purpose of pursuing national policy objectives, see also *US—Gambling*, Appellate Body Report (n. 19), n. 271.

[31] *US—Gambling*, Appellate Body Report (n. 19), n. 271; citing the panel *US—Gambling*, Panel Report (n. 19), paras. 314–317.

[32] Para 3 GATS preamble.

[33] See *United States—Measures Affecting the Production and Sale of Clove Cigarettes*, Appellate Body Report (4 April 2012) WT/DS406/AB/R, WTO Online Database doc no 12-1741, para. 95, on similar preamble of TBT: 'While the fifth recital [on progressive liberalization] clearly suggests that Members' right to regulate is not unbounded, the sixth recital [on the right to regulate] affirms that such a right exists while ensuring that trade-distortive effects of regulation are minimized.'

To answer this question, it must be recalled that the very nature of the international trade agreements is to constrain the WTO members' regulatory sovereignty.[34] Therefore, the WTO members' right to regulate may be preserved in the preamble's sense, even if the GATS prohibits a WTO member to pursue a regulatory objective. Accordingly, the GATS obligations do limit the WTO Members' sovereign right to regulate; for instance, to discriminate between nationals and foreigners (National Treatment, 'NT') as well as between foreigners (Most-Favoured-Nation treatment, 'MFN').[35] This must be acknowledged to appropriately interpret these GATS provisions.[36]

Moreover, it is flawed to categorize provisions into those that incorporate the purpose to safeguard the WTO members' right to regulate and others that represent the purpose of trade liberalization. For example, it is too simplistic to argue that the GATS scope as well as MFN and NT obligations are gateways to promote the liberalization of trade and that they must thus be interpreted broadly. In accordance with the same rationale, one may argue that the grounds of exception in Arts XIV and XIV*bis* GATS further the WTO members' rights to regulate, and that they must thus also be interpreted broadly. Such a one-sided interpretation would neglect that the divergent purposes have to be reconciled within all of all provisions and obligations of the GATS. The purposes pull on all of them—indeed, to a different extent depending on each provision.[37]

Consequently, the interpretation of the GATS's scope and all other provisions will take both purposes of the GATS into account. It will seek to reconcile both purposes, liberalizing trade and preserving the WTO members' right to regulate, sometimes leaning more towards the former, sometimes the latter, depending on other available interpretative means.

Last but not least, the adjudicating bodies may take supplementary means of interpretation into account. Only if the interpretation pursuant to Art 31 VCLT '(a) leaves the meaning ambiguous or obscure; or (b) leads to a result which is manifestly absurd or unreasonable', preparatory work of the treaty and the

---

[34] *China—Publications and Audiovisual Products* (n. 20), para. 222.

[35] ibid., p. 6. They also rightly point out that a uniform interpretation of the non-discrimination obligations across International economic law would not respect the differences of these fields, ibid., p. 3.

[36] Rightly emphasizing this aspect De Búrca (2002), pp. 190–191.

[37] Indeed, a commitment that is based on a positive list approach or qualified by an exemption or exception will serve the purpose of progressive liberalization more. This is demonstrated in *US—Clove Cigarettes* on Art 2.1 TBT, a general NT and MFN obligation. The TBT provides neither exemptions, nor exceptions. Against this background, the Appellate Body defined 'less favourable treatment' in Art 2.1 TBT narrower than in the GATT by incorporating regulatory considerations in its 'likeness' test (*US—Clove Cigarettes* (n. 33), paras. 169–176). The Appellate Body argued that in the GATT, contrary to the TBT, the balance between trade liberalization and the right to regulate was enshrined in the exceptions pursuant to Art XX GATT. Accordingly, there was no need for a narrower 'less favourable treatment' test in Art III(4) GATT (*US—Clove Cigarettes* (n. 33), para. 109).

circumstances of its conclusion may be used as interpretative means.[38] In the GATS's realm, available supplementary means are, for example, the Scheduling Guidelines,[39] the Sectoral classification list, and the CPC.[40,41] However, as far as the WTO members explicitly refer to them in their schedules of commitments or implicitly base their schedule's structure on them, they constitute contextual means of interpretation.[42]

3.1.2.2   Point of Departure to Interpret 'Essential Security Interests' and 'Public Order'

Even when applying these interpretative means, the interpretation of 'essential security interests' and 'public order' in Arts XIV*bis* and XIV GATS remains difficult. Both notions are intrinsically and intentionally vague and address sensitive areas of WTO member interests. This has two consequences.

First, the WTO adjudicating bodies recognize that they lack the means and mandate to question WTO members' preferences in these sensitive areas. Therefore, the adjudicating bodies provide members with wide discretion for establishing Arts XIV*bis*(1) and XIV(a) GATS. This, however, is a matter of burden of proof

---

[38] Dörr (2018b), para. 28. For example, in *US—Gambling*, Appellate Body Report (n. 19), para. 195, *China—Publications and Audiovisual Products* (n. 20), para. 400, the Appellate Body found these conditions established, whereas in *China—Certain Measures Affecting Electronic Payment Services*, Panel Report (16 July 2012) WT/DS413/R, WTO Online Database doc no 12-3729, para. 7.537, the panel did not.

[39] Council for Trade in Services, 'Guidelines for the Scheduling of Specific Commitments under the General Agreement on Trade in Services' S/L/92 ('Scheduling Guidelines'), which are a 'non-binding set of guidelines' (para. 1), and 'shall not modify any rights or obligations' (para. 3). They were based on the scheduling guidelines that were proposed by Secretariat to facilitate Uruguay Round negotiations.

[40] Group of Negotiations on Services, 'Services Sectoral Classification List' (Note by the Secretariat) MTN.GNS/W/120 ('Sectoral Classification List'). According to the Scheduling Guidelines, para. 23, the scheduled sectors should be, and in most cases are, based on the Sectoral Classification List. The Sectoral Classification List consists of 12 sectors and is in turn based on United Nations Statistics Division, 'Provisional Central Product Classification' ('CPC') (see Tuthill and Roy (2012), p. 167). After the cited provisional version of the CPC, the UN published several new versions of the CPC, including the most recent version 2.1 in 2015. However, WTO members still refer to the provisional version of the CPC for defining their schedules of commitments. Therefore, the following refers to 'CPC' as the provisional version of 1990.

[41] *US—Gambling*, Appellate Body Report (n. 19), paras. 178, 196, overruled the *US—Gambling*, Panel Report (n. 19), para. 6.82, holding that neither the Scheduling Guidelines, nor the Sectoral Classification List constitute context to the GATS. The Appellate Body applied them as supplementary means of interpretation, holding explicitly that the appeal did '*not* raise the question whether [they] constitute "supplementary means of interpretation"'. However, '[b]oth participants agree that they do, and we see no reason to disagree'.

[42] Similarly, Mavroidis (2020), who points out that even if the Sectoral Classification List itself is not seen as a contextual means in the sense of Art 31(2) VCLT, the WTO members' negotiation documents and concessions based on the Sectoral Classification List are.

in WTO dispute settlement. As a matter of legal obligation, every member is still bound by the GATS definition of 'essential security interests' and 'public order'. It is this definition, not the flexible adjudicating bodies' approach based on the burden of proof that the Screening Regulation incorporated into its screening ground 'security or public order'. Second and more importantly, 'essential security interests' and 'public order' are by definition highly member-specific. They depend on each WTO member's specific situation, society, and risk aversion.[43] This reflects the GATS's nature as an agreement that is mostly concerned with negative integration.[44]

Based on the above outlined interpretative means, the following will therefore focus on identifying criteria that are applicable to all WTO members for determining their 'essential security interests' and 'public order'. It will be shown that the nexus between the covered policy objective and the individual FDI at issue is the real constraining element for defining 'essential security interests' and 'public order'. Both Arts XIVbis(1) and XIV(a) GATS require the FDI to pose a certain degree of threat to the protected policy objective, in terms of probability and magnitude.[45] This further supports the conclusion reached in Sect. 3.1.1 that the prefix 'likely to affect' must also be interpreted in light of the GATS.

Accordingly, the following analysis will show that even broad interests that the EU and Member States concerns vis-à-vis foreign investors pursue qualify as essential security or public order interests to some extent. The element of threat, on the other hand, constitutes a high threshold for an individual FDI to fall under Arts XIVbis and XIV(a) GATS. Sections 3.1.3 and 3.1.4 will show that this limits the scope of the screening ground 'security or public order' significantly.

---

[43] In contrast to the ECJ, the WTO adjudicating bodies do not conclude from the notions' context as grounds of exception that they have to be interpreted narrowly. *European Communities—EC Measures Concerning Meat and Meat Products (Hormones)*, Appellate Body Report (16 January 1998) WT/DS26/AB/R and WT/DS48/AB/R, WTO Online Database doc no 98-0099, para. 104; Delimatsis (2014), p. 96. For the ECJ's case law see e.g. Case C-54/99 *Scientology* [2000] EU: C:2000:124, para. 17.

[44] Delimatsis (2007), p. 85, n. 5; Mavroidis (2007), pp. 11–12; Trachtman (2007), p. 641. Accordingly, it is recognized that WTO members have the right to determine their own level of protection of the interests listed in Art XIV GATS, including 'public order': *US—Gambling*, Appellate Body Report (n. 19), para. 308. See also *Korea—Measures Affecting Imports of Fresh, Chilled and Frozen Beef*, Appellate Body Report (11 December 2000) WT/DS161/AB/R and WT/DS169/AB/R, WTO Online Database doc no 00-5347, para. 176 (on Art XX(d) GATT 1994); *Dominican Republic—Measures Affecting the Importation and Internal Sale of Cigarettes*, Appellate Body Report (25 April 2005) WT/DS302/AB/R, WTO Online Database doc no 05-1669, para. 23; *Brazil—Measures Affecting Imports of Retreaded Tyres*, Appellate Body Report (3 December 2007) WT/DS332/AB/R, WTO Online Database doc no 07-5290, para. 210.

[45] Though related, the link 'necessary to' as required by the *chapeau* of Art XIVbis(1)(b) and Art XIV(a) GATS between the concrete WTO member measure and the protected interests is a different issue. This link is concerned with the concrete measure, here the screening and prohibition of FDI. The necessity test depends on the individual circumstances the FDI screening, and can thus not be assessed here.

3.1.3   'Essential Security Interests' Pursuant to Art XIVbis GATS

The component 'security' in the screening ground 'security or public order' refers to 'essential security interests' within the meaning of Art XIV*bis* GATS. Interpreting Art XIV*bis* GATS, and its counterparts in other WTO Agreements,[46] is one of the most controversial questions in the WTO. The nearly identically drafted Art XXI GATT 1994 is at the centre of this debate. The debate materialized in the disputes *US—Steel and Aluminium Products*, in which seven WTO members separately filed complaint against the US on its steel and aluminium import tariffs, which, in turn, invoked Art XXI(b)(iii) GATT 1994.[47] So far, only two panel reports shed light on the interpretation of 'essential security interests', *Russia—Traffic in Transit* on Art XXI(b) GATT[48] and *Saudi Arabia—Protection of IPR* on Art 73(b) TRIPS.[49] Both reports will play a crucial role in the following discussion.

The WTO members agreed that the GATS obligations are not subject to a general, open-ended national security exception. Art XIV*bis* GATS limits protected 'essential security interests'—for measures other than the non-disclosure of information—to an exhaustive list:

1. Nothing in this Agreement shall be construed:

    (a) to require any Member to furnish any information, the disclosure of which it considers contrary to its essential security interests; or

    (b) to prevent any Member from taking any action which it considers necessary for the protection of its essential security interests:

        (i) relating to the supply of services as carried out directly or indirectly for the purpose of provisioning a military establishment;

        (ii) relating to fissionable and fusionable materials or the materials from which they are derived;

        (iii) taken in time of war or other emergency in international relations; or

    (c) . . .

---

[46] See Art XXI GATT1994, Art 73 TRIPS, and Art III(1) of the Revised Agreement on Government Procurement.

[47] The seven WTO members are Turkey (DS564), China (DS 544), the EU (DS 548), Norway (DS 552), Russia (DS 554), India (DS 547), and Switzerland (DS 556). Mexico (DS 551) and Canada (DS 550) found a mutual solution with the US, and thus dropped their complaint. Though all distinct disputes, the same panelists were appointed; and the US communications are very similar, if not identical in all disputes. Panel reports were expected in Autumn 2020. For clarity and convenience, the following will refer to DS548 between the US and the EU only. The US filed complaint against the safeguard measures invoked by the complainants in the first disputes: China (DS 558), EU (DS 559), Russia (DS 566), Turkey (DS 561), and India (DS 585). The US filed no complaint against Switzerland.

[48] *Russia—Measures Concerning Traffic in Transit*, Panel Report (5 April 2019) WT/DS512/R, WTO Online Database doc no 19-2105.

[49] *Saudi Arabia—Measures concerning the Protection of Intellectual Property Rights*, Panel Report (16 June 2020) WT/DS567/R, WTO Online Database doc no 20-4200.

Accordingly, Art XIV*bis*(1)(b) GATS limits the protection of 'essential security interests' to the narrow list of Subparagraphs (i)–(iii).[50] A general discussion of what 'national security' or 'essential security interests' should be in today's world is thus from a WTO law perspective unnecessary.[51] Even WTO members arguing for an entirely self-judging Art XIV*bis* GATS recognize that these three subparagraphs limit the member's interpretation of 'essential security interests'.[52] The Screening Regulation adopted this exhaustive list as limiting the notion 'security' in its screening ground 'security or public order' by referring to Art XIV*bis* GATS.

To interpret 'security or public order' in the Screening Regulation, only Subparagraphs (i) and (ii) of Art XIV*bis*(b) GATS are relevant. Subparagraph (i) on the provisioning of military establishment addresses the EU's and Member States' interest to ensure that the investor will neither jeopardize their defence industry capacities, nor equip the investor's home country with capacities that may later be used against the EU and its Member States.[53] Moreover, all interests relating to nuclear infrastructure, technology, and inputs are covered by Subparagraph (ii). However, the interpretation of this subparagraph is relatively clear, and WTO members seem to agree that the protection of interests relating to fissionable and fusionable materials is of every member's highest priority. The following therefore omits to further analyze Subparagraph (ii), and focuses on Subparagraph (i).

Subparagraph (iii), on the other hand, is only remotely relevant to the Screening Regulation, and therefore also not further discussed in this book.[54] The Screening

---

[50] *Russia—Traffic in Transit* (n. 48), para. 7.65; Schloemann and Ohlhoff (1999), p. 442; Akande and Williams (2003), p. 384; Cottier and Delimatsis (2008), para. 19; Peter (2012), pp. 102–103; Mishra (2020b), p. 575; Ranjan (2020), p. 646; Weiß (2020), pp. 837–838.

[51] With a detailed discussion of the current shift from a 'Neoliberal Order' to a new 'Geoeconomic Order' in which economic and security considerations are increasingly mixed so that the concept of national security becomes broader, see Roberts et al. (2019), pp. 664–669. On broader concepts of 'national security', see also Gaukrodger and Gordon (2012), p. 502, and for a summary of different definition of (national) security, see Collins (2019), p. 3.

[52] See e.g. the US argumentation in *United States—Certain Measures on Steel and Aluminium Products*, US Responses to the Panel's First Set of Questions to the Parties (14 February 2020) WT/DS548, Office of the United State Trade Representative doc no DS548, paras. 103–108, 154–156. For recent contributions to the prominent, fierce controversy on the self-judging character of the WTO essential security exceptions see e.g. Voon (2019), pp. 47–48; Vidigal (2019), p. 203; Pinchis-Paulsen (2020), p. 109 (with a detailed discussion of the negotiation history of Art XXI GATT 1947 and 1994 from a US perspective); Ranjan (2020), pp. 648–651. See also Prazeres (2020), pp. 145–148, who explores ways for dealing with 'national security disputes' outside the WTO's DSB system.

[53] Art 4(1)(b), (c) Screening Regulation.

[54] Subparagraph (iii) is at focus in the recent and current disputes of *Russia—Traffic in Transit* (n. 48); *Saudi Arabia—Protection of IPR* (n. 49), and thus in literature. In *US—Steel and Aluminium Products*, a crucial issue is whether the overcapacities on the global steel and aluminium market constitute an 'other emergency in international relations'. The US nevertheless avoids to explicitly invoke Art XXI(b)(iii) GATT 1994 (counterpart to Art XIV*bis*(1)(b)(i) GATS). Otherwise the US may undermine its own argument that Art XXI GATT was self-judging (see *United States—Certain Measures on Steel and Aluminium Products*, US Second Written Submission (17 April 2020)

Regulation was neither 'taken in time of war or other emergency in international relations', nor specifically targeted at future FDI in these times.[55] Namely, the Screening Regulation did not target the Covid-19 or any similar crisis.[56] Moreover, one may argue that an 'other emergency in international relations' requires a conflict between states, whereas the Covid-19 crisis is rather a global health crisis and therefore is better addressed under 'public order'.[57]

Consequently, the following focuses on interpreting Subparagraph (i): 'essential security interests relating to the supply of services as carried out directly or indirectly for the purpose of provisioning a military establishment' ('essential security interests relating to provisioning a military establishment'). After having identified the defining elements of Art XIV*bis*(1)(b)(i) GATS, the following will assess whether these elements, and hence the screening ground 'security' in 'security or public order', cover the EU and Member States concerns vis-à-vis foreign investors.

3.1.3.1 Definition

It is still largely unclear how to define essential security interests relating to provisioning a military establishment.[58] The only two adjudicating body reports on a WTO security exception, *Russia—Traffic in Transit* and *Saudi Arabia—Protection of IPR*, deal with Subparagraph (iii).[59] Subparagraph (iii), however, addresses the most severe situation a state may be confronted with: war (or other emergency in international relations). Subparagraph (i), on the other hand, is related to military regardless of an acute emergency. Therefore, invoking Subparagraph (i) is subject to additional requirements compared to Subparagraph (iii). Most importantly, Subparagraph (i) requires a threat nexus between the specific service a WTO

WT/DS548, Office of the United State Trade Representative doc no DS548, para. 29). Nevertheless, Lester and Zhu (2019), pp. 1457–1459, list several other possible motivations behind the US measures, including the consideration that a certain level of steel production is required to supply the military. This motivation would fall under Art XXI(b)(ii) GATT 1994, counterpart to Art XIV*bis*(1)(b)(i) GATS.

[55] For this temporal element in Art XXI(b)(iii) GATT 1994, see *Russia—Traffic in Transit* (n. 48), paras. 7.70–76, 111–125.

[56] Mere political or economic differences do not yet constitute an emergency in international relations, ibid., para. 7.75. Agreeing Prazeres (2020), p. 140.

[57] On the definition element of conflict, see *Russia—Traffic in Transit* (n. 48), paras. 7.73, 76.

[58] So far, this question has been at issue only once when Sweden invoked Art XXI(b)(ii) of the former GATT 1947 to impose a quota on leather, plastic, and rubber boots. WTO members did not reach a conclusion, and Sweden eventually took back the measure. See Sweden, 'Import Restrictions on Certain Footwear' (Notification to the Council) L/4250 ('Sweden—Import Restrictions on Certain Footwear').

[59] *Russia—Traffic in Transit* (n. 48), para. 7.27 (on Art XXI(b)(iii) GATT 1994); *Saudi Arabia—Protection of IPR* (n. 49), para. 7.229 (on Art 73(b)(iii) TRIPS). The current WTO dispute *US—Steel and Aluminium Products* also deals with Subparagraph (iii), in the realm of Art XXI GATT 1994, see *US—Steel and Aluminium Products* (n. 54), para. 29.

member measure aims to protect and the essential security interest at issue ('relating to').

Defining essential security interests relating to provisioning military establishment starts with an analysis of the panel reports in *Russia—Traffic in Transit* and *Saudi Arabia—Protection of IPR*. Certainly, the reports deal with Arts XXI (b) GATT 1994 and 73(b) TRIPS generally, and not the counterpart of Art XIV*bis*(1) (b)(i), but (iii) GATS. However, the *chapeau* of all three provisions is similarly drafted.[60] Differences merely reflect the differences of their subjects, services, goods, and intellectual property. Moreover, all three articles provide the WTO members with a last resort to take measures for 'essential security interests' that would otherwise violate their WTO obligations. Hence, they have a similar purpose and context.[61] Certain differences will be addressed when they become relevant.

Therefore, the following will adapt the analytical framework applied in *Russia— Traffic in Transit* and *Saudi Arabia—Protection of IPR*, to define essential security interests relating to provisioning military establishment pursuant to Art XIV*bis*(1)(b) (i) GATS.[62] Given the lack of case law and scholar contributions, the following will propose new definitions of Subparagraph (i)'s key elements. They are based on the means of interpretation as provided by Arts 31 and 32 of the Vienna Convention on the Law of the Treaties, namely literal meaning, context, and object and purpose. Finally, it will be assessed whether the security element in 'security or public order' may meet the EU and Member States concerns vis-à-vis foreign investors.

---

[60] Art XXI GATT 1994 reads: "Nothing in this Agreement shall be construed . . . (b) to prevent any contracting party from taking any action which it considers necessary for the protection of its essential security interests; (i) relating to fissionable materials or the materials from which they are derived; (ii) relating to the traffic in arms, ammunition and implements of war and to such traffic in other goods and materials as is carried on directly or indirectly for the purpose of supplying a military establishment; (iii) taken in time of war or other emergency in international relations."

[61] See Cottier and Delimatsis (2008), para. 5.

[62] Generally, Appellate Body and panel reports do not constitute legally binding precedents. Nevertheless, they 'create legitimate expectations . . . and therefore should be taken into account where they are relevant to any dispute' (*Japan—Alcoholic Beverages II* (n. 25), para. 14, cited by *United States—Final Anti-dumping Measures on Stainless Steel from Mexico*, Appellate Body Report (30 April 2008) WT/DS344/AB/R, WTO Online Database doc no 08-2072, para. 158. Therefore, adopted panel and Appellate Body reports become 'part and parcel of the *acquis*' of the WTO legal order, Appellate Body reports being attributed with more importance (*US—Stainless Steel* (n. 62), para. 160). As a result, at least Appellate Body reports are *de facto* precedents. Panel reports are less important, but also create expectations, in particular if they are not appealed and adopted. On the nature of Appellate Body reports see Pauwelyn (2016), pp. 170–172, who rightly emphasizes the risk that the more importance previous reports have, the more a minority of well-equipped WTO members may shape WTO law by providing their views as (third-) parties to the dispute. See also recently Bacchus and Lester (2020), pp. 189–192, who argue that previous Appellate Body decisions are no *stare decisis*, but a matter of 'security and predictability of the multilateral trading system' (see Art 3.2 DSU).

3.1.3.1.1 Russia—Traffic in Transit and Saudi Arabia—Protection of IPR

The panel reports in *Russia—Traffic in Transit* and *Saudi Arabia—Protection of IPR* are the first WTO adjudicating body reports that interpret the notion 'essential security interests' pursuant to Art XXI(b)(iii) GATT 1994 and Art 73(b)(iii) TRIPS. While the appeal as well as the adoption of the panel report in *Saudi Arabia—Protection of IPR* have been suspended,[63] the panel report in *Russia—Traffic in Transit* was not appealed and adopted by the WTO Dispute Settlement Body ('DSB').[64] The DSB adoption demonstrates a certain approval of the report by WTO members. Accordingly, the panel report in *Saudi Arabia—Protection of IPR* largely follows the report in *Russia—Traffic in Transit*, and seeks to emphasize that the vast majority of the (third) parties to the dispute agreed on main aspects of the report in *Russia—Traffic in Transit*.

The following analysis therefore focuses on the panel report in *Russia—Traffic in Transit*, complemented, where appropriate, by elements of the report in *Saudi Arabia—Protection of IPR*. Moreover, the following concentrates on the aspects that are relevant to define essential security interests relating to provisioning a military establishment.

The Facts

The panel report in *Russia—Traffic in Transit* had to deal with the Russia-Ukraine crisis, starting in 2014 after the Ukraine signed the EU-Ukraine Association Agreement.[65] After the annexation of the 'Autonomous Republic of Crimea and the city of Sevastopol' by the Russian Federation,[66] a number of states imposed economic sanctions against Russian entities. In reaction, Russia imposed bans on certain goods from these states, including Ukraine, and restrictions on the transit of these goods.[67] According to the transit measures, Russia only allowed the transit of certain products from Ukraine to states such as Kazakhstan if undertaken via Belarus, not other border crossings. The transit measures also consisted of 'additional conditions related to identification seals and registration cards'.[68] In the dispute settlement process, Ukraine challenged these transit measures.[69] Russia invoked Art XXI(b)(iii) GATT 1994 and argued that the panel 'lacks jurisdiction'.[70]

---

[63] See communications from Saudi Arabia (WT/DS567/9) and Qatar (WT/DS567/9) both of 7 January 2022.

[64] Dispute Settlement Body, 'Russia—Traffic in Transit' (Adoption) WT/DS512/7.

[65] See summary of events in *Russia—Traffic in Transit* (n. 48), paras. 7.5–7.9; UN General Assembly, 'Resolution No 68/262. Territorial Integrity of Ukraine' (27 March 2014).

[66] UN General Assembly, 'Resolution No 71/205. Situation of Human Rights in the Autonomous Republic of Crimea and the City of Sevastopol (Ukraine)' (19 December 2016).

[67] *Russia—Traffic in Transit* (n. 48), paras. 7.10–7.17.

[68] ibid., para. 7.16.

[69] ibid., para. 7.1.

[70] ibid., para. 7.4.

In *Saudi Arabia—Protection of IPR*, severe diplomatic distortions were at issue between Qatar on the one, and Saudi Arabia and other countries in the Middle East on the other hand. Against this background, Saudi Arabia imposed political and economic sanctions against Qatar. From Saudi Arabia's perspective, the sanctions were supposed to incentivize Qatar to comply with its requests, namely to stop supporting terrorist and extremist activities to the detriment of Saudi Arabia.[71] This included not only closing all land, sea, and air ports, but allegedly also inhibiting a Qatari sports broadcaster to exert its broadcasting rights against violations by a Saudi Arabian broadcaster. Accordingly, Qatar challenged Saudi Arabian measures as violating TRIPS obligations to protect intellectual property rights. To defend its measures Saudi Arabia invoked Art 73(b)(iii) TRIPS.[72]

Aspects Relevant to the Interpretation of Art XIV*bis*(1)(b)(i) GATS
The panel report in *Russia—Traffic in Transit* contains some valuable guidance on the interpretation of 'essential security interests relating to provisioning a military establishment' in Art XIV*bis*(1)(b)(i) GATS.[73]

Most importantly, the panel establishes an analytical framework for assessing Art XXI(b)(iii) GATT 1994. First, assessing whether the situation at issue falls under Subparagraph (iii); second, determining the essential security interest at issue; third, determining whether both elements are sufficiently linked ('minimum requirement of plausibility'[74]).[75] The panel focused on the first step, while reducing the second and third step to a good faith test.[76] Most of the panel's first step analysis is irrelevant to interpret Subparagraph (i). However, in an *obiter dictum* the panel defined the nexus 'in relation to' between the Subparagraphs (i) and (ii) and the *chapeau* as a '"close and genuine relationship of ends and means" between the measure and the objective of the Member adopting the measure'.[77]

---

[71] *Saudi Arabia—Protection of IPR* (n. 49), paras. 2.27–2.29.

[72] For the concrete claims and invocation of both parties see ibid., paras. 3.1–3.4.

[73] For a comprehensive interpretation of *Russia—Traffic in Transit* (n. 48), see e.g. Boklan and Bahri (2020), p. 123.

[74] *Russia—Traffic in Transit* (n. 48), para. 7.138; *Saudi Arabia—Protection of IPR* (n. 49), para. 7.252.

[75] As summarized by *Saudi Arabia—Protection of IPR* (n. 49), para. 7.242.

[76] *Russia—Traffic in Transit* (n. 48), paras. 7.109–7.111, 7.132–7.133, 7.138; *Saudi Arabia— Protection of IPR* (n. 49), paras. 7.250, 7.252.

[77] *Russia—Traffic in Transit* (n. 48), para. 7.69, citing *United States—Import Prohibition of Certain Shrimp and Shrimp Products*, Appellate Body Report (12 October 1998) WT/DS58/AB/R, WTO Online Database doc no 98-3899, para. 136; *China—Measures Related to the Exportation of Various raw Materials*, Appellate Body Report (30 January 2012) WT/DS394/AB/R, WT/DS395/AB/R, and WT/DS398/AB/R, WTO Online Database doc no 12-0544, para. 355; *China—Measures Related to the Exportation of Rare Earths, Tungsten, and Molybdenum*, Appellate Body Report (7 August 2014) WT/DS431/AB/R, WT/DS432/AB/R, and WT/DS433/AB/R, WTO Online Database doc no 14-4626, para. 5.90.

Moving on to the second step, 'essential security interests', the panel held that the notion is 'evidently a narrower concept than "security interests"'.[78] Such interests were 'non-trade interests'[79] that relate to the 'quintessential functions of the state, namely, the protection of its territory and its population from external threats, and the maintenance of law and public order internally'.[80] The panel described the external dimension of the quintessential functions of the state also as defence and military interests.[81] Political and economic differences between WTO members did not in themselves constitute such interests.[82]

Despite providing these defining elements, the panel left it to WTO members to define their 'essential security interests', without elevating any concern to such a major security interest or misusing the leeway to circumvent WTO obligations.[83] The necessary level of articulating the 'essential security interests' rises, 'the further [the situation invoked by the WTO member] is removed from armed conflict, or a situation of breakdown of law and public order'.[84] Hence, the more remote the invoked situation is from the 'hard core'[85] of the subparagraphs assessed in the first step of analysis, the more burden the WTO member bears to establish that an essential security interest is at issue.

Finally, as the last step of analysis, the measures that were found to violate the GATT 1994 and for which Art XXI(b) GATT 1994 has been invoked as defence must not be implausible as to protecting the articulated essential security interest.[86]

The following will take the analytical framework, definitions, and substantiations as a point of departure for developing a test for the subparagraph at issue: essential security interests relating to provisioning a military establishment. Where necessary, alternatives to the panels' statements will be submitted.

3.1.3.1.2 Developing a Test for Subparagraph (i)

Subparagraph (i) of Art XIV*bis*(1)(b) GATS has so far not been at issue before the WTO adjudicating bodies. Only once, in 1975, still during the GATT years, Sweden invoked its GATT counterpart, Art XXI(b)(ii) GATT 1947, to adopt a quota on leather, plastic, and rubber boots. Sweden claimed that the shoe industry was vital to

---

[78] *Russia—Traffic in Transit* (n. 48), para. 7.130, cited by *Saudi Arabia—Protection of IPR* (n. 49), para. 7.249. See also Schloemann and Ohlhoff (1999), p. 445.

[79] *Russia—Traffic in Transit* (n. 48), para. 7.79, referring generally to the object and purpose of the WTO Agreement.

[80] ibid., para. 7.130, cited by *Saudi Arabia—Protection of IPR* (n. 49), para. 7.249.

[81] *Russia—Traffic in Transit* (n. 48), para. 7.75.

[82] ibid.

[83] ibid., paras. 7.131–7.133; *Saudi Arabia—Protection of IPR* (n. 49), paras. 7.249–7.250.

[84] *Russia—Traffic in Transit* (n. 48), para. 7.135.

[85] ibid., para. 7.136.

[86] ibid., para. 7.138; *Saudi Arabia—Protection of IPR* (n. 49), paras. 7.252–7.255.

meet its basic needs in times of a war or other international emergencies.[87] Though other WTO members expressed their doubts about this argumentation, there was no panel established, and thus no detailed discussion of the arguments.[88]

Therefore, the following develops a test of Subparagraph (i) based on its literal meaning, complimented by further interpretative means, and drawing upon the three steps analysis as developed by the panels in *Russia—Traffic in Transit* and *Saudi Arabia—Protection of IPR*.[89] It recognizes, but constrains the WTO members' wide discretion to determine their 'essential security interests relating to provisioning a military establishment'. The test will depart from a first step that defines 'services relating to provisioning a military establishment'. The second step to define the 'essential security interests' at issue will be complemented by a new third step that takes into account the nexus 'relating to' between Subparagraph (i) and the *chapeau* of Art XIV*bis*(1)(b) GATS. This three-pronged test would then be complemented by the last step, the necessity test as a minimum plausibility requirement. Focus, however, will lie on steps one to three, since they have not been at issue in case law yet.

Services Carried Out Directly or Indirectly for Provisioning Military Establishment

Subparagraph (i) of Art XIV*bis*(1)(b) GATS protects 'essential security interests relating to the supply of services as carried out directly or indirectly for the purpose of the provisioning a military establishment'. The interpretation of each central element, at least in part, hinges on individual WTO member preferences. Nevertheless, the elements also allow to define hard-core and more remote services falling under Subparagraph (i).

Starting from the literal meaning, an establishment may be defined as 'an organized body maintained for a state purpose', 'the ... personnel of a regiment, ship etc.' as well as '[a]n institution or business; the premises or personnel of this'.[90]

[87] Sweden—Import Restrictions on Certain Footwear (n. 58). For the argument why this did not constitute a Subparagraph (iii) defence, see the introduction to this section.

[88] GATT Council, 'Minutes of Meeting of 31 October 1975' C/M/109, pp. 8–9. Also addressing this case, Alford (2011), pp. 704–705. With a recent, but brief discussion of Subparagraph (i) in the context of cybersecurity, see Mishra (2020b), pp. 580–581. Without much substantiation, Mishra argues that Subparagraph (i) covers only a few cases, and is thus 'irrelevant' for the majority of cybersecurity measures.

[89] The *travaux préparatoires* as 'Supplementary Means of Interpretation' within the meaning of Art 32 VCLT do not offer any significant insights. Pinchis-Paulsen (2020), pp. 154–156, discusses different US proposals, but they provide no conclusive answer how to further substantiate the meaning of Subparagraph (i). Even if it did, the US proposals might not automatically be regarded as *travaux préparatoires*. They only represent the position of the US, but not of the entire WTO membership.

[90] Stevenson and Brown (2007), p. 866. See also '*peace establishment* reduced army etc. in time of peace. *war establishment* increased army etc. in time of war' (emphasis in original).

Military describes '*the* armed forces; or soldiers generally'.[91] Complemented by the context of Art XIV*bis*(1)(b) GATS, the central notion in subparagraph (i), 'military establishment' thus stands for the organized body of a country's armed forces comprising its personnel and premises.

Subparagraph (i) protects a state's interest to 'provisioning' these military establishments. This term means to supply the 'necessary resources (*for*)' the associated subject, here military establishment.[92] Provisioning thus describes the act of providing the military establishment with resources necessary to fulfil its functions. Both the concrete military functions and the necessary resources can only be defined by the WTO member itself. The most prominent, generally accepted function is the defence from external threats, traditionally war. To fulfil this function, some states choose to provide their military establishment with cutting-edge warfare technologies, while others rely on non-military resources. Hence, the definition of both military establishment and provisioning hinges on non-universal, individual WTO member preferences.

The same is valid for the last element of Subparagraph (i). The term 'the supply of services as carried out *directly or indirectly for the purpose of* provisioning a military establishment' opens the door to an indefinite range of services.[93] 'Indirectly' may include any purpose even remotely related to the provisioning of a military establishment. It thus depends on each WTO member to define a sufficiently indirect relationship.

Consequently, Subparagraph (i) is very open to individual WTO member considerations. At the same time, Subparagraph (i) may not encompass any service however indirect its relation to military establishment is, nor any purportedly military function or necessary resource to fulfil this function. Rather, WTO members will agree to a hard core of services that fall under Subparagraph (i), while other services are more remotely linked to military establishment.[94]

Against this background, three factors can be identified that determine whether a service belongs to the hard core and is thus definitely covered by Subparagraph (i), or whether it is more remote and subject to stricter review in the second step of Subparagraph (i). The factors result from the definitory space that each of the three central elements of Subparagraph (i) leaves to the WTO members.

---

[91] Stevenson and Brown (2007), p. 1781 (emphasis in the original). See also '*military-industrial complex* a country's military establishment and those industries producing arms or other military materials' (emphasis in the original).

[92] Stevenson and Brown (2007), p. 2384 (emphasis in the original).

[93] Hahn (1991), pp. 585 and 590, who also argues that the interpretation of direct and indirect is not more complicated than defining 'likeness' (Arts I(1), XVII GATS) or 'nullification' and 'impairment' (Art XXIII(3) GATS). Similarly, on Subparagraph (i) and dual-use digital services generally Mishra (2020b), pp. 580–581.

[94] In *Russia—Traffic in Transit* (n. 48), paras. 7.135–7.136, the panel hold that Russia acted in circumstances that were 'very close to the "hard core" of war or armed conflict'. Accordingly, under the *chapeau*, Russia did not need to establish its essential security interests too substantively.

First, an establishment constitutes a military establishment if it fulfils a *military function*. The less traditional or universal the military function at issue is, the less WTO members will agree that a military establishment evidently needs to be provisioned with services to fulfil this function (military function factor). Second, provisioning a military establishment means to provide the establishment with the *necessary resources* to fulfil its function. Hence, the less important the resource that a service should provide is to fulfil the military function, the less members will agree that the resource clearly falls in the scope of Subparagraph (i) (necessary resources factor). Third, the service at issue must be carried out *directly or indirectly* for provisioning the military establishment. Accordingly, the more indirectly the service at issue is related to the specific military function and resource, the less members will agree that the link between the service and the provisioning of the military establishment is sufficiently established (direct relation factor). The less a service fulfils these three factors, the more it becomes remote from the hard core of services.

The example of maintenance services for tanks illustrates the application of the three factors. Tanks are used inter alia to defend a state against external aggressions, namely war. They therefore serve the most traditional military function (military function factor). Moreover, in warfare tanks are a crucial resource to fulfil the military function of defending a state (necessary resources factor). Finally, maintenance of tanks is directly related to providing the military with tanks (direct relation factor). Hence, the maintenance services of tanks are hard-core services of Subparagraph (i). On the other hand, a much larger group of services will be more remote to the hard core of Subparagraph (i). Dual-use services, for instance, will usually fulfil the direct relation factor less, since they are also or even primarily carried out for a civilian purpose.

Nevertheless, as long as a service fulfils all three defining elements, the service falls under Subparagraph (i), whether belonging to the hard core of Subparagraph (i) or more remote. This distinction between hard- and non-hard-core services, however, becomes crucial when taking into account the relation to the overarching motive of Art XIV*bis*(1)(b) GATS: 'essential security interests'.

Relating to Essential Security Interests
Pursuant to Art XIV*bis*(1)(b)(i) GATS, the service provisioning military establishment must relate to 'essential security interests'. This requirement demonstrates the fundamental difference between Subparagraph (i) on the one, and Subparagraph (iii) on the other hand.

In time of war or other similar emergency, Subparagraph (iii) allows a WTO member to restrict trade in a particular service even if the service is in no functional relationship with the member's 'essential security interests'. A WTO member could, for instance, ban all trade with a certain state to end any interaction between both states' nationals and thereby preventing terrorism and extremism.[95] In the *chapeau*, the WTO member would have to cursorily establish why the prevention of terrorism

---

[95] This was Saudi Arabia's intention in *Saudi Arabia—Protection of IPR* (n. 49), paras. 7.284–7.285.

and extremism is essential to its security, and why a complete trade ban was necessary to pursue this essential security interest.[96] Accordingly, the panels in *Russia—Traffic in Transit* and *Saudi Arabia—Protection of IPR* could assess Subparagraph (i) first, and—separately—as a second and third step assess the WTO member's articulation of its 'essential security interests' and the necessity as link between this interest and the measure taken.

Under Subparagraph (i), however, the term 'relating to' requires an additional step that connects Subparagraph (i) with the *chapeau* term 'essential security interests'. The WTO member must establish why there is a relationship between the essential security interest and the specific service that provisions a military establishment. Otherwise, Art XIV*bis*(1)(b)(i) GATS would cover any non-hard-core service. WTO members could restrict trade in nearly every service and therefore frustrate their GATS rights and obligations. The purpose of Subparagraphs (i)–(iii) to narrow 'essential security interests' to an exhaustive list would fail.

As a result, the WTO member invoking Art XIV*bis*(1)(b)(i) GATS must first establish its essential security interest at issue, before second establishing its relation to the specific service at issue.

To summarize the case law on Art XIV*bis*(1)(b) GATS, 'essential security interests' are interests to maintain the quintessential functions of the state in their internal and external dimension. At the same time, Art XIV*bis*(1) GATS is no general law and order exception, but only addresses a 'breakdown' of law and public order.[97] The often proposed substantiation of 'essential security interests' as only non-trade or non-economic interests fails to provide additional substance.[98] Categorizing an interest as a non-trade objective depends on the perspective as exporter or importer. For example, import controls to rebalance a foreign trade deficit may be invoked to address geopolitical concerns of power relations between the states at issue and thus non-trade interests. Even in economic theory, where the distinction between economic and non-economic interests originates, non-economic interests are recognized as overlapping with other categories.[99]

Nevertheless, the definition of 'essential security interests' as interests to maintain the quintessential functions of the state, internally and externally, provides a wide

---

[96] In *Russia—Traffic in Transit* (n. 48), paras. 7.138–7.139; *Saudi Arabia—Protection of IPR* (n. 49), paras. 7.285–7.287, the necessity test was reduced to a test of good faith, and thus a plausibility control.

[97] *Russia—Traffic in Transit* (n. 48), para. 7.135. As will be shown in Sect. 3.1.4, even the broader Art XIV(a) GATS provides no general law and order exception.

[98] For this term see ibid., para. 7.79. Many authors also draw this distinction, e.g. Akande and Williams (2003), p. 390 ('purely economic reasons'); Cottier and Delimatsis (2008), para. 1. See also the EU's argument in *United States—Certain Measures on Steel and Aluminium Products*, EU Replies to the Questions from the Panel (14 February 2020) WT/DS548, European Commission Trade Dispute Settlement WTO cases doc no WT/DS548, para. 255 (also 'purely economic reasons').

[99] Krajewski (2003), pp. 12 and 18; Delimatsis (2007), p. 47. The latter cites Daerdorff (2000), pp. 70, 73, and 77–78. See also the US list of national security definitions of several WTO members, which all contain economic elements, *US—Steel and Aluminium Products* (n. 52), paras. 333–345.

frame for WTO members' determination. But—once determined—these interests become the benchmark for the following steps of analyzing Art XIV*bis*(1)(b) (i) GATS.[100]

The third step of analysis is the connection 'relating to' between services falling under Subparagraph (i) and the 'essential security interests'. This connection must be a close and genuine relationship.[101] In Subparagraph (i) this relationship can generally take two forms.[102] On the one hand, a state's 'essential security interests' may be affected because the supply of a service carried out for the military is disrupted, so that the service cannot provision the state's own military establishment anymore (first scenario). On the other hand, 'essential security interests' of one state (State A) may be undermined because the service at issue provisions another state's (State B) military establishment (second scenario). In the second scenario State A may for example take export control measures to prevent the transfer of military know-how to State B.

In both scenarios the close and genuine relationship between 'essential security interests' and a service provisioning a military establishment only exists if a service is so important for the provisioning of a military establishment that, if taken away (first scenario) or added (second scenario), an essential security interest of the WTO member is affected, in other words: threatened.[103]

At this point, the distinction between the hard and non-hard-core services of Subparagraph (i) becomes relevant. In case of a hard-core service, the WTO member will not need to specify the element of threat. These services are already sufficiently closely related to 'essential security interests'. However, the more a service becomes remote from the hard core of Subparagraph (i), the higher the threshold for establishing the element of threat becomes.

The element of threat consists of three cumulative criteria. They follow from the requirement of a genuine and sufficiently serious relationship between the essential security interest and the non-hard-core service of Subparagraph (i). The 'public order' exception in Art XIV(a) GATS gives further context to the criteria's definition. Footnote 5 to the GATS explicitly demands a 'genuine and sufficiently serious threat [that must be] posed to one of the fundamental interests of society'. Art XIV*bis*(1)(b) GATS, on the other hand, lacks such provision and addresses more sensitive interests of WTO members than Art XIV(a) GATS. Accordingly, the

---

[100] Similarly, in *Saudi Arabia—Protection of IPR* (n. 49), para. 7.281, the panel used the essential security interests as benchmark for the necessity test.

[101] See n. 77.

[102] 'In relation to' describes any kind of connection or relation, and is also defined as 'as regards', which in turn is defined as 'concerning' or 'with respect to' (see Stevenson and Brown (2007), pp. 2519 and 2511).

[103] Other authors deduce an element of threat from the *chapeau* alone, see Cottier and Delimatsis (2008), para. 20; and as part of a good faith reading of 'as it considers necessary' in Art XXI (b) GATT 1994, Akande and Williams (2003), pp. 389–390. More generally on the principle of good faith as guiding the interpretation of the *chapeau*, Weiß (2020), p. 846.

three criteria of threat will be similar to but less demanding than in the 'public order' exception.[104]

First, the service at issue must contribute to the invoked military function, which in turn must contribute to the essential security interest identified by the WTO member. Otherwise, there would be no causal relationship between service, military function, and the essential security interest at issue.

Second, the service must be irreplaceable or significantly difficult to replace. This criterion is not met if another available service can fulfil the same function, or another service provider can supply the same or an equally effective service, either directly or through training in a reasonable amount of time. The criterion's rationale is slightly different for the two scenarios covered by Subparagraph (i). In the first scenario, the state will still be capable of provisioning its military establishment to the extent itself deemed necessary because it can turn to another service or service supplier. In the second scenario, State B may use the service at issue for its military, but may equally use another service or service supplier. It is thus not *because of* the service at issue that State A's 'essential security interests' are threatened.

Third, there must be a certain probability that the threat materializes. Again, this element has slightly different meanings depending on the threat scenario at issue. In the first scenario, a sufficient relation between the essential security interest and the military establishment is only established if the supply of the service at issue is at risk. There must be a certain probability for the service supply to be interrupted or to severely malfunction, and thus for the military establishment to fulfil its function. In the second scenario, there must be a certain probability that State B will get access to and use the service at issue to the detriment of State A's 'essential security interests'. This criterion lowers the 'genuine threat' element known from Footnote 5 to the GATS to a minimum threshold of probability.

Only if a non-hard-core service of Subparagraph (i) fulfils these three criteria, will the third step of the test for Art XIV*bis*(1)(b)(i) GATS be met.[105]

As a fourth step, the concrete measure of issue must be necessary for protecting the essential security interest as substantiated by Subparagraph (i). In line with the panel reports in *Russia—Traffic in Transit* and *Saudi Arabia—Protection of IPR*, the necessity test is reduced to testing whether it is plausible that the WTO member took to the measure to in fact protect the essential security interest at issue.[106]

---

[104] For the detailed definition of 'public order', see Sect. 3.1.4.

[105] The burden of proof to establish these elements of threat, which is not at issue here, increases the more the service a WTO member wants to protect becomes remote from the hard-core services protected by Subparagraph (i).

[106] *Russia—Traffic in Transit* (n. 48), para. 7.138; *Saudi Arabia—Protection of IPR* (n. 49), paras. 7.242, 7.252.

3.1.3.1.3   Significant Limits for Non-hard-core Services of Subparagraph (i)

In sum, the notion of 'essential security interests' pursuant to Art XIV*bis*(1)(b)
(i) GATS defers its definition widely to WTO members, but also provides them
with significant limits. The provision requires a four-pronged test.

First, the service at issue must constitute a service provisioning a military
establishment. The service may either constitute the hard core of Subparagraph (i),
or become more remote from this hard core the more it fulfils three factors: the 'non-
traditional', 'indispensable resources', and 'indirect relation factor'. As a second
step, the 'essential security interests' at issue are determined, mostly based on the
WTO member's considerations. Third, the service must threaten 'essential security
interests'. Such threat is a minimum threshold, and is always established in case of
hard-core services of Subparagraph (i). The more the service becomes remote to this
hard core according the above three factors, the more a threat to the essential security
interest at issue must be established. Three criteria must be met: The service must
(i) contribute to a military function and the protection of the invoked essential
security interest, (ii) be irreplaceable or significantly difficult to replace, and (iii)
there must be a certain probability that the risk to the essential security interest
materializes. As a fourth step of analysis, the measure taken, here screening of an
individual FDI, must be necessary, hence plausible to protect the essential security
interest at issue.

With this test in mind, the discussion can now turn to applying these elements to
the EU and Member States concerns vis-à-vis foreign investors.

3.1.3.2   Consequences for Screening Regulation's Scope: Focus on Harmful Investor Concern Regarding Hard Core and Dual-Use Defence Sector

With the test for Subparagraph (i) of Art XIV*bis*(1)(b) GATS in mind, the discussion
can now turn to applying these elements to the EU and its Member States concerns
vis-à-vis foreign investors. Only to the extent the concerns fall under Subparagraph
(i), can the security element in 'security or public order' meet the EU and Member
States concerns.[107]

As shown, the focus of Art XIV*bis*(1)(b)(i) GATS lies on provisioning the
military with services. Hence, the security element in 'security or public order'
cannot meet EU and Member States concerns beyond military interests: the competition, reciprocity, and private information concern.

The harmful investor concern, on the other hand, may indeed be protected by
Subparagraph (i), and thus addressed by the security element in 'security or public
order'. The EU and Member States are concerned that an investor gains influence
over a domestic asset (M&A FDI), and uses this influence to shape the FDI target's

---

[107] For a definition of the concerns see Sect. 2.1.

business decisions in a way that is detrimental to public interest. This concern focuses on three concepts of sensitive assets: defence sector; critical infrastructure, technology, inputs; and strategic infrastructure, technology, and inputs. Only the first category of sensitive assets specifically addresses military interests and may thus fall under the security element of 'security or public order'.

Indeed, the defence sector, seems, at first sight, to coincide with the scope of Art XIV*bis*(1)(b)(i) GATS. Extrapolated from the services context, the security notion in accordance with Art XIV*bis*(1)(b)(i) GATS allows to screen FDI into firms that produce, possess, or operate (together referred to as 'provide') goods, services, infrastructure, technology, or inputs directly related to and indispensable for hard core military functions. No additional requirements apply, namely no threat requirement. Hence, even a remote, abstract risk suffices to screen, ultimately prohibit an investment. The hard core of the defence sector includes, for instance, firms that produce ammunition or tanks, possess technology exclusively applied for such production, or supply respective maintenance services.

However, the harmful investor concern regarding the defence sector also includes non-hard-core assets, namely dual-use assets. Such assets fall outside of the hard core of Subparagraph (i), since they only indirectly provision military establishment, and sometimes also fulfil a less traditional military function. Accordingly, the additional requirement of threat applies. The FDI target must therefore contribute to a certain military function that protects or threatens the essential security interest. In addition, the asset must be irreplaceable or significantly difficult to replace by another asset. Lastly, the Member State must establish a certain probability that the envisaged threat scenario will materialize. In particular the second and third criterion may not be satisfied by the EU's and the Member States' concerns.

According to the second criterion, the acquired firm must supply a service that may not be offered by another firm, either directly or through training in a reasonable amount of time. Moreover, the service must not be replaceable by a similar available service. In light of the EU and Member States harmful investor concern, this poses a high hurdle. Given the size of the EU market, many firms may be replaceable by other competitors or similar products.

The third criterion, probability for risk scenario to materialize, also constrains the screening ground's scope. EU or Member States must establish a certain probability that the investor will either disrupt the supply with a certain product that in turn disrupts a military establishment to fulfil its function, or that a third country will get access to and use the service at issue to the detriment of the EU's or a Member State's 'essential security interests'. Despite a seemingly unlikely worst-case scenario, there has been a few high-profile cases where a home country government induced an investor to disrupt the supply with a certain good.[108]

---

[108] See *EU—Energy Package* (n. 19), para. 7.1174. The EU invoked two examples to substantiate its defence under Art XIV(a) GATS in that, there were a threat to their energy security. The two examples were the oil embargo by the Organization of Arab Petroleum Exporting Countries in 1973 and the interruption of gas supplies to Ukraine in 2006 and 2009.

For example, the Member State may be concerned about an FDI in a firm developing artificial intelligence applications to identify specific persons by certain character traits from large databases. These applications are also, but not only used for military intelligence. The Member State is afraid that the foreign investor uses its influence on the acquired domestic firm to transfer the artificial intelligence application to its home country facilities. To meet the third criterion, the Member State must establish a certain probability that the FDI will cause harm to a concrete military function. Accordingly, the Member State must have a concrete reason to expect that either the acquired firm will cease to supply the artificial intelligence application to the Member State, or that the foreign investor will make the application available to its home country which may then use it against the Member State. For establishing the second criterion, no other equally effective application must be available to the Member State or the investor's home country. The alternative artificial intelligence application may also be supplied by a supplier from another state if the Member State can expect reliable supply.

Consequently, the EU and Member States harmful investor concern regarding the sensitive asset concept of the defence sector falls under the security element of 'security or public order'. For non-hard-core products to a military establishment such as dual-use products, a threat element must be established that constitutes a considerable hurdle, given the threat scenarios of concern. This last aspect supports the argument in Sect. 3.1.1 that the Screening Regulation's prefix *'likely to affect* security or public order' cannot override the Screening Regulation's reference to Art XIV*bis*(1)(b) GATS. The definition of 'essential security interests' pursuant to Art XIV*bis*(1)(b) GATS and the element of threat are inseparable. Besides, the notion 'likely to affect' probably poses a higher bar for FDI screening than the minimum element of threat developed above. This was certainly not the purpose behind the prefix 'likely to affect'.

The other concepts of sensitive assets critical and strategic infrastructure, technology, and inputs, lack the specific link to a military interest. In particular, the geopolitical dimension of and thus broader concept of security behind strategic assets does not qualify as an essential security interest. The security exception in Art XIV*bis*(1)(b) GATS is no open-ended concept, but exhaustively defined in its Subparagraphs (i)–(iii). Broader geopolitical interests may instead constitute fundamental interests of society and thus qualify as a public order interest.

In sum, the security element of the Screening Regulation's screening ground 'security or public order' allows the EU and Member States to meet their concerns vis-à-vis foreign investors only to a very small extent, completely excluding the competition, reciprocity, and private information concern. Nevertheless, the 'public order' element might significantly expand the Screening Regulation's scope.

3.1.4   'Public Order' Pursuant to Art XIV(a) GATS

The element of 'public order' in the screening ground 'security or public order' refers to the notion of 'public order' in Art XIV(a) GATS. Its meaning is also vague, but substantiated in Footnote 5:

> The public order exception may be invoked only where a genuine and sufficiently serious threat is posed to one of the fundamental interests of society.

Hence, in contrast to Art XIV*bis*(1)(b) GATS, the GATS explicitly provides two distinct defining elements to interpret 'public order': fundamental interests of society and a genuine and sufficiently serious threat.[109] As in the panel report *EU—Energy Package*, these will guide the following discussion.[110] The first element, fundamental interest of society, describes the interest that the WTO member must pursue to justify its measure pursuant to Art XIV(a) GATS. When screening FDI, the EU and its Member States must thus be able to invoke such fundamental interest of society. Second, this interest must be threatened by the concrete FDI at issue, similar to Art XIV*bis*(1)(b) GATS for non-hard-core services. Under Art XIV(a) GATS the threat must be genuine and sufficiently serious.

Section 3.1.4 will critically analyze the case law on both definitory elements, deduce common definitions from it, and, finally, apply them to the EU and Member States concerns vis-à-vis foreign investors.

3.1.4.1   Fundamental Interest of Society

Following Footnote 5 to the GATS, WTO Members must as a first requirement pursue a fundamental interest of society. This notion underwent some precision in the disputes *US—Gambling* and *EU—Energy Package*.[111]

---

[109] This definition replicates the ECJ's definition of 'public policy or public security' pursuant to Art 65(1)(b) TFEU, see *Scientology* (n. 43), para. 17 (on the former Art 73d(1)(b) EEC) which was already developed in Case C-36/75 *Rutili v Ministre de l'intérieur* [1975] EU:C:1975:137, para. 28, and thus before the GATS entered into force. Diebold (2008), pp. 62–63, therefore concludes that EU and WTO law should be interpreted analogously. However, given the much higher degree of integration in the EU this conclusion may not be so relentlessly drawn.

[110] *EU—Energy Package* (n. 19), para. 7.1144. The parties' appeal to this report is suspended due to the current impasse of the Appellate Body. In the only Appellate Body report on Art XIV(a) GATS so far, such a detailed analysis was neglected, since the interests at issue also fell under the other element in Art XIV(a) 'public morals', to which Footnote 5 to the GATS does not apply (*US—Gambling*, Appellate Body Report (n. 19), para. 298).

[111] The WTO adjudicating system does not follow legally binding precedents. Nevertheless, Appellate Body reports de facto have a similar status, and, less so, non-appealed, adopted panel reports; n. 62.

3.1.4.1.1   Case Law

The adjudicating bodies' approach to the definition of fundamental interests of society is highly deferential, leaving ample room for WTO members to define certain interests as fundamental.

This general hands-off approach manifests itself in two aspects. First, the concept of fundamental interests of society 'can vary in time and space, depending upon a range of factors, including prevailing social, cultural, ethical and religious values'.[112] The definition of fundamental interests of society may thus differ not only among, but even within WTO members.[113] Moreover, members only have to establish a minimum level of clarity why a certain interest should constitute a fundamental interest of society.[114] Member policies and laws may serve as indications.[115] Accordingly, in *EU—Energy Package* the panel took into account TFEU provisions and Commission communications seeking to secure energy supply for the EU's population.[116]

At the same time, case law only offers a few limits to the deferential understanding of fundamental interests of society. First and foremost, the WTO adjudicating bodies, referring to Footnote 5 to the GATS, hold that the 'public order' exception is no general law and order exception.[117] Moreover, in contrast to public morals, which refers to a community's 'standards of right and wrong conduct',[118] 'public order' is concerned with the impact on the society's functioning.[119] More concretely, the

---

[112] *US—Gambling*, Panel Report (n. 19), para. 6.461; *EU—Energy Package* (n. 19), para. 7.1153. *European Communities—Measures Prohibiting the Importation and Marketing of Seal Products*, Appellate Body Report (22 May 2014) WT/DS400/AB/R and WT/DS401/AB/R, WTO Online Database doc no 14-3051, para. 5.199, followed this substantiation for the definition of public morals in Art XX(a) GATT 1994. It thereby upheld *European Communities—Measures Prohibiting the Importation and Marketing of Seal Products*, Panel Report (25 November 2013) WT/DS400/R and WT/DS401/R, as modified by Appellate Body Report WT/DS400/AB/R and WT/DS401/AB/R, WTO Online Database doc no 13-6374, para. 7.380.

[113] *US—Gambling*, Panel Report (n. 19), para. 6.461, explicitly acknowledges the sensitivity for WTO members to define 'public morals' and 'public order'.

[114] *EU—Energy Package* (n. 19), para. 7.1153.

[115] *US—Gambling*, Panel Report (n. 19), paras. 6.466–6.467, upheld by *US—Gambling*, Appellate Body Report (n. 19), paras. 296, 298; *EU—Energy Package* (n. 19), para. 7.1154.

[116] *EU—Energy Package* (n. 19), para. 7.1154, n. 1923, e.g. Art 194 TFEU; Commission, 'European Energy Security Strategy' (Communication) COM (2014) 330 final.

[117] Implied by *US—Gambling*, Panel Report (n. 19), paras. 6.466–6.467, emphasizing that 'public order' refers only to fundamental interests of society, 'as reflected in public policy and law'; upheld by *US—Gambling*, Appellate Body Report (n. 19), paras. 296, 298.

[118] *US—Gambling*, Panel Report (n. 19), para. 6.465; upheld by *US—Gambling*, Appellate Body Report (n. 19), paras. 296, 298.

[119] Accordingly, the WTO adjudicating bodies held that the prevention of underage and pathological gambling tended to fall under public morals, while organized crime were rather a matter of 'public order'. The prevention of money laundering and of fraud schemes might fall under both concepts. See *US—Gambling*, Panel Report (n. 19), para. 6.469; upheld by *US—Gambling*, Appellate Body Report (n. 19), paras. 296, 298–299.

panel in *EU—Energy Package*, focusing on the functionality criterion, argued that disruptions of energy supply are 'potentially having severe social, economic and, ultimately, political consequences'. The disruption may prevent heating of households and industrial production.[120] The security of energy supply hence constituted a fundamental interest of society.[121]

Consequently, case law defers the definition of fundamental interests of society largely to WTO members, while maintaining certain restricting elements. WTO members must still establish a minimum level of clarity that a harm to the interests may have severe social, economic consequences. A WTO member's laws and policies may serve as an indication.

3.1.4.1.2 Developing the Case Law Further

Further substantiations of the WTO adjudicating bodies' broad definitory aspects are necessary. While many aspects are discussed, only two offer real substantiation to the definition of fundamental interests.

First, one may not compare Art XIV(a) GATS with the *ordre public* (Civil law) or public policy (Common law) exception in International Private Law ('IPL').[122] According to the IPL exception, jurisdictions have the right to deny recognition or enforcement of a judgment from another jurisdiction if it violates a fundamental principle of their legal order.[123] The comparison between IPL and GATS exceptions demonstrates that the international legal order knows very deferential concepts of grounds of exception.[124] For a parallel interpretation, however, the similarities are too little. The IPL exception protects fundamental legal, value-based principles, whereas the 'public order' exception in Art XIV(a) GATS seeks to ensure the functioning of a society from a more practical perspective. If an *ordre public* interest is violated, Art XIV(a) GATS would still require a severe impact on the society's functioning.

Second, as argued in the context of Art XIVbis GATS, the consideration that 'public order' only covered non-trade or non-economic objectives fails to offer any real additional substance.[125]

Third, the fact that an interest is also covered by Art XIVbis(1) or another Subparagraph of Art XIV GATS does not exclude the interest as falling under 'public order'. Instead, Art XIV(a) GATS may overlap with other grounds of exception, especially 'essential security interests', and health and environmental

---

[120] *EU—Energy Package* (n. 19), para. 7.1197; following the EU's argument.

[121] ibid., para. 7.1154.

[122] Krajewski (2003), p. 158; Cottier et al. (2008), para. 22.

[123] Case C-7/98 *Krombach* [2000] EU:C:2000:164, para. 37 (on the Brussels Convention).

[124] Similarly, but leaving further parallels open, Diebold (2008), pp. 56–57 and 64–65.

[125] See Sect. 3.1.3.1.2. Drawing this distinction Mavroidis (2005), p. 181; Cottier et al. (2008), para. 1; Bartels (2015), p. 95.

interests in Arts XIV*bis*(1)(b) and XIV(b) GATS. In particular, one may not distinguish between state interests and Art XIV*bis*(1)(b) GATS on the one hand, and societal interests and Art XIV(a) GATS on the other hand. State and societal interests are too deeply intertwined, and the exhaustive list in Art XIV*bis*(1)(b) GATS would overly limit WTO Members' rights to protect state interests.[126] While WTO Members will usually opt to invoke the more specific provisions of Arts XIV*bis*(1)(b) and XIV(b) and (c) GATS with more lenient requirements,[127] the Screening Regulation preferred the catch-all term 'public order' as its screening ground.

Rather, the focus should be laid on the functional concept of fundamental interests of society. The key criterion is whether a disruption of the interest at issue may have severe social or economic consequences.[128] To assess whether this criterion is met, two aspects can serve as—neither sufficient, nor necessary—indications. First, the member has laws and policies in place that attribute a high importance to the protection of the interest at issue. Hence, not every interest that is protected by laws and policies qualifies as fundamental. Otherwise, the notion of 'public order' would be reduced to a 'law and order' exception.[129] Second, the more people are affected by the disruption of an interest, the more important the interest may be.[130]

Another criterion substantiates fundamental interests of society negatively by carving out the interest to attain or enhance trade autonomy, for example reducing the dependency on the importation of a certain service by protecting its domestic production. The sensitive sector concept of strategic sectors pursues this interest to some extent. The WTO was created to enhance, not reduce international trade. If the grounds of exception to the GATS legitimized the protection of trade autonomy, they would allow WTO Members to pursue interests that their obligations were supposed to prohibit. Protecting trade autonomy as a 'public order' interest is hence not only fundamentally opposed to the WTO's spirit,[131] but would also undermine the WTO Member's rights and obligations.[132] This negative criterion, however, does

---

[126] *Contra* Krajewski (2003), p. 158; Cottier et al. (2008), para. 22.

[127] E.g. for the exception on health in Art XIV(b) GATS there is no threat requirement (Cottier et al. (2008), para. 32).

[128] Seemingly *contra* Grossman et al. (2013), p. 318, who argue that 'public order' is the most encompassing expression negotiators could choose, and that 'any regulatory intervention is presumably done to serve public order'. This understanding would equate 'public order' with public interest and thus contradict Footnote 5 to the GATS.

[129] *US—Gambling*, Panel Report (n. 19), para. 6.466–6.467, made clear that such 'law and order' understanding may be congruent with dictionary definition of 'order', but not with the additional requirements of Footnote 5 to the GATS.

[130] Diebold (2008), pp. 61–62.

[131] Schloemann and Ohlhoff (1999), p. 444.

[132] Of course, WTO members are still entitled to pursue such objectives, e.g. through decoupling their economies as currently China and the US (see Roberts et al. (2019), pp. 673–674). However, they may do so only as long as their measures do not violate their GATS obligations, or a specific

not apply to a case where trade autonomy is only a means to ultimately achieve another objective that is covered by Art XIV(a) GATS.

Therefore, WTO adjudicating bodies are generally right in deferring the definition of fundamental interests of society mostly to WTO Members. This deferential approach reflects the GATS's nature as an agreement that is mostly concerned with negative integration.[133] This is particularly valid for 'public order' as a diverse, dynamic concept of which the meaning depends on the society who is living in it.

Consequently, fundamental interests of society within the meaning of Art XIV (a) GATS are interests that are essential for the functioning of society. They can be manifold, depending on the invoking WTO member's society. Limits are in particular the fundamental status for society, which is well described by potentially severe social or economic consequences. A WTO member's legal framework may serve as an indication that a certain interest is fundamental for its society. The interest of trade autonomy is not covered.

3.1.4.1.3 Pursued Interests According to Concerns Vis-à-Vis Foreign Investors

The Screening Regulation's screening ground 'security or public order' can only meet the EU and Member States concerns vis-à-vis foreign investors if it significantly covers the interests pursued by the competition, reciprocity, harmful investor, and private information concern. Section 3.1.3 has already demonstrated that the security element of 'security or public order' covers the harmful investor concern regarding the defence sector, though with some hurdles for dual-use products. The other sensitive assets as well as the other three concerns generally are not covered by the security element. Therefore, it is crucial for assessing the Screening Regulation's effectiveness to analyze whether the 'public order' element of 'security or public order' covers the interests pursued by the other concerns. In other words, are these interests fundamental interests of society within the meaning of Art XIV(a) GATS?

As a starting point, the deferential definition of 'public order' allows to pursue a variety of interests that constitute fundamental interests of society. By adopting laws and policies, the EU and its Member States may indeed shape the status of interests as fundamental to society within the meaning of the GATS. Nevertheless, the definition criterion of severe social or economic consequences in case of disruption and the exclusion of the trade autonomy interest offer considerable guidance.

The EU and Member States competition concern is in principle covered. As argued above, the characterization of these interests as economic does not mean that they fall outside of the 'public order's' scope. Nevertheless, a harm to the interest in functioning competition must be of severe social or economic

---

provision allows them to (e.g. Art XIX GATT 1994, Agreement on Safeguards). For a similar line of argument see *Argentina—Financial Services*, Appellate Body Report (n. 19), para. 6.117.

[133] See Sect. 3.1.2.2.

consequences. Whether a harm to competition has such consequences is a long-time economic debate. Sceptics of free competition would even argue that the harm had in fact positive social and economic consequences. The GATS itself avoids taking sides.[134] According to the deferential approach to the definition of fundamental interests of society, however, the WTO member states' judgment becomes the benchmark. The EU and its Member States made competition a high priority of their cooperation. The entire internal market policy aims at ensuring and promoting competition. This is, for instance, mirrored in the TFEU rules on competition pursuant to Arts 101–107 and 119–20 TFEU and even in the TFEU's preamble.[135] Accordingly, for the EU and its Member States, a harm to these values may have severe social and economic consequences. However, to have such consequences, this harm must menace the system of competition as a whole. Only in this sense are competition fundamental interests of society within the meaning of Art XIV (a) GATS. This condition will gain importance when assessing the second element of 'public order': 'sufficiently serious threat'. Less important interests of competition may fall under Art XIV(c) GATS.[136]

The reciprocity concern, however, is not covered. The interest of reciprocal trade and investment relationships does not constitute an interest of society that, if harmed, has severe social or economic consequences. First, WTO members relied on reciprocity to negotiate and balance their GATS commitments, but the resulting obligations themselves apply regardless of reciprocity. Hence, WTO members waived their sovereign right to grant benefits on a reciprocal basis to the extent they undertook commitments.[137] Second, reciprocity is a political category of fairness and a negotiation tool in external policy. Accordingly, the EU and its Member States may accept a lower degree of market access for EU FDI into China than they accede to Chinese investors so that China agrees to more effective intellectual property protection. However, a lack of reciprocity has no severe social or economic consequences for the functioning of the EU and its Member States.

The harmful investor concern regarding the sensitive assets of critical and strategic infrastructure, technology, and inputs provides a mixed outcome. Critical infrastructure, technology, and inputs were defined as comprising assets, systems, technologies, or inputs essential for the maintenance of vital societal functions, health, safety, security, or economic or social well-being of people. This definition essentially mirrors the functional definition of fundamental interests. The Member States may therefore pursue a wide range of interests falling under the second group

---

[134] Cf. Krajewski (2001), p. 212, who argues that the WTO is not a general decision in favour of market economy.

[135] The respective part of the TFEU preamble provides: 'Recognising [*sic*] that the removal of existing obstacles calls for concerted action in order to guarantee steady expansion, balanced trade and fair competition'.

[136] For a more detailed discussion of this provision, see Sect. 4.3.7.2.

[137] Mavroidis (2005), p. 55, argues that reciprocity is no legal principle in GATT. A violation of a commitment did not give the affected party the right to in turn violate its own commitments. It had to refer the dispute to the Dispute Settlement System.

of sectors—for instance, securing energy supply, health services, telecommunication infrastructure, data storage and processing facilities and services. All these interests are, however, only covered to the extent they are protecting the essential, basic needs of the population. This aspect will become decisive under the second element of 'public order'.

The sensitive asset concept of strategic infrastructure, technology, and inputs, on the other hand, goes beyond the focus on vital societal functions. With this concern, EU and Member States pursue long-term industrial, economic, and geopolitical goals. This entails considerations to strengthen competitive advantages to facilitate building globally competitive domestic firms, as well as to protect or build certain assets of specific geopolitical importance. Therefore, the strategic asset concept at least in part aims at enhancing or protecting trade autonomy—an interest that, as analyzed above, does not constitute a fundamental interest of society. However, as far as other vital societal interests are pursued, these may qualify as fundamental interests of society.

Last but not least, the private information concern may also constitute a fundamental interest of society to the extent it addresses a significant part of the population or businesses. The fundamental value of protecting personal data for the EU and its Member States is inter alia reflected in Arts 8 and 17(1) CFR, as well as in the GDPR.[138] Nevertheless, these values are primarily individual interests. Here, the above-developed criterion of quantity comes into play. Only if a significant part of the population or businesses is affected, the individual interest becomes a fundamental interest of society.[139]

In sum, the 'public order' element in the screening ground 'security or public order' considerably covers the EU and Member States concerns vis-à-vis foreign investors as far as its first element, fundamental interest of society, is concerned. While the reciprocity concern is not covered, the harmful investor concern regarding critical assets in fact coincides with the concept of fundamental interest of society. The harmful investor concern is, however, not covered to the extent it addresses strategic assets and seeks to enhance or protect the EU's and Member States' trade autonomy. The competition and private information concerns pursue fundamental interests of the society only to the extent they address potential harm of large scale.

This rather positive conclusion for the screening ground's scope has, nonetheless, not yet addressed the core question for FDI screening: Is the concrete FDI at issue a matter of 'public order'? This aspect is addressed by its second element.

---

[138] Regulation (EU) 2016/679 of the European Parliament and of the Council of 27 April 2016 on the protection of natural persons with regard to the processing of personal data and on the free movement of such data, and repealing Directive 95/46/EC (GDPR) [2016] OJ L 119/1.

[139] See also on 'cyberthreats' generally, Mishra (2020a), p. 353.

3.1.4.2   Genuine and Sufficiently Serious Threat

Art XIV(a) GATS only protects a WTO member's fundamental interests of society if they are subject to a genuine and sufficiently serious threat. As will be demonstrated, this second element is the actual threshold for a WTO member to establish the ground of exception of 'public order'. The following discusses the first and only WTO case that dealt with this requirement, before substantiating it further and applying it to the EU and Member States concerns vis-à-vis third-country investors.

3.1.4.2.1   EU—Energy Package: Lenient Interpretation of 'Genuine Threat'

The panel report in *EU—Energy Package* is crucial for the interpretation of the second element of 'public order' for two reasons. First, it is so far the only WTO case law on the interpretation of genuine and sufficiently serious threat. It was appealed by both the EU and Russia. But due to the impasse of the Appellate Body the appeal's outcome is uncertain. Second, one of the challenged measures constitutes a narrow version of an FDI Screening mechanism.

Summary of the Case: A Quasi-FDI Screening Mechanism
The *EU—Energy Package* case dealt with several EU measures to regulate the internal market in natural gas, in particular the Directive 2009/73/EC on natural gas operations.[140] Among other measures, the Directive 2009/73/EC requires a certification for natural gas transmission system operators ('TSOs') to start their operations. In contrast to domestic TSOs, foreign controlled TSOs have to fulfil an additional criterion: they must establish that they will not put at risk the security of energy supply of the EU.[141] As the certification must be reassessed in case of a change in control, the certification requirement in fact constitutes an M&A FDI Screening mechanism.

The panel found this 'third-country certification measure' to violate the NT obligation in Art XVII GATS. To justify the violation, the EU invoked Art XIV (a) GATS and argued that the third-country certification measures was necessary to protect its 'public order'. More specifically, the EU argued that a foreign controlled TSO poses a genuine and sufficiently serious threat to the EU's security of energy supply, since the home country government may have the incentive and means to 'require or induce foreign controlled TSOs' to disrupt its gas supply.[142] This argument echoes the EU and its Member States harmful investor concern. The

---

[140] Directive 2009/73/EC of the European Parliament and of the Council of 13 July 2009 concerning common rules for the internal market in natural gas and repealing Directive 2003/55/EC [2009] OJ L 211/94.

[141] ibid., Arts 11(1),(3), 10(4)(b). Control is defined as 'the possibility of exercising decisive influence on an undertaking', ia through ownership or contractual arrangements (ibid., Art 2(36)).

[142] *EU—Energy Package* (n. 19), paras. 7.1171–7.1172.

panel rightly concluded that this argument refers to the element of genuine threat, addressing the notion 'sufficiently serious threat' later.[143]

Ultimately, the panel accepted the EU's defence under Subparagraph (a) of Art XIV GATS, but rejected it under its *chapeau*.[144] The EU could not show that it took similar measures against domestic TSOs that are also subject to foreign government influence due to business activities in these countries. The panel therefore concluded that addressing foreign TSOs only was applying the third-country certification measure 'in a manner which [constitutes] a means of arbitrary ... discrimination between countries'.[145]

The Panel's Interpretation and Lenient Application of 'Genuine and Sufficiently Serious Threat'

In the abstract, the panel interpreted the notion of genuine threat as 'a real, true and authentic possibility' that the purported threat materializes.[146] According to the panel, a (clearly) imminent threat or a 'significant degree of likelihood' would set the threshold too high.[147] 'Mere conjecture or speculation', 'an imaginary or very remote risk', and 'entirely hypothetical' would, on the other hand, constitute low degrees of likelihood.[148] The panel also held that a higher level of seriousness of the threat might reduce the required threshold of likelihood.[149]

The panel went on to apply these defining criteria rather cursorily. It proceeded in three steps to assess the EU's argument that foreign governments may instrumentalize TSOs to threaten the EU's security of energy supply. First, it held

---

[143] ibid., para. 7.1172.

[144] The panel also adopted a very deferential approach on the necessity test, in particular on the test of a reasonably available less restrictive measure, see Pogoretskyy and Talus (2020), p. 546 (on *EU—Energy Package* (n. 19), paras. 7.1229–7.1238). In the ambit of Art XX GATT 1994, the necessity test also loses importance, see Howse (2016), pp. 49–50. Sykes (2015), pp. 303–304 sees both elements, necessity test and *chapeau*, as counterweight to the deferential approach on the interests listed in Art XX GATT 1994.

[145] *EU—Energy Package* (n. 19), para. 7.1253: 'While we do not mean to imply that the same regulatory scheme should necessarily be applied with respect to foreign and domestically controlled TSOs, we believe that the European Union is required to adapt or "calibrate" its measure in a way so it addresses the threats posed by foreign governments requiring or inducing domestically controlled TSOs to undermine the European Union's security of energy supply as well. The lack of *any* assessment of threats posed by foreign governments requiring or inducing domestically controlled TSOs to undermine the European Union's security of energy supply, in our view, is not compatible with the cause or rationale of the third-country certification measure. Hence, this constitutes arbitrary and unjustifiable discrimination in violation of the *chapeau* of Article XIV of the GATS.' (emphasis in the original).

[146] ibid., para. 7.1168.

[147] ibid., paras. 7.1166–7.1168.

[148] ibid., paras. 7.1167–7.1168, 1189. On the difference between threat and risk in general in international law, Tsagourias (2017), p. 15.

[149] *EU—Energy Package* (n. 19), para. 7.1169.

that a foreign government had an incentive to induce firms controlled by its citizens to undermine the EU's security of energy supply.[150] Second, TSOs had a critical role for the EU's energy supply. Hence, the failure of one TSO to comply with its obligations had an impact on the EU's energy security as a whole.[151] Third, a foreign government had 'the means to require or induce' firms controlled by its citizens to comply with its own rather than the firm's commercial interests or legal obligations under EU law.[152] Mostly relying on these inferences and without demanding much evidence by the EU, the panel found a genuine threat that foreign governments required or induced foreign TSOs to undermine the EU's security of energy supply.[153]

Following the structure of Footnote 5 to the GATS, the panel then assessed whether the EU established a sufficiently serious threat. The panel held that this element required a threat of a certain magnitude or gravity.[154] It added that natural gas was far less fungible than oil, and that its supply infrastructure was fixed and of a finite quantity. Accordingly, if only one TSO interrupted its gas supply, the consequences would be significant.[155] Therefore, a sufficiently serious threat was found to be established.

Last but not least, the panel held that in this case a prudential regulatory framework could neither reduce the threat's likeliness, nor mitigate its gravity.[156] The fact that foreign controlled TSOs violated rules set by the regulatory framework for the natural gas market was the main argument to establish a threat in the first place.

---

[150] The EU only invoked two historical examples in which foreign governments took a similar measure: an oil embargo by the Organization of Arab Petroleum Exporting Countries in 1973 and the interruption of gas supplies to Ukraine in 2006 and 2009 (ibid., para. 7.1174). In both situations, however, the states interfered in 'their' firm's export of domestic products, not in a domestic firm's overseas production. Only the latter would match the allegation at issue in that, a foreign investor threatens the EU's energy security.

[151] ibid., para. 7.1181.

[152] ibid., paras. 7.1185–7.1187.

[153] It is important to note that for the case at issue the lenient interpretation of genuine threat had only limited consequences. The EU could not show that it took similar measures against domestic TSOs with business activities abroad. According to the panel, such domestic TSOs are, however, as susceptible to foreign government influence as foreign investors. The panel therefore concluded that only addressing foreign TSOs was arbitrary, and hence rejected the EU's defence under the *chapeau* of Art XIV(a) GATS; see ibid., para. 7.1253. This final conclusion might have affected the panel's generous application of its threat definition elements.

[154] ibid., paras. 7.1163, 7.1195.

[155] ibid., para. 7.1199.

[156] ibid., paras. 7.1179–7.1180, 7.1200–7.1201.

3.1.4.2.2   Further Elaborating the Definition of a Genuine and Sufficiently Serious Threat

The panel's definition of threat within the meaning of Art XIV(a) GATS as a real, true, and authentic possibility of a certain magnitude or gravity seems generally appropriate. However, further precision is necessary, particularly concerning the very lenient application of the definition of genuine threat to the facts.

Regarding the notion of genuine threat, it is uncertain whether WTO adjudicating bodies will adhere to the very lenient and cursory interpretation when confronted with a different set of facts. In principle, it is appropriate in the WTO context to set the probability threshold not too high. The few information exchange mechanisms and obligations between WTO Members may sometimes even justify to rely on inferences and assumptions.[157] Otherwise, the 'public order' exception may become a merely theoretical defence. Nevertheless, a genuine threat must require more than a causal relationship between the cause and the potential harm. If a threat's materialization is contingent on a human decision, namely of a government, there must be a real possibility that this decision will in fact be taken. Establishing that the decision maker has the (legal) means to take the decision is insufficient.

This seems to be ignored by the panel in *EU—Energy Package*. The panel concluded a genuine threat from its finding that a government generally has the possibility to induce a foreign investor and that an investor can disrupt natural gas supply through the acquired asset.

In addition, the panel seems to generally accept the argument that any foreign investor may be induced by its home country government to harm a certain host state interest, and thus genuinely poses a threat to a fundamental interest of society. This reasoning, however, legitimizes mistrust against foreign investors as a rule. This rule would undermine the GATS. Therefore, the standard of a genuine threat must be higher than the simple fact that a foreign government can induce an investor based in its country.

The notion sufficiently serious, on the other hand, was rightly defined as addressing both magnitude and gravity of the threat. The former describes an element of quantity, the latter a quality requirement. Both aspects are interrelated and important to limit the broad, deferential definition of fundamental interest of society. A certain magnitude is, for instance, reached if a large number of people are affected by the threat. To establish a certain level of gravity, the possible harm to the fundamental interest of society must be of a high intensity; in case of energy security, for example, the complete stop of energy supply. The panel rightly applied both elements when finding that TSOs relied on fixed infrastructure for a finite quantity of natural gas at a given time. An interruption of natural gas supply by one single TSO

---

[157] See Art XIV*bis*(1)(a) GATS on the non-disclosure of information for 'essential security interests'.

(quality element of threat) would thus affect large parts of the population and industry (quantity element).[158]

The natural gas example indicates a criterion for the seriousness of a threat for cases in which a society risks to be deprived of the access to a particular product. If the service of fundamental interest to society is supplied by a company holding a monopoly or large portion of market shares, a disruption of this firm's supplies will automatically have severe consequences.[159] By definition, a monopoly holding company has large market power that may not or only with great effort be substituted by another supplier—for legal, natural, or economic reasons. Particularly relevant in the FDI screening context are economic monopolies due to cutting-edge technologies, as well as natural monopolies because of capacity constraints for supply infrastructure. In the electricity, natural gas, petroleum, and water sector, for instance, suppliers rely on single transmission systems such as pipelines or grid. In all these cases of monopolies, the consumer's accommodation with the service of fundamental interest depends on the monopolist supplying this service. Once the monopolist stops its supply, the consumer is deprived of the service. This effect lasts for as long as the firm resumes the supply, since alternative suppliers do not exist in a monopolistic market.

The rationale for monopolies also applies to suppliers who hold a large portion of market shares. They are similarly difficult to be replaced by alternative suppliers.

As a result, in case an FDI threatens the supply with a service of fundamental interest to society, the seriousness of the threat may be presumed if the acquired domestic asset holds a monopoly or a large portion of market shares.

Finally, the prudential regulatory framework may be taken into account when determining whether a fundamental interest of society is threatened. As mentioned above, the panel in *EU—Energy Package* held that the regulatory framework could not mitigate a possible threat. In the case's context, this conclusion is correct. The presumption that an investor will not respect its legal obligations may not be rebutted by a regulatory framework that seeks to ensure service supply precisely through legal obligations. Beyond such fact settings, however, the prudential regulatory may indeed be taken into account for assessing a threat. The regulatory framework may create a factual structure that prevents or reduces the likeliness that a firm's non-compliance with the regulatory framework harms the fundamental interest at issue. A regulatory authority may, for example, have the power and resources to take over essential operations of the non-compliant firm. Hence, the threat would be less likely to materialize or to have less severe consequences. The first outcome rebuts the threat's genuineness, the latter its seriousness. Nevertheless, the WTO context

---

[158] *EU—Energy Package* (n. 19), para.7.1199.

[159] See Wolff (2009), pp. 190–191, on the notion of 'public policy or public security' pursuant to Art 65(1)(b) TFEU. *Wolff* argues that the ECJ only found a genuine and sufficiently serious threat in case of monopolist market structures. However, the analysis of the ECJ's case law will show that the ECJ seems to be willing to also find a genuine and sufficiently serious threat in other cases. Monopolistic market structures may not be more than an indicative criterion for finding a sufficiently serious threat. For a more detailed discussion see Sect. 3.2.2.

demands that the regulatory framework as a threat attenuating factor is used with caution. WTO members have the right to determine the level of protection they consider appropriate according to their specific situation, namely their resources and their society's risk aversiveness.[160]

All in all, the panel report in *EU—Energy Package* thus lied out important clarifications for the interpretation of genuine and sufficiently serious threat. Genuine and sufficiently serious threat means a real, true, and authentic possibility of a certain magnitude or gravity. These requirements must be taken seriously.[161] In particular, there must be concrete indications that the threat will materialize. The mere factual possibility is insufficient to satisfy the requirements of a genuine threat.

However, the panel report in *EU—Energy Package*, indicated an alternative approach to deal with the vague ground of exception of 'public order': the *chapeau*. Having leniently applied the definition to the facts, the panel rejected the EU's defence under the *chapeau* as an arbitrary discrimination between countries. One may therefore be tempted to neglect the complicated definition of fundamental interests of society and genuine and sufficiently serious threat, and focus on the *chapeau*. To reject this argument, a brief excursus on the other elements of Art XIV GATS is required.

It indeed seems that the WTO adjudicating bodies perceive the *chapeau* as the real bottleneck of the grounds of exception in Art XIV GATS. The *chapeau* prohibits arbitrary or unjustifiable, and thus not all discrimination when applying the measure at issue that pursues an interest listed in Art XIV GATS.[162] In *EU—Energy Package*, the panel found such discrimination and therefore dismissed a justification of the third-country certification measure under Art XIV(a) GATS.[163] This approach under Art XIV GATS is in line with WTO case law in general.[164]

On the other hand, the *chapeau* only addresses a measure's application. Thus, the measure itself remains in place. The respondent must only modify the application, meaning the factor that results in the unjustified or arbitrary discrimination ('modification measure').[165] In *EU—Energy Package*, for instance, the panel demanded

---

[160] See n. 44.

[161] Similarly, Diebold (2008), pp. 62–63.

[162] Ayres and Mitchell (2013), p. 251.

[163] *EU—Energy Package* (n. 19), para. 7.1253.

[164] See e.g. in the GATS realm *US—Gambling*, Appellate Body Report (n. 19), para. 369; *Argentina—Measures Relating to Trade in Goods and Services*, Panel Report (30 September 2015) WT/DS453/R, as modified by Appellate Body Report WT/DS453/AB/R, WTO Online Database doc no 15-5027, paras. 7.761–7.763 (the panel's finding on the *chapeau* was, contrary to other aspects, not appealed); as well as in the GATT 1994 realm *US—Shrimp* (n. 77), paras. 176, 184–186 (on Art XX(g) GATT 1994); *EC—Seal Products*, Appellate Body Report (n. 112), paras. 5.338–5.339 (on Art XX(a) GATT 1994). With the same conclusion on the *chapeau* as the actual bottleneck, Gaines (2001), pp. 743–744; Peter (2012), p. 122; Bartels (2015), p. 112.

[165] Howse (2016), p. 52. Accordingly, in *Argentina—Financial Services*, Appellate Body Report (n. 19), para. 6.156, the complainant Panama challenged the panel's finding that the measure at issue was 'necessary to secure compliance with laws or regulations' (Art XIV(c) GATS), even though the panel had followed Panama by finding that the measure at issue violated the *chapeau*.

that the EU adopted controls of domestic TSOs that operate on the EU and foreign markets—a call for a cohesive, but not identical policy framework for foreign and domestically controlled TSOs.[166] Effectively, the EU must thus either abolish the third-country certification measure, or introduce the same or another policy tool to also address the risk that domestic TSOs with business activities abroad pose.

As a consequence, the EU must either refrain from pursuing its policy interest or introduce new policy measures that may in turn create new restrictions to trade. Hence, the trade-restrictive measure may not only stay in place, but be complemented by a new trade restriction. As a result, the *chapeau* approach in fact encouraged trade restrictions. Moreover, a strict *chapeau* test has serious side effects. It also applies in cases where the WTO members pursue vital policy objectives that are clearly covered by the notion of 'public order' or other interests listed in Art XIV GATS. As the adoption of modification measures entails policy costs, a strict *chapeau* test also increases costs for clearly legitimate measures pursuing vital societal interests. In *EU—Energy Package*, such costs may, for example, occur due to additional measures against domestic TSOs, for the EU and its Member States themselves as well as for the domestic TSOs concerned.

These two aspects show that an overly broad understanding of 'public order', particularly of the element genuine threat, cannot be appropriately attenuated by the *chapeau* of Art XIV GATS. Therefore, an understanding of 'public order' that is generally deferential, especially regarding the determination of fundamental interests of society, while leaving significant meaning to the requirement of threat is not only formally in line with Art XIV(a) GATS, but also its broader context in Art XIV GATS.[167]

In sum, the element genuine and sufficiently serious threat, second element of 'public order' pursuant to Footnote 5 to the GATS, therefore serves as the real threshold to the 'public order' exception. The meaning of a real, authentic, and true possibility for the materialization of a threat of a certain magnitude or gravity has to be taken seriously to do justice to the notion of 'public order' in Art XIV(a) GATS.

3.1.4.2.3   Concerns Vis-à-Vis Foreign Investors

With these definitions in mind, the discussion can now turn to assessing to what extent the 'public order' element in the screening ground 'security or public order' covers the EU and Member States concerns vis-à-vis foreign investors when taking the element of threat into account. Section 3.1.4.1 concluded that the 'public order' element covers the harmful investor concern regarding critical and, in part, strategic assets, as well as the competition and private information concern to the extent they address potential harm of large scale.

---

[166] *EU—Energy Package* (n. 19), para. 7.1253.

[167] For a more detailed discussion of the other two elements of Art XIV(a) GATS, the necessity test and the chapeau, see Sect. 4.3.7.2.2.

To fulfil the conditions of the second element of 'public order' within the meaning of the GATS and thus screen specific FDI, the EU and Member States concerns vis-à-vis foreign investors must envisage FDI that poses a genuine and sufficiently serious threat to these interests.

The threat's first element, genuine, sets a relatively high threshold given the concerns at issue. Concrete facts may often not be available to prove a real possibility for the threat to materialize. Shareholder resolutions that prove an investor's plan to harm a public interest are unlikely; for example, the agreement to transfer critical technology know-how after the FDI. Similarly, earlier experiences may often lack; for instance, that the investor at issue had already transferred know-how after a similar previous transaction or that the home country government had already induced the investor to harm the FDI host state. Moreover, the fact that an investor A or foreign government B once posed a threat to a fundamental interest of society cannot establish that investor C or foreign government D will do the same.[168] Such general mistrust in foreign exporters and their governments is not covered by 'security or public order' interpreted in accordance with the GATS.

Combined with the second 'public order' element, sufficiently serious threat, the threshold becomes even higher. An FDI into a sector of fundamental interest of society that only affects the sector to a small extent will not pose a sufficiently serious threat. While the broad interest pursued by the FDI screening may constitute a fundamental interest of society, the concrete FDI at issue must threaten precisely the aspect that makes the interest a fundamental interest. For example, if a foreign investor acquires only one of many electricity suppliers in a city, the inhabitants' need for electricity will still be sufficiently satisfied in case the investor stops the acquired electricity supplier from providing electricity. Other electricity suppliers can take over. Hence, prohibiting the FDI would pursue the interest of securing the population's electricity needs. However, the concrete FDI is irrelevant to this goal, its prohibition does thus not pursue the 'public order' interest.

FDI in firms holding monopolies, on the other hand, will more easily result in sufficiently serious threats if the firms provide products that are fundamental to society. Therefore, the screening ground 'security or public order' widely covers FDI in natural monopoly, such as water, gas, electricity grid operators (not end suppliers as in the example), as well as technological monopoly sectors, including certain artificial intelligence and robotics applications, provided a genuine threat is established.

Nevertheless, the requirement of a sufficiently serious threat limits the EU and Member States ability in particular with regards to the competition and private information concern. Nearly no individual FDI will menace the system of competition in the internal market as a whole. Slightly more probable, but still rare is an FDI that gives the foreign investor access of private information of a significant part of the population or businesses.

---

[168] See n. 150 for the respective EU argument in *EU—Energy Package*.

All in all, the element of threat therefore reduces the scope of the 'public order' element in the screening ground 'security or public order' to a few, high-profile FDIs. The vast majority of FDI may not pose a genuine and sufficiently serious threat to a fundamental interest of society.

3.1.4.3 GATS Notion of 'Public Order': Unfit for the Vast Majority of FDI of Concern

The above discussion shows that the notion of 'public order' within the meaning of the GATS is unfit to address the vast majority of EU and Member States concerns vis-à-vis foreign investors—at least when assessing the screening of potential, concrete FDI. The EU and Member States reciprocity concern is not covered at all. The same may be said about the competition concern. Regarding the harmful investor and private information concern, the screening ground only covers a few, high-profile FDIs. The interest to enhance or protect a certain level of trade autonomy, as often included in the harmful investor concern about strategic assets, is not covered.

Similar to the conclusion under Art XIV*bis*(1)(b) GATS, it was shown that the element of threat is crucial to balance the deferential definition of fundamental interests of society, especially the aspect of a sufficiently serious threat. This further supports the argument in Sect. 3.1.1 that the protected interests are inseparable from the element of threat; and that therefore the Screening Regulation's prefix '*likely to affect* security or public order' cannot override the Screening Regulation's reference to Art XIV(a) GATS and its inherent probability nexus 'genuine threat'.

Consequently, the interpretation of 'public order' within the meaning of the GATS shows that the Screening Regulation's notion 'security or public order' is largely unfit as an FDI screening ground that intends to meet the EU and Member States concerns vis-à-vis foreign investors. The screening ground's scope is limited to a few, high-profile FDIs of concern.

3.1.5 'Security or Public Order' Pursuant to WTO Law: Appropriate Screening Ground Only in Parts

The Screening Regulation was, at least for many actors in the EU and Member States, adopted as a means to meet the EU and Member States concerns vis-à-vis foreign investors. Its screening ground 'security or public order' should therefore be expected to significantly cover these competition, reciprocity, harmful investor, and private information concerns. The screening ground's scope is determined by the GATS notions of 'essential security interests' (Art XIV*bis*(1)(b)(i) GATS) and 'public order' (Art XIV(a) GATS). The so defined screening ground of 'security or public order' misses this purpose.

The definitions of 'essential security interests' and 'public order' showed that the screening ground 'security or public order' is very open to a wide range of interests pursued. They only—but importantly—exclude the interest of reciprocity and enhancing or protecting trade autonomy, often included in the harmful investor concern about strategic assets.

However, the fact that a broad policy interest is covered does not mean that the screening ground covers any FDI screening that remotely contributes to this interest. Rather, the FDI must threaten this interest. The threshold of threat is not determined by the Screening Regulation's prefix *'likely to affect* security or public order', since the threat element is inseparable from the notions of 'essential security interests' and 'public order'.

The threshold of threat differs significantly between military-related and other interests. For FDI into targets that provide directly military-related products, such as tank production or maintenance, no additional element of threat must be established. For FDI into targets that produce dual-use products a minimum, but considerable threshold of threat applies. Both interests address the harmful investor concern on the defence sector. For all other concerns, as far as the pursued interests are covered, the element of threat reduces the screening ground's scope to a few, high-profile cases of FDI. The threat must be of a certain probability, and its potential effect shall be of a certain quantity and quality for the interest at issue.

As a result, the Screening Regulation seems a realistic option for only two groups of FDI targets. The first group of FDI targets consists of firms providing infrastructure, technology, or inputs that directly provision and are indispensable for generally recognized military functions. Screening FDI into firms providing dual-use items, on the other hand, remains difficult under the Screening Regulation. The second group of relevant FDI screening targets holds monopolies or large parts of market shares in a certain sensitive sector, for any disruption of their production will usually have a large effect in quantity and quality. However, the Member State must establish a real possibility that this threat scenario materializes.

In sum, EU and Member States therefore cannot meet large parts of their concerns vis-à-vis foreign investors with FDI Screening mechanisms based on the Screening Regulation and its screening ground 'security or public order'. Accordingly, the Screening Regulation does also not significantly raise barriers for foreign investors in the EU. Hence, the Screening Regulation also provides little leverage to achieve more favourable FDI treatment for EU investors from certain trading partners, notably China. The reciprocity concern vis-à-vis foreign investors is thus not even met through this indirect route.

Indeed, this result may come as a surprise. When arguing that the Screening Regulation was adopted precisely to meet the EU and Member States concerns vis-à-vis foreign investors, it appears contradictory that the regulation should now cover them only to a limited extent. However, the underlying assumption of this argument is flawed. As argued in Sect. 3.1.1, the object and purpose of the Screening Regulation is not to meet all EU and Member States concerns vis-à-vis foreign investors. In fact, the adoption and concrete design of the Screening Regulation was highly controversial. Accordingly, interpreting 'security or public order' in accordance with the GATS was a compromise—and the above conclusions demonstrate its costs for those who wanted to meet significantly more of the EU and Member States concerns vis-à-vis foreign investors. Nevertheless, the following Sect. 3.2 will show that the screening ground 'security or public order' is broader than the notions of 'public policy or public security'. The Screening Regulation does thus provide a broader option for FDI Screening mechanisms than those previously available to Member States.

3.2   FDI Screening Mechanisms Based on the TFEU Exception 'Public Policy or Public Security'

Section 3.1 concluded that FDI Screening mechanisms on the basis of the Screening Regulation meet the EU and Member States concerns vis-à-vis foreign investors only to a limited extent. Accordingly, it is worth considering the alternative legislative options for FDI Screening mechanisms that are available to Member States after the Screening Regulation. The most relevant option is an FDI Screening mechanism based on the screening ground 'public policy or public security' within the meaning of Art 65(1)(b) TFEU. Thus, for such an FDI Screening mechanism, the crucial question is: Does it cover more FDI of concern than the Screening Regulation and its screening ground 'security or public order'?

One is indeed inclined to presume that a ground of exception to a Fundamental freedom in EU law must evidently be narrower in scope than similar grounds of exception in WTO law. A higher level of harmonization might result in narrower grounds of exception.[169] Accordingly, FDI screening on the grounds of 'public policy or public security' within the meaning of Art 65(1)(b) TFEU would necessarily cover less FDI of concern than the screening ground 'security or public order' defined in accordance with the GATS. At the same time, however, one could also argue that the Fundamental freedoms as further reaching obligations than the GATS obligations must rely on broader grounds of exception than the GATS.

Without engaging in an in-depth comparative study, the following will define the notion 'public policy or public security' pursuant to Art 65(1)(b) TFEU to then assess whether an FDI Screening mechanism on this basis covers more FDI of concern than the Screening Regulation's screening ground 'security or public order'.

The analysis of the notion 'public policy or public security' departs from three main premises.[170] First, as a ground of exception to all Fundamental freedoms in the

---

[169] Munin (2010), p. 395.

[170] The following will cite a number of ECJ judgments and scholar contributions that were issued prior to the Treaty of Lisbon. Accordingly, they cite EEC or EC, not TFEU provisions. Nevertheless, the following will only highlight cases in which the difference between EEC and EC on the one, and TFEU on the other hand are relevant to the conclusion drawn from the judgments and contributions.

TFEU,[171] it is similarly interpreted under all of them.[172] Second, in accordance with the case law, the notion 'public policy or public security' is treated as one, not two grounds of exception. Third, the European Court of Justice ('ECJ') defines 'public policy or public security' as 'a genuine and sufficiently serious threat to a fundamental interest of society'[173]—a definition well-known from Footnote 5 to the GATS.[174] Only within these—in principle, strictly interpreted[175]—constraints may the Member States freely determine their fundamental interests.[176] The following is therefore also structured by the two core elements: fundamental interest of society and genuine and sufficiently serious threat.

Sections 3.2.1 and 3.2.2 will first define these two elements and apply them to FDI screening in the EU. On this basis, Sect. 3.2.3 will summarize that the screening ground 'public policy or public security' is even narrower in scope than 'security or public order' within the meaning of the Screening Regulation. Finally, Sect. 3.2.4 will address a particularity in EU law. Usually, the ground of exception 'public policy or public security' applies in an intra-EU context, since this is the primary scope of the Fundamental freedoms. The freedom of capital movement and its ground of exception Art 65(1)(b) TFEU, however, also apply to third-country investors. It is in this context that an FDI Screening mechanism on the screening ground 'public policy or public security' would apply. Section 3.2.4 will discuss different scholar contributions that are in favour of interpreting the exception ground 'public policy or public security' more broadly in a third-country context. Yet, it will be shown that this is not the case. The results reached in Sect. 3.2.3 thus remain valid.

---

[171] Arts 36, 45(3), 52(1), 62, and 65(1)(b) TFEU.

[172] Lübke (2006), p. 381; Leible and Streinz (2020), para. 17; Ress and Ukrow (2020c), para. 52. Sedlaczek and Züger (2018b), para. 3, emphasize that there are nevertheless certain differences depending on the context of each ground of exception.

[173] Settled case law, see only *Scientology* (n. 43), para. 17, citing *Rutili v Ministre de l'intérieur* (n. 109), para. 28; on the free movement of workers and former Art 48(3) EEC. Müller-Graff (2018), para. 10, nevertheless defines 'public policy' and 'public security' separately. Lübke (2006), p. 383, agrees, while rightly emphasizing that 'public security' is a part of the broader notion 'public policy'. Even from this perspective, a separate interpretation of both notions is therefore of no additional value to the theses submitted in this book.

[174] See Sect. 3.1.4. However, the book focuses on analyzing the EU's and Member States' flexibility to screen FDI, and thus omits a detailed comparative analysis of 'public order' pursuant to Art XIV (a) GATS on the one, and 'public policy or public security' pursuant to Art 65(1)(b) TFEU on the other hand.

[175] See e.g. *Scientology* (n. 43), para. 17. This principle is derived from the interpretative means of teleological interpretation and its instrument *effet utile*, both crucial to interpreting EU law, Wegener (2016a), para. 16. Support for the principle to interpret exceptions strictly is, however, on the retreat, in particular in national legal orders, see Rüthers et al. (2018), para. 820a. Discussing this principle generally in the context of delimiting the freedoms of capital movement and establishment Herz (2014), pp. 372–390.

The Appellate Body rejects the principle to interpret exceptions strictly, see n. 43.

[176] See e.g. Case C-503/99 *Commission v Belgium* [2002] EU:C:2002:328, para. 47, citing *Scientology* (n. 43), para. 17.

3.2.1   Fundamental Interest of Society

The first defining element of the notion 'public policy or public security' is the term 'fundamental interest of society'. The definition of fundamental interest of society pursuant to Art XIV(a) GATS was already so broad that an even broader interpretation under the notion 'public policy or public security' is nearly impossible. The following will therefore only briefly outline the ECJ's case law, provide some further clarification, and then assess the extent to which the EU and Member States concerns vis-à-vis foreign investors are covered.

3.2.1.1   ECJ Case Law: Little Clarity

The ECJ case law on defining fundamental interest of society provides little clarity. In only one judgment the ECJ indicates a general definition of fundamental interest of society. Moreover, just a few cases clearly define certain interests as fundamental to society. Instead, in most cases the ECJ leaves it open whether it is assessing a certain interest under the written ground of exception 'public policy or public security' or the unwritten ground of exception 'overriding reasons in the public interest'.[177] The latter concept is much broader. As a result, an interest that the ECJ found to be justified must not necessarily constitute a fundamental interest. It may as well 'only' qualify as a broader overriding reason in the public interest.[178] Yet, if the ECJ found that a certain interest did not fall under either of the grounds of exception, it is clear that the interest constitutes no fundamental interest of society.

Many of the below cited ECJ judgments dealt with 'Golden shares'. These are special rights that allow a state to exercise certain important controlling or managing rights in a firm beyond those that are regularly coming with the shares that the state

---

[177] See the key judgements *Dassonville* (n. 11); *Cassis de Dijon* (n. 11).

[178] The concepts of fundamental interest of society, and overriding reason in the public interest are fundamentally different. Given its purpose the latter is much broader. The ECJ introduced the unwritten ground of exception, overriding reasons in the public interest, to rebalance a rather expansive understanding of the Fundamental freedoms' scope. Prohibiting not only open, but also hidden discrimination, and even any restriction of free movement, the ECJ recognized that only a broader, unwritten ground of exception guarantees a sufficient degree of policy space for Member States. Overriding reasons in the public interest were thus created to be broader than the interests already protected by the written grounds of justification, for instance Art 65(1)(b) TFEU (for this history see e.g. Müller-Graff (2015), paras. 183–191; Kingreen (2016), paras. 37–48, 80–83). Today, however, the difference between both grounds of exception increasingly loses importance. Non-open discriminations or restrictions may be as intense barriers to the free movement as open discriminations. Moreover, the line between open and hidden discriminations is blurred. Scholars therefore increasingly argue that the unwritten ground of exception should apply to all forms of restriction of the Fundamental freedoms (see e.g. Dietz and Streinz (2015), p. 71; Schröder (2018), para. 34). Accordingly, the ECJ does often not specify the type of discrimination or restriction and then assesses whether the interest invoked by the defending Member State constitutes an overriding reason in the public interest.

holds in this firm.[179] For better understanding the background of each judgment, the cases are cited with a brief summary of the facts.

3.2.1.1.1 The Clear ECJ Judgments

As initially stated, the ECJ only once indicated a general definition of fundamental interests of society generally. In the judgment *Campus Oil* the ECJ held,

> It should be stated . . . that petroleum products, because of their exceptional importance as an energy source in the modern economy, are of fundamental importance for a country's existence, since not only its economy but above all its institutions, its essential public services and even the survival of its inhabitants depend upon them.[180]

The ECJ thus not only stated that the supply of petroleum products constitutes a fundamental interest of society. It also generally defined interests as fundamental for society if they are of fundamental importance for a country's economy, its institutions, its essential public services, or the survival of its inhabitants.

Applying these general criteria in subsequent judgments, the ECJ held that secure energy supply[181] and telecommunication[182] constitute fundamental interests of society. It is interesting to note that the ECJ referred to EC directives to argue that secure energy supply is of crucial importance to the EU.[183]

---

[179] According to such right, a state may e.g. have a veto right on a certain type of shareholder resolutions, or the right to appoint members to the supervisory board in a number that is disproportionate to the amount of capital shares or voting rights the state owns. For a detailed legal, as well as historical and political discussion see Weiss (2008).

[180] Case C-72/83 *Campus Oil* [1984] EU:C:1984:256, para. 34 (on obligation for importers to purchase a certain amount of petroleum from a state-owned refinery to maintain national refining capacity and thus supply with refinery products in Ireland).

[181] Case C-212/09 *Commission v Portugal* [2011] EU:C:2011:717, para. 82 (on Golden shares granting the right to appoint supervisory board members and veto power for certain shareholder resolutions); Case C-244/11 *Commission v Greece* [2012] EU:C:2012:694, para. 65 (on requirement of prior administrative approval for shares acquisitions over 20% or more, and on subsequent approval for certain shareholder resolutions, both for firms that own national infrastructure networks); specifically on natural gas *Commission v Belgium* [2002] (n. 176), paras. 46, 52 (on Golden share granting a ministerial right to veto certain shareholder resolutions); on petroleum Case C-463/00 *Commission v Spain* [2003] EU:C:2003:272, paras. 71, 73 (on requirement of prior administrative approval for shareholder resolutions that would let state shares in certain private firms fall under a certain threshold).

[182] *Commission v Spain* [2003] (n. 181), paras. 71, 73; Case C-244/11 *Commission v Greece* [2012] EU:C:2012:694, para. 65.

[183] *Commission v Portugal* [2011] (n. 181), para. 82: 'The importance attached by Member States and the European Union to the protection of a secure energy supply can, moreover, be seen, for example, with regard to oil, in Directive 2006/67 [today Council Directive 2009/119/EC of 14 September 2009 imposing an obligation on Member States to maintain minimum stocks of crude oil and/or petroleum products [2009] OJ L 265/9], and with regard to the natural gas sector in Directive 2003/55 [today Directive 2009/73/EC (n. 140)].'

On the other hand, the ECJ explicitly rejected economic grounds as a fundamental interest of society.[184] Accordingly, the ECJ excluded general financial interests, in particular securing a sufficient amount of taxes, as well as economic policy considerations such as strengthening the competitive structure of the market or modernizing and increasing the efficiency of means of production.[185] Also particularly relevant to screening FDI is the ECJ's judgment that the interest to securing the competitive structure attained through recent privatization did not constitute a fundamental interest of society.[186]

3.2.1.1.2   The Unclear ECJ Judgments

These few clear ECJ judgments are complemented by many decisions that leave it open whether a certain interest constitutes not only an overriding reason in the public interest, but also a fundamental interest of society.

In some judgments the ECJ listed public policy and public security in a list with other interests, without clarifying, however, whether the latter interests are part of public policy or public security. For instance, the ECJ held that 'the supply of . . . goods essential to the public as a whole, the continuity of public service, national defence, the protection of public policy and public security and health emergencies' may warrant restrictions of Fundamental freedoms.[187] Other judgments explicitly define interests as overriding reasons in the public interest—for example, the financial balance of social security systems, unfair competition and social dumping, as well as protecting workers.[188] Other examples are, according to the ECJ, preventing undistorted competition;[189] as well as protecting intellectual property,[190]

---

[184] The ECJ itself describes this as settled case law, e.g. Case C-367/98 *Commission v Portugal* [2002] EU:C:2002:326, para. 52 (on statutory limitations of foreign participation in certain reprivatized firms to 5–40% of the shares depending on the sector, as well as on approval requirements for domestic and foreign investments of a certain shares threshold).

[185] ibid., para. 52; Case C-274/06 *Commission v Spain* [2008] EU:C:2008:86, para. 44 (on state right to suspend voting rights of an investor who acquires more than 3% of the capital of an undertaking in the energy sector if the investor is a foreign public undertaking).

[186] Case C-174/04 *Commission v Italy* [2005] EU:C:2005:350, paras. 36–37 (on automatic suspension of voting rights of an investor who acquires more than 2% of the capital of undertakings in the electricity or natural gas sector if the investor is a public undertaking that fulfils certain conditions).

[187] Case C-326/07 *Commission v Italy* [2009] EU:C:2009:193, para. 45 (on special rights in joint stock companies in which the state holds shareholdings, inter alia the right to oppose an investment by which an investor acquires 5% of the voting rights).

[188] Case C-577/10 *Commission v Belgium* [2012] EU:C:2012:814, para. 45 (on the freedom of services (Art 56 TFEU) of foreign-established companies that are subject to registration requirements in Belgium).

[189] Joined Cases C-105 to 107/12 *Essent and Others* [2013] EU:C:2013:677, para. 58 (on prohibitions of certain restructuring measures by electricity and gas infrastructure companies).

[190] Joined Cases C-403 and 429/08 *Football Association Premier League and Others* [2011] EU:C:2011:631, para. 94 (on restrictions of the freedom of services through prohibiting the use of devices that decode exclusive football broadcasting to circumvent exclusive broadcasting rights).

the consumer,[191] or minority shareholders.[192] The ECJ also qualified ensuring the supply with services of general or strategic interest as overriding reasons in the public interest, in particular telecommunication services such as postal, telegraph, and telecommunication services.[193] According to case law, a Member State may secure the supply with these services by keeping a certain influence on the undertakings that supply these services—namely, if formerly public undertakings.[194]

However, these ECJ judgments do not allow any conclusion on the definition of 'public policy or public security'. Overriding reasons in the public interests do not necessarily constitute fundamental interests of society.[195]

On the other hand, interests that the ECJ explicitly rejected as overriding reasons in the public interest must a fortiori also be excluded from the narrower notion of 'public policy or public security'. Accordingly, the ECJ does not qualify the following interests as fundamental to society: protecting the banking sector, with the exception of the central banking system,[196] general 'interests of national economy',[197] as well as the interest to rebalance a lack of reciprocity in access to capital markets between the EU and third countries.[198] With the latter judgment, the ECJ clearly rejects the EU's and Member States' reciprocity concern.

Consequently, the unclear ECJ judgments only show which interests the ECJ does not define as interests of 'public policy or public security': protecting the banking sector (with the exception of the central banking system), general interests of national economy, and reciprocity. More generally, the ECJ qualifies many more interests as overriding reasons in the public interest than fundamental interests of society.

---

[191] *Essent and Others* (n. 189), para. 58, citing Case C-260/04 *Commission v Italy* [2007] EU: C:2007:508, para. 27 (on public concessions for betting services); Case C-393/05 *Commission v Austria* [2007] EU:C:2007:722, para. 52 (on the requirement for private inspection bodies of organically-farmed products to maintain a place of business or other permanent infrastructure in Austria).

[192] Case C-112/05 *Commission v Germany* [2007] EU:C:2007:623, para. 77 (on Volkswagen Act (Gesetz über die Überführung der Anteilsrechte an der Volkswagenwerk Gesellschaft mit beschränkter Haftung in private Hand), which gives public shareholders in Volkswagen more control than their shareholdings would be provided by general corporation laws).

[193] *Commission v Portugal* [2002] (n. 184), para. 47; *Commission v Spain* [2003] (n. 181), para. 66; Joined Cases C-282 and 283/04 *Commission v Netherlands* [2006] EU:C:2006:608, para. 38 (on Golden shares that the Netherlands provided for formerly public undertakings in the telecommunications sector, providing approval requirements for certain shareholder resolutions).

[194] *Commission v Netherlands* (n. 193), para. 38.

[195] See n. 178. See also Geiger (2013), pp. 233 and 239.

[196] *Commission v Spain* [2003] (n. 181), para. 70.

[197] Case C-201/15 *AGET Iraklis* [2016] EU:C:2016:972, paras. 96–98 (on state right to oppose employee mass layoffs based on certain criteria).

[198] Joined Cases C-436 and 437/08 *Haribo Lakritzen Hans Riegel* [2011] EU:C:2011:61, paras. 127–128 (on less favourable treatment in taxation of dividends from foreign sources compared to those from EU undertakings).

3.2.1.2   Interpreting Case Law: 'Public Policy or Public Security' Narrower Than Their GATS Counterpart

The summary of the ECJ's case law allows four main conclusions. First, an interest is fundamental to society if it is fundamental for a country's existence, and thus for the functioning of its institutions, its economy, and the survival of its inhabitants.[199] Second, this definition allows the Member States discretion to determine fundamental interests to their societies, but review is tighter than under Art XIV(a) GATS and the WTO adjudicating bodies. The ECJ therewith emphasizes its strict interpretation of the grounds of exception to the Fundamental freedoms. Third, the society is not affected in its fundamental interests by a mere violation of laws or individual rights.[200] Fourth, the notion 'public policy or public security' excludes economic grounds such as economic policy and competition considerations,[201] protecting the banking sector (with the exception of the central banking system), general interests of national economy, and reciprocity.[202]

As a result, the scope of fundamental interests within the meaning of 'public policy or public security' is narrower, not broader than the scope of 'public order' pursuant to Art XIV(a) GATS. Most importantly, it does not only exclude the interest of reciprocity, but also certain competition policy considerations—namely, enhancing the competitive structure of a market, or securing it after privatization.

---

[199] *Campus Oil* (n. 180), para. 34. Similarly Geiger (2013), pp. 230–231. See also Wojcik (2015b), para. 19; Ress and Ukrow (2020c), para. 53.

[200] See Kemmerer (2010), pp. 248 and 254.

[201] See e.g. Martini (2008), p. 319; Kemmerer (2010), p. 254 (on saving or strengthening employment); Herrmann (2019), pp. 446–447 (on preserving an existing market structure in a specific sector); Hindelang and Hagemeyer (2017), p. 887. The exclusion of economic grounds remains elusive. As already argued for the notions of 'essential security interests' and 'public order' pursuant to the GATS, the line between economic and non-economic interests is too blurred to offer interpretative guidance. See Sect. 3.1.3.1.2.

[202] There are several additional criteria discussed to further substantiate the notion 'public policy or public security' in light of EU and Member States concerns vis-à-vis foreign investors. Some exclude protectionist interests (see e.g. Nettesheim (2008), p. 763; Hindelang and Hagemeyer (2017), p. 887). Some note that the interests the ECJ defined as fundamental interests of society all provide one common characteristic: they are grid-bound or, slightly broader, network industries (Wolff (2009), pp. 192–193, joined by Geiger (2013), pp. 233–234). Both proposals have deficiencies. On the one hand, generally excluding protectionism skips the necessary discussion of what concrete interest is protectionist. Protecting is a certain interest is only 'protectionist' if its protection is illegitimate for some reason. On the other hand, the fact that the supply of an interest is network-bound is an indication, but no necessary characteristic of a fundamental interest to society. Another valuable criterion are laws and policies of the EU and its Member States through which the fundamental importance of an interest may be demonstrated (see already in n. 183, cf. e.g. *Commission v Portugal* [2011] (n. 181), para. 82. For further concrete interests that are argued to be fundamental interests of society see e.g. Wolff (2009), pp. 189–195; Geiger (2013), pp. 232–242.

3.2.1.3 Consequences for FDI Screening Mechanisms: Narrower Scope

The above developed definition and criteria for fundamental interests of society within the meaning of Art 65(1)(b) TFEU show that the scope of FDI Screening mechanisms on the grounds of 'public policy or public security' is slightly narrower than those on the screening ground 'security or public order'.

To begin with, the screening ground 'public policy or public security' cannot meet the competition concern. Considerations of strengthening or maintaining a certain competition or market structure are no fundamental interest of society within the meaning of Art 65(1)(b) TFEU. Accordingly, from an EU law perspective, foreign government influence, namely subsidies, that distort the internal market are not fundamental to the EU's or a Member State's existence either.

Moreover, the ECJ explicitly held that considerations of reciprocity are not covered by the notion fundamental interests within the meaning of 'public policy or public security'. The second EU and Member States concern vis-à-vis foreign investors is therefore also not met.

The harmful investor concern is but less covered by fundamental interests of society within the meaning of Art 65(1)(b) TFEU compared to the scope of the screening ground 'security or public order'. Only the first two sensitive asset concepts are covered: defence sector, and critical infrastructure, technology, and inputs. While defence interests are certainly fundamental to the EU's and Member States' existence, the notion critical as defined in accordance with Directive 2008/114/EC for the purposes of this book well reflects the definition of fundamental interests of society. As under Art XIV(a) GATS, the scope of 'public policy or public security' regarding the harmful investor interests on critical assets will largely be determined by the element of threat. The sensitive asset concept of strategic infra-structure, technology, and inputs, on the other hand, is not covered by the EU law notion of fundamental interests of society. As already mentioned above, consider-ations of enhancing competitive advantages do not constitute fundamental interests of society. Moreover, FDI screening to achieve long-term industrial, economic, and geopolitical goals may be strategically helpful, but not vital to basic state functions.[203]

The private information concern is covered to the extent it exceeds the sphere of individual rights, becoming a societal interest. Thus, as under Art XIV(a) GATS, a significant part of the population must be affected.[204] This threshold will become

---

[203] With the same result, but based on the consideration that they are purely economic interests, Martini (2008), p. 319. Martini rejects the objective of industrial policy and supporting national champions as fundamental interest of society. See also Kemmerer (2010), p. 253, who rejects the objective to secure and create employment, since they were individual interests that do not constitute fundamental interests of society.

[204] Geiger (2013), p. 238, classifies the protection of business secrets as fundamental interest of society, arguing that the existence of business secrets is a constitutive element of a productive economic environment. Nevertheless, the protection of business rights stays an individual right that is a priori not protected by 'public policy or public security'.

crucial for the second element of 'public policy or public security': genuine and sufficiently serious threat.

Consequently, an FDI Screening mechanism on the grounds of 'public policy or public security' covers less interests than the Screening Regulation's notion 'security or public order'. The notion fundamental interests of society excludes not only the reciprocity concern, but also the competition and harmful investor concern regarding strategic infrastructure, technologies, and inputs. Nevertheless, FDI Screening mechanisms based on 'public policy or public security' may have advantages compared to the Screening Regulation's screening ground if the required element of threat is less demanding and therefore allows more individual FDI screening.

3.2.2   Genuine and Sufficiently Serious Threat

The second element of 'public policy or public security' as defined by settled ECJ case law is a genuine and sufficiently serious threat,[205] or paraphrased a 'real, specific and serious risk'.[206] A Member State's measure is justified on the grounds of 'public policy or public security' if it not only pursues a fundamental interest of society, but also addresses a threat to this interest.

As under Arts XIV*bis* and XIV(a) GATS, the second element of 'public policy or public security' significantly limits a rather broad understanding of fundamental interest of society. The term genuine and sufficiently serious threat consists of two elements that describe different threat dimensions. A genuine threat stands for the *probability* that the risk at issue materializes. Following the ECJ judgment *Albore*, that component may be paraphrased as a real and specific threat.[207] A sufficiently serious threat means that the envisaged risk must have a *significant detrimental effect* on the fundamental interest at issue. The risk must thus be serious in relation to the interest at issue.

3.2.2.1   ECJ Case Law Poses High Threshold of Genuine Threat

The ECJ interprets a genuine and sufficiently serious threat strictly. In its judgments on Golden shares and similar cases, the ECJ has never been called upon assessing whether there was a genuine and sufficiently serious threat in a concrete case. Instead, it had to deal with legislative acts that abstractly allowed a national administration to restrict capital movement. Accordingly, the question before the

---

[205] See n. 173.
[206] Case C-423/98 *Albore* [2000] EU:C:2000:401, paras. 22, 24, in which Art 65(1)(b) TFEU was not directly at issue. Instead, the ECJ generally referred to Art 73d EEC, and held that 'public security' and the proportionality required a 'real, specific and serious risk'.
[207] ibid.

ECJ was whether the legislative acts sufficiently ensured that the administrative restrictions would only be taken in case of a genuine and sufficiently serious threat. While concrete findings on the component sufficiently serious threat are lacking, the ECJ signalled a restrictive understanding of the term genuine.

In the judgments on Golden shares and similar cases, the ECJ had to deal with legislation that allowed the administration to intervene in management decisions of certain undertakings, for example the sale of shares to a private investor. The legislation defined certain criteria according to which the authorities were allowed to intervene and thus restrict the freedom of capital movement. The ECJ held that these criteria must sufficiently mirror the requirement of a genuine and sufficiently serious threat to be justified under Art 65(1)(b) TFEU. In other words, concrete legislative criteria must limit the administrative actions to cases in which a genuine and sufficiently serious threat is established.[208] Otherwise, the criteria would allow the administration too wide discretion for determining whether a capital movement poses a genuine and sufficiently serious threat to a fundamental interest of society.[209] Accordingly, the Member States must prove that the screening criteria are appropriate to achieve the pursued objective to protect threatened fundamental interests of society.[210]

Such a proof requires 'precise evidence'.[211] The ECJ indicated that it may suffice for establishing a genuine threat to cite past examples of foreign investors who were induced by foreign governments. In *Commission v Italy (March 2009)*, for example, Italy defended its measure to control foreign acquisitions by citing past cases in which investors were linked to terror organizations or disrupted energy supply. The

---

[208] For instance in *Commission v Italy* [March 2009] (n. 187), para. 40, the ECJ held: 'A preliminary point to note is that the criteria examined here determine the circumstances in which the powers of the State to oppose the acquisition of certain shareholdings or the conclusion of certain agreements of shareholders in the companies concerned may be exercised. It is apparent from the Court's case-law that the use of such powers may be contrary to the free movement of capital . . . The point at issue in this case is whether those criteria fix conditions that make it possible to vindicate the exercise of such powers.' This is confirmed by Case C-244/11 *Commission v Greece* [2012] EU:C:2012:694, para. 78: 'the nine evaluation criteria listed in [a Greek law allowing authorities to refuse certain shareholding acquisitions] do not cover cases of real and sufficiently serious threats to the security of supply and cannot, therefore, be considered to be of direct relevance to the intended objective.'

[209] In *Commission v Italy* [March 2009] (n. 187), para. 53, the ECJ held: 'The general and abstract nature of those criteria is incapable of ensuring that the special powers will be exercised in accordance with the requirements of Community law.' Similarly, Case C-244/11 *Commission v Greece* [2012] EU:C:2012:694, para. 77: 'Neither the general reference . . . to "general interest criteria" nor the nine evaluation criteria which are listed merely by way of example . . . make it possible to determine the specific objective circumstances in which the power to oppose the acquisition of holdings is capable of being exercised.'

[210] *Commission v Italy* [March 2009] (n. 187), para. 49; *Commission v Portugal* [2011] (n. 181), para. 85; Joined Cases C-52 and 113/16 *SEGRO* [2018] EU:C:2018:157, paras. 84–85.

[211] Case C-161/07 *Commission v Austria* [2008] EU:C:2008:759, paras. 36–37 (on restriction of economic activity of EU citizens from certain Member States by additional conditions and registration requirements).

ECJ held that the Italian measure might have been justified if the legislative criteria were more precisely linked to these threats.[212] Moreover, the ECJ held that genuine does not mean immediate threat. A Member State is therefore allowed to act before the threat becomes immediate.[213] While this shows a certain latitude in the interpretation of a genuine threat,[214] the ECJ does not reduce the meaning of genuine to abstract risks. Mere prudential measures are therefore not covered.

More concretely, the ECJ held, for instance, that a genuine threat to a fundamental interest of society is not established only by the fact that an investor acquires 10% of capital shares, significant influence,[215] or that the investor is controlled by a foreign state.[216]

Contrary to the WTO adjudicating bodies, the ECJ therefore adopts a rather restrictive understanding of genuine threat, namely by requiring precise evidence for such threat. An abstract assumption of risk is insufficient. At the same time, the ECJ clarified that genuine did not mean immediate, and showed a certain latitude when the Member State faced difficulties to prove a concrete threat. Precise ECJ case law on the element sufficiently serious threat is lacking.

3.2.2.2 Developing Case Law Further

In the analyzed case law the ECJ adopted an interpretation of genuine, as in real and specific, threat that respects the literal meaning of genuine. It also appropriately reflects the EU's level of integration, in particular the crucial importance of the Fundamental freedoms to the internal market. At the same time, the ECJ avoids a too restrictive interpretation by rejecting an understanding of genuine as immediate. Nevertheless, the interpretation of sufficiently serious threat remains unclear.

The term sufficiently serious addresses the impact that the threat has if it materializes. As already argued for the definition of 'public order' pursuant to Art XIV (a) GATS, the term serious combines two dimensions. On the one hand, it describes the threat's impact on the fundamental interest of society at issue in a quantitative manner, thus the threat's magnitude. On the other hand, seriousness expresses the quality or gravity of the impact the materialized threat would have on the fundamental interest. Both dimensions are interrelated in that, a particularly large

---

[212] *Commission v Italy* [March 2009] (n. 187), paras. 49–52.

[213] Case C-543/08 *Commission v Portugal* [2010] EU:C:2010:669, paras. 86–87 (on Golden shares in privatized electricity supplier that provide state with management rights disproportionate to its capital shares).

[214] Herrmann (2019), pp. 449–450, referring to *Scientology* (n. 43), paras. 20–21.

[215] *Commission v Italy* [March 2009] (n. 187), para. 48; Case C-244/11 *Commission v Greece* [2012] EU:C:2012:694, paras. 69–70.

[216] *Commission v Spain* [February 2008] (n. 185), paras. 43, 45. The ECJ's approach is well illustrated in Case C-244/11 *Commission v Greece* [2012] EU:C:2012:694, para. 70: 'However, the scheme at issue produces its effects before the company has even adopted a decision, namely without a risk being established, even a potential one, of interference with the security of supply.'

magnitude of threat allows for a lower level of gravity to constitute a sufficiently serious threat, and *vice versa*.[217]

As developed under Art XIV(a) GATS, in case of the risk that a society might be deprived of the access to a particular product produced by a specific firm, one may presume that the threat is sufficiently serious if the firm holds a monopoly or a large portion of market shares.[218]

Another substantiating criterion concerns both the genuineness and seriousness of a threat. As discussed under Art XIV(a) GATS, the threat may be mitigated by a prudential regulatory framework.[219] On the one hand, a regulatory framework may prevent a threat from materializing at all; in which case the threat would not be genuine. On the other hand, the framework may mitigate the impact of the materialized threat, for example by giving authorities the possibility to intervene and guarantee the supply of the product of fundamental interest. In the context of Art XIV(a) GATS, it was argued that a WTO member may itself determine its aversiveness and thus the effectiveness of its regulatory framework. The EU, however, provides a much higher level of integration, and therefore more harmonization on the Member States' aversiveness to risk. Therefore, the ECJ may indeed second-guess a Member State's assessment of whether a regulatory framework guarantees a sufficient level of protection for the fundamental interest at issue.[220]

Consequently, the threat components of genuine and sufficiently serious pose a high threshold to protect a fundamental interest of society within the meaning of Art 65(1)(b) TFEU. The higher degree of harmonization in the EU than in the WTO results in less deference to the Member States when establishing a genuine and sufficiently serious threat. This particularly applies to the element of genuine threat and the mitigating criterion of the regulatory framework. Hence, the element of threat in 'public policy or public security' is more demanding than in the screening ground 'security or public order' as defined in accordance with Art XIV(a) GATS, even more so compared to the threat element in 'essential security interests' pursuant to Art XIV*bis*(1)(b) GATS.

3.2.2.3   Consequences for FDI Screening Mechanisms: Significantly Higher Hurdles

Having defined the threat element of 'public policy or public security', the discussion may now turn to analyzing its effects on the scope of an FDI Screening mechanism on this screening ground.

---

[217]See Sects. 3.1.4.2.1 and 3.1.4.2.2.

[218]See Sect. 3.1.4.2.2.

[219]See e.g. the Commission's argument in *Commission v Portugal* [2010] (n. 213), paras. 75–76. However, the argument was invoked in the context of the measure's proportionality. The ECJ did not address the Commission's argument in its findings.

[220]For the term 'second-guessing' WTO member policy choices, see Howse (2016), p. 53.

Section 3.2.1 found that 'public policy or public security' covers the EU and Member States concerns vis-à-vis foreign investors only partly. Regarding the harmful investor concern only the sensitive assets of defence sector, and critical infrastructure, technology, and inputs are covered. In addition, the private information concern is covered. However, there must be a real and specific possibility that the FDI will cause a harm of a certain magnitude and gravity to the interest at issue.

As already stated under Art XIV(a) GATS, the Member States will in many cases not be able to point at a real and specific possibility, but rather abstract risks. For example, in only a few, high-profile cases of FDI will a Member State have 'precise evidence'[221] that a foreign investor will impose its interests on the FDI target in a way that harms the fundamental Member State interest at issue.[222] Providing past examples may only satisfy the burden of proof if these examples are comparable to the FDI, investor and investor's home country at issue. Even more than the WTO adjudicating bodies, the ECJ will demand that the EU and its Member States lay out how the foreign investor and possibly its home country will exert their influence. Consequently, in the vast majority of cases the FDI will not pose a genuine threat.[223]

Even if a genuine threat is established, the genuineness must relate to a sufficiently serious threat for the fundamental interest of society at issue. Here, similar conclusions as under Art XIV(a) GATS apply.

Last but not least, both the genuineness and seriousness of a threat may be attenuated by a regulatory framework—namely, by an authority that has enough power and resources to intervene in case of a disruption to the interest at issue. In the EU context the ECJ may more easily find that the regulatory framework in fact mitigates a risk, so that a threat is no longer genuine or sufficiently serious. This aspect is particularly relevant to FDI in the network-based industries of basic supplies such as electricity, water, petroleum, and natural gas. Often, powerful supervisory authorities exist in these sectors. They may be capable of guaranteeing the supply even against the interests of the supplier, possibly influenced by the foreign investor.

Consequently, the element of a genuine and sufficiently serious threat significantly limits the scope of FDI Screening mechanisms based on the screening ground 'public policy or public security' within the meaning of Art 65(1)(b) GATS. These limits go beyond the limitations posed by the element of threat in the notion 'public order' pursuant to Art XIV(a) GATS. In addition, the element of threat in 'public policy or public security' is clearly narrower than the threat element in Art XIV*bis*(1) (b) GATS that the screening ground 'security or public order' provides for defence interests.

---

[221] *Commission v Austria* [2008] (n. 211), paras. 36–37.

[222] See Sect. 3.1.4.2.3.

[223] Similarly Geiger (2013), p. 246.

3.2.3 'Public Policy or Public Security' as Screening Ground: Significantly Narrower Than 'Security or Public Order'

The analysis of the notion 'public policy or public security' pursuant to Art 65(1) (b) TFEU in light of FDI screening in the EU showed that FDI Screening mechanisms based on this notion would cover less FDI of concern than the Screening Regulation's screening ground 'security or public order'.

First, the element of fundamental interests of society excludes more concerns than Art XIV(a) GATS. Besides the reciprocity concern and parts of the harmful investor concern on strategic assets, Art 65(1)(b) TFEU also excludes the EU and Member States harmful investor concern regarding strategic assets entirely and their competition concern.

Second, for those concerns that are covered by the notion of fundamental interests, the threat requirement further narrows the scope of 'public policy or public security' as a screening ground—again, more strictly than Art XIV(a) GATS. Most importantly, the ECJ demands more precise evidence for establishing a genuine threat posed by the foreign investor.

Given its small scope, an FDI Screening mechanism on the grounds of 'public policy or public security' does not meet the reciprocity concern through the indirect route either. It fails to significantly raise barriers for foreign investors in the EU, and hence to provide the EU with considerable leverage to achieve more favourable FDI treatment for EU investors from certain trading partners, in particular China.

In sum, FDI Screening mechanisms based on the screening ground 'public policy or public security' pursuant to Art 65(1)(b) TFEU would fulfil the purpose of meeting the EU and Member States concerns vis-à-vis foreign investors even less than an FDI Screening mechanism based on the Screening Regulation and its screening ground 'security or public order'.

3.2.4 Broader Interpretation of 'Public Policy or Public Security' in Third-Country Settings?

So far, the discussion has ignored that the screening ground 'public policy or public security' pursuant to Art 65(1)(b) TFEU would be part of an FDI Screening mechanism that only addresses FDI from third countries, not from other Member States.[224] Several authors argue that in such a third-country setting a different rationale applies than in intra-EU contexts. If their argument proves valid, the definition of 'public policy or public security' may be modified and become a

---

[224] Section 2.4.2 defined *Foreign* direct investment for the purposes of this book. As an exception for the purposes of this section, however, third-country FDI means the FDI that, pursuant to the freedom of capital movement, is not intra-EU capital movement. The difference of intra-EU and third-country capital movement will be discussed in more detail in Sect. 4.2.5.

more lenient requirement. FDI Screening mechanisms on the grounds of 'public policy or public security' would then be able to meet more of the EU and Member States concerns vis-à-vis foreign investors, and the above reached conclusion would need to be adjusted.

It is correct that the meaning of 'public policy or public security' is also determined by its context as ground of exception to the Fundamental freedoms. To leave as much room as possible for the free movement of goods, services, people, and capital in the EU internal market, the ECJ interprets the notion of 'public policy or public security' strictly.[225] Hence, one may argue that such strict interpretation is only in accordance with the Fundamental freedoms' purpose if goods, services, people, and capital move inside the internal market. Once the movement involves crossing the EU's external border, a broader interpretation may be more appropriate.

The issue of interpreting the notion of 'public policy or public security' more broadly in third-country settings addresses for the first time the central question of FDI screening and the Fundamental freedoms: Does third-country FDI enjoy Fundamental freedom protection, and, if so, to what extent do the Fundamental freedoms allow less favourable treatment of third-country FDI compared to intra-EU FDI? This wider context of FDI Fundamental freedom protection must be taken into account when answering the question of interpreting 'public policy or public security' more broadly in a third-country setting. Before discussing this question, the following will therefore briefly outline its wider context.

3.2.4.1   The Fundamental Freedom Protection of Third-Country FDI: Broader Interpretation of Art 65(1)(b) TFEU as One of Several Issues

The protection of third-country FDI by the Fundamental freedoms is decided at many different levels. While several Fundamental rights guaranteed in the CFR[226] as well as the freedom of establishment pursuant to Arts 49, 54 TFEU provide some protection,[227] the central provision of protection for third-country FDI is the freedom of capital movement in Art 63(1) TFEU. In Art 63(1) TFEU less favourable treatment of third-country FDI is discussed at three different levels.

First, the question of different treatment arises when determining the scope of the freedom of capital movement. On the one hand, third-country FDI could as a principle be accorded less protection.[228] On the other hand, the scope of Art 63

---

[225] See n. 175.

[226] In particular the freedom to choose an occupation (Art 15(1) and (3) CFR), to conduct a business (Art 16 CFR), the right to property (Art 17 CFR), and the right to equality (Art 20 CFR).

[227] For the protection of foreign investors who are formally established in the EU through Arts 49, 54 TFEU, see Sects. 4.2.2 and 4.2.3.

[228] Schön (2005), pp. 496–497; Smit (2012), pp. 392–394, discuss but reject different degrees of protection for intra- and third-country capital movement.

(1) TFEU regarding third-country FDI could be limited by the freedom of establishment in that, whenever a third-country FDI qualifies as an establishment within the meaning of Art 49 TFEU, the freedom of capital movement does not apply.[229]

Second, the notion of prohibited restrictions may be narrowed in case of third-country FDI. One may, for example, limit the scope of Art 63(1) TFEU to discriminations, rejecting the ECJ's broad interpretation of restriction.[230,231] Alternatively, one may focus on the discrimination standard.[232] For instance, third-country FDI and intra-EU FDI could generally be treated as incomparable. Their different treatment could thus not constitute a restriction within the meaning of the freedom of capital movement. For a more modest modification, the comparability of third-country and intra-EU FDI could be subject to higher standards of likeness.[233]

A third way to take the particularities of third-country FDI into account is to interpret the grounds of exception differently than in an intra-EU setting. This approach may take the form of exceptionally applying the unwritten ground of

---

[229] See in detail in Sect. 4.2.

[230] On the notion of restriction, see e.g. Case C-135/17 *X [Sociétés intermédiaires établies dans des pays tiers]* [2019] EU:C:2019:136, para. 55: 'It follows from the Court's settled case-law that the measures prohibited as restrictions on the movement of capital include those which are such as to discourage non-residents from making investments in a Member State or to discourage that Member State's residents from doing so in other States'. See also *Essent and Others* (n. 189), para. 39: 'Article 63(1) TFEU generally prohibits restrictions on movements of capital between Member States'. This finding nevertheless does not allow the conclusion that the ECJ argues for a narrower notion of restriction in third-country contexts, since the judgments dealt with intra-EU cases only.

[231] Clostermeyer (2011), p. 315, who limits the notion of prohibited restriction within the meaning of Art 63(1)(b) TFEU in third-country contexts to discriminatory measures, but only for internal regulatory tax law measures, not for non-tax measures and measures addressing transactions. One may also treat every measure that discriminates against FDI as a mere non-discriminatory restriction. This would give Member States more flexibility to restrict FDI if one follows the prevailing view that (open) discriminations may only be justified by written grounds of exception. If so, classifying a discrimination as a restriction would allow the Member States to justify these measures also on the broader grounds of overriding reasons in the public interest. (See n. 177, 178).

[232] Indicating this as a possibility Case C-446/04 *Test Claimants in the FII Group Litigation* [2006] EU:C:2006:774, para. 170. However, the ECJ seems to have given up this view, provided that the ECJ had ever seriously adopted it. While the ECJ rather focuses on the possibility to interpret the grounds of exception more broadly, some AGs continue to argue for a higher standard of discrimination in third-country contexts, see *Haribo Lakritzen Hans Riegel* (n. 198), para. 119, in comparison with Joined Cases C-436 and 437/08 *Haribo Lakritzen Hans Riegel* [2010] Opinion of AG Kokott, EU:C:2010:668, para. 112. See also *X [Sociétés intermédiaires établies dans des pays tiers]* (n. 230), para. 68, in which the ECJ argues that intra-EU and third-country settings do not as such justify differential treatment. With a different interpretation of the ECJ's case law and in favour of modifying the discrimination standard in third-country contexts Sedlaczek and Züger (2018a), para. 4. Without reference to case law suggesting that intra-EU and third-country cases are not comparable, Schnitger (2005), p. 494; Schön (2005), pp. 512–513 (on tax havens). *Contra* Hindelang (2009), pp. 196–198.

[233] In favour of this approach, Lübke (2015), para. 76.

exception overriding reasons in the public interest to open discriminations.[234] Moreover, the grounds of exception could be generally understood more broadly. This approach is in line with the ECJ's jurisprudence in the realm of different taxation regimes for third-country and intra-EU dividend flows. Only in this context, the ECJ held:

> [I]t may be that a Member State will be able to demonstrate that a restriction on capital movements to or from non-member countries is justified for a particular reason in circumstances where that reason would not constitute a valid justification for a restriction on capital movements between Member States.[235]

The ECJ took a similar approach in other cases on tax measures that mostly dealt with the interpretation of overriding reasons in the public interest. The ECJ's main argument is the different legal context in third-country settings caused by less harmonization and cooperation, especially regarding tax information exchange mechanisms.[236] Accordingly, the ECJ recognizes that to prevent tax evasion the Member States must have the flexibility to take more restrictive measures into account vis-à-vis foreign firms compared to EU firms, including denying a tax advantage completely.

It is important to note that this consideration is an issue of proportionality.[237] Contrary to what some authors conclude, the ECJ did not admit certain Member State interests as fundamental interests of society in third-country contexts, but

---

[234] Of course, this argument relies on the presumption that the unwritten ground of exception is not applicable to open discrimination anyway. On this condition, Herrmann (2019), p. 447, argues that the ECJ might exceptionally apply the unwritten ground of exception to open discrimination in a third-country context.

[235] *Test Claimants in the FII Group Litigation* [2006] (n. 232), para. 171, following Case C-446/04 *Test Claimants in the FII Group Litigation* [2006] Opinion of AG Geelhoed, EU:C:2006:240, para. 121. See also Case C-101/05 *Skatteverket v A* [2007] EU:C:2007:804, paras. 60–62 (on a Member State's possibility to refuse tax advantages on incoming dividends from foreign undertakings because the authorities lack access to the same information exchange mechanisms as in an intra-EU context); Case C-540/07 *Commission v Italy* [2009] EU:C:2009:717, paras. 69–73 (on Member State's possibility to treat dividends paid to foreign shareholders differently because the authorities lack access to the same information exchange mechanisms as in an intra-EU context); *Haribo Lakritzen Hans Riegel* (n. 198), paras. 119–120.

[236] *Skatteverket v A* (n. 235), paras. 61–62.

[237] Several scholars generalize the ECJ's approach and argue that the proportionality requirement may be more lenient towards Member States in a third-country setting, see Hindelang (2009), p. 242; Kemmerer (2010), p. 289; Clostermeyer (2011), pp. 323–324; Lübke (2015), para. 76; as well as arguably Bayer and Ohler (2008), p. 25; Wojcik (2015a), para. 66. Bayer and Ohler propose to lower the burden of proof for Member States' ('reduzieren der Kontrolldichte'). Less clear on whether also to accept other grounds of exception Ress and Ukrow (2020a), para. 230.

excluded them in intra-EU settings.[238] Even less did the ECJ indicate that the threshold of a genuine and sufficiently serious threat may be lowered.[239]

In sum, if one recognizes a difference in the protection of third-country and intra-EU capital movement, this difference may be given effect at three different levels: the scope of the freedom of capital movement, its notion of prohibited restriction, and the grounds of exception. Interpreting the ground of exception 'public policy or public security' more broadly is thus only one of several gateways through which third-country FDI may receive less Fundamental freedom protection than intra-EU FDI.

3.2.4.2 Broader Interpretation of Art 65(1)(b) TFEU: Inappropriate Gateway for Taking Third-Country Particularities into Account

With the wider Fundamental freedom context in mind, the discussion can now turn to assessing whether the ground of 'public policy or public security' within the meaning of Art 65(1)(b) TFEU should be interpreted more broadly in a third-country setting. Even provided that third-country FDI should receive less protection by the freedom of capital movement, literal meaning, context, and purpose of 'public policy or public security' pursuant Art 65(1)(b) TFEU weigh against a broader interpretation in third-country settings.

According to the literal meaning, Art 65(1)(b) TFEU applies to all measures that fall under the scope of the freedom of capital movement. Neither Art 63(1), nor Art 65(1)(b) TFEU indicate any differentiation between intra-EU and third-country cases. Indeed, at the same time, the literal meaning does also not explicitly exclude a different interpretation.[240]

More importantly, however, Arts 63–66 TFEU demonstrate that the particular interests of EU and Member States that are arising from the freedom of capital movement's *erga omnes* effect should be addressed by other provisions than Art 65 (1)(b) TFEU and its broader interpretation in third-country settings. Arts 64, 65(4) and 66 TFEU all provide specific grounds of exception for third-country settings. Particularly relevant to FDI screening are Art 64(2) and (3) TFEU. They give the EU the right to restrict the freedom of capital movement in relation to third-country FDI—without any substantial requirements.[241] This grants the EU enough

---

[238] Kotthaus (2012), p. 116; Geiger (2013), p. 185, n. 672; Sedlaczek and Züger (2018a), para. 5; Herrmann (2019), p. 448, interpret the ECJ's jurisprudence as implying that additional grounds of justification may be applicable in a third-country context. Wolff (2009), pp. 211–213, argues for a broader understanding of overriding reasons in the public interest, namely for the protection of competition and employment.

[239] Kemmerer (2010), p. 292, nevertheless suggests a broader interpretation of Art 65(1)(b) TFEU, in particular a broader interpretation of fundamental interest of society.

[240] Kemmerer (2010), pp. 264–265 and 271–272; Geiger (2013), p. 231, argue that the wording of Art 65(1)(b) TFEU is sufficiently open to a differentiation.

[241] See Sect. 4.2.5.

flexibility to act at the international stage despite the *erga omnes* effect of the freedom of capital movement.[242] Accordingly, it is not appropriate to interpret 'public policy or public security' more broadly in order to fulfil the same purpose.

Some may argue against this contextual argument that the above-mentioned provisions, except Art 65(4) TFEU on tax measures, only provide the EU with further flexibility in third-country FDI settings, not the Member States. Following this argument, only a broader interpretation of 'public policy or public security' would also give Member States additional flexibility to restrict the freedom of capital movement in third-country settings.[243] However, this argument implies that Arts 63–66 TFEU recognize a specific need of the Member States to adopt measures in third-country settings. This assumption is wrong. On the contrary: The competence to regulate FDI lies in principle with the EU. This is additionally demonstrated by the EU's exclusive Common commercial policy competence pursuant to Art 207 (1) TFEU that since the Treaty of Lisbon also includes FDI.

Consequently, the wording of Arts 63(1) and 65(1)(b) TFEU, their context, and their purpose show that the written ground of exception 'public policy or public security' within the meaning of Art 65(1)(b) TFEU fulfils the same classic function of justification in intra-EU as well as third-country contexts as its counterparts do for all other Fundamental freedoms. This conclusion is also in the interest of a coherent interpretation of 'public policy or public security'.[244]

At the same time, this conclusion still permits to take the particularities of third-country capital movement into account. First, the lower level of harmonization and cooperation between Member States and third-countries may more often result in a genuine and sufficiently serious threat for a fundamental interest of society. For example, if a Member State has information about EU, but not about foreign investors due to an EU cooperation mechanism, only the foreign investors will pose a particular threat. This, however, is simply the consequence of applying the above-developed general standards of Art 65(1)(b) TFEU to the facts.[245] Second, as outlined above, there are other gateways available for better adapting the freedom of capital movement to the particularities of third-country settings. The most prominent gateway, delimiting the freedom of capital movement from the freedom of establishment, will be addressed in Sect. 4.2.

Consequently, the above conclusions on the scope of FDI Screening mechanisms based on the screening ground 'public policy or public security' remain valid—its

---

[242] There is consensus that the purpose of Art 64(2) and (3) TFEU is inter alia that the EU maintains a certain flexibility to restrict third-country capital movement for keeping room of manoeuvre in international negotiations, see e.g. Hindelang (2009), p. 300; Ress and Ukrow (2020b), para. 22.

[243] Kemmerer (2010), p. 276, but still on Art 58(1)(b) EC. In the EC, however, the EU's exclusive competence for the Common commercial policy did not yet include FDI.

[244] See the other grounds of exception in Arts 36(1), 45(3), 52(1), and 62 TFEU, and for the coherent interpretation of 'public policy or public security' under all Fundamental freedoms n. 172.

[245] See the ECJ's argument of different legal contexts between the EU and third countries in Sect. 3.2.4.1.

scope is considerably smaller than that of the Screening Regulation's screening ground 'security or public order'.

3.3   FDI Screening Mechanism Options Largely Unfit to Address the Concerns Vis-à-Vis Foreign Investors

This chapter has shown that none of the currently available legislative options for FDI Screening mechanisms allows Member States to meet their concerns vis-à-vis foreign investors to a significant extent. This is valid—to different degrees—for FDI Screening mechanisms on the screening grounds of 'security or public order' in accordance with the Screening Regulation, 'public policy or public security' within the meaning of Art 65(1)(b) TFEU, as well as 'essential security interests' pursuant to Art 346(1)(b) TFEU.

FDI Screening mechanisms on the grounds of 'security or public order' have the broadest scope to screen FDI. While they, like the other options, fail to meet the reciprocity concern, the other concerns may at least be met to a small extent in few, high-profile cases of FDI. Meeting the harmful investor concern is a realistic option in particular for two groups of FDI targets. The first group of FDI targets consists of firms providing infrastructure, technology, or inputs that directly provision and are indispensable for generally recognized military functions. Nevertheless, screening FDI into firms providing dual-use items remains difficult under the Screening Regulation. The second group of relevant FDI screening targets holds monopolies or large parts of market shares in a certain sensitive sector, for any disruption of their production will usually have a large effect in quantity and quality. However, the Member State must establish a real possibility that this threat scenario materializes.

In comparison, an FDI Screening mechanism on the grounds of 'public policy or public security' allows to meet EU and Member States concerns vis-à-vis foreign investors to an even lesser extent. Most importantly, the competition concern and the harmful investor concern regarding strategic assets are largely excluded from the notion of 'public policy or public security'. An FDI Screening mechanisms on the grounds of 'essential security interests' within the meaning of Art 346(1)(b) TFEU is even more limited in scope. It only covers narrow military interests, and thus also fails to considerably meet the EU and Member States concerns vis-à-vis foreign investors.

In addition, given their small scope, none of the FDI Screening mechanism options may significantly raise barriers for foreign investors in the EU. As a result, they cannot provide the EU with considerable leverage to achieve more favourable FDI treatment for EU investors from certain trading partners, in particular China. The reciprocity concern may therefore not even be met through this indirect route.

In sum, all current options for FDI Screening mechanisms in the EU fail to significantly meet the EU and Member States concerns vis-à-vis foreign investors. The available screening grounds are too narrow: from the broadest, 'security or public order' within the meaning of the Screening Regulation and Arts XIV*bis*(1) (b) and XIV(a) GATS, to 'public policy or public security' (Art 65(1)(b) TFEU), to the narrowest 'essential security interests' (Art 346(1)(b) TFEU). Those actors in the EU and Member States who wanted the Screening Regulation to allow them to significantly meet all the EU and Member States concerns vis-à-vis foreign investors may therefore be disappointed. The screening ground 'security or public order' was a compromise—and the above conclusions demonstrate its costs.

Therefore, a second question naturally arises: Do the EU and Member States have the flexibility to adopt FDI Screening mechanisms on broader grounds than 'security or public order'?

References

Akande D, Williams S (2003) International adjudication on national security issues: what role for the WTO? Virginia J Int Law 43:365–404

Alford RP (2011) The self-judging WTO security exception. Utah Law Rev:697–760

Ayres G, Mitchell AD (2013) General and security exceptions under the GATT 1994 and the GATS. In: Carr I, Bhuiyan JH, Alam S (eds) International trade law and the WTO. Federation Press, Annandale, pp 226–268

Bacchus J, Lester S (2020) The rule of precedent and the role of the appellate body. J World Trade 54:183–198

Bartels L (2015) The chapeau of the general exceptions in the WTO GATT and GATS agreements: a reconstruction. Am J Int Law 109:95–124. https://doi.org/10.5305/amerjintelaw.109.1.0095

Bayer W, Ohler C (2008) Staatsfonds ante portas. ZG:12–31

Bhala R, Witmer E (2020) Interpreting interpretation: textual, contextual, and pragmatic interpretative methods for international trade law. Connecticut J Int Law 35:62–132

Bismuth R (2020) Reading between the lines of the EU regulation establishing a framework for screening FDI into the Union. In: Bourgeois JHJ (ed) EU framework for foreign direct investment control. Kluwer Law International, Alphen aan den Rijn, pp 103–114

Boklan D, Bahri A (2020) The first WTO's ruling on national security exception: balancing interests or opening Pandora's box? World Trade Rev 19:123–136. https://doi.org/10.1017/S1474745619000430

Clostermeyer M (2011) Staatliche Übernahmeabwehr und die Kapitalverkehrsfreiheit zu Drittstaaten: Europarechtliche Beurteilung der §§ 7 Abs. 2 Nr. 6 AWG, 53 AWV. Nomos, Baden-Baden

Collins A (2019) Introduction: what is security studies? In: Collins A (ed) Contemporary security studies, 5th edn. Oxford University Press, Oxford, pp 1–10

Cottier T, Delimatsis P (2008) Art XIVbis GATS. In: Wolfrum R, Stoll P-T, Feinäugle C (eds) WTO – trade in services. Martinus Nijhoff, Leiden

Cottier T, Schneller L (2014) The philosophy of non-discrimination in International Trade Regulation. In: Kamperman Sanders A (ed) The principle of national treatment in international economic law: trade, investment and intellectual property. Elgar, Cheltenham, pp 3–33

Cottier T, Delimatsis P, Diebold NF (2008) Art XIV GATS. In: Wolfrum R, Stoll P-T, Feinäugle C (eds) WTO – trade in services. Martinus Njihoff, Leiden

Cremona M (2020) Regulating FDI in the EU legal framework. In: Bourgeois JHJ (ed) EU framework for foreign direct investment control. Kluwer Law International, Alphen aan den Rijn, pp 31–55

Daerdorff AV (2000) The economics of government market intervention, and its international dimension. In: Bronckers MCEJ (ed) New directions in international economic law: essays in honour of John H. Jackson. Kluwer Law International, The Hague, pp 70–85

De Búrca G (2002) Unpacking the concept of discrimination in EC and international trade law. In: Barnard C, Scott J (eds) The law of the single European market: unpacking the premises. Hart, Oxford, pp 181–195

de Kok J (2019) Towards a European framework for foreign investment reviews. Eur Law Rev 44: 24–48

Delimatsis P (2007) International trade in services and domestic regulations: necessity, transparency, and regulatory diversity. Oxford University Press, Oxford

Delimatsis P (2014) Who's afraid of necessity? And why it matters? In: Lim AH, de Meester B (eds) WTO domestic regulation and services trade: putting principles into practice. Cambridge University Press, Cambridge, pp 95–109

Diebold NF (2008) The morals and order exceptions in WTO law: balancing the toothless tiger and the undermining mole. J Int Econ Law 11:43–74. https://doi.org/10.1093/jiel/jgm036

Dietz S, Streinz T (2015) Das Marktzugangskriterium in der Dogmatik der Grundfreiheiten. EuR:50–73. https://doi.org/10.5771/0531-2485-2015-1-50

Dörr O (2018a) Art 31 VCLT. In: Dörr O, Schmalenbach K (eds) Vienna Convention on the law of treaties: a commentary, 2nd edn. Springer, Berlin

Dörr O (2018b) Art 32 VCLT. In: Dörr O, Schmalenbach K (eds) Vienna Convention on the law of treaties: a commentary, 2nd edn. Springer, Berlin

Gaines S (2001) The WTO's reading of Article XX Chapeau: a disguised restriction on environmental measures. Univ Pa J Int Econ Law 22:739–862

Gaukrodger D, Gordon K (2012) Foreign government-controlled investors and host country investment policies: OECD perspectives. In: Sauvant KP, Sachs LE, Jongbloed WS (eds) Sovereign investment: concerns and policy reactions. Oxford University Press, Oxford, pp 496–511

Geiger F (2013) Beschränkungen von Direktinvestitionen aus Drittstaaten. Nomos, Baden-Baden

Grossman GM, Horn H, Mavroidis PC (2013) National treatment. In: Horn H, Mavroidis PC (eds) Legal and economic principles of world trade law: economics of trade agreements, border instruments, and national treasures. Cambridge University Press, Cambridge, pp 205–346

Hahn M (1991) Vital interests and the law of GATT: an analysis of GATT's security exception. Mich J Int Law 12:558–620

Herrmann C (2019) Europarechtliche Fragen der deutschen Investitionskontrolle. Zeitschrift für europarechtliche Studien 22:429–476. https://doi.org/10.5771/1435-439X-2019-3-429

Herz B (2014) Unternehmenstransaktionen zwischen Niederlassungs- und Kapitalverkehrsfreiheit: Grundlegung einer Abgrenzungslehre. Nomos, Baden-Baden

Hilf M, Goettsche G (2003) The relation of economic and non-economic principles in international law. In: Griller S (ed) International economic governance and non-economic concerns: new challenges for the international legal order. Springer, Wien, pp 5–46

Hindelang S (2009) The free movement of capital and foreign direct investment: the scope of protection in EU law. Oxford University Press, Oxford

Hindelang S, Hagemeyer TM (2017) Enemy at the Gates?: Die aktuellen Änderungen der Investitionsprüfvorschriften in der Außenwirtschaftsverordnung im Lichte des Unionsrechts. EuZW:882–890

Howse R (2016) The World Trade Organization 20 years on: global governance by judiciary. Eur J Int Law 27:9–77. https://doi.org/10.1093/ejil/chw011

Hudec RE (1998) GATT/WTO constraints on national regulation: requiem for an 'Aim and Effects' test. Int Lawyer 32:619–649

Jaeckel L (2020) Art 346 AEUV. In: Grabitz E, Hilf M, Nettesheim M (eds) Das Recht der Europäischen Union: EUV/AEUV, 71st edn. CH Beck, Munich

Kemmerer M (2010) Kapitalverkehrsfreiheit und Drittstaaten. Nomos, Baden-Baden

Kingreen T (2016) Arts 34–36 AEUV. In: Calliess C, Ruffert M (eds) EUV/AEUV: Das Verfassungsrecht der Europäischen Union mit Europäischer Grundrechtecharta, 5th edn. CH Beck, Munich

Korte S (2019) Regelungsoptionen zum Schutz vor Fremdabhängigkeiten aufgrund von Investitionen in versorgungsrelevante Unternehmen. WiVerw (GewA):79–141

Kotthaus J (2012) Binnenmarktrecht und externe Kapitalverkehrsfreiheit. Nomos, Baden-Baden

Krajewski M (2001) Verfassungsperspektiven und Legitimation des Rechts der Welthandelsorganisation (WTO). Duncker & Humblot, Berlin

Krajewski M (2003) National regulation and trade liberalization in services: the legal impact of the general agreement on trade in services on National Regulatory Autonomy. Kluwer Law International, The Hague

Leible S, Streinz R (2020) Art 36 AEUV. In: Grabitz E, Hilf M, Nettesheim M (eds) Das Recht der Europäischen Union: EUV/AEUV, 71st edn. CH Beck, Munich

Lester S, Zhu H (2019) A proposal for 'Rebalancing' to deal with 'National Security' trade restrictions. Fordham Int Law J 42:1451–1474

Lübke J (2006) Der Erwerb von Gesellschaftsanteilen zwischen Kapitalverkehrs- und Niederlassungsfreiheit. Nomos, Baden-Baden

Lübke J (2015) § 5 Die binnenmarktliche Kapital- und Zahlungsverkehrsfreiheit. In: Müller-Graff P-C (ed) Europäisches Wirtschaftsordnungsrecht. Nomos, Baden-Baden

Martini M (2008) Zu Gast bei Freunden?: Staatsfonds als Herausforderung an das europäische und internationale Recht. DÖV:314–322

Mavroidis PC (2005) The general agreement on tariffs and trade: a commentary. Oxford University Press, Oxford

Mavroidis PC (2007) Highway XVI re-visited: the road from non-discrimination to market access in GATS. World Trade Rev 6:1–23. https://doi.org/10.1017/S1474745606003077

Mavroidis PC (2020) The regulation of international trade, Volume 3: The general agreement on trade in services. MIT Press, Cambridge

Mishra N (2020a) Privacy, cybersecurity, and GATS Article XIV: a new frontier for trade and internet regulation? World Trade Rev 19:341–364. https://doi.org/10.1017/S1474745619000120

Mishra N (2020b) The trade: (cyber)security dilemma and its impact on global cybersecurity governance. J World Trade 54:567–590

Moberg A, Hindelang S (2020) The art of casting political dissent in law: The EU's framework for the screening of foreign direct investment. Common Mark Law Rev 57:1427–1460

Müller-Graff P-C (2015) Art 34 AEUV. In: von der Groeben H, Schwarze J, Hatje A (eds) Europäisches Unionsrecht: Vertrag über die Europäische Union - Vertrag über die Arbeitsweise der Europäischen Union - Charta der Grundrechte der Europäischen Union, 7th edn. Nomos, Baden-Baden

Müller-Graff P-C (2018) Art 52 AEUV. In: Streinz R (ed) EUV/AEUV: Vertrag über die Europäische Union und Vertrag über die Arbeitsweise der Europäischen Union, 3rd edn. CH Beck, Munich

Munin N (2010) Legal guide to GATS. Kluwer Law International, Alphen aan den Rijn

Nettesheim M (2008) Unternehmensübernahmen durch Staatsfonds: Europarechtliche Vorgaben und Schranken. ZHR 172:729–767

Pauwelyn J (2016) Minority rules: precedent and participation before the WTO Appellate Body. In: Olsen HP, Jemielniak J, Nielsen L (eds) Establishing judicial authority in international economic law. Cambridge University Press, Cambridge, pp 141–172

Peter S (2012) Public interest and common good in international law. Helbing Lichtenhahn, Basel

Pinchis-Paulsen M (2020) Trade multilateralism and U.S. National Security: the making of the GATT security exceptions. Mich J Int Law 41(109). https://doi.org/10.36642/mjil.41.1.trade

Pogoretskyy V, Talus K (2020) The WTO Panel Report in EU–Energy Package and its implications for the EU's gas market and energy security. World Trade Rev 19:531–549. https://doi.org/10.1017/S1474745619000260

Prazeres TL (2020) Trade and national security: rising risks for the WTO. World Trade Rev 19: 137–148. https://doi.org/10.1017/S1474745619000417

Ranjan P (2020) National security exception in the General Agreement on Tariffs and Trade (GATT) and India–Pakistan Trade. J World Trade 54:643–665

Ress G, Ukrow J (2020a) Art 63 AEUV. In: Grabitz E, Hilf M, Nettesheim M (eds) Das Recht der Europäischen Union: EUV/AEUV, 71st edn. CH Beck, Munich

Ress G, Ukrow J (2020b) Art 64 AEUV. In: Grabitz E, Hilf M, Nettesheim M (eds) Das Recht der Europäischen Union: EUV/AEUV, 71st edn. CH Beck, Munich

Ress G, Ukrow J (2020c) Art 65 AEUV. In: Grabitz E, Hilf M, Nettesheim M (eds) Das Recht der Europäischen Union: EUV/AEUV, 71st edn. CH Beck, Munich

Roberts A, Choer Moraes H, Ferguson V (2019) Toward a geoeconomic order in international trade and investment. J Int Econ Law 22:655–676. https://doi.org/10.1093/jiel/jgz036

Rüthers B, Fischer C, Birk A (2018) Rechtstheorie: Mit juristischer Methodenlehre, 10th edn. CH Beck, Munich

Schloemann H, Ohlhoff S (1999) 'Constitutionalization' and dispute settlement in the WTO: national security as an issue of competence. Am J Int Law 93:424–451

Schnitger A (2005) Die Kapitalverkehrsfreiheit im Verhältnis zu Drittstaaten: Vorabentscheidungsersuchen in den Rs. van Hilten, Fidium Finanz AG und Lasertec. IStR:493–504. https://doi.org/10.5771/9783845292724

Schön W (2005) Der Kapitalverkehr mit Drittstaaten und das internationale Steuerrecht. In: Gocke R (ed) Körperschaftsteuer, internationales Steuerrecht, Doppelbesteuerung: Festschrift für Franz Wassermeyer zum 65. Geburtstag. CH Beck, Munich, pp 489–522

Schröder W (2018) Art 36 AEUV. In: Streinz R (ed) EUV/AEUV: Vertrag über die Europäische Union und Vertrag über die Arbeitsweise der Europäischen Union, 3rd edn. CH Beck, Munich

Sedlaczek M, Züger M (2018a) Art 64 AEUV. In: Streinz R (ed) EUV/AEUV: Vertrag über die Europäische Union und Vertrag über die Arbeitsweise der Europäischen Union, 3rd edn. CH Beck, Munich

Sedlaczek M, Züger M (2018b) Art 65 AEUV. In: Streinz R (ed) EUV/AEUV: Vertrag über die Europäische Union und Vertrag über die Arbeitsweise der Europäischen Union, 3rd edn. CH Beck, Munich

Smit D (2012) EU freedoms, Non-EU countries and company taxation. Kluwer Law International, Alphen aan den Rijn

Stevenson A, Brown L (2007) Shorter Oxford English Dictionary on historical principles, 6th edn. Oxford University Press, Oxford

Sykes AO (2015) Economic 'Necessity' of international law. Am J Int Law 109:296–326. https://doi.org/10.5305/amerjintelaw.109.2.0296

Trachtman JP (2007) The international economic law revolution and the right to regulate. Cameron May, London

Tsagourias N (2017) Risk and the use of force. In: Ambrus M, Rayfuse RG, Werner W (eds) Risk and the regulation of uncertainty in international law. Oxford University Press, Oxford, pp 13–37

Tuthill L, Roy M (2012) GATS classification issues for information and communication technology services. In: Burri M, Cottier T (eds) Trade governance in the digital age: World Trade Forum. Cambridge University Press, Cambridge, pp 157–178

Velten J (2020) The investment screening regulation and its screening ground 'Security or Public Order'. CTEI Working Paper Series. https://repository.graduateinstitute.ch/record/298429. Accessed 2 Feb 2022

Vidigal G (2019) WTO adjudication and the security exception: something old, something new, something borrowed - something blue? Leg Issues Econ Integr 46:203–224

Voon T (2019) Can international trade law recover? The security exception in WTO law: entering a new era. Am J Int Law 113:45–50. https://doi.org/10.1017/aju.2019.3

Wegener B (2016a) Art 19 EUV. In: Calliess C, Ruffert M (eds) EUV/AEUV: Das Verfassungsrecht der Europäischen Union mit Europäischer Grundrechtecharta, 5th edn. CH Beck, Munich

Wegener B (2016b) Art 346 AEUV. In: Calliess C, Ruffert M (eds) EUV/AEUV: Das Verfassungsrecht der Europäischen Union mit Europäischer Grundrechtecharta, 5th edn. CH Beck, Munich

Weiss M (2008) Goldene Aktien im Lichte der Rechtsprechung des EuGH: Unter besonderer Berücksichtigung des harmonisierten Übernahmerechts. Nomos, Baden-Baden

Weiß W (2020) Adjudicating security exceptions in WTO law: methodical and procedural preliminaries. J World Trade 54:829–852

Wojcik K-P (2015a) Art 63 AEUV. In: von der Groeben H, Schwarze J, Hatje A (eds) Europäisches Unionsrecht: Vertrag über die Europäische Union - Vertrag über die Arbeitsweise der Europäischen Union - Charta der Grundrechte der Europäischen Union, 7th edn. Nomos, Baden-Baden

Wojcik K-P (2015b) Art 65 AEUV. In: von der Groeben H, Schwarze J, Hatje A (eds) Europäisches Unionsrecht: Vertrag über die Europäische Union - Vertrag über die Arbeitsweise der Europäischen Union - Charta der Grundrechte der Europäischen Union, 7th edn. Nomos, Baden-Baden

Wolff J (2009) Ausländische Staatsfonds und staatliche Sonderrechte: Zum Phänomen 'Sovereign Wealth Funds' und zur Vereinbarkeit der Beschränkung von Unternehmensbeteiligungen mit Europarecht. Berliner Wissenschafts-Verlag, Berlin

Chapter 4
Flexibility for FDI Screening on Broader Grounds Than 'Security or Public Order'

Chapter 3 demonstrated that the current legislative options for FDI Screening mechanisms in the EU cannot meet large parts of the EU and Member States concerns vis-à-vis foreign investors. The options' screening grounds circling around the notions of security and public order are too narrow to cover the concerns. This conclusion is even valid for the broadest available screening ground, 'security or public order' within the meaning of the Screening Regulation, which is limited by the meaning of 'essential security interests' and 'public order' pursuant to Arts XIV*bis*(1)(b) and XIV(a) GATS. This chapter therefore asks whether the EU and its Member States have the flexibility to adopt FDI Screening mechanisms on broader grounds than 'security or public order'.

FDI Screening mechanisms primarily regulate the establishment[1] of foreign investors in the EU through M&A FDI. In principle, every State has the right to regulate the establishment in its own territory. Accordingly, States even have the right to discriminate between investors from third countries, or between third country investors and domestic investors.[2] However, States may have—unilaterally

---

[1] In this sense, 'establishment' is used in an untechnical way, neither referring to Art 49 TFEU, nor any specific notion of International economic law.

[2] *Canada—Administration of the Foreign Investment Review Act*, GATT Panel Report (7 February 1984) BISD 30S/140, para. 5.1, the only decision of a WTO adjudicating body where a cross-sector FDI Screening mechanism was at issue. The US challenged Canada's practice to conclude investor agreements under the screening mechanism that stipulate performance requirements for the investor. Today, such performance requirements are prohibited under the TRIMs Agreement. See also Working Group on the Relationship between Trade and Investment, 'Modalities for Pre-establishment Commitments Based on GATS-type, Positive List Approach' (Note by the Secretariat) WT/WGTI/W/120, para. 2; Cottier and Schneller (2014), pp. 5–6.

© The Author(s), under exclusive license to Springer Nature Switzerland AG 2022   127
J. Velten, *Screening Foreign Direct Investment in the EU*, EYIEL Monographs -
Studies in European and International Economic Law 26,
https://doi.org/10.1007/978-3-031-05603-1_4

or vis-à-vis other States—committed to market access and non-discrimination obligations that limit these rights. Indeed, in EU primary law and International economic law, the EU and its Member States have undertaken obligations to admit FDI to their market. Most importantly, the EU and its Member States unilaterally committed to the freedom of capital movement from third countries vis-à-vis foreign investors (Art 63(1) TFEU). In addition, the EU and its Member States concluded several international agreements, in particular the GATS, that additionally limit their flexibility to screen FDI.

Therefore, to assess the EU and its Member States' flexibility to screen FDI on broader grounds than 'security or public order', this chapter will analyze the legal limitations posed by EU primary law and International economic law. For both, the following analysis will first determine the obligations the EU and its Member States have to admit foreign investors on the internal market. Only to the extent such obligations exist will it be necessary to also assess the grounds of exception to these obligations. In other words, the EU and its Member States have the flexibility to screen FDI on broader grounds than 'security or public order' to the extent one of the following two conditions is met: The EU and its Member States have no obligation to admit FDI on its internal market, or, in case such an obligation exists, the relevant obligation is subject to an exception that is broader in scope than the Screening Regulation's screening ground 'security or public order'.

Both conditions depend on the concrete personal and substantial scope of FDI Screening mechanisms. Do they apply to all M&A FDI or only FDI beyond a certain threshold? How exactly are foreign investors defined? From the perspective of capturing the EU and Member States concerns vis-à-vis foreign investors as much as possible, Sect. 2.4.3 defined these cornerstones of FDI Screening mechanisms broadly. So defined FDI Screening mechanisms cover all M&A FDI and a large group of foreign investors (country of legal organization, seat, or ultimately controlling persons).[3] This chapter will find that EU primary law and International economic law pose different, inconsistent limits to adopt so defined FDI Screening mechanisms. It will identify the personal and substantial scope of FDI Screening mechanisms as the most important parameter that shapes the EU's and Member States' options to adopt FDI screening on broader grounds than 'security or public order'.

More concretely, the first section of this chapter, Sect. 4.1, will assess who in the EU has the competence to screen FDI on broader grounds than 'security or public order'—the EU or its Member States. Sections 4.2 and 4.3 will then examine the EU's and Member States' obligations to admit FDI pursuant to EU primary law and International economic law. This includes an analysis of relevant grounds of exception to the extent the EU and Member States have obligations to admit FDI. Both sections identify policy options for FDI Screening mechanisms on broader grounds than 'security or public order' that comply with EU primary law and International economic law respectively. The options' scopes differ according to the personal and

---

[3]For the definitions in detail Sects. 2.4.1 and 2.4.2.

substantial scope the FDI Screening mechanism may have. They must all compromise in one way or another on the extent to which EU and Member States concerns vis-à-vis foreign investors are met.

Last, Sect. 4.4 combines the findings to identify the EU's and Member States' potential legislative options for FDI Screening mechanisms on broader grounds than 'security or public order' that comply with both EU primary law and International economic law. Much will depend on the personal and substantial scope of the envisaged FDI Screening mechanism.

To be sure, this chapter thus focuses on the EU's and its Member States' flexibility to screen FDI beyond the Screening Regulation's scope. However, it does not assess—but allows inferences on—whether the Screening Regulation complies with EU and International economic law.

4.1 Competence for FDI Screening Mechanisms: EU or Member States?

This section examines who has the competence for adopting FDI Screening mechanisms on broader grounds than 'security or public order'—the EU, the Member States, or both. Given the broader screening ground, the competence must reach beyond simply harmonizing the TFEU ground of exception in Art 65(1)(b), 'public policy or public security'.[4]

---

[4]This book will thus not specifically address a possible Member State competence for 'national security', 'public policy or public security', and 'essential security interests' pursuant to Art 4(2), sentences 2 and 3 TEU; Arts 65(1)(b) TFEU and 346(1)(b) TFEU. It is controversial whether these provisions allow Member States to take own measures in areas that fall under the Common commercial policy. See on Art 4(2), sentences 2 and 3 TEU, Art 65(1)(b) TFEU in favour of a carve-out from other EU competences Benyon (2010), p. 98; Dimopoulos (2011), p. 77; Schmitt (2013), p. 282; Bings (2014), p. 91; Obwexer (2015b), para. 10.

Arguing against Art 65(1)(b) TFEU as a ground of exception to EU competences from Art 207 TFEU, Puig (2013), pp. 158–159. Apparently in favour, the German government when adopting a prior version of the German FDI screening mechanisms in German Foreign Trade and Payments Ordinance (Außenwirtschaftsverordnung), as amended as of 25 August 2021, secs 55–59, see German Federal Government (2008), Drucksache 16/7668, p. 3. The ECJ case law is inconsistent. Earlier judgments explicitly found that Art 36 EEC (now Art 36 TFEU) is a ground of exception for Member States to derogate from EU law, not a reservation of competence, see Case C-35/76 *Simmenthal Spa v Ministero delle finanze* [1976] EU:C:1976:180, para. 14; Case C-5/77 *Tedeschi v Denkavit* [1977] EU:C:1977:144, paras. 33–35; Case C-72/83 *Campus Oil* [1984] EU: C:1984:256, para. 32. In Opinion 2/15 *EU-Singapore Free Trade Agreement* [2017] EU:C:2017: 376, paras. 100–101, 103, the ECJ seems to open a door to generally reserve Member States' competence in the areas of 'public policy or public security'. This may also be seen in light of the new identity clause in Art 4(2) TEU (formerly very narrow Art F(1) TEU 1992, and Art 6(3) TEU 1997). With a more detailed discussion, focusing on possible restrictions of the free movement of EU citizens pursuant to Art 21 TFEU, see Guastaferro (2012), pp. 290–299.

The EU based the Screening Regulation on its exclusive Common commercial policy competence pursuant to Arts 3(1)(e), 207(2) TFEU. Alternatively, one may find an appropriate legal basis for adopting FDI Screening mechanisms in the internal market provisions, more precisely Art 64(2) and (3) TFEU on the freedom of capital movement.[5] This alternative would mean a shared competence for FDI Screening mechanisms between the EU and Member States.[6]

The following sections will analyze why the screening of FDI in principle falls under both Arts 3(1)(e), 207(2), as well as Art 64(2) and (3) TFEU. To determine whether the adoption of FDI screening rules is a matter of exclusive EU or shared competence between EU and Member States, the last section will determine when one legal basis overrules the other.

4.1.1   Common Commercial Policy Pursuant to Arts 3(1)(e), 207(2) TFEU

FDI Screening mechanisms have three important characteristics that at the same time are also key determinants whether a measure falls under the Common commercial policy pursuant to Arts 3(1)(e) and 207(2) TFEU. FDI Screening mechanisms are (i) unilateral restrictions (ii) vis-à-vis foreign, not EU investors that (iii) address incoming FDI in the phase of market entry and to a small extent after market entry.[7] The ECJ judgment on the EU-Singapore FTA clarified that measures fulfilling these three characteristics fall under Art 207(2) TFEU, and therefore in the EU's exclusive competence.[8] The following therefore only briefly applies the developed standards in *EU—Singapore Free Trade Agreement* to the facts of FDI Screening mechanisms.

Art 207(2) TFEU demonstrates that the EU's Common commercial policy competence not only covers the more prominent contractual, but also autonomous trade policy. Autonomous trade policy measures are internal legal acts that the EU adopts autonomously, meaning without participation of other actors, but which nevertheless shape external trade relationships.[9] Regulatory measures such as FDI Screening mechanisms meet this definition.

---

[5]The following will cite some ECJ judgments and scholar contributions that were issued prior to the Treaty of Lisbon. Accordingly, they cite EEC or EC, not TFEU provisions. Nevertheless, the following will only highlight cases in which the difference between EEC and EC on the one, and TFEU on the other hand are relevant to the conclusion drawn from the judgments and contributions. See also Chap. 3, n. 170.

[6]Sections 4.2.2 and 4.2.3 will show that FDI falls under the freedom of capital movement. For the purposes of this section, this result is presumed.

[7]See anti-circumvention rules that address investors who are already established in the EU, Art 3(6) Screening Regulation.

[8]*EU-Singapore Free Trade Agreement* (n. 4).

[9]Weiß (2020), para. 64.

Moreover, the Common commercial policy includes measures with regard to FDI as defined in the realm of the freedom of capital movement, and for the purposes of this book.[10] It does not differentiate between the phases of establishment and post-establishment. As a result, the Common commercial policy competence also encompasses FDI Screening mechanisms insofar as they address the post-establishment phase for circumvention control.[11]

Last but not least, the measure at issue must relate specifically to international trade. In other words, the measure must be 'intended to promote, facilitate or govern trade', and 'must have direct and immediate effects on trade'.[12] Despite its neighbouring terms 'promote or facilitate', the definition's notion 'govern' also includes legal acts that restrict trade, for example to protect the EU of certain trade effects.[13] Consequently, screening FDI governs trade within the meaning of Art 207(1) TFEU. The FDI Screening mechanisms are also supposed to have direct and immediate consequences on trade with third countries.[14] They raise the barriers for FDI market access significantly, whether by *ex ante* authorization requirement or *ex post* prohibition right.[15]

---

[10] See FDI definition in Sect. 2.4.1. One may read Art 207(1) TFEU as requiring FDI to have a special relation to trade in goods or services ('and the *commercial aspects of* intellectual property, *foreign direct investment*, the achievement of uniformity in measures of liberalisation [*sic*]', emphasis added). The German and French version of Art 207(1) TFEU, however, demonstrate that the term 'commercial aspects' only qualifies intellectual property, not FDI. The German version reads: 'und für die Handelsaspekte des geistigen Eigentums, die ausländischen Direktinvestitionen, die Vereinheitlichung der Liberalisierungsmaßnahmen'. In French the same provision reads: 'et les aspects commerciaux de la propriété intellectuelle, les investissements étrangers directs, l'uniformisation des mesures de libéralisation'. See also Cottier and Trinberg (2015b), para. 60.

[11] *EU-Singapore Free Trade Agreement* (n. 4), para. 87.

[12] Settled case law, see Case C-414/11 *Daiichi Sankyo and Sanofi-Aventis Deutschland* [2013] EU: C:2013:520, para. 51; Case C-137/12 *Commission v Council* [2013] EU:C:2013:675, para. 57; *EU-Singapore Free Trade Agreement* (n. 4), paras. 36, 84.

[13] Schmitt (2013), pp. 152–153. See also Case C-411/06 *Commission v Parliament and Council* [2009] EU:C:2009:518, para. 62, in which the protection of health and environment from trade effects is considered part of the Common commercial policy. The fact that trade restrictive measures also fall under Art 207(1) TFEU is also demonstrated by numerous anti-dumping measures, e.g. on subsidized imports Regulation (EU) 2016/1036 of the European Parliament and of the Council of 8 June 2016 on protection against dumped imports from countries not members of the European Union [2016] OJ L 176/21; Regulation (EU) 2016/1037 of the European Parliament and of the Council of 8 June 2016 on protection against subsidised imports from countries not members of the European Union [2016] OJ L 176/55.

[14] The ECJ confirmed this view in a judgment on an international agreement that sought to create a single registration system for appellations of origin and geographical indications, Case C-389/15 *Commission v Council (Revised Lisbon Agreement)* [2017] EU:C:2017:798, paras. 70–71. Aim of the single registration system was to facilitate trade by creating a harmonized registration mechanism instead of distinct mechanisms in all member states of the treaty at issue.

[15] For the two possible FDI Screening mechanisms designs, see Sect. 2.4.3. This conclusion does not necessarily apply to the Screening Regulation, since it only provides Member States with options for FDI Screening mechanisms, without itself raising concrete barriers. On this, see e.g. Cremona (2020), pp. 43–45.

Consequently, the FDI Screening mechanisms provide a sufficiently specific relation to trade with third countries, and therefore fall under the EU's Common commercial policy.[16] Accordingly, the EU might be exclusively competent to adopt FDI Screening mechanisms.[17]

4.1.2 Shared Internal Market Competence Pursuant to Arts 63(1), 64(2) and (3) TFEU

Besides Arts 3(1)(e) and 207(2) TFEU, adopting FDI Screening mechanisms may also be based on the internal market competence in Arts 63(1) and 64(2) and (3) TFEU in conjunction with Art 4(2)(a) TFEU. This competence is shared between EU and Member States in that, Member States may themselves take legislative action to the extent that the EU has not exercised its own competence (Art 2(2) TFEU).

One may argue that with the Screening Regulation the EU has exercised its own competence and thereby taken the policy field of FDI screening out of the Member States hands. If so, Arts 63(1) and 64(2) and (3) TFEU would assign the competence to adopt *any* FDI Screening mechanisms exclusively to the EU. However, one may also argue that the Member States have preserved the competence for FDI Screening mechanisms on broader screening grounds than those provided in the current Screening Regulation. The following will set this argument aside, and focus on the question whether FDI Screening mechanisms do fall under the shared competence of Arts 63(1) and 64(2) and (3) TFEU at all.

Art 63(1) TFEU prohibits all restrictions on the movement of capital, not only between Member States, but also between Member States and third countries (*erga omnes* effect). Accordingly, a provision that regulates third-country capital

---

[16] With the same conclusion Tietje (2007), p. 8; Herrmann (2010), pp. 209–210; Hindelang and Maydell (2010), p. 72; Schill (2010), p. 520; Bungenberg (2011), p. 39; Schmitt (2013), p. 155; Weiß (2020), para. 43. Dismissing a sufficiently specific relation to trade, Günther (2018), p. 29 (but ultimately nevertheless in favour of Art 207(2) TFEU as the correct legal basis); Geiger (2013), pp. 83–84 (without much argumentation). Korte (2019), pp. 106–107, argues that the competence for FDI Screening mechanisms remains with the Member States. The FDI Screening mechanism's centre of gravity lies on Art 64(2) and (3) TFEU, instead of Art 207(2) TFEU. According to Korte, Art 64(2) and (3) TFEU apply; and the EU has not exercised its competence entirely by adopting the Screening Regulation, thereby omitting a blocking effect.

[17] Indeed, even in areas of exclusive competence, the EU may empower the Member States to adopt own legal acts (Art 2(1) TFEU). On possible forms of empowerment see Calliess (2016a), para. 10; Nettesheim (2020), para. 19.

movement may also fall under the shared internal market competences.[18] Moreover, Art 64(2) and (3) TFEU explicitly classify certain measures on third-country capital movement, in particular on FDI, as aspects of the freedom of capital movement. Pursuant to Art 64 TFEU, such measures must be adopted in accordance with the ordinary legislative procedure of Art 294 TFEU (Art 64(2) TFEU), or, in case of a step backwards as regards the liberalization of capital movement, unanimously by the Council after consulting the Parliament (Art 64(3) TFEU). Pursuant to Art 4(1) and (2) TFEU, these competences are shared competences between EU and Member States.[19]

Screening FDI restricts the movement of capital from third countries within the meaning of Arts 63(1) and 64(2) and (3) TFEU to the extent that the FDI includes foreign capital inflows into the EU.[20] Accordingly, one may also argue that FDI screening falls in the shared competence of EU and Member States, not in the EU's exclusive competence pursuant to Art 207(2) TFEU.[21]

4.1.3 Reconciling the Conflict Between Exclusive Common Commercial Policy and Shared Internal Market Competences

Sections 4.1.1 and 4.1.2 showed that a priori FDI Screening mechanisms can fall under the EU's exclusive Common commercial policy competence as well as the internal market competence shared between EU and Member States. The following assesses whether one competence nevertheless overrides the other.

Generally, lawmakers must choose the legal basis for a legal act based 'on objective factors that are amenable to judicial review; these include the purpose and content of that measure'.[22] If the legal act has a twofold purpose or twofold

---

[18] Regarding the Screening Regulation, Herrmann (2019), pp. 462–463, argues that only the freedom of establishment applies, not the freedom of capital movement. Accordingly, Art 64(2) and (3) TFEU must also fail to apply. *Contra* Moberg and Hindelang (2020), pp. 1440–1442.

[19] Obwexer (2015a), para. 12; Korte (2019), p. 103.

[20] Bings (2014), p. 85, argues that Art 64(2) and (3) TFEU cover only market access, but not FDI protection after establishment. Similarly, Strik (2014), p. 30, who categorizes investment protection as falling under the freedom of establishment. Dimopoulos (2011), p. 84, argues that market access falls under the Common commercial policy, while investment protection is covered by Art 63(1) TFEU. Both views find no basis in the wide definition of restriction of capital movement within the meaning of Art 63(1) TFEU. For the ECJ's jurisprudence on the notion of restriction see Chap. 3, n. 230.

[21] If correct, the Screening Regulation may be subject to an action for annulment pursuant to Art 263(2) TFEU, since it would have been based on the wrong legal basis. See Günther (2018), p. 18; Bast (2020), para. 30.

[22] Settled case law, see e.g. Case C-48/14 *Parliament v Council* [2015] EU:C:2015:91, para. 29, with further references.

content, one has first to determine the main or predominant purpose or content. Only if unsuccessful, may a dual legal basis apply.[23]

FDI Screening mechanisms on the grounds of 'public policy or public security' within the meaning of Art 65(1)(b) TFEU harmonize the Member States' application of a ground of exception to the freedom of capital movement in Art 63(1) TFEU. Insofar an FDI Screening mechanism must be based on Art 64(2) or (3) TFEU—at least in combination with Art 207(2) TFEU.[24]

The focus of this chapter, however, lies on FDI Screening mechanisms beyond the screening ground 'public policy or public security' within the meaning of Art 65(1)(b) TFEU. Insofar, the rule of a main or predominant purpose or content offers no guidance for choosing between Art 207(2) and 64(2), (3) TFEU as a legal basis. In particular, FDI Screening mechanisms intend to both protecting the internal market from certain external threats and regulating external trade. For example, the harmful investor concern is not only about protecting domestic assets from foreign investors, but also preventing certain domestic assets to be exported abroad.[25]

Therefore, a delimitation of the Common commercial policy and internal market competences must be sought at a more general level.[26] Mainly three arguments are discussed.

---

[23] See e.g. *Commission v Council* (n. 12), para. 53, with further references: 'If examination of that measure reveals that it pursues a twofold purpose or that it has a twofold component and if one of those is identifiable as the main or predominant purpose or component, whereas the other is merely incidental, that measure must be based on a single legal basis, namely that required by the main or predominant purpose or component.'

[24] On this issue in detail see Cremona (2020), pp. 34–50, 53–54. She argues that the harmonization of Member State public order or public policy interests must (also) be based on an internal market competence, citing as an example Directive 2004/38/EC of the European Parliament and of the Council of 29 April 2004 on the right of citizens of the Union and their family members to move and reside freely within the territory of the Member States [2004] OJ L 158/77, arts 27–33. She goes on to argue that in the realm of the Common commercial policy this might require a dual legal basis together with Art 207(2) TFEU.

[25] Referring to the internal market purpose, on the one hand, and the external trade purpose, on the other hand, misses the purpose of Arts 63, 64(2), (3), 207(2) TFEU anyway. Art 207(2) TFEU also encompasses trade-restrictive measures, and Art 63(1) TFEU, due to its *erga omnes* effect, is also about external policies. The grounds of exception in Arts 64(2) and (3) TFEU want to equip the EU with flexibility vis-à-vis capital movement from foreign States. Bröhmer (2016b), para. 2; Ress and Ukrow (2020b), para. 4. For a more detailed analysis of the object and purpose of Art 64 TFEU, see Sect. 4.2.5.1. Clostermeyer (2011), pp. 102, 108, 114–116, differentiates between both competences according to the measure type. Contractual trade policy with third countries falls under Art 207(1) TFEU, while autonomous measures in 'non-economic areas' fall under the internal market competence pursuant to Arts 63(1), 64(2), (3) TFEU. Schill (2019), pp. 107–108, seems to argue that capital restricting measures to protect Union and Member State interests fall under Art 64(2) and (3) TFEU. Nevertheless, he claims that the Screening Regulation falls under Art 207(2) TFEU, since it is part of the EU's overall trade strategy to achieve more favourable treatment of EU investors in third countries.

[26] Müller-Ibold (2010), p. 113; Bings (2014), pp. 87–89, opine for a parallelism of Arts 207(2), and 63 (1), 64 (2) and (3) TFEU. However, they omit discussing the resulting conflict of divergent competences and legislative procedure. Seemingly of the same opinion, Strik (2014), pp. 83–85.

First, Art 207(1) TFEU, amending Art 133 EC, may constitute the more recent provision that supersedes Art 64(2) and (3) TFEU.[27] The predecessor provision of Art 64(2) and (3) TFEU exists already since the Maastricht Treaty as Art 73c EEC and later Art 57 EC. However, the Lisbon Treaty also slightly amended Art 64(2) and (3) TFEU. It moved the second sentence of Art 57(2) EC to a new paragraph 3 of Art 64 TFEU. Neither one of the provisions may thus be said to be more recent and thereby superseding the other.

Second, one may understand one provision as *lex specialis* vis-à-vis the other provision. Some argue that Arts 63(1), and 64(2) and (3) TFEU are more specific than the Common commercial policy competence, since the former explicitly address the movement of capital and the protection of the internal market.[28] On the other hand, more scholars argue that Common commercial policy as an external policy competence for unilaterally regulating third country relations is more specific than Arts 63(1), and 64(2) and (3) TFEU.[29] However, not only the Common commercial policy, but also Art 64(2) and (3) TFEU apply exclusively to third-country capital movement. Arguing that the third-country relation characterizes the specificity of Art 207(2) TFEU therefore misses the core of Art 64(2) and (3) TFEU. Nevertheless, if Art 63(1), and 64(2) and (3) TFEU are *lex specialis* to Art 207 (2) TFEU, the latter would be deprived of its meaning to the extent that it covers regulating FDI through autonomous legal acts. Hence, the *lex specialis* argument fails to offer any added value for the delimitation of the Common commercial policy and internal market competence.[30]

The third argument, the object and purpose of both competences, gives real guidance on delimiting Arts 64(2), (3) and 207(2) TFEU. The Treaties provide the EU with the exclusive competence for external commercial policy to create a common policy landscape that allows to more effectively pursue EU and Member States interests in international trade negotiations.[31] One important element of these negotiations are the conditions for foreign investors in the EU and third countries—namely, market access and investor protection.[32] Therefore, it is in the interest of a concise and unified external commercial policy that the EU is also competent for regulating the market access for foreign investors through autonomous legal acts pursuant to Art 207(2) TFEU.[33] This consideration weighs in favour of Art

---

[27] Benyon (2010), p. 83; Schmitt (2013), pp. 279–280.

[28] Addressing, but rejecting this argument Clostermeyer (2011), p. 102; Geiger (2013), p. 78.

[29] Benyon (2010), p. 83; Cottier and Trinberg (2015b), paras. 64–65; Weiß (2020), para. 40.

[30] With the same conclusion Günther (2018), p. 27.

[31] Cottier and Trinberg (2015a), para. 2; Günther (2018), p. 31.

[32] Cottier and Trinberg (2015b), para. 50. See e.g. Section 8.4 CETA and Section 8.8-12 EU-Singapore Agreement addressing market access for establishments of foreigners, of which the definition encompasses FDI, but is different than in Art 49 TFEU.

[33] Schmitt (2013), pp. 280–281; Cottier and Trinberg (2015b), para. 65. Insofar, the principle of interpreting exclusive EU competences restrictively (see Calliess (2016b), para. 14), must stand back behind the purpose of a unified Common commercial policy.

207(2) TFEU overriding the shared internal market competence, and thus for an exclusive competence of the EU for FDI Screening mechanisms on broader grounds than 'public policy or public security'.[34]

It is important to note that this conclusion does only address the issue of competence. Art 64(3) TFEU, as a ground of exception to the freedom of capital movement, still requires a special legislative procedure in case of a step backwards in capital movement liberalization pursuant to Art 64(3) TFEU. This higher burden for de-liberalizing capital movement regulation is a direct consequence of the substantial content of Art 64(2) and (3) TFEU.[35]

Consequently, Art 207(2) TFEU gives the EU exclusive competence for FDI Screening mechanisms beyond 'public policy or public security' pursuant to Art 65(1)(b) TFEU, and thus also beyond 'security or public order' within the meaning of the Screening Regulation. The following will thus only assess the *EU's* flexibility to adopt broader FDI Screening mechanisms.

4.2   Flexibility for FDI Screening Mechanisms Pursuant to EU Law

Section 4.1 showed that the EU has exclusive competence to adopt FDI Screening mechanisms beyond the screening ground 'security or public order'. For exercising this competence EU primary law poses significant limits. The Fundamental freedoms of the TFEU and Fundamental rights of the CFR provide investment rights not only to EU, but also to foreign investors. Relevant limits for FDI screening may derive especially from the freedoms of capital movement and establishment (Arts 63(1) and 49 TFEU) as well as the fundamental rights to freely choose an occupation and to conduct a business, the right to property and to non-discrimination (Arts 15(1) and (3), 16, 17(1), and 21(2) CFR).

Though Fundamental rights are increasingly important as limits to EU and Member States legal acts, they only pose minimum limits to third-country measures such as FDI screening. Most importantly, they may all be restricted to meet

---

[34] Also in favour of an exclusive EU competence for FDI Screening mechanisms, but without taking the special procedural rules of Art 64(3) TFEU into account, Cottier and Trinberg (2015b), Art 207 AEUV, para. 65; Günther (2018), p. 31; Weiß (2020), paras. 40, 43; and without addressing Art 64(2) and (3) TFEU Tietje (2007), p. 8; Herrmann (2010), p. 209; Bungenberg (2011), p. 39. Puig (2013), pp. 150–152, argues that the internal market competence applies to the extent Art 64(2) and (3) TFEU apply. This should avoid deriving these provisions of their meaning. The same result is achieved by the approach chosen here when still requiring the special legislative procedure pursuant to Art 64(3) TFEU. In favour of a dual legal basis of Arts 207(2) and 64(2) TFEU, Moberg and Hindelang (2020), p. 1445.

[35] See also Tietje (2009), p. 14. One may therefore describe Art 64(2) and (3) TFEU as a condition to exercise the Common commercial competence in Art 207(2) TFEU ('Wahrnehmungskompetenz'), see Nettesheim (2009), p. 391. For a detailed discussion of whether FDI Screening mechanisms constitute a step backwards in liberalization, see Sect. 4.2.5.

objectives of general interest recognized by EU law (Art 52(1) CFR). The notion of objectives of general interest is much broader than the exceptions to the Fundamental freedoms 'public policy or public security' (Art 65(1)(b) TFEU) and 'essential security interests' (Art 346(1)(b) TFEU). The following will therefore focus on the limits to screening FDI posed by the Fundamental freedoms, and only briefly outline the limits set by the Fundamental rights.

The limits deriving from the freedoms of capital movement and establishment depend first and foremost on their scope of application regarding foreign investors and third-country FDI. If the freedoms of capital movement or establishment apply, the EU's flexibility to adopt FDI Screening mechanisms is limited to the grounds of exception provided to these Fundamental freedoms. This book submits an analysis of both aspects, the freedoms of capital movement and establishment's scope of application and their grounds of exception. It does, however, not discuss the second prong of the Fundamental freedom test: restriction. FDI Screening mechanisms pass this test. In both cases, Case 1 and Case 2, FDI Screening mechanisms impede the FDI or at least render it less attractive,[36] in other words discourage foreign investors from making investments.[37,38] A detailed discussion is therefore not necessary.

It will be shown that the protection of foreign investors by the Fundamental freedoms is highly fragmented.[39] The fragmentation primarily stems from the different personal scopes of the freedoms of capital movement and establishment. While the freedom of capital movement a priori applies to EU and foreign investors (*erga omnes* effect), the freedom of establishment only covers EU-established investors.

This has important consequences for the EU's flexibility adopt FDI Screening mechanisms on broader grounds than 'security or public order'. Their personal and substantial scope determines the limits that are set by EU primary law. Different options offer different flexibility, but all compromise on the extent to which the EU and Member States may meet their concerns vis-à-vis foreign investors. Accordingly, the following discussion requires a high degree of differentiation.[40]

Against this background, the following will first briefly confirm that not only the Member States, but also the EU are bound by the Fundamental freedoms (Sect. 4.2.1). Sections 4.2.2 and 4.2.3 will then in turn analyze the personal and substantial

---

[36] Both notions of restriction are settled case law for Art 49 TFEU, see e.g. Case C-563/17 *Associação Peço a Palavra and Others* [2019] EU:C:2019:144, para. 54.

[37] This notion of restriction is settled case law for Art 63(1) TFEU, see e.g. Joined Cases C-52 and 113/16 *SEGRO* [2018] EU:C:2018:157, para. 65.

[38] On the definition of Case 1 and 2 of FDI Screening mechanisms see Sect. 2.4.3.

[39] For the definition of FDI and Foreign investors as well as the differences between the latter and the notion of EU-established investor in Art 54(1) TFEU, see Sect. 2.4.2.

[40] The following will cite a number of ECJ judgments and scholar contributions that were issued prior to the Treaty of Lisbon. Accordingly, they cite EEC or EC, not TFEU provisions. Nevertheless, the following will only highlight cases in which the difference between EEC and EC on the one, and TFEU on the other hand are relevant to the conclusion drawn from the judgments and contributions. See also Chap. 3, n. 170 and in this chapter n. 5.

scope of the freedoms of capital movement and establishment. An analysis of the freedoms' personal scope will demonstrate the fragmented protection of foreign investors. Due to the inconsistent personal scopes, the delimitation of the freedoms' substantial scope becomes crucial. After having developed a delimitation test, a complex picture emerges to determine whether legislation falls under the freedoms of capital movement and/or establishment. Section 4.2.4 will summarize these findings for FDI Screening mechanisms, and conclude that they, depending on their design, at least in part fall under the freedom of capital movement. Hence, the scope of the grounds of exception to the freedom of capital movement becomes crucial.

Chapter 3 already concluded that 'public policy or public security' within the meaning of Art 65(1)(b) TFEU fails to offer the EU and the Member States enough flexibility to meet their concerns vis-à-vis foreign investors. Accordingly, Sect. 4.2.5 focuses on the flexibility to screen FDI provided by Art 64(2) and (3) TFEU. From a substantial perspective, this flexibility is nearly limitless. Therefore, Sect. 4.2.6 will at last briefly outline possible additional limits deriving from the Fundamental rights.

Section 4.2.7 will summarize the flexibility the EU has to adopt FDI Screening mechanisms beyond the screening ground 'security or public order' within the meaning of the Screening Regulation. It depends mainly on the personal and substantial scope of FDI Screening mechanisms. Thus, Sect. 4.2.7 will identify the different FDI Screening mechanism design options, and analyze the option's shortcomings to meet the EU and Member States concerns vis-à-vis foreign investors.

4.2.1   EU Legislator as Addressee of the Fundamental Freedoms

The EU's flexibility to exert its exclusive competence on FDI Screening mechanisms may only be limited by the Fundamental freedoms if the EU is bound by them.

While this is not evident from the Fundamental freedoms' wording, this interpretation finds strong support in their object and purpose. The Fundamental freedoms' purpose is to complete the internal market and, to this end, protect its participants.[41] This purpose may be jeopardized by not only Member State, but also EU measures—even though the EU may be less likely to discriminate among Member States.[42] Consequently, for effectively fulfilling their purpose, the Fundamental freedoms must also apply to EU legislation.[43]

---

[41] Terhechte (2020), para. 40.

[42] Pache (2015), para. 44.

[43] This is accordance with the vast majority of case law and literature. On the freedoms of capital movement and establishment, the most relevant in the FDI screening context, see e.g. Case C-247/08 *Gaz de France - Berliner Investissement* [2009] EU:C:2009:600, para. 53. On Arts 34–35 TFEU Joined Cases C-154 and 155/04 *National Association of Health Stores and Others* [2005] EU:

Nevertheless, the ECJ only rarely annuls EU secondary law for breaching primary law for two reasons.[44] First, the ECJ sometimes finds an EU measure to promote, rather than restrict trade. Accordingly, the ECJ finds no prohibited restriction of the Fundamental freedom.[45] Moreover, when assessing a measure's proportionality, the ECJ generally grants the EU wide discretion.[46]

Consequently, the EU's flexibility to adopt FDI Screening mechanisms beyond the grounds of 'security or public order' is limited by the Fundamental freedoms. This conclusion is not significantly attenuated by the ECJ's lenient approach to review EU legislation. FDI Screening mechanisms clearly restrict, rather than promote trade. Moreover, the ECJ's lenient approach may not modify the main parameters that determine the EU's flexibility to adopt FDI Screening mechanisms: the personal and substantial scope of the freedoms of capital movement and establishment, and the scope of Art 64(2) and (3) TFEU. Substantial notions in the Fundamental freedoms only have one legal meaning, whether applying to Member States or the EU measures. As the following focuses on defining these substantial notions, the ECJ's lenient proportionality test is only of little relevance to the conclusion reached below. If the Fundamental freedoms do not apply, the proportionality test does neither.

4.2.2 Personal Scope of Freedoms of Capital Movement and Establishment

Section 4.2.1 concluded that the EU is bound by the Fundamental freedoms. Accordingly, the discussion can now turn to the limits the freedoms of capital movement and establishment pose to the EU's flexibility to adopt FDI Screening mechanisms. These limits depend first of all on whether the foreign investors fall in the freedoms' personal scope.

Section 2.4.2 defined foreign investors broadly to best capture the EU and Member States concerns vis-à-vis foreign investors. Accordingly, foreign investors were defined as (i) constituted or otherwise organized under the laws of a third

---

C:2004:848, para. 47; Case C-549/15 *E.ON Biofor Sverige* [2017] EU:C:2017:490, para. 45. Generally, see e.g. Mortelmans (2002), p. 1337; Sørensen (2011), p. 340; Forsthoff (2020a), para. 131. Zazoff (2011), in particular p. 229, argues that the EU is exceptionally bound by the Fundamental freedoms when acting to positively harmonize and liberalize the internal market.

[44] Syrpis (2015), pp. 467–468.

[45] E.g. acceptance regime for vegetables according to a set catalogue of vegetable species as promoting trade, Case C-59/11 *Association Kokopelli* [2012] EU:C:2012:447, para. 81.

[46] See e.g. Case C-491/01 *British American Tobacco (Investments) und Imperial Tobacco* [2002] EU:C:2002:741, paras. 122–123; *National Association of Health Stores and Others* (n. 43), paras. 46, 50 (both on Art 34 TFEU). See also Syrpis (2015), p. 468, who cites Fritzsche (2010), p. 380, to demonstrate that the ECJ's approach to review such discretion is still inconsistent.

country; (ii) having their registered office, central administration, or principal place of business in a third country; or (iii) being ultimately controlled by at least one person of a third country. At the same time, it was found that FDI is typically following two scenarios of legal organization. Either, the FDI is undertaken by an entity that was formed in accordance with the law of a third country, has its registered seat and central administration in a third country, and has no substantial business activities in the EU (Scenario 1). Or, the FDI is undertaken by an SPV, which is formed in accordance with the law of a Member State, has its registered seat and central administration in the EU, and had no prior business activity (EU SPV; Scenario 2). In both scenarios, a foreign State may itself be the investor or stand behind the investor.

The freedoms of capital movement and establishment only pose limits to the EU's flexibility to screen FDI to the extent the Fundamental freedoms protect these categories of foreign investors. Hence, if the freedom of establishment, for example, excludes one of these investor categories and the FDI Screening mechanism only applies to this group, the freedom of establishment does not limit the EU's flexibility to adopt a screening ground broader than 'security or public order'.

Section 4.2.2.1 will generally define the personal scope of both freedoms of capital movement and establishment by examining the necessary link the foreign investor must have with the EU. Section 4.2.2.2 will analyze, more specifically, whether foreign States and 'their' public undertakings may benefit from the Fundamental freedoms. The EU and Member States concerns vis-à-vis foreign investors are particularly high for FDI of these investors. If they are excluded from the Fundamental freedoms' personal scope, FDI Screening mechanisms may at least screen these FDI without any Fundamental freedom limits.

As Sects. 4.2.2.1 and 4.2.2.2 will conclude that certain foreign investors are outside the personal scope of the freedoms of capital movement and establishment a third question arises: If the FDI investor falls outside, but the FDI target and/or its owners fall within the freedoms' scope, does the FDI as such benefits from the freedoms' protection? If so, the foreign investor who is in theory outside the freedoms' personal scope becomes an indirect beneficiary via other transaction parties. Accordingly, the freedoms' restrictive personal scope would in fact be without major consequences. The EU's flexibility to adopt FDI Screening mechanisms would thus nevertheless be limited by the freedoms of capital movement and establishment—to the extent FDI is covered by their substantial scope. The question of the foreign investor as indirect beneficiary will be addressed in Sect. 4.2.2.3.

4.2.2.1 Sufficient Link Between Foreign Investor and EU

The personal scope of the freedoms of capital movement and establishment depends first of all on a sufficient link that the foreign investor must have with the EU. There are fundamental differences between both freedoms.

4.2.2.1.1 Freedom of Capital Movement Pursuant to Art 63(1) TFEU

According to the wording of Art 63(1) TFEU, the freedom of capital movement requires no geographical link between the investor as a person and the EU.[47] Instead, the focus lies on the capital as an object. Consequently, the personal scope of the freedom of capital includes a priori all possible subjects of rights and obligations.[48]

4.2.2.1.2 Freedom of Establishment Pursuant to Arts 49 and 54 TFEU

The personal scope of the freedom of establishment, on the other hand, is limited to EU citizens and EU Companies as defined in Arts 49(1) and 54 TFEU.[49] The necessary link between foreign investor and EU has a formal and, for secondary establishments such as FDI, substantial element.

For qualifying as an EU Company within the meaning of Art 54 TFEU, a company must be formed in accordance with the law of a Member State, and have either their registered office, central administration, or principal place of business in the EU (EU Company, all other companies: Non-EU Companies). This definition defines many more companies as EU Companies than investors are defined as EU investors for the purposes of this book.[50] Most importantly, in contrast to the definition chosen here, Art 54(1) TFEU considers a company an EU Company regardless of it being controlled by foreign citizens.[51]

Accordingly, the foreign investor in Scenario 1 fails to establish a sufficient link to the EU, since he is constituted under third-country laws and has his registered seat and administration in a third country. Only the investors in Scenario 2 of typical FDI transactions, EU SPVs, are EU Companies, and thus fall in the personal scope of the freedom of establishment.[52] The EU SPV's control by a foreign parent company, even a foreign State, is irrelevant.

---

[47] This is the largely prevailing opinion. Nevertheless *contra* Kingreen (2016), para. 34.

[48] Herz (2014), p. 39, who rightly emphasizes that the freedom of capital movement nevertheless also includes the subject behind the capital movement in the protection.

[49] Art 54 TFEU uses the term company and firm. The following will use the term company as umbrella term.

[50] Cf definition of foreign and EU investors in Sect. 2.4.2.

[51] Widely prevailing opinion in case law and among scholars, see Joined Cases C-504 and 613/16 *Deister Holding* [2017] EU:C:2017:1009, para. 84; as well as Bayer and Ohler (2008), pp. 20–21; Korte (2016b), para. 12; Tiedje (2015b), paras. 23–24; Ego (2017), para. 24; Forsthoff (2020c), para. 22. Smit (2012), pp. 365–366, argues that both the primary and secondary establishment must be 'situated' in the territory of a Member State. If this relates to the below discussed aspect of 'established' within the meaning of Art 49(2) TFEU, this is correct.

[52] The following terms SPVs that fulfil the requirements in Art 54(1) TFEU as EU SPVs.

From this formal perspective, it also seems irrelevant that the SPV investor has no business activity in the EU. However, when taking into account the conjunction with Art 49(1) TFEU, this substantial aspect becomes crucial. In case of a secondary establishment, Art 49(1), sentence 2 TFEU provides that the natural person or company undertaking the secondary establishment must be 'established' in the EU.[53] Thus, if an FDI constitutes a secondary establishment, only an investor established in the EU falls in the personal scope of the freedom of establishment.

At first sight, it seems obvious that a company's FDI constitutes a secondary establishment, since the SPV as an existing company founds another company to further its business purpose. Following this criterion of legal control, every FDI that qualifies as an establishment[54] constitutes a *secondary* establishment.[55] Nevertheless, some argue that a company can only constitute a primary establishment and thus engage in a secondary establishment if it exercises business activity.[56] Accordingly, the typical SPV, which has not exercised any business activity before the FDI, but assumes activities through the FDI, would itself not constitute a primary establishment, but undertakes its primary establishment through the FDI. Hence, for the investor in this transaction to fall into the personal scope of the freedom of establishment, the SPV would not need to be established in the EU.[57]

However, this understanding must be rejected. It confuses the delimitation of primary and secondary establishment with the more fundamental question of whether a company generally requires an actual business to benefit from the freedom of establishment.[58] Therefore, the criterion of legal control applies: a company's FDI

---

[53] Jung (2019), paras. 16–17. *Contra* Tiedje (2015b), para. 30, who reads the requirement of a 'real and continuous link' into Arts 54 and 49(1) TFEU, see n. 61, 58. He thus nevertheless reaches the same result.

[54] On the definition of establishment within the meaning of Art 49(1) TFEU, see Sect. 4.2.3.2.

[55] This approach is arguably the prevailing opinion in literature, see Tiedje (2015a), para. 40; Ego (2017), paras. 34–36; Müller-Graff (2018a), paras. 23–24; Herrmann (2019), p. 440; Forsthoff (2020b), para. 63. See also Herz (2014), p. 51; Jung (2019), paras. 17–18. Of course, an M&A FDI only constitutes a secondary establishment if the acquiring company obtains a shareholding that gives the investor sufficient influence on the target. For a detailed discussion of the freedom of establishment's substantial scope, in particular the necessary level of influence, see Sect. 4.2.3.2.

[56] Lübke (2006), pp. 204–205; Forsthoff (2020b), para. 63.

[57] Lübke (2006), pp. 204–205.

[58] This fundamental question is discussed under the notion of 'genuine establishment'. Accordingly, genuine economic activity is sometimes considered as a requirement for the substantial scope of the freedom of establishment, see Case C-196/04 *Cadbury Schweppes und Cadbury Schweppes Overseas* [2006] EU:C:2006:544, para. 54; Case C-378/10 *VALE* [2012] EU:C:2012:440, para. 34. Other judgments emphasize that pursuing a genuine economic activity is precisely not a precondition to Art 49 TFEU, see Case C-212/97 *Centros* [1999] EU:C:1999:126, paras. 29–30; Case C-208/00 *Überseering* [2002] EU:C:2002:632, paras. 48, 73; Case C-167/01 *Inspire Art* [2003] EU:C:2003:512, para. 139; Case C-106/16 *Polbud - Wykonawstwo* [2017] EU:C:2017:804, paras. 40–42. For scholar contributions see e.g. Kindler (2012), p. 888; Roth (2012), p. 1744; Ego (2017), para. 29; Jung (2019), para. 16; Forsthoff (2020b), paras. 24–25.

always constitutes a secondary establishment—provided the FDI substantially qualifies as an establishment. Consequently, the FDI investor, in Scenario 2 the EU SPV, must be established in the EU within the meaning of Art 49(1), sentence 2 TFEU.[59]

One may presume that an EU Company within the meaning of Art 54(1) TFEU is established in the EU. Based on this point of departure, 'established in the EU' must be defined negatively. Companies are not established in the EU if they are solely or predominantly integrated in a third-country economy.[60] This is determined by the place of their business activities.[61] SPVs have no own business activity, but are integrated in a larger group of companies. Hence, if this group of companies is solely or predominantly integrated in a third-country economy, the same applies to the SPV (Non-EU Established SPV). According to this negative definition of 'established in the EU', EU SPVs in the context of FDI screening are not established in the EU. They constitute Non-EU Established SPVs.[62]

This has important consequences for the EU's flexibility to screen FDI. On the one hand, the book's definition of foreign investors in light of the EU and Member States concerns vis-à-vis foreign investors is incompatible with the definition of the personal scope pursuant to Art 54(1) TFEU. Nevertheless, in both typical transaction scenarios of FDI, the freedom of establishment does not apply, since the investors do not fall in the freedom's personal scope. If the FDI is undertaken by a Non-EU Company within the meaning of Art 54(1) TFEU, the investor directly falls outside

---

[59] In these cases, founding the SPV constitutes the primary establishment, even if a company that does not fulfil Art 54(1) TFEU is founder and does thus not fall under the freedom of establishment. Company transformations or changing a company's registered seat would, however, constitute a primary establishment, Ego (2017), para. 34.

[60] Jung (2019), para. 17; Forsthoff (2020c), para. 24.

[61] Business activity is a broad term. A company may e.g. be considered having business activities in the EU if it undertakes considerable exports or FDI in the internal market; cf Tiedje (2015b), para. 29, who uses these criteria to substantiate the requirement of a genuine economic activity (see n. 58).

[62] Others favour a positive definition of 'established in the EU', see Lackhoff (2000), p. 197; Frenz (2012), paras. 2301, 2298; Tiedje (2015b), paras. 29–31. This approach, however, often collides with the requirement of a genuine business activity to qualify as an establishment (see n. 58). Müller-Graff (2018a), paras. 31–32, e.g. draws the connection to genuine economic activity. The position of AG La Pergola in Case C-212/97 *Centros* [1998] Opinion of AG La Pergola, EU: C:1998:380, para. 12, remains unclear. He substantiated the criterion 'principal establishment ... outside the Community' with the requirement of an 'effective and continuous link with the economy of a Member State'. Essentially, both approaches may be boiled down to the controversy around the correct interpretation of the notion 'real and continuous link' as used by General Programme for the abolition of restrictions on freedom of establishment [1962] OJ L 36/7; see Forsthoff (2020c), para. 24, on the negative definition, and Frenz (2012), para. 2301, n. 314; Tiedje (2015b), para. 30; Müller-Graff (2018a), para. 31, on the positive definition. The discussion is also closely related to the discussion on genuine business activity as a requirement for the freedom of establishment (see n. 58) as well as the problem of misusing the freedom of establishment by 'wholly artificial arrangements which do not reflect economic reality'; see e.g. Joined Cases C-398 and 399/16 *X* [2018] EU:C:2018:110, para. 46. For scholar contributions e.g. Ringe (2011); Tridimas (2011); Saydé (2014), p. 138; Forsthoff (2020a), paras. 302–323; Klöpfer (2016).

the personal scope of Arts 49 and 54 TFEU (Scenario 1). If the FDI is undertaken by an EU SPV, the SPV is not established in the EU as required for secondary establishments pursuant to Art 49(1), sentence 2 TFEU.

At the same time, the freedom of capital movement provides no particular requirements for a company to fall in its personal scope. Therefore, foreign investors who undertake FDI in the two typical FDI scenarios fall in the personal scope of the freedom of capital movement, but not of the freedom of establishment.

4.2.2.2   Foreign States and Public Undertakings

Apart from these freedom-specific considerations, the Fundamental freedoms may, in addition, exclude foreign States and 'their' public undertakings from their personal scopes in general. The Treaties provide several arguments for why such investors may not benefit from Fundamental freedom protection.

The most important argument derives from the Fundamental freedoms' purpose. Besides competition law and sectoral policies, the Fundamental freedoms are one of three pillars to complete the internal market.[63] They should create and secure an area of free movement of goods, persons, services, and capital. To facilitate and control the completion of the internal market, the Fundamental freedoms were granted the status as individual rights. Individuals are, as Member States, part of the EU legal order and its internal market, and therefore should have the means to enforce their rules, especially through the Fundamental freedoms.[64] Accordingly, the Fundamental freedoms are not directed against state interference as the German Fundamental rights (*Grundrechte*). Instead, they are means to complete the internal market.[65]

This consideration is crucial for assessing whether States generally, and foreign states and public undertakings more specifically, are beneficiaries of the Fundamental freedoms. Some scholars argue that foreign States may not fall in the Fundamental freedoms' personal scope, since not even Member States do (a fortiori conclusion).[66] Therefore, the following will first assess whether and, if so, why Member States are beneficiaries of the Fundamental freedoms.

---

[63] For this categorization see Terhechte (2020), para. 40. In particular, the (undistorted) competition is therefore not only an objective, but also an integral part of the internal market, as shown by Protocol (No 27) on the Internal Market and Competition shows, Schröder (2018), para. 24. Hence, the objective of a common internal market is at the interface between Fundamental freedoms and EU competition law, O'Keeffe and Bavasso (2000), p. 543.

[64] Case C-26/62 *Van Gend en Loos* [1963] EU:C:1963:1, pp. 12–13.

[65] Bayer and Ohler (2008), p. 21; Rauber (2019), p. 95.

[66] Bognar (1997), pp. 248–249; Wolff (2009), p. 141.

4.2.2.2.1 Member States in the Personal Scope of the Fundamental Freedoms

It is controversial whether Member States are beneficiaries of the Fundamental freedoms.[67] While functional arguments weigh in favour of a large group of Fundamental beneficiaries, the literal meaning of several provisions weighs against it.

First and foremost, the often-found categorization of Fundamental freedoms as an individual right or subjective right against public authorities (*subjektiv-öffentliches Recht*) may not be transposed to States.[68] Certainly, by definition, States stand opposite individuals, subjective rights are invoked against States. This alone, however, is insufficient to exclude Member States from the personal scope of Fundamental freedoms. As initially stated, the Fundamental freedoms' purpose is not defending individuals against certain State actions, but to achieve a functioning internal market. Invoking Fundamental freedoms against state measures is only one means to achieve this purpose. Opening the personal scope of Fundamental freedoms may enhance the Fundamental freedoms' contribution to this end. Therefore, the Fundamental freedoms' purpose is blind to the formalistic assessment whether a Member State acts, or a sufficiently separate company or individual.[69] From this functional perspective, Member States should therefore fall in the personal scope of the Fundamental freedoms.

This functional approach is coherent with the overarching concept of the internal market. Its second pillar, EU competition law, also looks at the difference between Member State and undertaking from a functional perspective.[70] Arts 101 to 109 TFEU impose strict competition law disciplines according to functional criteria in that, they do not apply to non-economic, public activities, regardless of the acting

---

[67] In favour of Member States as beneficiaries Storr (2001), pp. 273, 300; Crones (2002), p. 27. See also Ehlers (2014), paras. 46–47, who argues that Art 54(2) TFEU requires a legally structured organization. *Contra* Member States as beneficiaries of the Fundamental freedoms Bognar (1997), pp. 248–249; Bayer and Ohler (2008), p. 20; Wolff (2009), pp. 140–141; Rauber (2019), pp. 97–98. See also Hindelang (2009), p. 207. In contrast to Wolff's interpretation, Case C-174/04 *Commission v Italy* [2005] Opinion of AG Kokott, EU:C:2005:138, para. 23, does not necessarily imply that the Fundamental freedoms exclude Member States from their personal scope. At issue were public undertakings on which measures were imposed by a Member State other than the Member State controlling the public undertaking. Therefore, she argued, beneficiary and addressee of the Fundamental freedom did not coincide in the same person, and the public undertaking could invoke the freedom of capital movement. Ohler (2002), Art 56 EGV, para. 228, argues that the ECJ has left it open whether Member States may *invoke* Fundamental freedoms. The ECJ's judgment he cites to underpin his argument, however, deals with the question to what extent Member States are *bound by* the Fundamental freedoms (Case C-78/98 *Commission v Belgium* [2000] EU:C:2000:497, paras. 20–25).

[68] For this definition of Fundamental freedoms see Cremer (2015), p. 40; Frenz (2016), para. 218.

[69] Similarly on the freedom of establishment Rauber (2019), pp. 97–98.

[70] For categorizing the TFEU competition law as means to complete the internal market, see Terhechte (2020), para. 40.

entity's legal organization.[71] This supports the above argument that the internal market, and thus the Fundamental freedoms as one of its pillars, is about liberalizing economic activities, regardless of the actor.

However, the described, pure functional approach is limited by the literal meaning of some provisions. Already the central norm Art 26(2) TFEU expresses a fundamental difference. It promotes the free movement of goods, services, and capital, apparently regardless of the actor moving these elements, while also seeking to liberalize the free movement of persons. Member States, however, are not persons. Hence, Member States must at least be excluded from the personal scope of person-related freedoms, notably the freedom of establishment.

Other provisions draw a distinction between beneficiaries of the Fundamental freedoms on the one and Member States on the other hand—namely, provisions of the freedom of establishment: Arts 49 ('nationals of a Member State'), 54-(1) ('companies or firms formed in accordance with the law of a Member State'),[72] and 55 TFEU ('nationals of the other Member States'). Pursuant to Art 62 TFEU, Art 54(1) TFEU also applies to the object- and person-related freedom of services.[73] Even the object-related freedom of goods draws a formal distinction between Member States and other market actors in Art 37 TFEU.[74]

As the latter provision on an object-related Fundamental freedom only addresses a minor aspect of the freedom of goods, it is outweighed by the strong functional argument made above. Object-related freedoms as the freedoms of goods and capital movement remain primarily concerned with liberalizing the object itself, regardless of the actor behind. Member States therefore fall in their personal scope, as long as the activity substantially falls in the freedoms' scope. Person-related Fundamental freedoms, however, exclude Member States from their scope—unless Member

---

[71] See e.g. Mestmäcker and Schweitzer (2012), paras. 11, 16–22; Schröter et al. (2015), paras. 84–88.

[72] Member States and their subdivisions ('Gebietskörperschaften') are not 'formed in accordance with the law of a Member State' within the meaning of Art 54(1) TFEU, but by their constitution, see with the same conclusion Rauber (2019), pp. 97–98. In Germany e.g. not only the Federal State as such, but also the Bundesländer as well as municipalities and their legal associations ('Landkreise', 'Bezirke') are part of the State and thus excluded from the scope of Art 54(2) TFEU; with a similar conclusion Bayer and Ohler (2008), p. 20, ('mittelbare Staatsverwaltung'); Forsthoff (2020c), para. 12.

[73] For categorizing the freedom of services as object- and person-related, see Kluth (2016), paras. 1–2; Randelzhofer and Forsthoff (2020), para. 4. Another provision in the realm of the freedom of services is Art 56(1) TFEU ('nationals of Member States').

[74] Even the genesis of the seemingly clearly object-related freedom of capital movement may provide arguments against Member States as beneficiaries of the Fundamental freedoms. Originally, Art 67(1) EEC read 'restrictions on the movement of capital *belonging to persons resident in Member States*' (emphasis added). In the same vein, Art 1(1) of the Directive on Capital movement provides 'restrictions on movements of capital taking place between persons resident in Member States'. Accordingly, both legal acts distinguished between Member States and market actors. By adopting Art 73b EEC, today Art 63(1) TFEU, Member States only sought to eliminate the principle that beneficiaries of the freedom of capital movement must be EU residents; see Wojcik (2015a), para. 10.

States organize their economic activity in distinct entities that are sufficiently remote from the Member State's sphere (public undertakings).[75,76]

Consequently, Member States only fall in the personal scope of object-related Fundamental freedoms, in particular the freedom of capital movement. On the other hand, they are not beneficiaries of the person-related Fundamental freedoms, namely the freedom of establishment, unless they act through a separate entity within the meaning of Art 54(2) TFEU.

4.2.2.2.2   Foreign States as Beneficiaries of the Fundamental Freedoms

Having established that Member States fall inside the scope of object-related, but not person-related Fundamental freedoms, the discussion may now turn to foreign States as Fundamental freedom beneficiaries.

Of course, the above arguments against Member States as beneficiaries of Fundamental freedoms also apply to foreign States, for they derive from their general nature as States. Therefore, foreign States also fall outside the scope of person-related Fundamental freedoms, namely the freedom of establishment.

In addition, the interpretative rules in Arts 34 and 36 VCLT for international treaties offer another argument against foreign States as beneficiaries of person- *and* object-related Fundamental freedoms.[77] Pursuant to Art 34 VCLT, international treaties do in principle not create obligations or rights for a State without its consent.

---

[75]This is consensus among ECJ and scholars, regardless of the precise delimitation between State und public undertaking, Case C-174/04 *Commission v Italy* [2005] EU:C:2005:350, para. 32 (on the freedom of capital movement); *Atomausstieg*, German Federal Constitutional Court (Bundesverfassungsgericht) Judgment [2016] 1 BvR 2821/11, BVerfGE 143, 246, para. 195; Badura (1997), p. 299; Manthey (2001), p. 105; Storr (2001), pp. 298–300; Lübke (2006), p. 157; Weller (2008), p. 863; Clostermeyer (2011), p. 179; Kainer (2015), para. 26; Ruthig and Storr (2015), p. 55; Müller-Graff (2018b), para. 5.

[76]To be sure, this conclusion regarding person-related Fundamental freedoms respects the principle of neutrality on state ownership as laid down in Art 345 TFEU. Member States may still choose to conduct certain activities in public, not privatized manners, and rely on the Fundamental freedoms (Case C-646/15 *Trustees of the P Panayi Accumulation & Maintenance Settlements* [2016] Opinion of AG Kokott, EU:C:2016:1000, paras. 23–24. In the realm of the freedoms of establishment and services, this is demonstrated by Art 54(2) TFEU (for the freedom of services in conjunction with Art 62 TFEU). Pursuant to this provision, a public undertaking is also sufficiently separate from the Member State if the 'entity . . ., under national law, possesses rights and obligations that enable it to act in its own right within the legal order concerned, notwithstanding the absence of a particular legal form' (Case C-646/15 *Trustees of the P Panayi Accumulation & Maintenance Settlements* [2017] EU:C:2017:682, para. 29). Key criterion for a separate entity is thus the capability to act distinctly from the Member State, not privatization. Member States therefore remain free in their decision to nationalize or privatize their activities in order to benefit from Fundamental freedom protection (Wolff (2009), pp. 138–139, citing Case C-174/04 *Commission v Italy* [2005] Opinion of AG Kokott, EU:C:2005:138, paras. 24–25).

[77]Bognar (1997), p. 248; Bayer and Ohler (2008), p. 20; Hindelang (2009), p. 207; Wolff (2009), p. 141; Ress and Ukrow (2020a), para. 120. Without citing this argument, also Wojcik (2015a), para. 10.

Pursuant to Art 36(1) VCLT, parties to a treaty may nevertheless create rights for another State if the parties manifested their intention to do so.[78] It is here where the initially replicated a fortiori argument becomes relevant.[79] If the Member States themselves are no beneficiaries of person-related Fundamental freedoms, why should they grant such rights to foreign States? More importantly, the EU Treaties fail to manifest their intention to extend Fundamental freedom protection, whether person- or object-related, to other States.

Therefore, foreign States are excluded from the personal scope of all Fundamental freedoms, whether person- or object-related. Yet, when foreign States undertake FDI in the EU, they will often act through public undertakings, however these may be defined. It is therefore crucial to also evaluate whether these foreign undertakings are beneficiaries of the Fundamental freedoms.

4.2.2.2.3   Foreign Public Undertakings as Beneficiaries of the Fundamental Freedoms

For assessing whether foreign public undertakings fall in the personal scope of the Fundamental freedoms, two aspects are important. First, the last argument on foreign states as beneficiaries of the Fundamental freedoms must be recapitulated. Second, additional functional arguments are discussed that derive from the Fundamental freedoms themselves.

The conclusion that foreign States are neither beneficiaries of the person-related, nor of the object-related Fundamental freedoms was based on the rule of interpretation in Arts 34 and 36 VCLT: The Fundamental freedoms do not manifest their intent to protect foreign States. However, the Fundamental freedoms indeed express the intent that companies within the meaning of Art 54 TFEU may fall in the personal scope of the Fundamental freedoms, as long as they are not 'non-profit making'.[80] This is regardless of private or public ownership. The Fundamental freedoms hence adopt a functional approach. Therefore, to the extent foreign States act through companies within the meaning of Art 54(1) and (2) TFEU, they may be

---

[78] Proelss (2018b), para. 16.

[79] See n. 66.

[80] Art 54(2) TFEU also excludes all regional subdivisions of States as created by the constitution. This follows from the wording of Art 54(2) TFEU: 'formed in accordance with the law of a Member State' (see n. 72). Some scholars deal with the entire issue of foreign States and public undertakings as beneficiaries of the Fundamental freedoms when defining non-profit companies in the realm of Art 54(2) TFEU, see e.g. Manthey (2001), pp. 111–112; Clostermeyer (2011), pp. 178–179; Forsthoff (2020c), para. 12. Also explicitly in favour of defining the personal scope of the freedom of capital movement in accordance with Art 54(2) TFEU, Ehlers (2014), paras. 46–47; Gramlich (2017), para. 14.

beneficiaries of the Fundamental freedoms. Insofar, the argument derived from Arts 34 and 36 VCLT fails to apply.[81]

However, the fundamental decision to protect companies regardless of the public ownership is contingent on another crucial principle in the EU Treaties: EU public undertakings are subject to the strict competition rules pursuant to Arts 101 and 102 TFEU.[82] Art 106(1) TFEU obliges Member States to 'neither enact nor maintain in force any measure contrary to the rules contained in the Treaties, in particular to those rules provided for in Article 18 and Articles 101 to 109'. Pursuant to Art 106 TFEU, a public undertaking is 'any entity engaged in an economic activity, irrespective of its legal form and the way in which it is financed'[83] on which the public authorities may exert dominant, meaning majority influence.[84] Accordingly, a *foreign* public undertaking is an undertaking on which a foreign State exerts dominant influence.[85]

Foreign States and thus foreign public undertakings are not subject to Art 106 and the strict competition rules in Arts 101 and 102 TFEU. As a result, in contrast to EU

---

[81] In addition, the argument of Arts 34 and 36 VCLT is only valid for States; not for (public) entities that the VCLT considers sufficiently distinct from States (Proelss (2018a), para. 12). The delimitation of State and undertaking is controversial, see with a presentation of positions and arguments, e.g. Dereje (2015), in particular pp. 88ff, 198ff. In the context of FDI screening, Bayer and Ohler (2008), p. 21, argue that States include all legally non-distinct divisions of States, as well as undertakings that exercise public functions or rights. The discussion is similar to the controversy on the delimitation of governmental and non-governmental organizations within the meaning of Art 34 ECHR, see *Islamic Republic of Iran Shipping Lines v Turkey*, ECHR Judgment [2007] Case 40998/98, 2007-V ECHR 327, paras. 78–81. Given the here chosen focus on the argument derived from Art 54(1) TFEU, a further discussion of the definition of public undertakings in international law is omitted.

[82] It may seem appropriate to also cite Art 107(1) TFEU as another functional argument. However, this provision prohibits state aid to all undertakings, public and private. As a result, Art 107(1) TFEU would only allow the conclusion that every foreign undertaking would be excluded from the personal scope of the Fundamental freedoms, since they may benefit from state aid. This conclusion, however, would reach too far. The alternative conclusion that only those undertakings that have in fact received state aid are excluded from the freedoms' personal scope would also be flawed. EU undertakings that have benefited from state aid may also still invoke their Fundamental freedoms.

[83] Settled ECJ case law Case C-49/07 *MOTOE* [2008] EU:C:2008:376, para 21; Case C-74/16 *Congregación de Escuelas Pías Provincia Betania* [2017] EU:C:2017:496, para. 41.

[84] See e.g. Mestmäcker and Schweitzer (2012), paras. 37–42; Klotz (2015), paras. 9–12. The element of influence derives from Commission Directive 2006/111/EC of 16 November 2006 on the transparency of financial relations between Member States and public undertakings as well as on financial transparency within certain undertakings [2006] OJ L 318/17. Transparency Directive, art 2(b), sentence 1 defines an undertaking as public if 'the public authorities may exert directly or indirectly a dominant influence by virtue of their ownership of it, their financial participation therein, or the rules which govern it'. Art 2(b), sentence 2 clarifies that dominant influence means a majority influence, in particular by majority of voting rights.

[85] At the same, the TFEU deems undertakings on which a States exerts influence below the threshold of dominant influence to pose no, or a sufficiently low risk to competition. Therefore, these undertakings fall in the personal scope of the Fundamental freedoms, even if influenced by foreign States.

public undertakings, foreign public undertakings may not fall in the personal scope of the Fundamental freedoms.

As repeatedly emphasized, both undistorted competition and Fundamental freedoms are indispensable pillars to complete the internal market.[86] The free movement of objects and persons promoted by the Fundamental freedoms, on the one hand, and undistorted competition ensured by Arts 106 and 101 to 102 TFEU, on the other hand, complement each other.[87] Both instruments are two sides of the same coin.[88] Only to the extent that the interplay between both instruments works, does EU law treat private and public undertakings equally.[89] For foreign public undertakings this interplay is incomplete. Foreign States in their role as owners of foreign public undertakings are not subject to Art 106 TFEU. The risk foreign public undertakings pose to competition through their public owners is not attenuated.[90] Therefore, foreign public undertakings may not benefit from the Fundamental freedoms.[91]

This conclusion meets counterarguments at least regarding the object-related freedom of capital movement. Some argue that literal meaning and *effet utile* weigh against excluding foreign public undertakings from the personal scope of the freedom of capital movement.[92] These arguments are unconvincing.

Certainly, the wording of Art 63(1) TFEU only addresses capital as an object, not the person moving the capital. This object-related nature of the freedom of capital movement, however, does not justify to neglect the personal dimension of capital movement completely. Simply omitting any reference to the person behind the capital, does not mean to discard the general Fundamental freedom element of personal scope.[93]

---

[86] See n. 63.

[87] Terhechte (2020), para. 41.

[88] For the metaphor of 'the other side of the same coin', see *Commission v Italy* [2005] Opinion of AG Kokott (n. 76), para. 25. Adopting this metaphor Kainer (2015), para. 26. Similarly, Burgi (1997), p. 298; Bayer and Ohler (2008), pp. 17–18, 21; Clostermeyer (2011), p. 179. *Contra* Storr (2001), p. 293, who argues that Art 106(1) TFEU (on Art 86(1) EEC) only provides a negative principle of not favouring public 'their' public undertakings over public undertakings of other Member States and private undertakings. The provision would, however, not make any positive claim to grant rights to public undertakings.

[89] See also Schweitzer (2011), p. 92, without the here proposed reservation.

[90] Storr (2001), p. 285, rightly points out that every State action, and thus every action of public undertakings, must by law serve the public interest.

[91] Taking foreign public ownership into account when assessing possible grounds of exception to the Fundamental freedoms is no adequate alternative to the approach proposed here; suggesting this approach Bayer and Ohler (2008), p. 21. This alternative solution would pose the burden on Member States to justify the restrictions of foreign public undertaking activities. It would also neglect the main reason why Member State public undertakings benefit from the fundamental reasons that does not apply to third-foreign public undertakings: Art 106 TFEU.

[92] Wolff (2009), p. 139, who nevertheless goes on to exclude from the freedom of capital movement transactions with foreign States or state funds that may be instrumentalized by foreign States.

[93] Wolff (2009), p. 139; Clostermeyer (2011), p. 178. *Commission v Italy* [2005] (n. 75), para. 32, seems to support the argument of a neutral wording, but the ECJ had to deal with Member States, not foreign public undertakings.

According to the *effet utile* argument, the object and purpose of the freedom of capital movement demands the protection of every capital movement irrespective of the person moving the capital. Yet, this argument overly emphasizes one object and purpose of the freedom of capital, while neglecting others as well as the freedom's context as only one instrument to complete the internal market. First, Art 106 TFEU demonstrates that the interest to complete the internal market includes fair competition by regulating risks posed by public undertakings. If the freedom of capital movement protects foreign public undertakings, which are not subject to Art 106 TFEU, the freedom would pursue its liberalizing interest while jeopardizing its overall aim to complete the internal market as promoted by the TFEU.

Second, the interest to protect the capital brought into the EU by foreign public undertakings may still be protected by the freedom of capital of the other parties to the capital transaction. Insofar foreign public undertakings would enjoy indirect protection through the freedom of capital movement.[94] Excluding foreign public undertakings from the personal scope of the freedom of capital movement does therefore not automatically mean that the freedom leaves the FDI unprotected. It rather implies that the particular interests of foreign public undertakings regarding their capital are only protected to the extent they overlap with other transaction parties who fall into the personal scope of the freedom of capital movement.

Consequently, foreign States and foreign public undertakings are generally excluded from the personal scope of Fundamental freedoms. From an EU law perspective, the EU thus seems to have wide flexibility to screen FDI of these investors—without prejudice to their indirect protection through other parties of the transaction.

4.2.2.3   Indirect Fundamental Freedom Protection for Foreign Investors?

The previous discussion focused on the foreign investor as beneficiary of the Fundamental freedoms. It was shown that foreign States and foreign public undertakings are generally excluded from the personal scope of the Fundamental freedoms, person- and object-related (Sect. 4.2.2.2). In addition, Non-EU Companies within the meaning of Art 54(1) TFEU and, in case of secondary establishment, Non-EU Established SPVs are excluded from the personal scope of the freedom of establishment (Sect. 4.2.2.1). Nevertheless, if other parties to the transaction fall in the personal scope of the freedoms of establishment or capital movement, the FDI may, overall, still receive Fundamental freedom protection. The foreign investors would be protected indirectly, and the FDI Screening mechanisms would nevertheless need to comply with the Fundamental freedoms.

---

[94] A different conclusion applies only if the limited personal scope also constitutes a general exception to the Fundamental freedom at issue. For a detailed discussion see Sect. 4.2.2.3.

The indirect Fundamental freedom protection of an a priori excluded foreign investors hinges on two aspects. First, the action of selling or disinvesting company shares could be excluded from the substantial scope of the freedoms of capital movement and establishment because the freedoms do not protect this negative dimension of economic activity. In this case, the other FDI transaction parties are substantially not protected by Arts 49 and/or 63(1) TFEU. As a result, indirect Fundamental freedom for the foreign States, foreign public undertakings, Non-EU Companies, and Non-EU Established SPVs would fail. However, as will be shown, the freedoms of capital movement and establishment both protect this negative freedom dimension.

Second, the purpose behind excluding one transaction party, here the investor, from the personal scope of a Fundamental freedom may require to exclude the entire transaction from the Fundamental freedom protection. The exclusion of the foreign investor from the Fundamental freedom's personal scope would hence constitute a general exemption from the Fundamental freedom's applicability.[95] Insofar, the conclusions for the freedom of establishment as a person-related freedom differ from those reached for the object-related freedom of capital movement.

4.2.2.3.1   Freedom of Establishment

The freedom of establishment protects the negative dimension of establishment, but as a person-related Fundamental freedom generally excludes FDI with personally excluded investors from its scope.

In contrast to its wording, Art 49 TFEU protects the positive and negative dimension of establishment. EU nationals and companies have, on the one hand, the right to take up and pursue business activities as self-employed persons, to set up and manage undertakings, as well as to set up secondary establishments. On the other hand, the freedom of establishment also protects EU nationals and companies in dissolving companies or disinvesting of company shareholdings that constitute an establishment within the meaning of Art 49 TFEU.[96,97] Setting up and dissolving, or

---

[95] Wolff (2009), p. 143 ('*Bereichsausnahme*'). For the instruments of Golden shares and other state rights in FDI targets, a policy alternative to FDI screening, Art 345 TFEU may constitute a general exemption from the Fundamental freedoms. See e.g. Joined Cases C-105 to 107/12 *Essent and Others* [2013] EU:C:2013:677, para. 53 (not as separate ground of justification, but as an overriding reason in the public interest). In favour of Art 345 TFEU as a ground of exemption ('*Bereichsausnahme*'), Lübke (2006), pp. 349–352. Wolff (2009), pp. 131–136, argues that Art 345 TFEU only exempts the decision for or against privatization from the Fundamental freedoms' scope. See also recently with a summary of the discussion and in favour of Art 345 TFEU as an overriding reason in the public interest, Haraldsdóttir (2020), pp. 19–21 (interpreting case law as following the 'retained powers formula').

[96] On the threshold that defines a shareholding as establishment within the meaning of Art 49 TFEU, see Sect. 4.2.3.2.

[97] Case C-436/00 *X and Y* [2002] EU:C:2002:704, paras. 35–38; Case C-268/03 *De Baeck* [2004] EU:C:2004:342, paras. 20–21. See also Lübke (2006), p. 208; Herz (2014), pp. 183–184 (positive and negative dimension of freedom of establishment must be protected).

investing in and disinvesting of an establishment constitute two sides of the same coin. Without the right to dissolve an establishment, the right to set up the establishment in the first place would be significantly devalued.[98]

Nevertheless, the focus of the freedom of establishment lies on its positive dimension. The negative freedom of establishment of some parties to an establishment transaction may not indirectly provide positive freedom to set up an establishment to a person or company that is personally excluded from Art 49 TFEU. As a person-related freedom, the freedom of establishment has a particular interest not to grant protection to excluded companies, even indirectly. Given the strong personal element of Art 49 TFEU, other parties to the transaction who fall into the personal scope of Arts 49 and 54 TFEU have no legitimate interest to expect protection for their transaction with a personally excluded transaction party.[99] This conclusion is supported by the Fundamental freedoms' nature as subjective rights merely as means to complete the internal market.[100] Hence, when interpreting the freedom of establishment the broader consequences for the internal market must be taken into account. Art 54 TFEU and the broader context and purpose of the freedom of establishment clearly states that foreign States, foreign public undertakings, Non-EU Companies, and Non-EU Established SPVs in case of secondary establishment should not enjoy the protection of the freedom of establishment when accessing the internal market. This decision may not be undermined by indirectly protecting this group of foreign investors through other parties to the transaction.

Consequently, the freedom of establishment does not provide foreign States, foreign public undertakings, Non-EU Companies, and Non-EU Established SPVs in case of secondary establishment with indirect protection by protecting other parties to the transaction who fall into the personal scope of Arts 49 and 54 TFEU.

4.2.2.3.2   Freedom of Capital Movement

Besides its protection of Non-EU Companies and Non-EU Established SPVs in case of secondary establishment, the object-related freedom of capital movement is also more open to an indirect protection of foreign investors who do not fall in its personal scope—foreign States and foreign public undertakings.

The freedom of capital movement seeks to liberalize capital flows regardless of the capital's origin and destination. This purpose represents the fundamental difference compared to person-related Fundamental freedoms. Certainly, the protection of capital is not entirely detached from the person who moves the capital. But the freedom of capital movement prioritizes the protection of capital over person. As a consequence, from the perspective of Art 63(1) TFEU, protecting the acquisition of shares is as important as their sale. More generally, investment is as worthy

---

[98] Similarly, Herz (2014), p. 184.

[99] With this argument in the realm of the freedom of capital movement, Wolff (2009), p. 143.

[100] See introduction to Sect. 4.2.2.2.

protecting as disinvesting, since capital flows in both cases. Therefore, the freedom of capital movement protects all other parties to the FDI transaction as well.

As a result, the indirect protection of foreign States and foreign public undertakings, as under the freedom of establishment, depends on the second hurdle: Does their exclusion from the Fundamental freedoms' personal scope constitute a general exception from Fundamental freedom protection?[101] The wording of Art 63(1) TFEU seems clear. Every capital movement between Member States and third states is protected. Only non-profit activities are carved out—an exception that is irrelevant to the FDI screening context.[102] The characteristic of foreign State or foreign public undertaking is an investor-, person-specific trait. It is thus secondary to the object-related freedom of capital movement. Concluding from such secondary characteristic a general exception to the freedom of capital movement would undermine the crucial difference between person- and object-related Fundamental freedoms. Foreign States and foreign public undertakings may therefore receive indirect protection by other transaction parties who fall in the personal scope of Art 63(1) TFEU.

To be sure, this conclusion does not undermine excluding foreign States and foreign public undertakings from the personal scope of object-related Fundamental freedoms in the first place. Excluding these investors from the personal scope means denying Fundamental freedom protection to *their interests*. Indirect protection through Art 63(1) TFEU complies with this rationale. If indirectly protected, foreign states and foreign public undertakings are only protected to the extent that their interests overlap with the interests of other, personally protected transaction parties.[103] As a result, only the interests of personally protected transaction parties are protected.

Consequently, personally excluded foreign States and foreign undertakings may receive indirect Fundamental freedom protection. This conclusion is, however, subject to one caveat: the substantial protection of the concrete capital movement at issue. This depends on the delimitation of the freedoms of capital movement and establishment—a question that will be discussed in Sect. 4.2.3.

4.2.2.4   Limited Personal Scope with Minor Consequences for the EU's Flexibility to Screen FDI

In sum, the above analysis has shown that the personal scopes of the freedoms of capital movement and establishment are highly inconsistent.

---

[101] In favour Wolff (2009), p. 143. *Contra* Ohler (2002), Art 56 EGV, p. 234, (regarding Member States), and apparently Hindelang (2009), pp. 206–207 by emphasizing the indirect protection of foreign investors.

[102] See e.g. Case C-271/09 *Commission v Poland* [2011] EU:C:2011:855, paras. 40–42, in which the ECJ rejects a 'non-economic' activity based on a narrow definition. Generally for a definition of non-profit, e.g. Storr (2001), pp. 276–282.

[103] For this argument see Sect. 4.2.2.2.3.

The freedom of capital movement protects primarily the object capital, and therefore a priori every person who moves such capital, whether EU citizen or foreign national. Nevertheless, two exceptions apply. Art 63(1) TFEU excludes foreign States and foreign public undertakings from its personal scope. These actors are only protected indirectly via the other party of the transaction, but may not themselves invoke the freedom of capital movement.

The freedom of establishment's personal scope, on the other hand, is much further limited. First, as under Art 63(1) TFEU, foreign States and foreign public undertakings are excluded. Second, the freedom of establishment's personal scope, in stark contrast to Art 63(1) TFEU, further excludes 'foreigners' from its scope. This exclusion applies to all Non-EU Companies within the meaning of Art 54(1) TFEU. Additionally, in the case of secondary establishments, namely FDI, Art 49 TFEU also excludes EU Companies that are not EU-Established. In all these cases, Art 49 TFEU does exclude the entire transaction from its scope, meaning that it does not even protect the excluded actors indirectly via the other transaction party.

Consequently, the freedom of establishment excludes all foreign investors that are relevant to FDI Screening mechanisms: Non-EU Companies (Scenario 1) and Non-EU Established SPVs (Scenario 2). The freedom of capital movement, however, protects all relevant foreign investors, at least indirectly.

This has important consequences for the EU's flexibility to adopt FDI Screening mechanisms on broader grounds than 'security or public order'. For avoiding that FDI Screening mechanisms must comply with the Fundamental freedoms, one may be inclined to only apply the mechanisms to foreign investors who are excluded from the freedom of establishment. So designed FDI Screening mechanisms could encompass Non-EU Companies and Non-EU Established SPVs, and thus all foreign investors of concern. Their personal scope could also be more limited; for example, to foreign States and/or foreign public undertakings only. Nonetheless, however designed, the FDI Screening mechanism would need to comply with Art 63(1) TFEU. This result would only change if Art 63(1) TFEU does by substance not apply to FDI generally, or at least to a certain group of FDI that the FDI Screening mechanism addresses. As initially stated, the personal and substantial scope of FDI Screening mechanisms thus becomes the parameter that determines the EU's and Member States' flexibility to screen FDI on broader grounds than 'security or public order'.

4.2.3   Substantial Scope of the Freedoms of Capital Movement and Establishment

The analysis of the personal scopes of the freedoms of capital movement and establishment in Arts 49 and 63(1) TFEU concluded that the EU's flexibility to adopt FDI Screening mechanisms depends on the substantial scope of the freedom of capital movement.

From a substantial perspective, the EU and Member States are concerned with FDI. FDI was defined as investment that is aiming to establish or maintain lasting and direct links between the investor and FDI target by giving the investor effective participation in the management or control of the FDI target.[104] As will be shown, the freedom of capital movement applies to FDI. Hence, combined with its wide personal scope, the freedom of capital movement has the potential to significantly limit the EU's flexibility to screen FDI. However, it is controversial whether under certain circumstances the freedom of establishment overrides the freedom of capital movement. Only to the extent the freedom of establishment does so, the freedom of capital movement will not apply—and the EU's flexibility to adopt FDI Screening mechanisms on broader grounds than 'security or public order' becomes wider.

Indeed, the freedom of establishment can only override the freedom of capital movement to the extent it applies, at least substantially. Accordingly, the following Sects. 4.2.3.1 and 3.2.3.2 will first define the substantial scopes of both the freedoms of capital movement and establishment. The analysis will focus on M&A, not greenfield FDI, since only the former is subject to FDI Screening mechanisms as defined in Sect. 2.4.3. It will find that for M&A FDI Arts 49 and 63(1) TFEU significantly overlap. Insofar, the freedom of establishment could thus override the freedom of capital movement. This question will be discussed in Sect. 4.2.3.3. After analyzing the respective ECJ case law and scholar contributions, an own test will be developed for delimiting the freedoms of capital movement and establishment. This test will, together with the findings on the freedoms' personal scope in Sect. 4.2.2, be applied to assess the EU's flexibility to adopt FDI Screening mechanisms in the following Sect. 4.2.4.

When delimiting the freedoms of capital movement and establishment in light of the EU's flexibility to adopt FDI Screening mechanisms, one important aspect must be kept in mind. As initially stated, the freedom of establishment may only override the freedom of capital movement if it in fact applies, not personally, but substantially. Hence, to the extent an FDI Screening mechanism applies to FDI that qualifies as capital movement, but not establishment, the question of delimiting both freedoms does not even arise. Insofar, as will be discussed in detail in Sect. 4.2.4, the EU's flexibility to adopt FDI Screening mechanisms will always be limited by the freedom of capital movement, regardless of the discussion around the delimitation of Arts 49 and 63(1) TFEU.[105] This consideration adds another layer to design the FDI Screening mechanisms' substantial scope in a way that allows the EU wide flexibility on adopting a broader screening ground than 'security or public order'.

Before Sect. 4.2.3.5 concludes this section by summarizing the results, Sect. 4.2.3.4 will briefly analyze whether any of the results to the delimitation of the

---

[104] For the definition of FDI for the purposes of this book, see Sect. 2.4.1.

[105] Indeed, the delimitation of both freedoms will nevertheless be important at the level of individual FDI cases. If an FDI is prohibited based on an FDI Screening mechanism, the investor may invoke his Fundamental freedoms as a defence before courts. The delimitation of the freedoms of capital movement and establishment will decide over the investor claim's success.

freedoms of capital movement and establishment change if one takes into account the other party of the transaction as potential beneficiary of the freedoms.

4.2.3.1 Capital Movement Within the Meaning of Art 63(1) TFEU

The freedom of capital movement in Art 63(1) TFEU primarily protects cross-border[106] capital movement, regardless of the person moving the capital. It is thus an object-related Fundamental freedom for production factors.[107]

The subject of protection, capital movement, is neither defined in primary or secondary law, nor ECJ case law.[108] In light of the freedom of capital movement's purpose to effectively allocate capital as a production factor, literature defines capital movement as any cross-border transfer of monetary or physical capital.[109] Often, the definition includes the purpose of investment as the 'primary'[110] or 'typical'[111] motivation behind the capital transfer, or the transfer being 'concerned with the investment of the funds'.[112] However, this subjective criterion is usually intended to delimit the freedom of capital movement from the freedom of establishment already at definition level.[113] It is yet possible—and preferable—to define capital movement

---

[106]For a detailed analysis of the cross-border element, see Spies (2015), pp. 60–65.

[107]Lübke (2006), pp. 156, 158, 160. Critical Herz (2014), pp. 39–40, who cites Ohler (2006), p. 692, to argue that the distinction between person- and object-related Fundamental freedoms is overrated. According to Herz, Art 63(1) TFEU obviously also took into account the person behind the capital movement. Nevertheless, the purpose of the freedom of capital movement is focused on the object capital, not the person behind. The freedom of capital's purposes of effective allocation of capital and a functioning and stable monetary union (see in more detail in Sect. 4.2.3.3.2) show that the free movement of the object capital is the freedom's prime purpose. The distinction of object- and person-related Fundamental freedoms emphasizes this purpose.

[108]Bröhmer (2016a), para. 10.

[109]Lübke (2015), paras. 26, 31. Sceptical on the criterion of one-sidedness Frenz (2012), para. 3590.

[110]Bröhmer (2016a), para. 10.

[111]Ress and Ukrow (2020a), para. 131.

[112]The ECJ used this criterion for delimiting the freedom of capital movement from other Fundamental freedoms, see Joined Cases C-286/82 and 26/83 *Luisi and Carbone v Ministero dello Tesoro* [1984] EU:C:1984:35, para. 21; Case C-308/86 *Lambert* [1988] EU:C:1988:405, para. 10. Today, the ECJ cites Council Directive 88/361/EEC of 24 June 1988 for the implementation of Article 67 of the Treaty [on the former European Communities Treaty] (Capital Movement Directive) [1988] OJ L 178/5, for defining capital movement, see e.g. Case C-452/04 *Fidium Finanz* [2006] EU:C:2006:631, paras. 41–42; Case C-317/15 *X v Staatssecretaris van Financiën* [2017] EU:C:2017:119, para. 27. Case C-318/07 *Hein Persche* [2008] Opinion of AG Mengozzi, EU:C:2008:561, paras. 29–30, rightly points out that the ECJ did never intend for the subjective criterion of investment or remuneration to exhaustively define capital movement within the meaning of Art 63(1) TFEU.

[113]See for a summary of these positions Herz (2014), p. 38. Ego (2017), para. 690, additionally demands that capital movement must be more than a single transaction of goods and services. Kotthaus (2012), pp. 33–34, rightly points out that this consideration simply excludes the

distinctively, without a subjective element aimed at delimiting Art 63(1) TFEU from Art 49 TFEU.

The Capital Movement Directive is recognized to have indicative value for defining capital movement within the meaning of Art 63(1) TFEU.[114] Annex I to the Capital Movement Directive defines capital movement as inter alia FDI 'in its widest sense', portfolio and real estate investments, as well as securities, financial loans, and credits. Art 64(1) and (2) TFEU support this definition for FDI, including in the form of real estate investments, since they list both forms of capital movement as possible targets to restrict the freedom of capital movement.

Hence, the freedom of capital movement widely covers cross-border business transactions, in particular FDI.

4.2.3.2   Establishment Within the Meaning of Art 49 TFEU

The freedom of establishment protects business activities in the form of cross-border primary or secondary establishment.[115] The following will briefly introduce the general concept of establishment, before focusing on defining establishment through acquiring or merging with another company.

4.2.3.2.1   General Concept of Establishment

Pursuant to Art 49(2) TFEU, establishment is defined as to 'take up and pursue activities as self-employed persons and to set up and manage undertakings, in particular companies' within the meaning of Art 54(2) TFEU. Accordingly, Art 49(2) TFEU adds a functional meaning to the, at first sight, static and formal concept of establishment: the function to independently pursue business activities.[116] Hence, the freedom of establishment circles around the criterion of a person's business activity; it is a person-related Fundamental freedom.[117]

The ECJ added to this definition. It held that an establishment within the meaning of Art 49 TFEU is 'the actual pursuit of an economic activity through a fixed establishment in another Member State for an indefinite period'.[118] For companies this requires 'actual establishment' in a Member State 'and the pursuit of genuine

---

remuneration for goods and services from the substantial scope of the freedom of capital movement, but is no constitute definitory element of capital movement.

[114]Capital Movement Directive (n. 112). Its status as guidance for defining capital movement is settled case law, see n. 151.

[115]For the definition of secondary establishment see Sect. 4.2.2.1.2.

[116]Tiedje (2015a), para. 1.

[117]Lübke (2006), p. 158. For a *critique* of the distinction between person- and object-related Fundamental freedoms, see Herz (2014); Ohler (2006), n. 107.

[118]Case C-221/89 *Factortame* [1991] EU:C:1991:320, para. 20; *Cadbury Schweppes und Cadbury Schweppes Overseas* (n. 58), para. 54; *VALE* (n. 58), para. 34.

economic activity there'.[119] Accordingly, the freedom of establishment seeks to protect participation in the economic life of the EU 'on a stable and continuous basis', 'to profit therefrom'.[120] This ultimately aims at enabling undertakings to freely choose their business site on purely commercial criteria.[121] The motivation of profit-making may also be subordinate to other motivations.[122]

This definition addresses two aspects that are particularly relevant to FDI screening. First, one might argue that FDI with the sole purpose of transferring know-how or politically influencing the FDI host state falls outside the scope of the freedom of establishment. However, even if true, the investor will always at least have a subordinate profit-making motivation, and thus fall in the substantial scope of the freedom of establishment. Second, the definition criteria seem an appropriate tool to address the problem of misuse of the freedom of establishment. If a company does not meet the seat requirements provided by Art 54(1) TFEU and instrumentalizes an SPV for undertaking an FDI only to benefit from the protection of Art 49 TFEU, this may be considered a circumvention of the requirements in Art 54(1) TFEU. Yet, Sect. 4.2.2 already showed that SPVs fall outside the personal scope of the freedom of establishment pursuant to Art 49(1), sentence 2 TFEU when undertaking an FDI anyway because they are usually only or predominantly integrated in a third-country economy.[123] Therefore, the aspect of misuse and circumvention of the freedom of establishment is not further discussed here.[124]

Thus, generally, an establishment is the self-employed pursuit of an economic activity on a stable and continuous basis. Pursuing such an activity can take any form. This includes the acquisition of shares in or assets of another company (share or asset deal), as well as a merger with another company resulting in a certain shareholding in the target company.[125] The following will refer to both cases as M&A transactions.

---

[119] *VALE* (n. 58), para. 34, with further references to case law. On the notion of a genuine economic activity as a—disputed—general requirement for an establishment see n. 58.

[120] Case C-55/94 *Gebhard* [1995] EU:C:1995:411, para. 25, in the broader context of delimiting the freedom of establishment to the free movement of workers and services.

[121] Tiedje (2015c), para. 4.

[122] See Tiedje (2015a), para. 62; Müller-Graff (2018a), para. 13; Forsthoff (2020b), para. 22. All definition criteria presented in this paragraph may be seen as following directly from the literal meaning of Art 49 TFEU ('activities as self-employed persons'). They are thus not simply negative criteria to delimit the freedom of establishment from other Fundamental freedoms. Nevertheless, many scholars define establishment by delimitation only, see e.g. Ego (2017), para. 27; Müller-Graff (2018a), para. 11.

[123] See Sect. 4.2.2.1.2.

[124] The general concept of misusing EU law is more relevant for other EU companies as well as when circumventing secondary law. For case law and scholar contributions on this concept; see n. 62.

[125] See e.g. Lübke (2006), para. 43.

4.2.3.2.2   Defining Establishment in Case of Partial M&A Transactions

An EU Company within the meaning of Art 54(1) TFEU may establish a secondary establishment by an M&A transaction merging with or acquiring another company.[126] If the M&A results in a 100% ownership for the investor, the M&A clearly constitutes an establishment. If, however, the investor acquires only parts of the target company (partial M&A), it is less clear from which threshold a partial M&A transaction constitutes an establishment within the meaning of Art 49 TFEU. The question thus is: What is the threshold beyond which such a partial M&A constitutes a self-employed pursuit of an economic activity on a stable and continuous basis?

ECJ Case Law: Hidden Hints
The ECJ only implicitly defines a threshold for a partial M&A to constitute establishment within the meaning of Art 49 TFEU. Delimiting Arts 49 and 63(1) TFEU, the ECJ held that 'national legislation intended to apply only to those *shareholdings which enable the holder to exert a definite influence on a company's decisions and to determine its activities* falls within the scope of the freedom of establishment'.[127] In contrast to the notion 'decisive influence' as in public undertaking pursuant to Art 106 TFEU,[128] the elements of 'definite influence' and 'determining the company's activities' does not require a controlling influence as in majority.[129] Hence,

---

[126]For the notion of EU and Non-EU Company see Sect. 4.2.2.1.2.

[127]*Associação Peço a Palavra and Others* (n. 36), para. 43 (emphasis added). This is settled case law, based on Case C-251/98 *Baars* [2000] EU:C:2000:205, para. 22.

[128]See Sect. 4.2.2.2.3, n. 84.

[129]This is the prevailing interpretation of the ECJ's case law in literature, see e.g. Kemmerer (2010), p. 170; Smit (2012), pp. 52–54; Geiger (2013), p. 136; Herz (2014), p. 246; Patzner and Nagler (2014), p. 732; Lübke (2006), para. 106; Spies (2015), pp. 435–436; Bröhmer (2016a), para. 31; Hindelang and Hagemeyer (2017), p. 885; Forsthoff (2020a), para. 101. Only Müller-Graff (2003), p. 936; Weller (2008), p. 862, demand a 50% shareholding, or, alternatively, additional contractual arrangements that guarantee a similar level of control. The ECJ has emphasized the difference between control and definite influence, see ia Case C-81/09 *Idryma Typou* [2010] EU:C:2010:622, paras. 51–52. Nevertheless, the above cited ECJ's case law is frequently referred to when using the term controlling shareholding ('Kontrollbeteiligung'), see Martini (2008), p. 318; Lecheler and Germelmann (2010), p. 130; Tountopoulos (2013), p. 34; Unger (2015), p. 67; Wojcik (2015a), para. 65; Ego (2017), para. 702; Hindelang and Hagemeyer (2017), p. 885. The term controlling shareholding is prone to misunderstanding control as majority control, as may be seen in Patzner and Nagler (2014), p. 732, who use this expression, cites ECJ case law, and then demands a shareholding of at least 50% in a company for an establishment within the meaning of Art 49 TFEU. Also unclear in Martini (2008), p. 318. In fact, the German version of definite influence in case law is generally misleading. Mostly, definite influence is translated as 'sicherer Einfluss'. Sometimes, however, the same English and French term ('influence certaine') is translated as 'bestimmender' (e.g. Case C-524/04 *Test Claimants in the Thin Cap Group Litigation* [2007] EU:C:2007:161, para. 27), 'bestimmter' (e.g. Case C-244/11 *Commission v Greece* EU:C:2012:694, paras. 21, 23), or even 'gewisser Einfluss' (*Überseering* (n. 58), para. 77). 'Bestimmender' seems to require a higher level of influence than 'gewisser'.

according to settled case law, the ECJ finds an establishment in case of a partial M&A if the transaction gives the investor definite influence on the target company and lets her determine the target's activities.[130] As both terms overlap and complement each other, the following will deal with them together under the term 'definite influence'.

Defining Definite Influence
The notion definite influence is not open to concrete numerical thresholds, but may only be defined by soft criteria.

Whether an investor's influence on the target company is definite depends on the applicable national law, as well as the contractual arrangements and facts in the specific case, such as special voting agreements[131] or the overall distribution of shares.[132,133] As these criteria cannot universally be expressed by a numerical threshold, the ECJ case law is inconsistent in this respect.[134] For example, the ECJ

---

[130] See Case C-251/98 *Baars* [2000] EU:C:2000:205, para. 22: 'So, a national of a Member State who has a holding in the capital of a company established in another Member State which gives him definite influence on the company's decisions and allows him to determine its activities is exercising his right of establishment.' Similarly, *Überseering* (n. 58), para. 77; Case C-81/09 *Idryma Typou* [2010] EU:C:2010:622, para. 47; Case C-244/11 *Commission v Greece* [2012] EU:C:2012:694, para. 21. This also is the widely prevailing opinion in literature, see e.g. Geiger (2013), pp. 135–136; Ress and Ukrow (2020a), para. 315. Apparently *contra* Case C-35/11 *Test Claimants in the FII Group Litigation* [2012] Opinion of AG Jääskinen, EU:C:2012:483, para. 114, who argues that the centre of gravity shifts to the freedom of establishment when voting rights go beyond the threshold of 10%. As voting rights of 10% do not constitute a definite influence (see cited ECJ judgments in n. 139), AG Jääskinen thus seems to argue that the investor's definite influence on the target company is no necessary condition for an establishment within the meaning of Art 49 TFEU.

[131] Case C-298/05 *Columbus Container Services* [2007] EU:C:2007:745, para. 31.

[132] Case C-326/07 *Commission v Italy* [2009] EU:C:2009:193, para. 38; Case C-81/09 *Idryma Typou* [2010] EU:C:2010:622, para. 51. Generally, there are different notions of 'shares' in corporations: shares of nominal or currently valued capital as well as shares in voting rights. Judgments and scholar contributions usually seem to refer to shares of nominal capital. These capital shares are typically corresponding with the capital holder's shares of voting rights. Therefore, the following also refers to shares in nominal capital. When it comes to determining the investor's influence, not only voting rights among shareholders, but also voting rights in other contexts such as in the supervisory board become relevant.

[133] Case C-207/07 *Commission v Spain* [2008] EU:C:2008:428, para. 33; Roth (2009), pp. 268–269; Smit (2012), pp. 52–54. See also Krolop (2008), p. 16, who suggests a threshold of 30% of the voting rights for a definite influence citing the notion of control pursuant to German Securities Transaction Act (Wertpapierübertragungsgesetz) s 29; Herz (2014), p. 247, who stresses the possibilities of contractual arrangements.

[134] Moreover, the ECJ has no competence to interpret Member State law and therefrom derive a concrete threshold. This is stressed by *Associação Peço a Palavra and Others* (n. 36), para. 36. Tountopoulos (2013), p. 34, states in his note on Case C-244/11 *Commission v Greece* [2012] EU:C:2012:694, that Greek law requires additional factors in order for a 20% capital shares to give the investor definite influence on the target company. He adds that the parties obviously implied a sufficient degree of influence, and therefore did not submit this aspect to the ECJ for decision. Spies (2015), pp. 444–445, highlights that this approach based on national law means in third-country

found the holding of 20%,[135] 25%,[136] 26.5%,[137] and of more than 34%[138] of the target's capital to give definite influence on a company. On the other hand, the ECJ excludes definite influence in case of a 10% shareholding, still emphasizing that this depends on the circumstances of the case.[139] Nevertheless, these difficulties do not justify to skip an abstract definition of definite influence,[140] and directly address the delimitation of the freedom of establishment from the freedom of capital movement.[141]

When defining definite influence, the general definition of establishment must be taken into account. The investor's possibility to definitely influence the target company must allow him to pursue an economic activity on a stable and continuous basis,[142] in other words an entrepreneurial activity.[143] This in turn must create a stable and continuous link to the host state's economy generally.[144]

Obviously, not any possibility for the investor to influence the target company's decisions satisfies the standard of definite influence.[145] At the same time, Advocate General ('AG') Sánchez-Bordona rightly stated that definite influence constitutes a lower threshold than 'determining or decisive influence'. Rather, definite influence meant 'influence that can be used to play an active part in the management of the

---

cases to interpret third-country corporate law. In cases of International private law, this, however, is a typical scenario. The court then seeks an expert opinion on the relevant foreign law question.

[135] Case C-244/11 Commission v Greece [2012] EU:C:2012:694, paras. 23–24.

[136] Case C-492/04 *Lasertec* [2007] EU:C:2007:273, paras. 21–22; Case C-382/16 *Hornbach-Baumarkt* [2018] EU:C:2018:366, para. 29.

[137] Joined Cases C-504 and 613/16 *Deister Holding* [2017] EU:C:2017:1009, para. 82.

[138] Case C-311/08 *SGI* [2010] EU:C:2010:26, paras. 34–35 (34 and 65% of capital); Case C-686/13 *X v Skatteverket* [2015] EU:C:2015:375, para. 24 (45% of capital and voting rights); *Associação Peço a Palavra and Others* (n. 36), para. 44 (45 and 61% of capital).

[139] *Commission v Italy* [March 2009] (n. 132), para. 48; Case C-282/12 *Itelcar* [2013] EU:C:2013:629, para. 22; Case C-47/12 *Kronos International* [2014] EU:C:2014:2200, para. 35.

[140] Tiedje (2015a), para. 25, nevertheless declares it settled case law that an investor holding 20% of a company's capital may exert definite influence within the meaning of Art 49 TFEU.

[141] Nevertheless choosing this approach Schön (2015), p. 566 (for the later English version see Schön (2016), p. 229), who adopts the lawmaker's perspective, and thus bases his assessment on the intention behind the Member State's measure. He argues that, insofar, the delimitation of the freedoms of capital movement and establishment requires looking back and forth between the purpose of Art 49 TFEU, on the one hand, and the intention behind the Member State measure, on the other hand.

[142] Case C-251/98 *Baars* [2000] EU:C:2000:205, para. 22. With a detailed analysis whether the investor's influence must be objectively possible or subjectively intended, see Lübke (2006), pp. 208–210. Lübke argues against a subjective approach due to a lack of legal certainty. It would be impossible to find an establishment in the moment of the M&A for a legal observer.

[143] Ohler (2002), Art 56 EGV, para. 113; Schön (2015), p. 566.

[144] Schön (2000), p. 11, therefore names a shareholder with definite influence an 'entrepreneur-shareholder' and contrasts this category to an 'investment-shareholder'.

[145] Clostermeyer (2011), pp. 181–182.

company'.[146] Differently put, important strategic decisions require the investor's approval—or, in other words, his veto right.[147] In case of a veto right, the company's management must coordinate with the investor and maybe modify the envisaged decision in the investor's interest in order to obtain her approval. At the same time, the investor cannot take and implement decisions on his own, regardless of the management's and other shareholders' positions. Hence, the investor's business ideas and strategies shape the target company's activities and strategy, without determining them. This suffices to satisfy the freedom of establishment's core element to personally pursue an economic activity.[148]

Against this background, the definition of definite influence consists of two elements: (i) important decisions that (ii) cannot be taken without the investor.

Important Decisions

There are two categories of important decisions: constitutive and strategic decisions.

First, decisions are important if they affect the constitution, and thus existence of the company. This category includes amending the company's articles of association and voting the company's board members (executive and supervisory boards).[149] Similarly important are the company's dissolution, its merger or demerger with or

---

[146]Case C-563/17 *Associação Peço a Palavra and Others* [2018] Opinion of AG Sánchez-Bordona, EU:C:2018:937, para. 50. For ECJ judgments and scholar contributions that reject an interpretation in the sense of control, see n. 129.

[147]Lübke (2006), p. 213; Nettesheim (2008), p. 754; Hindelang (2009), p. 85; Clostermeyer (2011), p. 187; Spies (2015), pp. 429–430. For a non-legal perspective, see UNCTAD, 'World Investment Report 2016: Investor Nationality: Policy Challenges' (New York, 2016), p. 129. Demanding more than a veto right Martini (2008), p. 318; Voland (2009), p. 523; Geiger (2013), p. 139.

[148]Herz (2014), p. 248, with some reservations, proposes to interpret definite influence in accordance with the notion 'decisive influence' in Council Regulation (EC) No 139/2004 of 20 January 2004 on the control of concentrations between undertakings (Merger Regulation) [2004] OJ L 24/1, art 3(2) (on the prior version Council Regulation (EEC) No 4064/89 of 21 December 1989 on the control of concentrations between undertakings [1989] OJ L 395/1, art 3(3). However, as analyzed above, decisive and definite influence have different meanings. Moreover, the object and purpose of the Merger Regulation also weigh in favour of a higher level of influence required by decisive as compared to definite influence. The Regulation seeks to identify a level of influence that enables the merged companies to coordinate market behaviour to the detriment of competition. This requires a controlling influence. Some aspects of Merger Regulation, art 3(2) are nevertheless useful to interpret definite influence, see n. 154.

[149]This is also implied by those scholars who directly define definite influence by blocking minority pursuant to German Stock Corporation Act (Aktiengesetz) s 179(1) and (2), see e.g. Case C-31/11 *Scheunemann* [2012] EU:C:2012:481, 26, 29; Roth (2009), p. 269. For appointing members of executive and supervisory board, Hindelang (2009), p. 85, quoting Tiedje and Troberg (2003), para. 29. The latter contribution refers to the definition of FDI within the meaning of the Capital Movement Directive (n. 112). From the perspective of Hindelang, this quote is correct, since he argues that the notion of establishment and FDI are congruent, Hindelang (2009), p. 86.

from other companies, the transfer of the undertaking, and the company headquarters' transfer abroad.[150]

The second category of important decisions are strategic, not day-to-day, operative decisions that determine the target company's business activity. The distinction between strategic and day-to-day operative decisions stems from the characteristic of corporations, in which the management conducts day-to-day business in the interest of the corporation's good, widely independent from any shareholders involvements.[151] Nevertheless, some of these shareholders are considered to exert definite influence on the corporation. As a result, an investor's influence on a company's day-to-day decision may not determine whether an investor generally has a definite influence on the target company within the meaning of Art 49 TFEU. Instead, strategic operative decisions are the decisions that shape the entrepreneurial business activity that the establishment is founded to pursue, in particular its future development. Such a decision will typically have a significant effect on the market value of a company. The effect on the market value is therefore a good proxy to determine whether a decision is of strategic operative importance.

For further substantiating the definition of important strategic operative decisions, one may refer to the notion 'inside information' in the Market Abuse Regulation, which relies on the same rationale.[152] Pursuant to Art 17(1) of the Market Abuse Regulation certain important inside information about the company must be disclosed to the public. These are information that if disclosed 'would be likely to have a significant effect' on the company's market value and that 'a reasonable investor would be likely to use as part of the basis of his or her investment decision'.[153] Inside information in this sense include control and profit transfer agreements; acquisition, merger or mandatory offers; procurement of equity and debt capital; important investment with impact on the company value; and changes in personnel on high management levels.[154] Accordingly, all decisions to take or accept these measures significantly affect a company's value, and are thus of strategic operative importance within the meaning of Art 49 TFEU. This assessment may also be transposed to non-publicly traded companies by applying a hypothetical test.

Consequently, important decisions for defining definite influence within the meaning of Art 49 TFEU are, on the one hand, decisions that concern the company's

---

[150] Case C-326/07 *Commission v Italy* [2009] EU:C:2009:193, paras. 39, 4.

[151] Rightly emphasized by Krolop (2008), p. 8.

[152] Regulation (EU) No 596/2014 of the European Parliament and of the Council of 16 April 2014 on market abuse (Market Abuse Regulation) [2014] OJ L 173/1.

[153] Market Abuse Regulation (n. 152), art 7(1)(a), (4).

[154] Kumpan (2018), Art 7, para. 14. These are mainly the same decisions that are considered to be relevant to the notion 'decisive influence' within the meaning of Merger Regulation (n. 148), art 3(2). See on the Merger Regulation, e.g. Körber (2012), paras. 34–35. Insofar, Herz is right in proposing to interpret definite influence in accordance with Merger Regulation, art 3(2), see n. 148.

constitution and, on the other hand, important strategic operative decisions as defined in Art 7(1) and (4) of the Market Abuse Regulation.

That Cannot Be Taken Without the Investor

For an investor to exert definite influence on the target company within the meaning of Art 49 TFEU, other company actors must not be able to take the above-defined important decisions without the investor. As initially pointed out, the level of influence depends on a case-by-case basis, namely national corporate laws and contractual arrangements. The following will identify certain universal criteria that may be taken into account when determining whether a decision cannot be taken without the investor.

Starting from the idea that it should be impossible to take the decision without the investor, the threshold of blocking minority seems an appropriate criterion for definite influence. Hence, all shareholders who can veto an important decision have definite influence over the target company. Share thresholds that result in a blocking minority depend on national corporate law, sometimes modified by a company's articles of association[155] or workers co-determination.[156] In Germany, for instance, amending a company's articles of association requires 25% of the shares represented at the shareholder meeting.[157] The threshold may be lowered by the articles of association. As attendance to shareholder meetings of larger companies is usually low, the threshold of 25% of represented shares may already be reached by shareholders owning much less shares. For example, if only 60% of shares are represented at a shareholder meeting, shares of 15% would already constitute a blocking minority. Other blocking minorities in favour of a shareholder may be stipulated by the company's articles of association or contractual arrangements. This includes different majority rules for important decisions that in fact result in a veto right for the investor, such as appointing executive board members.[158]

Moreover, the investor may have specific rights that give him a definite influence on important decisions; for example, the power to appoint a certain number of supervisory board members.

---

[155] In German Stock Corporation Act (n. 149) several sections offer flexibility for amending statutory majority rules: e.g. ss 77(1) (executive board appointment), 101(2) (power to appoint supervisory board members), 122(1) and (2) (resolutions by shareholder meetings).

[156] The rights of worker co-determination are limited to corporations and cooperatives with more than 2000 employees. They affect the supervisory board's composition as well as its majority requirements, see Habersack (2019), § 108, paras. 21–22.

[157] German Stock Corporation Act (n. 149), s 179(1), sentence 1; (2), sentence 1.

[158] Pursuant to German Stock Corporation Act (n. 149), ss 84, 108, appointing an executive board member requires a decision of the supervisory board with a simple majority, see Spindler (2019), § 84, paras. 21–22.

On the other hand, the right to call a shareholder meeting or to modify its agenda are only of minor importance for influencing a company's business activities.[159] Therefore, these rights do not qualify the investor's influence as definite influence on the target company within the meaning of Art 49 TFEU.

Consequently, the main criterion for finding that an investor has definite influence is the investor's blocking minority regarding important decisions. The investor may also have specific rights such as the power to appoint a certain number of supervisory board members.

4.2.3.2.3 Partial M&A Transactions as Establishment If They Give Definite Influence

To summarize, a partial M&A constitutes an establishment within the meaning of Art 49 TFEU if the investment gives the investor definite influence on the target company. Definite influence means that important decisions cannot be taken without the investor. There are two categories of important decisions: company constitution, for example amending the articles of association, and strategic operative decisions that significantly affect the company's value interpreted as in the notion inside information pursuant to Art 7(1) and (4) Market Abuse Regulation. A decision cannot be taken without the investor in particular in cases of veto rights or a blocking minority. If, for instance, the German Stock Corporations Act applies, the investor obtains definite influence on the company when acquiring 25% of its shares.[160] Due to usually low representation at shareholder meetings, this threshold typically decreases to 20% of the shares.

4.2.3.2.4 The Freedom of Capital Movement Notion of FDI in Art 49 TFEU

Having defined establishment through partial M&A pursuant to Art 49 TFEU, the discussion may now turn to identifying the overlap between the substantial scope of the freedoms of capital movement and establishment. Section 4.2.3.1 showed that the freedom of capital movement applies to FDI, and that FDI, if at all a Fundamental freedom notion, is a notion of the freedom of capital movement.[161] M&A FDI is defined as enabling the shareholder to participate effectively in the management or control of the FDI target, while an establishment pursuant to Art 49 TFEU requires

---

[159] In German law these rights require 20% of company shares, for modifying the shareholder meeting agenda shares worth €500,000, see German Stock Corporation Act (n. 149), s 122(1) and (2).

[160] Clostermeyer (2011), p. 187.

[161] Dimopoulos (2011), p. 82, mixes both notions by formulating 'establishment of FDI'.

the investor's definite influence on the target company.[162] It is controversial whether these definitions are congruent, and thus if every M&A FDI constitutes an establishment within the meaning of Art 49 TFEU.[163]

The better arguments weigh in favour of the establishment notion definite influence to require a higher threshold of influence than the FDI notion effective participation. Their literal meanings already indicate different thresholds. While transition from effective to definite is certainly fluent, one may nevertheless draw a line of increasing influence from effective, to definite, to decisive or determining participation or influence.[164] On this line, effective participation conveys influence as in direct communicative influence, definite influence lets the company actually take the investor's position into account, and decisive influence entails the investor's power to decide or control every important decision.[165]

Moreover, the context of Art 64(1) and (2) TFEU also weighs in favour of a different level of influence between establishment and FDI. The provision lists FDI, including real estate investments, and establishment as alternatives. Accordingly, if

---

[162]For the FDI definition see Sect. 2.4.1. It is congruent with the Capital Movement Directive (n. 112).

[163]The ECJ favours a stricter notion of influence for establishment than for FDI, implied by contrasting the definitions of establishment and FDI, see e.g. *Commission v Italy* [March 2009] (n. 132), paras. 34–35; *Idryma Typou* (n. 129), paras. 47–49. Spies (2015), p. 438, n. 2329, argues that Case C-35/11 *Test Claimants in the FII Group Litigation* [2012] EU:C:2012:707, para. 102, explicitly equated both notions. However, given the other above-cited judgments, this may not be concluded from the phrase 'It is apparent from that provision [Art 64(1) TFEU] that Article 63 TFEU on the free movement of capital covers, in principle, capital movements involving establishment or direct investment. The latter terms relate to a form of participation in an undertaking through the holding of shares which confers the possibility of effectively participating in its management and control'. The prevailing opinion in literature also is in favour of definite influence being more narrow than the FDI notion, see Case C-446/04 *Test Claimants in the FII Group Litigation* [2006] Opinion of AG Geelhoed, EU:C:2006:240, para. 119; Clostermeyer (2011), p. 185; Kotthaus (2012), p. 62; Puig (2013), p. 140; Herz (2014), p. 291; Wojcik (2015a), para. 64; de Kok (2019), p. 29. Also Lübke (2015), para. 43, formerly with the opposite opinion in Lübke (2006), p. 214. Apparently also Smit (2012), p. 65; Tiedje (2015a), para. 31; Korte (2016a), para. 39, who all stress that they refer to FDI that gives a definite influence, and thus imply FDI that does not give such level of influence. For the same level of influence Hindelang (2009), p. 85 ('essentially' the same level). Also implied by Roth (2009), pp. 267–268; and apparently Nettesheim (2008), p. 754, who lists both definite influence and effective participation as alternative definitions. *Test Claimants in the FII Group Litigation* [2012] Opinion of AG Jääskinen (n. 130), paras. 114–115, also seems to imply the same level of influence for both notions when arguing that the centre of gravity shifts to the freedom of establishment when voting rights go beyond the threshold of 10%. The question of overlapping definitions of FDI and establishment are closely linked with the delimitation of the freedoms of capital movement and establishment. Regarding this question, some argue that only the freedom of establishment applies for FDI, thereby implying that an FDI fulfils the conditions of an establishment pursuant to Art 49 TFEU.

[164]See also *Associação Peço a Palavra and Others*, Opinion of AG Sánchez-Bordona (n. 146), para. 50. *Contra* Hindelang (2009), p. 87, who rightly differentiates between decisive or definitive and definite influence, but does not see the difference between effective and definite influence.

[165]For the distinction between effective participation and the power to influence decisions in a certain manner, see also *Commission v Italy* [March 2009] (n. 132), paras. 38–39.

establishment and FDI would require the same threshold of investor influence, the term establishment in Art 64(1) and (2) TFEU would essentially be deprived of its scope of application. It would only apply in the trivial cases in which establishment does not come with movement of capital: a self-employed person who establishes herself, funded by her own means only, without acquiring financial assets, such as a company or real estate.[166]

Hence, the notion definite influence within the meaning of Art 49 TFEU requires a higher level of investor influence than the notion effective participation that is required to qualify as FDI. As a result, every establishment in the form of M&A constitutes an FDI, and thus capital movement within the meaning of Art 63(1) TFEU; but not every FDI constitutes an establishment within the meaning of Art 49 TFEU.

4.2.3.3   Delimiting the Freedoms of Capital Movement and Establishment: Parallel or Exclusive Application in Light of the *Erga Omnes* Effect of Art 63(1) TFEU

Section 4.2.3.2 showed the overlap of the substantial scopes of Arts 49 and 63(1) TFEU regarding FDI. A priori, the freedom of capital movement includes all M&A FDI, whereas the freedom of establishment only encompasses M&A FDI to the extent the investor obtains definite influence on the target company. Accordingly, an investor may be able to invoke both Fundamental freedoms in case of an M&A FDI that gives him definite influence on the target company. If the FDI qualifies as establishment, but the investor is excluded from the freedom of establishment's personal scope, the freedom of capital movement could nevertheless apply—and thus fulfil a 'catch-all function'.

However, due to different contexts, and objects and purposes of both freedoms, in particular their diverging personal scopes, it is disputed whether a catch-all function of the freedom of capital movement adequately expresses the delimitation of both freedoms. Most importantly, one might be inclined to argue that the limited personal scope of the freedom of establishment only takes effect if the freedom of establishment overrides the freedom of capital movement. Before engaging in this discussion, several clarifications are necessary.

First, the following departs from the understanding that the delimitation of Arts 49 and 63(1) TFEU is undertaken at the applicatory, not definitory level. As shown in Sects. 4.2.3.1 and 4.2.3.2, establishment within the meaning of Art 49 TFEU and capital movement pursuant to Art 63(1) TFEU can be defined independently from each other. The definition of capital movement, for instance, is not supplemented by the subjective element that the capital movement is made with the purpose to invest

---

[166]With this example Ohler (2002), Art 57 EGV, para. 11; Hindelang (2009), p. 86.

funds.[167] This element would have intended to delimit both freedoms at definitory level. Independent substantial scopes of both freedoms are also in line with the TFEU. For example, Art 64(1) and (2) TFEU list both FDI and establishment as capital movement that may be restricted.[168] Moreover, both freedoms protect different aspects of a specific business activity. These freedom-specific interests would be negated if by definition only one freedom applies.[169]

Second, the issue of delimiting the freedoms of capital movement and establishment only arises if by definition both freedoms substantially apply to a specific situation. If an FDI does not give the investor definite influence on the FDI target: the freedom of establishment does not apply, the issue of delimitation does not arise, and the freedom of capital movement may not be overridden by the freedom of establishment. Hence, the freedom of capital movement applies. This will become crucial when assessing the EU's flexibility to adopt FDI Screening mechanisms. To the extent the FDI Screening mechanisms apply to FDI that gives the investors less than definite influence on the FDI target, they address situations in which only the freedom of capital movement applies. Such FDI Screening mechanisms will therefore always need to comply with the freedom of capital movement—regardless of how to delimit both freedoms. Section 4.2.4 will further elaborate this aspect in light of the conclusions reached below.

Third, a delimitation test at the applicatory level must not necessarily conclude that one freedom (always) overrides the other. On the contrary, it will be shown that the TFEU in most cases favours a parallel applicability of the freedoms of capital movement and establishment.

Fourth, determining that one freedom applies exclusively requires a delimitation criterion.[170] Section 4.2.3.2 has already shown that the freedom of establishment only applies if the investor may exert definite influence on the target company. Hence, definite influence as the delimitation criterion would result in an exclusive applicability of the freedom of establishment over the freedom of capital movement.[171]

---

[167] See Sect. 4.2.3.1 and n. 112.

[168] Hindelang (2009), p. 111; Kotthaus (2012), p. 63; Geiger (2013), p. 150; Lübke (2015), para. 47; Schön (2015), p. 560; Tiedje (2015a), para. 23; Ress and Ukrow (2020a), para. 318. It is sometimes unclear whether these authors argue on the definitory or applicatory level. *Contra* Herz (2014), pp. 320–321, who argues that the term 'establishment' in Art 64(1) and (2) TFEU does not refer to the notion of establishment within the meaning of Art 49 TFEU. However, the TFEU will not define the term establishment differently in so similar contexts.

[169] Lübke (2006), pp. 232–233; Lübke (2015), para. 47.

[170] With a detailed analysis of all delimitation criteria that are being discussed in case law and literature, see Herz (2014), pp. 238–257.

[171] Presenting this as the delimitation criterion Müller-Graff (2003), p. 936; Nettesheim (2008), pp. 753–754; Kotthaus (2012), p. 58; Geiger (2013), p. 147; Gosch and Schönfeld (2015), p. 760; Ego (2017), paras. 701–705. Spies (2015), p. 467, makes this delimitation criterion one part of her proposed delimitation test.

Fifth, it will be shown that the issue of delimiting the freedoms of capital movement and establishment becomes particularly important in cases in which the freedom of establishment does personally not apply. Section 4.2.2 showed that Arts 49 and 54 TFEU exclude Non-EU Companies, Non-EU Established SPVs undertaking FDI, foreign States, and foreign public undertakings. Art 63(1) TFEU, on the other hand, protects these investors, at least indirectly. In these cases, the freedom of capital movement applies personally and substantially, whereas the freedom establishment denies the investor its substantial protection for personal reasons. This contradiction will accompany the discussion: Should the freedom of establishment override the freedom of capital movement at least in cases in which an FDI qualifies as an establishment, but the investor falls outside the personal scope of the freedom of establishment? Or, should the freedom of capital movement be assigned a catch-all function for cases in which the freedom of establishment fails to apply personally?[172] Investments that qualify as establishment, but which are undertaken by investors falling outside the freedom of establishment's personal scope, Non-EU Companies, Non-EU Established SPVs undertaking FDI, foreign States, and foreign public undertakings, will in the following be termed 'Third-country cases'.

Against this background, the following will first analyze the ECJ's case law on the delimitation of Arts 49 and 63(1) TFEU. In a second step, the discussion will develop a delimitation test, building on ECJ case law, scholar contributions, and primary law arguments.

4.2.3.3.1   Making Sense of Case Law on Delimiting the Freedoms of Capital Movement and Establishment

With its judgment *Baars* of 13 April 2000 and numerous subsequent judgments, the ECJ significantly contributed to delimit the freedoms of capital movement and establishment.[173] The vast majority of these judgments dealt with the overlap of Arts 49 and 63(1) TFEU in case of M&A investments. Nevertheless, unresolved questions and aspects worthy of criticism remain. The following outlines the ECJ's test to delimit the freedoms of capital movement and establishment, identifies the ECJ's stance on a parallel or exclusive relationship between the two, and finally determines the applied delimitation criterion.[174]

---

[172] This catch-all function will only fail in the improbable case in which the FDI is solely set up with capital from the host state; Tiedje (2015a), para. 31, n. 47. Another example of establishment in which cross-border capital movement is missing is an establishment without any starting capital, e.g. an artist without assets, see Schön (2015), p. 562. More generally, one can thus state that nearly all establishments rely on capital movement, Forsthoff (2020b), para. 128.

[173] Case C-251/98 *Baars* [2000] EU:C:2000:205. For a summary of case law that demonstrates the earlier lack of clarity, see Nettesheim (2008), pp. 742–747.

[174] For the ECJ's case law on interpreting the grounds of exception in third-country contexts, see Sect. 3.2.4. The ECJ does not generally interpret these grounds more broadly, but admits that there might be cases in which a measure could fail the proportionality test in intra-EU, but pass it in third-country cases.

The ECJ's Delimitation Test for Arts 49 and 63(1) TFEU
The ECJ has a well-established test when confronted with cases that relate to the freedoms of capital movement and establishment. If an individual is restricted in moving capital or establishment, the restriction is based on a measure, which is itself legislation or is based on legislation. The ECJ's delimitation test departs from the purpose of this legislation,[175] and identifies three types.[176]

First, legislation can intend to exclusively apply to shareholdings that give the investor definite influence on the target company's decisions. In this case, the freedom of establishment applies. According to the ECJ, the measure's effect on the freedom of capital movement was solely an 'unavoidable consequence' that does 'not warrant an independent examination in light of' Art 63(1) TFEU.[177] This result remains valid in third-country contexts in which the freedom of establishment is personally not applicable.[178]

The second type of legislation is intended to exclusively apply to portfolio investment, and thus investment that is solely aimed at investing funds, not influencing the target company in its business activity. To this second legislation type, the ECJ exclusively applied the freedom of capital movement.[179]

Third, legislation that addresses capital movement irrespective of the shareholding and the degree of investor influence on the target company fell under both Arts

---

[175] *Commission v Italy* [March 2009] (n. 132), para. 33;*Test Claimants in the FII Group Litigation* [2012] (n. 163), para. 90; *Associação Peço a Palavra and Others* (n. 36), para. 43. The ECJ uses the term 'national legislation'. However, there is no reason why the same approach should not be applied to EU legislation. Therefore, the following uses the general term 'legislation'.

[176] The ECJ itself describes this as settled case law, see e.g. *Associação Peço a Palavra and Others* (n. 36), para. 43. Applying this test, the ECJ concludes the exclusive applicability of Art 49 TFEU e.g. in *Cadbury Schweppes und Cadbury Schweppes Overseas* (n. 58), paras. 32–33; *Commission v Italy* [March 2009] (n. 132), para. 39; *Commission v Greece* (n. 129), paras. 23–25. In the past, some scholars assumed that this case law were specific to tax law cases, see Krolop (2008), p. 16; Scharf (2008), p. 22. Case C-112/05 *Commission v Germany* [2007] EU:C:2007:623, para. 13; *Commission v Greece* (n. 129), paras. 21–25, both on Golden shares regulation, rebutted this assumption. Nevertheless, Hindelang and Hagemeyer (2017), p. 886, still doubt that this case law may be transposed to other than tax law cases, since it is exclusive Member State competence and crucial for Member States to secure tax revenue. According to Hindelang and Hagemeyer, the ECJ therefore wanted to avoid a unilateral liberalization of capital movement vis-à-vis third-countries that affects Member States' tax revenues. For the definition of definite influence as the definitory criterion of an establishment through M&A within the meaning of Art 49 TFEU, see Sect. 4.2.3.2.2.

[177] *Commission v Italy* [March 2009] (n. 132), para. 39. Similarly, *Lasertec* (n. 136), paras. 25, 28 (also 'primarily affects'); *Cadbury Schweppes und Cadbury Schweppes Overseas* (n. 58), para. 33. In *Lasertec* the ECJ adds that Art 49 TFEU were 'primarily affected', and the restriction of Art 63(1) TFEU an 'unavoidable consequence'.

[178] *Test Claimants in the Thin Cap Group Litigation* (n. 129), paras. 101–104; *Lasertec* (n. 136), para. 27; *Scheunemann* (n. 149), paras. 34–35. On the delimitation of the freedom of services from Art 63(1) TFEU, *Fidium Finanz* (n. 112), para. 50.

[179] Following this rationale, in Joined Cases C-436 and 437/08 *Haribo Lakritzen Hans Riegel* [2011] EU:C:2011:61, paras. 36–38, the ECJ only assesses and applies Art 63(1) TFEU. The ECJ applies the same rationale in many judgments, see e.g. *X v Skatteverket* (n. 138), para. 19.

49 and 64(1) TFEU.[180] Therefore, this third type of legislation addresses two sorts of cases. On the one hand, cases of capital movement within the meaning of Art 63(1) TFEU only. On the other hand, cases that qualify as both capital movement and establishment pursuant to Art 49 TFEU.[181]

Most cases deal with the third legislation type. In its judgments on FDI screening, golden shares, and similar measures, the ECJ applies either both,[182] or focuses on one of the freedoms for procedural reasons of legal or economic nature.[183,184]

In third type tax legislation, the ECJ adds a further prong to the delimitation test: the facts of the individual case.[185] The ECJ only applies the freedom of establishment if the investment at issue qualifies as an establishment, meaning an investment that gives the investors definite influence on the target company. Otherwise, it applies the freedom of capital movement. Many scholars misinterpret this case law as indicating that the ECJ favours an exclusive application of the freedom of establishment.[186]

---

[180] *Idryma Typou* (n. 129), para. 49; *Test Claimants in the FII Group Litigation* [2012] (n. 163), para. 93; *X v Skatteverket* (n. 138), para. 19. Korte (2016a), para. 35, interprets this case law as focusing on the legislative intent only for third category legislation, but for the other categories on the shareholdings at issue. However, Korte's references to Bünning (2014), p. 1778; Forsthoff (2020b), para. 129, do not support this thesis.

[181] Pointing out these possible sets of facts Schön (2015), pp. 558–559. Spies (2015), p. 254, argues that in the first and second legislation category the legislative intent and the affected sets of facts are usually the same. Accordingly, the ECJ's subjective approach came to the same conclusion.

[182] *Columbus Container Services* (n. 131), paras. 29–33, 55–57; *Commission v Spain* [July 2008] (n. 133), paras. 36–39, 61–62; *Commission v Italy* [March 2009] (n. 132), para. 38.

[183] *Commission v Germany* [2007] (n. 176), paras. 15–16 (the Commission could not establish a definite influence for the case at issue). With the same interpretation Hindelang (2009), pp. 90–95; Kemmerer (2010), p. 169; Geiger (2013), pp. 144–145; Schön (2015), pp. 572–573.

[184] Earlier ECJ judgments on Golden shares and similar regulations also belong in the category of judgments that only apply Art 63(1) TFEU, e.g. Case C-503/99 *Commission v Belgium* [2002] EU: C:2002:328, paras. 58–59 (the ECJ examines Art 49 TFEU apparently only because it was invoked by the Commission, and for its conclusion refers to its conclusions on Art 63(1) TFEU); Case C-367/98 *Commission v Portugal* [2002] EU:C:2002:326, paras. 21–26, 36, 56 (the Commission claimed a violation of both Arts 49 and 63(1) TFEU, but the ECJ only examined Art 63(1) TFEU, and held that 'there is no need for a separate examination' in light of Art 49 TFEU); *Commission v Italy* [2005] (n. 75), paras. 26–29 (in both cases the Commission only claimed a violation of Art 63(1) TFEU); Case C-274/06 *Commission v Spain* [2008] EU:C:2008:86, paras. 1, 7, 16. Herz (2014), pp. 231–232, also sees these judgments as indifferent to the issue of delimitation of Arts 49 and 63(1) TFEU.

[185] *Test Claimants in the FII Group Litigation* [2012] (n. 163), para. 94; *Kronos International* (n. 139), para. 37, with further references. Its judgments on investment screening, Golden shares, and similar legislation arouse in abstract preliminary ruling procedures pursuant to Art 267 TFEU. There was thus no case at issue to assess. There are only two exceptions. In *Idryma Typou* (n. 129), paras. 47–52, 60, the ECJ could have, but omitted to assess the case at issue. However, as the submitted questions were limited to abstract issues. One may thus not conclude that the ECJ rejected transposing the tax case law to other contexts such as FDI screening. In *Associação Peço a Palavra and Others* (n. 36), paras. 43–44, the ECJ did assess the individual case only by basing its interpretation of an abstract law on the more specific tender specifications that were applied in the case at issue.

[186] Kemmerer (2010), pp. 166–168; Geiger (2013), p. 146; Lübke (2015), para. 46; Schön (2015), pp. 576–577; Bröhmer (2016a), Art 63 AEUV, paras. 28, 35; Herz (2014), p. 252, even argues that

However, the ECJ in fact confuses two levels of analysis. The Court starts by abstractly assessing the compliance of legislation with Arts 49 and 63(1) TFEU, but leaves the delimitation question open, and ends up examining whether this legislation *in concreto* violates the Fundamental freedom of an individual; in other words, whether the individual legal action is successful.[187] These ECJ judgments on tax cases may therefore not generally define the ECJ's test to delimit the freedoms of capital movement and establishment.

Consequently, the above summary of the ECJ's case law based on the three legislation types remains valid. The ECJ's test for delimiting the freedoms of capital movement and establishment relies on the intent of the legislation on which the restricting measure at issue is based.[188] At the same time, it is much less clear whether the ECJ in fact favours an exclusive or parallel application of (one of) the freedoms. The following will first argue that the legislative intent as a method for delimiting the freedoms of capital movement and establishment is, if applied at applicatory, not definitory level, an adequate method to delimit the Arts 49 and 63(1) TFEU. Second, it will show that the ECJ's case law indicates an in principle parallel application of Arts 49 and 63(1) TFEU.

Point of Departure for Delimiting Arts 49 and 63(1) TFEU: Intent of Legislation

The ECJ case law on delimiting the freedoms of capital movement and establishment departs from the legislative intent. This point of departure may be misleading, but for delimiting Arts 49 and 63(1) TFEU at the applicability level appropriate.

Some argue that the ECJ's delimitation test was inconsistent with the Fundamental freedoms' nature as subjective, individual rights.[189] Indeed, this criticism is correct as far as the legislative intent, at definitory level, determines the (potentially) applicable Fundamental freedom.[190] Any Fundamental freedom assessment must depart from the individual who invokes the Fundamental freedom against a certain measure. Only this approach places the individual as beneficiary of the Fundamental freedom at the centre.[191] When abstractly assessing whether a legislation complies with the Fundamental freedom, the key question thus becomes: Which economic

---

the ECJ in fact undertakes an assessment of the individual case only, without intending to develop a general delimitation test.

[187] Explicitly in *Test Claimants in the FII Group Litigation* [2012] (n. 163), para. 99: 'A company resident in a Member State *may therefore rely on that provision* [Art 63(1) TFEU] *in order to call into question the legality of such rules*, irrespective of the size of its shareholding in the company paying dividends established in a third country' (emphasis added). Replicated by *Kronos International* (n. 139), para. 52. Ohler (2002), Art 56 EGV, para. 64, also seems to support this understanding.

[188] Gosch and Schönfeld (2015), p. 757, and arguably Ress and Ukrow (2020a), para. 318, also understand the legislative intent as the single delimitation method.

[189] Müller-Graff (2003), p. 935; Hindelang (2009), pp. 99–100; Herz (2014), pp. 251–252. Explicitly in favour Schön (2015), pp. 577–578.

[190] *Contra* Schön (2015), pp. 566–567.

[191] Müller-Graff (2003), p. 935; Clostermeyer (2011), p. 184.

activities does the legislation objectively affect, rather than subjectively intend to address? The affected economic activities are then to be defined pursuant to the Fundamental freedoms' substantial and personal scope. Only if a measure affects economic activities that constitute both capital movement and establishment, the question of delimiting Arts 49 and 63(1) TFEU arises. To the extent the measure affects economic activities that only constitute capital movement, but not establishment, only the freedom of capital movement can apply. Hence, there is no room for delimiting Arts 49 and 63(1) TFEU.[192]

Nevertheless, if found that both freedoms may apply to a specific situation, the legislative intent may still provide a method to delimit the freedoms of capital movement and establishment at applicatory level. Insofar the scholars' criticism must be rejected.

The critics argue that by delimiting both freedoms based on the legislative intent the legislator might itself determine which Fundamental freedom applies.[193] Interestingly, others argue the exact opposite: If the ECJ can only take the measure's objective content into account, the legislator might artificially separate the measure into several parts to which respectively only one Fundamental freedom applies. In such cases, the ECJ had to be able to take the legislator's intent into account to ensure proper application of the Fundamental freedoms.[194] In comparison, the costs of legislators determining the applicable Fundamental freedom by artificial measure design seems higher than the risk that they determine the applicable Fundamental freedom by their intent. Therefore, the ECJ should be able to take the legislative intent into account when delimiting the Fundamental freedoms.[195]

Consequently, the ECJ's approach to depart from the legislative intent is to be rejected for determining whether Arts 49 and 63(1) TFEU may apply at definitory level. If, however, by definition both the freedoms of capital movement and

---

[192] This was already indicated by the second clarification in the introduction to this section. Similarly without much argumentative effort, de Kok (2019), p. 29; Zwartkruis and de Jong (2020), p. 456. Lübke (2015), para. 38, applies a similar test. Also Spies (2015), pp. 142, 154–157, but as part of a two-tier test. According to her test, both the case at issue and the legislative intent should fall under the Fundamental freedom's scope. For abstractly assessing legislation without a case at issue, Spies takes into account whether the legislation restricts one or both freedoms. This, however, confuses the applicability of a Fundamental freedom and, as a second step, its restriction by a concrete measure.

[193] Hindelang (2009), p. 100; Herz (2014), pp. 250–251.

[194] Schön (2015), p. 578. See also Spies (2015), pp. 251, 270–272, who seeks to meet the concern by demanding an overall assessment of the legislation's content and its design in Member State law. According to Spies, the legislative intent should not be the basis for delimiting Arts 49 and 63(1) TFEU, at least in cases on taxation, since taxation remains exclusive Member State competence. However, the particularities of taxation for Member States may be taken into account when applying the test.

[195] Case C-164/12 *DMC* [2014] EU:C:2014:20, paras. 32–34. Gosch and Schönfeld (2015), p. 757, argue that the ECJ adds considerations of the legislation's impact to its purpose method to avoid that policy makers disguise their purpose. Herz (2014), p. 250, also sees the risks of a formal purpose-based approach and therefore criticizes the ECJ's case law.

establishment apply, the ECJ is right in taking into account the legislative intent as the method to delimit both freedoms. Based on this method, a variety of delimitation criteria may be applied, for example the intent to regulate market access. This allows a nuanced delimitation test.[196]

Exclusive or Parallel Applicability of Arts 49 and 63(1) TFEU?

Regardless of the level at which the ECJ exactly deals with delimiting the freedoms of capital movement and establishment, its stance on the freedoms' relation remains unclear. While the ECJ's earlier case law seemed to indicate an exclusive applicability of the freedom of establishment, the judgment *Test Claimants in the FII Group Litigation (2012)* may have marked a turning point. Several aspects imply that the ECJ, at least now, favours a generally parallel application of both freedoms.[197]

In several judgments the ECJ exclusively applied the freedom of establishment if the legislation was solely intended to address investments that gave the investor definite influence on the target company. At the same time, the freedom of establishment, by definition, can only apply in case of a definite influence. Consequently, the ECJ exclusively applied the freedom of establishment whenever it was by definition applicable.[198] Therefore, many scholars conclude that the ECJ is in favour of an exclusive applicability of Art 49 TFEU, overriding Art 63(1) TFEU.[199]

---

[196] One may even assume that the ECJ bases its case law on such an understanding without making the theoretical background transparent, arguably with similar understandings Lübke (2015), para. 38; Forsthoff (2020b), para. 129. Therefore, it would be misleading to present the legislative intent as the only delimitation criterion, and on this basis dismissing the ECJ's case law, see Müller-Graff (2003), p. 935.

[197] Other judgments seem to be indifferent to the issue of delimitation of Arts 49 and 63(1) TFEU. Often, the ECJ assesses Art 63(1) TFEU, and either omits any reference to Art 49 TFEU, or holds that an examination of Art 49 TFEU was not necessary, Case C-302/97 *Konle* [1999] EU:C:1999: 271, para. 22; Case C-423/98 *Albore* [2000] EU:C:2000:401, para. 22; Case C-452/01 *Ospelt und Schlössle Weinberg* [2003] EU:C:2003:493, para. 24; Case C-364/01 *Barbier* [2003] EU:C:2003: 665, paras. 58, 75; Case C-235/17 *Commission v Hungary* [2019] EU:C:2019:432, para. 53. In another case the ECJ primarily examined Art 49 TFEU and only briefly addressed Art 63(1) TFEU, Case C-345/05 *Commission v Portugal* [2006] EU:C:2006:685, paras. 13–18, 44–45. With a more detailed analysis of some of these cases, all regarding real estate transactions, see Herz (2014), pp. 213–230, who interprets these judgments as mostly indifferent on how to delimit Arts 49 and 63(1) TFEU.

[198] For ECJ judgments see n. 198. Regarding real estate investment for establishment purposes, the ECJ tends to a parallel applicability of Arts 49 and 63(1) TFEU. Insofar, Art 63(1) TFEU is a 'corollary' to Art 49 TFEU, see *Konle* (n. 197), para. 22; Joined Cases C-515, 519 to 524, and 526 to 540/99 *Reisch and Others* [2002] EU:C:2002:135, paras. 28–29.

[199] With this interpretation all scholars who understand the ECJ as applying Art 49 TFEU exclusively in case of a definite influence, see n. 171. Also Hindelang (2009), p. 108; Smit (2012), pp. 461–464; Tietje (2014), para. 33; Lübke (2015), para. 44; Ress and Ukrow (2020a), para. 318. As this results in an exclusive application of Art 49 TFEU, the label 'gravity approach' would be misleading; with the same conclusion Geiger (2013), p. 147. Clostermeyer (2011), p. 208, nevertheless uses the label 'gravity approach'.

This reading may not be refuted by the ECJ's case law on third type legislation, in which the ECJ applies both freedoms. If a measure intends to regulate both establishments and mere capital movement, it simply addresses two sets of facts. On the one hand, M&A that only qualifies as capital movement; on the other hand, M&A that qualifies as establishment and capital movement. Applying both freedoms is necessary to cover both situations.[200]

The judgment *Test Claimants in the FII Group Litigation (2012)*, however, indicates a parallel application of Arts 49 and 63(1) TFEU—at least in cases in which the investor is excluded from the personal scope of the freedom of establishment. *Test Claimants in the FII Group Litigation (2012)* and subsequent judgments dealt with legislation on taxing dividends and loan interests that moved from or to third countries within a company group, regardless of the level of influence between the companies.[201] Accordingly, the measures intended to regulate the taxation of establishments pursuant to Art 49 TFEU as well as mere capital movement within the meaning of Art 63(1) TFEU. If the ECJ had taken the individual case into account as in the other judgments on tax law, it would have concluded that the freedom of establishment applied. However, the company at issue was a Non-EU Company. Hence, following the test of taking the individual case into account, no Fundamental freedom would have applied. Against this background, the ECJ held that an otherwise non-protected investor must indeed be able to rely on the freedom of capital movement—unless the measure at issue related to the conditions of market access to the internal market.[202] For justifying this caveat, the ECJ argued that applying the freedom of capital movement must 'not enable economic operators who do not fall within the limits of the territorial scope of freedom of establishment to profit from that freedom'.[203]

In other words, the ECJ held that the freedom of capital movement applies in case of third type legislation even if (i) the company at issue in the individual case constitutes an establishment, and (ii) is personally excluded from the freedom of

---

[200]Lübke (2015), para. 45.

[201] *Test Claimants in the FII Group Litigation* [2012] (n. 163), paras. 96–103; *Kronos International* (n. 139), paras. 39–52, both on taxing dividends. In *Itelcar* (n. 139), paras. 16–24, the ECJ extends this strand of case law to taxation of interests received from shareholder loans.

[202] *Test Claimants in the FII Group Litigation* [2012] (n. 163), para. 97. If dividends and loan interests are taxed, the company on which the taxes are imposed must already have been granted market access, *Test Claimants in the FII Group Litigation* [2012] (n. 163), para. 100; *Kronos International* (n. 139), para. 54. In tax law cases outside third-country context, the ECJ omits to refer to the exception for legislation that intends to regulate market access, see e.g. *X v Skatteverket* (n. 138), paras. 23–24; *Deister Holding* (n. 51), paras. 81–84. Market access as delimitation criterion also emerges when delimiting Art 63(1) TFEU from the freedom of services, see Case C-580/15 *Van der Weegen and Others* [2017] EU:C:2017:429, para. 29; and ii) 'Delimitation Criterion'.

[203] *Kronos International* (n. 139), para. 53. *Test Claimants in the FII Group Litigation* [2012] Opinion of AG Jääskinen (n. 130), para. 122; paraphrases this consideration by opining that the personally limited scope of Art 49 TFEU may not be extended to third-countries 'through the backdoor'.

establishment—unless (iii) the legislation regulates market access.[204] Certainly, this case law had Non-EU Companies in mind. However, the rationale may be transposed to all other investors who fall outside the freedom of establishment, but inside the scope of freedom of capital movement: Non-EU Established SPVs, foreign States, and foreign public undertakings ('Third-country cases').[205]

Consequently, for third type legislation, at least in tax law cases, the ECJ assigns a catch-all function to the freedom of capital movement. Such a catch-all function is only possible if, as a principle, the freedoms of capital movement and establishment apply parallelly. The parallel applicability must, according to *Test Claimants in the FII Group Litigation (2012)*, only give way to the exclusive applicability of Art 49 TFEU if the legislation intends to regulate market access.

One may therefore read this case law as indicating a parallel application of the freedoms of capital movement and establishment generally, regardless of the legislation type.[206] Two additional arguments support this conclusion. First, the relation of Arts 49 and 63(1) TFEU may not depend on whether a legislation plays in the ambit of tax law or another field of law.[207] Second, if the freedoms apply parallelly at the individual case level as in *Test Claimants in the FII Group Litigation (2012)*, they must also apply parallelly at the abstract legislation level.[208] The ECJ's rationale for assigning the freedom of capital movement a catch-all function if the freedom of establishment does personally not apply is valid at both levels.[209]

In sum, it may be concluded that the ECJ, as a principle, favours the parallel applicability of the freedoms of capital movement and establishment. As an exception, the freedom of establishment applies exclusively when the legislation regulates market access—even if the freedom of establishment is personally not applicable.[210,211]

---

[204] *Test Claimants in the FII Group Litigation* [2012] (n. 163), paras. 96–103. For the subsequent judgments see n. 201. The term Non-EU Company was defined as a company that does not meet the requirements of Art 54(1) TFEU, see Sect. 4.2.2.1.2.

[205] See introduction to this Sect. 4.2.3.3.

[206] See also Spies (2015), pp. 241–242. Hindelang and Hagemeyer (2017), p. 885, still understand ECJ case law as applying Art 49 TFEU exclusively.

[207] Scharf (2008), p. 22. *Contra* Hindelang and Hagemeyer (2017), p. 886, since the policy area of direct taxation is particularly sensitive for Member States, see n. 176.

[208] Nevertheless, in *Test Claimants in the FII Group Litigation* [2012] (n. 163), paras. 98–99, the ECJ explicitly stated that Art 49 TFEU remains exclusively applicable in case of first type legislation (legislation that only addresses shareholdings giving the investor a definite influence on the target company).

[209] For these considerations see ibid., paras. 97–100.

[210] With the same understanding of ECJ case law Spies (2015), pp. 243–244, who finds corporate, business, and commercial law to often provide market access rules.

[211] With a similar conclusion Spies (2015), pp. 242–243, who expects that the ECJ will increasingly consider the legislative intent, not the individual case. Spies rightly infers that this would lead to more parallel applicability of Arts 49 and 63(1) TFEU, since the ECJ consulted the individual case to avoid parallel application.

Transposed to FDI Screening mechanisms, the ECJ case law might conclude that neither the freedom of establishment, nor the freedom of capital movement applies. If FDI Screening mechanisms are intended to exclusively apply to M&A FDI that gives the investor definite influence on the target company (first type legislation) or to FDI generally (third type legislation category), neither Art 49, nor Art 63(1) TFEU would apply. The freedom of capital movement would not apply, since the FDI Screening mechanisms regulate foreign investor market access; the freedom of establishment would not apply because the foreign investors fall outside its personal scope.[212]

ECJ Case Law: Three Main Features for the Delimitation of Arts 49 and 63(1) TFEU

In sum, one may summarize the ECJ case law on the delimitation of the freedoms of capital movement and establishment as being characterized by three main features.

First, according to the ECJ, the delimitation should depart from the legislative intent. Legislation may intend to regulate only M&A that gives the investor definite influence on the target company (first type legislation), only M&A that gives the investor less than definite influence (second type legislation), or M&A irrespective of the level of influence the investor gains (third type legislation). Second, at least in case of third type legislation, the freedoms of capital movement and establishment apply, as a principle, parallelly. As an exception, the freedom of establishment overrides the freedom of capital movement. Third, the exception applies if two delimitation criteria are met: the M&A investor falls outside of the personal scope of Arts 49, 54(1) TFEU, and the legislation regulates market access. While the ECJ focuses on Non-EU Companies as investors who are personally excluded from the freedom of establishment, it may be presumed that the ECJ would transpose its case law also on all other Third-country cases.

This case law is to be rejected to the extent it assesses the legislative intent to determine whether Arts 49 and 63(1) TFEU apply at definitory level. Instead, any Fundamental freedom assessment must depart from the individual who invokes the Fundamental freedom against a certain measure. When abstractly assessing whether a legislation complies with the Fundamental freedom, the analysis must thus depart from the situations that the legislation objectively affects, and whether the freedoms may apply to these situations. As will be further discussed below, this has significant consequences for the relevance of a delimitation test for FDI Screening mechanisms. Indeed, at applicatory level, the ECJ is right in taking into account the measure's purpose as the delimitation method.

Against this background, the following will develop a comprehensive test for delimiting the freedoms of capital movement and establishment, focusing on legislation that regulates M&A. To this end, the following will assess in detail whether

---

[212] See Sect. 4.2.2.4. With a similar application of the ECJ case law to FDI Screening mechanisms, de Kok (2019), p. 29.

the second and third main features of ECJ case law are appropriate: Arts 49 and 63(1) TFEU apply as a principle parallelly, but as an exception the former is overriding the latter in case the two mentioned delimitation criteria are met—the legislation applies to investors who are excluded from the freedom of establishment's personal scope, and the legislation regulates market access.

4.2.3.3.2 Developing a Delimitation Test

Delimiting the freedoms of capital movement and establishment is crucial for determining to what extent policy makers are limited when adopting legislation that regulates M&A—namely, FDI Screening mechanisms. If the legislation exclusively applies to Third-country cases, Fundamental freedom limits can only derive from the freedom of capital movement. It is therefore indispensable to determine whether the freedom of capital movement in fact applies in such cases, or whether it is overridden by the—substantially, but not personally applicable—freedom of establishment.

The test for delimiting the freedoms of capital movement and establishment departs from two premises. First, both freedoms can, by definition, apply parallelly to a specific situation. The investment enabling the investor to exert definite influence on the company's business decisions constitutes not only capital movement pursuant to Art 63(1) TFEU, but also an establishment within the meaning of Art 49 TFEU. Second, when abstractly assessing which Fundamental freedoms may apply to a legislation, one must first assess which situations the legislation objectively affects, not subjectively intends to address.

As a consequence of the second premise, there are three categories of legislation, in parallel to the ECJ's three legislation types. The first category objectively affects only investments that give the investor less than definite influence on the target company. Hence, by definition only the freedom of capital can apply; the affected investment falls outside of the freedom of establishment's substantial scope. The second category only affects investments that give the investor definite influence on the company. Therefore, by definition, Arts 49 and 63(1) TFEU may apply to all affected situations. Third and last, the legislation may affect situations in which, by definition, only Art 63(1) TFEU applies, as well as situations in which Arts 49 and 63(1) TFEU apply—namely, if the legislation affects FDI generally.

As already stated, a delimitation test can only apply to situations in which by definition both Fundamental freedoms may apply.[213] The delimitation test is therefore only relevant to the second category of legislation that exclusively applies to situations of investments giving the investor definite influence on the company. As will be further elaborated in Sect. 4.2.4, this has important consequences for the EU's flexibility to adopt FDI Screening mechanisms: The following delimitation test

---

[213] See second clarification in introduction to this Sect. 4.2.3.3.

is only relevant to FDI Screening mechanisms that fall into the second category of legislation, and thus not to mechanisms that apply to FDI generally.

Against this background, the following will first determine the relation between the freedoms of capital movement and establishment at applicatory level, hence their parallel or exclusive applicability. It will be argued that as a principle both freedoms apply parallelly. However, this may cause contradictions due to the diverging personal scopes of both freedoms in Third-country cases. In these cases, the freedom of establishment is therefore exceptionally overridden by the freedom of capital movement. Finally, delimitation method and criterion will be determined to develop a fully-fledged delimitation test.

The Principle: Parallel Relation Between Arts 49 and 63(1) TFEU

Literal meaning, context, and object and purpose of the freedoms of capital movement and establishment weigh in favour of their parallel application.[214]

To begin with, the freedom of capital movement may not generally override the freedom of establishment. As practically every establishment comes with capital movement,[215] such an exclusive applicability of Art 63(1) TFEU would reduce the freedom of establishment's scope to a limited number of cases.[216]

Moreover, the mutual references in Arts 49(2) and 65(2) TFEU weigh in favour of applying the freedoms of capital movement and establishment parallelly.[217] The only message that may reasonably be inferred from Art 49(2) TFEU is that the freedom of capital movement can also apply if a transaction constitutes an establishment within the meaning of Art 49 TFEU.[218] The reference of Art 49(2) TFEU to

---

[214]The arguably predominant opinion in literature is in favour of an entirely parallel relation of Arts 49 and 63(1) TFEU, Hindelang (2009), p. 114; Wolff (2009), pp. 168–170; Kemmerer (2010), pp. 170–171; Clostermeyer (2011), p. 219; von Wilmowsky (2014), para. 55; Lübke (2015), para. 149; Wojcik (2015a), para. 66. As will be shown below, other scholars argue for an, in principle, parallel applicability that exceptionally gives way to the exclusive applicability of the Art 49 TFEU.

In favour of the exclusive applicability of Art 49 TFEU Bröhmer (2016a), para. 35, as well as originally Ohler (1997), p. 1801, who now is in favour of a parallel applicability of both freedoms, except in third-country cases, Ohler (2002), Art 56 EGV, paras. 118–119. In addition, all those who see definite influence as a delimitation criterion between both freedoms are in fact in favour of the exclusive applicability of Art 49 TFEU, Tiedje (2015a), para. 25.

[215]See Sect. 4.2.3.2.4.

[216]Lübke (2006), p. 230; Herz (2014), p. 309. See also Herz (2014), pp. 275–276, on the historical arguments weighing against an exclusive applicability of the freedom of establishment.

[217]Geiger (2013), pp. 151–152. On the other hand, Bachlechner (1998), p. 531; Mülbert (2001), p. 2089, argue that Arts 49(2) and 65(2) TFEU result in an infinite chain of references that cannot provide any argument to the relation between Arts 49 and 63(1) TFEU. This argumentation, however, ignores that the provisions address different levels of assessment, scope of application (Art 49 TFEU) on the one and ground of exception on the other hand (Art 65(2) TFEU), Herz (2014), pp. 323–324.

[218]The relevant part of Art 49(2) TFEU reads: 'subject to the provisions of the Chapter relating to capital'. The alternative reading, applying the freedom of capital movement exclusively, would deprive the freedom of establishment of its meaning.

'provisions of the Chapter relating to capital' more concretely relates to the grounds of exception in Arts 64 to 66 TFEU.[219] Similarly, Art 65(2) TFEU references the 'restrictions on the right of establishment which are compatible with the Treaties', and thus accepts that both freedoms are applied parallelly. On the one hand, this provides additional grounds of exception to the freedom of capital movement—presupposing that Art 63(1) TFEU is applicable. On the other hand, Art 65(2) TFEU references the grounds of exception to the freedom of establishment, and is thus implying that Art 49 TFEU also applies.[220]

In addition, Art 64 TFEU weighs in favour of a parallel applicability of Arts 49 and 63(1) TFEU. The provision offers an additional ground of exception to the freedom of capital movement for inter alia FDI and establishment from third countries. If, however, the freedom of capital movement did not apply to establishment in the first place, Art 64 TFEU would be deprived of its meaning.[221]

As a final contextual argument, Arts 49 and 63(1) TFEU protect different market activities or aspects thereof. Accordingly, the notions of restriction and grounds of exception in both freedoms are tailored to their respective subject.[222] Only a parallel applicability of Arts 49 and 63(1) TFEU would ensure an effective implementation of these specificities.

A similar argument can be made for the object and purpose of both freedoms.[223] While the freedom of capital movement protects the object capital (object-related freedom), the freedom of establishment focuses on the person that seeks an establishment (person-related freedom).[224] FDI falls under both freedoms to the extent it gives the investor definite influence on the target company. Effectively achieving the purpose of both Arts 49 and 63(1) TFEU requires their parallel applicability. However, it will be shown that this *effet utile* argument has its constraints.

---

[219] Müller-Graff (2003), p. 934; Geiger (2013), pp. 142–143; Hindelang (2009), p. 89. *Contra* Herz (2014), pp. 322–323, who develops an *argumentum e contrario* arguing that Art 49(2) TFEU, in contrast to Art 65(2) TFEU, does precisely not reference the grounds of exception. While this may be concluded from the provisions' explicit wording, the literal meaning and context of Art 49(2) TFEU make clear that the reference is indeed of an even wider scope. It includes the grounds of exception as well as the scope of application of the freedom of capital movement.

[220] Herz (2014), pp. 324–325; Schön (2015), p. 560; Ego (2017), para. 697. Smit (2012), p. 452, however, turns this argument around. He reads Art 65(2) TFEU primarily in light of Third-country cases. In these cases, he argues, Art 65(2) TFEU should ensure that the restrictions to the freedom of establishment apply even though the freedom of establishment is not applicable.

[221] See for scholars with the same line of argument n. 168.

[222] Lübke (2015), paras. 48, 78. In particular, Art 65(2) TFEU demonstrates that the freedom of capital movement recognizes the grounds of exception of Arts 50–53 TFEU as tailored to establishment situations. On this basis, Müller-Graff (2003), p. 933, even argues that Art 63(1) TFEU vis-à-vis Art 49 TFEU only had collateral significance. This understanding, however, neglects Art 49(2) TFEU and the fact that all Fundamental freedom purposes are in principle equally ranked.

[223] Hindelang (2009), pp. 110–111; Clostermeyer (2011), p. 215; Lübke (2015), para. 47; Schön (2015), p. 560.

[224] In favour of also taking this element into account when delimiting Arts 49 and 63(1) TFEU; Schön (2015), p. 561. Criticizing this approach Herz (2014), p. 265.

The above arguments show that, as a principle, the freedoms of capital movement and establishment apply parallelly. This includes their grounds of exception, meaning that if the restriction of one freedom is justified, the restriction of the other freedom will also be justified.[225]

The Exception: Exclusive (Non-)Applicability of Art 49 TFEU in Third-Country Cases?

The parallel applicability of both freedoms is challenged in Third-country cases. The diverging personal scopes of Arts 49 and 63(1) TFEU create a complex picture of conflicting purposes.

Practically every establishment includes capital movement. Hence, a person that engages in establishment can always enjoy Fundamental freedom protection, even though the freedom of establishment does not apply due to its limited personal scope pursuant to Arts 49 and 54 TFEU.[226] Is this a circumvention of Arts 49 and 54 TFEU that should be corrected by the freedom of establishment exceptionally overriding the freedom of capital movement? If so, a personally not applicable Fundamental freedom, the freedom of establishment, would override another, personally and substantially applicable freedom, the freedom of capital movement. Accordingly, the capital movement FDI that also constitutes establishment would not enjoy Fundamental freedom protection. The *erga omnes* effect of Art 63(1) TFEU would insofar be nullified.[227] The following will assess how to resolve this conflict of purposes.[228]

---

[225] Müller-Graff (2003), p. 934. On applying the grounds of exception of one freedom in the ambit of the other freedom Dimopoulos (2011), pp. 82–83.

[226] Unger (2015), p. 68, concludes that this would make the freedom of capital movement a 'pseudo freedom of establishment' ('unechte Niederlassungsfreiheit'). Spies (2015), pp. 199–200, cites Opinion 1/94 *Accords annexés à l'accord OMC* [1994] EU:C:1994:384, para. 81, to stress that it was a deliberate decision to limit the personal scope of Art 49 TFEU. She rightly concludes that this understanding collides with the *erga omnes* effect of Art 49 TFEU. This is why she argues that Art 49 TFEU should override Art 63(1) TFEU if the legislation at issue at least almost exclusively applies to entrepreneurial shareholding within the meaning of Art 49 TFEU, Spies (2015), p. 467. Herz (2014), pp. 414–415, is also in favour of an exclusive applicability of Art 49 TFEU in third-country cases due to the conflicting interests.

[227] Geiger (2013), p. 154; Tietje (2014), para. 33. See also Hindelang (2009), p. 111, who equates FDI and establishment and therefore bases his argument here on the assumption that Art 49 TFEU would override Art 63(1) TFEU in each case of FDI (see Sect. 4.2.3.2.4). *Contra* Roth (2009), p. 267, who is afraid of undermining the purpose Arts 49 and 54 TFEU if interpreting Art 63(1) TFEU too broadly.

[228] Under Art 65(2) TFEU another conflict materializes if Arts 49 and 63(1) TFEU apply parallelly in Third-country cases. The conflict may, however, be resolved by other means than applying Art 49 TFEU exclusively. Art 65(2) TFEU provides that restrictions allowed under Arts 49–55 TFEU must also be allowed under Arts 63–66 TFEU. Hence, technically, the freedom of establishment's grounds of exception apply to restrictions of Art 63(1) TFEU, except in Third-country cases. In these cases Art 49 TFEU, and thus its grounds of exception, are not applicable. Consequently, foreign investors enjoy a higher level of Fundamental freedom protection than EU Companies generally. To resolve this conflict, one may apply the freedom of establishment's grounds of exception analogically also in Third-country cases (see Herz (2014), p. 364; Lübke (2015), para.

Before all, this conflict demonstrates that an exclusive application of Art 49 TFEU should be considered with caution. Indeed, besides the above outlined arguments in favour of a generally parallel applicability of both freedoms, several arguments weigh against the freedom of establishment overriding the freedom of capital movement in Third-country cases.

A first argument, however, is little convincing. Some argue that the TFEU provided sufficient means to avoid an overly intrusive *erga omnes* effect of Art 63(1) TFEU. Arts 64, 65(4) and 66 TFEU sufficiently addressed the particularities of Third-country cases by providing additional grounds of exception for capital movements from third countries.[229] However, Arts 64(3) and 65(4) TFEU set a high obstacle to restricting third-country capital movement. In case of a step backwards in liberalization, the Council must decide unanimously.[230] The freedom of establishment, on the other hand, does not apply and therefore fails to set any obstacle to restricting the third-country establishment. Accordingly, measures restricting establishment would be adopted by the majority rule in Parliament and Council in the ordinary legislative procedure pursuant to Arts 207(2) and 294 TFEU. Therefore, Arts 64(3) and 65(4) TFEU fail to provide the EU with the regulatory flexibility that is comparable to a situation in which Art 49 TFEU overrides Art 63(1) TFEU completely. The same applies to the ground of exception in Art 66 TFEU because it also deviates from the ordinary legislative procedure.[231]

A further argument provides another inappropriate alternative to applying the freedom of establishment exclusively in Third-country cases. The conflicts in Third-county cases could also be resolved by modifying the notion of restriction or the interpretation of the grounds of exception to reduce the level of protection in Third-country cases. This, however, would only shift the problem to another level in the

---

149). Others read Art 65(2) TFEU as implying that Art 49 TFEU overrides Art 63(1) TFEU in Third-country cases. They argue that the limited personal scope of Arts 49 and 54 TFEU is a 'restriction' within the meaning of Art 65(2) TFEU. This, however, overstretches the term 'restriction' (cf Hindelang (2009), p. 112; Wolff (2009), pp. 166–167). If a company does not fall in the personal scope of the freedom of establishment, hindering its investment will not 'restrict' its freedom of establishment, since it does not even apply. Last but not least, Smit (2012), p. 453, reads Art 65(2) TFEU as a general collision rule that, negatively, ensures that foreign investments are not treated more favourable than intra-EU investments (see also in n. 220).

[229] Clostermeyer (2011), p. 218 (only referring to Art 64(1) and (2) TFEU); Lübke (2015), para. 150. Similarly, Case C-101/05 *Skatteverket v A* [2007] EU:C:2007:804, paras. 31–33, when arguing for an equal protection of intra- and extra-EU capital movement.

[230] See in detail Sect. 4.2.5.

[231] An additional argument against Arts 64, 65(4) and 66 TFEU as sufficient means to address third-country contexts seems to be the competence for the EU only, not the Member States. However, the EU has exclusive competence on internal measures regulation FDI anyway, see Sect. 4.1.3.

assessment of the freedom of capital movement. The problem is better and more transparently addressed at the applicatory level.[232]

The only clear contextual argument that weighs in favour of applying Arts 49 and 63(1) TFEU parallelly in Third-country cases derives from Art 64 TFEU. As argued above, in case of an exclusive applicability of Art 49 TFEU, Art 64 TFEU would be deprived of its meaning to the extent that it includes measures on establishment.[233]

Finally, teleological arguments remain. Generally, the freedoms of capital movement and establishment intend to protect different aspects of market activities. Only a parallel applicability would fully achieve this purpose. Accordingly, some scholars argue that a catch-all function of the freedom of capital movement in Third-country cases is necessary for Art 63(1) TFEU to express its intent to the maximum—a classic *effet utile* argument.[234] But what exactly is the intent of Art 63(1) TFEU, in particular of its *erga omnes* effect?

As a point of departure, the *effet utile* is no isolated interpretative means, but an annex to the object and purpose of a norm,[235] which fluently transcends into other interpretative means, namely, contextual considerations.[236] Those who argue with the *effet utile* for a catch-all function of Art 63(1) TFEU therefore presume that the freedom of capital and its *erga omnes* effect intend to protect the movement of capital to the fullest extent possible, even at the expense of a divergent purpose incorporated in Arts 49 and 54 TFEU for Third-country cases. This presumption is wrong.

Generally, the freedom of capital movement intends to promote the free and effective allocation of capital in the internal market. This shall contribute to achieve a competitive and prosperous economy and hence the well-being of EU citizens.[237] In addition, Arts 1(2) and 3(2) TEU and Art 26(2) TFEU show that the freedom of capital movement ultimately serves to build an EU-wide social market economy and create 'an ever closer union among the peoples of Europe'. Hence, despite its third-

---

[232] On the different gateways for taking the particularities of third-country contexts into account, see Sect. 3.2.4.

[233] *Contra* the contextual argument of Art 64 TFEU Lecheler and Germelmann (2010), p. 132. They argue Art 64 TFEU, as Art 66 TFEU, might apply as a legal competence basis even if Art 63(1) TFEU does not apply, since it is overridden by Art 49 TFEU.

[234] Scharf (2008), p. 14; Hindelang (2009), p. 111; Kemmerer (2010), p. 170; Kotthaus (2012), p. 63; Geiger (2013), p. 154; Schuelken and Sichla (2019), p. 1408. In the same vein, Hindelang (2013), p. 81, when he is seeking to preserve a last bit of free movement right ('einen Rest materieller Freiheitsverbürgung'). He thus wrongly insinuates that if one Fundamental freedom overrides another, this would already undermine the Fundamental rights as a whole.

[235] Herz (2014), pp. 331–332. On this issue generally Wegener (2016), para. 16; Rüthers et al. (2018), para. 820c.

[236] Similarly, Lübke (2006), p. 167.

[237] Schön (1997), pp. 745–746; Spies (2015), p. 28; Ress and Ukrow (2020a), para. 10. Also Lübke (2015), para. 9, who concludes that Art 63(1) TFEU protected the expectation of return from investing funds.

country scope, the freedom of capital movement still primarily aims at completing the internal market.[238]

This primary focus of Art 63(1) TFEU is neglected by those who argue that the freedom of capital movement intends to protect all capital movement regardless of its origin, even to the effect of undermining the freedom of establishment's limited personal scope. Often, this position is further substantiated by an economic argument. As third-country capital movement contributed to a competitive and prosperous EU economy, its full protection were in the interest of the internal market's overall purpose.[239] However, the underlying economic assumption is wrong, at least for FDI. FDI does not necessarily contribute to a host state economy's growth and development.[240] Therefore, it is too simple to argue that capital import promotes the economic development in the EU, and that the *effet utile* of Art 63(1) TFEU must thus win over conflicts with the freedom of establishment.[241]

Instead, the freedom of capital movement's protection of third-country capital movement has a purpose that is different from its primary purpose focused on the internal market. Combined with the EU's goal to establish the Euro as a common currency pursuant to Art 3(4) TEU, the *erga omnes* effect of Art 63(1) TFEU intends to contribute to an internationally competitive currency. This aims at strengthening the EU as a monetary union and global financial hub.[242]

Consequently, the freedom of capital movement's purpose is more focused on completing the internal market than realizing complete liberalization of third-country capital movement.[243] This conclusion is further supported by Art

---

[238] Cf Herz (2014), pp. 335–338; Ress and Ukrow (2020a), Art 63 AEUV, paras. 11, 13, highlight the importance of Art 63(1) TFEU for the internal market.

[239] See Hindelang (2009), pp. 27–29. See also Lübke (2006), pp. 232–233, who, in Lübke (2015), para. 10, also emphasizes the additional purpose of Art 63(1) TFEU in third-country contexts that is, to strengthen the monetary union. Moreover, Spies (2015), pp. 37–39, who at the same time indicates her doubts. Herz (2014), p. 337, labels the opinion simplistic that the purpose of Art 63(1) TFEU is the effective capital allocation ('unterkomplex').

[240] See economic analysis in Sect. 2.2.

[241] Nevertheless, adopting this argument Hindelang (2009), pp. 112–113; Geiger (2013), pp. 173–176, 182. Hindelang uses this argument as the main reason to argue for a parallel applicability of Arts 49 and 63(1) TFEU.

[242] Geiger (2013), pp. 178–182; Herz (2014), pp. 342–345; Spies (2015), pp. 32–35; Ress and Ukrow (2020a), Art 63 AEUV, para. 19. In the same vein, *Skatteverket v A* (n. 229), para. 31; Joined Cases C-436 and 437/08 *Haribo Lakritzen Hans Riegel* [2010] Opinion of AG Kokott, EU:C:2010: 668, para. 110. For a presentation of minority viewpoints that see the *erga omnes* effect as a mere political goal, without creating individual rights for foreigners, see Hindelang (2009), pp. 24–27. Also highlighting the different purposes for intra-EU and third-country capital movement, Roth (2009), p. 262.

[243] Similarly, Lecheler and Germelmann (2010), p. 132. On this basis, Herz (2014), pp. 345, 358, 414–415, even argues that the limited purpose of Art 63(1) TFEU regarding third-country capital movement weighs in favour of according less protection to third-country capital movement than to intra-EU capital movement generally. Also based on this argumentation, Hertz concludes that Art 49 TFEU may override Art 63(1) TFEU in Third-country cases. However, this conclusion would transform a limited purpose of protection into no protection at all, and therefore goes too far.

64 TFEU. Arts 63 to 66 TFEU provide far more grounds of exception to restrict third-country than EU-internal capital movement.

In sum, assigning Art 63(1) TFEU a catch-all function for establishments of investors who fall outside the personal scope of Arts 49 and 54 TFEU would mean to realize the *erga omnes* effect at all costs. At the same time, the presented contextual and teleological arguments weigh in favour of a parallel applicability of Arts 49 and 63(1) TFEU to the widest extent possible.

Herz seeks to resolve this dilemma by applying a rule-exception model to the detriment of the freedom of capital movement.[244] He argues that granting Fundamental freedom protection to foreigners constitutes an exception to the rule that only EU citizens and companies enjoy Fundamental freedoms protection. Herz adds that this rule-exception model would be undermined if Art 63(1) TFEU is assigned a catch-all function in case Art 49 TFEU does personally not apply.[245] Accordingly, the freedom of establishment must override the freedom of capital movement in Third-country cases. However, this outcome significantly limits the freedom of capital movement's applicability. It thus ignores the above-discussed arguments in favour of a parallel applicability of both freedoms. They constitute the reason Herz is missing when he finds that the TFEU provided no reason for making the exception a rule.[246]

A more appropriate application of the rule-exception model that takes the conflicting interests into account is offered by a less intrusive solution. As a point of departure, the freedoms of capital movement and establishment apply parallelly. The freedom of capital movement is assigned a catch-all function even in Third-country cases.[247] Exceptionally, this parallel applicability gives way to an exclusive (non-)application of the freedom of establishment if a parallel application would *significantly undermine* the freedom of establishment's limited personal scope. It is argued that the freedom of establishment is significantly undermined by a catch-all function of Art 63(1) TFEU *if a business activity relates to the freedom's core function*. This is the only approach that reconciles the limited personal scope of Arts 49 and 54 TFEU on the one hand, and the *erga omnes* effect of Art 63(1) TFEU on the other hand.[248] On this basis, the following will develop a delimitation test.

---

[244] Herz (2014), pp. 372–390, who also presents a detailed analysis of the rule-exception-model in legal doctrine. In particular, Herz emphasizes that this model requires to first identify all possible interpretations of an exception, and then choose the interpretation that results in the exception's narrowest scope, Herz (2014), p. 392.

[245] Herz (2014), p. 402.

[246] Herz (2014), p. 407.

[247] For the definition of Non-EU Company, see Sect. 4.2.2.1.

[248] Smit (2012), pp. 478–482, submits a low-threshold delimitation criterion. The legislation would need to have a sufficient causality link to Arts 49 and 63(1) TFEU. If the legislation had such link to both, Arts 49 and 63(1) TFEU might apply parallelly. Smit denies this link only if it were too indirect or tenuous. However, this criterion is very imprecise, and fails to address the real conflict of parallel application: the limited personal scope of Arts 49 and 54 TFEU.

Developing the Delimitation Test: Applying Art 49 TFEU Exclusively According to the Delimitation Criterion 'Personal, Entrepreneurial Activity'
Before developing the delimitation test for Arts 49 and 63(1) TFEU in Third-country cases by defining the freedom of establishment's core function, it should be recalled when this delimitation test comes into play.

When assessing the Fundamental freedoms with which a legislation must comply, the delimitation test must start with identifying the situations that the legislation objectively affects.[249] As long as the legislation also affects investments that give the investor less than definite influence, the freedom of capital movement definitely applies. Insofar, the issue of delimitation does not even arise, and the legislation must comply with the freedom of capital movement. For legislation, however, that only affects investments that give the investor definite influence, the delimitation of Arts 49 and 63(1) TFEU becomes crucial.

As for the second step of the delimitation test, the above analysis showed that the freedom of establishment should, as an exception, override the freedom of capital movement only if two criteria are met. First, the investors affected by the legislation must fall outside the personal scope of the freedom of establishment. Only in such Third-country cases are the conflicting purposes between Arts 49 and 63(1) TFEU so significant that they justify an exclusive application of Art 49 TFEU. Second, the freedom of establishment must be affected in its core function.

The following will argue that the core of Art 49 TFEU is best described by legislation that intends to regulate the 'personal entrepreneurial activity' of the investor. Before, some arguments against this approach will be addressed, and the delimitation method outlined.

Criticism on the Delimitation Test

Besides those already discussed above, there are three other main arguments against exceptionally applying the freedom of establishment exclusively.[250]

First, some argue that a (personally) non-applicable Fundamental freedom could not override a personally and substantially applicable freedom.[251] Clostermeyer additionally argues that the freedom of capital movement had a catch-all function that must prevail. like Art 2(1) of the *Grundgesetz*.[252] However, such comparison lacks the basis. The Fundamental freedom function to complete the internal market is

---

[249] See introduction to ii).

[250] The following arguments are sometimes also invoked against the above-discussed exclusive applicability of Art 49 TFEU generally or in third-country contexts. As they would not have affected the above-reached outcome, these arguments are more relevant here and are thus addressed in the following.

[251] Clostermeyer (2011), pp. 217–218.

[252] Clostermeyer (2011), pp. 218–219. For the catch-all function of Art 2(1) *Grundgesetz*, see e.g. Kahl (2013), paras. 35–39.

incomparable to the nature of Fundamental rights as a defence against state action.[253] Moreover, it has been shown that the limited personal scope of Arts 49 and 54 TFEU has to be taken into account to do justice to the freedom of establishment's purpose.[254]

Second, it is argued that applying the freedom of establishment exclusively would cause a paradox: The Fundamental freedom protection should not decrease, the higher the degree of investor influence through M&A becomes.[255] Yet, there simply is no logical basis for this argument. Indeed, there are numerous reasons why more personal engagement of foreigners results in less Fundamental freedom protection.[256]

Third, oftentimes the delimitation of Arts 49 and 63(1) TFEU is rejected on the grounds of an imprecise delimitation criterion.[257] Certainly, precision and legal certainty are fundamental. However, this is no valid argument to reverse a conclusion reached by numerous interpretative means.

Having addressed these three arguments against the proposed delimitation test, the discussion now turns to developing the delimitation method and then identifying the delimitation criterion.

Delimitation Method: Assessing the Legislative Intent

The delimitation method comes into play at the second step of the delimitation test. Before, it was determined which Fundamental freedoms by definition apply to the situations that are objectively affected by the legislation at issue. A legislation may affect situations in which substantially both Arts 49 and 63(1) TFEU, but personally only Art 63(1) TFEU may apply. If so, the delimitation method helps to determine whether the freedom of establishment exceptionally overrides the freedom of capital movement.

The delimitation method cannot rely on the individual case at issue. Such an approach provides no added-value to assessing the Fundamental freedom limits to abstract legislation. Beyond the individual case, there are two possible delimitation

---

[253] See already in Sect. 4.2.2.2.

[254] Spies (2015), pp. 201–202. The ECJ reaches the same result, see n. 202.

[255] With this argument e.g. Schraufl (2007), p. 606; Geiger (2013), pp. 154–155 (both labelling this effect a paradox); Hindelang and Hagemeyer (2017), p. 885; Ress and Ukrow (2020a), para. 314. Wojcik (2015a), para. 66, also criticizes the 'odd' result of a decreasing Fundamental freedom protection with increasing investor influence. Herz (2014), p. 334, sees a more general paradox. He argues that Fundamental freedoms are directives for optimizing freedom. Herz concludes that it would be contrary to this nature if an allowed restriction of one Fundamental freedom also restricts another freedom. At least in the relation between Arts 49 and 63(1) TFEU, however, precisely this consequence is provided by Art 49(2) and 65(2) TFEU.

[256] See also Nettesheim (2008), p. 751; Roth (2009), p. 267.

[257] Against the delimitation criterion of definite influence—which would mean the exclusive applicability of Art 49 TFEU—Geiger (2013), p. 152; Lübke (2015), para. 47. On the difficulty to precisely identify the legislative intent in the realm of taxation, Schön (2015), pp. 579–580.

methods: the purpose of the legislation or of the activities objectively affected by the legislation.

Two arguments weigh against assessing the purpose of the objectively affected activities.[258] First, the purpose of the activity depends on the investor. Therefore, the purpose is difficult to assess, especially at the moment of the investment itself, even more so when dealing with abstract legislation.[259] The same conclusion is valid for an objectified purpose.[260] Second, the purpose behind an investment can change over time, with the strange result of varying applicable Fundamental freedoms.

More appropriate as delimitation method is the legislative intent. As repeatedly emphasized, the freedoms of capital movement and establishment pursue different purposes. These purposes complement each other for M&A that constitutes FDI and establishment at the same time. In other words, they address different aspects of the same business activity. Liberalizing capital movement does not equate with liberalizing establishment. The legislative intent as a delimitation method can best capture this relation between Arts 49 and 63(1) TFEU.

While legislative intent may also result in some uncertainty, the uncertainty may be limited to an acceptable degree by relying on the legislation's wording and the official explanation accompanying the legislation. At the same time, assessing a legislative intent must go beyond these formal elements to prevent that the legislator itself determines the applicable Fundamental freedom.[261]

The legislative intent is therefore the better method to delimit the freedoms of capital movement and establishment in case a legislation affects situations to which substantially both freedoms may apply, but personally only the freedom of capital movement does.

Delimitation Criterion: 'Personal, Entrepreneurial Activity'

The delimitation method must be complemented by a delimitation criterion that determines when to exceptionally apply the freedom establishment to override the freedom of capital movement. In other words, the criterion must define when the catch-all function of the freedom of capital movement should exceptionally not apply. As was concluded above, the parallel applicability of both freedoms should only give way to the freedom of establishment if the latter's core function is affected. Against this background, it is obvious to define the delimitation criterion from the perspective of the freedom of establishment. What is the freedom of establishment's core function that justifies to exceptionally deviate from the parallel applicability of

---

[258] Generally against this delimitation method Ohler (2002), Art 56 EGV, para. 120; Hindelang (2009), p. 111; Herz (2014), pp. 240–241. See also Lecheler and Germelmann (2010), p. 131. Clostermeyer (2011), p. 183, also dismisses this delimitation method in the realm of defining establishment.

[259] Herz (2014), pp. 240–241; Spies (2015), p. 230.

[260] Lübke (2015), para. 37; on real estate acquisitions, Bachlechner (1998), pp. 530–531.

[261] See i) 'Point of Departure for Delimiting Arts 49 and 63(1) TFEU'.

Arts 49 and 63(1) TFEU? In case law and literature different criteria are discussed. It will be shown that 'personal, entrepreneurial activity' is the best suited criterion.

First and foremost, the criterion 'definite influence' is not a suitable delimitation criterion. As key criterion for defining establishment within the meaning of Art 49 TFEU, it would simply result in the exclusive applicability of the freedom of establishment in all cases of M&A in Third-country cases.[262]

Some scholars propose criteria that implicitly presume a core of each Fundamental freedom without defining it. For instance, when seeking an activity's centre of gravity, one must first define where the core of Arts 49 and 63(1) TFEU lies. Otherwise, the poles for the gravity test are missing.[263] The same applies when assessing which Fundamental freedom is directly and which merely indirectly affected.[264]

In recent judgments the ECJ seems to apply the delimitation criterion of market access. If legislation intends to regulate the market access of Non-EU Companies, the freedom of establishment must override the freedom of capital movement, even though the former is personally not applicable.[265] If, on the other hand, the regulation intends to regulate Non-EU Companies after market access, the freedom of capital movement (also) applies. This latter conclusion would for example apply in the case of dividend tax measures.[266] Accordingly, the ECJ seems to see the personal market access as the core of the freedom of establishment.[267]

However, the criterion of market access is inappropriate to delimit the freedoms of capital movement and establishment for two reasons. First, it reminds one of the complex definition of the notion 'restriction' in Art 49(1) TFEU and the Fundamental freedoms generally. The ECJ defines it broadly as any 'measure liable to *hinder or make less attractive the exercise' of the freedom of establishment*. Accordingly, market access will probably be similarly defined.[268] If so, any legislation may at least indirectly also intend to regulate the market access of Non-EU Companies.[269] As a

---

[262] See introduction to this Sect. 4.2.3.3.

[263] In favour of a gravity test Cremer (2015), p. 46; Kingreen (2016), para. 30.

[264] Hindelang (2009), p. 112, sees both approaches as ultimately the same.

[265] *Test Claimants in the FII Group Litigation* [2012] (n. 163), para. 100, and subsequent judgments, see n. 202. Also Dimopoulos (2011), p. 84, who repeatedly stresses that Art 63(1) TFEU applies only to the capital movement related to the FDI, not the FDI itself. Given that the Capital Movement Directive (n. 112) explicitly defines FDI as capital movement, this statement is misleading. However, he is right in differentiating between liberalizing the capital movement and the establishment as a distinct business activity.

[266] *Test Claimants in the FII Group Litigation* [2012] (n. 163), para. 100.

[267] See also Spies (2015), pp. 222–223, who argues that sector-specific prudential regulation, business and corporate laws contain such market access rules.

[268] *Gebhard* (n. 120), para. 37.

[269] This is also demonstrated by the attempt of Spies (2015), pp. 246–247, to interpret the ECJ's case law. At last, she defines the criterion market access as the requirement of a significantly negative impact on market access ('wesentliche negative Auswirkungen auf den Marktzugang')—a very broad criterion.

result, the freedom of establishment would widely override the freedom of capital movement; a result contrary to the principle of their parallel applicability.[270] Second and more importantly, the delimitation criterion market access neglects situations after market access that include activities the freedom of establishment specifically intends to protect. For example, regulations governing the practice of professions relate to the core of the freedom of establishment, but do not govern market access. More concrete examples are requirements for the director's nationality, or for the production and workplace.

Another possible core element of the freedom of establishment vis-à-vis the freedom of capital movement may be a long-term engagement in the host country.[271] Yet, it is part of both freedoms. The Capital Movement Directive, for instance, defines FDI inter alia as serving 'to establish or to maintain *lasting* and direct links' between investor and target company.[272] In addition, simply investing funds may also have a long-term goal, especially if invested to obtain the dividends deriving from the investment.

Instead, the appropriate delimitation criterion is whether the legislation intends to regulate personal, entrepreneurial activity. The entrepreneurial[273] and personal element[274] of an investment activity describe the core element of the freedom of establishment vis-à-vis the freedom of capital movement. In contrast to Art 63(1) TFEU, Art 49 TFEU requires a stable and fixed personal integration into the host state's economy. Only this allows a person to become a market participant, and its business activity to benefit from the host state's economy.[275] The entrepreneurial element describes the actual pursuit of a business activity through an M&A transaction. The personal element highlights the individual as beneficiary of the person-related freedom of establishment in contrast to the object-related freedom of capital movement.

Accordingly, the first legislative intent that would lead to an exclusive applicability of Art 49 TFEU is to regulate risks lying in the person of the investor. The legislator must thus intend to prevent or shape the integration of a particular person into its economy. Though an indication, not every legislation that specifically addresses foreign investors will regulate risks lying in their person.[276] For example,

---

[270]This consequence causes criticism in literature of market access as delimitation criterion, see Kingreen (2016), paras. 65, 68, with further references.

[271]Spies (2015), p. 463, proposes to assess the notion 'long-term' in accordance with Council Directive 2011/96/EU of 30 November 2011 on the common system of taxation applicable in the case of parent companies and subsidiaries of different Member States [2011] OJ L 345/8, art 3(2) (b), and on this basis sets a threshold of two years.

[272]Capital Movement Directive (n. 112), Annex I.

[273]Ohler (2002), Art 56 EGV, para. 113; Schön (2015), p. 566.

[274]Similarly, Ohler (2002), Art 56 EGV, para. 119.

[275]Ohler (2002), Art 56 EGV, para. 109. Similarly, Lecheler and Germelmann (2010), p. 131, who then identify the stable integration in the host state's internal market as delimitation criterion without providing further substantiation.

[276]Nevertheless, adopting this argument Ohler (2002), Art 56 EGV, para. 119.

a notification requirement for takeover bids will primarily intend to protect the capital market, not to regulate any personal element of the bidder.[277] Similarly, capital-related market access restrictions such as regulations on the amount of capital in- and outflows have no person-related purpose. Legislation that, on the other hand, fulfils the delimitation criterion is, for instance, regulation seeking to guarantee that a company is reachable for authorities and courts, or that entrepreneurs meet basic requirements of reliability.[278] Other examples are personal market access restrictions that seek to regulate the number of market participants in a certain sector. This category also includes legislation that regulates the number of either shareholders or shares a shareholder can hold in order to ensure a sufficient level of influence for another shareholder. Typical examples for such regulation are golden share rules.

The second legislative intent that would lead to an exclusive applicability of Art 49 TFEU is regulating the entrepreneurial aspect of business activity. The point of departure for this category is that liberalizing a certain capital movement does not mean to also liberalize the underlying establishment, thus the business activity the capital movement was meant to fund. Non-EU Companies may not invoke the freedom of capital movement to invalidate legislation that intends to regulate the entrepreneurial aspect of their activity in the EU. Such entrepreneurial aspects are, for instance, regulating how to exercise a certain profession such as qualification and minimal supply requirements, or environmental and consumer protection. On the other hand, legislation that regulates a company's internal organization, in particular of corporations, does not specifically address the concrete business activity for which an establishment is undertaken, but rather how to organize a business generally. Such legislation does therefore not intend to regulate the entrepreneurial aspect of a business activity.

Consequently, the delimitation criterion 'personal, entrepreneurial activity' most appropriately describes the core of the freedom of establishment vis-à-vis the freedom of capital movement. Hence, if a legislation primarily intends to regulate the personal and/or entrepreneurial aspect of business activity, the freedom of establishment overrides the freedom of capital movement. The notion of 'primarily' refers to a gravity test. If the legislation also intends to regulate other aspects, a gravity test determines which intent is at the centre of the legislation. This test may be based on the legislation's wording and the official accompanying explanation.

4.2.3.3.3   Summarizing the Delimitation Test for Arts 49 and 63(1) TFEU

In sum, the proposed test for delimiting the freedoms of capital movement and establishment consists of three elements when assessing whether a specific legislation must comply with the freedoms of capital movement, establishment, or both.

---

[277] See e.g. German Securities Transaction Act (n. 133), ss 10–11.

[278] See e.g. German Trade, Commerce and Industry Regulation Act (Gewerbeordnung), s 35.

As a first step, one must identify the situations the legislation objectively affects. There are three categories of legislation. The first category only affects investments that give the investor less than definite influence on the target company. Hence, only the freedom of capital can apply; the issue of delimitation does thus not even arise. The second category only affects investments that give the investor definite influence on the company. Here, the delimitation test becomes crucial because, by definition, both Arts 49 and 63(1) TFEU may apply to all affected situations. Third and last, the legislation may affect situations in which, by definition, only Art 63(1) TFEU applies, as well as situations in which Arts 49 and 63(1) TFEU may apply. Thus, the legislation in parts affects situations in which the delimitation does not arise. The policy makers' flexibility to adopt such legislation is therefore limited by the freedom of capital movement anyway. Hence, the delimitation of Arts 49 and 63(1) TFEU is much less relevant.[279]

The second step departs from the understanding that, as a principle, Arts 49 and 63(1) TFEU apply parallelly. If, however, the legislation applies only to Third-country cases, meaning investors who are excluded from the personal scope of the freedom of establishment, Non-EU Companies, Non-EU Established SPVs, foreign states, and/or foreign public undertakings,[280] the freedom of capital movement may exceptionally give way to the personally non-applicable freedom of establishment.

As a third step, one then looks at the legislative intent (delimitation method). If the legislation intends to regulate the personal and/or entrepreneurial aspect of a Non-EU Company's business activity, the freedom of capital movement is overridden by the freedom of establishment. Hence, neither the freedom of capital movement, nor the personally inapplicable freedom of establishment apply. As a result, the policy maker's flexibility to adopt the legislation is not limited by the Fundamental freedoms.

4.2.3.4 The Non-Investor Perspective: Jeopardizing the Delimitation Test?

Before applying the developed delimitation test to FDI Screening mechanisms, one last aspect must be considered. So far, the discussion focused on the investor's perspective on the FDI transaction. This perspective was also the basis to conclude that the delimitation of the freedoms of capital movement and establishment becomes crucial in only one of three possible legislation categories: if the legislation exclusively applies to investments that give the investor definite influence on the target company. In this case, the legislation exclusively addresses situations in which, by definition, both the freedoms of capital movement and establishment may apply. If, in Third-country cases, the freedom of establishment overrides the freedom of capital movement, no Fundamental freedom applies.

---

[279] It remains relevant when applying the legislation, cf n. 105.

[280] For their definition see Sect. 4.2.2.4.

When now taking the non-investor perspective, the conclusion might be different. Often, in case of M&A, investors acquire their shareholding from different shareholders who individually possess shareholdings that give them less than definite influence on the target company. Thus, even if an investor in sum acquires a shareholding that gives definite influence on the target company, at the individual transaction level the shareholdings will often not qualify as establishment. Thus, one might argue that the legislation does in fact not exclusively apply to investments that give the investor definite influence on the company. Accordingly, taking the non-investor perspective, the sellers' freedom of capital movement would apply anyway, and delimiting Arts 49 and 63(1) TFEU loses relevance.[281]

However, the single transactions must be seen as one integrated investor transaction for setting up an establishment. Otherwise, one M&A establishment would often not constitute an establishment pursuant to Art 49 TFEU, but consist of several capital movements within the meaning of Art 63(1) TFEU. If so, the limited personal scope of the freedom of establishment loses any effect. This would significantly undermine Arts 49 and 54 TFEU. Therefore, the investor's perspective must prevail over the seller's perspective.

This restriction of the sellers' freedom of capital movement is acceptable for two reasons. First, the consequences are limited to cases in which the core of the freedom of establishment is affected. As shown above, the freedom of establishment only overrides the freedom of capital movement in Third-country cases and if the legislation at issue intends to regulate the investor's personal, entrepreneurial activity. In all other cases, the freedoms of capital movement and establishment apply parallelly, and the seller remains protected by Art 63(1) TFEU.

Second, as stressed several times, the Fundamental freedoms' nature as subjective rights is only a means to complete internal market.[282] Therefore, restricting the sellers' freedom of capital movement is acceptable in the interest of other internal market interests. Accordingly, the interest to limit the establishment of investors who are excluded from the personal scope of the freedom of establishment may override the freedom of capital movement in case the core of the freedom of establishment is affected.

With the same arguments, one may neglect the freedom of capital movement of other shareholders or potential investors that are not involved in the transaction, but may be affected; for example, by in- or decreasing shareholding values.[283]

Last but not least, one may also adopt the seller's perspective to assess the freedom of establishment's personal scope. Accordingly, the freedom of establishment could apply because the seller, in contrast to the investor, falls in the personal scope. However, it was argued in Sect. 4.2.2.3 that the freedom of establishment, in

---

[281] The sellers' disinvestment is also protected by the freedom of capital movement Sect. 4.2.2.3. This even applies if the investor is a foreign State or foreign public undertaking, and as such excluded from the personal scope of Art 63(1) TFEU.

[282] For this argument see in particular Sect. 4.2.2.3.

[283] Lübke (2015), para. 45.

contrast to the freedom of capital movement, does not provide such indirect protection to investors that are personally excluded from its scope. If an establishment transaction involves a personally excluded investor, the entire transaction is excluded from the freedom of establishment's scope. Hence, the non-investor perspective on the freedom of establishment has no consequence.

In sum, the non-investor perspective can thus not change the above developed test to delimit the freedoms of capital movement and establishment.

4.2.3.5 Arts 49 and 63(1) TFEU: Widely Overlapping Substantial Scopes for FDI, Exclusive Applicability of Art 49 TFEU in Third-Country Cases

This section has shown that the substantial scopes of the freedoms of capital movement and establishment widely overlap, and that both freedoms apply parallelly, with an exception in Third-country cases.

The freedom of capital movement applies to all FDI, while the freedom of establishment in case of M&A FDI only applies if the investor obtains definite influence on the FDI target. The notion of definite influence is narrower than the FDI notion 'possibility to participate effectively in a company's management or control'. Therefore, every establishment in the form of M&A constitutes capital movement within the meaning of Art 63(1) TFEU; but not every M&A FDI constitutes an establishment within the meaning of Art 49 TFEU.[284]

If a specific investment qualifies as capital movement and establishment, as a principle, both the freedoms of capital movement and establishment apply. However, as an exception, the freedom of capital movement does not apply to a measure if (i) the investor in Third-country cases is excluded from the freedom of establishment's personal scope and (ii) the legislation on which the measure is based primarily intends to regulate the personal, entrepreneurial activity behind an investment.

When abstractly assessing which Fundamental freedom applies to a legislation, one must first identify the situations to which the legislation objectively applies. To the extent the legislation applies to investments that only qualify as capital movement, but not as establishment, the issue of delimiting both freedoms does not arise. By definition, the freedom of establishment does not apply. Hence, such legislation must always comply with the freedom of capital movement, regardless of the delimitation test and the legislation's intent.

---

[284] With the rare exception of cases in which the establishment requires no cross-border capital movement.

4.2.4 Applying the Findings to FDI Screening Mechanisms: Two Policy Options

The analysis of the freedoms of capital movement and establishment's personal and substantial scopes showed that the EU's flexibility to adopt FDI Screening mechanisms on broader grounds than 'security or public order' pursuant to EU primary law depends on the mechanisms' personal and substantial scope.

Section 4.2.2 concluded that an FDI Screening mechanism only falls outside the personal scope of the freedom of establishment if it exclusively applies to Non-EU Companies, Non-EU Established SPVs, foreign States, and/or foreign public undertakings (together referred to as Third-country cases). Nevertheless, such mechanism still needs to comply with the freedom of capital movement, since any foreign investor falls at least indirectly in its personal scope. As a result, an FDI Screening mechanism may only avoid limitations of both Fundamental freedoms if the freedom of capital movement does substantially not apply.

Section 4.2.3 demonstrated that whether an FDI Screening mechanism falls in the substantial scopes of the freedoms of capital movement and establishment, again, depends on the investors and investments the mechanism covers. If the FDI Screening mechanism applies to FDI generally, and thus also affects FDI that *does not give* the investor definite influence on the FDI target, the freedom of capital movement always applies substantially. Hence, the FDI Screening mechanism must comply at least with the freedom of capital movement.

A different conclusion may only be reached if the FDI Screening mechanism exclusively applies to FDI that *does give* the investor definite influence on the FDI target. This depends on the above developed delimitation test. As a point of departure, the FDI Screening mechanism must meet two criteria. First, substantially, the FDI Screening mechanism must only apply to M&A FDI that gives the investor definite influence. Second, personally, they must only apply to Third-country cases, in other words FDI by investors who are personally excluded from the freedom of establishment's personal scope, namely Non-EU Companies and/or Non-EU Established SPVs. Accordingly, the FDI Screening mechanism would apply only to cases in which by definition substantially both, but personally only the freedom of capital movement applies.

Following the delimitation test, the freedom of capital movement would be overridden by the freedom of establishment if the FDI Screening mechanism intends to regulate the investor's personal, entrepreneurial activity. FDI Screening mechanisms fulfil this condition. They intend to regulate risks deriving from the investors' conduct, aims, and their relations to home country governments. The mechanisms thus seek to prevent risks posed by the investor as a person. As a result, an FDI Screening mechanism that meets the two design criteria is not limited by the freedoms of capital movement and establishment.

Consequently, the EU has two policy options for designing an FDI Screening mechanism that goes beyond the screening ground 'security or public order'.

First, the FDI Screening mechanism may be limited to FDI that gives the investor definite influence on the FDI target, and to Non-EU Companies, Non-EU Established SPVs, foreign States, and/or foreign public undertakings. The personal limitation still allows the EU to screen FDI in the two most typical FDI scenarios: Non-EU Companies and Non-EU Established SPVs. The substantial limitation, however, results in serious shortcomings to meet the EU and Member States concerns vis-à-vis foreign investors. The EU and Member States are also concerned about investors who obtain less than definite influence on the FDI target—namely, with respect to the harmful investor and private information concern. The possibility to actively participate in the management and control of a domestic asset suffices. Limiting FDI Screening mechanisms to FDI that gives the investor definite influence on the domestic asset will not meet these concerns.

Even if the EU settled with limiting the FDI Screening mechanism to cases of establishment, it would be difficult to cast the distinction between FDI and establishment into law. A universal numerical threshold for definite influence shareholdings is lacking. A solution might be to adopt the abstract definition of definite influence as benchmark, combining it with a statutory rebuttable assumption that M&As fulfil this requirement if they lead to a shareholding of above 25% of shares.

Nevertheless, the EU might accept the shortcomings of this first policy option if this allows to more broadly and precisely define a screening ground that meets the EU and Member States concerns vis-à-vis foreign investors.

As a second option, the EU may design the FDI Screening mechanism in a way that all groups of FDI and foreign investors are included. Thus, the EU and Member States concerns vis-à-vis foreign investors would be entirely covered. As this option includes all groups of FDI, the freedom of capital movement applies. Further including all groups of foreign investors, not only investors who are personally excluded from the freedom of establishment, also means that the freedom of establishment applies. Hence, a so designed FDI Screening mechanism must comply with the freedoms of capital movement and the freedom of establishment. As a result, the EU's flexibility to adopt a screening ground beyond 'security or public order' depends on the available grounds of exception. Chapter 3 has already shown that the grounds of 'public policy or public security' pursuant to Art 65(1)(b) TFEU are insufficient to meet the EU and Member States concerns vis-à-vis foreign investors. However, the most relevant ground of exception remains: Art 64(2) and (3) TFEU. Pursuant to Art 49(2) TFEU it also applies to the freedom of establishment.

4.2.5   Art 64(2) and (3) TFEU: Wide Substantial Flexibility to Regulate FDI with High Procedural Hurdles

If the freedoms of capital movement and establishment apply to an FDI Screening mechanism, the EU's flexibility to adopt a broader screening ground than 'security or public order' is determined by the scope of Art 64(2) and (3) TFEU. Art 64 TFEU provides a ground of exception to restrict certain 'movement of capital to or from third countries'. Pursuant to Art 49(2) TFEU, this ground of exception justifies a restriction of not only the freedom of capital movement, but also the freedom of establishment.[285]

The relevant passages of Art 64(2) and (3) TFEU for justifying an FDI Screening mechanism read as follows:

(2) Whilst endeavouring to achieve the objective of free movement of capital between Member States and third countries to the greatest extent possible and without prejudice to the other Chapters of the Treaties, the European Parliament and the Council, acting in accordance with the ordinary legislative procedure, shall adopt the measures on the movement of capital to or from third countries involving direct investment . . . establishment . . .

(3) Notwithstanding paragraph 2, only the Council, acting in accordance with a special legislative procedure, may unanimously, and after consulting the European Parliament, adopt measures which constitute a step backwards in Union law as regards the liberalisation [*sic*] of the movement of capital to or from third countries.

Accordingly, Art 64(2) and (3) TFEU provide grounds of exception to the *erga omnes* effect of the freedom of capital movement in certain policy areas—namely, third-country FDI and establishment within the meaning of Art 49 TFEU.[286] However, the grounds of exception are only available to EU, not Member States measures. If the measures constitute 'a step backwards in Union law', they must be adopted in a special legislative procedure, unanimously by the Council after consulting the Parliament. This constitutes a high procedural hurdle.[287]

The following will first define the term 'movement of capital to or from third countries', which determines the scope of Art 64(2) and (3) TFEU. It will then argue that substantially Art 64(2) and (3) TFEU provide the EU with wide flexibility to adopt measures on third-country FDI and establishment. In particular, the ground of exception reaches beyond the measures allowed by the grandfathering clause in Art 64(1) TFEU. Third, the discussion will turn to defining the term 'a step backwards in Union law', determining when the high procedural hurdle of Art 64(3) TFEU

---

[285] See Sect. 4.2.3.3.2 'The principle'.

[286] On the congruency between the term establishment in Art 64(2) TFEU and Art 49 TFEU see n. 168.

[287] The nearly identical, predecessor provision Art 57(2) EC served e.g. as a legal basis for Council Decision 2008/801/EC of 25 September 2008 on the conclusion, on behalf of the European Community, of the United Nations Convention against Corruption [2008] OJ L 287/1, as well as several conclusions on the EU's Neighbourhood policy, see with further examples Bröhmer (2011), Art 64 AEUV, fn. 23.

applies. Fourth and last, these general conclusions will be applied to FDI Screening mechanisms to determine the EU's flexibility for their adoption.

4.2.5.1 'Movement of Capital to or from Third Countries'—What Is Third-Country Capital Movement?

While the freedom of capital movement generally applies regardless of the capital's and investor's origin, its grounds of exception indeed draw a line between intra-EU and third-country capital movement.[288] Art 64 TFEU only applies to 'movement of capital to or from third countries' involving FDI, establishment, financial services, and securities. But when does capital moves to or from third countries? In other words: What is third-country capital movement? It will be shown that this definition is different from the definition of Third-country cases as defined above in accordance with the definition of foreignness pursuant to Arts 49 and 54 TFEU. The freedoms of capital movement and establishment define foreignness differently.

As a point of departure, the nature of the freedom of capital movement and the wording 'move' weigh in favour of tracing the actual capital flows to determine the capital's foreignness. Accordingly, third-country capital movement would require that the object capital crosses the border between a third country and the EU. However, it is impossible to trace the capital until its origins, since the capital movement FDI, for example, consists of many different forms of capital, including loans, securities, and physical capital. Instead, the capital's origin and destination must be approximated through another criterion: the persons who exchange the capital.

For natural persons, this criterion is relatively easy to substantiate. Their place of residency must decide. The person's location is likely to be the location where the capital is coming from.[289]

For juridical persons and companies, however, the assessment is more complex. First, it is unclear how to define a company's residence. The notion EU Company as defined in Art 54(1) TFEU represents a company's nationality, not residency.[290] Second, coming from the rationale to trace down the capital to its origins, it would be overly simplistic to merely assessing the company that is acting as transaction party. This becomes particularly evident when considering large company networks that often use SPVs to undertake FDI and other forms of capital movement. Therefore, the capital's origin and destination are determined by the persons who control the company.[291]

---

[288] The other grounds of exception for third-country capital movement are Arts 65(4) and 66 TFEU.

[289] See also OECD, 'Benchmark Definition of Foreign Direct Investment' (Paris, 2008), para. 117. See also Lübke (2006), p. 277.

[290] For definition of EU Company within the meaning of Art 54(1) TFEU, see Sect. 4.2.2.1.2.

[291] The OECD defines SPVs as residents, but also includes the controlling entities in the FDI relationship, see OECD, 'Benchmark Definition of Foreign Direct Investment' (n. 289), para. 315.

This is in line with the object and purpose of Art 64 TFEU. The ground of exception was inter alia intended to preserve the EU's and its Member States' flexibility for third-country capital movement restrictions in three areas.[292] First, Member States and EU wanted to maintain reservations they had undertaken in multi- and plurilateral capital movement agreements, especially the OECD Code of Liberalization of Capital Movements ('OECD Code of Capital Movements'). Under the OECD Code of Capital Movements, Germany and France, for instance, reserved ownership requirements in the air and maritime transport sector. Second, even beyond these reservations, the EU and its Member States wanted to—and did— maintain certain ownership requirements, in particular in the air and maritime transport, and energy sector.[293] Both ownership requirements look at the controlling persons. Last but not least, the EU wanted third to keep the flexibility to only liberalize third-country capital movement to the extent third countries liberalize their capital markets. Such reciprocity requirements are also often based on the foreign ownership or control of companies.

For fulfilling this purpose, Art 64 TFEU must define third-country capital movement based on the persons who control it. Otherwise, the above-listed measures could not be justified. This can be shown by an example: If applying Art 54(1) TFEU as the rule to determine the capital movement's origin, the transaction parties' registered office, central administration, or principal place of business would decide over their third-country definition. Accordingly, if an EU SPV fully acquires an EU airline, the transaction would remain intra-EU capital movement—even if owned and controlled by foreign nationals. Hence, Art 64 TFEU would not apply. However, it is exactly the banning or screening of transactions like these in accordance with ownership requirements that Art 64 TFEU was supposed to allow.

Therefore, Art 64 TFEU must define third-country capital movement with regards to companies by referring to the controlling persons.[294] In accordance with the definition for natural persons, the controlling person's residence not nationality decides.

For an indication of how to define the notion of 'control' reference may be made to the definition of *Foreign* Direct investment in this book in accordance with Directive 2009/73/EC, art 2(36), on the internal market in natural gas:

> '[C]ontrol' means any rights, contracts or any other means which, either separately or in combination and having regard to the considerations of fact or law involved, confer the possibility of exercising decisive influence on an undertaking, in particular by

---

[292]For the following three aspects see Bakker (1996), pp. 233–234, 246–247; Smit (2012), pp. 645–648.

[293]See summary in Commission (2003), pp. 325–326.

[294]*Contra* Hindelang (2009), p. 78. He argues that the definition of third-country capital movement based on foreign control would introduce 'the theory of seeking to determine the nationality of a company by the nationality of its shareholders' 'by the backdoor' (Hindelang (2009), p. 77, n. 188). This argument is flawed. It is derived from Art 54(1) TFEU, which rejects such control theory to define EU Companies. Art 64 TFEU, however, applies the control theory to identify capital from third countries. The rationales behind both definitions are thus different.

(a) ownership or the right to use all or part of the assets of an undertaking; or
(b) rights or contracts which confer decisive influence on the composition, voting or decisions of the organs of an undertaking.[295]

Consequently, third-country capital movement within the meaning of Art 64(2) and (3) TFEU means that one of the transaction parties at issue, if natural persons, is a resident in a third country, if companies, is controlled by a resident in a third country.

4.2.5.2   No Significant Substantial Limits

The grounds of exception in Art 64(2) and (3) TFEU seem to pose no additional substantial limits to the EU's flexibility to regulate third-country capital movement as long as the measures relate to FDI, establishment, financial services, and securities. There are, however, two aspects that require closer attention: the relation of Art 64(2) and (3) TFEU to Art 64(1) TFEU, and the possible substantial limits posed by a proportionality requirement.

4.2.5.2.1   Art 64(2) and (3) TFEU Limited to Grandfathered Measures Pursuant to Art 64(1) TFEU?

Some scholars submit that the substantial scope of Art 64(2) and (3) TFEU is significantly narrowed by its reference to Art 64(1) TFEU. Accordingly, Art 64(2) and (3) TFEU only allowed the EU to adopt measures in policy areas that were already addressed by EU or Member States measures in accordance with Art 64(1) TFEU.[296] The grandfathering clause in Art 64(1) TFEU allows the EU and its Member States to maintain certain restrictions on foreign capital movement that existed on 31 December 1993, or in the case of Bulgaria, Estonia, and Hungary on 31 December 1999:

> The provisions of Article 63 shall be without prejudice to the application to third countries of any restrictions which exist on 31 December 1993 under national or Union law adopted in respect of the movement of capital to or from third countries involving direct investment . . . establishment . . . In respect of restrictions existing under national law in Bulgaria, Estonia and Hungary, the relevant date shall be 31 December 1999.

For supporting their proposal on a narrow scope of Art 64(2) and (3) TFEU, the scholars quote *Skatteverket v A*, in which the ECJ held:

> Article 57(2) EC must be read in conjunction with Article 57(1) and simply permits the Council to adopt measures on those categories of capital movements and the national or

---

[295] See Sect. 2.4.2.

[296] Puig (2013), p. 152; Herrmann (2019), pp. 462–463. In both cases, however, the scholars discuss Art 64(2) and (3) TFEU in their capacity as possible competence basis in contrast to Art 207(1) and (2) TFEU. Herrmann and Puig might come to different conclusions for the substantial scope of Art 64(2) and (3) TFEU as grounds of exception to the *erga omnes* effect of Art 63(1) TFEU.

Community restrictions for which paragraph 1 expressly provides cannot be relied on against the Council.[297]

However, these scholars misinterpret the judgment. The ECJ only held that Art 64(2) and (3) TFEU do not generally carve out third-country FDI, establishment, and the other addressed capital movements from the prohibition in Art 63(1) TFEU. The Member States cannot invoke their individual measures in accordance with Art 64(1) TFEU against EU measures pursuant to Art 64(2) and (3) TFEU to justify their own new measures.[298] Instead, Art 64(2) TFEU must be read in conjunction with Art 64(1) TFEU to conclude that beyond the grandfathered measures pursuant to Art 64(1) TFEU the addressed categories of third-country capital movement may be restricted by the EU only.

While the literal meaning of Art 64(2) and (3) TFEU fails to offer any further arguments; context, and object and purpose weigh against a narrow, standstill reading of Art 64(2) and (3) TFEU.

If the EU were to adopt new measures only to the extent of the grandfathered EU and Member State measures pursuant to Art 64(1) TFEU, the EU's ground of exception would depend on individual Member State choices—choices made before 1993. First, it is improbable that the scope of a ground of exception for the EU is determined by individual, uncoordinated Member State decisions. Second, the ground of exception would be significantly limited if the EU's scope of action were limited to policy areas that were relevant before 1993. Types of and risks by third-country capital movement are evolving over time. The EU's flexibility provided by Art 64(2) and (3) TFEU would therefore become increasingly irrelevant.

Moreover, the object and purpose of Art 64(2) and (3) TFEU, aside Arts 65(4) and 66 TFEU, is to provide the EU with the necessary leverage in international negotiations to further liberalize capital movement at the global level. As the EU liberalized its internal market for foreign capital unilaterally, other states may lack incentives to offer the same treatment to EU capital. The EU may recreate such incentives by adopting third-country capital restrictions to later reduce them in exchange for a globally higher level of capital movement liberalization. A narrow standstill reading of Art 64(2) and (3) could not deliver on this purpose.[299]

---

[297] *Skatteverket v A* (n. 229), para. 34.

[298] This becomes much clearer when reading the French and German version of ibid. The French version reads: 'En effet, le paragraphe 2 de l'article 57 CE doit être lu en combinaison avec le paragraphe 1 du même article et se limite à permettre au Conseil d'adopter des mesures relatives auxdites catégories de mouvements de capitaux, sans que les restrictions nationales ou communautaires dont le maintien est explicitement prévu par ce paragraphe 1 puissent lui être opposées.' The judgment's German version provides: 'Art 57 Abs. 2 EG ist nämlich in Verbindung mit Abs. 1 dieses Artikels zu lesen und beschränkt sich darauf, dem Rat zu erlauben, Maßnahmen für diese Kategorien von Kapitalbewegungen zu beschließen, ohne dass ihm die einzelstaatlichen oder gemeinschaftlichen Beschränkungen, deren Beibehaltung in diesem Abs. 1 ausdrücklich vorgesehen ist, entgegengehalten werden könnten.'

[299] Similarly, Korte (2019), p. 126. See also Wojcik (2015b), para. 15; Bröhmer (2016b), para. 9; Ress and Ukrow (2020b), paras. 4, 22. Arguably also Hindelang (2009), p. 300.

Consequently, Art 64(2) and (3) TFEU provide the EU with a ground of exception to Art 63(1) TFEU without additional limits, in particular for measures on third-country FDI and establishment. The EU may thus widely deviate from the prohibition of Art 63(1) TFEU in third-country contexts.[300] The only other substantial limit that the EU may then be confronted with is the principle of proportionality.[301]

4.2.5.2.2   Proportionality Requirement as a Substantial Limit to Art 64(2) and (3) TFEU?

A proportionality test would considerably constrain the EU's flexibility to regulate foreign capital movement in the forms of FDI, establishment, financial services, and securities. To start with, one must differentiate between two types of proportionality tests. On the one hand, a proportionality test may aim at balancing the public interest behind an EU measure against individual rights and interests, for example of foreign investors and EU target companies (individual interest proportionality test). On the other hand, another type of proportionality test, as similarly provided for by the subsidiarity principle pursuant to Art 5(3) TEU, intends to maintain the competence distribution between EU and Member States (competence proportionality test). Art 64(2) and (3) only incorporate a competence proportionality test.

Pursuant to Art 64(2) TFEU, the EU shall adopt measures on third-country capital movement 'without prejudice to the other Chapters of the Treaties'. Among others, this phrase references the principle of proportionality in Art 5(4) TEU. This provision requires a competence proportionality test.[302] The EU measure 'shall not exceed what is necessary to achieve the objectives of the Treaties', by content and form. Accordingly, the EU's measure adopted pursuant to Art 64(2) and (3) TFEU must be proportionate in relation to the Member States' interest to regulate foreign capital movement nationally. For instance, if a *directive* for *FDI* Screening mechanisms in the energy sector is sufficient to protect the EU's interest of energy security, the EU shall not instead adopt a cross-sector FDI screening *regulation*. The ECJ grants the EU legislator broad discretion for its competence proportionality assess-

---

[300] This is the predominant opinion in literature, see Smit (2012), pp. 787–788; Wojcik (2015b), para. 1; Schön (2016), p. 233; Bröhmer (2016b), para. 3; Sedlaczek and Züger (2018), para. 7; Korte (2019), p. 126; Cremona (2020), pp. 37–38; Ress and Ukrow (2020b), paras. 4–5.

[301] Similarly, Art 64(2) and (3) TFEU reference the principle of subsidiarity pursuant to Art 5(3) TEU when providing 'without prejudice to the other Chapters of the Treaties'. However, at least in the realm of regulating FDI, the subsidiarity principle does not apply. The EU has the exclusive competence pursuant to Art 207(2) TFEU anyway (see Sect. 4.1). Pursuant to Art 5(3) TEU, the subsidiarity principle is limited to 'areas which do not fall within [the EU's] exclusive competence'.

[302] Streinz (2018), para. 44; Bast (2020), para. 67.

ment.[303] Hence, the threshold for meeting the competence proportionality test in Art 64(2) and (3) TFEU is low.

On the other hand, Art 64(2) and (3) TFEU do not incorporate an individual interest proportionality test that weighs the EU measure against individual rights and interests.[304] First, such test does not follow from the referenced Art 5(4) TEU. As argued above, this provision is limited to a competence proportionality test.[305] Second, the phrase 'whilst endeavouring to achieve the objective of free movement of capital between Member States and third countries to the greatest extent possible' is only a political, programmatic call on EU legislators. It is not a substantial legal limit to the ground of exception in the form of an individual interest proportionality test.[306] Third, given the lack of any hint in the wording of Art 64(2) and (3) TFEU, one may not otherwise read an individual interest proportionality test into Art 64(2) and (3) TFEU.[307]

Besides, there is no need for artificially reading the individual interest proportionality test into Art 64(2) and (3) TFEU or referring to it as a general principle of EU law. Since the adoption of the Lisbon Treaty, an individual interest proportionality test usually applies as a consequence of the Fundamental right protection pursuant to the CFR.[308] Freedoms like the freedoms to choose an occupation and to conduct a business (Arts 15(1), 16 CFR), the right to property (Art 17 CFR) and to non-discrimination (Arts 20, 21(2) CFR) all provide a minimum level of protection—also to foreign investors. Accordingly, the ECJ transposed its case law on the individual interest proportionality test as a general principle of EU law into the assessment of the Fundamental rights.[309]

Indeed, incorporating the individual interest proportionality test into the Fundamental rights assessment is even legally required. Only against the background of the concrete Fundamental right(s) at issue will the proportionality test be applied appropriately. While the ECJ usually applied a highly deferential proportionality

---

[303] Generally, the ECJ grants the EU legislator 'broad discretion' when determining the proportionality of exercising its competence through legislation. Hence, the ECJ only reviews decisions for 'manifest errors', see e.g. Case C-358/14 *Poland v Parliament and Council* [2016] EU:C:2016: 323, paras. 78–79; Case C-643/15 *Slovakia v Council* [2017] EU:C:2017:631, paras. 123–124, 245–246.

[304] See also Hindelang (2009), pp. 303–304.

[305] Streinz (2018), para. 44; Bast (2020), para. 67. Nevertheless, Wojcik (2015b), para. 21, reads a proportionality test into the reference to Art 5(4) TEU that weighs the public interests behind the EU measure against individual interests and the general interest of capital liberalization.

[306] Sedlaczek and Züger (2018), para. 23.

[307] *Contra* Ress and Ukrow (2020b), para. 26, who argue that even though Art 64(2) and (3) TFEU lack the term 'requisite' as in Art 65(1)(b) TFEU, the proportionality principle must apply.

[308] Streinz (2018), para. 44; Bast (2020), para. 68.

[309] See e.g. Joined Cases C-92 and 93/09 *Volker and Markus Schecke and Eifert* [2010] EU:C:2010: 662, paras. 45–46, 74; Joined Cases C-293 and 594/12 *Digital Rights Ireland and Seitlinger and Others* [2014] EU:C:2014:238, para. 46. For case law before the CFR had gained explicit legally binding status, see e.g. Joined Cases C-453/03, 11, 12, and 194/04 *ABNA and Others* [2005] EU: C:2005:741, paras. 67–68.

test when referring to the general principle of EU law, it significantly tightened its review when Fundamental rights were at stake. For example, in *Digital Rights Ireland and Seitlinger and Others*, the ECJ held

> where interferences with fundamental rights are at issue, the extent of the EU legislature's discretion may prove to be limited, depending on a number of factors, including, in particular, the area concerned, the nature of the right at issue guaranteed by the Charter, the nature and seriousness of the interference and the object pursued by the interference.[310]

Only in the unlikely case in which no Fundamental right applies will the general principle of proportionality step in.[311]

Therefore, Art 64(2) and (3) TFEU only incorporate a competence proportionality test pursuant to Art 5(4) TFEU. The 'gap' of an individual interest proportionality test weighing the EU measure against individual rights is filled by the Fundamental rights granted by the CFR. Such an individual interest proportionality test does thus not follow from Art 64(2) and (3), and hence poses no substantial limit to their grounds of exception.

In sum, the grounds of exception in Art 64(2) and (3) TFEU therefore pose no significant substantial limits, neither through its relation to Art 64(1) TFEU, nor by an in-depth proportionality test.

4.2.5.3   Procedural Limits for Measures 'Which Constitute a Step Backwards' in Liberalization

Nevertheless, Art 64(2) and (3) TFEU may, depending on the EU measure at issue, pose significant procedural limits for restricting foreign capital movement.

As a principle, EU measures restricting foreign capital movement in the form of FDI, establishment, financial services, and securities shall be taken in accordance with the ordinary legislative procedure pursuant to Art 294 TFEU. This requires inter alia the qualified majorities of Council and Parliament (Art 64(2) TFEU). In case of a step backwards in the liberalization of third-country capital movement, a special legislative procedure applies instead (Arts 289 (2), 297 (1) TFEU). The Council must adopt the measure unanimously after consulting the Parliament (Art 64(3) TFEU). If FDI Screening mechanisms constitute a step backwards in liberalization, the EU would hence face a significant procedural hurdle for their adoption.

As a starting point, only EU law can determine the benchmark for assessing whether a measure constitutes a step backwards in relation to the prior degree of

---

[310] *Digital Rights Ireland and Seitlinger and Others* (n. 309), para. 74. See also Case C-508/13 *Estonia v Parliament and Council* [2015] EU:C:2015:403, paras. 28–40.

[311] Bast (2020), para. 68.

capital movement liberalization.[312] This follows from the wording of Art 64(3) TFEU 'a step backwards in Union law' as opposed to 'national or Union law' referred to by Art 64(1) TFEU.[313] Moreover, it would be difficult to determine the benchmark of liberalization through Member State rules (liberalization level in one, the majority, or in nearly all Member States).

Consequently, a step backwards in liberalization requires an assessment of the planned EU measure's effect on the liberalization of third-country capital movement achieved through EU law. Ress and Ukrow rightly depart from the understanding that a direct or indirect, factual or potential effect suffices to find a step backwards in liberalization.[314] But the question remains: What exactly is the benchmark for determining the step backwards: primary and secondary, or only secondary law?

Hindelang argues for the former. Accordingly, the benchmark for a step backwards in foreign capital movement liberalization is the level achieved through Arts 63(1) and 64 TFEU, hence the complete liberalization of capital movement.[315] Accordingly, any new EU measure that does not exclusively promote trade would constitute a step backwards in liberalization, and would thus fall under Art 64(3) TFEU.[316]

The predominant opinion in literature, on the other hand, only takes secondary law into account, leaving the principle of complete liberalization in Art 63(1) TFEU and Member States rules aside.[317] As a consequence, if a secondary law benchmark is missing, there is no step backwards in liberalization, and Art 64(2) TFEU applies.[318]

The better arguments weigh in favour of secondary law as benchmark. In opposition to Hindelang's argument, the literal meaning of the phrase 'a step backwards in Union law' in Art 64(3) TFEU does not necessarily reference secondary and primary law, namely Art 63(1) TFEU.[319] Instead, the literal meaning of Art 64(3) TFEU is also open to the interpretation that 'Union law' only references secondary law.

This second reading is strongly supported by a contextual argument. Reading Art 64(3) TFEU as also referencing primary law and thus Art 63(1) TFEU significantly narrows the scope of Art 64(2) TFEU. Compared to the complete liberalization of

---

[312]This seems to be consensus in literature, see Ohler (2002), Art 57 EGV, para. 22; Hindelang (2009), pp. 300–301; Sedlaczek and Züger (2018), para. 20; Korte (2019), p. 127.

[313]Ohler (2002), Art 57 EGV, para. 22; Hindelang (2009), pp. 300–301.

[314]Ress and Ukrow (2020b), para. 24. Agreeing Hindelang (2009), p. 300; Sedlaczek and Züger (2018), para. 20.

[315]Hindelang (2009), pp. 300–301, n. 174. Similarly, Günther (2018), p. 20.

[316]Some authors may at least allow measures that harmonize grandfathered Member State restrictions Korte (2019), p. 129, sees the harmonization of grandfathered Member State restrictions as the prime example for Art 64(2) TFEU.

[317]Sedlaczek and Züger (2018), para. 20; Korte (2019), p. 127. Implied by Ohler (2002), Art 57 EGV, para. 22.

[318]Ohler (2002), Art 57 EGV, para. 22; Sedlaczek and Züger (2018), para. 20.

[319]Hindelang (2009), pp. 300–301.

foreign capital movement through Art 63(1) TFEU any measure that does not exclusively promote trade constitutes a step backwards. Hence, Art 64(3) TFEU, normatively the exception to Art 64(2) TFEU, would in fact become the norm.[320] Hence, the EU would, as a norm, need to adopt third-country capital movement restrictions by unanimity in the Council after mere consultation of the Parliament—a severe deviation from the ordinary legislative procedure pursuant to Art 294 TFEU.

To avoid this result, one must read the term 'a step backwards in Union law' as setting only EU secondary law as the benchmark. Thus, if there is no secondary law in a certain policy area, a new EU measure cannot constitute a step backwards in the liberalization of foreign capital movement. In these cases Art 64(2) TFEU and the ordinary legislative procedure pursuant to Art 294 TFEU apply. In case of a step backwards in liberalization, however, Art 64(3) TFEU and its special legislative procedure apply.

4.2.5.4   Consequences for FDI Screening Mechanisms: Additional Flexibility with Limitations

With these general conclusions in mind, the discussion can now turn to the concrete case of FDI Screening mechanisms. While substantial limits deriving from Art 64(2) and (3) TFEU are negligible, the procedural limits the EU may face when adopting FDI Screening mechanisms are high. In addition, if FDI Screening mechanisms are to be justified by Art 64(2) and (3) TFEU, its scope provides important design implications.

It was shown that from a substantial perspective, even if the freedom of capital movement and the freedom of establishment apply, the EU has wide flexibility to adopt FDI Screening mechanisms beyond 'security or public order' within the meaning of the Screening Regulation. Most importantly, the competence proportionality test required by Art 5(4) TEU does not pose any considerable limits to broader FDI Screening mechanisms, by directive or regulation.

From a procedural perspective, however, the EU faces much higher hurdles. Certainly, as a principle, the EU must adopt foreign capital movement restricting measures in accordance with the ordinary legislative procedures pursuant to Art 294 TFEU. But a new FDI Screening mechanism now constitutes a step backwards in the liberalization of FDI capital movement. The Screening Regulation has become the benchmark of capital movement liberalization for incoming FDI. Accordingly, the benchmark is optional FDI screening in Member States on the grounds of 'security or public order' as defined by the Screening Regulation.[321] FDI Screening mechanisms on broader grounds would therefore reduce the liberalization of incoming FDI. In other words, by adopting the Screening Regulation based on a narrow screening ground, the EU itself set a high bar for regulating incoming FDI.

---

[320] Sedlaczek and Züger (2018), para. 20.

[321] For the definition of the screening ground see Sect. 3.1.

As a result, the EU would need to adopt broader FDI Screening mechanisms in accordance with the special legislative procedure laid out in Art 64(3) TFEU. The FDI Screening mechanisms must be adopted by the Council unanimously after consulting the Parliament. The requirement of unanimity in the Council constitutes a high hurdle for adopting new FDI Screening mechanisms. Each Member State must agree with their adoption.

Last but not least, Art 64(3) TFEU only applies to the extent the FDI Screening mechanism affects third-country FDI within the meaning of the freedom of capital movement. For entirely relying on Art 64(3) TFEU, the FDI Screening mechanism must thus only apply to foreign investors who are controlled by a resident of a third country. For the definition of 'controlled' one may refer to Directive 2009/73/EC, art 2(36). The EU would thus need to refrain from the definition of foreign investors that was found to be best capturing the EU and Member States concerns vis-à-vis foreign investors. The FDI Screening mechanism could not also define foreign investors according to their place of legal organization or seat location.[322]

In sum, Art 64(3) TFEU gives the EU wide flexibility to adopt FDI Screening mechanisms with considerable constraints. From a procedural perspective, the EU, represented by the Council, must overcome high hurdles to adopt FDI Screening mechanisms on broader grounds than 'security or public order' as defined in the Screening Regulation. In addition, the EU would also need to limit the FDI Screening mechanism's personal scope to foreign investors who are controlled by a resident of a third country.

Nevertheless, such an FDI Screening mechanism could define an appropriate screening ground beyond 'security or public order' without constraints. Only the Fundamental rights pursuant to the CFR may provide additional substantial limits. These limits will be briefly discussed below.

The flexibility pursuant to Art 64(2) and (3) TFEU thus goes much further than any other available ground of exception to the freedoms of capital movement and establishment—namely, the unwritten ground of 'overriding reasons in the public interest'.[323] While providing much wider flexibility than 'public policy or public security' within the meaning of Art 65(1)(b) TFEU, the unwritten ground of exception is still significantly limited in two ways. First, the interests that may be pursued are limited, in particular so called 'economic interests' are excluded.[324] Second, it is still prevailing opinion that the unwritten ground of exception does not apply to open discriminations. FDI Screening mechanisms, however, openly discriminate against third-country FDI vis-à-vis intra-EU FDI. Therefore, this book does not further discuss the unwritten ground of exception 'overriding reasons in the public interest'.

---

[322] For the definition of Foreign investor see Sect. 2.4.2.

[323] See the key judgements Case C-8/74 *Dassonville* [1974] EU:C:1974:82; Case C-120/78 *Rewe v Bundesmonopolverwaltung für Branntwein* [1979] EU:C:1979:42 (hereafter *Cassis de Dijon*), as well as the related analysis in Sect. 3.2.1.

[324] See analysis in Sect. 3.2.1.1.2.

4.2.6 Excursus: Fundamental Rights as Minor Limitations to FDI Screening Mechanisms

As repeatedly highlighted, regardless of the applicable Fundamental freedoms, the Fundamental rights pursuant to the CFR pose additional, but minor limitations to the EU's flexibility to adopt FDI Screening mechanisms. In the context of FDI screening, four Fundamental rights are particularly relevant that also apply to foreigners: the freedoms to freely choose an occupation (Art 15(1) and (3) CFR) and to conduct a business (Art 16 CFR), as well as the rights to property (Art 17(1) CFR) and to non-discrimination (Art 21(2) CFR).

However, pursuant to Art 52(1) CFR:

> Subject to the principle of proportionality, limitations [to the Fundamental rights] may be made only if they are necessary and genuinely meet objectives of general interest recognised [sic] by the Union or the need to protect the rights and freedoms of others.[325]

For assessing the EU's flexibility to adopt FDI Screening mechanisms, the most relevant part of Art 52(1) CFR is the phrase 'objectives of general interest recognised [sic] by the Union'. This phrase shows that even if foreign investors may invoke Fundamental rights, the EU has the flexibility to adopt FDI Screening mechanisms to meet objectives of general interest, provided the measure meets an individual interest proportionality test.[326]

Objectives of general interest recognized by the Union are inter alia provided in Art 3 TEU.[327] Accordingly, the EU may adopt FDI Screening mechanisms to pursue interests such as sustainable development, economic growth, protecting and improving the environment, promoting scientific and technological advance (all in Art 3(3) TEU), as well as promoting EU interests in international relations (Art 3(5) TEU). This list of interests that are all relevant FDI screening criteria already shows how broadly the EU may define an FDI screening ground that still complies with the Fundamental rights.

Certainly, the FDI Screening mechanism must also be proportionate vis-à-vis the concrete Fundamental right at issue. The mechanism must genuinely meet and be necessary to meet its objectives. However, this limit is a minimum requirement compared to the limitations provided by the Fundamental freedom grounds of exception 'public policy or public security' (Art 65(1)(b) TFEU) and 'essential security interests' (Art 346(1)(b) TFEU).[328]

---

[325] This ground of exception applies to all relevant Fundamental rights, Ashiagbor (2014), para. 15.35; Everson and Gonçalves (2014), paras. 16.51–16.52; Torremans (2014), paras. 17.64–17.65. On Art 21 CFR Kilapatrick (2014), paras. 21.32–21.39, 21.81, who seems to imply that Art 52(1) CFR applies to Art 21(2) CFR. However, there is no reason why Art 52(1) CFR should not allow the discrimination between EU citizens and third-country nationals.

[326] See Sect. 4.2.5.2.2.

[327] Lenaerts (2012), p. 391; Peers and Prechal (2014), para. 52.47.

[328] More detailed on the proportionality test in Art 52(1) TFEU, see e.g. Peers and Prechal (2014), paras. 52.65–52.82.

Consequently, the Fundamental rights only pose minor substantial limitations to the EU's flexibility to adopt FDI Screening mechanisms. Subject to the mechanism's proportionality, the EU may pursue a wide array of general interests that goes far beyond the TFEU notions of 'public policy or public security' and 'essential security interests', as well as the screening ground 'security or public order' within the meaning of the Screening Regulation.

4.2.7 Wide EU Flexibility for FDI Screening Mechanisms Beyond 'Security or Public Order'—But Compromises on Their Personal and Substantial Scopes

Section 4.2 revealed a complex picture of Fundamental freedom protection for foreign investors and FDI, and thus for the EU's flexibility to adopt FDI Screening mechanisms on broader grounds than 'security or public order' within the meaning of the Screening Regulation.

The freedoms of capital movement and establishment differ significantly in their personal scopes, but widely overlap at the substantial level. At the same time, Art 64(2) and (3) TFEU offer an in substance wide, but in procedural terms narrow ground of exception to the freedom of capital movement, and, by way of Art 49(2) TFEU, to the freedom of establishment. Moreover, Art 64(2) and (3) TFEU only apply to FDI from foreign investors who are controlled by a resident in a third country, not those who are foreign by place of legal organization or seat location.

Against this background, the EU essentially has two options for adopting an FDI Screening mechanism on broader grounds than 'security or public order' within the meaning of the Screening Regulation.[329]

As a first option, the FDI Screening mechanism may be limited to (i) foreign investors who are Non-EU Companies, Non-EU Established SPVs, foreign States, and/or foreign public undertakings, and (ii) FDI that gives the investor definite influence on the target company. The first requirement ensures that the FDI Screening mechanism only applies to investors who are excluded from the personal scope of the freedom of establishment. The second requirement makes the FDI Screening mechanism exclusively applicable to capital movement that also qualify as establishment within the meaning of Art 49 TFEU. If these two requirements are fulfilled, the EU's flexibility to adopt FDI Screening mechanisms is not limited by any Fundamental freedom. However, the option omits to cover FDI that gives the

---

[329] A third option may be FDI Screening mechanisms based on the unwritten ground of exception of 'overriding reasons in the public interest'. However, as discussed, this ground of exception is significantly limited in two ways. First, the interests that may be pursued are still narrow, in particular regarding 'economic interests' as defined by the ECJ. Second, it is still prevailing opinion that the unwritten ground of exception does not apply to open discriminations. FDI Screening mechanisms, however, openly discriminate against third-country FDI vis-à-vis intra-EU FDI.

investor less than definite influence on the FDU target. Hence, the EU and Member States concerns vis-à-vis foreign investors are not fully met.

To avoid this shortcoming, the EU could follow a second option. It may only limit the FDI Screening mechanism's scope personally, more concretely to investors who are controlled by a resident in a third country. If so, the EU may—pursuant to the Fundamental freedoms—freely determine the FDI Screening mechanism's screening ground. Art 64(3) TFEU gives the EU, in substance, a limitless ground of exception. From a procedural perspective, however, the EU must overcome high hurdles. The FDI Screening mechanism must be adopted, after consulting the Parliament, by the Council—with unanimity.

For both options, substantial limits are only posed by the Fundamental rights. These limits constitute minor limitations, for they allow the EU to pursue a wide array of general interests that goes far beyond the scope of the Screening Regulation's notion 'security or public order', as well as the TFEU notion of 'public policy or public security' in Art 65(1)(b) TFEU. Hence, the FDI Screening mechanism must only be proportionate to achieve its objectives. This test leaves the EU wide flexibility.

Consequently, the EU may freely determine a screening ground beyond 'security or public order' pursuant to EU primary law if it accepts one of two shortcomings. On the one hand, it may accept that the FDI Screening mechanisms does not apply to all FDI, but only FDI that gives the investor definite influence on the FDI target. On the other hand, the EU may need to overcome the high procedural hurdle of unanimity in the Council. Given the controversies when negotiating the Screening Regulation, it will politically be even more difficult to unite all Member State positions around an FDI Screening mechanism on a broader screening ground. Nevertheless, from an EU law perspective, it is important to state: If the EU does not adopt a broad FDI Screening mechanism that significantly covers the EU and Member States concerns vis-à-vis foreign investors, this would be more due to lacking political majorities, than to legal limitations.

Nevertheless, in sum, pursuant to EU law, the EU has important legislative options for FDI Screening mechanisms beyond the screening ground of 'security or public order' as defined in the Screening Regulation. It remains to be seen whether these options are compliant with International economic law.

4.3 Flexibility for FDI Screening Pursuant to International Economic Law

The options for FDI Screening mechanisms on broader grounds than 'security or public order' within the meaning of the Screening Regulation are only viable if they are also compliant with International economic law. The EU is not only subject to international law,[330] but shall also, by its own standards, contribute 'to the strict observance ... of international law'.[331]

FDI Screening mechanisms primarily regulate the establishment[332] of foreign investors in the EU through M&A FDI. As a principle of international law, States have the right to control the establishment of foreign investors as they deem appropriate, even on discriminatory grounds. However, in agreements of International economic law, States may have committed to letting foreign investors establish themselves in their territory, vis-à-vis other States or investors.[333] To assess the EU's flexibility to adopt FDI Screening mechanisms on broader grounds than 'security or public order' it is therefore also necessary to assess EU obligations pursuant to International economic law.

Section 4.3.1 will identify the sources of International economic law that may contain EU obligations to admit FDI to the internal market. This includes a brief overview of agreements concluded by Member States and their potential effects on the EU's flexibility to adopt FDI Screening mechanisms. Section 4.3.2 will outline how international agreements to which the EU itself is party may limit the EU's flexibility to screen FDI. The section will focus on EU FTAs, the recent EU-UK Trade and Cooperation Agreement, and a possible EU-China CAI, as well as WTO agreements (GATT 1994, TRIMs and TRIPS Agreement, GATS).

While all these sources of International economic law significantly limit the EU's flexibility to adopt FDI Screening mechanisms, the GATS will be identified as the most relevant for the theses submitted in this book. On the one hand, the GATS contains EU commitments vis-à-vis all WTO members, especially all those that are at the centre of the EU and Member States concerns vis-à-vis foreign investors. On the other hand, the GATS provisions are often reflected in the relevant FTAs, and may therefore inform their interpretation. The following sections will therefore assess the EU's GATS obligations in more detail.

To start with, Sect. 4.3.3 will analyze the GATS's scope and conclude that the GATS largely covers FDI and FDI Screening mechanisms. The GATS contains general obligations for WTO members as well as further reaching obligations that only apply if committed to sector-by-sector by the individual WTO member (specific commitments). Section 4.3.4 will identify the relevant specific EU commitments, including assessing the EU's sector commitments that are particularly relevant in the FDI screening context: electricity and artificial intelligence. Before doing so, Sect. 4.3.4 will conclude that the National Treatment ('NT') obligation in Art XVII GATS has the largest potential to limit the EU's flexibility to screen FDI on broader

---

[330] Art 47 TEU.

[331] Art 3(5) TEU.

[332] Here and in the following sections, 'establishment' is used in an untechnical way, neither referring to Art 49 TFEU, nor any specific notion of International economic law. It overlaps, but must not necessarily be identical with the notion of FDI.

[333] In German scholarship, the German FDI screening measures are usually found to be compliant with Public international law; see for the most detailed discussion, Geiger (2013), ch 8; more briefly Tietje (2007), pp. 4, 9; Martini (2008), pp. 320–321; Nettesheim (2008), pp. 738–739.

grounds than 'security or public order'. However, it will also be shown that its consequences are considerably limited by a lack of EU sector-specific commitments for FDI relevant to the EU and Member States concerns vis-à-vis foreign investors.

In addition, the general obligation to treat services and service suppliers of one WTO member not less favourable than services and service suppliers of any other country is crucial. Section 4.3.5 will find that this Most-favoured-nation ('MFN') treatment obligation in Art II(1) GATS considerably limits the EU's flexibility to screen FDI in accordance with the concerns vis-à-vis investors from certain specific countries.

After a short summary of the obligations FDI Screening mechanisms may violate in Sect. 4.3.6, Sect. 4.3.7 will then assess the EU's remaining flexibility to screen FDI even if it violates GATS obligations: the grounds of exception. Following the purpose of this chapter to assess the EU's flexibility to adopt FDI Screening mechanisms on broader grounds than 'security or public order', Sect. 4.3.7 will look beyond the grounds of exception in Arts XIV*bis*(1)(b) and XIV(a) GATS. Instead, the section will focus on broader grounds of exception that may justify a discrimination between third countries: Arts V(1) and XIV(c) GATS. Broader grounds of exception that generally justify a NT violation, the discrimination between foreign and domestic investors, are not available.

Last, Sect. 4.3.8 will summarize the conclusions, and apply them to FDI Screening mechanisms. It will identify policy options for FDI Screening mechanisms beyond the grounds of 'security or public order' that comply with International economic law and considerably meet the EU and Member States concerns vis-à-vis foreign investors. Much will depend on the personal and substantial scope of the FDI Screening mechanism as well as some possible screening criteria.

4.3.1 Relevant International Economic Law: Agreements on FDI Establishment to Which the EU Is Party

The EU's flexibility to adopt FDI Screening mechanisms can be limited by International economic law in many ways. The following will explain why the following will focus on EU agreements that cover the establishment of foreign investors or, in other words, the admission of FDI into the EU. It will, however, omit a detailed discussion of agreements that primarily cover post-establishment investor treatment, as well as agreements concluded by Member States.

4.3.1.1 Exclusion by Content: Agreements Covering the Establishment of Foreign Investors

When assessing the EU's flexibility to regulate FDI, one of the first possible limitations that comes to mind is international investment law, namely Bilateral

Investment Treaties ('BITs'). In the EU, the EU itself as well as Member States have BITs in place.[334] BITs concluded by the EU are named Investment Protection Agreements ('IPAs'), which are often negotiated with, but concluded separately from FTAs.[335] However, the relevance of BITs and IPAs for the EU's flexibility to adopt FDI Screening mechanisms is limited.

Simplified, one may say that FDI Screening mechanisms primarily regulate the establishment of foreign investors, while Member State BITs and IPAs mostly cover the post-establishment phase. While this distinction is not always clear-cut, it nevertheless shows that overlaps of FDI Screening mechanisms, on the one hand, and Member State BITs and IPAs, on the other hand, are limited.[336]

Traditionally, Member State BITs focused on protecting existing investment and thus on the post-establishment phase, not on further liberalizing the establishment of foreign investors as such. Therefore, Member States have rarely undertaken clear obligations to admit establishments of foreign investor to their market.[337] The focus on the post-establishment phase is even clearer for EU IPAs. They protect investment only to the extent it is operated, and thus not the phase of establishment itself. Such protection is especially accorded through fair-and-equitable treatment standards, provisions on expropriation, and investor rights to damages, including investor-state arbitration mechanisms.[338] EU obligations for liberalizing the

---

[334] In accordance with Regulation (EU) No 1219/2012 of the European Parliament and of the Council of 12 December 2012 establishing transitional arrangements for bilateral investment agreements between Member States and third countries (BIT Transition Regulation) [2012] OJ L 351/40, arts 3, pp. 7–11, there are still around 1300 Member State BITs in place; and new ones are being negotiated. See Commission, 'Report on the Application of Regulation (EU) No 1219/2012 establishing transitional arrangements for bilateral investment agreements between Member States and third countries' COM (2020) 134 final, pp. 2–4, on Member State BITs with third countries that Member States kept in place after the Lisbon Treaty, as well as on the number of authorization requests for new BITs. For an overview of all Member State BITs currently in place or negotiated, see Commission, 'List of the Bilateral Investment Agreements referred to in Article 4(1) of Regulation (EU) No 1219/2012 of the European Parliament and of the Council establishing transitional arrangements for bilateral investment agreements between Member States and third countries: Notices of Member States' OJ C 198/1 (2019). The BITs are progressively replaced with new agreements concluded by the EU (BIT Transition Regulation (n. 334), art 3, recitals 5–6).

[335] This approach ensures that only the IPA must be ratified by Member States, while the FTA can be adopted more quickly. Only the IPA-covered fields portfolio investment and state-investor arbitration tribunals are fields of mixed competence (*EU-Singapore Free Trade Agreement* (n. 4), paras. 238, 244, 293, 304). The EU FTAs with Singapore and Vietnam are recent examples of this approach.

[336] This assumption is also implied by de Melo (2020), p. 600.

[337] Martini (2008), p. 321; Commission, 'Towards a Comprehensive European International Investment Policy' (Communication) COM (2010) 343 final, p. 5; Alschner (2013), pp. 469–470. Alschner also highlights one Member State BIT that includes pre-establishment protection, Art 4(2) of the 2005 Belgium-Luxembourg-Democratic Republic of the Congo BIT, see Alschner (2013), n. 70.

[338] See e.g. the definitions of scope in Art 2.1.1(b) of the EU-Vietnam IPA ('This Chapter applies to ... investors with respect to the *operation* of their covered investment.' (emphasis added). The EU-Singapore IPA takes a slightly different approach by first limiting covered investors to persons

establishment of foreign investors, on the other hand, are part of EU FTAs—without typical investment law elements such as investor-state arbitration.[339] These obligations will be further analyzed in Sect. 4.3.2.

Certainly, in some cases FDI Screening mechanisms also address the post-establishment phase. As stated in Sect. 4.2.2, FDI that is relevant to FDI Screening mechanisms is typically taking place in two scenarios: either by Non-EU Companies (Scenario 1) or by Non-EU Established SPVs that were founded by Non-EU Companies only to undertake the FDI (Scenario 2).[340]

For the foreign investor in Scenario 2, the EU SPV constitutes an investment that he operates when undertaking the FDI that then becomes subject to FDI screening. Accordingly, prohibiting the FDI at issue may violate the foreign investor's post-establishment rights linked to his first investment: establishing the SPV. However, the investor established the SPV knowing that subsequent FDI may be subject to the FDI Screening mechanism. His establishment and any subsequent establishment by the SPV were thus contingent on the possible limits posed by the FDI Screening mechanism. It is therefore unlikely that the investor could invoke post-establishment rights against the screening of the SPV's subsequent FDI.[341]

In Scenario 1 the FDI is the foreign investor's establishment. Post-establishment rights are therefore irrelevant. This conclusion arguably even applies to Case 2 FDI Screening mechanisms, which generally authorize incoming FDI while reserving the authorities' right to prohibit an individual investment.[342] In these cases the investor was never admitted a full establishment that he could defend by post-establishment rights. The same rationale applies when the authorities authorize the FDI, but impose orders of mitigation measures to remedy risks as part of the FDI screening process.

Consequently, though necessary to be taken into account, post-establishment rights will not pose significant limitations to FDI Screening mechanisms. Accordingly, Member States BITs and EU IPAs are only little relevant to the EU's flexibility to adopt FDI Screening mechanisms. The following therefore omits discussing both further.

---

who have made an investment (Art 1.2.2), and including the limitation to the post-establishment phase into the substantial obligations; see e.g. NT obligation in Art 2.3.1, which is limited 'to the operation, management, conduct, maintenance, use, enjoyment and sale or other disposal of their investments'. Cf Titi (2018), pp. 7–8.

[339] In Art 8.2.1(f) EU-Vietnam FTA; Art 8.8(d) EU-Singapore FTA; Art 7.9(a) EU-South Korea FTA, the FTAs all exclude Investor-State arbitration for establishment disputes.

[340] For the terms Non-EU Company and Non-EU Established SPV, see Sect. 4.2.2.1.1.

[341] The EU SPV itself will often not qualify as an investor of the other party to the agreement, since it is already established in the EU. Thus, many EU SPVs do not constitute an investor within the meaning of the BIT or IPA.

[342] See definition of FDI Screening mechanism in Sect. 2.4.3.

4.3.1.2   Exclusion by Party: Agreements to Which the EU Is Party

In addition to the exclusion based on content, the following will also limit its scope to agreements to which the EU is party, excluding relevant Member State agreements, namely the OECD Code of Capital Movements.

4.3.1.2.1   Agreements Concluded by the EU or the EC

The EU and its predecessor, the EC, concluded several agreements with third countries in the realm of International economic law that may limit the EU's flexibility to screen FDI. Most important in the realm of FDI screening are the WTO agreements, namely the GATS, as well as FTAs such as CETA, and the EU-Vietnam and EU Korea FTAs.

For assessing the legal effect of these agreements, one has to differentiate between the external perspective vis-à-vis the other parties to the agreement, and the internal perspective vis-à-vis EU law.[343]

From the external perspective, by their own effect, the WTO agreements and FTAs are binding on the EU as a party to these agreements. The EU is not only party to the FTAs itself concluded, but also to the agreements concluded by the EC— namely, the WTO-Agreement and all associated agreements in its Annexes 1 to 3. The EU succeeded the EC as original member to the WTO (Arts XI(1), XIV (1) WTO-Agreement).[344],[345] The legally binding effect follows either from the agreements themselves, see for example Art II(1) WTO-Agreement, or from the universal principle of international law *pacta sunt servanda*.[346] Hence, vis-à-vis the other parties to the agreements the EU is limited in adopting FDI Screening mechanisms that violate its agreement obligations.

In addition, from the internal perspective, EU law itself binds the EU to comply with its obligations in international agreements. International agreements concluded

---

[343] Herrmann and Streinz (2014), para. 57. This is also highlighted by Case C-104/81 *Kupferberg* [1982] EU:C:1982:362, para. 13, when stating that by complying with an international agreement the Member States do not only fulfil an obligation vis-à-vis the 'non-member country concerned but also and above all in relation to the Community which has assumed responsibility for the due performance of the agreement'.

[344] In the WTO both the EU and Member States are members ('parallel membership'). This is due to the mixed competences between EC and Member States at the time of conclusion of the WTO-Agreement. The ECJ found that the EC only had the competence to conclude the GATT, but not GATS and TRIPS (see *Accords annexés à l'accord OMC* (n. 226), paras. 34, 47, 54, 98, 71, 105. Even with the extended EU Common commercial policy, the lines of competences between EU and Member States remain blurred, see e.g. Herrmann and Streinz (2014), paras. 61–72. The parallel membership is therefore still necessary.

[345] Both the EU (Art 47 TEU) and the EC (Art 210 EEC, Art 281 EC) have or had legal personality, and therefore could and did conclude international agreements in their own capacity.

[346] See Art 26 and recital 3 to the VCLT. See also Schmalenbach (2018), para. 4.

by the EU, and EC, are an 'integral part' of the EU legal order.[347] Accordingly, Art 216(2) TFEU provides that agreements concluded by the EU are binding upon the EU (and its Member States).[348] The same applies to agreements concluded by the EC as the EU's predecessor. The agreements have primacy over EU secondary law.[349] As a result, EU secondary law, such as an FDI Screening mechanism, must comply with WTO agreements and FTAs concluded by the EU and EC.[350]

Another, very controversial question is whether the ECJ can review secondary law on the basis of international agreements. In other words: Can the agreements be relied upon before the ECJ to invalidate an EU measure? Another similar question is: Can individuals invoke a violation of the agreement before the ECJ?[351] For the purpose of this book, however, this controversy may be neglected. This book only seeks to assess the EU's—legal—flexibility to adopt FDI Screening mechanisms. While it would certainly raise political costs for the EU if the ECJ could annul its FDI Screening mechanisms, the legal conclusion remains the same. The EU must, of course, comply with its external and internal legal obligations.[352]

Therefore, the EU is bound by the WTO agreements and FTAs to which it is party. Thus, obligations deriving from these agreements limit the EU's flexibility to adopt FDI Screening mechanisms.

---

[347] Case C-181/73 *Haegeman* [1974] EU:C:1974:41, paras. 3–5, on the TRIPS, but the reasoning is applicable to all WTO agreements.

[348] Art 228(7) EEC and Art 300(7) EC provided the same effect for the EC before the Lisbon Treaty.

[349] Case C-308/06 *Intertanko and Others* [2008] EU:C:2008:312, para. 42, with further references. The ECJ based its reasoning on Art 300(7) EC, today Art 216(2) TFEU. See also Rosas (2008), pp. 77–78; Herrmann and Streinz (2014), para. 112.

[350] See e.g. on a bilateral trade agreements *Kupferberg* (n. 343), paras. 11–12.

[351] Joined Cases C-659/13 and 34/14 *C&J Clark International* [2016] EU:C:2016:74, para. 84. In settled case law the ECJ often denies its jurisdiction for reviewing secondary law on the basis of international agreements, see e.g. *Intertanko and Others* (n. 349), paras. 43–45. Only if the agreement is directly applicable and has direct effect, does the ECJ review whether the secondary law at issue violates the agreement. In principle, the ECJ denies direct applicability and effect for WTO-Agreements (Case C-149/96 *Portugal v Council* [1999] EU:C:1999:574, paras. 42–48; Case C-377/02 *Van Parys* [2005] EU:C:2005:121, para. 39; Joined Cases C-120 an 121/06 P *FIAMM and Others v Council and Commission* [2008] EU:C:2008:476, para. 111). One exception to this rule on WTO law applies if the EU measure itself expressly refers to WTO law (see *Portugal v Council* [1999] (n. 351), para. 49; *Van Parys* (n. 351), para. 40; *C&J Clark International* (n. 351), para. 87). This exception's condition is arguably met by the Screening Regulation, which references Arts XIV(a) and XIV*bis*(1)(b) GATS, see also Sect. 3.1.1. On the other hand, the ECJ seems to recognize direct applicability and effect of bilateral agreements (*Kupferberg* (n. 343), paras. 11–12; Maresceau (2013), p. 698). At least in objective annulment proceedings, it is unconvincing that the ECJ rejects to review secondary law on the basis of international law that is binding upon the EU, see Thym (2009), para. 459; Herrmann and Streinz (2014), para. 125. With a detailed analysis of this controversy, see e.g. Jacobs (2011); de La Rochère (2013); Lenaerts (2014).

[352] Of course, the ECJ has the competence to review the application of the Screening Regulation's screening ground 'security or public order' even if it references Arts XIV*bis*(1)(b) and XIV (a) GATS.

4.3.1.2.2   Member State Agreements with Third Countries

Aside from agreements concluded by the EU or EC, the Member States themselves have agreements with third countries in place that may not legally but factually limit the EU's flexibility to screen FDI. While Member State BITs were already excluded from further analysis due to their focus on post-establishment rights, another important legal source may be the OECD Code of Capital Movements.

From the EU's perspective, the OECD Code of Capital Movements is merely a legal instrument of an international organization, the OECD, to which certain Member States, but not itself are a member. In fact, only 22 Member States are members in the OECD. The EU itself has a special observer-status.[353] Legally, the EU is therefore not party to, and thus not bound by the OECD Code of Capital Movements.

However, for the 22 Member States that are OECD members, the OECD Code of Capital Movements is, as a decision of the OECD Council, legally binding.[354] Pursuant to Art 2(a), (b)(iv) in conjunction with List A of Annex A to the OECD Code of Capital Movements, the OECD members must admit FDI of other OECD members to their markets. OECD members also committed not to discriminate between OECD members when adopting their liberalization measures (Art 9 OECD Code of Capital Movements). An EU FDI Screening mechanism that contradicts these OECD obligations may comply with the EU's legal obligations, but drive Member States into breaking their obligations vis-à-vis other OECD members. In other words, vis-à-vis the EU, a Member State is obliged to follow the FDI Screening mechanisms. Vis-à-vis the OECD, the Member State must comply with the OECD Code of Capital Movements.

Accordingly, one may argue that the EU's flexibility to screen FDI is factually limited by the OECD Code of Capital Movements. However, this conclusion is attenuated by two aspects.

First, the 22 Member States that are OECD members have two possibilities to deviate from their commitment to liberalize FDI inflows. First, they may invoke reservations to their commitments that they lodged pursuant to Art 2(b) of the OECD Code of Capital Movements at the time of the OECD Code of Capital Movements' adoption.[355] Member States have lodged such reservations for example in the accountancy, legal services, and real estate sectors.[356] Second, Art 3 of the OECD Code of Capital Movements provides a 'public order and security' exception.

---

[353] OECD Convention, Supplementary Protocol No 1.

[354] Art 5(a) of the OECD Convention.

[355] With a view to progressively abolishing these reservations on FDI, OECD members are not allowed to lodge new reservations on FDI. This prohibition only applies to the capital movements listed in List A of Annex A, and therefore not only to FDI, but also e.g. to the sale of real estates and the admission of certain foreign securities. OECD members may always add reservations regarding capital movement listed in List B of Annex A, e.g. building or purchasing real estate.

[356] See list of reservations in Annex B of e.g. Austria, Belgium, Czech Republic, France, and Germany.

Accordingly, OECD members may deviate from their commitments to take action they 'consider necessary' for 'public order and security' reasons.[357] The phrase 'it considers necessary' demonstrates that the ground of exception is self-judging, and therefore provides the OECD members with wide discretion to determine their interests of 'public order and security'—of course, within the limits of the phrase's meaning.

Second, and most importantly, the countries at focus of the EU and Member States concerns vis-à-vis foreign investors are non-OECD members. Neither China, nor Brazil, India, Iran, or Russia are members of the OECD. One may expect that the FDI Screening mechanisms will mainly be applied against investors from these states. Therefore, in the individual case at issue, the 22 Member States that are OECD members will usually not violate their OECD obligations.[358]

For these reasons, the following will omit a further analysis of the OECD Code of Capital Movements obligations of the 22 Member States that are OECD members.

4.3.1.3 Focus on EU Agreements Liberalizing the Establishment of Foreign Investors

Consequently, the following sections will focus on agreements with third countries concluded by the EU that do not merely protect the post-establishment phase of investments, but liberalize the establishment of foreign investors. As already indicated, these conditions especially apply to bi-, pluri-, and multilateral trade agreements.

4.3.2 International Economic Law Obligations on Foreign Investor Establishment

Two main sources of International economic law liberalize the establishment of foreign investors in the EU: FTAs and other bi- or plurilateral agreements on the one, and multilateral WTO agreements on the other hand. The following will provide an overview of EU obligations in both agreement categories. It will focus on identifying

---

[357] Art 3 OECD Code of Capital Movements: 'The provisions of this Code shall not prevent a Member from taking action which it considers necessary for: i) the maintenance of public order or the protection of public health, morals and safety; ii) the protection of its essential security interests; iii) the fulfilment of its obligations relating to international peace and security.'

[358] A third aspect is that the OECD Code of Capital Movements has no enforcement mechanism such as the dispute settlement mechanisms of panels and Appellate Body in the WTO. Direct consequences for Member States violating the OECD Code of Capital Movements are therefore limited. However, the EU would act against its own principles if accepting that its FDI Screening mechanism drives Member States into violating the OECD Code of Capital Movements. See Art 3(5) TEU: 'shall contribute to . . . the strict observance . . . of international law'.

obligations that may significantly limit the EU's flexibility to adopt FDI Screening mechanisms on broader grounds than 'security or public order'.

4.3.2.1   Bi- and Plurilateral Agreements

The EU has concluded numerous agreements with third countries that cover foreign investor establishment, namely FTAs.[359] The new generation of preferential trade agreements is going far beyond classic trade agreements on goods trade. In particular, they are also covering trade through commercial presence, in other words establishment, and thus FDI.

As repeatedly stated, FDI Screening mechanisms apply to situations in which a foreign investor seeks to establish an enterprise in the EU that qualifies as an FDI. FDI as defined in the realm of FDI screening is an investment of any kind by an investor aiming to establish or to maintain lasting and direct links between the investor and the FDI target.[360] FTAs define their scope for liberalizing investment based on the same or a very similar definition, usually under the notion 'establishment'.[361]

This section will outline the EU's limits to FDI screening pursuant to FTAs based on two examples of the EU's general approach on FTAs: CETA and the EU-Vietnam FTA. CETA, on the one hand, is the prime example of future FTAs with like-minded developed countries, whether as integrated FTA-IPA agreements or separated in two different agreements. The EU-Vietnam FTA, on the other hand, is a recent example of FTAs that may be concluded with countries with which a deep level of economic integration is not feasible or wanted. The section will focus on substantial obligations, omitting an analysis of state and investor rights to enforce them.[362] The outline of the EU commitments in CETA and the EU-Vietnam FTA give an indication of how FTAs limit the EU's flexibility to adopt FDI Screening mechanisms generally.

In addition, this section will address the consequences of two important, recent developments: the provisional application of the EU-UK Trade and Cooperation Agreement as well as the 'Agreement in Principle' on an EU-China CAI.[363] Especially the EU-China CAI has the potential to significantly limit the EU's flexibility to

---

[359] For a list and summary of the 35 major trade agreements see Commission, 'Report on Implementation of EU Free Trade Agreements: 1 January 2018 - 31 December 2018' COM (2019) 455 final, pp. 2–3.

[360] See definition in Sects. 2.4.1 and 2.4.3.

[361] See e.g. Arts 8.2.1(f) EU-Vietnam FTA; 8.8(d) EU-Singapore FTA; 7.9(a) EU-South Korea FTA.

[362] The most prominent tool, Investor-State arbitration, is usually limited to post-establishment rights, see n. 339.

[363] Commission, 'EU-China Comprehensive Agreement on Investment: The Agreement in Principle' (30 December 2020) <https://trade.ec.europa.eu/doclib/cfm/doclib_section.cfm?sec=120> accessed 2 February 2022.

adopt FDI Screening mechanisms. China is at the centre of the EU and Member States concerns vis-à-vis foreign investors. Therefore, the entire purpose of FDI Screening mechanisms would be at stake if the EU-China CAI required the EU to exclude Chinese investors from their personal scope.

4.3.2.1.1   EU-Vietnam FTA

The EU-Vietnam FTA liberalizes FDI significantly. Its Section B of Chapter 9 on 'Liberalisation [*sic*] of Investment' liberalizes 'establishment'. Establishment in this sense is defined as 'the setting up, including the acquisition, of a juridical person ... with a view to establishing or maintaining lasting economic links'.[364] This definition mirrors the definition of FDI within the meaning of FDI Screening mechanisms.[365]

Based on this scope, the EU commits, pursuant to Art 8.5.1 EU-Vietnam FTA, to according:

> to investors of the other Party and to their enterprises, with respect to establishment in its territory, treatment no less favourable than that accorded, in like situations, to its own investors and to their enterprises.[366]

This NT commitment thus prohibits to screen FDI of Vietnamese investors,[367] without also screening FDI of EU investors.[368] This has the potential to undermine

---

[364] Art 8.2.1(f) EU-Vietnam FTA.

[365] The definition excludes the operation of the establishment, since this would address investment protection after the establishment, which is only covered by the EU-Vietnam IPA.

[366] Art 8.2.1(h) EU-Vietnam FTA defines investor as 'a natural person or a juridical person of a Party that seeks to establish ..., is establishing or has established an enterprise in the territory of the other Party'. '"Juridical person of a Party" means a juridical person of the Union or a juridical person of Viet Nam, set up in accordance with the domestic laws and regulations of the Union or its Member States, or of Viet Nam, respectively, and engaged in substantive business operations ... in the territory of the Union or of Viet Nam, respectively' (Art 8.2.1(j) EU-Vietnam FTA). '"juridical person" means any legal entity duly constituted or otherwise organised under applicable law, whether for profit or otherwise, and whether privately-owned or governmentally-owned, including any corporation, trust, partnership, joint venture, sole proprietorship or association'. (Art 8.2.1 (i) EU-Vietnam FTA).

[367] For easier reading the more untechnical terms 'Vietnamese investor' and 'EU investor' are used instead of 'investor of Vietnam' or 'investor of the EU', see for these terms Art 8.2(j), (l) EU-Vietnam FTA.

[368] In Art 8.4 EU-Vietnam FTA, the EU also commits to grant investors from Vietnam market access. Art 8.4 EU-Vietnam FTA is drafted similarly to Art XVI GATS. As is argued under Art XVI GATS, the screening of FDI on the basis of qualitative, not quantitative criteria does not constitute a market access restriction within the meaning of Art XVI GATS, and thus most likely neither within the meaning Art 8.4 EU-Vietnam FTA. See Sect. 4.3.4.1. Moreover, Art 8.19 EU-Vietnam FTA on 'Domestic Regulation' provides certain soft, procedural obligations for 'licensing requirements' and 'qualification requirements', such as the objectivity and transparency of criteria. FDI Screening mechanisms may qualify as such requirements. However, the softer obligations in Art 8.19 EU-Vietnam FTA can only apply if the entire measure is not discriminatory, and thus already prohibited by the NT obligation in Art 8.5.1 EU-Vietnam FTA. Again, the same issue arises under

the fundamental rationale of FDI Screening mechanisms: screening foreign, not domestic investors.

In addition, the EU's NT commitment applies not only to privately, but also publicly owned investors.[369] This is important to note considering the EU and Member States competition, harmful investor, and private information concerns regarding state-owned or -influenced investors. Yet, the EU chose another path to address its concerns about state influence. In Chapters 10 and 11 of the FTA, the parties commit to subject their SOEs to certain competition laws to ensure minimum market distortions, and decision-taking based on commercial considerations. Moreover, they commit to non-discrimination between private and public, domestic and foreign goods and service suppliers.[370] This attenuates the EU's concern that Vietnamese investors are under state influence when deciding to establish themselves in the EU or later in the operation of their establishment.

Nevertheless, the impact of the EU's NT commitment in Art 8.5.1 EU-Vietnam FTA is less significant than it seems at first sight. It is subject to four caveats.

First, the entire Chapter 8 does not apply to certain sectors—namely, audio-visual services, the 'production of or trade in arms, munitions and war material', and 'services supplied and activities performed in the exercise of governmental authority'.[371]

Second, the NT obligation in Art 8.5.1 EU-Vietnam FTA only applies in sectors to which the parties specifically committed (positive list approach). The EU committed to NT of Vietnamese investors in a wide array of sectors, for instance for computer and related services. At the same time, the EU maintained significant flexibilities in other sectors—for example, in the realm of energy services, meaning pipeline transportation of fuels; wholesale trade services, retail sales, and distribution services of fuels, electricity, and water.[372]

Third, Art 17.13(b) EU-Vietnam FTA provides the EU with a security exception nearly identical to Arts XXI(b) GATT 1994, and XIV*bis*(1)(b) GATS. Therefore, the—limited—EU flexibilities already analyzed in Sect. 3.1 apply.

Fourth, the EU-Vietnam FTA, as all EU new generation preferential trade agreements, is generally more open to public interest considerations when weighed against investment liberalizing interests. In several provisions the parties emphasize that the commitments they enter into are without prejudice to their right to regulate.[373] It is important to stress that these provisions do not constitute a ground of

---

Art VI(5) GATS, which will be discussed in more detail in Sect. 4.3.4.3. Therefore, the following discussion is limited to the NT commitment. In addition, in Art 8.6.1 EU-Vietnam FTA, the EU commits to treat investors from Vietnam not less favourable than investors of any other country— however, only relating to the operation of the establishment, not the establishment itself.

[369] See again the definition of 'juridical person' in Art 8.2.1(i) in conjunction with (h), cited in n. 366.

[370] See in particular Arts 10.3.3, 11.4.1, 11.5 EU-Vietnam FTA.

[371] Art 8.3.2(a), (b), (f) EU-Vietnam FTA.

[372] See EU schedule of commitments in Appendix 8-A-2 to the EU-Vietnam FTA.

[373] See e.g. Arts 8.1.2 and 13.2.1(b) EU-Vietnam FTA.

exception for which the regulating party bears the burden of proof. Instead, they may determine the interpretation of the party's commitments, including the scope of the EU's NT obligation vis-à-vis Vietnamese investors in Art 8.5.1 EU-Vietnam FTA. Accordingly, one may invoke the EU's right to regulate to argue that a measure affects EU and Vietnamese investors not 'in like situations'. Thus, the measure would not violate the EU's commitment to NT. This may also provide the EU with more flexibility for screening FDI of Vietnamese investors, but not EU investors, at least in some situations.

Nevertheless, while these four caveats have an attenuating effect, the EU-Vietnam FTA significantly limits the EU's flexibility to screen FDI of Vietnamese investors, in particular due to the EU's commitment to NT in Art 8.5.1 EU-Vietnam FTA.

4.3.2.1.2   CETA

In many ways CETA takes a different approach than the EU-Vietnam FTA. Most importantly, CETA incorporates FTA and IPA into one agreement,[374] and provides a much deeper integration. This deeper integration also manifests itself in more investment liberalization. Namely two provisions determine the EU's flexibility to screen FDI vis-à-vis Canada.[375]

First, as in the EU-Vietnam FTA, the EU commits to NT of Canadian investors[376] regarding their establishment.[377] In CETA, however, the parties agreed to a negative

---

[374]This is namely demonstrated by the definition of investor in Art 8.1 CETA as an investor who 'seeks to make, is making or has made an investment' (cf Titi (2018), p. 7). With the integration of FTA and IPA the parties did not expand the investor rights regarding investment protection and investor-state arbitration to the pre-establishment phase. This is explicitly stated by Art 8.2.4 CETA. These additional investor rights in the realm of investment protection do therefore not limit the EU's flexibility to screen FDI.

[375]As in the EU-Vietnam FTA, the commitment to granting market access to foreign investors in Art 8.4.1 CETA is drafted similarly to Art XVI GATS. Therefore, the commitment does arguably not prohibit FDI Screening mechanism, which are based on qualitative, not quantitative criteria; see n. 368 and Sect. 4.3.4.1. Similarly, the EU's obligations on 'Domestic Regulation' in Art 12.13 CETA do not apply, since the FDI Screening mechanisms already constitute NT discrimination pursuant to Art 8.6.1 CETA; see also n. 368 and Sect. 4.3.4.3. Accordingly, Canada schedules its own FDI screening mechanism, the Investment Canada Act (as amended) 1985, as a reservation to NT, not Domestic regulation (Reservation I-C-1 in Canada's schedule to Annex I). Admittedly, the same reservation is scheduled to Market access. The Market access reservation, however, is due to the Economic needs test that is also included in the Investment Canada Act.

[376]For easier reading the following uses the more untechnical terms 'Canadian investor' and 'EU investor' instead of 'investor of Canada or 'investor of the EU', see for these terms Art 8.1 CETA.

[377]As CETA integrates FTA and IPA, the scope of its investment chapter does not differentiate between establishment and operation. Instead, Art 8.1 CETA generally defines investment as 'every kind of asset that an investor owns or controls, directly or indirectly, that has the characteristics of an investment, which includes a certain duration and other characteristics such as the commitment of

list approach. This means liberalizing investment across all sectors, unless a party schedules a reservation.[378] Art 8.6.1 CETA provides:

> Each Party shall accord to an investor of the other Party and to a covered investment, treatment no less favourable than the treatment it accords, in like situations to its own investors and to their investments with respect to the establishment, acquisition, expansion ... of their investments in its territory.

Accordingly, since FDI Screening mechanisms screen foreign and thus Canadian investors, but not EU investors, they would violate the EU's NT obligation. Apart from a few generally exempted sectors,[379] the EU scheduled a number of (sub)sector reservations to its NT commitment.[380] Nevertheless, the EU's NT obligation covers a wide array of sectors.

Second, the parties in CETA also committed to treat investors of the other party not less favourable than investors of any other country—unlike under the EU-Vietnam FTA also regarding the investors' establishment. Art 8.7.1 CETA provides

> Each Party shall accord to an investor of the other Party and to a covered investment, treatment no less favourable than the treatment it accords in like situations, to investors of a third country and to their investments with respect to the establishment, acquisition, expansion... of their investments in its territory.

Pursuant to this MFN obligation, the EU can only screen FDI of Canadian investors if it also screens any investor of another country in a like situation. This significantly raises the barriers to adopt FDI Screening mechanisms vis-à-vis Canadian investors.

At the same time, CETA, like the EU-Vietnam FTA, emphasizes the parties' right to regulate,[381] and provides exceptions to the parties' commitments.[382] The grounds of exception go beyond those provided in the EU-Vietnam FTA. In addition to a security exception that is nearly identical with Arts XXI GATT 1994 and XIV*bis*

---

capital or other resources, the expectation of gain or profit, or the assumption of risk'. Art 8.1 CETA then adds a non-exhaustive list of examples.

[378] Nevertheless, the parties also exempted a small number of sectors generally from their invest-ment liberalization commitments. The EU exempted audio-visual services, Canada cultural indus-tries (Art 8.2.3 CETA). Regarding establishment and the acquisition of establishments, the parties further exempted the sectors of air transport services and activities as governmental authority (Art 8.2.2 CETA).

[379] Pursuant to Art 8.2.2 these services are air services and related services, as well as 'activities carried out in the exercise of governmental authority'. They are thus similar to those excluded in the EU-Vietnam FTA, except for audiovisual services.

[380] In its schedule to Annex II the EU namely scheduled exceptions for investment liberalization for public utilities; the collection, purification, and distribution of water; certain business services such as legal and telecommunication services; cultural, educational, social, and health services; as well as certain transport and energy services.

[381] See preamble and Arts 23.2 and 24.3 CETA.

[382] Interestingly, however, in the chapter on liberalizing investment the right to regulate is only explicitly addressed for the section of investment protection, and thus not regarding the NT and MFN obligations for investor establishment in Arts 8.6.1 and 8.7.1 CETA; see Art 8.9.1 CETA.

GATS,[383] CETA also incorporates the other general GATT 1994 exception in Art XX, and adds a third exception that is nearly identical with Art XIV GATS.

Last but not least, CETA also addresses concerns about state ownership and influence on investors by providing rules on competition, and requiring inter alia SOEs to take decisions based on commercial considerations; without discriminating between private and public market actors, as well as domestic and foreign goods and service providers.[384]

All in all, especially the EU's NT commitment in CETA significantly limits its flexibility to screen Canadian investors—in even more sectors than committed to in the EU-Vietnam FTA.

4.3.2.1.3 Recent Developments: EU-UK Trade and Cooperation Agreement and EU-China CAI

The EU-Vietnam FTA and CETA seem less illustrative for EU commitments on establishment liberalization vis-à-vis the United Kingdom and China to which the EU has special relations. The United Kingdom is a former Member State. China, on the other hand, is not only an important trading partner, but also a 'systemic rival' who is a main focus of the EU and Member States concerns vis-à-vis foreign investors.[385] Vis-à-vis both countries recent developments have led to new agreements: The EU-UK Trade and Cooperation Agreement and an agreement in principle on an EU-China CAI. Given the EU and Member States concerns vis-à-vis Chinese investors, the latter is of paramount importance.

EU-UK Trade and Cooperation Agreement
The EU-UK Trade and Cooperation Agreement, despite its special character as post-EU membership agreement, constitutes in its most relevant parts for this book an FTA. This is particularly true in the realm of investment liberalization.

Provisionally applicable as of 1 January 2021,[386] its chapter on services and investment includes the establishment of investors of the other party.[387] As in CETA, the parties, in Art SERVIN.2.3, commit to NT for the establishment of investors:

---

[383] Art 28.6 CETA.

[384] See namely Arts 17.2, 17.3, 18.4, 18.5 CETA.

[385] For the notion 'systemic rival' see Commission and High Representative of the Union for Foreign Affairs and Security Policy, 'EU-China - A Strategic outlook' (Joint Communication) JOIN (2015), pp. 1, 5, reaffirmed by European Council, 'Conclusions of European Council Meeting (1 and 2 October 2020)' EUCO 13/20, para. 26.

[386] Art FINPROV.11(2) EU-UK Trade and Cooperation Agreement, only until 28 February 2021 if not subsequently agreed otherwise or ratified before.

[387] Art SERVIN.1.2(h), (j) EU-UK Trade and Cooperation Agreement.

> Each Party shall accord to investors of the other Party and to covered enterprises treatment no less favourable than that it accords, in like situations, to its own investors and to their enterprises, with respect to their establishment and operation in its territory.[388]

The EU-UK Trade and Cooperation Agreement also follows a negative list approach that by default extends the NT obligation to all sectors, except where explicitly excluded. As the EU scheduled only a few reservations—much less than in CETA—its NT commitment covers the wide majority of sectors.[389] As in CETA, but in contrast to the EU-Vietnam FTA, the parties furthermore commit to MFN treatment in Art 2.4(1) EU-UK Trade and Cooperation Agreement.

Both commitments are again limited by grounds of exception that reflect Arts XX and XXI GATT 1994, Arts XIV and XIV*bis* GATS,[390] as well as by the emphasis of the parties' right to regulate in Art SERVIN.1.1(2) of the EU-UK Trade and Cooperation Agreement.

As a result, regarding the liberalization of investor establishment, the EU's commitments vis-à-vis the United Kingdom are comparable to those in CETA, but go beyond the EU-Vietnam FTA. Therefore, the following will include the United Kingdom in the category of an FTA partner country.

EU-China CAI

In the context of FDI screening, the EU and China's agreement on concluding the EU-China CAI is even more important. If the EU-China CAI significantly limits the

---

[388] As in the EU-Vietnam FTA and CETA, the EU also commits to granting market access to foreign investors in Art SERVIN.2.2 EU-UK Trade and Cooperation Agreement. This provision is drafted similarly to Art XVI GATS. Therefore, the commitment does arguably not prohibit FDI Screening mechanism, which are based on qualitative, not quantitative criteria, see n. 368 and Sect. 4.3.4.1. Similarly, the EU's obligations on 'Domestic Regulation' in Arts SERVIN.5.2-5.11 EU-UK Trade and Cooperation Agreement do not apply, since the FDI Screening mechanisms already constitute NT discrimination pursuant to Art SERVIN.2.3 EU-UK Trade and Cooperation Agreement; see also n. 368 and Sect. 4.3.4.3.

[389] E.g., across sectors for privatized public utilities (Annex SERVIN-2 Reservation No 1(a) of the EU-UK Trade and Cooperation Agreement); arms, munition, and war materials (Annex SERVIN-2, Reservation No 1(e)); as well as in the subsectors of legal services (Annex SERVIN-1 Reservation No 2(a)); auditing services (Annex SERVIN-1 Reservation No 2(d)); railway passenger transportation (Annex SERVIN-2 Reservation 20(d)). In addition, different Member States added reservations in different sectors. The sectors transport and certain related services, audiovisual services, national maritime cabotage, and inland waterways transport are entirely exempted from commitments in the title 'Services and Investment'.

[390] Art EXC.1(1) EU-UK Trade and Cooperation Agreement incorporates Art XX GATT 1994 and Art EXC.1(2) is nearly identical to Art XIV GATS. Art EXC.4 reflects Art XXI GATT 1994 and Art XIV*bis* GATS, with Art EXC.4(b)(i) having a slightly broader wording than its WTO counterparts: ...*connected to* the production of or traffic in arms, ammunition and implements of war and to such production, traffic and transactions *in other goods and materials, services and technology, and to economic activities*, carried out directly or indirectly for the purpose of supplying a military establishment (emphasis added).

EU's flexibility to adopt FDI Screening mechanisms vis-à-vis China, the entire purpose of FDI screening in the EU may be undermined.

At the moment of writing, the EU and China have reached an 'Agreement in Principle' on the EU-China CAI,[391] but its ratification in the EU was still on hold in particular due to differences between EU and China over China's treatment of the Uyghur population.[392] Nevertheless, the agreement has been substantially agreed and published.[393] The following will identify the commitments that, in the near future, may limit the EU's flexibility to adopt FDI Screening mechanisms vis-à-vis China. Given the uncertainty around the EU-China CAI's ratification, the following will not be based on a detailed analysis of the submitted sector-specific commitments in the EU's schedule but will, insofar, rely on the Commission's summary.[394]

The negotiated EU-China CAI is an investment liberalization and protection agreement that covers the establishment and post-establishment phase.[395] As in the trade agreements analyzed above, the most important provision for the EU's flexibility to adopt FDI Screening mechanisms is the NT obligation.[396] In Art 4(1) of Section II of the EU-China CAI, the parties commit to accord NT to investors of the other party with respect to establishment and its operation, unless they scheduled a reservation for a certain measure or sector (negative list approach). As the definition of establishment reflects the notion of FDI,[397] the EU's NT obligation may forbid the EU to adopt FDI Screening mechanisms that screen foreign, thus Chinese investors, but not EU investors.[398] Moreover, given the negative list approach, the EU's NT commitment may cover a wide array of sectors. If comparable to its commitments

---

[391] Commission, 'Agreement in Principle on EU-China CAI' (n. 363).

[392] See e.g. Ni (2021).

[393] See 'EU-China Comprehensive Agreement on Investment (CAI): list of sections', <https://trade.ec.europa.eu/doclib/press/index.cfm?id=2237> accessed 2 February 2022.

[394] Commission, 'Agreement in Principle on EU-China CAI' (n. 363).

[395] See Art 1(1) of Section II EU-China CAI, and the definition of establishment and operation in Art 2 of Section I EU-China CAI.

[396] As in the EU-Vietnam FTA, CETA, and the EU-UK Trade and Cooperation Agreement, the EU also commits to granting market access to foreign investors in Art 2 of Section II EU-China CAI. As in the other agreements, the provision is drafted similarly to Art XVI GATS. Therefore, the commitment does arguably not prohibit FDI Screening mechanism, which are based on qualitative, not quantitative criteria, see n. 368 and Sect. 4.3.4.1. Similarly, the EU's obligations on 'Domestic Regulation' in Section III EU-China CAI do not apply, since the FDI Screening mechanisms already constitute NT discrimination pursuant to Art 4(1) EU-China CAI; see also n. 368 and Sect. 4.3.4.3.

[397] See Art 2 of Section I EU-China CAI: '"establishment" means the setting up, including the acquisition [footnote 1], of an enterprise in China or in the EU respectively with a view to establishing or maintaining lasting economic links'. Footnote 1 adds: 'The term "acquisition" shall be understood as including capital participation in an enterprise with a view to establishing or maintaining lasting economic links.' For the definition of FDI for the purposes of this book see Sect. 2.4.1.

[398] For easier reading the untechnical terms 'Chinese investor' and 'EU investor' are used instead of 'investor of China' or 'investor of the EU', see for these terms Art 2 of Section II EU-China CAI.

vis-à-vis Canada and the United Kingdom, the EU's flexibility to screen FDI of Chinese investors may be significantly limited.

As already concluded with regard to the other agreements, this conclusion is only slightly attenuated by three aspects: the emphasis on the parties' right to regulate,[399] a small number of sectors that are completely exempted from the investment liberalization obligations,[400] and grounds of exception that reflect those in WTO law.[401]

However, the Commission emphasizes that it did not commit to more than it had already agreed to in the WTO, namely in the GATS. Indeed, this statement is already at odds with the agreement's negative list approach to the NT obligation, since its counterpart in Art XVII GATS follows a positive list approach.[402] Nevertheless, the Commission announces: 'The policy space in the sensitive sectors (such as energy, infrastructure, ... or public services ...) is well preserved.'[403] Due to the limited available information, this book will follow the Commission's assessment. It thus assumes that the EU NT commitments in the EU-China CAI do not exceed the EU's WTO obligations, namely its sector-specific commitments to NT in Art XVII GATS. The EU's flexibility to adopt FDI Screening mechanisms vis-à-vis China is therefore still mainly determined by the GATS, which will be assessed below.

Last but not least, it is interesting to note that the EU-China CAI follows the EU's approach in the EU-Vietnam FTA to address competition, harmful investor, and private information concerns regarding state-owned or -influenced investors. The agreement omits a differentiation between private and public enterprises. Instead, it focuses on rules that require public enterprises to act based on non-discriminatory treatment and according to commercial considerations.[404]

Consequently, but subject to the two caveats initially defined, the EU's NT obligation in the EU-China CAI limits the EU's flexibility to adopt FDI Screening mechanisms that meet the EU and Member States concerns vis-à-vis investors from China. However, these limits do not seem to exceed the EU's relevant WTO obligations—especially its sector-specific commitments to NT in Art XVII GATS. They will be discussed in more detail below. Thus, the EU-China CAI does not add additional significant limitations, but merely reinforces the EU's limits to adopt broader FDI Screening mechanisms that already existed before.

---

[399] See preamble and Art 1(2) of Section I EU-China CAI.

[400] Art 1(2) of Section II EU-China CAI exempts audio-visual services, certain air transport services, and activities supplied in the exercise of governmental authority from investment liberalization obligations.

[401] See Art 4(1) and (2) of Section VI EU-China CAI, which reflect Art XIV GATS and incorporate Art XX GATT 1994. Art 10 of Section VI EU-China CAI reflects the security exceptions in Art XXI GATT 1994 and Art XIVbis GATS, with a slightly broader wording than its WTO counterparts; cf Art EXC.4(b)(i) of the EU-UK Trade and Cooperation Agreement as analyzed in n. 390.

[402] See in more detail Sects. 4.3.4.2 and 4.3.4.4.

[403] Commission, 'Agreement in Principle on EU-China CAI' (n. 363), p. 2.

[404] Art 3bis(3) of Section II EU-China CAI.

4.3.2.1.4   FTAs as Significant Limits for EU FDI Screening Mechanisms Vis-à-vis Partner Countries—EU-China CAI as an Outlier

The overview of the EU's bi- and plurilateral agreements showed a highly complex picture of EU obligations to liberalize foreign establishment. The obligations differ greatly among FTA partner countries. Nevertheless, the analysis indicated that FTAs significantly limit the EU's flexibility to adopt FDI Screening mechanisms on broader grounds than 'security or public order'.

The analysis of the EU-Vietnam FTA and CETA showed that the EU has extensively liberalized the establishment of investors from Vietnam and Canada. Namely, NT obligations significantly limit the EU's flexibility to screen FDI of these investors. Certainly, exempted and reserved (sub)sectors, grounds of exception, and the emphasis of the parties' right to regulate attenuate the liberalization to some extent. Nevertheless, a general cross-sector FDI screening beyond the grounds of 'security or public order' seems difficult to reconcile with the EU's commitments. Last but not least, the agreements demonstrate that the EU seeks to address concerns of public ownership and influence by promoting efficient competition rules, not by excluding public or publicly influenced actors from their markets.

As argued in the introduction, this conclusion based on the examples of the EU-Vietnam FTA and CETA may be extrapolated to other present and future bi- and plurilateral FTAs and other agreements that include FTA chapters. This was confirmed by the EU-UK Trade and Cooperation Agreement. The agreement follows the approach in CETA. However, given the UK's particular status as a former Member State, the EU commits to NT for investment liberalization in even more sectors. In addition, this finding further emphasizes that the EU's NT commitments differ greatly among FTAs based on a different sector coverage. Thus, it is very difficult to consistently identify sectors in which the EU may still discriminate against investors from all FTA partner countries.

As a result, one may more generally conclude that the EU's flexibility to adopt FDI Screening mechanisms on broader grounds than 'security or public order' is significantly limited vis-à-vis all FTA partner countries. This has important consequences for designing a legislative option of FDI Screening mechanisms that complies with International economic law: If the EU nevertheless adopts FDI Screening mechanisms on broader grounds than 'security or public order', it would need to exclude investors of FTA partner countries from their personal scope.

In the EU-China CAI, however, the EU has opted for a different route than in its FTAs. While it also limits the EU's flexibility to adopt FDI Screening mechanisms, the EU's commitments do, according to the Commission, not exceed those undertaken in the WTO, namely in the GATS. Thus, for assessing the EU's limits to adopt FDI Screening mechanisms pursuant to the EU-China CAI, it is sufficient to analyze the EU's WTO commitments, namely its sector-specific commitments to NT pursuant to Art XVII GATS. This will be done in the following.

Finally, the analysis showed that the EU's relevant bi- and plurilateral agreements often adopt provisions that reflect WTO law, namely the GATS. Consequently, the

GATS analysis in the following sections is also relevant to the interpretation of the EU's commitments in many other agreements of International economic law.

4.3.2.2 WTO Agreements: GATS with the Potential to Widely Liberalize FDI

In the WTO the EU has undertaken commitments that limit its flexibility to screen FDI vis-à-vis 136 other WTO members.[405] The EU is, as all of its Member States, a full member of the WTO, and as such bound by WTO law.[406] WTO law consists of the WTO-Agreement and its Annexes 1 to 4.[407] The annexes include inter alia the GATT 1994, based on the GATT 1947, the TRIMs Agreement, the TRIPS Agreement, and the GATS. These agreements focus on the different trade elements: goods, services, and IP rights. Investment, on the other hand, is only covered to the extent it is relevant to these elements. As a result, WTO investment rules are highly fragmented.

The following will briefly assess these agreements' potential to limit the EU's flexibility to adopt FDI Screening mechanisms. It will conclude that the GATT 1994, as well as the TRIMs and TRIPS Agreements only limit the EU's flexibility of how to design the FDI screening process, namely by prohibiting certain requirements that may be imposed on the investor as a condition to receive FDI authorization. Only the GATS, however, liberalizes the establishment of foreign investors, and is thus directly relevant to the EU's flexibility to adopt FDI Screening mechanisms on broader grounds than 'security or public order'.

4.3.2.2.1 Agreements on Trade in Goods: GATT 1994 and TRIMs Agreement

The WTO agreements on trade in goods provide some limits on measures that are often imposed on foreign investors to attenuate home country concerns: local content and performance requirements. These measures require the investor to operate her facility in the host country in a way that includes purchasing or using domestically produced goods.

The GATT 1994 limits the WTO members' flexibility to adopt quantitative restrictions, tariffs, other duties and charges, as well as internal domestic policies regarding the trade in goods through outright prohibitions, MFN, and NT obligations.[408] The NT obligation in Art III(4) GATT 1994, as the most important

---

[405] Overall, the WTO has 164 members, reduced by the EU and its Member States, 136 members remain.

[406] See Arts II(1), XI(1), XIV(1) WTO-Agreement, and n. 344.

[407] Art II(1), (2) WTO-Agreement.

[408] Arts I(1), III(1), (2), (4), XI(1), XIII GATT 1994.

obligation in this context, prohibits WTO members to adopt policies affecting the trade in goods that discriminate between goods of domestic origin on the one and imported goods on the other hand. Such policies may even be measures that do 'not directly regulate goods, or the importation of goods'.[409] Accordingly, the WTO adjudicating bodies have found that local content measures violate Arts III(4) or XI (1) GATT 1994 if they require investors to purchase or use only domestic products, or a certain amount of these products in their production.[410] Investment requirements on employment, subsequent domestic investment, and research and development, however, do not violate GATT obligations.[411]

The GATT 1994 is complemented by the TRIMs Agreement. The agreement applies to 'investment measures related to trade in goods only'.[412] In so doing, its scope broadly overlaps with the GATT 1994.[413] Importantly, however, Art 2.2 TRIMs Agreement explicitly states that certain investment measures always violate Arts III(4) or XI(1) GATT 1994.[414] The list of prohibited investment measures contains local content and performance requirements, as well as trade-balance requirements.[415] More concretely, WTO members are prohibited to adopt four groups of measures: requirements to purchase or use products of domestic origin

---

[409] *China—Measures Affecting Trading Rights and Distribution Services for Certain Publications and Audiovisual Entertainment Products*, Appellate Body Report (21 December 2009) WT/DS363/ AB/R, WTO Online Database doc no 09-6642, para. 227.

[410] See e.g. *India—Certain Measures Relating to Solar Cells and Solar Modules*, Panel Report (24 February 2016) WT/DS456/R, as modified by Appellate Body Report WT/DS456/AB/R, WTO Online Database doc no 15-6724, paras. 7.195–7.198 (on requirements to use a minimum amount of domestically produced auto parts and components); already on Art III(4) GATT 1947, *Canada— FIRA* (n. 2), paras. 5.8–5.11 (on investor undertakings to purchase goods of Canadian origin and from Canadian suppliers; investors committed deliberately to these undertakings in order to improve their chances for authorization in the Canadian FDI screening procedure). For further examples of panel reports see *China—Publications and Audiovisual Products* (n. 409), n. 432.

[411] *Canada—FIRA* (n. 2), para. 5.21.

[412] Art 1 TRIMs Agreement.

[413] *Brazil—Certain Measures Concerning Taxation and Charges*, Panel Report (30 August 2017) WT/DS472/R and WT/DS497/R, as modified by Appellate Body Report WT/DS472/AB/R and WT/DS497/AB/R, WTO Online Database doc no 17-4582, para. 7.39. The overlap is mainly due to the fact that the TRIMs Agreement merely clarifies that the prohibition of quantitative restrictions and NT discrimination in Arts XI(1) and III(4) GATT 1994 also applies to investment-related measures.

[414] *Canada—Measures Relating to the Feed-in Tariff Program*, Appellate Body Report (6 May 2013) WT/DS412/AB/R and WT/DS426/AB/R, WTO Online Database doc no 13-2400, paras. 5.24, 5.26, 5.94, 5.103; *Brazil—Taxation*, Panel Report (n. 413), para. 7.40. On appeal, in *Brazil— Certain Measures Concerning Taxation and Charges*, Appellate Body Report (13 December 2018) WT/DS472/AB/R and WT/DS497/AB/R, WTO Online Database doc no 18-7793, paras. 5.62–5.64, 5.77–5.79, the Appellate Body also focused on assessing Art III(4) GATT 1994. Regarding Art 2(1) TRIMs Agreement, it held that Brazil did not submit any further arguments. One may therefore argue that the Appellate Body upheld the panel's characterization of the relation between GATT 1994 and TRIMs Agreement.

[415] Trade-balance requirements seek to ensure that the host state's balance of imports and exports is intact, and therefore require the investor to import and/or export goods of a certain value.

or source; quantitative limits to purchase or use of imported products; quantitative limits to import products; and restrictions of product exports.[416] These measures are only allowed if the WTO member may invoke a ground of exception pursuant to Art 3 TRIMs Agreement, which references Arts XX and XXI GATT 1994. Requirements to (not) transfer technology, on the other hand, are arguably not prohibited under the TRIMs, and therefore allowed beyond the provided grounds of exception.[417]

As a result, WTO members are considerably limited in imposing goods trade-related measures on investors as part of FDI screening procedures. This restriction even applies if prohibited measures are not imposed by authorities, but incorporated in undertakings the investor deliberately commits to in the course of the FDI screening procedure.[418]

Nevertheless, GATT 1994 and TRIMs Agreement only limit WTO members' flexibility to regulate investment to the extent their measures favour domestic goods over foreign goods, in one way or another. The establishment or investment protection measures as such are not covered.[419] Before the WTO and TRIMs Agreement era, this was confirmed by the panel in *Canada—FIRA*. Having this decision in mind, the WTO members did not expand the scope of the TRIMs to establishment of foreign investors generally.[420] Though expressing the desire to 'facilitate investment across international frontiers', this desire was not put into concrete legal obligations.[421] Indeed, some WTO members strongly opposed against further liberalizing foreign investor establishment. This opposition also materialized in the failure to conclude a multilateral investment agreement, and advance with the WTO Multilateral Framework on Investment.[422]

---

[416] Annex to TRIMs Agreement. See e.g. *Canada—Feed-In Tariff Program* (n. 414), para. 7.111 (on a minimum local content requirement on electricity generators using solar and windpower technologies); *India—Solar Cells*, Panel Report (n. 410), para. 7.63 (on local content requirement to use specific local goods to be eligible for bidding in a national solar energy bidding process). India's appeal in India—Solar Cells did not further address the TRIMs Agreement (*India—Certain Measures relating to Solar Cells and Solar Modules*, Appellate Body Report (16 September 2016) WT/DS456/AB/R, WTO Online Database doc no 16-4918, para. 5.12).

[417] Trebilcock et al. (2013), p. 584.

[418] *Canada—FIRA* (n. 2), paras. 5.4–5.6, arguing that the investor does so only to raise her chances that the screening authority authorizes the investment.

[419] Chaisse (2012), p. 163; Heinemann (2012), p. 854, n. 54. In *Brazil—Taxation*, Brazil did not raise this issue by arguing that 'pre-market' measures directed at producers not goods are not covered by Art III GATT 1994. In this sense, the notion 'pre-market' was only intended to differentiate between producer- and good-related measures (see *Brazil—Taxation*, Panel Report (n. 413), paras. 7.61–7.70; *Brazil—Taxation*, Appellate Body Report (n. 414), para. 5.80).

[420] Similarly, Trebilcock et al. (2013), p. 584. Otherwise important developing countries would not have agreed to the TRIMs Agreement, see their 'Draft Declaration on Trade-Related Investment Measures' as paraphrased in Croome (1999), p. 222.

[421] Croome (1999), pp. 116–117, 219–223, 267–268; Heinemann (2012), p. 85, n. 51.

[422] On the failure to conclude the Multilateral Investment Treaty within the OECD, see e.g. Böhmer (1998), p. 267. On the later developments and discussion around a multilateral set of investment

Therefore, neither the GATT 1994, nor TRIMs Agreement restrict the WTO members' flexibility to regulate the establishment of foreign investors. The EU thus maintains its flexibility to adopt FDI Screening mechanisms.[423] Nevertheless, the agreements limit the EU's flexibility to impose content and performance requirements as conditions for authorizing or not prohibiting the FDI. This may have some attenuating effect on the EU's and Member States' flexibility to shape the FDI screening process in accordance with their concerns vis-à-vis foreign investors.

4.3.2.2.2 TRIPS Agreement

Another WTO agreement that is relevant to FDI screening is the TRIPS Agreement. Similar to the GATT 1994 and TRIMS Agreement, the TRIPS Agreement provides certain restrictions on requirements that are sometimes imposed during the FDI screening process, yet not on the adoption of the FDI Screening mechanism itself.

The TRIPS Agreement provides a multilateral framework for the protection of intellectual property rights, and does not explicitly address investment. Parts II to IV of the TRIPS Agreement provide a minimum level of absolute intellectual property protection regarding availability, scope, use, enforcement, acquisition, and maintenance of intellectual property rights.[424] For instance, Art 28(2) TRIPS Agreement provides that patent owners shall have the right to assign the patent or conclude licensing contracts. The agreement protects intellectual property rights further by means of negative integration. Arts 3(1) and 4 TRIPS Agreement generally prohibit discriminatory practices with regard to the protection of intellectual property rights through NT and MFN obligations.[425]

At the same time, the TRIPS Agreement recognizes the particular importance of other public interests that may weigh against protecting intellectual property. Accordingly, Art 7 TRIPS Agreement states that the protection of intellectual property rights should contribute to inter alia 'the transfer and dissemination of technology ... in a manner conducive to social and economic welfare'. In addition, Art 8 TRIPS Agreement ensures that WTO members reserve the right to adopt measures necessary for certain public interests, including the socio-economic and technological development. In contrast to other WTO agreements, the TRIPS

---

rules in the WTO, see e.g. Sauvé (2006), p. 325; Wolf (2008), pp. 74–80. Current plurilateral Structural Discussions on a multilateral framework on investment facilitation for development focus on procedures and cooperation, excluding the fundamental issues of market access and investment protection (see WTO members Afghanistan and others, 'Joint Ministerial Statement on Investment Facilitation for Development' WT/L/1072/Rev.1).

[423] With the same result Lecheler and Germelmann (2010), p. 103; Geiger (2013), p. 286; Fassion and Natens (2020), pp. 123–124, 131–132.

[424] Cf Malbon et al. (2014), para. 1.05.

[425] See e.g. Elfring (2009), paras. 1–3. See also Malbon et al. (2014), paras. 3.03–3.07.

obligations are therefore relatively open to taking public interest considerations into account.[426]

Consequently, the TRIPS Agreement, as the GATT 1994 and the TRIMs Agreement, does not limit the WTO members' flexibility to adopt FDI Screening mechanisms as such. It does not address the establishment of foreign investors.

Nevertheless, the TRIPS Agreement limits the WTO members' flexibility to impose intellectual property requirements on the foreign investor as part of the FDI screening process. This becomes important if the EU and Member States want to address their concern that a foreign investor may transfer know-how to his home country.[427] The prohibition to transfer or license certain know-how may violate Art 28(2) TRIPS Agreement, which provides the right to assign and license patent rights. The prohibition may also violate the non-discrimination obligations in Arts 3(1) and 4 TRIPS Agreement, especially when discriminating between different WTO members. However, the EU and Member States keep more flexibility than the screening ground 'security or public order' within the meaning of the Screening Regulation provides. Arts 7 and 8 TRIPS Agreement allow to pursue technological development, socio-economic effects, and other public interests of vital importance.[428]

In sum, the TRIPS Agreement does not address the issue of investor establishment, and therefore does not affect the EU's flexibility to adopt FDI Screening mechanisms as such. Nonetheless, the TRIPS Agreement limits to some extent restrictions of intellectual property rights that the EU and Member States may want to impose on foreign investors as conditions to authorizing or not prohibiting the FDI. This affects the EU's and its Member States' flexibility to shape the FDI screening process in accordance with their concerns vis-à-vis foreign investors on know-how transfer.

4.3.2.2.3 GATS

In contrast to the other WTO agreements analyzed so far, the GATS explicitly covers the establishment of foreign investors—for the purpose of trading services. It therefore has the potential to widely limit the EU's flexibility to adopt FDI Screening mechanisms.

---

[426]Malbon et al. (2014), paras. 7.15–7.22, argue that Art 7 TRIPS Agreement, in conjunction with inter alia Art 8 TRIPS Agreement, provides context to the agreement's interpretation ('any ambiguities in the Agreement are to be read in favour of an interpretation of TRIPS provisions that advances the social and economic conditions of all [WTO] [m]embers'). Malbon et al. (2014), paras. 8.08–8.10, also read Art 8 TRIPS Agreement as ensuring that TRIPS Agreement provisions are interpreted not only from a pure trade perspective, but in light of all principles addressed in Art 8 TRIPS Agreement.

[427]For a summary of the EU and Member States concerns vis-à-vis foreign investors, see Sect. 2.1.

[428]Also emphasizing this flexibility of WTO members to impose 'investment-policy-related measures on foreign patent-holders', Trebilcock et al. (2013), p. 529.

Art II(2) GATS defines the scope of the GATS as encompassing four modes of trade in services. Mode three is 'the supply of a service ... by a service supplier of one Member, through commercial presence in the territory of any other Member' (Art II(2)(c) GATS). Pursuant to Art XXVIII(d)(i) GATS a '"commercial presence" means any type of business or professional establishment including through ... the acquisition ... of a juridical person'. The GATS thus covers the establishment of foreign investors through M&A FDI. The additional requirement to 'supply of a service' through the M&A FDI will be fulfilled by most investors. In fact, the vast majority of companies at least also supplies a service, for instance maintenance services for their manufactured goods. Thus, the GATS constitutes a multilateral agreement that widely liberalizes FDI, at least to the extent it qualifies as commercial presence within the meaning of the GATS.

For all modes of service supply the GATS provides two types of obligations: general obligations and specific commitments. Generally, WTO members must inter alia accord MFN treatment when admitting the establishment of foreign investors (Art II(1) GATS).[429] This may significantly limit the EU's flexibility to adopt FDI Screening mechanisms that focus on particular countries. As specific commitments, the GATS provides market access and NT obligations (Arts XVI and XVII GATS). Broadly put, the market access obligation prohibits the WTO members to adopt an exhaustive list of quantitative market access restrictions, whereas the NT obligation requires to treat foreign investors not less favourable than domestic investors. However, the specific commitments only apply to the extent the respective WTO member has committed to them sector by sector (positive list approach). The EU has undertaken specific commitments in a wide array of sectors.[430]

At the same time, the GATS also provides grounds of exception that a WTO member may invoke to justify a violation of its GATS obligations. Besides the already analyzed exceptions of 'public order' (Art XIV(a) GATS) and 'essential security interests' (Art XIVbis(1)(b) GATS),[431] Art XIV GATS provides further exceptions. Art XIV(c) GATS, for example, exceptionally allows measures necessary to secure compliance with laws or regulations, relating inter alia to privacy and

---

[429] Adlung and Mattoo (2008), p. 64.

[430] WTO Member schedules are based on Art XX GATS. The following will refer to commitments of the EU. This is meant to include those commitments that were originally undertaken by the Member States before the EU obtained exclusive competence for Common commercial policy pursuant to Art 207(1) TFEU. Today, only Bulgaria, Croatia, and Romania maintain their own schedule. All other Member States commitments were merged into the 'EU Schedule', with differing terms, limitations, conditions, and qualifications among Member States in some cases. In the following, this book will refer to the 'EU commitments' as comprising all Member state commitments as scheduled in the 'EU Schedule'. Accordingly, when saying the EU committed to NT or Market access in certain sectors, this would include all Member States. This is in line with the EU's competence for trade policy pursuant to Art 207, para. 1 TFEU. Referring to EU commitments as in the EU Schedule, this book will, however, exclude the commitments of Bulgaria, Croatia, and Romania. Including their additional three schedules would further complicate the already complex and fragmented EU commitments.

[431] Arts XIV(a) and XIVbis(1)(b) GATS, for their analysis see Sect. 3.1.

safety. However, these grounds of exception are by definition narrow. Moreover, they are subject to further restrictions. First, the WTO member's measure must be 'necessary' to protect the listed interest. Second, the measure must fulfil the requirements in the *chapeau* of Art XIV GATS in that, the measure must not be applied in a manner that constitutes 'a means of arbitrary or unjustifiable discrimination. . ., or a disguised restriction of trade'.

Therefore, it is crucial to first assess the precise limits to the EU's flexibility to adopt FDI Screening mechanisms posed by the general and specific commitments: the MFN, Market access, and NT obligations in Arts II(1), XVI, and XVII GATS. Only to the extent these provisions limit the EU's flexibility to adopt FDI Screening mechanisms the grounds of exception become relevant. These aspects will be assessed in Sects. 4.3.3 to 4.3.8. The analysis may also inform the interpretation of the EU's commitments in its bi- and plurilateral agreements on the liberalization of establishment, since they are often similarly drafted. Indeed, when doing so, their different contexts and purposes must be taken into account.

4.3.2.3 Focus on the Multilateral GATS as Legal Limitation to the EU's Flexibility to Screen FDI

In sum, the overview of the EU's bi- and plurilateral agreements, as well as WTO agreements showed that the EU FTAs, as well as the GATS limit the EU considerably in adopting FDI Screening mechanisms on broader grounds than 'security or public order' within the meaning of the Screening Regulation.

FTAs, on the one hand, significantly limit the EU's flexibility to adopt broader FDI Screening mechanisms, especially by the NT obligation on investor establishment. However, the EU concluded FTAs only with a small number of third countries, such as Canada, the UK, and Vietnam. With the countries at particular focus of the concerns vis-à-vis foreign investors (Brazil, India, Iran, and Russia), on the other hand, the EU has no such FTAs in place—except since recently with China, subject to final adoption of the EU-China CAI. While the recent compromise on an EU-China CAI certainly grants China the status as a major EU trading partner, the EU stayed, according to the Commission, within the limits of its WTO commitments. Therefore, vis-à-vis countries of particular concern, it is still WTO law that determines the EU's flexibility to adopt FDI Screening mechanisms on broader grounds than 'security or public order'. Nonetheless, the analysis showed that FDI Screening mechanisms may need to exclude investors from other FTA partner countries to comply with the EU's FTA commitments.

The GATS, on the other hand, also provides important obligations for foreign investor establishment, though not as far reaching as the FTAs. However, these obligations limit the EU's flexibility to adopt FDI Screening mechanisms vis-à-vis all other 136 WTO members. This includes the countries of particular concern— even China, as the EU-China CAI does not exceed the EU's WTO commitments. In addition, many GATS provisions are reflected in the FTAs, most importantly the sector-specific approach, the NT obligation, and the grounds of exception. Their interpretation may therefore inform the FTA analysis—while taking into account their different contexts and purposes. The EU's obligations pursuant to the GATS are thus of utmost importance.

Last but not least, the other WTO agreements—GATT 1994, TRIMs, and TRIPS Agreement—only pose limits to the restrictions EU and Member States may impose as conditions in the FDI screening process. Namely, FDI Screening mechanisms may not impose content and performance requirements that affect goods trade.

Given the particular relevance of the GATS, the following analysis will further assess the concrete GATS obligations that may limit the EU's flexibility to adopt FDI Screening mechanisms on broader grounds than 'security or public order'. Section 4.3.3 will start with a detailed discussion of the GATS's scope. Sections 4.3.4 to 4.3.6 will then identify the GATS obligations that may limit the EU's flexibility to adopt FDI Screening mechanisms. Against this background, Sect. 4.3.7 will address relevant grounds of exception beyond 'public order' and 'essential security interests' pursuant to Arts XIV(a) and XIV*bis*(1)(b) GATS.

Finally, Sect. 4.3.8 will summarize the results and outline the policy options the EU has to adopt FDI Screening mechanisms on broader grounds than 'security or public order' that comply with WTO law and International economic law more generally. Much will depend on the personal and substantial scope of the FDI Screening mechanism as well as the envisaged screening criteria.

4.3.3   The Scope of the GATS

The constraining effect of the GATS on the EU's flexibility to adopt FDI Screening mechanisms beyond the screening ground 'security or public order' depends on the GATS's exact scope.[432] The scope is defined in Art I(1) GATS:

This Agreement applies to measures by Members affecting trade in services.

This definition includes three elements: (i) 'measures' (ii) 'affecting' (iii) 'trade in services'. The latter element is further defined as the supply of a service through four different modes (Art I(2) GATS). These modes include the supply of a service through 'commercial presence' (Mode three) by acquisition of a juridical person— the most relevant to FDI Screening mechanisms.[433]

Art XXVIII(c) GATS adds an illustrative list of measures falling in the GATS's scope:

(c) 'measures by Members affecting trade in services' include measures in respect of

---

[432] In *Canada—Certain Measures Affecting the Automotive Industry*, Appellate Body Report (31 May 2000) WT/DS139/AB/R and WT/DS142/AB/R, WTO Online Database doc no 00-2170, para. 152, the Appellate Body called this the 'threshold question' of the GATS.

[433] See Arts I(2)(c) and XXVIII(d)(i) GATS.

   (i) the purchase, payment or use of a service;

  (ii) the access to and use of, in connection with the supply of a service, services which are required by those Members to be offered to the public generally;

 (iii) the presence, including commercial presence, of persons of a Member for the supply of a service in the territory of another Member.

FDI screening and thus FDI Screening mechanisms regulate the establishment of foreign investors, in other words their 'commercial presence'. They might therefore fall under subparagraph (iii).

To confirm this presumption, the following sections will define the three elements of Art I(1) GATS: measures, affecting, and trade in services. The interpretation will be—as for all other relevant GATS provisions in the following sections—based on the interpretative means as outlined in Sect. 3.1.2.1. A particular focus will lie on the question whether the FDI Screening mechanism as a general law falls in the GATS's scope. Section 4.3.3.4 will summarize the results.

4.3.3.1 Measures

To fall in the GATS's scope, FDI Screening mechanisms must constitute a 'measure' within the meaning of Art I(1) GATS.[434]

Measure is further defined in Art XXVIII(a) GATS. The provision states that measures can take any form, including a law, regulation, procedure, or administrative decision. However, Art XXVIII(a) GATS does not cover measures that leave total discretion over their adoption to another actor. Hence, an EU directive or regulation that let the Member States decide over their implementation would not qualify as a measure within the meaning of Art I(1) GATS.[435] It is interesting to note that the Screening Regulation itself would therefore not qualify as a measure within the meaning of the GATS because it defers the adoption and application of an FDI Screening mechanism entirely to the Member States.[436]

---

[434] A similar, but different question is whether the adjudicating bodies have jurisdiction over a measure. This depends on the interpretation of Art 3.3 DSU. It provides that 'measures taken by another Member' should be promptly settled. The Appellate Body held: 'In principle, any act or omission attributable to a WTO Member can be a measure of that Member for purposes of dispute settlement proceedings.' (*United States—Sunset Review of Anti-Dumping Duties on Corrosion-Resistant Carbon Steel Flat Products from Japan*, Appellate Body Report (15 December 2003) WT/DS244/AB/R, WTO Online Database doc no 03-6603, para. 81). It suffices that instruments have general or prospective application, irrespective of their application to particular instances. There are two main arguments. First, WTO law also protects the security and predictability of future trade. Second, from a judicial economy perspective, it seems overly burdensome to oblige WTO members to litigate only single instances of concrete measure application, rather than the underlying abstract measure. See *US—Corrosion-Resistant Steel Sunset Review* (n. 434), para. 82, with further references to panel reports.

[435] See *European Union and its Member States—Certain Measures Relating to the Energy Sector*, Panel Report (10 August 2018) WT/DS476/R, WTO Online Database doc no 18-5025, paras. 7.387–7.389.

[436] Art 3, para. 1, recital 8 of Screening Regulation.

Most importantly, however, an FDI Screening mechanism as defined in Sect. 2. 4.3, as well as the final administrative prohibition of an individual FDI do qualify as measures within the meaning of Art I(1) GATS.

4.3.3.2   Affecting

A more complicated question is whether these measures are 'affecting' the trade in services. While this is evident for each individual prohibition of FDI, it is much less clear for the FDI Screening mechanism in general. The notion of affecting comprises two aspects.

On the one hand, it decides over the necessary nexus between the measure at issue and the trade in services: Must the measure directly regulate the supply of services, or are indirect effects on the trade in services enough? The Appellate Body follows the latter approach, finding that the meaning of affecting is 'wider in scope than such terms as "regulating" or "governing"'.[437] It is thus sufficient if a measure 'regulates other matters but nevertheless affects trade in services'.[438] As FDI Screening mechanisms are even directly regulating the establishment of a commercial presence, they are affecting trade in the sense of this first aspect of affecting.

On the other hand, the notion affecting decides over the degree of effect the measure at issue must have on trade in services in order to fall in the scope of the GATS. The measure must modify the conditions of competition.[439] The GATS itself makes clear that abstract measures may fulfil this requirement by, for instance, stating that domestic regulation measures of general application can affect trade

---

[437] *European Communities—Regime for the Importation, Sale and Distribution of Bananas*, Appellate Body Report (9 September 1997) WT/DS27/AB/R, WTO Online Database doc no 97-3593, para. 220.

[438] ibid., paras. 217, 220, citing and upholding *European Communities—Regime for the Importation, Sale and Distribution of Bananas (Complaint by the United States)*, Panel Report (22 May 1997) WT/DS27/R/USA, as modified by Appellate Body Report WT/DS27/AB/R, WTO Online Database doc no 97-2070, para. 7.285. The Appellate Body also held: 'In our view, the use of the term "affecting" reflects the intent of the drafters to give a broad reach to the GATS. The ordinary meaning of the word "affecting" implies a measure that has "an effect on", which indicates a broad scope of application.' Based on this understanding, the Appellate Body also argues that the GATS scope is not limited by the scope of GATT 1994 (*EC—Bananas III*, Appellate Body Report (n. 437), para. 221; *Canada—Autos*, Appellate Body Report (n. 432), paras. 159–160). It is in this sense that the Appellate Body also refers to the interpretation of Art III(4) GATT1994 as context for interpretation, *Argentina—Measures Relating to Trade in Goods and Services*, Appellate Body Report (14 April 2016) WT/DS453/AB/R, WTO Online Database doc no 16-2077, para. 6.109. For the issue of delimitation between GATT 1994 and GATS, see Sect. 4.3.3.3.1, in particular n. 450.

[439] *EC—Bananas III (US)*, Panel Report (n. 438), para. 7.281, n. 469, based on the preparatory work for the GATS in Group of Negotiations on Services, 'Definitions in the Draft General Agreement on Trade in Services' (Note by the Secretariat) MTN.GNS/W/139, para. 12: 'The term "affecting" has been interpreted in Article III of the GATT to mean an effect on the competitive relationship between like products, not on the subsequent trade volumes in those products'.

(Art VI(1) GATS).[440] Two Panel decisions give further guidance on the interpretation.[441]

In *EU—Energy Package* the measure at issue subjected the supply of gas pipeline services to a certificate, which was granted if inter alia the investment did not put the energy supply in the EU at risk.[442] The Panel held: 'As the third-country certification measure sets out the requirements for TSOs [gas transmission system operators] to be certified and hence permitted to supply pipeline transport services in the EU territory, it therefore affects trade in such pipeline transport services.'[443] In *Argentina—Financial Services* the Panel held that a measure affects trade in services if it affects a supplier's decision to establish a commercial presence.[444] At issue was an authorization for exchanging domestic into foreign currency when the investor wants to repatriate the investment. The authorization was granted if certain requirements were met. The Panel held that such an authorization requirement for repatriation already affects the investor's decision to establish a commercial presence.[445]

The panel's decision in *Argentina—Financial Services* needs further clarification. Even though its result is reasonable, any measure even remotely related to trade in services may affect an investor's decision to establish a commercial presence. Even a WTO member's aggressive policy in bilateral trade conflicts, for instance, could fulfil this condition. Instead, the determinant criterion for affecting trade in services is a minimum degree of modifying the competitive conditions of a foreign service supplier. In addition, the service supplier must be affected in its specific function as a service supplier, not merely as a person that happens to be in the WTO member's territory.

Before applying this understanding to FDI Screening mechanisms, it should be recalled that the mechanisms can take two forms. On the one hand, the mechanism may generally ban incoming FDI with the possibility of authorizing a specific FDI in an individual administrative decision ('Case 1'). On the other hand, the mechanism may generally authorize incoming FDI with the possibility for the government to prohibit an individual investment ('Case 2'). Legally, this uncertainty manifests itself in a statutory condition precedent to the contract between investor and asset.[446]

---

[440] Nettesheim (2008), p. 739, seems to oppose this view by stating that only the individual FDI prohibition can violate the GATS obligations; agreeing with Nettesheim, Geiger (2013), p. 283.

[441] On the nature of WTO adjudicating bodies' reports as precedents, see Chap. 3, n. 62.

[442] Directive 2009/73/EC of the European Parliament and of the Council of 13 July 2009 concerning common rules for the internal market in natural gas and repealing Directive 2003/55/EC [2009] OJ L 211/94, art 11(3)(b): 'granting certification will not put at risk the security of energy supply of the Member State and the Community'.

[443] *EU—Energy Package* (n. 435), para. 7.1067.

[444] *Argentina—Measures Relating to Trade in Goods and Services*, Panel Report (30 September 2015) WT/DS453/R, as modified by Appellate Body Report WT/DS453/AB/R, WTO Online Database doc no 15-5027, para. 7.112.

[445] ibid., paras. 7.110–7.112.

[446] See definition of FDI Screening mechanisms in Sect. 2.4.3.

Case 1 FDI Screening mechanisms resemble the third-country certification measure in *EU—Energy Package*. In both cases, the establishment of a commercial presence is subject to an authorization that is granted if certain qualitative criteria are met. In this scenario, the WTO member sets the non-admission of FDI as the rule, which puts the burden of proof for the admission criteria on the investor. This burden directly modifies the conditions of competition for foreign investors. Case 1 FDI Screening mechanisms therefore affect the trade in services.

Case 2 FDI Screening mechanisms are less intensive restrictions of trade. As long as the WTO member does not decide to prohibit the investment, there is no direct effect on FDI. Nevertheless, the statutory condition precedent to the investment contract modifies the conditions of competition. For instance, such a legally manifested uncertainty results in less competitive financing conditions for the investment compared to a situation in which the FDI is not subject to such condition precedent. Less competitive financing conditions in turn affect, for instance, the prize an investor is able to pay to acquire the FDI target. Thus, Case 2 FDI Screening mechanisms are affecting trade in services.

Consequently, the individual FDI prohibition decision as well as Case 1 and 2 FDI Screening mechanisms in general are affecting trade in services, and thus fall in the scope of the GATS. The Screening Regulation, on the other hand, does not qualify as a measure within the meaning of Art I(1) GATS, since it leaves the adoption of FDI Screening mechanisms in the discretion of the Member States.

4.3.3.3 Trade in Services

The last element necessary to establish that a measure falls in the scope of the GATS is 'trade in services'. The element comprises three different aspects. First, there must be a supply of a *service* that could be affected, meaning that the investor must supply a service through its FDI. Second, the FDI must qualify as one *mode of supply*—namely, as 'commercial presence' within the meaning of Art I(2)(c) GATS.[447] Third, this *trade* in services must actually or potentially take place so that a measure can be said to affect trade in services.

---

[447] One could argue that FDI screening also affects all other modes of supply, since FDI may also be undertaken to supply services through the other modes. For instance, it will most likely increase intra-firm services trade between the investor's foreign establishment and its newly acquired commercial presence. This would constitute supply mode one (Art I(2)(a) GATS). Even investment-related movement of natural persons may be affected (see Descheemaeker (2016), pp. 272–274). It might be argued that FDI Screening mechanisms affect these modes indirectly within the broad meaning of 'affecting' as elaborated in Sect. 4.3.3.2. However, the investor's and FDI Screening mechanisms' evident purpose is to supply or address Mode Three trade. The other effects are thus very remote. Considering these mechanisms as also 'affecting' all other modes of supply would thus result in a too broad understanding of 'affecting' limiting the WTO members' right to regulate too much.

4.3.3.3.1   Supply of a Service Through FDI

As a first requirement, the FDI Screening mechanisms must affect FDI that is undertaken to supply services in the host country. Hence, either the FDI target asset must supply services that the investor continues to supply, or the investor intents to supply new services through the target. The FDI is thus not a service in itself. Irrelevant are also services that the investor plans to supply from its own home state establishments to the acquired asset (intra-firm trade).

It is here where the GATS for the first time really proves its nature as a multilateral agreement widely liberalizing FDI. M&A FDI, the focus of FDI Screening mechanisms, targets an entire firm or asset with all its business activities. Accordingly, even if the FDI focuses on the asset's production of a certain good, it also acquires all other asset activities, including service supply. Hence, objectively, the investor undertakes the FDI to supply these services.

In fact, arguably all modern firms supply services. A domestic robot manufacturer will, for example, probably also supply 'Engineering and Integrated engineering services', 'Consultancy services related to the installation of computer hardware' and 'Software implementation services', 'R&D services on natural sciences', as well as 'Services incidental to manufacturing'.[448] In addition, even classic manufacturing companies, such as car producers, offer many goods-related services, such as engineering, installation, operation, maintenance, and financial services.[449] When taking other internal services into account, such as human resources, cafeteria services to employees, and IT maintenance, the scope seems to become unbelievably broad.

As a result, nearly all M&A FDI constitute FDI to supply a service, and thus trade in services—provided the other requirements are met, in particular that the FDI constitutes a commercial presence within the meaning of Art XXVIII(d) GATS.

But are all these services really relevant to determine whether an investor undertakes an FDI to supply a service? This question is very specific to commercial presence as trade, in particular M&A FDI. Only in these cases may investors be considered to supply all business activities that are performed by the FDI target. It seems that this question has not been addressed in scholarship so far.[450]

---

[448] In the above listed order: Sectors 1. A. (e) and (f), B. (a) and (b), C. (a) and F. (i) of the Sectoral Classification List and EU Schedule.

[449] See also Abu-Akeel (1999), pp. 192–194.

[450] Though related, this question is different to the delimitation of trade in goods and trade in services. The latter issue often emerges in the context of a seemingly goods-related measure, such as tariffs or taxes based on goods import. In these cases, one could argue that the targeted good also entails a service, or that distribution service suppliers are affected because their opportunities to distribute this good are distorted. For the first example see *Canada—Certain Measures Concerning Periodicals*, Appellate Body Report (30 June 1997) WT/DS31/R/AB, WTO Online Database doc no 97-2653; *China—Publications and Audiovisual Products* (n. 409). For the second example see *EC—Bananas III*, Appellate Body Report (n. 437); *Canada—Autos*, Appellate Body Report (n. 432). On this subject see also Abu-Akeel (1999), pp. 194–196; Trebilcock et al. (2013), p. 494; Mavroidis (2016), p. 353.

A broad interpretation of trade in services through commercial presence would considerably restrain the WTO members' right to regulate. The broader the GATS's scope is defined, the broader the GATS's obligations become. This is particularly valid for the general obligations such as the MFN obligation in Art II(1) GATS, since they always apply.[451]

To start with, not every service supplied by the investor or the target should define the M&A FDI as trade in services. Otherwise, essentially every measure that affects M&A FDI, directly or indirectly, would fall in the scope of the GATS. This would overly constrain the WTO members' right to regulate. Instead, only services that are characteristic to the investor's or target's business purpose should define an FDI in the target as supplying a service—only such characteristic services are thus 'Trade-defining services'.

Indicators for the characteristic status of services are whether these services are defined as a business purpose in the involved company's articles of association, and how much financial turnover these services account for. The definition also applies regardless of whether a service is supplied externally (inter-firm trade) or internally (intra-firm trade), as long as they are supplied by the target itself and not by the investor's foreign establishment to the target.[452] Intra-firm trade must be covered, since the GATS wants to enhance all forms of trade. However, the definition excludes internal services that are evidently not relevant to determine whether the FDI is trade in services—namely, internal human resources and IT services, as well as restaurant and cafeteria services to employees.[453] Otherwise, again, every M&A FDI would be trade in services.

Consequently, an M&A FDI may only constitute trade in services if the investor and/or the target supplies services that are characteristic for their business purpose, externally or internally. Most modern manufacturing firms will supply Trade-defining services, such as engineering, installation, consultancy, operation, maintenance, and financial services. M&A FDI in these firms may therefore constitute trade in services.[454] This is, of course, still subject to two further conditions: the FDI

---

[451] For MFN obligations there is the possibility to schedule sector-specific exemptions. These are, however, designed to expire after ten years (Art II(2) GATS and para. 6 of Annex on Article II Exemptions).

[452] See also on the possibly applicable trade mode for intra-firm trade, n. 447.

[453] This situation is slightly different for hospitals which usually also supply restaurant services to their customers. These may be seen as part of a medical treatment and thus hospital services, since they typically respect a certain diet depending on the patient's health status. Hence, their characterization ultimately depends on the WTO member's schedule of commitments.

[454] A related aspect is whether manufacturing itself can constitute a service, if done on a fee or contract basis for another firm (see 884-886 CPC; Council for Trade in Services, 'Energy Services' (Background Note by the Secretariat) S/C/W/311 ('Background Note on Energy Services 2010'), paras. 52(a), 78(b)). Not only is this distinction generally acknowledged in the WTO for drawing the line between trade in services and goods (Yanovich (2011), p. 32). The EU also approves it implicitly by also referring to 'Services incidental to manufacturing' in 1.F. (i) in the EU Schedule, but not to manufacturing in itself.

constitutes a 'commercial presence', and there is in fact trade in services that can be affected by the measure.

4.3.3.3.2   FDI as Commercial Presence

The GATS defines trade in services as the supply of a service through four different modes. The most relevant mode for FDI Screening mechanisms is Mode three, for which Art I(2)(c) GATS provides that trade in services is the supply of a service

> by a service supplier of one Member, through commercial presence in the territory of any other Member.[455]

Accordingly, there are two elements of 'Mode three trade': the mode itself, commercial presence, and the cross-border element of service supply from one WTO member to another member.

Commercial presence is thus, as the term itself indicates, about supplying a service through *presence* in the territory of the WTO member where the consumer is located.[456] Commercial presence is defined as 'any type of business or professional establishment, ... for the purpose of supplying a service'. Art XXVIII (d) GATS provides an illustrative list of forms to establish a commercial presence, including through acquisition. However, the provision fails to clarify whether a partial acquisition is also covered.[457] Moreover, if it is covered, the threshold is unclear from which acquired shares qualify as a commercial presence. This is crucial for FDI Screening mechanisms, since they apply to M&A FDI generally, and thus also to partial M&A transactions.[458]

The broader context of Art XXVIII(d) GATS weighs in favour of partial M&A transactions as commercial presence through acquisition. First, the list in Art XXVIII (d) is merely illustrative so that the missing enumeration of partial acquisition does not necessarily have indicative value. Second, it would be contrary to the purpose of Arts I(2)(c) and XXVIII(d) GATS to accept the total acquisition of a firm, but not a partial acquisition that in fact gives the investor the same rights.[459]

The last argument further indicates that the threshold for a partial M&A to qualify as commercial presence should be approximated to the influence an investor gains with a complete acquisition of a firm. Hence, contrary to the definition of establishment within the meaning of Art 49 TFEU, the investor would need to obtain

---

[455] Art I(2)(c). For other affected modes of trade, see n. 449, 447.

[456] Services supplied through mode four (Art I(2)(d) GATS) are also supplied through presence in the territory of another WTO member.

[457] For trade in financial services, this has been clarified in the Understanding on Financial Services, sec D(2): '"Commercial presence" means an enterprise within a Member's territory for the supply of financial services and *includes wholly- or partly-owned subsidiaries*' (emphasis added).

[458] See for the similar issue of partial M&A transactions as establishment within the meaning of Art 49 TFEU, Sect. 4.2.3.2.2.

[459] Seemingly in favour of only total acquisition, Feinäugle (2008), para. 17.

influence that allows her to own or control the firm.[460] This conclusion is supported by the cross-border element in Art I(2)(d) GATS, and the definitions of 'juridical person (of another Member)' in Art XXVIII(f), (m) and (n) GATS. A commercial presence only qualifies as Mode three trade if it serves the purpose to supply a service by a service *supplier of one WTO member to another member*. Therefore, the commercial presence must qualify as the commercial presence *of the foreign service supplier*.[461] Accordingly, the FDI target must become the commercial presence of the foreign investor through the M&A. This is only the case if the investor gets to own or control the commercial presence within the meaning of Art XXVIII (n) GATS.[462]

Art XXVIII(n) GATS provides that a company is:

  (i) 'owned' by persons of a Member if more than 50 per cent of the equity interest in it is beneficially owned by persons of that Member;
 (ii) 'controlled' by persons of a Member if such persons have the power to name a majority of its directors or otherwise to legally direct its actions.

As a result, the partial M&A of an existing domestic firm only falls within the scope of the GATS if the foreign investor acquires more than 50% of the shares, or if the acquired shares allow the investor to legally direct the actions of the target. The minimum threshold to establish a commercial presence for the GATS is thus significantly higher than the threshold for FDI as well as establishment within the meaning of Art 49 TFEU. A blocking minority for important business decisions is not enough. The conclusions under Art 49 TFEU are, however, insofar applicable as an investor may also gain control by statutory or contractual provisions that grant him the right to name a majority of the target firm's directors. Control is also established if the investor has the right to take all important business decisions on its own. As under Art 49 TFEU, business decisions are important if they would constitute insider information within the meaning of Art 7 para. 1(a), 4 of the Market Abuse Regulation.[463]

---

[460] For the definition under EU primary law, see Sect. 4.2.3.2.2.

[461] Following this argument, a foreign investor A from Member Y could acquire 30% of the shares in a firm established in the EU, in which investor B from Member Z holds the other 70%. Even if one could argue that a 30% shareholding qualifies as a permanent presence and thus a commercial presence, A would not supply a service through this presence. Controlling only 30% of the shares, A does neither own, nor control the firm. For the purposes of the GATS, services supplied by the firm would be services supplied by Z.

[462] Descheemaeker (2016), p. 272 relies directly on Art XXVIII(m) and (n) GATS to define commercial presence. Chang et al. (1999), p. 100, implies this by citing the GATS definitions of 'ownership' and 'control'. Art XXVIII(m) and (n) GATS are, however, primarily aimed at defining the origin of a service. This is, for instance, to determine the application of the denial-of-benefits clause in Art XXVII(c) GATS or of a Member-specific exemption to the MFN obligation. In the same vein, *EC—Bananas III (US)*, Panel Report (n. 438), para. 7.295.

[463] See for the arguments to refer to Art 7 para. 1(a), 4 of the Market Abuse Regulation (n. 152), as well as for the thresholds of investor influence for FDI and establishment within the meaning of Art 49 TFEU Sect. 4.2.3.2.

This has important consequences for FDI Screening mechanisms. They will only affect trade in services to the extent they address FDI that gives the investor the right to own or control the acquired firm in a majority sense. This is, for instance, the case for M&A FDI by which the foreign investor obtains 50% of the shares in a host state target firm. Hence, the notions of FDI and commercial presence are incongruent.[464]

4.3.3.3   (Potential) Trade in Services

Having established that FDI Screening mechanisms address the supply of a service through commercial presence to some extent, it must finally be assessed whether FDI Screening mechanisms affect *trade in services*.

Generally, it suffices that the measure at issue, here the FDI Screening mechanism, affects potential trade in services. Thus, it is enough if service suppliers can potentially enter the market at any time. These suppliers would also be affected by the measure, not only those that already trade the affected services.[465]

As a consequence, FDI Screening mechanisms will largely affect (potential) trade in services. Without having assessed any sector in detail, it may be assumed that most firms in the EU could be taken over by foreign investors, and thus become commercial presences for foreign investors to supply services. This trade in services through commercial presence is affected by FDI Screening mechanisms.

4.3.3.4   FDI Screening Mechanisms Largely Fall in the GATS's Scope

All in all, FDI Screening mechanisms largely are measures affecting trade in services within the meaning of Art I(1) GATS. The GATS proves to be a multilateral agreement that widely liberalizes FDI. FDI falls in the GATS's scope to the extent it gives the investor controlling, majority influence on the FDI target and serves to supply a service. The vast majority of FDI will fulfil the last requirement. Either the investor or the FDI target will at least also supply services that are characteristic to the investor's or target's business purpose (Trade-defining services). Hence, the GATS may significantly limit the EU's flexibility to adopt FDI Screening

---

[464] For definition of FDI for the purpose of this book see Sect. 2.4.1. In contrast, Hoekman (1995), fn. 5, seems to equate FDI and commercial presence.

[465] See *EC—Bananas III (US)*, Panel Report (n. 438), para. 7.320, upheld by *EC—Bananas III*, Appellate Body Report (n. 437), paras. 225–228; *Argentina—Financial Services*, Panel Report (n. 444), paras. 7.88–7.94. The panel in *Argentina—Financial Services* correctly held that the Appellate Body in *Canada—Autos* did not reject the approach developed in *EC—Bananas III*. Having determined that there was in fact trade in wholesale trade services of motor vehicles, the Appellate Body in Canada—Autos upheld its prior finding. It only emphasized that the Panel would have had to assess whether the conditions of competition for these services were in fact affected. See *Canada—Autos*, Appellate Body Report (n. 432), paras. 157, 163–165; *Argentina—Financial Services*, Panel Report (n. 444), paras. 7.95–7.96.

mechanisms on broader grounds than 'security or public order' within the meaning of the Screening Regulation.

FDI Screening mechanisms only fall outside the GATS's scope to the extent they apply to FDI that does not qualify as commercial presence, meaning FDI that gives the investor less than controlling, majority influence on the FDI target. It is interesting to note that the notion of commercial presence thus differs not only from the notion of FDI, but also from establishment in Art 49 TFEU. Both require a lower threshold of investor influence.[466]

One may be inclined to translate this limit of the GATS's scope into a legislative option for FDI Screening mechanisms. However, this limit only states that the GATS does not apply for FDI that gives the investor *less* than majority influence on the FDI target. Incorporating this limitation into FDI Screening mechanisms is no viable policy option in light of the EU and Member States concerns vis-à-vis foreign investors. The risk of harmful investor influence, for instance, increases, not decreases with higher influence on the FDI target.

Even though FDI Screening mechanisms thus largely fall in the GATS's scope, the EU's flexibility to adopt them will only be limited to the extent the mechanisms in fact violate GATS obligations. This will be assessed in the following.

4.3.4 Relevant Specific GATS Commitments: National Treatment, Market Access, and Domestic Regulation

The GATS only limits the EU's flexibility to adopt FDI Screening mechanisms on broader grounds than 'security or public order' to the extent it provides obligations that the FDI Screening mechanisms would violate. One main source of these obligations may be the far reaching specific commitments to market access (Art XVI GATS), NT (Art XVII GATS), and domestic regulation (Art VI(5) GATS).[467] WTO members undertake these specific commitments by service sector in their schedules (Art XX(1) GATS). Before assessing whether the EU has undertaken relevant sector-specific commitments, it will first be discussed to what extent these commitments may in fact limit the flexibility to adopt FDI Screening mechanisms.

4.3.4.1 Art XVI GATS: Market Access Obligation

At first sight, the most obvious limit to FDI Screening mechanisms seems to derive from the WTO member's commitment to grant market access to services and service suppliers of other WTO members pursuant to Art XVI GATS.

---

[466] See Sect. 4.2.3.2.

[467] In the following, this book will refer to 'EU commitments' and the EU Schedule as explained in n. 430.

Before starting this analysis, it should be recalled that FDI Screening mechanisms authorize (Case 1 mechanisms) or prohibit (Case 2 mechanisms) FDI in accordance with certain qualitative criteria.[468] To address the EU and Member States concerns vis-à-vis foreign investors, the screening criteria relate to the investor and the risk he may pose to certain public interests, such as competition, energy and water supply, private information, or future industrial policy goals. If the government decides that an FDI meets one of these criteria, it will not admit the investment. Accordingly, the admission of FDI depends on an individual government decision based on certain legal criteria.

Against this background, it is crucial to understand that the market access obligation does not generally prohibit market access restrictions. Instead, Art XVI (2) GATS exhaustively lists specific prohibited market access restrictions, and thus defines 'Market access' for GATS purposes narrowly.[469] Particularly relevant to FDI Screening mechanisms are Art XIV(2)(a) and (f) GATS:

(a) limitations on the number of service suppliers whether in the form of numerical quotas, monopolies, exclusive service suppliers or the requirements of an economic needs test;

(f) limitations on the participation of foreign capital in terms of maximum percentage limit on foreign shareholding or the total value of individual or aggregate foreign investment.

One might argue that either the adoption of an FDI Screening mechanism as such or at least the administrative decision to deny FDI the admission based on the mechanism may violate one or both provisions.

4.3.4.1.1   FDI Screening Mechanism as Legislative Measure

Depending on the design, an FDI Screening mechanism could violate either Art XVI (2)(a) or (f) GATS. Adopting a mechanism to screen M&A FDI above a certain threshold of shareholding percentage may constitute a limitation on the participation of foreign capital (Art XVI(2)(f) GATS). Similarly, one may argue that the FDI Screening mechanism limits the number of service suppliers by screening an FDI that qualifies as a commercial presence of foreign investors (Art XVI(2)(a) GATS). As the rationale behind both provisions is similar, they will be analyzed together.

In general, Art XIV(2)(a) to (f) GATS have to be interpreted narrowly, since they are drafted exhaustively and narrowly.[470] In addition, the NT obligation

---

[468] For the definition of Case 1 and Case 2 FDI Screening mechanisms see Sect. 2.4.3.

[469] *United States—Measures Affecting the Cross-Border Supply of Gambling and Betting Services*, Appellate Body Report (7 April 2005) WT/DS285/AB/R, WTO Online Database doc no 05-1426, para. 215; *Argentina—Financial Services*, Appellate Body Report (n. 438), paras. 7.387–7.390. See also e.g. Delimatsis and Molinuevo (2008), paras. 2, 22, who rightly conclude that Market access in the GATS is a legally defined concept, and does not refer to the commonly used term 'establishment' or 'admission'.

[470] See also Pauwelyn (2005), pp. 158–159, additionally arguing with the context Art VI GATS and the GATS preamble provide for Art XVI GATS.

compliments the protection of the pre-establishment phase with regard to discriminatory measures. A broad interpretation of Art XIV(2)(a) to (f) GATS is thus not the only way to ensure a high degree of liberalization.

Moreover, FDI Screening mechanisms at issue do not constitute 'Economic needs tests' as understood by Art XVI(2)(a) to (d) GATS. As the name suggests, Economic needs tests assess whether the host state economically needs a specific (supply mode of) service; for instance, the need for a restaurant or taxi in relation to the population density and existing competitors.[471] The tests are thus concerned with the categories of demand and supply.[472] FDI Screening mechanisms, by contrast, are based on qualitative criteria relating to the investor, in GATS terms the service supplier. Therefore, only mechanisms that include industrial policy considerations on future economic needs may partially fall under Art XVI(a) GATS.[473]

The explicit mentioning of the notion Economic needs test in Art XVI(a) to (f) GATS also shows that approval procedures other than such tests are not covered. Similarly, the Scheduling Guidelines state that approval procedures such as qualification, technical, and licensing requirements based on a service's quality or a service supplier's qualification[474] should not be scheduled under Art XVI GATS 'as long as they do not contain any of the limitations specified in Article XVI'.[475] Accordingly, the Scheduling Guidelines imply that general service supplier qualification requirements do not fall under Art XVI GATS. In the same vein, the Scheduling Guidelines list the authorization for real estate purchase according to economic, social, and welfare interests as an example for an NT, not Market access restriction.[476] As a result, the FDI Screening mechanisms at issue do not constitute Economic needs tests.[477]

---

[471] Scheduling Guidelines, para. 12; Mavroidis (2007), p. 4. For an example in Mode four, see the Canadian immigration test based on a labour market test, Canada, 'Mode 4 Commitments and Economic Needs Tests' (Communication from Canada to the Committee on Specific Commitments) S/CSC/W/47.

[472] Krajewski (2003), p. 89.

[473] For the possibility of an ecology impact test falling partially under Art XVI(2)(a) GATS, see ibid.

[474] For the categorization of service quality and service supplier qualification in light of the relationship to Art VI GATS, Pauwelyn (2005), p. 153.

[475] Scheduling Guidelines, para. 10. Indeed, the Scheduling Guidelines also seem to find that the Market access obligation is violated if the right to supply a service is uncertain. Uncertainty might exist where the FDI depends on the government's individual admission decision. However, the Scheduling Guidelines (para. 8) only finds this to be the case if a license is granted 'on a discretionary basis', meaning without setting any criteria. In the same vain, Council for Trade in Services, 'Economic Needs Test' (Note by the Secretariat) S/CSS/W/118, paras. 6–7. Complemented by Addendums 1 and 2, the Secretariat Note lists all 'economic needs' tests that WTO members scheduled.

[476] Scheduling Guidelines, Annex 2, Attachment 1, para. XI. Annex 2 Attachment 1, para. VIII also lists authorization requirements for non-residents as restrictions of NT, not Market access.

[477] This applies to the vast majority of FDI Screening mechanisms in light of the concerns vis-à-vis foreign investors. The only exception would be screening mechanisms on the grounds of industrial

Moreover, FDI Screening mechanisms do not provide a specific quantitative threshold within the meaning of Art XVI(2)(a) and (f) GATS. Rather, FDI Screening mechanisms screen only M&A FDI above a certain shareholding percentage based on certain qualities lying in the investor's person. Therefore, reaching the shareholding threshold does not result in a service ban, but only in a lower probability of getting the opportunity to supplying the service. However, these considerations of effect are invalid in the ambit of Art XVI(2)(f) and Art XVI GATS.[478] Whether or not a foreign investor is allowed to establish a commercial presence depends on the supplier's qualities, not a fix quantitative threshold.

FDI Screening mechanisms do also not constitute a 'zero quota' for supplying a service through commercial presence. As previously argued, the number of admitted foreign service suppliers is determined on a case-by-case basis based on qualitative criteria relating to the service supplier. This also applies to a Case 1 FDI Screening mechanism where the access for foreign investors is blocked by default, since it ultimately also depends on the government's admission decision. Accordingly, the mechanisms may not be compared to the facts in *US—Gambling*. In this case the Appellate Body found that a complete ban of internet gambling amounts to a 'zero quota' and hence falls under Art XVI(2)(a) GATS.[479] An FDI Screening mechanism does not completely ban any kind of service, mode or method of supply. It does thus not amount to such 'zero quota'.

Last but not least, the WTO members' schedules do not provide further guidance. The schedules could serve as context to interpret Art XVI(2) GATS, if they reveal a common understanding of WTO members' entries in their commitments.[480] Indeed, there are numerous entries of 'authorization' or 'permission' measures as horizontal exceptions to commitments under both the Market access column[481] and NT column.[482] However, the majority of WTO members seems to use the Market access column as the general column for horizontal exceptions to Market access and

---

policy that also take future economic needs into account in that, they would assess the future supply and demand for a specific service or service supplier. Council for Trade in Services, 'Mode 3 – Commercial Presence' (Background Note by the Secretariat) S/C/W/314, paras. 57–58, states that some WTO members scheduled some FDI Screening mechanisms as 'economic needs tests', implying that not all FDI screening mechanisms constitute such tests.

[478] *US—Gambling*, Appellate Body Report (n. 469), para. 232, held that the term 'in the form of' in Art XVI(2)(a) GATS should not be understood 'to have the effect of'. The Appellate Body thus saw the risk of a too expansive interpretation of the list in Art XVI(2) GATS when taking into account a measure's effect.

[479] ibid., para. 251. For a limitation on national service suppliers constituting 'zero quotas', and thus a limitation of the number of suppliers, see also Krajewski (2003), p. 86. He analyzes that such interpretation is in line with the WTO members' scheduling practice.

[480] Cf Krajewski (2003), p. 86, who consults the WTO members schedules to interpret the notion 'numerical quotas' in Art XVI(2)(a) GATS.

[481] For instance, Finland (EU Schedule, p. 9), Ireland (EU Schedule on Financial Services, GATS/SC/31/Suppl.4/Rev.1, p. 15), Poland (EU Schedule, pp. 10–11) and Slovenia (EU Schedule, p. 11).

[482] Austria, Czech Republic (both EU Schedule, p. 11), Germany, Finland, Ireland (all EU Schedule, p. 12), Poland, Sweden and Slovakia (all EU Schedule, p. 13).

NT. They schedule both clear quantitative exceptions and merely NT-incompliant approval mechanisms in the Market access column.[483] Regardless of the reasons,[484] the practice has no legal consequences. Pursuant to Art XX(2) GATS, any exception to Market access also applies to NT. Therefore, one may not draw the conclusion that WTO members consider authorization and permission measures scheduled in the Market access column in fact as Market access measures within the meaning of Art XVI(2) GATS. They may also constitute NT violations.

Consequently, the FDI Screening mechanisms at issue are no Market access restrictions within the meaning of Art XVI(2) GATS. Though to some extent resulting in a limitation of the number of suppliers or of foreign participation (Art XVI(2)(a) and (f) GATS), the limitation is not general and quantitative, but a qualitative case-by-case decision.

4.3.4.1.2 Individual Screening Decision

The individual, administrative decision of not admitting an investment does also not constitute a violation of Art XVI(2)(a) and (f) GATS. Otherwise, every negative decision based on qualification, technical, or licensing requirements would amount to a quantitative limitation within the meaning of Art XVI(2) GATS. This would not only undermine the restrictive notion of Market access. In addition, the Scheduling Guidelines do not consider qualification, technical and licensing requirements to be restrictions within the meaning of Art XVI(2) GATS.[485]

This conclusion is also in line with the wide understanding of Market access measures in *US—Gambling*. An individual negative administrative decision on the investment's admission is not a 'zero quota' in the sense of the Appellate Body

---

[483] See for example Cyprus on limitations on Market access (EU Schedule, p. 7): 'The permission of the Central Bank is required for the participation of any non-resident in a corporate body or partnership in Cyprus. Foreign participation in all sectors/subsectors included in the Schedule of Commitments is normally limited up to 49 per cent.' Accordingly, Cyprus bans all foreign participations above 49%, and requires permission for all other investments. France, under limitations on Market access, schedules the authorization of foreign investment as well as a fix limitation of foreign participation in newly privatized companies (EU Schedule, pp. 8–9). With a similar exception Italy and Portugal (EU Schedule, p. 10). Slightly different is Malta's entry where a requirement of a legal form ('local company') is combined with a prior permission requirement (EU Schedule, p. 10). See also Canada (Canada's schedule of specific GATS commitments, p. 2): 'The acquisition of control of a Canadian business by a non-Canadian is subject to approval'. This refers to its 'economic needs' test which may take economic needs considerations into account, too, e.g. product variety and effects on competition (Investment Canada Act (n. 375) sec 20(c), (d)). See, last but not least, China did e.g. not commit to the establishment of foreign companies branches generally (China's schedule of specific GATS commitments, p. 1).

[484] Reasons may be uncertainty about the legal nature of the measure or convenience to put all relevant exceptions to its specific commitments in one column. See also Krajewski (2003), p. 84, who terms such scheduling practice 'simply a scheduling mistake'.

[485] Scheduling Guidelines, para. 10.

decision. It is not comparable to a complete ban of internet gambling without the possibility to an exceptional approval.[486]

Consequently, FDI Screening mechanisms based on qualitative criteria such as competition, energy and water supply, and private information protection are no Market access restrictions within the meaning of the GATS. In the end, the admission of service suppliers cannot be measured by numbers, but is based on a qualitative criterion in case-by-case decisions. An exception may apply to FDI Screening mechanisms criteria based on concrete future economic needs.

4.3.4.2 Art XVII GATS: National Treatment Obligation

Nevertheless, the FDI Screening mechanisms could still violate the NT obligation. Pursuant to Art XVII GATS the NT, if committed to, requires that:

> each Member shall accord to services and service suppliers of any other Member, in respect of all measures affecting the supply of services, treatment no less favourable than that it accords to its own like services and service suppliers.

According to the conclusions reached in Sect. 4.3.3, the FDI Screening mechanisms at issue are measures affecting trade in services. They also affect 'the supply of services' within the meaning of Art XVII GATS because this notion is defined as 'trade in services' (Art I(2) GATS).[487] Hence, FDI Screening mechanisms fulfil this first element of Art XVII(1) GATS.

In addition, to constitute a violation of Art XVII GATS, FDI Screening mechanisms would also need to (i) differentiate between 'like' services and service suppliers to (ii) accord one part of the comparison group 'less favourable treatment'. The following will assess these two requirements in turn.

4.3.4.2.1 *De Jure* Differentiation Between Like Foreign and Domestic Investors

First, FDI Screening mechanisms must differentiate between like services and service suppliers. As will be shown, it results in an irrebuttable presumption of 'likeness' if a measure differentiates between services and service suppliers solely

---

[486] *US—Gambling*, Appellate Body Report (n. 469), para. 251.

[487] *Argentina—Financial Services*, Panel Report (n. 444), para. 7.474, thus comes to the conclusion that 'affecting the supply of services' is closely linked to 'affecting trade in services'. Accordingly, *China—Measures Affecting Trading Rights and Distribution Services for Certain Publications and Audiovisual Entertainment Products*, Panel Report (12 August 2009) WT/DS363/R, as modified by Appellate Body Report WT/DS363/AB/R, WTO Online Database doc no 09-3798, para. 7.970; *EU—Energy Package* (n. 435), para. 7.736, held that the case law on the meaning of 'affecting' under Art I(1) GATS is applicable.

based on their origin—in other words, if it differentiates *de jure*.[488] This is crucial when assessing the violation of NT by FDI Screening mechanisms, since the mechanisms explicitly differentiate between foreign and domestic suppliers.

To constitute *de jure* differentiation pursuant to Art XVII GATS, a measure must differentiate solely based on the origin of services and service suppliers. The origin of service suppliers for GATS purposes is defined in Arts XXVIII(g) and (k) to (n) GATS. Pursuant to Art XXVIII(m)(i) GATS, a 'juridical person of another Member' means a juridical person which is

> constituted or otherwise organized under the law of that other Member, and is engaged in substantive business operations in the territory of that Member or any other Member.[489]

The GATS criterion of origin is thus the country of the firm's constitution and substantive business operations.[490] As shown in Sect. 2.4.2, the FDI Screening mechanisms, on the other hand, apply another criterion to determine the investor's foreignness. They alternatively assess either the country of the firm's constitution or of its registered seat, or the nationality of its beneficial owners. Nevertheless, it would be too formalistic to conclude that the FDI Screening mechanisms do not differentiate solely based on the service supplier's origin within the meaning of the GATS. All provided criteria are only a different, but common form to determine a firm's origin. Hence, the FDI Screening mechanisms do constitute *de jure* discrimination with respect to the investors as service suppliers.

The same conclusion is valid for the other comparison group in Art XVII GATS: supplied services.[491] Art XXVII(f) GATS shows that the origin of services is defined by the origin of their supplier. Therefore, by referring to the investor's, thus supplier's origin only, the FDI Screening mechanisms also differentiate between the affected services solely based on their origin.

---

[488]This book will use the terminology of *de jure* and *de facto* discrimination. The latter is the broadest term to describe non-origin-based discrimination. There is, however, other terminology, such as formal and factual, explicit and implicit, as well as direct and indirect discrimination, see also Ehring (2002), p. 921, fn. 3. It is not always clear whether such different terminology stands for a different meaning. At least the term of indirect discrimination is narrower than a purely effect-based approach. Indirect discrimination compares the trade restrictive effects of the differentiating measure based on a non-origin criterion to the effects of the same measure, but hypothetically differentiating based on origin, Eeckhout (2001), pp. 233–234; Krajewski (2003), p. 108. De Búrca (2002), p. 187; on the other hand, defines indirect discrimination as a measure that results in disadvantageous treatment of one group over the other. Her approach is therefore limited to the differential effects, and could thus also be termed factual discrimination.

[489]To be sure, the definition of a 'juridical person of another Member' for commercial presence pursuant to Art XXVIII(m)(ii) GATS is not at issue here. This provision only defines when an already established commercial presence constitutes the establishment of a foreign service supplier. On this basis, it can then be assessed whether the WTO member in which the foreign service supplier is so established violated any GATS obligation vis-à-vis supplier.

[490]*Argentina—Financial Services*, Appellate Body Report (n. 438), para. 6.40, also refers to Arts XXVIII(f), (g), and (k) through (n) GATS to define origin within the meaning of the MFN and NT obligation.

[491]ibid., para. 6.38.

Consequently, FDI Screening mechanisms differentiate *de jure* between domestic and foreign services and service suppliers within the meaning of Art XVII GATS.

The following argues that this conclusion results in the irrebuttable presumption that the compared domestic and foreign services and service suppliers are like. By differentiating between services and service suppliers solely based on their origin, the measure taking WTO member itself makes the *prima facie* case for likeness. The acting member apparently assumes that the services and service suppliers are like in all characteristics except their origin.[492] If not, why would a WTO member differentiate solely based on origin?

Certainly, one might consider that this is because the measure-taking WTO member considers the differentiation criterion of origin to be a reliable proxy that is easier to cast into law or administer than the actual, underlying differentiation criterion. Accordingly, one could argue that if the acting WTO member can show that the origin is really a proxy for another legitimate criterion of differentiation, the presumption of likeness may be rebutted. The Appellate Body report in *Argentina—Financial Services* seems to support this rationale. Faced with a differentiation between 'cooperative' and 'uncooperative' WTO members for tax transparency purposes, the Appellate Body accepted a rebuttal of likeness on two grounds. First, the defendant can rebut the complainant's *prima facie* case that 'origin is indeed not the exclusive basis for the distinction'.[493] Second, the defendant can present arguments and evidence that demonstrate the 'unlikeness' of services and service suppliers, and thereby rebut the presumption of likeness itself.[494]

However, it is doubtful that this decision may be read as accepting a rebuttal of the presumption of likeness for cases of *de jure* discrimination. First, in these cases the first rebuttal option is unavailable. If the origin is the explicit criterion of differentiation, there is no room for establishing that origin 'is indeed not the exclusive basis'. Even if foreign services and service suppliers were 'unlike' according to any other differentiation criterion, the measure cannot but treat all foreign services and service suppliers the same way. Such first rebuttal option only makes sense if the differentiation criterion seems *de facto* to relate exclusively to origin; such as cooperative and non-cooperative WTO members. Panel reports, to which the Appellate Body itself refers, support this interpretation. When dealing with *de jure* distinction, none of the panel reports mentioned the first rebuttal option.[495]

---

[492] Regan (2006), p. 202.

[493] *Argentina—Financial Services*, Appellate Body Report (n. 438), para. 6.45.

[494] ibid. It is remarkable that this threshold is rather low to rebut the presumption of likeness. The respondent must not demonstrate that the domestic and foreign services and service supplies are not like.

[495] ibid., para. 6.36. On Art III(2) GATT 1994: *Argentina—Measures Affecting the Export of Bovine Hides and the Import of Finished Leather*, Panel Report (19 December 2000) WT/DS155/R, WTO Online Database doc no 00-5282, paras. 11.168–11.170; *China—Measures Affecting Imports of Automobile Parts*, Panel Report (18 July 2008) WT/DS339/R, WT/DS340/R, and WT/DS342/R, as modified by Appellate Body Report WT/DS339/AB/R, WT/DS340/AB/R, and WT/DS342/AB/R,

The second rebuttal option, demonstrating the 'unlikeness' of the services and service suppliers, is not available either. If the only differentiating criterion is origin, the measure would treat even those services and service suppliers differently that are identical according to the supposedly underlying differentiation criteria.[496] Accordingly, the origin as a proxy necessarily leads to false positives. In other words, in these cases the WTO member would treat services and service suppliers differently *solely based on their origin*. This is explicitly prohibited by Art XVII GATS.

All this only allows one conclusion: Art XVII GATS prohibits the differentiation based on origin whether as an actual differentiation criterion or as proxy for an underlying consideration.[497] The likeness of services and service suppliers is presumed; the presumption cannot be rebutted. By committing to the NT obligation in the GATS, the WTO members agreed to refrain from the criterion of origin as proxy for differentiating between supposedly unlike services and service supplier. Accordingly, they also accepted to bear the costs of this loss of regulatory flexibility. If origin is used as a proxy, the WTO members must cast the actual differentiation criterion into law. To be sure, *Argentina—Financial Services* may still be in line with this conclusion. If the Appellate Body had been confronted with an explicit *de jure* differentiation, it might have ruled differently.

Consequently, the EU and its Member States cannot rebut the presumption of likeness between EU and foreign investors. Hence, FDI Screening mechanisms treat like services and service suppliers differently.

4.3.4.2.2 Less Favourable *Treatment*

Nevertheless, differentiating *de jure* between like services and service suppliers, here foreign and domestic investors, only violates Art XVII GATS if this differentiation also results in less favourable treatment of one part of the comparison group.

WTO Online Database doc no 08-3275, para. 7.216. On Art III(4) GATT 1994: *Canada—Certain Measures Affecting the Automotive Industry*, Panel Report (11 February 2000) WT/DS139/R and WT/DS142/R, as modified by Appellate Body Report WT/DS139/AB/R and WT/DS142/AB/R, WTO Online Database doc no 00-0455, paras. 2.15–2.18, 10.74; *Argentina—Measures Affecting the Importation of Goods*, Panel Report (22 August 2014) WT/DS438/R, WT/DS444/R, and WT/DS445/R, as modified by Appellate Body Report WT/DS438/AB/R, WT/DS444/AB/R, and WT/DS445/AB/R, WTO Online Database doc no 14-4794, paras. 6.274–6.275. On Art I(1) GATT 1994: *Colombia—Indicative Prices and Restrictions on Ports of Entry*, Panel Report (27 April 2009) WT/DS366/R, WTO Online Database doc no 09-1865, para. 7.355; *United States—Certain Measures Affecting Imports of Poultry from China*, Panel Report (29 September 2010) WT/DS392/R, WTO Online Database doc no 10-4731, paras. 7.430–7.431.

[496] *Indonesia—Certain Measures Affecting the Automobile Industry*, Panel Report (2 July 1998) WT/DS54/R, WT/DS55/R, WT/DS59/R, and WT/DS64/R, WTO Online Database doc no 98-2505, para. 14.113, cited by *Colombia—Ports of Entry* (n. 495), para. 7.182. See also Ortino (2004), pp. 124–135, including a summary of relevant case law.

[497] Regan (2006), pp. 201–202; Ortino (2008), p. 198. See also Ortino (2004), pp. 135, 148. Seemingly *contra* Delimatsis and Hoekman (2018), p. 277.

Section 4.3.3 found that FDI Screening mechanisms affect trade in services within the meaning of Art I(1) and thus Art XVII GATS, either by prohibiting FDI by default (Case 1) or by generally authorizing FDI subject to an exceptional prohibition combined with a statutory condition precedent to the investment contract (Case 2). In both cases the investment is not automatically banned, but only to a preliminary and possibly an in-depth assessment according to certain screening criteria to then decide whether to authorize or prohibit the FDI.[498]

Pursuant to Art XVII(3) GATS, treating like services and service suppliers less favourable means to modify the conditions under which the services and service suppliers are competing. This principle calls for an economic assessment of less favourable treatment according to which the measure at issue must distort the conditions of competition between like services and service suppliers. The adjudicating bodies usually engage in high-level econometric considerations of competitive opportunities, avoiding any clear economic test.[499]

Nevertheless, the economic test that seems to provide the theoretical background to the adjudicating bodies' approach is an asymmetric impact test. To assess the measure's effect on the conditions of competition, the asymmetric impact test compares the impact of the measure on the entire group of services and service suppliers of one or certain WTO members to the impact on the entire group of like services and service suppliers of any other country.[500] The impact on a single or only a few transactions is not enough.[501] An actual trade effect is not needed.[502] Hence, the asymmetric impact test finds a discrimination if—overall—services and service suppliers of one or certain WTO members receive less favourable treatment.

In *EU—Energy Package* the panel substantiated this definition for a quasi-FDI screening measure.[503] It found that a measure puts an additional burden on a natural gas transmission system operator ('TSO') if it allows the TSO to supply his service only after an authority has assessed whether he puts at risk the security of energy supply. Hence, as only foreign not domestic TSOs had to undergo this assessment,

---

[498] See Sect. 2.4.3.

[499] See e.g. *China—Certain Measures Affecting Electronic Payment Services*, Panel Report (16 July 2012) WT/DS413/R, WTO Online Database doc no 12-3729, paras. 7.712, 7.725.

[500] Accordingly, the test assesses two groups. On the one hand, it compares the number of all foreign services and service suppliers that *receive* beneficial treatment to the number of all their domestic counterparts. On the other hand, it compares the number of all foreign services and service suppliers that *do not receive* beneficial treatment to the number of all their domestic counterparts. See e.g. *EC—Bananas III (US)*, Panel Report (n. 438), paras. 7.334–7.335. See also on less favourable treatment under the MFN obligation in Art II(1) GATS *Canada—Autos*, Appellate Body Report (n. 432), para. 174, criticizing the panel for not conducting such asymmetric impact test.

[501] Otherwise, the test for finding a modification of the conditions of competition would constitute a diagonal impact test or non-restriction test. Such test finds a measure discriminatory if it has a less favourable impact on one or a few transactions of the protected comparison group. See Ehring (2002), pp. 924–927; Diebold (2010), pp. 41–42.

[502] Ehring (2002), p. 961.

[503] For a detailed discussion of this case see already Sect. 3.1.4.2.1.

the panel concluded that the EU accorded less favourable treatment to foreign TSOs.[504]

Indeed, FDI Screening mechanisms place even higher burdens on foreign investors to supply their services through commercial presence. FDI is subject to either, in Case 1, a general authorization requirement or, in Case 2, the possibility of an exceptional prohibition combined with a statutory condition precedent to the investment contract. As already argued for establishing a trade effect of FDI Screening mechanisms, both aspects place considerable burdens on the foreign investors, inter alia due to uncertainty and less competitive financing opportunities.[505] In addition, in both cases the FDI screening procedure is combined with a preliminary assessment and possibly an in-depth investigation based on certain screening criteria, such as a possible risk to the security of energy supply as dealt with in *EU—Energy Package*. All of these burdens on foreign investors modify the conditions of competition vis-à-vis domestic investors.

Therefore, FDI Screening mechanisms treat foreign investors less favourable than domestic investors.

4.3.4.2.3   FDI Screening Mechanisms as *De Jure* Discrimination

Consequently, FDI Screening mechanisms constitute *de jure* discrimination, and thus violate the NT obligation.[506]

Accordingly—to the extent of having committed to NT—the EU may only adopt FDI Screening mechanisms on broader grounds than 'security or public order' within the meaning of the Screening Regulation and thus Arts XIV*bis*(b) and XIV (a) GATS if they can be justified based on other grounds of exception, namely those in Art XIV GATS. However, to this end, the EU would need to invoke a policy rationale that consistently justifies the different treatment of domestic investors, on the one hand, and foreign investors from all other WTO members, on the other hand. A consistent rationale must thus explain why to treat EU investors differently than investors from countries as different as Brazil, Canada, China, Iran, Russia, and the US. Moreover, even if there were such consistent policy rationale, it would also need to be covered by a ground of exception in Art XIV GATS. Given the similar policy environment in the EU and, for example, the US and Canada, it seems highly unlikely that the EU could provide such a consistent policy rationale that meets the EU and Member States concerns vis-à-vis foreign investors, and falls under an exception in the exhaustive list in Art XIV GATS.[507]

---

[504] *EU—Energy Package* (n. 435), para. 7.1128.

[505] See Sect. 4.3.3.2.

[506] Given this clear *de jure* discrimination, a further discussion of possible *de facto* discrimination of investors from certain countries, such as China, Iran, and Russia, is omitted.

[507] For details on the nature and requirements of Art XIV GATS, see Sect. 4.3.7.

In sum, the NT obligation in Art XVII GATS therefore poses a significant hurdle to adopt FDI Screening mechanisms on broader grounds than 'security or public order'. Nevertheless, these consequences are at least in part attenuated by the NT obligation's nature as a specific commitment based on different service sectors. This will be further discussed in Sect. 4.3.4.3.

4.3.4.3 Art VI GATS: Obligations for Domestic Regulation

Before addressing the EU's sector-specific commitments, the limits provided by the last relevant specific commitment must be briefly assessed. Art VI GATS might limit the EU's flexibility to adopt FDI Screening mechanisms on broader grounds than 'security or public order' by a variety of procedural and substantial obligations for domestic regulation—a term defined neither in the GATS, nor in subsequent agreements or reports.

The procedural obligations of Art VI GATS will most likely be fulfilled by FDI Screening mechanisms. EU primary law will demand the same, if not a higher standard, of measure administration.[508] In addition, Art VI(4) GATS gives the Council for Trade in Services a mandate to establish disciplines for qualification requirements and procedures, technical standards, and licensing requirements. However, it has not adopted any discipline that would be relevant to FDI Screening mechanisms.[509] In the absence of such disciplines, Art VI(5) GATS provides minimum obligations for licensing and qualification requirements and technical standards if they nullify or impair specific commitments. Such measures must be

---

[508] See e.g. the respective provisions Art 3(2)–(3), (5) Screening Regulation on administration and judicial review of decisions.

[509] The only success of the mandate for the Council for Trade in Services so far is the adoption of Council for Trade in Services, 'Disciplines on Domestic Regulation in the Accountancy Sector' (Decision by the Council) S/L/64 ('Disciplines on Domestic Regulation in Accountancy Sector'). Large scale, multilateral negotiations within the framework of Art VI(4) GATS came to a halt in 2017 when a Joint initiative of 59 WTO members, including China, the EU and its Member States, as well as Russia, chose to move forward on a plurilateral level (Ministerial Conference, 'Disciplines on Domestic Regulation' (Communication from certain WTO members) WT/MIN(17)/7/Rev.2, WT/GC/190/Rev.2. This decision came after WTO members disagreed on concluding multilateral negotiations that they relaunched within the Working Party on Domestic Regulation. Negotiation development and hurdles are well described by Working Party on Domestic Regulation, 'Disciplines on Domestic Regulation pursuant to GATS Article VI:4' (Chairman's Progress Report) S/WPDR/W/45, replicated in Council for Trade in Services, 'Negotiations on Trade in Services' (Report by the Chairman to the Trade Negotiations Committee) TN/S/36. See also Gari (2020), pp. 67–69. Now, the Joint Initiative is developing procedural rules for domestic regulation, such as timely, transparent, and objective administration. The initiative excludes substantial aspects e.g. substantial definitions (except of 'authorization') or requirements for a general 'necessity test'. The WTO members committed to inscribe the negotiation results in their Additional commitments pursuant to Art XVIII GATS on an MFN basis (see WTO members Albania and others, 'Joint Statement on Services Domestic Regulation' WT/L/1059). The access to the respective Reference Draft Paper (INF/SDR/W/1/Rev.1, dated 12 December 2019) is restricted.

applied in a manner that inter alia is not more burdensome than necessary (Art VI(5) (i) and (4)(b) GATS). Art VI(5) GATS indicates a four-pronged test: First, there must be a relevant specific commitment; second, the measure must nullify or impair this commitment; third, the measure's application, not the measure itself, must respect Art VI(4)(a) to (c) GATS, inter alia it must be not more burdensome than necessary; and, fourth, the measure could not reasonably be expected at the time the specific commitment at issue was made (Art VI(5)(ii) GATS).

Provided FDI Screening mechanisms constitute licensing or qualification requirements, namely the necessity test 'not more burdensome than necessary' could constitute a considerable limit to the EU's flexibility to adopt them. However, Art VI(5) does not apply to measures that are already outright prohibited on other grounds, namely by the NT obligation.

Art XVII GATS prohibits all discriminatory 'measures affecting the supply of services'. The provision does thus not distinguish between internal and external, or pre- and post-establishment measures.[510] Consequently, Art XVII GATS comprises all domestic regulation within the meaning of Art VI(5) GATS, and, if discriminatory, prohibits it. Already prohibited, these discriminatory measures cannot also fall under the softer requirements for applying a measure in Art VI(5) GATS. Only the grounds of exception in Arts XIV and XIV*bis* GATS could justify a violation of Art XVII GATS. Accordingly, once it is established that a measure is discriminatory, only Art XVII GATS, and not Art VI(5) GATS applies.[511] The line between both provisions is thus drawn by the definition of discrimination in the NT obligation.[512]

Therefore, as FDI Screening mechanisms violate the NT obligation, the additional requirements of Art VI(5) GATS regarding a measure's application do not apply. Art VI GATS does thus not pose any considerable limits to the adoption of FDI Screening mechanisms by the EU.

4.3.4.4 The EU's Sectoral Commitments

The analysis of relevant specific commitments showed that the EU's flexibility to adopt FDI Screening mechanisms may be restricted only but significantly by the NT obligation in Art XVII GATS.[513] The NT obligation prohibits the explicit differentiation between domestic and foreign investors; the core element of FDI Screening mechanisms. However, the NT obligation only applies to the extent the EU has undertaken to comply with it. The EU's undertakings of specific commitments are listed in its Schedule of Specific Commitments in the GATS ('EU Schedule') by service sectors and subsectors and trade mode pursuant to Art I(2) GATS.

---

[510]Pauwelyn (2005), p. 149.

[511]Cossy (2008), pp. 351–352; Krajewski (2008), Art VI, para. 2.

[512]Muller (2017), p. 464.

[513]The following assessment focuses on the EU commitments as included in the EU Schedule, excluding Bulgaria, Croatia, and Romania, which maintain their own schedules, see n. 430.

Overall, the EU has undertaken a limited, but large number of NT commitments in Mode three trade. Therefore, general cross-sector FDI Screening mechanisms will violate at least some EU commitments to NT, and thus be GATS-inconsistent. Sector-specific FDI Screening mechanisms, on the other hand, remain a viable option.

This book cannot provide a comprehensive analysis of all EU NT commitments that may restrict its flexibility to screen FDI. However, it will submit a test to determine whether the EU, or any other WTO member, has committed to NT for an individual FDI. An exemplary analysis of two service sectors will show that the EU Schedule generally seems to leave considerable room for FDI Screening mechanisms in sectors that are at the centre of the concerns vis-à-vis foreign investors. The first example will deal with a critical infrastructure sector, the electricity transmission and distribution sector, and the second example will represent more economic, industrial policy concerns by analyzing sector commitments with respect to services using artificial intelligence.

4.3.4.4.1   Test to Determine Relevant NT Sector Commitments for FDI

An FDI target is usually supplying more than one service. Therefore, it is difficult to determine whether a specific FDI falls under a sector-specific commitment to NT for Mode three trade. Before developing a test to determine the relevant NT commitments for an FDI, it is important to recall the concept of Trade-defining services that was established above to assess whether an FDI constitutes trade in services.

It was argued that a commercial presence through M&A FDI only constitutes trade in services if the investor or FDI target supplies services that are characteristic to the investor's and/or target's business purpose. These services were termed Trade-defining services. Otherwise, every commercial establishment through M&A FDI would constitute trade in services, since every firm supplies some kind of services, such as internal human resources services. Nevertheless, the potential of trade in services through M&A FDI is large. For instance, an FDI already constitutes trade in services if the target is a car manufacturer, but also supplies maintenance services.[514]

This approach has important implications for assessing the WTO members' specific commitments to accord NT to M&A FDI.[515] Only the services that were found to determine whether or not an FDI falls in the scope of the GATS also determine the WTO members' relevant specific commitments. Consequently, the assessment of specific commitments is limited to FDI's Trade-defining services.

---

[514]For a detailed discussion of the scope of the GATS, see Sect. 4.3.3.3.1.

[515]The following will refer to M&A FDI generally. Of course, M&A FDI only falls in the GATS's scope if it constitutes a commercial presence, and thus gives the investor controlling influence on the FDI target. See Sect. 4.3.3.3.2.

Despite this limitation, M&A FDI usually constitutes trade in more than one service.[516] So how to define which service determines a WTO member's specific commitments—the commitments to all supplied Trade-defining services sectors or maybe only to an even further narrowed notion of core service sectors?[517]

WTO members undertake specific commitments in their schedule by service sector, mode of supply, and specific commitment (Art XX GATS). More concretely, the WTO members divide their schedules in several sectors, each consisting of several subsectors, usually based on the Sectoral classification list, which was originally based on the CPC.[518] Accordingly, the Trade-defining services of an M&A FDI may fall under different sectors in a WTO member's schedule of commitments. For instance, if a foreign investor acquires a domestic supplier that offers data analysis services, this supplier will most likely supply Data processing services as well as Data base services (843, 844 CPC).[519] It may additionally supply Software implementation services (842 CPC), R&D services on natural sciences (851 CPC), as well as Technical testing and analyzing services (8676 CPC). At least if the EU has committed to NT in all of these sectors for Mode three trade, the EU must accord NT to the investor in this specific FDI.

But must the EU also accord NT to the investor, if it has committed to only a part of these services? The more services sectors are relevant to determine a WTO member's commitments regarding an M&A FDI, the more likely it is that the WTO member has overall no commitment to award NT to the investor. In other words, one missing service sector could result in the FDI not being subject to the WTO member's specific commitments at all. One could argue that this understanding would frustrate the existing commitments in all other sectors relevant to the FDI at issue.[520]

The first aspect of this discussion is the concrete scope of a sector commitment. A schedule's sector entry may also include other services that are, from this service's perspective, ancillary. This depends on the interpretation of each individual entry. Entries in the schedule of commitments are interpreted in the same way as GATS provisions, pursuant to the general rules of interpretation in Arts 31 and 32 VCLT.

---

[516] In *China—Electronic Payment Services* (n. 499), para. 7.55, the US used the notion 'integrated services' to describe Electronic payment services ('EPS') as one service integrating several other services that are covered by other sectors in the Sectoral Classification List. As such, according to the US, EPS should only fall under Subsector 7.B.d of the Sectoral Classification List ('All payment and money transmission services'). Entries in Subsectors like 7.B.k and l of the Sectoral Classification List would thus be irrelevant (7.B.k: 'Advisory and other auxiliary financial services'; 7.B.l: 'Provision and transfer of financial information and financial data processing and related software by providers of other financial services').

[517] For the elements of 'core' and 'ancillary' services, see e.g. *China—Publications and Audiovisual Products*, Panel Report (n. 487), paras. 7.1195, 7.1201.

[518] See Chap. 3, n. 40.

[519] In the EU Schedule in the sector of Data base services (844 CPC), Subsector 1.B. (d) also includes the maintenance and repair of data, at least for the purpose of data bases.

[520] See similar argument of the US based on the Understanding on Financial Services, para. 8, in *China—Electronic Payment Services* (n. 499), para. 7.532.

The schedule as a whole and other GATS provisions are contextual means of interpretation within the meaning of Art 31(1) VCLT. The Sectoral classification list and the CPC may serve as additional interpretative means (Art 32 VCLT).[521] The same applies to the Scheduling Guidelines.[522] As stated above, a detailed discussion of the entire EU Schedule would go too far. However, the EU Schedule gives guidance for cases in which the FDI includes several sectors, while the specific sector commitments remain silent on possible ancillary services.

The EU Schedule demonstrates that only some (sub-)sector commitments include ancillary services. This is, for example, true for the transport,[523] construction,[524] and financial services sectors.[525] However, the fact that the schedule of commitments explicitly mentions ancillary services as part of a few main core services only shows that this is an exception to the rule. Typically, ancillary services are scheduled separately. Accordingly, the schedule shows that ancillary services should only be considered to share the commitment status with their core service if explicitly defined together.

If core and ancillary services are not scheduled as one (sub-)sector, the principle of mutual exclusivity of sectors and subsectors applies. It argues against consolidating several services sectors in favour of a core service. The principle of mutual

---

[521] See Sect. 3.1.2.1. This is of course different if WTO members explicitly refer to the Sectoral Classification List or the CPC, see e.g. EU Schedule, Sector 3 on Construction and related engineering services.

[522] See Chap. 3, n. 14.

[523] EU Schedule, Subsector 11.A. (f): 'Supporting services for maritime transport' (similar in nearly all other subsectors) as an independent listing of an ancillary service to maritime transport. Moreover, Subsector 11.H of the EU Schedule defines a second type of ancillary services: 'Services auxiliary to all modes of transport: cargo-handling, storage and warehouse services, freight transport agency services, other'. This combination of two kinds of ancillary services is remarkable. The only possible interpretation is that transport specific ancillary services go under Subsector 11.H, whereas transport unspecific services that also support the core transport service go under Subsector 11.A. (f).

[524] The EU Schedule by referring to 511 of CPC lists 'Pre-erection work at construction sites' as independent subsector. At the same time, by referring to 512 and 513 CPC it lists 'General construction work for buildings' and 'General construction work for civil engineering'. The commitments of some countries are split between these related sectors (see e.g. Finland, Latvia, and Slovenia). Though understood as a separate subsector, one could refer to the pre-erection services as an ancillary or supporting service to the general construction services.

[525] For the majority of Member States the EU refers to the sector definitions in Art 5(a) of the Annex on Financial Services which are very similar to the sectors in the Sectoral Classification List. Several subsectors include services that may as well be scheduled as independent services. E.g. para. 5(a)(xv) describes 'Provision and transfer of financial information, and financial data processing and related software by suppliers of other financial services' and thus carves out services that would otherwise be included in Computer business services (Subsector 1.B. (a)–(c) of the EU Schedule). A similar carve out is undertaken for auxiliary services in general in para. 5(a)(xvi) ('Advisory, intermediation and other auxiliary financial services on all the activities listed in subparagraphs (v) through (xv)').

exclusivity was developed by the Appellate Body.[526] The Appellate Body stated that a specific service cannot fall within two different sectors or subsectors at the same time depending on the core service at issue. The principle ensures clear WTO member obligations, especially in a situation 'where ... [a WTO member] made a full commitment in one of those sectors and a limited, or no, commitment, in the other'.[527] Based on this principle, panels rejected the idea of ancillary and core services. In *China—Electronic Payment Services*, the panel rejected the US argument that the electronic payment services are 'Payment and money transmission services' (Subsector 7.B(d) of the Sectoral classification list) and as such core services that include several other ancillary services that could also fall under other subsectors.[528] According to the panel, this would mean that the ancillary services, inter alia 'Advisory and other auxiliary financial services'(Subsector 7.B (k) of the Sectoral classification list), could in some cases fall under payment and money transmission services, and sometimes be considered separately under their own entry. This 'result ... is difficult to reconcile with the Appellate Body's clarification that a specific service cannot fall within two different sectors or subsectors'.[529]

Accordingly, the principle of mutual exclusivity of sectors and subsectors prevents the same services from being considered as core services to other service sectors in some instances, and in other instances as 'stand-alone services' in independent (sub-)sectors.[530] Therefore, sector and subsector entries in a WTO member's schedule do not contain ancillary services, unless they explicitly provide otherwise. This generally weighs against defining certain core Trade-defining services and others that are ancillary to them to determine whether a WTO member has undertaken a specific NT commitment regarding a specific M&A FDI. Instead, the member would need to have committed to NT in every Trade-defining service (sub-) sector of an M&A FDI.

The Scheduling Guidelines support such a narrow understanding of the WTO members' commitments. They state that a commitment in one mode of supply should not implicitly cause an obligation in another mode to which the WTO

---

[526] *US—Gambling*, Appellate Body Report (n. 469), para. 180; *EU—Energy Package* (n. 435), para. 7.325.

[527] *US—Gambling*, Appellate Body Report (n. 469), para. 180.

[528] These other sectors were Subsectors 7.B. (k) and (l) of the Sectoral Classification List. See *China—Electronic Payment Services* (n. 499), para. 7.528: 'In the United States' view, these "aspects" include such elements as the provision of the underlying physical network and wiring; fraud protection; authorization routing, authorization decision solutions, global clearing management, exception handling solutions, automated calculation of the net financial position of a sender/ receiver of financial transactions based on the desired currency and settlement service option selected by each party; and, the creation and execution of the transfer order for each financial institution participating in the value day payment activity.'

[529] ibid., para. 7.529. In a similar vein, *China—Publications and Audiovisual Products*, Panel Report (n. 487), paras. 7.1195, 7.1201.

[530] See *China—Electronic Payment Services* (n. 499), para. 7.517.

member did not explicitly commit.[531] The same rationale is followed on sector commitments when stating:

> They [the commitments] do not imply a right for the supplier of a committed service to supply uncommitted services which are inputs to the committed service.[532]

Applied to the case of a foreign investor supplying a service through M&A FDI, this means that a WTO member only has specific commitments vis-à-vis the individual M&A FDI if all the supplied services are committed to, not only to a certain core service. Thus, if the FDI target, for example, provides data processing services that build on client data stored at the target's own premises (data base services), the WTO member would need to have commitments in both sectors.

Consequently, for specific commitments to apply to an M&A FDI, there must be commitments in all sectors of Trade-defining services of the FDI. There is no place for attaching some services to a supposedly core service, and then only assessing whether the WTO member at issue committed to this core service sector. Only this understanding fully respects the importance of a sector-based commitment approach. WTO members may, however, define service sectors in their schedules of commitments as encompassing certain ancillary services.

This understanding gives the WTO members much more flexibility for regulating commercial presences through M&A FDI—for instance, by FDI Screening mechanisms that violate the NT obligation. A missing sector commitment to one of several Trade-defining services of an FDI results in no specific commitment for the *entire* FDI.[533] Accordingly, in order to determine the EU's flexibility to screen FDI in a certain industry, it is enough to identify one or two of the industry's key service sectors. Even if the EU may generally have committed to NT in numerous sectors, for maintaining the flexibility to adopt FDI Screening mechanisms in this industry it would be enough to have not committed to certain sectors that FDI of concern typically also affects. With this test in mind, the discussion can now turn to the two exemplary sectors: electricity transmission and distribution, as well as artificial intelligence services.

4.3.4.4.2 Electricity Transmission and Distribution Services

The electricity transmission and distribution services sectors are particularly relevant to FDI screening because they relate to critical infrastructure, which is at the centre

---

[531] Scheduling Guidelines, para. 35: 'Where a service transaction requires in practical terms the use of more than one mode of supply, coverage of the transaction is only ensured when there are commitments in each relevant mode of supply.'

[532] Scheduling Guidelines, para. 25.

[533] Following this rationale, the foreign investor could also agree to dismantle the uncovered sectors from her FDI to rely on the EU's specific commitments for the rest of the FDI. Such dismantlement could also be requested during the screening procedure as a mitigation measure; for the procedure pursuant to FDI Screening mechanisms see Sect. 2.4.3.

of the EU and Member States harmful investor concern.[534] On the one hand, electricity is of utmost importance for the functioning of society. On the other hand, the electricity transmission and distribution services sectors are particularly susceptible to disruptions of supply. If the EU has undertaken no specific commitments for electricity transmission and distribution services for Mode three trade and NT, the EU keeps the flexibility to screen FDI this sector.

Determining the EU's commitments in this sector, however, is complicated. There is no specific schedule entry for this sector. In fact, the WTO members' commitments in the entire energy sector are highly fragmented, since energy services were not negotiated during the Uruguay Round.[535] Even the line between trade in services and goods is blurred. The production of electricity as a good[536] does not constitute a service, unless it is produced on account of a third party on a fee or contract basis.[537] Moreover, it is difficult to determine which activities are so closely linked to the electricity production that they, too, are excluded from trade in services.[538] The EU lists only two electricity specific sectors in its GATS schedule: pipeline transport services of fuel as possible input for electricity production[539] and 'Services incidental to energy distribution' ('Incidental energy distribution services').[540,541] Other related services are listed as general services—for example, construction and related engineering services, as well as storage services.[542]

The most relevant sector entry for electricity transmission and distribution services is Incidental energy distribution services. But does distribution in this sense

---

[534] See the failed acquisition of shares in the transmission network operator 50 Hertz by the Chinese SOE State Grid Corporation of China, Heide (2018).

[535] In the realm of investment and electricity services, the Energy Charter Treaty is another important source of International economic law. However, the treaty does not cover market access and is thus less relevant to the thesis submitted in this book, cf Sect. 4.3.1.1.

[536] This is the opinion of most WTO members, see Background Note on Energy Services 2010 (n. 454), para. 32, n. 36. See also electricity as a good in 171 CPC as well as all goods listed in Annex I to the CPC ('Energy Related Products'), such as the input goods coal (110 CPC) and uranium (130 CPC). The European Energy Charter and EU law also categorize electricity as a good, see Cottier et al. (2011), p. 215. These authors also point out that goods and services are unsuitable terms to define energy, and thus support a distinct definition of energy sectors, Cottier et al. (2011), pp. 220, 222–223.

[537] For this understanding of the definition of trade in services, see n. 454.

[538] Yanovich (2011), p. 32.

[539] Subsector 11.G of the EU Schedule and Sectoral Classification List; 7131 CPC. The CPC, to which only Lithuania refers, defines this sector as 'Transportation via pipeline of crude or refined petroleum and petroleum products and of natural gas.' The definition of this subsector was dealt with in *EU—Energy Package* (n. 435), paras. 7.292–7.238, regarding the schedule of Croatia, Hungary, and Lithuania. It was found to 'encompass[es] the transportation or transmission of natural gas through transmission pipelines', but to exclude supply or supply services, and LNG services.

[540] Subsector 1.F. (j) of the EU Schedule and Sectoral Classification List, 887 CPC.

[541] In the wider energy sector, the EU Schedule and Sectoral Classification List also list 'Services incidental to mining' (883, 5115 CPC).

[542] In the here followed order: Subsectors 3.A.–E., 4.B.–C., 11.H. (b) of the Sectoral Classification List.

also include transmission? One way of defining distribution is in delimitation of transmission. Accordingly, transmission would be electricity delivery over high voltage lines from generators to distribution companies and large industrial consumers, and distribution the delivery of electricity to end-consumers through low voltage lines.[543] If so, EU commitments to Incidental energy distribution services would not result in commitments to energy transmission services.

Nevertheless, distribution may also be understood more broadly. A WTO Secretariat Background note on the energy sector first adopts the same contrasting definition, but then also provides that electricity 'is distributed to consumers via transmission and distribution grids'.[544] More importantly, 887 CPC defines Incidental energy distribution services as 'transmission and distribution services on a fee or contract basis of electricity ... to household, industrial, commercial and other users'.[545] As explained above, the CPC served as the basis for the Sectoral classification list, and is therefore a supplementary means to interpret the WTO members' schedules.[546] Some Member States have even explicitly referred to the definition in 887 CPC.[547] Consequently, a broader interpretation of distribution seems to be more in line with the EU's understanding of its schedule.

The vast majority of Member States has undertaken no specific commitments for Incidental energy distribution services. The EU is thus not significantly constrained in screening FDI into assets that supply such services. This conclusion applies regardless of the fact that two Member States, Latvia and to some extent Lithuania, have NT commitments in the subsector of Incidental energy distribution services.[548] The commitments of only two Member States cannot bind the EU as a whole. Nevertheless, the EU must take into account these Member States' commitments

---

[543] Background Note on Energy Services 2010 (n. 454), para. 28. The EU defines transmission as 'the transport of electricity on the extra high-voltage and high-voltage interconnected system with a view to its delivery to final customers or to distributors, but does not include supply' (Directive 2009/72/EC of the European Parliament and of the Council of 13 July 2009 concerning common rules for the internal market in electricity and repealing Directive 2003/54/EC [2009] OJ L 211/55, art 2(3); and, replacing it as of 31 December 2020, Directive (EU) 2019/944 of the European Parliament and of the Council of 5 June 2019 on common rules for the internal market for electricity and amending Directive 2012/27/EU [2019] OJ L 158/125, art 2(34)). Distribution is defined as 'the transport of electricity on high-voltage, medium-voltage and low-voltage distribution systems with a view to its delivery to customers, but does not include supply' (Directive 2009/72/EC (n. 543), art 2(5); Directive (EU) 2019/944 (n. 543), art 2(28)).

[544] Council for Trade in Services, 'Energy Services' (Background Note by the Secretariat) S/C/W/ 52, para. 8 (emphasis added).

[545] Emphasis added.

[546] See Chap. 3, n. 40, 41.

[547] Latvia, Hungary, Lithuania, and Slovenia. Insofar, 887 CPC even constitutes a contextual interpretative means.

[548] Only Latvia fully committed to NT for Energy distribution services in Mode three trade, while Lithuania limited its commitment to the gas sector, both referring to the 887 CPC definition. Hungary and Slovenia only committed to NT in Mode three trade for consultancy services relating to this sector.

when adopting its measures—for example, by granting a reservation in favour of these Member States.

As a result, in the electricity transmission and distribution sector, the EU has not committed to NT for potential M&A FDI. Every supplier of electricity transmission and distribution services will also supply services incidental to these services that will also often constitute Trade-defining services for the FDI. Hence, a missing commitment to NT in the subsector of Incidental energy distribution services results in no commitment to NT for the entire FDI. This follows from the above developed standard for assessing WTO member commitments for M&A FDI.

4.3.4.4.3 Artificial Intelligence Services

The second exemplary sector to assess the EU's specific commitments to NT that may limit its flexibility to adopt FDI Screening mechanisms is the 'Artificial intelligence sector'. Indeed, the term Artificial intelligence sector ('AI sector') is—deliberately—misleading. AI is 'the ability of a digital computer or computer-controlled robot to perform tasks commonly associated with intelligent beings . . ., such as the ability to reason, discover meaning, generalize or learn from past experience'.[549] Hence, AI is not a service, but a technology that is applied to supply specific services, and is marketed and sold as such.[550] The term AI sector is, nonetheless, chosen here to highlight that some of EU and Member States concerns vis-à-vis foreign investors are not directly translatable in GATS sector terms.

For assessing the EU's commitments on AI services, the analysis must turn to the services that apply AI—thus adopting a functional approach.[551] These sectors are numerous: financial technology (so called Fintech) services, medical diagnosis, and voice or handwriting recognition,[552] facial recognition,[553] online search engines, car

---

[549] WTO, 'World Trade Report 2018: The Future of World Trade: How digital technologies are transforming global commerce' (Geneva, 2018) <https://www.wto.org/english/res_e/publications_e/wtr18_e.htm> accessed 2 February 2022, 30, citing Copeland (2021).

[550] Irion and Williams (2019), p. 19. This form of AI is called 'Applied AI', in contrast to 'Strong AI' and cognitive simulation, both of which are less relevant, see Copeland (2021).

[551] A functional approach was e.g. also supported by the EC during the e-commerce negotiations at the WTO, Council for Trade in Services, 'Classification in the Telecom Sector under the WTO-GATS Framework' (Communication from the EC) S/CSC/W/44. In para. 1 the EC state: 'Rather, this Communication is based on the premise that *telecommunications services do not cover* economic activities or *services which require telecommunications services for their transport or delivery* and the supply of which is subject to specific commitments undertaken in other relevant sectors.' (emphasis added). Indeed, the context of the distinction from the telecommunications sector and AI is evidently different, since telecommunications activities are recognized as services, whereas AI as such is only a technology.

[552] Copeland (2021).

[553] Irion and Williams (2019), p. 24.

autopilots,[554] machine learning, and real-time bidding for online advertisement.[555] All these services fall under separate service sectors, such as 'Financial data processing',[556] 'Medical and dental services',[557] 'Data processing services',[558] or 'Advertising services'.[559] Though controversial, the adjudicating bodies understand these sectors as technology neutral.[560] Accordingly, commitments to these sectors also encompass services applying new technologies, even if not anticipated at the moment of commitment[561]

The following will not analyze any EU NT commitment to AI-relevant services sectors, but focus on some sectors where AI is particularly prevalent and advanced. This is, for example, true for the above-mentioned Financial data processing services, Medical and dental services, and Data processing services. The latter sector could serve as a catch-all term in the absence of function-specific sectors, since the characteristic of AI applying services is to process data. The EU's NT commitments in Mode three of these sectors differ and are highly fragmented among Member States.

In the Medical and dental services sector, only 16 Member States committed to NT without reservations. Even more Member States inscribed additional reservations in the Market access column, which is, pursuant to Art XX(2) GATS, applicable to NT as well. In the Financial data processing sector the commitments are even more fragmented, since only 17 Member States adhered to the 'Understanding of Commitments in Financial Services' (Understanding on Financial services), and scheduled their commitments accordingly.[562] The seven other Member States chose to schedule their commitments based on the Sectoral classification list, with further differences among them.[563] The Member States that adhered to the Understanding on Financial services committed to Market access and NT subject to certain

---

[554] Irion and Williams (2019), p. 19.

[555] Irion and Williams (2019), p. 19.

[556] Art 5(a)(xv) of the Annex on Financial Services.

[557] Subsector 1.A. (h) of the EU Schedule and Sectoral Classification List.

[558] Subsector 1.B. (c) of the EU Schedule and the Sectoral Classification List.

[559] Irion and Williams (2019), p. 19, Subsector 1.F. (a) of the EU Schedule and the Sectoral Classification List.

[560] Pauletto (2008), p. 531; Irion and Williams (2019), p. 19. This reading is supported by the Appellate Body decisions US—Gambling, Appellate Body Report (n. 469), paras. 198–201, 208; China—Publications and Audiovisual Products (n. 409), paras. 363–365, 368–370, where the services at issue were classified according to the service provided, not their method of supply: electronic and internet.

[561] Closely related are the recently relaunched talks on trade-related aspects of e-commerce by a group of WTO members; see WTO members Albania and others, 'Joint Statement on Electronic Commerce' WT/L/1056. The group includes inter alia China and Russia, but not India.

[562] On the sui generis legal status of the Understanding on Financial services, see von Bogdandy and Windsor (2008), paras. 1–3.

[563] Cyprus, Estonia, Malta, Latvia, Lithuania, Poland, and Slovenia. Bulgaria, Croatia, and Romania maintain their own schedules, see n. 430.

reservations.[564] The right to subject commercial presence to an authorization mechanism is, however, only reserved by the Czech Republic, France, Portugal, and Slovakia.[565] In the catch-all sector Data processing services, the EU committed to NT except Malta.[566] Moreover, Slovakia scheduled a licensing exception under Market access, which also applies to its NT commitment.[567]

Consequently, a general answer on the EU's flexibility to screen FDI regarding AI technology is impossible. At least, in the catch-all sector Data processing services the EU has undertaken wide reaching NT commitments. In other, more function-specific sectors that rely on AI technology, commitments are so fragmented amongst WTO members that a harmonized solution is difficult. This and the fact that AI is a technology, not a service, show that FDI Screening in order to safeguard AI technology has significant shortcomings from a GATS perspective. Other technology-based instruments, such as patent laws, business secrecy, and technology export control may be better suited. If FDI Screening mechanisms remains the chosen policy means to meet the concerns regarding AI technology, the EU would need to identify particular AI-intense sectors, and achieve a more harmonized commitment structure among Member States.

4.3.4.5 *De Jure* NT Discrimination Preventing Cross-Sector FDI Screening Mechanisms

The analysis of the specific commitments showed that only the NT obligation poses a significant limit to adopting FDI Screening mechanisms on broader grounds than 'security or public order' within the meaning of the Screening Regulation. FDI Screening mechanisms violate the NT obligation *de jure* because they only apply to

---

[564]Hungary horizontally scheduled important exceptions on the transfer of information, especially personal data (EU Schedule on Financial services, paras. 8–12).

[565]Only France scheduled that exception in the NT column: 'In addition to French credit institutions, issues denominated in French francs may be lead managed only by French subsidiaries (under French law) of non-French banks which are authorised, based on sufficient means and commitments in Paris of the candidate French subsidiary of a non-French bank.' The following other Member States scheduled exceptions to Market access, which may also apply to NT pursuant to Art XX (2) GATS. E.g. Czech Republic provides: 'Banking services may be provided only by Czech established banks or branches of foreign banks having a licence granted by the Czech National Bank in agreement with the Ministry of Finance. The granting of the licence is based on the consideration of criteria which are applied consistently with GATS. Mortgage loan services may be provided only by Czech established banks.' The Slovakian exception is similarly drafted. Portugal scheduled a modified economic-needs test based on a contribution to 'increase the national banking system's efficiency' and 'to produce significant effects on the internationalization of the Portuguese economy'.

[566]Malta and Slovakia. The latter through a license requirement under the Market access column which may also serve as a reservation under NT (Art XX(2) GATS).

[567]'For mode 3 and with regard to on-line information and/or data processing (including transaction processing): license is required.'

foreign investors. Other important specific commitments do not apply to FDI Screening mechanisms. On the other hand, FDI Screening mechanisms do not constitute Market access limitations within the meaning of Art XVI(2) GATS. They are based on qualitative, not quantitative criteria. Art VI(5) GATS, on the other hand, only provides further obligations for non-discriminatory domestic regulation.

The violation of the NT obligation by FDI Screening mechanisms, however, has less consequences than one might expect. The NT obligation only limits the EU's flexibility to adopt FDI Screening mechanisms in sectors for which the EU has committed to NT. Given the EU's specific commitments in a wide array of sectors, a general cross-sector FDI Screening mechanism will violate at least some of the EU's commitments. Yet, sector-specific mechanisms remain a viable option.

Admitting an FDI means admitting the supply through commercial presence of all characteristic services supplied by the acquired FDI target and/or the investor (Trade-defining services). It was argued that if a commitment to NT in only one of the Trade defining services sectors is lacking, the EU has no obligation to grant NT to the FDI as a whole. Only this understanding fully respects the GATS's sector-based commitment approach. As a result, it is more likely that, despite wide sector commitments to NT, an FDI also supplies a Trade-defining service for which the EU has undertaken no NT commitment. Therefore, the EU would not need to respect NT; the FDI Screening mechanisms could not violate the NT obligation. Hence, for assessing its flexibility to adopt sector-specific FDI Screening mechanisms, the EU could focus on a limited number of sectors that are often affected by FDI of concern.[568]

The exemplary assessment of two relevant sectors showed that the EU kept wide flexibility to screen FDI in the sectors of electricity transmission and distribution. A technology-specific FDI Screening, which for example focuses on AI, on the other hand, is less promising because it is at odds with the service sector-based GATS system. It is thus difficult for the EU to assess relevant specific commitments for FDI in this 'sector'.

Last but not least, given the EU and Member States concerns vis-à-vis foreign investors, the EU will not be able to present a consistent policy rationale that justifies the screening of all foreign investors, including so fundamentally different countries like China and the United States, while excluding all EU investors. The grounds of exception in Art XIV GATS beyond 'security or public order' within the meaning of Arts XIV*bis*(1)(b) and XIV(a) GATS will therefore not allow the EU to justify a violation of Art XVII GATS.

These conclusions have important implications for the substantial scope of FDI Screening mechanisms. A general cross-sector FDI Screening mechanism will violate the EU's NT commitments. A viable alternative may be sector-specific

---

[568] According to this approach, it may be effective from a policy perspective to leave unclear classification issues open. This may leave more room to WTO members to invoke uncommitted services sectors in order to prove that they are not bound by NT for a specific FDI.

screening mechanisms that take the EU's concrete sector commitments into account. Its sector scope could be much broader than the EU's sector commitments appear to be, since the EU must have committed to NT through Mode three trade in all services sectors that the FDI supplies and the investor is planning to supply via the FDI.

4.3.5 General Obligation: Most-Favoured Nation Clause

In addition, the EU's flexibility to adopt FDI Screening mechanisms on broader grounds than 'security or public order' may be limited by the EU's general GATS obligations. These apply also to FDI for which the EU has undertaken no specific commitment to NT. The most important general obligation is the MFN clause. It prohibits discrimination between third countries; discrimination the EU may want to incorporate in FDI Screening mechanisms to meet the EU and Member States concerns vis-à-vis foreign investors.[569]

Art II(1) GATS provides:

> With respect to *any measure covered by this Agreement*, each Member shall accord immediately and unconditionally to services and service suppliers of any other Member *treatment no less favourable* than that it accords to *like* services and service suppliers of any other country.[570]

Like the NT obligation, the MFN obligation has three elements: the measure falling in the GATS's scope (in conjunction with Art I(1) GATS), the 'likeness' of services and service suppliers, and 'less favourable treatment'. In contrast to the NT obligation, however, the MFN obligation follows a very restrictive negative list approach: Every WTO member has to comply with the MFN clause, unless it scheduled an exemption pursuant to Art II(2) GATS. The EU Schedule reserves no exemption relevant to FDI Screening.

As concluded above, FDI Screening mechanisms constitute measures affecting trade in services within the meaning of Art I(1) GATS to the extent the M&A FDI gives the investor a controlling influence, and the FDI thus constitutes a commercial presence for supplying a service. Insofar, FDI Screening mechanisms are measures covered by the GATS.[571]

Less evident is whether the FDI Screening mechanisms treat services and service suppliers from one WTO member less favourable than like services and service suppliers from any other country. The less favourable treatment may result from a differentiation between like third-country services and service suppliers based on their origin, either explicitly, *de jure*, or implicitly, *de facto*. The MFN obligation—as the NT obligation—prohibits both forms of discrimination.[572]

---

[569] See fourth cornerstone of FDI Screening mechanisms as defined in Sect. 2.4.3.

[570] Emphasis added.

[571] See Sect. 4.3.3.

[572] *EC—Bananas III*, Appellate Body Report (n. 437), para. 234; Adlung (2016), p. 67.

Of course, this book cannot analyze all possible ways of how FDI Screening mechanisms may *de jure* or *de facto* violate the MFN obligation. Nevertheless, the above conclusions on the EU's FTA obligations vis-à-vis certain third countries as well as the cornerstones of FDI Screening mechanisms developed in Sect. 2.4.3 allow to identify some potential differentiations in FDI Screening mechanisms that deserve a more detailed analysis. The definitions and conclusions developed under the NT obligation of Art XVII GATS on likeness and less favourable treatment also become relevant here.[573]

4.3.5.1   *De Jure* Discrimination of Investors from Non-FTA Countries

Section 4.3.2.1 showed that the EU has significantly limited its flexibility to screen FDI vis-à-vis its FTA partner countries Vietnam and Canada. It was also argued that this conclusion may be extrapolated to other present and future FTAs, and that the EU's flexibility to screen FDI is thus generally significantly limited vis-à-vis FTA partner countries, including the United Kingdom as a former Member State. Therefore, the EU may be inclined to exclude investors from FTA partner countries to avoid violating its bilateral obligations. To this end, FDI Screening mechanisms would need to explicitly differentiate between investors from FTA partner countries on the one and all other third countries on the other hand.[574]

Such differentiation would constitute a differentiation purely based on origin, and thus a *de jure* differentiation. In these cases, as already concluded under the NT obligation in Sect. 4.3.4.2.1, the likeness of compared services and service suppliers is presumed. Applied to FDI screening this means the comparison of foreign investors and the services supplied through the FDI target. This presumption cannot be rebutted. Moreover, as discussed in Sect. 4.3.4.2.2, it constitutes less favourable treatment of one investor group vis-à-vis another investor group if only the former is subject to FDI Screening mechanisms.[575]

As a result, the FDI Screening mechanisms would violate the MFN to the extent they differentiate between investors from FTA parties and from other third countries.

---

[573] See Sects. 4.3.4.2.1 and 4.3.4.2.2. Despite their different context, the NT and MFN provisions' basic notions likeness and less favourable treatment are to be interpreted similarly. Arts II(1) and XVII GATS 'share the essential nature of anti-discrimination provisions' (*Argentina—Financial Services*, Appellate Body Report (n. 438), para. 6.105). In Argentina—Financial Services, the Appellate Body also emphasizes the parallel understanding by assessing likeness and less favourable treatment pursuant to Arts II(1) and XVII GATS in the same paragraph (*Argentina—Financial Services*, Appellate Body Report (n. 438), paras. 6.18ff, 6.101ff). See also Zdouc (2004), p. 416.

[574] The EU-China CAI will, according to the Commission, not exceed the EU's WTO commitments. A different treatment of Chinese investors is thus unlikely.

[575] In *EU—Energy Package*, the panel held that a measure constitutes less favourable treatment if it subjects only one group of like investors to a security of energy assessment (*EU—Energy Package* (n. 435), para. 7.1096).

4.3.5.2 *De Facto* Discrimination of Investors from Countries of Concern

The EU and Member States concerns vis-à-vis foreign investors also indicate a *de facto* discrimination of investors from specific third countries according to four differentiation criteria: home country protection of IP rights, private information, and competition, as well as home country influence on business activities.[576]

The first three criteria relate to the legal protection of substantial interests. Insofar, the EU could argue that only its own or comparable laws guarantee a sufficient level of protection of these interests. Accordingly, to the extent foreign investors are subject to laws in their home country that constitute less protection, they may undermine the EU's protection of IP rights, private information, and competition. Consequently, the FDI Screening mechanisms may focus on investors from home countries that the EU considers to provide less protection.

More concretely, regarding IP right protection, the EU could argue that a foreign investor who is subject to inferior IP protection laws in its home country may, if IP rights are transferred to the investor, not respect these rights to the extent EU law requires.[577] Similarly, if a foreign investor's home country accords private information less protection than the EU, private information transfer to the foreign investor may jeopardize the EU's protection of this information.

In the realm of competition, the rationale is a little more complex. According to the EU and Member States competition concern, a foreign investor may receive state aid by its home country—namely, through access to funding that is more favourable than offered under market conditions. As a result, the investor may distort competition. This, according to the EU and Member State rationale, could have been avoided if the foreign investor and its home country had to respect EU competition laws. With the already described shortcomings, this competition concern is often boiled down to focusing on SOEs.[578] Accordingly, the FDI Screening mechanisms could, for instance, focus on foreign investors from third countries with less stringent competition rules than those provided for public undertakings in Arts 106 and 107 TFEU.

A vaguer consideration, on the other hand, is that some foreign governments exert more influence on 'their' investors than others. This consideration does not seek to protect a specific interest in itself, but describes a higher risk to other interests that FDI Screening mechanisms want to protect.[579] Following this rationale, FDI Screening mechanisms may focus on investors from countries where governmental influence on investors is assumed to be high, in particular China, Iran, and Russia. For influence on SOEs, the EU could again refer to the level of competition protection through Arts 106 and 107 TFEU as differentiation criterion. These provisions also

---

[576] See also Sect. 2.4.3.

[577] This consideration does not apply where the investor has the right to exploit the asset's intellectual property rights, e.g. in case of a complete acquisition or an exploitation agreement.

[578] For the competition concern, the rationale behind, and its shortcomings, see Sect. 2.1.1.

[579] Cf the harmful investor concern Sect. 2.1.3.

seek to ensure a certain independency of SOE business decisions from public interest interference. Another basis for differentiation may be corporate governance models in the investors' home countries that ensure that business decisions, whether of private investors or SOEs, are taken based on commercial, not public interest or political considerations.[580]

All these differentiation rationales would result in FDI Screening mechanisms that in fact differentiate between investors based on their home countries. This differentiation may manifest itself in more screening of FDI from these countries than FDI from other countries—for example, authorities could more often open an in-depth investigation, or more often prohibit investments from these countries. So designed or applied FDI Screening mechanisms may thus constitute *de facto* discrimination.

For *de facto* discrimination, these investors must be like other non-screened investors and the treatment must be less favourable within the meaning of Art II (1) GATS.

4.3.5.2.1   Like Service Suppliers

FDI Screening mechanisms only discriminate within the meaning of Art II(1) GATS if they treat services and service suppliers less favourable than other *like* services and service suppliers. As FDI Screening mechanisms focus on investor-, not service-related criteria, the following will focus on the likeness of investors only.[581] Since the differentiations at issue here are *de facto*, not *de jure* differentiations, it is more complex to establish likeness.

From the GATS perspective, the FDI constitutes a commercial presence to supply a service. Hence, not the FDI itself is the service, but the services supplied by the FDI target company, complemented by services that the investor plans to additionally supply through the FDI target. If the FDI reaches the threshold of commercial presence, it constitutes service trade; hence, the investor becomes a service supplier.[582] Accordingly, FDI Screening mechanisms must not discriminate against such service suppliers from certain WTO members, compared to any like service suppliers from other third countries.

---

[580]The EU has adopted a similar approach in its bilateral trade and investment agreements with countries that have a strong public sector. See e.g. the Art 3bis of Section II EU-China CAI and Chapters 10 and 11 of the EU-Vietnam FTA, and their brief analysis in Sect. 4.3.2.1.3 'EU-China CAI'.

[581]The likeness criterion also comprises two more layers: the likeness of services across the supply modes pursuant to Art I(2) GATS as well as the relation between the likeness of services and the likeness of service suppliers. However, as FDI Screening mechanisms focus on the investors and thus service suppliers only, and apply across sectors, the following will concentrate on the likeness of service suppliers.

[582]See Sect. 4.3.3.3.

In WTO case law it is established that every likeness analysis departs from four criteria: the product's end-uses in a given market; consumers' tastes and habits; the product's properties, nature, and quality; and product classification.[583] The latter criterion plays only a minor role in the GATS because the available services classifications, the Sectoral classification list and the more detailed CPC,[584] are much less precise than the harmonized system for the good classification in the GATT.[585] Moreover, in the GATS's ambit, the products' properties, nature, and, quality may be translated into the services' properties, nature, and qualities, as well as the service suppliers' characteristics and qualifications.[586]

The adjudicating bodies only apply these criteria to the extent they affect the competitive relationship between services and service suppliers.[587] In other words,

---

[583] These criteria stem from Working Party on Border Tax Adjustment, 'GATT Working Party Report' BISD 18S/97, para. 18. The criteria have been reiterated in decisions ever since, see e.g. *Japan—Customs Duties, Taxes and Labelling Practices on Imported Wines and Alcoholic Beverages*, GATT Panel Report (10 November 1987) BISD 34S/83, para. 5.6, on Art III(2) GATT; *European Communities—Measures Affecting Asbestos and Asbestos-Containing Products*, Appellate Body Report (12 March 2001) WT/DS135/AB/R, WTO Online Database doc no 01-1157, para. 101, on Art III(4) GATT, adding tariff classification; and, finally, transposing it to Arts II(1) and XVII(1) GATS, subject to qualifications, *Argentina—Financial Services*, Appellate Body Report (n. 438), paras. 6.30–6.31.

[584] On both see Chap. 3, n. 40.

[585] Cossy (2008), p. 334, giving the example of cardiologists and dermatologists being in the same subsector of specialized medical services. See also Wolfrum (2008), para. 37; Delimatsis and Hoekman (2018), p. 285. While *EC—Bananas III (US)*, Panel Report (n. 438), para. 7.289, still relied on the CPC to some extent, *Argentina—Financial Services*, Appellate Body Report (n. 438), para. 6.32, simply lists the CPC as one possible criterion without further assessment. Mattoo (1997), p. 128, rightly argues that an indication for the 'unlikeness' of services is established if the services at issue are not in the same CPC classification.

[586] On Art 2.1 TBT, *United States—Measures Affecting the Production and Sale of Clove Cigarettes*, Appellate Body Report (4 April 2012) WT/DS406/AB/R, WTO Online Database doc no 12-1741, para. 117, held that regulatory concerns may effect the criteria of physical characteristics and consumer preferences.

[587] *Argentina—Financial Services*, Appellate Body Report (n. 438), para. 6.34; *Argentina—Financial Services*, Panel Report (n. 444), para. 7.163. Apparently with the same conclusion, yet without undertaking an analysis of the competitive relationship *EU—Energy Package* (n. 435), paras. 7.419, 7.421. The Appellate Body has rejected a non-economic understanding of likeness that would apply the above-listed four criteria regardless of them affecting the competitive relationship of services and service suppliers (see *China—Electronic Payment Services* (n. 499), para. 7.700; *Argentina—Financial Services*, Appellate Body Report (n. 438), para. 6.22). At the same time, in *Argentina—Financial Services* the Appellate Body stated that it was 'not called upon to pronounce in this appeal on the relevance and weight of specific criteria for determining whether service suppliers and the services provided are "like"' (*Argentina—Financial Services*, Appellate Body Report (n. 438), para. 6.33). Given its prior emphasis of the competitive relationship, this Appellate Body statement could only have in mind the definition of the degree of a competitive relationship that is necessary to establish likeness. Non-economic criteria could thus impinge on a supposedly economic test. This gives the adjudicating bodies additional flexibility to determine the results of a market-based 'likeness' test (see also *Argentina—Financial Services*, Appellate Body Report (n. 438), para. 6.26). The remarks on the characteristics of services and service suppliers in *Argentina—Financial*

the market place determines whether services and service suppliers are like.[588] Assessing likeness accordingly results in a large group of like foreign investors. The comparison group consists not only of other service suppliers that supply the same services as the FDI target company, but also of all potential investors that *could* become service suppliers; for example, by establishing a commercial presence through M&A. Hence, any foreign firm equipped with the financial means to acquire a sufficient number of shares of a domestic service supplier to establish a commercial presence constitutes a potential service supplier.[589]

Given the differentiation criteria that FDI Screening mechanisms may apply, the protection of IP rights, private information, and competition, as well as foreign government influence on investors, one may be inclined to argue that foreign investors from countries with, for example, a weak protection of private information are unlike investors from countries with private information protection similar to the EU. Following the adjudicating bodies' understanding of likeness, however, such inferior protection of private information does only rarely impinge on the competitive relationship between investors. In only a few cases will a consumer in the market place base his choice between two services on whether the home country of the investors behind the service supplier provides privacy information protection similar to the EU. This is even less so for the other differentiation criteria of competition and IP rights protection, and foreign government influence.

Consequently, the FDI Screening mechanism would differentiate between *like* foreign investors of different third countries within the meaning of Art II(1) GATS when differentiating between foreign investors based on the four differentiation criteria of home country protection of IP rights, private information, and competition, as well as foreign government influence on investors.

4.3.5.2.2 Less Favourable Treatment

According to the second core element of Art II(1) GATS, the FDI Screening mechanisms only discriminate if they treat one part of like foreign investors less favourable than the other part of this comparison group.

As already argued under the NT obligation in Art XVII GATS in Sect. 4.3.4.2.2, applying FDI screening only to one group of like investors constitutes less favourable treatment of this group vis-à-vis those investors who are not subject to the mechanism.[590]

Services, Appellate Body Report (n. 438), para. 6.39, must be read against this background. Nevertheless, Grossman et al. (2013), pp. 307–312, argue for the concept of 'policy likeness'.

[588] The adjudicating bodies also dismissed a subjective approach that takes the possibly legitimate regulatory intent behind the measure at issue into account (see *EC—Bananas III*, Appellate Body Report (n. 437), para. 241).

[589] See also the definition of (potential) trade in services, in Sect. 4.3.3.3.3.

[590] See also Sect. 4.3.5.1, in particular n. 575.

According to the differentiation criteria listed above, the FDI Screening mechanisms screen FDI (more) if the investor's home country protects IP rights, private information, and competition less than the EU, as well as if the home country is perceived to exert high influence on business decisions. Accordingly, only investors whose home countries fulfil these criteria are subject to screening, while FDI of other third-country investors is not or less screened—at least on these grounds. Hence, the investors from home countries that meet the screening criteria are treated less favourable than investors from all other third countries. It makes no difference whether this effect results from the FDI Screening mechanism's design or its application.

Consequently, FDI Screening mechanisms violate the MFN obligation if they, by design or application, differentiate between foreign investors based on their home countries level of protection for IP rights, private information, and competition, as well as state influence on business decisions in their home countries.

4.3.5.2.3 An Alternative Approach to the Non-discrimination Test

The above discussion of the non-discrimination test pursuant to Art II(1) GATS focused on the economic understandings of likeness and less favourable treatment as applied by the adjudicating bodies. However, recent case law and literature signal an understanding of likeness that is more open to non-economic criteria of likeness, in particular to international standards.[591] Therefore, the following will briefly introduce an alternative understanding of likeness based on international standards as additional likeness criteria. In the future, this may considerably increase the EU's flexibility to adopt FDI Screening mechanisms that today would violate the MFN obligation.

The alternative understanding of likeness and less favourable treatment departs from the rationale that the MFN obligation allows differentiation between third countries as long as it is based on harmonized differentiation criteria. Such harmonization must not only take place within the WTO.[592] Alternatively, other

---

[591] Another long-time debate is whether the non-discrimination test should instead assess whether the intention behind the measure at issue was discriminatory. The most discussed subjective approach is the 'aims-and-effects test', which the Appellate Body rightly rejected for Arts II (1) and XVII(1) GATS in *EC—Bananas III*, Appellate Body Report (n. 437), para. 241; and for the non-discrimination obligation in the GATT 1994 in *European Communities—Measures Prohibiting the Importation and Marketing of Seal Products*, Appellate Body Report (22 May 2014) WT/DS400/AB/R and WT/DS401/AB/R, WTO Online Database doc no 14-3051, paras. 5.90, 5.93, 5.117 (on Arts I(1) and III(4) GATT 1994). The GATS does not provide the means to determine whether the regulatory intent behind a measure is legitimate or discriminatory. The adjudicating bodies are not called to fill this void, which is highly sensible for WTO members. Some authors nevertheless favour an understanding based on an objectivized regulatory intent (see the discriminatory intent account e.g. Cossy (2008), pp. 344, 348; widely agreeing Pauwelyn (2008), pp. 362–363).

[592] See the harmonization mandate for the Council for Trade in Services in Art VI(4) GATS, which so far only led to the Disciplines on Domestic Regulation in Accountancy Sector (n. 509), and the plurilateral joint initiative following Ministerial Conference, 'Communication from Certain Members on Domestic Regulation' (n. 509).

organizations may set international standards that qualify as admissible harmonized, non-economic criteria for likeness in Art II(1) (and Art XVII) GATS.[593]

Recent case law indicated openness to such an approach. In *Argentina—Financial Services*, Argentina differentiated between countries that it categorized as cooperative and non-cooperative regarding the exchange of tax information. To justify the categorization, Argentina referred vaguely to tax information exchange standards developed by the Global Forum on Transparency and Exchange of Information for Tax Purposes ('Global Forum'), the Financial Action Task Force ('FATF'), and the OECD.[594]

The panel then considered these organizations' standards and statements as facts in two ways. First, it used statements of the Global Forum and OECD to find that the conditions of competition between financial institutions are affected if some of them are and other are not subject to tax information exchange between their home and host countries.[595] Second, the panel found that the objective to protect 'national tax collection systems against harmful tax practices' is of 'vital importance' based on standards and resolutions by OECD, Global Forum, and G20. The panel thus implied that standards and resolutions of these organizations may establish the legitimacy of a policy objective within the meaning of the GATS.[596]

On appeal the Appellate Body rejected the panel's conclusions, but omitted a detailed discussion of the definition and role of international standards in the GATS. Instead, it used the neutral term 'international instruments'.[597] Nevertheless, one may argue that, if the Appellate Body had wanted to, it would have used the opportunity to generally reject international standards as an element to interpret the non-discrimination obligations. By not doing so, the Appellate Body may have wanted to signal its openness to a more important role of international standards in Arts II(1) and XVII GATS. This is also in line with a current scholar movement, which, at the same time, also emphasizes the need for transparent and inclusive standard-setting processes.[598]

Indeed, in order to qualify as international standards within the meaning of the GATS, standards and their standard-setting organizations must meet certain criteria. One crucial criterion is that the standard-setting organization must be 'open to all

---

[593] In Arts VI(5)(b) and VII(5) GATS, the GATS itself accepts international standards to be taken into account when assessing domestic regulation and the recognition of another WTO member's standards or criteria for authorization, licensing, or certification of service suppliers.

[594] For a description of both organizations see *Argentina—Financial Services*, Panel Report (n. 444), paras. 2.55–2.62.

[595] ibid., paras. 7.509–7.516, 7.665–7.671.

[596] ibid., 7.671.

[597] *Argentina—Financial Services*, Appellate Body Report (n. 438), paras. 5.2, 29.

[598] See e.g. Pauwelyn (2014), p. 739; Gari (2016), p. 589; Mavroidis and Wolfe (2017), p. 1. De Meester (2008), pp. 646–647, discusses the financial regulation standards developed by the Basel Committee on Banking Supervision as elements of an MFN assessment.

WTO members'.[599] This condition seems, for example, to be fulfilled by the International Organization for Standardization ('ISO') as well as the International Electrotechnical Commission ('IEC'). Their statutes provide a formal application process only.[600] Moreover, the TBT repeatedly defines own terms by explicitly referring to ISO/IEC standards.[601] ISO and IEC standards may therefore serve as an additional likeness criterion for assessing non-discrimination pursuant to Art II (1) GATS.

A particularly relevant standard in the context of FDI screening in the EU is the ISO/IEC standard 27701:2019 on security techniques for privacy information management. The standard ensures a certain level of private information security. Accordingly, for meeting the concern regarding private information protection, the FDI Screening mechanism could differentiate based on whether the investors are certified with the ISO/IEC standard 27701:2019, instead of on the investor home country's private information protection laws. If the standard is admitted as a likeness criterion in Art II(1) GATS, the FDI Screening mechanisms will not violate the MFN obligation. The investors between whom the mechanism differentiates would be considered unlike. Nonetheless, it remains doubtful whether the EU and its Member States would find their concern regarding private information protection sufficiently met by an FDI Screening mechanism that screens foreign investors based on whether they are certified with the ISO/IEC standard 27701:2019. Even Huawei,

---

[599] See Art VI(5)(b) GATS and Footnote 3 to the GATS: 'international bodies whose membership is open to the relevant bodies of at least all Members of the WTO'. Art VII(5) GATS, on the other hand, does not reference Footnote 3, but also references 'relevant intergovernmental and non-governmental organizations'. Nevertheless, only a common definition of relevant organization for both provisions makes sense. This is even more so, since Annex 1 to the TBT, para. 4, also uses the term 'open to the relevant bodies of at least all Members'. On the interpretation of this term in the realm of the TBT, see *United States—Measures Concerning the Importation, Marketing and Sale of Tuna and Tuna Products*, Appellate Body Report (16 May 2012) WT/DS381/AB/R, WTO Online Database doc no 12-2620, paras. 364, 384–386. Further criteria for international standards that may also apply in the GATS realm are listed in Committee on Technical Barriers to Trade, 'Decision on the Committee on Principles for the Development of International Standards, Guides and Recommendations with relation to Articles 2, 5 and Annex 3 of the Agreement' (Annex 4 to Second Triennal Review of the Operation and Implementation the Agreement on Technical Barriers to Trade) G/TBT/9.

[600] International Organization for Standardization, 'ISO Statutes' (Geneva, 2018) <https://www.iso.org/publication/PUB100322.html> accessed 2 February 2022, arts 3.1 and 3.2; International Electrotechnical Commission, 'IEC Statutes and Rules of Procedure' (as amended, Geneva, 2001) <https://www.iec.ch/members_experts/refdocs/> accessed 2 February 2022, art 4.

[601] See e.g. Annex 1 to the TBT, which defines certain terms by reference to International Organization for Standardization and International Electrotechnical Commission, 'ISO/IEC Guide 2:1991: General Terms and Their Definitions concerning Standardization and Related Activities' (Geneva, 1991) <https://www.iso.org/standard/19713.html> accessed 2 February 2022. ISO/IEC Guide 2:1991 has now been updated to International Organization for Standardization and International Electrotechnical Commission, 'ISO/IEC Guide 2:2004: Standardization and Related Activities—General Vocabulary' (as amended, Geneva, 2004) <https://www.iso.org/standard/39976.html> accessed 2 February 2022.

a Chinese firm at the centre of the EU's and Member States' private information concern, was certified with the ISO/IEC standard 27701:2019.[602]

As it is also uncertain whether the adjudicating bodies would except international standards as a likeness criterion, the following will continue on the basis of the conclusions reached in Paragraphs i) and ii). They concluded that FDI Screening mechanisms differentiating between foreign investors based on the level of protection of IP rights, private information, and competition in their home countries violate the MFN obligation.

4.3.5.3 FDI Screening Mechanisms as *De Jure* and *De Facto* MFN Discrimination

In sum, FDI Screening mechanisms may violate the MFN obligation in Art II (1) GATS on several grounds when taking into account the EU's obligations vis-à-vis FTA partner countries as well as the EU and Member States concerns vis-à-vis foreign investors from certain specific third countries. On the one hand, if FDI Screening mechanisms differentiate between investors from FTA parties and other third countries, they constitute *de jure* MFN discrimination. On the other hand, FDI Screening mechanisms constitute *de facto* discrimination to the extent they differentiate between foreign investors based on the level of protection of IP rights, private information, and competition in their home countries, as well as a higher level of home country government influence on business decisions.

Therefore, the EU may only adopt FDI Screening mechanisms to the extent they do not provide these two types of differentiation. Insofar the EU's flexibility to adopt FDI Screening mechanisms on broader grounds than 'security or public order' is limited. However, the EU preserves this flexibility to the extent it may invoke relevant grounds of exception. In contrast to FDI Screening mechanisms violating the NT obligation, consistent justification rationales and relevant grounds of exception are available—namely, Arts VI(1) and XIV(c) GATS. They will be discussed in Sect. 4.3.7.

---

[602] According to Huawei's own statement, the British Standards Institution certified Huawei to respect the ISO 27701 standard (Huawei press release, 30 December 2019, <https://www.huawei.com/en/press-events/news/2019/12/huawei-ma5800-code-evaluation-build-engineering-assessment> accessed 2 February 2022. For the data protection concerns regarding Huawei, see Financial Times (2019) (paywall).

4.3.6 Preliminary Result: Wide GATS Scope, Significant Limitations from the NT Obligation, Potential MFN Violation

The previous sections on the GATS allow five main conclusions that have significant implications for the EU's flexibility to adopt FDI Screening mechanisms beyond the grounds of 'security or public order' pursuant to International economic law.

First, the GATS widely liberalizes FDI, but only to the extent it qualifies as commercial presence—thus FDI that gives the investor controlling, majority influence on the FDI target. As nearly all investors and/or FDI targets will supply services that are, together with other business activities such as manufacturing, characteristic to their business purpose (Trade-defining services), the FDI will usually qualify as trade in services.[603] Thus, overall, a large part of FDI qualifies as trade in services through commercial presence.

Second, FDI Screening mechanisms that address M&A FDI qualifying as commercial presence are measures affecting trade in services within the meaning of Art I (1) GATS. Not only the individual FDI prohibition, but also the FDI Screening mechanisms themselves fall into the scope of the GATS.

Third, FDI Screening mechanisms violate the NT obligation in Art XVII GATS. By differentiating explicitly between foreign and domestic investors, FDI Screening mechanisms even constitute *de jure* discrimination. Therefore, the EU's flexibility to adopt FDI Screening mechanisms beyond the screening ground of 'security or public order' is significantly limited. Resorting to the grounds of exception beyond Arts XIV*bis*(1)(b) and XIV(a) GATS is not an option. The EU cannot invoke any policy rationale that consistently explains the differentiation between all foreign investors from Brazil and Canada, to China, Iran, and the United States, on the one hand, and all domestic investors, on the other hand. Moreover, even if there were such consistent policy rationale, it would arguably not fall under the exhaustive list in Art XIV GATS.

Fourth, the consequences arising from the NT obligation are attenuated. While a general cross-sector FDI Screening mechanism will violate one of the EU's many NT commitments, sector-specific mechanisms remain a viable option. A commitment to NT for a specific FDI requires a commitment to Mode three trade in all Trade-defining services sectors. If the EU has no commitments in certain services sectors that are typically supplied by FDI targets of concern, whether classic manufacturing or new IT services companies, the screening of FDI in these targets would not violate the EU's NT obligation. An assessment of EU commitments in two exemplary sectors showed that the EU kept wide flexibility to screen FDI in targets that supply electricity transmission and distribution services. A technology-specific FDI Screening, for example regarding AI technologies, on the other hand, is less promising, since it is at odds with the sector-based GATS system.

---

[603] For the definition of Trade-defining services see Sect. 4.3.3.3.1.

Fifth, the general MFN obligation significantly limits the EU's flexibility to adopt FDI Screening mechanisms that differentiate in two ways. On the one hand, mechanisms that only apply to investors non-FTA partner countries, excluding investors from FTA partner countries. On the other hand, FDI Screening mechanisms that, by design or application, screen investors only or more who are not from countries with an inferior level of protection of IP rights, private information, and competition, as well as a from countries with a higher level of government influence on business decisions. Still, for FDI Screening mechanisms so violating the MFN obligation, the grounds of exception may apply.

These conclusions have significant implications for how the EU may design the scope of FDI Screening mechanisms beyond the grounds of 'security or public order'.

Most importantly, Art XVII GATS prevents the EU from adopting general cross-sector FDI Screening mechanisms—vis-à-vis all WTO members. They will violate the EU sector-specific commitments to NT with respect to Mode three trade. Nevertheless, sector-specific mechanisms remain a viable alternative to meet the EU and Member States concerns vis-à-vis foreign investors. The EU could identify certain services sectors that FDI targets of concern usually supply. For example, the screening of FDI in the electricity transmission and distribution sector remains possible.

Finally, such sector-specific FDI Screening mechanisms may only differentiate based on the investor's home country status as FTA partner country and certain country-specific concerns vis-à-vis foreign investors to the extent relevant grounds of exception apply. This will be assessed in the following Sect. 4.3.7.

4.3.7   Relevant Grounds of Exception for MFN Violation: Arts V(1) and XIV(c) GATS

Sections 4.3.3 to 4.3.6 showed that the GATS limits the EU's flexibility to adopt FDI Screening mechanisms on broader grounds than 'security or public order' within the meaning of the Screening Regulation and thus Arts XIV*bis*(b) and XIV(a) GATS. These limits derive inter alia from the MFN obligation pursuant to Art II(1) GATS. On the one hand, the FDI Screening mechanism may violate Art II(1) GATS *de jure* by explicitly differentiating between investors from FTA partner and other third countries. On the other hand, FDI Screening mechanisms may *de facto* discriminate against foreign investors from home countries with protection of IP rights, private information, and competition that the EU considers inferior to its own level of protection, as well as from countries with an allegedly higher level of government influence on business decisions.

Designing or applying FDI Screening mechanisms in these two ways is GATS inconsistent—unless the EU may justify the violation based on a ground of exception. Section 3.1 already showed that the grounds of exception in Arts XIV(a) and

XIV*bis*(1)(b) GATS fail to considerably cover the EU and Member States concerns vis-à-vis foreign investors, especially due to the necessary element of threat. However, the GATS may offer other grounds of exception that cover the above described differentiations: Arts V(1) and XIV(c) GATS.

Art V(1) GATS may allow the EU to discriminate between FTA and non-FTA partner countries, and XIV(c) GATS may justify discrimination based on different levels of IP rights, private information, and competition protection, as well as foreign government influence.

4.3.7.1 Art V(1) GATS: Differentiating Between FTA Partners and Other Third Countries

Art V(1) GATS may give the EU the right to differentiate between foreign investors from FTA partner and from other third countries. The provision offers WTO members the possibility to further liberalize trade in Regional Trade Agreements ('RTAs') without obliging these members to extend the agreed preferential treatment to other WTO members.[604] In order words, Art V(1) GATS constitutes an exception to the MFN obligation in Art II(1) GATS.[605]

The ground of exception is subject to three requirements. First, the RTA must (further) liberalize trade between the parties, without raising new barriers of trade vis-à-vis other WTO members (Art V(1) and (4) GATS). Second, the RTA must have substantial sectoral coverage (Art V(1)(a) GATS). Third, the RTA must eliminate substantially all NT discrimination between the parties (Art V(1) (b) GATS). Since Art V(1) GATS provides an exception to GATS provisions, the liberalization requirements in Art V(1)(b) GATS are limited to trade in services only.

The present work cannot provide an in-depth analysis that assesses whether all EU FTAs meet these three requirements. The EU itself suggests that its FTAs are RTAs within the meaning of Art V(1) GATS by having notified them to the WTO pursuant to Art V(7) GATS. Moreover, much weighs in favour of recent EU FTAs fulfilling the three requirements of liberalization, substantial sector coverage, and elimination of substantially all NT discrimination.

---

[604] *Canada—Autos*, Panel Report (n. 495), para. 10.271.

[605] ibid., paras. 10.265, 10.271. See also on the parallel GATT provision, Art XXIV(5) GATT 1994, *Peru—Additional Duty on Imports of Certain Agricultural Products*, Appellate Body Report (20 July 2015) WT/DS457/AB/R, WTO Online Database doc no 15-3716, para. 5.116. Here, the Appellate Body held: 'In our view, the references in paragraph 4 to facilitating trade and closer integration are not consistent with an interpretation of Article XXIV as a broad defence for measures in FTAs that roll back on Members' rights and obligations under the WTO covered agreements.' This may be read as weighing against Art XXIV(5) GATT 1994, and thus Art V (1) GATS, as a general exception to the MFN obligation. However, in *Peru—Agricultural Products*, Peru was found to have violated its obligations to reduce customs pursuant to Art II(b) GATT 1994, not the MFN obligation. Nevertheless, If WTO law wants to give WTO members the right to conclude—and respect—additional RTAs, it must provide an exception to the MFN obligation. Otherwise, this aim would be undermined.

The first condition to liberalize trade will be fulfilled by the EU FTAs because they provide further services trade liberalization than the prior *status quo* under WTO law and other International economic law.[606] It is less clear, however, whether the EU FTAs also meet the two other requirements on substantial sector coverage and elimination of NT discrimination.

According to the second requirement, the EU FTA must have substantial sectoral coverage, quantitatively and qualitatively.[607] Footnote 1 to the GATS further clarifies that this criterion comprises the number of sectors, the affected volume of trade, and the modes of supply. Regarding the modes of supply, the RTA may provide different levels of liberalization among modes, but must not exclude any mode 'a priori'.[608] This applies to the commitments of both FTA parties.[609] Only little light has been shed on defining the term 'substantial'. In *Turkey—Textiles* the Appellate Body interpreted the similar GATT notion in Art XXIV(8)(a) GATT 1994 to be 'not the same as *all* the trade, and also ... considerably more than merely *some* of the trade'.[610] This is supposed to offer some degree of flexibility to WTO members.[611]

Recent FTAs make use of this flexibility, while still providing substantial sector coverage. In CETA, for instance, Canada and the EU excluded from the services chapters certain air transport services, audio-visual services for the EU, and cultural industries for Canada.[612] In the EU-Vietnam FTA, the EU and Vietnam excluded the same sectors, adding the minor subsectors of services relating to nuclear materials; production of arms, munition, war material.[613] All other services sectors, however, are a priori covered by both FTAs.[614]

---

[606]This requirement was also briefly discussed in *Peru—Agricultural Products* (n. 605), para. 5.112. Under this requirement, Adlung (2020), pp. 493, 498, addresses GATS-minus RTAs that stipulate obligations that in scope are inferior to the respective GATS obligations, for example excluding the awarding of subsidies from the NT obligation. However, this issue is better addressed under Art V(1)(b) GATS, namely whether eliminating NT discrimination between the RTA parties with the exception of subsidies constitutes the elimination of substantially all NT discrimination.

[607]Cottier and Molinuevo (2008), para. 11.

[608]Cottier and Molinuevo (2008), para. 19.

[609]Cottier and Molinuevo (2008), para. 24.

[610]*Turkey—Restrictions on Imports of Textile and Clothing Products*, Appellate Body Report (22 October 1999) WT/DS34/AB/R, WTO Online Database doc no 99-4546, para. 48 (emphasis in the original).

[611]ibid.

[612]Arts 8.2.2(a), 9.2.2(e)), 8.3.3, 9.2.2(b) and (c) CETA. Canada and the EU also excluded all activities carried out in the exercise of governmental authority (Arts 8.2.2(b), 9.2.2(a) CETA).

[613]Arts 8.3(a), (d)–(e), 8.9(a) EU-Vietnam FTA. For the investment chapter, the parties also excluded services performed in the exercise of governmental authority (Art 8.3.2(f) EU-Vietnam FTA).

[614]This book does not submit a full analysis of all sector commitments in CETA and the EU-Vietnam FTA. It may be expected that the parties to the EU FTAs commit to NT vis-à-vis the other FTA party at least in those sectors in which they also committed to NT under the GATS.

Hence, these FTAs do not only cover all modes of service supply,[615] but also the vast majority of services sectors, only excluding certain subsectors. This suffices to meet the requirement of substantial sector coverage. As already argued in Sect. 4.3.2.1, one may extrapolate this conclusion to other modern EU FTAs.

The third requirement demands the absence or elimination of substantially all NT discrimination in the covered sectors within the meaning of Art XVII GATS.[616] FTAs, on the other hand, often define NT differently. For instance, both CETA and the EU-Vietnam FTA define NT as no less favourable treatment of service suppliers and services of the other party than that accorded to its own service suppliers and services—*in like situations*.[617] Art XVII GATS, however, uses the criterion 'like services' and 'like service suppliers'. Moreover, in contrast to the GATS, EU FTAs exclude subsidies from the NT obligation.[618] Nevertheless, while not eliminating *all* NT discrimination, the EU FTAs eliminate considerably more than just some NT discrimination. Thus, one may expect that at least more recent EU FTAs, which are similar to CETA and the EU-Vietnam FTA, also meet the third requirement of Art V (1) GATS, eliminating substantially all NT discrimination within the meaning of Art XVII GATS.[619]

Consequently, more recent EU FTAs will generally meet the requirements of Art V(1) GATS. Thus, in FDI Screening mechanisms the EU may differentiate *de jure* between foreign investors from FTA partner and other third countries, subject to a more detailed analysis of each FTA with respect to the three requirements of Art V (1) GATS.

4.3.7.2 Art XIV(c) GATS: Justifying *De Facto* Discrimination of Investors from Countries of Concern

Art XIV(c) GATS, on the other hand, may preserve the EU's flexibility to adopt FDI Screening mechanisms that discriminate *de facto* against foreign investors from home countries with protection of IP rights, private information, and competition that the EU considers inferior to its own level of protection, as well as from countries with an allegedly higher level of government influence on business decision.

---

[615] The EU-China CAI, on the other hand, is limited to investment, and does thus only cover Mode three trade (commercial presence). Accordingly, it would not fulfil the requirements of Art V (1) GATS.

[616] Also emphasized by Adlung (2020), p. 494. See also *Canada—Autos*, Panel Report (n. 495), para. 10.270.

[617] Paraphrased in accordance with Arts 8.6(1) and (2), 9.3, 10.6.2(a) CETA for establishment, cross-border trade, and temporary personal presence; Art 8.5 EU-Vietnam FTA for establishment.

[618] See Arts 8.15.5(b) and 9.2.2(g) CETA.

[619] With a detailed discussion of the possible discrepancy between the notions of NT discrimination, see Adlung (2020), pp. 503–506.

Art XIV(c) GATS is, as Art XIV(a) GATS, a general exception to WTO members' GATS obligations. Embedded in the general requirements of Art XIV GATS, it provides:

Art XIV. General Exceptions
   Subject to the requirement that such measures are not applied in a manner which would constitute a means of arbitrary or unjustifiable discrimination between countries where like conditions prevail, or a disguised restriction on trade in services, nothing in this Agreement shall be construed to prevent the adoption or enforcement by any Member of measures:

(a) . . .
(b) . . .
(c) necessary to secure compliance with laws or regulations which are not inconsistent with the provisions of this Agreement including those relating to:

   (i) the prevention of deceptive and fraudulent practices or to deal with the effects of a default on services contracts;
  (ii) the protection of the privacy of individuals in relation to the processing and dissemination of personal data and the protection of confidentiality of individual records and accounts;
 (iii) safety.

Given the term 'including those relating to', the list in Subparagraphs (i) to (iii) is evidently non-exhaustive.[620] As a result, Art XIV(c) GATS seems to open a door to a variety of regulatory considerations, as long as they are based on 'laws or regulations which are not inconsistent' with the GATS.

The assessment of Art XIV(c) GATS is two-tiered. The measure at issue, here the FDI Screening mechanism or its application, must first be provisionally justified under the specific exception in Art XIV(c) GATS. Second, the measure must satisfy the requirements of the *chapeau* of Art XIV GATS.[621] The *chapeau* only addresses the measure's application, not the legality of the measure itself ('such measures are not applied in a manner which').[622] For assessing the EU's abstract flexibility to adopt FDI Screening mechanisms, it is therefore enough to focus on the first tier: Under which conditions would an FDI Screening mechanism be provisionally justified that differentiates between investors on the basis of IP rights, private information, and competition protection, as well as the level of government influence on business decisions in their home countries?

The following will base the legal standards to interpret Art XIV(c) GATS mostly on the panel report in *Argentina—Financial Services*, the most recent GATS case on Art XIV(c) GATS. Though the legal standards applied by the panel were not appealed, the Appellate Body nevertheless signalled agreement with the panel's approach.[623] The Appellate Body only raised concerns on minor issues, which will

---

[620] See also Krajewski (2003), p. 158.

[621] *US—Gambling*, Appellate Body Report (n. 469), para. 292.

[622] Krajewski (2003), p. 161.

[623] Panama stated that the legal standards for Art XIV(c) GATS were 'well-developed', and therefore only appealed the standards' application; *Argentina—Financial Services*, Appellate Body Report (n. 438), paras. 6.157, 6.200, 6.221.

be addressed to the extent they are necessary for assessing the general limits of Art XIV(c) GATS to FDI Screening mechanisms. The following analysis will also consult case law on Art XX(d) GATT 1994. Both provisions Art XIV(c) GATS and Art XX(d) GATT 1994 are to be interpreted similarly.[624]

Point of departure for any analysis under Art XIV(c) GATS are those aspects of the measure that resulted in violating the GATS obligations.[625] Accordingly, the present analysis starts from the FDI Screening mechanisms' discrimination on the basis of IP rights, private information, and competition protection, and level of government influence on business decisions. Discrimination is justified under Art XIV(c) GATS if (i) it is designed to secure compliance with laws and regulations that are not in themselves inconsistent with the GATS, and (ii) if the measures are necessary to secure such compliance.[626] The following will define these requirements in turn, and apply them to the possible MFN discriminations of FDI Screening mechanisms.

4.3.7.2.1   To Secure Compliance with GATS-Consistent Laws and Regulations

First, Art XIV(c) GATS requires that the measure must be designed to secure compliance with laws and regulations that are GATS-consistent.

Laws and regulations within the meaning of Art XIV(c) GATS may pursue a variety of policy objectives, not only those mentioned in the non-exhaustive list in Subparagraphs (i) to (iii).[627] The WTO member must invoke a concrete rule that protects a certain public interest and that its measure seeks to ensure compliance with. This rule may either follow from one concrete provision in a law or a regulation, or from a comprehensive legal framework consisting of several instruments.[628] The WTO member must provide the texts of the relevant laws and regulations.[629] This further clarifies that it is not enough to merely invoke policy objectives derived from broad, allegedly common values or interests. Moreover, the rule must be consistent with the GATS. Hence, it must not, for instance, discriminate against foreign services or service supplier or between them. Yet, any rule is to be considered GATS-consistent until proven otherwise.[630]

---

[624] *US—Gambling*, Appellate Body Report (n. 469), para. 291; *Argentina—Financial Services*, Panel Report (n. 444), para. 7.590. See also *India—Solar Cells*, Appellate Body Report (n. 416), paras. 5.110–5.111, which cites *Argentina—Financial Services*, Appellate Body Report (n. 438), on Art XIV(c) GATS to interpret Art XX(d) GATT 1994.

[625] *Argentina—Financial Services*, Appellate Body Report (n. 438), para. 6.168.

[626] *Argentina—Financial Services*, Panel Report (n. 444), para. 7.593.

[627] Krajewski (2003), pp. 158–159.

[628] *India—Solar Cells*, Appellate Body Report (n. 416), para. 5.111.

[629] *Argentina—Financial Services*, Panel Report (n. 444), para. 7.609.

[630] *US—Gambling*, Appellate Body Report (n. 469), para. 138; *Dominican Republic—Measures Affecting the Importation and Internal Sale of Cigarettes*, Appellate Body Report (25 April 2005)

In addition, the measure must be *designed* to secure compliance with the invoked rule. This only constitutes a minimum threshold to ensure a minimum nexus between the measure and the rule.[631] It is enough for the invoking WTO member to show that the measure is 'not incapable of' securing compliance with the measure.[632]

When applying these defining elements to the discriminating aspects of FDI Screening mechanisms a heterogeneous picture emerges. FDI Screening mechanisms that are based on IP rights and private information protection may contribute to ensure that foreign investors comply with concrete rules. For IP right protection such rules are for example provided in Directive 2004/48/EC on the enforcement of IP rights; Directive (EU) 2015/2436 on trademarks; or Directive (EU) 2019/790 on copyrights.[633] To protect private information, the EU could invoke the GDPR.[634] From these directives and regulations, the EU could therefore deduce rules that FDI Screening mechanism seeks to ensure compliance with.

To protect competition, however, such a concrete rule is not available. The EU and Member States competition concern is about foreign investors with easier access to financial funding than EU investors, in particular through home country state subsidies. This might distort competition in the EU.[635] Accordingly, the EU may compare EU and home country competition rules to assess the risk of competition distortion through the FDI. The EU may then screen investors from home countries with allegedly lower competition protection standards. This, however, is not a consideration that is protected by Art XVI(c) GATS. Art XIV(c) GATS protects measures that seek to secure compliance with specific rules—by which the relevant service suppliers are bound. The relevant EU competition laws, Arts 106 and

---

WT/DS302/AB/R, WTO Online Database doc no 05-1669, para. 111 (on Art XX(d) GATT 1994); *Argentina—Financial Services*, Panel Report (n. 444), paras. 7.620, 7.625. See also Mishra (2020), p. 352.

[631] The requirement of 'designed to' follows from the literal meaning of 'measures necessary to secure compliance with', see *Mexico—Tax Measures on Soft Drinks and Other Beverages*, Appellate Body Report (6 March 2006) WT/DS308/AB/R, WTO Online Database doc no 06-0914, para. 72.

[632] *Colombia—Measures Relating to the Importation of Textiles, Apparel and Footwear*, Appellate Body Report (7 June 2016) WT/DS461/AB/R, WTO Online Database doc no 16-3060, paras. 5.134–5.135.

[633] Directive 2004/48/EC of the European Parliament and of the Council of 29 April 2004 on the enforcement of intellectual property rights, in the corrected version [2004] OJ L 195/16; Directive (EU) 2015/2436 of the European Parliament and of the Council of 16 December 2015 to approximate the laws of the Member States relating to trade marks [2015] OJ L 336/1; Directive (EU) 2019/790 of the European Parliament and of the Council of 17 April 2019 on copyright and related rights in the Digital Single Market and amending Directives 96/9/EC and 2001/29/EC [2019] OJ L 130/92.

[634] Regulation (EU) 2016/679 of the European Parliament and of the Council of 27 April 2016 on the protection of natural persons with regard to the processing of personal data and on the free movement of such data, and repealing Directive 95/46/EC (GDPR) [2016] OJ L 119/1. Mishra (2020), p. 352, raises doubts whether the GDPR adequacy rules on third countries' data protection laws are non-discriminatory, citing Kuner (2019).

[635] For a detailed discussion of this concern see Sect. 2.1.2.

107 TFEU, however, do only apply to EU public undertakings and Member States, not to foreign undertakings and third countries. Another EU rule that applies to foreign investors and/or third countries and may attenuate the concern of competition distortions by foreign investors does not exist either. Consequently, the EU cannot invoke any rule that an FDI Screening mechanism would seek to ensure compliance with when differentiating between foreign investors based on their home countries' competition rules.

This is even more true for the discrimination based on foreign government influence on business decisions in the investor's home country. There is no EU rule that prohibits foreign investors to be influenced by foreign governments. To the extent the competition rules in Arts 106 and 107 TFEU may approximate this concern, they do, as just argued, not apply to foreign investors and their home country governments.

Hence, FDI Screening mechanisms that discriminate based on competition rules and government influence on business decisions in foreign investors' home countries cannot be justified by Art XIV(c) GATS. Only FDI Screening mechanisms that discriminate between foreign investors based on their home countries' level of protection of IP rights and private information can invoke concrete EU rules they seek to ensure compliance with. Insofar, FDI Screening mechanisms that violate the MFN obligation in Art II(1) GATS may thus be justified under Art XIV(c) GATS— if they pass its necessity test.

4.3.7.2.2   Necessity Test

The second requirement to provisionally justify a measure under Art XIV(c) GATS is that the measure must be *necessary* to secure compliance with the invoked rule. In *India—Solar Cells* the Appellate Body outlines the necessity test as follows:

> [A] determination of whether a measure is 'necessary' entails a more in-depth and holistic examination of the relationship between the inconsistent measure and the relevant laws or regulations. This involves, in each case, a process of 'weighing and balancing' a series of factors, including: the extent to which the measure sought to be justified contributes to the realization of the end pursued . . .; the relative importance of the societal interest or value that the 'law or regulation' is intended to protect; and the trade-restrictiveness of the challenged measure. In most cases, a comparison between the challenged measure and reasonably available alternative measures should then be undertaken.[636]

Accordingly, for deciding whether a measure is necessary to secure compliance with a specific rule, one must assess four factors: the importance of the objective pursued,

---

[636] *India—Solar Cells*, Appellate Body Report (n. 416), para. 5.59 (footnotes omitted, on Art XX (d) GATT 1994), citing *Korea—Measures Affecting Imports of Fresh, Chilled and Frozen Beef*, Appellate Body Report (11 December 2000) WT/DS161/AB/R and WT/DS169/AB/R, WTO Online Database doc no 00-5347, paras. 162–164, 166; *Colombia—Textiles* (n. 632), paras. 5.71–5.74; *EC—Seal Products*, Appellate Body Report (n. 591), para. 5.169. These are also cited by *Argentina—Financial Services*, Panel Report (n. 444), paras. 7.659–7.660.

the contribution of the measure to the objective, the measure's trade-restrictiveness, and the availability of less trade-restrictive, reasonably available measures.[637] In a final assessment these four factors have to be weighed and balanced to conclude whether or not a measure is necessary within the meaning of Art XIV(c) GATS.

The Importance of the Policy Objective Pursued
The importance of the policy objective pursued by the rule that the measure at issue seeks to secure compliance with is at least obvious for those interests that are mentioned in the subparagraphs of Art XIV(c) GATS.[638] Therefore, 'the protection of the privacy of individuals' (Art XIV(c)(ii) GATS), and thus the protection of private information is of high importance.[639] The protection of IP rights is equally important, since the parallel provision of Art XIV(c) in GATT 1994, Art XX(d), also lists patents, trademarks, and copyrights as interests that compliance measures may protect.

Contributing to Securing Compliance
Moreover, the measure at issue must contribute to its objective that is, to secure compliance with a specific rule. Hence, the question is not (only) whether the measure contributes to the overall policy objective, for example private information protection, but whether it contributes to ensure compliance with the specific rule at issue.[640] Given the term contributing, it is enough if the measure secures partial compliance.[641] Yet, 'the greater the contribution, the more easily a measure might be

---

[637] In *Argentina—Financial Services*, Appellate Body Report (n. 438), para. 6.221, the Appellate Body cautioned against a too 'disaggregated and compartmentalized' assessment of these factors, in particular if multiple measures are at issue. Nevertheless, for identifying factors that may limit the EU's flexibility to screen FDI, such a compartmentalized approach is indispensable.

[638] In *Argentina—Financial Services*, Panel Report (n. 444), paras. 7.662–7.682, the panel also relied on decisions and reports of other international fora such as the OECD and the Financial Action Task Force to conclude that protecting the tax collection system and fighting against harmful tax practices is of utmost importance to Argentina.

[639] Mishra (2020), p. 354.

[640] *Argentina—Financial Services*, Appellate Body Report (n. 438), paras. 6.227, 229; citing *Korea—Various Measures on Beef*, Appellate Body Report (n. 636), para. 163 (on Art XX (d) GATT 1994). The contribution of the measure must be based on a qualitative or quantitative assessment, instead of simple inferences (*Argentina—Financial Services*, Appellate Body Report (n. 438), para. 6.234).

[641] Cottier et al. (2008), para. 40, who cite *Korea—Measures Affecting Imports of Fresh, Chilled and Frozen Beef*, Panel Report (31 July 2000) WT/DS161/R and T/DS169/R, as modified by Appellate Body Report WT/DS161/AB/R and WT/DS169/AB/R, WTO Online Database doc no 00-3025, para. 658. This reference, however, does not support the conclusion of 'partial compliance'. The panel only argued that it was enough if the measure at issue was in part designed to secure compliance, but, in other parts, pursued different objectives. Nevertheless, *Argentina—Financial Services*, Appellate Body Report (n. 438), para. 6.234, also emphasizes the term contribution.

considered to be "necessary"'.[642] Assessing *ex ante* whether the foreign investor will respect laws regarding IP rights and private information, FDI Screening mechanisms are contributing to securing compliance with these laws.

Trade-Restrictiveness

The third factor of the necessity test evaluates the measure's trade-restrictiveness. This factor is particularly important, since measures with little trade-restrictive effect are more easily considered necessary.[643] Trade bans and measures that amount to a trade ban are the most trade-restrictive form a compliance measure can take.[644] Information requirements, on the other hand, constitute a low level of trade-restrictiveness, even if the authorities may deny trade authorization in case the information is not provided.[645] For evaluating the trade-restrictiveness of a measure one must also take into account the potential trade-deterring effect the measure has— for instance, through higher taxes for foreign services.[646] These defining aspects show that the trade-restrictiveness depends on the specific design, structure, and operation of the measure.[647] It is thus difficult to abstractly evaluate the trade-restrictiveness of FDI Screening mechanisms. However, some determinants can be identified.

FDI Screening mechanisms only constitute a trade ban to the extent a concrete FDI screening leads to a prohibition of the investment. The mechanism as such, however, is less trade-restrictive. As already discussed, there are two possibilities of FDI Screening mechanism design: mechanisms generally prohibiting incoming FDI with the possibility of authorizing a specific FDI in an individual administrative decision (Case 1), and mechanisms generally authorizing FDI with the possibility for exceptional prohibition (Case 2). In Case 2, the mechanism is combined with a statutory condition precedent to the investment contract.[648] In both cases, the FDI Screening mechanism is thus more than simply a requirement to provide additional information. The mechanism rather imposes an authorization requirement on FDI that is based on a qualitative assessment of the foreign investor. This in itself restricts trade.[649] However, the trade-restrictive effect will ultimately depend on how much

---

[642] *Korea—Various Measures on Beef*, Appellate Body Report (n. 636), para. 163.

[643] ibid. (on Art XX(d) GATT 1994); *Argentina—Financial Services*, Panel Report (n. 444), para. 7.727.

[644] *Argentina—Financial Services*, Appellate Body Report (n. 438), para. 6.238; citing *Brazil—Measures Affecting Imports of Retreaded Tyres*, Appellate Body Report (3 December 2007) WT/DS332/AB/R, WTO Online Database doc no 07-5290, para. 150 (on Art XX(d) GATT 1994).

[645] *Argentina—Financial Services*, Panel Report (n. 444), paras. 7.720–7.723.

[646] ibid., para. 7.719.

[647] ibid., para. 7.688, though on how to determine whether the measure contributes to the compliance objective.

[648] See Sects. 4.3.3.2 and 2.4.3.

[649] See also the assessment of FDI Screening mechanisms modifying the conditions of competition in Sect. 4.3.4.2.2.

the mechanism is in fact used to prohibit or restrict FDI. The more the FDI Screening mechanism is used, the more it creates uncertainty, and thus a trade-deterring effect.

Consequently, one may conclude that FDI Screening mechanisms generally have a medium trade-restrictive effect, depending on their concrete design and operation.[650]

No Reasonably Available Alternative Measure

The last factor that must be taken into account when assessing a compliance measure's necessity is whether an alternative, less-restrictive measure is reasonably available.

The WTO member itself determines the level of protection that it deems appropriate for the interest at issue.[651] This may even be a zero-risk level of protection.[652] Alternative measures must therefore achieve the same level of protection.[653] Nevertheless, it would be too simple to argue that *ex post* measures can never fulfil the same level of protection as *ex ante* measures. Measures such as *ex post* investigations, prosecution, fines, and record-keeping may be as protective as *ex ante* measures.[654] Often, an alternative to specific, trade-restrictive *ex ante* measures is general policing, which is usually more targeted.[655] If a WTO member wants to argue that an alternative is not reasonably available because the costs are too high, it must provide specific evidence. Nevertheless, it is in any case WTO-inconsistent to avoid costs of policing measures by shifting them entirely on importers or exporters.[656]

With these general guidelines in mind, the discussion can turn to concrete alternative measures to FDI Screening mechanisms to secure the same level of protection to IP rights and private information. There are large differences between both fields of law, and reasonably alternative measures depend on the concrete design and operation of the FDI Screening mechanism. However, it is possible to

---

[650] See for a similar conclusion on the certification requirement for foreign-controlled natural gas transmission system operators *EU—Energy Package* (n. 435), paras. 7.1227–7.1228. According to the panel, the trade-restrictiveness of such a measure will ultimately depend on its application.

[651] On Art XIV(a) GATS: *US—Gambling*, Appellate Body Report (n. 469), para. 308, citing *Korea—Various Measures on Beef*, Appellate Body Report (n. 636), para. 176 (on Art XX (d) GATT 1994). See also on Art XX GATT 1995: *Dominican Republic—Import and Sale of Cigarettes* (n. 630), para. 23; *Brazil—Retreaded Tires* (n. 644), para. 210.

[652] Cottier et al. (2008), para. 41. Often, however, the adjudicating bodies find that the measure at issue does not exclude any risk of non-compliance, but seeks to significantly reduce the risk. This makes it then easier to list alternative measures. See e.g. *Korea—Various Measures on Beef*, Appellate Body Report (n. 636), para. 178.

[653] *Argentina—Financial Services*, Panel Report (n. 444), paras. 7.732–7.736.

[654] *Korea—Various Measures on Beef*, Appellate Body Report (n. 636), paras. 178–180.

[655] ibid., para. 172.

[656] ibid., para. 181.

identify two measures of which one is definitely not, and another may be a reasonably available alternative to FDI Screening mechanisms.

First, it is insufficient to argue that IP and private information laws are compulsory and therefore in themselves sufficient to secure compliance with them. The whole rationale behind FDI Screening mechanisms is that the foreign investor fails to respect these obligations.[657]

Second, alternative policing measures may constitute a reasonably available alternative to an FDI Screening mechanism. Certainly, no policing measure will completely eliminate risks to IP rights and private information protection; but FDI Screening mechanisms will neither. FDI Screening mechanisms are in fact imprecise risk assessment procedures, in which many different FDI aspects are reviewed in a short period of time. Thus, even strict screening mechanisms will not eliminate, but only attenuate risks. The benchmark of the level of protection that an alternative measure must fulfil is therefore significantly attenuated. In addition, policing measures, usually undertaken by specialized regulatory agencies, are more targeted at the pursued policy objective, here IP rights and private information protection. They therefore may be seen as better contributing to securing compliance with IP and private information laws.

Policing that may provide a similar level of protection may, for instance, consists of a registration requirement for FDI that affects IP rights and private information, ongoing regulatory surveillance, and finally a strict sanctioning mechanism in case of non-compliance that, at the same time, incentivizes compliance in the first place. Nevertheless, in contrast to FDI Screening mechanisms, policing measures do not allow to completely prohibit FDI.[658] Insofar, the level of protection may thus be described as higher than the listed alternatives. But, as stated above, even the FDI Screening mechanism does not eliminate, but only attenuates the risk of IP rights and private information protection violations. This level of protection may also be ensured by ongoing regulatory control and other available sanctions.

Consequently, policing may be a reasonably available measure to FDI Screening mechanisms that is less trade-restrictive and contributes even better to securing compliance with IP and private information protection laws. The ultimate result, however, depends on the design and operation of the concrete FDI Screening mechanism.

---

[657] Similarly, *EU—Energy Package* (n. 435), paras. 7.1237, 1227, in which the panel found that an EU statute requiring gas transmission operators ('TSOs') not to comply with foreign law that undermines the EU's energy security does not provide the same level of energy security protection than an *ex ante* screening mechanism of foreign-controlled TSOs that sought to assess the possible effect of foreign government interference on the EU's energy security.

[658] A disinvestment order is first nearly impossible, since disinvestment is highly complex and requires an alternative investor who acquires the foreign investor's shares. Second, a disinvestment order may fail to meet its objective because the foreign investor may already have violated IP rights and private information protection before the disinvestment.

Weighing and Balancing

The above four-factor analysis assessed the necessity of FDI Screening mechanisms to secure FDI investor compliance with IP and private information protection laws. While the conclusions ultimately depend on the concrete design and operation of the mechanisms, the analysis could nevertheless determine certain cornerstones for the necessity test of FDI Screening mechanisms under Art XIV(c) GATS. These cornerstones are, as the last step of the necessity test, to be weighed and balanced in order to determine whether the relationship is sufficiently close between the measure FDI Screening mechanism, on the one hand, and the specific rule the measure seeks to ensure compliance with, thus relevant IP and private information laws, on the other hand.

The analysis found that FDI Screening mechanisms pursue policy objectives of high importance, and contribute to securing foreign investor compliance with IP and private information protection laws. Moreover, they may be categorized as medium trade-restrictive. However, specifically targeted policing measures such as FDI registration requirements, ongoing regulatory surveillance, and strict sanctioning mechanisms may be reasonably alternative measures that are less trade-restrictive and contribute better to securing compliance with IP and private information protection laws. Weighed and balanced, these factors therefore weigh against the necessity of FDI Screening mechanisms to secure compliance with IP and private information protection laws. In principle, policing may be a more appropriate measure.

Consequently, an abstract assessment of FDI Screening mechanisms under Art XIV(c) GATS indicates that the mechanisms fail the necessity test to the extent they discriminate between foreign investors based on the level of IP and private information protection in their home countries. The final conclusion whether an FDI Screening mechanism meets the necessity test in Art XIV(c) GATS, however, depends on its concrete design and operation beyond the broad six cornerstones of the FDI Screening mechanism as identified in Sect. 2.4.3.

Nevertheless, the constraining elements of the necessity test identified here allow to conclude that justification of an MFN discrimination based on the level of IP and private information protection in their home countries is unlikely. To ensure compliance with the GATS, the EU may therefore refrain from designing FDI Screening mechanisms as discriminating according to these two differentiation criteria. Instead, the EU may concentrate on targeted policing measures such as FDI registration requirements, ongoing regulatory surveillance, and strict sanctioning mechanisms.

4.3.7.2.3   Art XIV(c) GATS: No Promising Ground of Exception for MFN Discrimination

As a result, Art XIV(c) GATS, though depending on the FDI Screening mechanism's concrete design and operation, does not constitute a promising resort for the EU to differentiate between foreign investors based on IP rights, private information, and competition protection, and home country government influence.

Regarding the protection of competition laws and foreign government influence, the EU cannot invoke any rule that attenuates their concern and binds foreign investors or their home country governments. Hence, there simply is no rule FDI Screening mechanisms could secure compliance with. This must be kept in mind when assessing the EU's proposal of new FDI screening mechanism at EU level for (partial) EU target acquisitions that are facilitated by foreign subsidies.[659]

With respect to MFN discrimination on the grounds of IP rights and private information protection, the necessity test of Art XIV(c) GATS poses high barriers to FDI Screening mechanisms. Regulatory policing is a less trade restrictive, reasonably available, alternative measure that contributes even better to protecting IP and private information laws. FDI registration requirements, ongoing regulatory surveillance, and strict sanctioning mechanisms may be better targeted and, therefore, better address risks that FDI poses.

Consequently, the EU does not have the flexibility to adopt FDI Screening mechanisms that differentiate between foreign investors based on their home countries' protection of competition and their home country governments' influence on business decisions. The same conclusion is typically valid for a differentiation based on IP rights and private information protection, with the caveat of the concrete design and operation.

In general, the EU therefore only preserves the flexibility to adopt FDI Screening mechanisms that discriminate between foreign investors from FTA and non-FTA partner countries.

4.3.8 The Implications for FDI Screening Mechanisms

Section 4.3 showed that the EU's flexibility to adopt FDI Screening mechanisms on broader grounds than 'security or public order' within the meaning of the Screening Regulation is limited by International economic law in different ways. This has important implications on how to design the scope of FDI Screening mechanisms.

Relevant sources of International economic law are, first and foremost, agreements that the EU concluded with third countries that contain EU obligations on the establishment of foreign investors, not those obligations usually contained in Member States BITs and EU IPAs on the post-establishment phase of investments. Against this background, it was found that mainly two legal sources significantly limit the EU's flexibility to adopt FDI Screening mechanisms: FTAs and the GATS.

---

[659] See Commission, 'Proposal for a Regulation of the European Parliament and of the Council on foreign subsidies distorting the internal market' COM (2021) 223 final, and discussion in Sect. 2. 3.2.

FTAs prohibit NT discrimination, and thus the screening of investors from FTA partner countries, but not of EU investors. This was shown by the examples of CETA and the EU-Vietnam FTA, as well as the EU-UK Trade and Cooperation Agreement. Though apparently also true for the EU-China CAI, the EU's commitments do, according to the Commission, not exceed its commitments in the WTO. Thus, for the EU's NT commitment vis-à-vis China the assessment of the limits posed by WTO law, namely the GATS, applies. Vis-à-vis FTA partner countries, however, the EU's flexibility to adopt FDI Screening mechanisms that screen investors from these countries on broader grounds than 'security or public order' is significantly limited. In order to avoid a violation of its FTAs, the EU may therefore exclude FTA partners from the FDI Screening mechanisms' personal scope. It was further shown that this would be in compliance with the GATS. Even though a differentiation between investors from FTA and non-FTA partner countries constitutes an MFN violation pursuant to Art II(1) GATS, the MFN discrimination will in most cases be justified by Art V(1) GATS. In particular, EU FTAs will generally meet the requirement of Art V(1) GATS to eliminate substantially all NT discrimination. This was at least shown for more recent FTAs, again based on the examples CETA and EU-Vietnam FTA.

The GATS limits the EU's flexibility to adopt FDI Screening mechanisms vis-à-vis all other WTO members, and thus 136 countries, in two ways.

First, FDI Screening mechanisms constitute *de jure* discrimination against foreign investors, and thus violate the NT obligation in Art XVII GATS. While the EU only committed to NT in a limited—but large—number of sectors, general cross-sector screening mechanisms will nevertheless violate the wide-reaching EU NT commitments. In addition, a cross-sector FDI Screening mechanism could also not be based on a broader ground of exception than 'security or public order' within the meaning of the Screening Regulation. The EU lacks a consistent rationale that could explain the general differentiation between foreign and domestic investors.

Nevertheless, sector-specific FDI Screening mechanisms remain a viable, NT-compliant option. The EU may identify sectors for which it has not undertaken sector-specific NT commitments in Mode three trade. If focusing on services sectors, the identification of potential sectors for FDI screening is relatively easy. The EU already avoids a violation of its NT obligation if it is lacking a specific commitment in only one service sector that the FDI target supplies and that is characteristic to its and/or the investor's business purpose. In accordance with this approach, it could, for example, be demonstrated that the EU preserved wide flexibility to screen FDI in the electricity sector, since the EU has no commitments for electricity transmission and distribution services. If the EU wants to protect other sectors for which it has undertaken commitments, it must consider to withdraw the respective commitments pursuant to Art XXI GATS. This, however, requires compensatory adjustment of other WTO members.

Second, the GATS limits the EU's flexibility to adopt FDI Screening mechanisms that differentiate between investors from different third countries. The MFN obligation in Art II(1) GATS prohibits the EU to focus on investors from home countries with protection of IP rights, private information, and competition that the EU considers inferior to its own level of protection, as well as from countries with an allegedly higher level of government influence on business decisions. Moreover, an appropriate ground of exception on broader grounds than 'security or public order' is lacking. Namely, Art XIV(c) GATS comes with significant shortcomings.

On the one hand, it does not allow differentiation based on the protection of competition and government influence on business decisions. The relevant EU competition laws, for example Arts 106 and 107 TFEU, do not bind foreign investors and third countries. Accordingly, the EU cannot secure compliance of foreign investors with these laws. This must also be kept in mind when assessing the EU's proposal for screening FDI that is facilitated by foreign subsidies.[660] On the other hand, FDI Screening mechanisms will typically not be necessary to secure compliance with IP rights and private information laws. FDI registration requirements, ongoing regulatory surveillance, and strict sanctioning mechanisms may constitute reasonably alternative measures that are better targeted and less trade-restrictive than FDI Screening mechanisms.[661]

Overall, the GATS therefore significantly limits the EU's flexibility to adopt FDI Screening mechanisms on broader grounds than 'security or public order' within the meaning of the Screening Regulation. Only sector-specific FDI Screening mechanisms are a viable, GATS-compliant option. Their sector scope is determined by the EU's sector-specific commitments to NT in Mode three trade. At the same time, the GATS indicates alternative policy means to meet the EU and Member States concerns vis-à-vis foreign investors: more stringent and precise regulatory measures such as FDI registration requirements and ongoing regulatory surveillance.

Last but not least, GATT 1994, TRIMs, and TRIPS Agreement limit the EU's flexibility to impose conditions on the FDI authorization during the screening procedure. GATT 1994 and TRIMs Agreement prohibit certain trade-related content and performance requirements, and the TRIPS Agreement certain restrictions on IP rights transfer.

The final section of this chapter, Sect. 4.4, will combine these conclusions with those reached in the analysis of EU law in Sects. 4.1 and 4.2 to generally assess the EU's flexibility to adopt FDI Screening mechanisms on broader grounds than 'security or public order' within the meaning of the Screening Regulation.

---

[660] ibid.

[661] A definite conclusion depends on the concrete design and operation of the FDI Screening mechanism that cannot be given here.

4.4   Legal Limitations for FDI Screening Mechanisms According to Four Scope Variables

The conclusions in the previous sections now allow a comprehensive answer to the second main question that this book asked at its outset: Do the EU and Member States have the flexibility to adopt broader FDI Screening mechanisms than the current FDI Screening mechanisms based on screening grounds circling around the notions of security and public order? The answer is: in parts.

Section 4.2 had concluded that the current options for FDI Screening mechanisms fail to considerably cover the EU and Member States concerns vis-à-vis foreign investors. Even the broadest available screening ground, 'security or public order' within the meaning of the Screening Regulation, is too narrow. This chapter therefore examined the legal limitations posed by EU primary law and International economic law for the EU or Member States to adopt FDI Screening mechanisms on broader grounds that better meet their concerns vis-à-vis foreign investors.

To begin with, it is only the EU who has the competence to adopt FDI Screening mechanisms on broader grounds. This follows from the Common commercial policy in Art 207(2) TFEU. Indeed, this competence collides with the shared internal market competence of the freedom of capital movement pursuant to Arts 63(1) and 64(2) and (3) TFEU in conjunction with Art 4(2)(a) TFEU because the freedom of capital movement, due to its *erga omnes* protection, also protects FDI from third countries and thus not only 'classic' internal market cases. Nevertheless, the EU's competence for Common commercial policy must override the internal market competence to ensure a concise and unified external commercial policy for regulating the market access of foreign investors. This collision already is a harbinger of the conflicts that may arise from the *erga omnes* protection of the freedom of capital movement.

Turning to such substantial legal limitations, both EU primary law and International economic law provide significant protection to FDI and Foreign investors resulting in major legal limitations for FDI Screening mechanisms on broader grounds than 'security or public order'.

EU primary law, meaning the Fundamental freedoms of establishment and capital movement, narrow the potential legislative options for FDI Screening mechanisms on broader grounds than 'security or public order' essentially to two options.[662] Both available options compromise on the extent to which the EU may meet the EU and Member States concerns vis-à-vis foreign investors. On the one hand, the FDI Screening mechanism may be limited to (i) foreign investors who are Non-EU Companies, Non-EU Established SPVs, foreign States, and/or foreign public undertakings, and (ii) FDI that gives the investor definite influence on the target company. If so, the EU may define the screening ground as it deems appropriate. Low hurdles

---

[662] A third option may be FDI Screening mechanisms based on the unwritten ground of exception of 'overriding reasons in the public interest'. However, this option has other significant shortcomings, and was thus not further discussed in this book. See n. 329.

are only posed by the proportionality test of the Fundamental rights. However, while the personal scope encompasses all relevant foreign investors, substantially a significant portion of FDI is not covered: FDI that gives the investor less than definite influence on the FDI target.

A second policy option meets this shortcoming, but comes with another. The EU may also only limit the FDI Screening mechanism's personal scope to investors who are controlled by a third-country resident. As an indication how to define the notion of 'controlled' one may refer to Directive 2009/73/EC, art 2(36). Substantially, this second option significantly meets the EU and Member States concerns vis-à-vis foreign investors. The option also allows the EU to define the screening ground as it deems appropriate, except for minor Fundamental rights limits. Moreover, the personal scope based on control will cover most of the relevant foreign investors. Finally, the second option, in contrast to the first option, covers FDI generally. From a procedural perspective, however, the EU must overcome high hurdles: The FDI Screening mechanism must be adopted, after consulting the Parliament, by the Council—with unanimity.

Given the diverging stakeholder positions during the Screening Regulation's adoption, such unanimity seems unlikely. The first option thus seems the only feasible policy option for FDI Screening mechanisms on broader grounds than 'security or public order'.

International economic law further limits both options for FDI Screening mechanisms on broader grounds than 'security or public order'.[663]

First, both EU law policy options must be narrowed to sector-specific FDI Screening mechanisms to ensure GATS compliance. General cross-sector mechanisms violate the EU's GATS commitments to NT in Art XVII GATS. The sector coverage depends on a more detailed assessment of the EU's sector commitments to NT for Mode Three trade. The analysis has shown that the identification of such sectors is relatively easy, unless the FDI Screening mechanism is technology-, and not sector-centred. The EU has the flexibility to screen a specific FDI if it lacks a commitment in only one service sector that the FDI target or investor supplies and that is characteristic to its and/or the investor's business purpose. Following this approach, it was shown that the EU may, for instance, adopt an FDI Screening mechanism in the electricity sector.

Second, since FDI Screening mechanisms violate at least modern EU FTAs, their personal scope may be limited to investors from non-FTA partner countries. However, such a limitation in personal scope is only GATS-consistent to the extent the FTA eliminates substantially all NT discrimination. This will usually be the case for modern EU FTAs, but does apparently not apply to the EU-China CAI. Based on the information available at the time of writing, the agreement, if concluded, will not

---

[663] The analysis of International economic law was limited to EU FTAs and WTO agreements. For the reasons discussed in Sect. 4.3.1, Member States BITs, EU IPAs, and the OECD Code of Capital Movements are less relevant, and were thus not further analyzed.

considerably exceed the EU's WTO commitments. Therefore, the agreement seems to fail to pose additional limits to those already provided by the GATS.[664]

Third, the GATS limits the EU's flexibility to adopt FDI Screening mechanisms that, by design or application, differentiate between investors based on a lower level of IP rights, private information, and competition protection in their home countries, as well as based on an allegedly higher level of government influence on business decisions.[665] This significantly limits the EU's flexibility to meet the EU and Member States concern vis-à-vis certain specific countries—most importantly, China.

Fourth, GATT 1994, TRIMs, and TRIPS Agreement limit the EU's flexibility to impose conditions on the FDI authorization during the screening procedure—namely, content and performance requirements related to trade in goods, and certain restrictions on IP rights transfer.

In sum, only the EU, not the Member States, has the flexibility to adopt FDI Screening mechanisms on broader grounds than 'security or public order'—their scope can, however, not fully meet the EU and Member States concerns vis-à-vis foreign investors.

Last but not least, the GATS may help to identify alternative policy means to meet EU and Member States concerns vis-à-vis foreign investors. The analysis of the ground of exception for compliance measures in Art XIV(c) GATS indicated three less trade restrictive alternatives: FDI registration requirements, ongoing regulatory surveillance, and strict sanctioning mechanisms. These policing measures may even better target the concrete EU and Member States concerns vis-à-vis foreign investors. Certainly, the measures will not completely eliminate the EU and Member States concerns. However, FDI Screening mechanisms will neither. In fact, FDI Screening mechanisms are rather imprecise risk assessment procedures pursuant to which a variety of authorities reviews many different aspects of an investment in a short period of time. In comparison, the described policing measures by specialized authorities may at least in some sectors be more targeted and effective to meet the EU and Member States concerns vis-à-vis foreign investors.

References

Abu-Akeel AK (1999) Definition of trade in services under the GATS: legal implications. George Wash J Int Law Econ 32:189–210

Adlung R (2016) International rules governing foreign direct investment in services: investment treaties versus GATS. J World Invest Trade 17:47–85. https://doi.org/10.1163/22119000-01701002

---

[664] This conclusion is based on the negotiated EU-China CAI, published on 22 January 2021, and Commission, 'Agreement in Principle on EU-China CAI' (n. 363), p. 2.

[665] Depending on the concrete design and operation of the FDI Screening mechanism, the GATS may to some extent allow differentiation based on IP rights and private information protection.

Adlung R (2020) WTO/GATS-alien framework provisions in RTAs – a closer look. World Trade Rev 19:493–510. https://doi.org/10.1017/S1474745619000235

Adlung R, Mattoo A (2008) The GATS. In: Mattoo A, Stern RM, Zanini G (eds) A handbook of international trade in services. Oxford University Press, Oxford, pp 48–83

Alschner W (2013) Americanization of the BIT Universe: the influence of Friendship, Commerce and Navigation (FCN) treaties on modern investment treaty law. Goettingen J Int Law 5:455–486

Ashiagbor D (2014) Art 15 – freedom to choose an occupation. In: Peers S, Hervey TK, Kenner J, Ward A (eds) The EU charter of fundamental rights: a commentary. Hart, Oxford

Bachlechner M (1998) Liegenschaftserwerb und Kapitalverkehrsfreiheit. Zeitschrift für europarechtliche Studien 1:519–534

Badura P (1997) Das öffentliche Unternehmen im europäischen Binnenmarkt. ZGR:291–305

Bakker A (1996) The liberalization of capital movements in Europe: The Monetary Committee and Financial Integration 1958 - 1994. Kluwer Academic, Dordrecht

Bast J (2020) Art 5 EUV. In: Grabitz E, Hilf M, Nettesheim M (eds) Das Recht der Europäischen Union: EUV/AEUV, 71st edn. CH Beck, Munich

Bayer W, Ohler C (2008) Staatsfonds ante portas. ZG:12–31

Benyon FS (2010) Direct investment, national champions and EU treaty freedoms: from Maastricht to Lisbon. Hart, Oxford

Bings SL (2014) Neuordnung der Außenhandelskompetenzen der Europäischen Union durch den Reformvertrag von Lissabon. Nomos, Baden-Baden

Bognar Z (1997) Europäische Währungsintegration und Außenwirtschaftsbeziehungen: Eine Analyse des gemeinschafts- und völkerrechtlichen Rahmens der europäischen Außenwährungsbeziehungen. Nomos, Baden-Baden

Böhmer A (1998) The struggle for a multilateral agreement on investment; an assessment of the negotiation process in the OECD. German Yearb Int Law 41:267–298

Bröhmer J (2011) Art 64 AEUV. In: Calliess C, Ruffert M (eds) EUV/AEUV: Das Verfassungsrecht der Europäischen Union mit Europäischer Grundrechtecharta, 4th edn. CH Beck, Munich

Bröhmer J (2016a) Art 63 AEUV. In: Calliess C, Ruffert M (eds) EUV/AEUV: Das Verfassungsrecht der Europäischen Union mit Europäischer Grundrechtecharta, 5th edn. CH Beck, Munich

Bröhmer J (2016b) Art 64 AEUV. In: Calliess C, Ruffert M (eds) EUV/AEUV: Das Verfassungsrecht der Europäischen Union mit Europäischer Grundrechtecharta, 5th edn. CH Beck, Munich

Bungenberg M (2011) The division of competences between the EU and its Member States in the area of investment politics. In: Bungenberg M, Griebel J, Hindelang S (eds) International investment law and EU law. Springer, Berlin, pp 29–42

Bünning M (2014) 'Im Anwendungsbereich der Niederlassungsfreiheit ist keine Berufung auf die Kapitalverkehrsfreiheit möglich': Anmerkung zu Bundesfinanzhof, Urteil vom 6 März 2013, I R 10/11. BB:303

Burgi M (1997) Die öffentlichen Unternehmen im Gefüge des primären Gemeinschaftsrechts. EuR:261–290

Calliess C (2016a) Art 2 AEUV. In: Calliess C, Ruffert M (eds) EUV/AEUV: Das Verfassungsrecht der Europäischen Union mit Europäischer Grundrechtecharta, 5th edn. CH Beck, Munich

Calliess C (2016b) Art 3 AEUV. In: Calliess C, Ruffert M (eds) EUV/AEUV: Das Verfassungsrecht der Europäischen Union mit Europäischer Grundrechtecharta, 5th edn. CH Beck, Munich

Chaisse J (2012) The regulation of trade-distorting restrictions in foreign investment law: an investigation of China's TRIMs compliance. Eur Yearb Int Econ Law:159–187. https://doi.org/10.1007/978-3-642-23309-8_5

Chang P, Karsenty G, Mattoo A, Richtering J (1999) GATS, the modes of supply and statistics on trade in services. J World Trade 33:93–115

Clostermeyer M (2011) Staatliche Übernahmeabwehr und die Kapitalverkehrsfreiheit zu Drittstaaten: Europarechtliche Beurteilung der §§ 7 Abs. 2 Nr. 6 AWG, 53 AWV. Nomos, Baden-Baden

Commission (2003) The European Economy: 2003 Review. European Economy 6. Commission, Brussels

Copeland BJ (2021) Artificial Intelligence. Encyclopedia Britannica. https://www.britannica.com/technology/artificial-intelligence. Accessed 2 Feb 2022

Cossy M (2008) Some thoughts on the concept of 'likeness' in the GATS. In: Panizzon M, Pohl N, Sauvé P (eds) GATS and the regulation of international trade in services: world trade forum. Cambridge University Press, Cambridge, pp 327–357

Cottier T, Molinuevo M (2008) Art V GATS. In: Wolfrum R, Stoll P-T, Feinäugle C (eds) WTO – trade in services. Martinus Njihoff, Leiden

Cottier T, Schneller L (2014) The philosophy of non-discrimination in international trade regulation. In: Kamperman Sanders A (ed) The principle of national treatment in international economic law: trade, investment and intellectual property. Elgar, Cheltenham, pp 3–33

Cottier T, Trinberg L (2015a) Art 206 AEUV. In: von der Groeben H, Schwarze J, Hatje A (eds) Europäisches Unionsrecht: Vertrag über die Europäische Union - Vertrag über die Arbeitsweise der Europäischen Union - Charta der Grundrechte der Europäischen Union, 7th edn. Nomos, Baden-Baden

Cottier T, Trinberg L (2015b) Art 207 AEUV. In: von der Groeben H, Schwarze J, Hatje A (eds) Europäisches Unionsrecht: Vertrag über die Europäische Union - Vertrag über die Arbeitsweise der Europäischen Union - Charta der Grundrechte der Europäischen Union, 7th edn. Nomos, Baden-Baden

Cottier T, Delimatsis P, Diebold NF (2008) Art XIV GATS. In: Wolfrum R, Stoll P-T, Feinäugle C (eds) WTO – trade in services. Martinus Njihoff, Leiden

Cottier T et al (2011) Energy in WTO law and policy. In: Cottier T (ed) The prospects of international trade regulation: from fragmentation to coherence. Cambridge University Press, Cambridge, pp 211–244

Cremer W (2015) Die Grundfreiheiten des Europäischen Unionsrechts. JURA:39–55

Cremona M (2020) Regulating FDI in the EU legal framework. In: Bourgeois JHJ (ed) EU framework for foreign direct investment control. Kluwer Law International, Alphen aan den Rijn, pp 31–55

Crones L (2002) Grundrechtlicher Schutz von juristischen Personen im europäischen Gemeinschaftsrecht. Nomos, Baden-Baden

Croome J (1999) Reshaping the world trading system: a history of the Uruguay Round, 2nd edn. Kluwer Law International, The Hague

De Búrca G (2002) Unpacking the concept of discrimination in EC and international trade law. In: Barnard C, Scott J (eds) The law of the single European market: unpacking the premises. Hart, Oxford, pp 181–195

de Kok J (2019) Towards a European framework for foreign investment reviews. Eur Law Rev 44: 24–48

de La Rochère JD (2013) L'effet direct des accords internationaux. In: ECJ (ed) The Court of Justice and the Construction of Europe: analyses and perspectives on sixty years of case-law: La Cour de Justice et la construction de l'Europe: Analyses et Perspectives de Soixante Ans de Jurisprudence. TMC Asser, The Hague, pp 637–658

De Meester B (2008) Testing European prudential conditions for banking mergers in the light of most favoured nation in the GATS. J Int Econ Law 11:609–647. https://doi.org/10.1093/jiel/jgn020

de Melo ML (2020) Protection of domestic investors under the WTO and international investment regimes. World Trade Rev 19:589–604. https://doi.org/10.1017/S1474745620000142

Delimatsis P, Hoekman B (2018) National tax regulation, voluntary international standards, and the GATS: Argentina–financial services. World Trade Rev 17:265–290. https://doi.org/10.1017/S1474745617000635

Delimatsis P, Molinuevo M (2008) Art XVI GATS. In: Wolfrum R, Stoll P-T, Feinäugle C (eds) WTO – trade in services. Martinus Njihoff, Leiden

Dereje J (2015) Staatsnahe Unternehmen: die Zurechnungsproblematik im Internationalen Investitionsrecht und weiteren Bereichen des Völkerrechts. Nomos, Baden-Baden

Descheemaeker S (2016) Ubiquitous uncertainty: the overlap between trade in services and foreign investment in the GATS and EU RTAs. Leg Issues Econ Integr 43:265–293

Diebold NF (2010) Non-discrimination in international trade in services: 'likeness' in WTO/GATS. Cambridge University Press, Cambridge

Dimopoulos A (2011) EU foreign investment law. Oxford University Press, Oxford

Eeckhout P (2001) Constitutional concepts for free trade in services. In: De Búrca G, Scott J (eds) The EU and the WTO: legal and constitutional issues. Hart, Oxford, pp 211–236

Ego A (2017) Europäische Niederlassungsfreiheit. In: Goette W, Habersack M, Kalss S (eds) Münchener Kommentar zum Aktiengesetz: Band 7, 4th edn. CH Beck, Munich

Ehlers D (2014) § 7 Allgemeine Lehren. In: Ehlers D, Becker U (eds) Europäische Grundrechte und Grundfreiheiten, 4th edn. De Gruyter, Berlin

Ehring L (2002) De Facto discrimination in WTO law: national and most-favored-nation treatment - or equal treatment? J World Trade 36:921–977

Elfring K (2009) Art 3 TRIPS. In: Stoll P-T, Busche J, Arend K (eds) WTO – trade-related aspects of intellectual property rights. Martinus Njihoff, Leiden

Everson M, Gonçalves RC (2014) Art 16 – freedom to conduct a business. In: Peers S, Hervey TK, Kenner J, Ward A (eds) The EU charter of fundamental rights: a commentary. Hart, Oxford

Fassion J, Natens B (2020) The EU proposal for FDI control: the WTO on the sidelines? In: Bourgeois JHJ (ed) EU framework for foreign direct investment control. Kluwer Law International, Alphen aan den Rijn, pp 121–134

Feinäugle C (2008) Art XXVIII GATS. In: Wolfrum R, Stoll P-T, Feinäugle C (eds) WTO – trade in services. Martinus Njihoff, Leiden

Financial Times (2019) What are the main security risks of using Huawei for 5G? https://www.ft.com/content/8b48f460-50af-11e9-9c76-bf4a0ce37d49. Accessed 2 Feb 2022

Forsthoff U (2020a) Art 45 AEUV. In: Grabitz E, Hilf M, Nettesheim M (eds) Das Recht der Europäischen Union: EUV/AEUV, 71st edn. CH Beck, Munich

Forsthoff U (2020b) Art 49 AEUV. In: Grabitz E, Hilf M, Nettesheim M (eds) Das Recht der Europäischen Union: EUV/AEUV, 71st edn. CH Beck, Munich

Forsthoff U (2020c) Art 54 AEUV. In: Grabitz E, Hilf M, Nettesheim M (eds) Das Recht der Europäischen Union: EUV/AEUV, 71st edn. CH Beck, Munich

Frenz W (2012) Handbuch Europarecht: Band 1: Europäische Grundfreiheiten, 2nd edn. Springer, Berlin

Frenz W (2016) Europarecht, 2nd edn. Springer, Berlin

Fritzsche A (2010) Discretion, scope of judicial review and institutional balance in European law. Common Mark Law Rev 47:361–403

Gari G (2016) Is the WTO's approach to international standards on services outdated? J Int Econ Law 19:589–605. https://doi.org/10.1093/jiel/jgw059

Gari G (2020) Recent developments on disciplines on domestic regulations affecting trade in services: convergence or divergence? In: Hoffmann RT, Krajewski M (eds) Coherence and divergence in services trade law. Springer, Cham, pp 59–94

Geiger F (2013) Beschränkungen von Direktinvestitionen aus Drittstaaten. Nomos, Baden-Baden

German Federal Government (2008) Antwort der Bundesregierung auf Kleine Anfrage: Europarechtliche Beurteilung der geplanten Änderung des Außenwirtschaftsgesetzes. Bundesdrucksache, Berlin

Gosch D, Schönfeld J (2015) Kapitalverkehrsfreiheit und Drittstaaten - Ein (vorläufiger) Zwischenstand. IStR:755–759

Gramlich L (2017) Art 63 AEUV. In: Pechstein M, Nowak C, Häde U (eds) Frankfurter Kommentar zu EUV, GRC und AEUV. Mohr Siebeck, Tübingen

Grossman GM, Horn H, Mavroidis PC (2013) National treatment. In: Horn H, Mavroidis PC (eds) Legal and economic principles of world trade law: economics of trade agreements, border instruments, and national treasures. Cambridge University Press, Cambridge, pp 205–346

Guastaferro B (2012) Beyond the exceptionalism of constitutional conflicts: the ordinary functions of the identity clause. Yearb Eur Law 31:263–318. https://doi.org/10.1093/yel/yes022

Günther V (2018) Der Vorschlag der Europäischen Kommission für eine Verordnung zur Schaffung eines Rahmens für die Überprüfung ausländischer Direktinvestitionen in der Europäischen Union: Investitionskontrolle in der Union vor dem Hintergrund kompetenzrechtlicher Fragen. Beiträge zum Transnationalen Wirtschaftsrecht 157:1

Habersack M (2019) §§ 95–116 AktG. In: Goette W, Habersack M, Kalss S (eds) Münchener Kommentar zum Aktiengesetz: Band 2, 5th edn. CH Beck, Munich

Haraldsdóttir K (2020) The nature of neutrality in EU law: Article 345 TFEU. Eur Law Rev 45:3–24

Heide D (2018) Nach 50Hertz – Bundesregierung wehrt sich gegen weitere Übernahme aus China. https://www.handelsblatt.com/politik/deutschland/sicherheitsbedenken-nach-50hertz-bundesregierung-wehrt-sich-gegen-weitere-uebernahme-aus-china/22858764.html?ticket=ST-1488581-LNjdVpvWA51nohcplElP-ap6. Accessed 2 Feb 2022

Heinemann A (2012) Government control of cross-border M&A: legitimate regulation or protectionism? J Int Econ Law 15:843–870. https://doi.org/10.1093/jiel/jgs030

Herrmann C (2010) Die Zukunft der mitgliedstaatlichen Investitionspolitik nach dem Vertrag von Lissabon. EuZW:207–212

Herrmann C (2019) Europarechtliche Fragen der deutschen Investitionskontrolle. Zeitschrift für europarechtliche Studien 22:429–476. https://doi.org/10.5771/1435-439X-2019-3-429

Herrmann C, Streinz R (2014) § 11 Die EU als Mitglied der WTO. In: von Arnauld A (ed) Europäische Außenbeziehungen. Nomos, Baden-Baden

Herz B (2014) Unternehmenstransaktionen zwischen Niederlassungs- und Kapitalverkehrsfreiheit: Grundlegung einer Abgrenzungslehre. Nomos, Baden-Baden

Hindelang S (2009) The free movement of capital and foreign direct investment: the scope of protection in EU law. Oxford University Press, Oxford

Hindelang S (2013) Die steuerliche Behandlung drittstaatlicher Dividenden und die europäischen Grundfreiheiten: Die teilweise (Wieder-)Eröffnung des Schutzbereiches der Kapitalverkehrsfreiheit für Dividenden aus drittstaatlichen Direktinvestitionen – zugleich eine Besprechung des Urteils in der Rechtssache Test Claimants in the FII Group Litigation II. IStR:77–81. https://doi.org/10.1515/9783110525687-001

Hindelang S, Hagemeyer TM (2017) Enemy at the Gates?: Die aktuellen Änderungen der Investitionsprüfvorschriften in der Außenwirtschaftsverordnung im Lichte des Unionsrechts. EuZW:882–890

Hindelang S, Maydell N (2010) Die Gemeinsame Europäische Investitionspolitik – Alter Wein in neuen Schläuchen? In: Bungenberg M, Griebel J, Hindelang S (eds) Internationaler Investitionsschutz und Europarecht. Nomos, Baden-Baden, pp 11–80

Hoekman B (1995) Assessing the general agreement on trade in services. In: Martin W, Winters LA (eds) The Uruguay Round and the developing economies. World Bank, Washington, pp 327–364

Irion K, Williams J (2019) Prospective policy study on artificial intelligence and EU trade policy. https://www.ivir.nl/projects/prospective-policy-study-on-artificial-intelligence-and-eu-trade-policy/. Accessed 2 Feb 2022

Jacobs FG (2011) The internal legal effects of the EU's international agreements and the protection of individual rights. In: Arnull A, Barnard C, Dougan M, Spaventa E (eds) A constitutional order of states?: Essays in EU law in honour of Alan Dashwood. Hart, Oxford, pp 13–33

Jung P (2019) Art 54 AEUV. In: Becker U, Hatje A, Schoo J, Schwarze J (eds) EU-Kommentar, 4th edn. Nomos, Baden-Baden

Kahl W (2013) § 124 Die allgemeine Handlungsfreiheit. In: Bauer H, Merten D, Papier H-J (eds) Handbuch der Grundrechte: Band V: Grundrechte in Deutschland - Einzelgrundrechte II. CF Müller, Heidelberg

Kainer F (2015) § 4 Die binnenmarktliche Niederlassungsfreiheit der Unternehmen. In: Müller-Graff P-C (ed) Europäisches Wirtschaftsordnungsrecht. Nomos, Baden-Baden

Kemmerer M (2010) Kapitalverkehrsfreiheit und Drittstaaten. Nomos, Baden-Baden

Kilapatrick C (2014) Art 21 – non-discrimination. In: Peers S, Hervey TK, Kenner J, Ward A (eds) The EU charter of fundamental rights: a commentary. Hart, Oxford

Kindler P (2012) Der reale Niederlassungsbegriff nach dem VALE-Urteil des EuGH. EuZW:888–892

Kingreen T (2016) Arts 34–36 AEUV. In: Calliess C, Ruffert M (eds) EUV/AEUV: Das Verfassungsrecht der Europäischen Union mit Europäischer Grundrechtecharta, 5th edn. CH Beck, Munich

Klöpfer M (2016) Missbrauch im Europäischen Zivilverfahrensrecht. Mohr Siebeck, Tübingen

Klotz R (2015) Art 106 AEUV. In: von der Groeben H, Schwarze J, Hatje A (eds) Europäisches Unionsrecht: Vertrag über die Europäische Union - Vertrag über die Arbeitsweise der Europäischen Union - Charta der Grundrechte der Europäischen Union, 7th edn. Nomos, Baden-Baden

Kluth W (2016) Art 57 AEUV. In: Calliess C, Ruffert M (eds) EUV/AEUV: Das Verfassungsrecht der Europäischen Union mit Europäischer Grundrechtecharta, 5th edn. CH Beck, Munich

Körber T (2012) Art 3 FKVO. In: Immenga U, Mestmäcker E-J (eds) Wettbewerbsrecht: EU-Wettbewerbsrecht, 5th edn. CH Beck, Munich

Korte S (2016a) Art 49 AEUV. In: Calliess C, Ruffert M (eds) EUV/AEUV: Das Verfassungsrecht der Europäischen Union mit Europäischer Grundrechtecharta, 5th edn. CH Beck, Munich

Korte S (2016b) Art 54 AEUV. In: Calliess C, Ruffert M (eds) EUV/AEUV: Das Verfassungsrecht der Europäischen Union mit Europäischer Grundrechtecharta, 5th edn. CH Beck, Munich

Korte S (2019) Regelungsoptionen zum Schutz vor Fremdabhängigkeiten aufgrund von Investitionen in versorgungsrelevante Unternehmen. WiVerw (GewA):79–141

Kotthaus J (2012) Binnenmarktrecht und externe Kapitalverkehrsfreiheit. Nomos, Baden-Baden

Krajewski M (2003) National regulation and trade liberalization in services: the legal impact of the general agreement on trade in services on national regulatory autonomy. Kluwer Law International, The Hague

Krajewski M (2008) Art VI. In: Wolfrum R, Stoll P-T, Feinäugle C (eds) WTO – trade in services. Martinus Njihoff, Leiden

Krolop K (2008) Staatliche Einlasskontrolle bei Staatsfonds und anderen ausländischen Investoren im Gefüge von Kapitalmarktregulierung, nationalem und internationalem Wirtschaftsrecht: Anmerkungen zum Referentenentwurf eines 13. Gesetzes zur Änderung des Außenwirtschaftsgesetzes. Humboldt Forum Recht:1–19

Kumpan C (2018) VO (EU) Nr 596/2014. In: Hopt KJ, Kumpan C, Merkt H, Roth M (eds) Handelsgesetzbuch: Mit GmbH & Co., Handelsklauseln, Bank- und Börsenrecht, Transportrecht (ohne Seerecht), 38th edn. CH Beck, Munich

Kuner C (2019) The internet and the global reach of EU law. In: Cremona M, Scott J (eds) EU law beyond EU borders: the extraterritorial reach of EU law. Oxford University Press, Oxford, pp 112–145

Lackhoff K (2000) Die Niederlassungsfreiheit des EGV - nur ein Gleichheits- oder auch ein Freiheitsrecht? Duncker & Humblot, Berlin

Lecheler H, Germelmann CF (2010) Zugangsbeschränkungen für Investitionen aus Drittstaaten im deutschen und europäischen Energierecht. Mohr Siebeck, Tübingen

Lenaerts K (2012) Exploring the limits of the EU charter of fundamental rights. Eur Const Law Rev 8:375–403. https://doi.org/10.1017/s1574019612000260

Lenaerts K (2014) Direct applicability and direct effect of international law in the EU legal order. In: Lannon E, Govaere I, van Elsuwege P, Adam S (eds) The European Union in the world: essays in honour of Professor Marc Maresceau. Martinus Njihoff, Leiden, pp 45–64

Lübke J (2006) Der Erwerb von Gesellschaftsanteilen zwischen Kapitalverkehrs- und Niederlassungsfreiheit. Nomos, Baden-Baden

Lübke J (2015) § 5 Die binnenmarktliche Kapital- und Zahlungsverkehrsfreiheit. In: Müller-Graff P-C (ed) Europäisches Wirtschaftsordnungsrecht. Nomos, Baden-Baden

Malbon J, Lawson C, Davison MJ (2014) The WTO agreement on trade-related aspects of intellectual property rights: a commentary. Elgar, Cheltenham

Manthey NV (2001) Bindung und Schutz öffentlicher Unternehmen durch die Grundfreiheiten des europäischen Gemeinschaftsrechts. Lang, Frankfurt am Main

Maresceau M (2013) The Court of Justice and Bilateral Agreements. In: ECJ (ed) The Court of Justice and the Construction of Europe: analyses and perspectives on sixty years of case-law: La Cour de Justice et la construction de l'Europe: Analyses et Perspectives de Soixante Ans de Jurisprudence. TMC Asser, The Hague, pp 693–717

Martini M (2008) Zu Gast bei Freunden?: Staatsfonds als Herausforderung an das europäische und internationale Recht. DÖV:314–322

Mattoo A (1997) National treatment in the GATS: corner-stone or Pandora's box? J World Trade 31:107–135

Mavroidis PC (2007) Highway XVI re-visited: the road from non-discrimination to market access in GATS. World Trade Rev 6:1–23. https://doi.org/10.1017/S1474745606003077

Mavroidis PC (2016) The regulation of international trade. MIT Press, Cambridge

Mavroidis PC, Wolfe R (2017) Private standards and the WTO: reclusive no more. World Trade Rev 16:1–24. https://doi.org/10.1017/S1474745616000379

Mestmäcker E-J, Schweitzer H (2012) Art 106 Abs 1 AEUV. In: Immenga U, Mestmäcker E-J (eds) Wettbewerbsrecht: EU-Wettbewerbsrecht, 5th edn. CH Beck, Munich

Mishra N (2020) Privacy, cybersecurity, and GATS Article XIV: a new frontier for trade and internet regulation? World Trade Rev 19:341–364. https://doi.org/10.1017/S1474745619000120

Moberg A, Hindelang S (2020) The art of casting political dissent in law: the EU's framework for the screening of foreign direct investment. Common Mark Law Rev 57:1427–1460

Mortelmans K (2002) The relationship between the treaty rules and community measures for the establishment and functioning of the internal market – towards a concordance rule. Common Mark Law Rev 39:1303–1346

Mülbert P (2001) Konzeption des europäischen Kapitalmarktrechts für Wertpapierdienstleistungen. WM:2085–2102

Muller G (2017) Troubled relationships under the GATS: tensions between market access (Article XVI), national treatment (Article XVII), and domestic regulation (Article VI). World Trade Rev 16:449–474. https://doi.org/10.1017/S1474745616000471

Müller-Graff P-C (2003) Einflußregulierung in Gesellschaften zwischen Binnenmarktrecht und Eigentumsordnung. In: Habersack M, Hommelhoff P, Hüffer U, Schmidt K (eds) Festschrift für Peter Ulmer zum 70. Geburtstag am 2. Januar 2003. De Gruyter, Berlin, pp 929–954

Müller-Graff P-C (2018a) Art 49 AEUV. In: Streinz R (ed) EUV/AEUV: Vertrag über die Europäische Union und Vertrag über die Arbeitsweise der Europäischen Union, 3rd edn. CH Beck, Munich

Müller-Graff P-C (2018b) Art 54 AEUV. In: Streinz R (ed) EUV/AEUV: Vertrag über die Europäische Union und Vertrag über die Arbeitsweise der Europäischen Union, 3rd edn. CH Beck, Munich

Müller-Ibold T (2010) Foreign investment in Germany: restrictions based on public security concerns and their compatibility with EU law. Eur Yearb Int Econ Law:103–122. https://doi.org/10.1007/978-3-540-78883-6_5

Nettesheim M (2008) Unternehmensübernahmen durch Staatsfonds: Europarechtliche Vorgaben und Schranken. ZHR 172:729–767

Nettesheim M (2009) Kompetenzen. In: von Bogdandy A, Bast J (eds) Europäisches Verfassungsrecht: Theoretische und dogmatische Grundzüge, 2nd edn. Springer, Dordrecht, pp 389–439

Nettesheim M (2020) Art 2 AEUV. In: Grabitz E, Hilf M, Nettesheim M (eds) Das Recht der Europäischen Union: EUV/AEUV, 71st edn. CH Beck, Munich

Ni V (2021) EU parliament 'freezes' China trade deal over sanction. The Guardian. https://www.theguardian.com/world/2021/may/20/eu-parliament-freezes-china-trade-deal-over-sanctions. Accessed 2 Feb 2022

O'Keeffe D, Bavasso A (2000) Four freedoms, one market and national competence: in search of a dividing line. In: O'Keeffe D (ed) Judicial review in European Union law: Libor Amicorum in honour of Lord Slynn of Hadley. Libor Amicorum Lord Slynn. Kluwer Law International, The Hague, pp 541–556

Obwexer W (2015a) Art 4 AEUV. In: von der Groeben H, Schwarze J, Hatje A (eds) Europäisches Unionsrecht: Vertrag über die Europäische Union - Vertrag über die Arbeitsweise der Europäischen Union - Charta der Grundrechte der Europäischen Union, 7th edn. Nomos, Baden-Baden

Obwexer W (2015b) Art 4 EUV. In: von der Groeben H, Schwarze J, Hatje A (eds) Europäisches Unionsrecht: Vertrag über die Europäische Union - Vertrag über die Arbeitsweise der Europäischen Union - Charta der Grundrechte der Europäischen Union, 7th edn. Nomos, Baden-Baden

Ohler C (1997) Die Kapitalverkehrsfreiheit und ihre Schranken. WM:1801

Ohler C (2002) Europäische Kapital- und Zahlungsverkehrsfreiheit: Kommentar zu den Artikeln 56 bis 60 EGV, der Geldwäscherichtlinie und Überweisungsrichtlinie. Springer, Berlin

Ohler C (2006) Zulässige Versagung der Erlaubnis zur gewerbsmäßigen Kreditvergabe: Anmerkung zu EuGH, Urteil vom 3 Oktober 2006, Rs C-452/04 (Fidium Finanz). EuZW:691–693

Ortino F (2004) Basic legal instruments for the liberalisation of trade: a comparative analysis of EC and WTO law. Hart, Oxford

Ortino F (2008) The principle of non-discrimination and its exceptions in GATS: selected legal issues. In: Kern A, Andenæs MT (eds) The world trade organization and trade in services. Martinus Njihoff, Leiden, pp 173–204

Pache E (2015) § 10 Grundfreiheiten. In: Schulze R, Zuleeg M, Kadelbach S, Beljin S (eds) Europarecht: Handbuch für die deutsche Rechtspraxis, 3rd edn. Nomos, Baden-Baden

Patzner A, Nagler J (2014) Regelung eines Mitgliedstaats zur Beseitigung der Doppelbesteuerung von Gewinnausschüttungen - Kronos International Inc./FA Leverkusen: Anmerkung zu EuGH, Urt. v. 11.9.2014, C-47/12, Kronos International Inc./FA Leverkusen. IStR:731–733

Pauletto C (2008) Comment: digital trade: technology versus legislators. In: Panizzon M, Pohl N, Sauvé P (eds) GATS and the regulation of international trade in services: world trade forum. Cambridge University Press, Cambridge, pp 530–533

Pauwelyn J (2005) Rien ne Va Plus? Distinguishing domestic regulation from market access in GATT and GATS. World Trade Rev 4:131–170. https://doi.org/10.1017/S1474745605002351

Pauwelyn J (2008) Comment: the unbearable lightness of likeness. In: Panizzon M, Pohl N, Sauvé P (eds) GATS and the regulation of international trade in services : world trade forum. Cambridge University Press, Cambridge, pp 358–369

Pauwelyn J (2014) Rule-based trade 2.0? The rise of informal rules and international standards and how they may outcompete WTO treaties. J Int Econ Law 17:739–751. https://doi.org/10.1093/jiel/jgu042

Peers S, Prechal S (2014) Article 52 – scope and interpretation of rights and principles. In: Peers S, Hervey TK, Kenner J, Ward A (eds) The EU charter of fundamental rights: a commentary. Hart, Oxford, pp 1498–1565

Proelss A (2018a) Art 34 VCLT. In: Dörr O, Schmalenbach K (eds) Vienna Convention on the Law of Treaties: a commentary, 2nd edn. Springer, Berlin

Proelss A (2018b) Art 36 VCLT. In: Dörr O, Schmalenbach K (eds) Vienna Convention on the Law of Treaties: a commentary, 2nd edn. Springer, Berlin

Puig RV (2013) The scope of the new exclusive competence of the European Union with regard to 'foreign direct investment'. Leg Issues Econ Integr 40:133–162

Randelzhofer A, Forsthoff U (2020) Art 56, Art 57 AEUV. In: Grabitz E, Hilf M, Nettesheim M
    (eds) Das Recht der Europäischen Union: EUV/AEUV, 71st edn. CH Beck, Munich
Rauber J (2019) Zur Grundrechtsberechtigung fremdstaatlich beherrschter juristischer Personen:
    Art. 19 Abs. 3 GG unter dem Einfluss von EMRK, EU-GRCh und allgemeinem Völkerrecht.
    Mohr Siebeck, Tübingen
Regan DH (2006) Regulatory purpose and 'like products' in Article III:4 of the GATT (with
    additional remarks on Article III:2). In: Bermann GA (ed) Trade and human health and safety.
    Cambridge University Press, Cambridge, pp 190–223
Ress G, Ukrow J (2020a) Art 63 AEUV. In: Grabitz E, Hilf M, Nettesheim M (eds) Das Recht der
    Europäischen Union: EUV/AEUV, 71st edn. CH Beck, Munich
Ress G, Ukrow J (2020b) Art 64 AEUV. In: Grabitz E, Hilf M, Nettesheim M (eds) Das Recht der
    Europäischen Union: EUV/AEUV, 71st edn. CH Beck, Munich
Ringe W-G (2011) Sparking regulatory competition in European company law: the impact of the
    Centros line of case law and its concept of 'abuse of law'. In: de La Feria R, Vogenauer S (eds)
    Prohibition of abuse of law: a new general principle of EU law? Hart, Oxford, pp 107–126
Rosas A (2008) The European Court of Justice and public international law. In: Wouters J,
    Nollkaemper A, de Wet E (eds) The Europeanisation of international law: the status of
    international law in the EU and its Member States. TMC Asser, The Hague, pp 71–85
Roth W-H (2009) Investitionsbeschränkungen im deutschen Außenwirtschaftsrecht: Europa- und
    völkerrechtliche Probleme. ZBB 21:257–336
Roth GH (2012) Das Ende der Briefkastengründung? - Vale contra Centros. ZIP:1744–1745
Rüthers B, Fischer C, Birk A (2018) Rechtstheorie: Mit juristischer Methodenlehre, 10th edn. CH
    Beck, Munich
Ruthig J, Storr S (2015) Öffentliches Wirtschaftsrecht. CF Müller, Heidelberg
Sauvé P (2006) Multilateral rules on investment: is forward movement possible? J Int Econ Law 9:
    325–355. https://doi.org/10.1093/jiel/jgl011
Saydé A (2014) Defining the concept of abuse of union law. Yearb Eur Law 33:138–162. https://
    doi.org/10.1093/yel/yeu021
Scharf D (2008) Die Kapitalverkehrsfreiheit gegenüber Drittstaaten. Beiträge zum Transnationalen
    Wirtschaftsrecht 76:1
Schill SW (2010) Der Schutz von Auslandsinvestitionen in Deutschland im Mehrebenensystem:
    deutsches, europäisches und internationales Recht. AöR 135:498–540
Schill SW (2019) The European Union's foreign direct investment screening paradox: tightening
    inward investment control to further external investment liberalization. Leg Issues Econ Integr
    46:105–128
Schmalenbach K (2018) Art 26 VCLT. In: Dörr O, Schmalenbach K (eds) Vienna Convention on
    the Law of Treaties: a commentary, 2nd edn. Springer, Berlin
Schmitt R (2013) Die Kompetenzen der Europäischen Union für ausländische Investitionen in und
    aus Drittstaaten. Utz, Munich
Schön W (1997) Europäische Kapitalverkehrsfreiheit und nationales Steuerrecht. In: Schön W
    (ed) Gedächtnisschrift für Brigitte Knobbe-Keuk. Dr Otto Schmidt, Cologne, pp 743–777
Schön W (2000) Das Bild des Gesellschafters im Europäischen Gesellschaftsrecht. RabelsZ 64:1–
    37
Schön W (2015) Kapitalverkehrsfreiheit und Niederlassungsfreiheit. In: Ackermann T, Köndgen J
    (eds) Privat- und Wirtschaftsrecht in Europa: Festschrift für Wulf-Henning Roth zum 70.
    Geburtstag. CH Beck, Munich, pp 551–581
Schön W (2016) Free movement of capital and freedom of establishment. Eur Bus Organ Law Rev
    17:229–260. https://doi.org/10.1007/s40804-016-0051-1
Schraufl M (2007) Die Auswirkungen der Konkurrenz zwischen Niederlassung- und
    Kapitalverkehrsfreiheit auf Drittstaatensachverhalte im Steuerrecht. RIW:603
Schröder M (2018) Art 26 AEUV. In: Streinz R (ed) EUV/AEUV: Vertrag über die Europäische
    Union und Vertrag über die Arbeitsweise der Europäischen Union, 3rd edn. CH Beck, Munich

Schröter H, Zurkinden P, Lauterburg BC (2015) Vorb zu Artt 101 bis 105. In: von der Groeben H, Schwarze J, Hatje A (eds) Europäisches Unionsrecht: Vertrag über die Europäische Union - Vertrag über die Arbeitsweise der Europäischen Union - Charta der Grundrechte der Europäischen Union, 7th edn. Nomos, Baden-Baden

Schuelken T, Sichla B (2019) Außenwirtschaftsrechtlicher Schutz vor drittstaatlichen Investitionen in Kritische Infrastrukturen: Notwendiger Schutz berechtigter Interessen oder Verstoß gegen das Europarecht? NVwZ:1406–1410

Schweitzer H (2011) Sovereign wealth funds: market investors or 'imperialist capitalists'? The European response to direct investment by non-EU state-controlled entities. Eur Yearb Int Econ Law:79–120. https://doi.org/10.1007/978-3-642-14432-5_4

Sedlaczek M, Züger M (2018) Art 64 AEUV. In: Streinz R (ed) EUV/AEUV: Vertrag über die Europäische Union und Vertrag über die Arbeitsweise der Europäischen Union, 3rd edn. CH Beck, Munich

Smit D (2012) EU freedoms, non-EU countries and company taxation. Kluwer Law International, Alphen aan den Rijn

Sørensen KE (2011) Reconciling secondary legislation and the treaty rights of free movement. Eur Law Rev 36:339–361

Spies K (2015) Die Kapitalverkehrsfreiheit in Konkurrenz zu den anderen Grundfreiheiten. LexisNexis, Wien

Spindler G (2019) §§ 76–94. In: Goette W, Habersack M, Kalss S (eds) Münchener Kommentar zum Aktiengesetz: Band 2, 5th edn. CH Beck, Munich

Storr S (2001) Der Staat als Unternehmer: Öffentliche Unternehmen in der Freiheits- und Gleichheitsdogmatik des nationalen Rechts und des Gemeinschaftsrechts. Mohr Siebeck, Tübingen

Streinz R (2018) Art 5 EUV. In: Streinz R (ed) EUV/AEUV: Vertrag über die Europäische Union und Vertrag über die Arbeitsweise der Europäischen Union, 3rd edn. CH Beck, Munich

Strik P (2014) Shaping the single European market in the field of foreign direct investment. Hart, Oxford

Syrpis P (2015) The relationship between primary and secondary law in the EU. Common Mark Law Rev 52:461–487

Terhechte JP (2020) Art 3 EUV. In: Grabitz E, Hilf M, Nettesheim M (eds) Das Recht der Europäischen Union: EUV/AEUV, 71st edn. CH Beck, Munich

Thym D (2009) Auswärtige Gewalt. In: Bogdandy A von, Bast J (eds) Europäisches Verfassungsrecht: Theoretische und dogmatische Grundzüge, 2nd edn. Springer, Dordrecht, pp 441–488

Tiedje J (2015a) Art 49 AEUV. In: von der Groeben H, Schwarze J, Hatje A (eds) Europäisches Unionsrecht: Vertrag über die Europäische Union - Vertrag über die Arbeitsweise der Europäischen Union - Charta der Grundrechte der Europäischen Union, 7th edn. Nomos, Baden-Baden

Tiedje J (2015b) Art 54 AEUV. In: von der Groeben H, Schwarze J, Hatje A (eds) Europäisches Unionsrecht: Vertrag über die Europäische Union - Vertrag über die Arbeitsweise der Europäischen Union - Charta der Grundrechte der Europäischen Union, 7th edn. Nomos, Baden-Baden

Tiedje J (2015c) Vorb Artt 49–55. In: von der Groeben H, Schwarze J, Hatje A (eds) Europäisches Unionsrecht: Vertrag über die Europäische Union - Vertrag über die Arbeitsweise der Europäischen Union - Charta der Grundrechte der Europäischen Union, 7th edn. Nomos, Baden-Baden

Tiedje J, Troberg P (2003) Art 43 EG. In: von der Groeben H (ed) Kommentar zum Vertrag über die Europäische Union und zur Gründung der Europäischen Gemeinschaft: Band 1, 6th edn. Nomos, Baden-Baden

Tietje C (2007) Beschränkungen ausländischer Unternehmensbeteiligungen zum Schutz vor 'Staatsfonds' – Rechtliche Grenzen eines neuen Investitionsprotektionismus. Policy Pap Transnatl Econ Law 26:1

Tietje C (2009) Die Außenwirtschaftsverfassung der EU nach dem Vertrag von Lissabon. Beiträge zum Transnationalen Wirtschaftsrecht 83:1

Tietje C (2014) § 10 Niederlassungsfreiheit. In: Ehlers D, Becker U (eds) Europäische Grundrechte und Grundfreiheiten, 4th edn. De Gruyter, Berlin

Titi C (2018) The evolution of substantive investment protections in recent trade and investment treaties. https://ictsd.iisd.org/themes/global-economic-governance/research/the-evolution-of-substantive-investment-protections-in. Accessed 2 Feb 2022

Torremans P (2014) Art 17 – right to property. In: Peers S, Hervey TK, Kenner J, Ward A (eds) The EU charter of fundamental rights: a commentary. Hart, Oxford

Tountopoulos V (2013) Niederlassungsfreiheit: Genehmigungserfordernis für Beteiligung an Niederlassungsfreiheit: Genehmigungserfordernis für Beteiligung an 'strategischen Aktiengesellschaften' – Nachträgliche Kontrolle der Beschlussfassung: Anmerkung zu EuGH, Urt v. 8. 11. 2012 – C-244/11 (Kommission/Griechenland). EuZW:32–34

Trebilcock MJ, Howse R, Eliason A (2013) The regulation of international trade, 4th edn. Routledge, London

Tridimas T (2011) Abuse of rights in EU law: some reflections with particular reference to financial law. In: de La Feria R, Vogenauer S (eds) Prohibition of abuse of law: a new general principle of EU law? Hart, Oxford, pp 169–192

Unger S (2015) Anmerkung zu EuGH, Urt. v. 11.9.2014, C-47/12 (Kronos International Inc./ Finanzamt Leverkusen). EuZW:67–68

Voland T (2009) Freitag, der Dreizehnte – Die Neuregelungen des Außenwirtschaftsrechts zur verschärften Kontrolle ausländischer Investitionen. EuZW:519–523

von Bogdandy A, Windsor J (2008) Understanding of commitments on financial services. In: Wolfrum R, Stoll P-T, Feinäugle C (eds) WTO – trade in services. Martinus Njihoff, Leiden

von Wilmowsky P (2014) § 12 Freiheit des Kapital- und Zahlungsverkehrs. In: Ehlers D, Becker U (eds) Europäische Grundrechte und Grundfreiheiten, 4th edn. De Gruyter, Berlin, pp 470–503

Wegener B (2016) Art 19 EUV. In: Calliess C, Ruffert M (eds) EUV/AEUV: Das Verfassungsrecht der Europäischen Union mit Europäischer Grundrechtecharta, 5th edn. CH Beck, Munich

Weiß W (2020) Art 207 AEUV. In: Grabitz E, Hilf M, Nettesheim M (eds) Das Recht der Europäischen Union: EUV/AEUV, 71st edn. CH Beck, Munich

Weller M-P (2008) Ausländische Staatsfonds zwischen Fusionskontrolle, Außenwirtschaftsrecht und Grundfreiheiten ZIP:857–865

Wojcik K-P (2015a) Art 63 AEUV. In: von der Groeben H, Schwarze J, Hatje A (eds) Europäisches Unionsrecht: Vertrag über die Europäische Union - Vertrag über die Arbeitsweise der Europäischen Union - Charta der Grundrechte der Europäischen Union, 7th edn. Nomos, Baden-Baden

Wojcik K-P (2015b) Art 64 AEUV. In: von der Groeben H, Schwarze J, Hatje A (eds) Europäisches Unionsrecht: Vertrag über die Europäische Union - Vertrag über die Arbeitsweise der Europäischen Union - Charta der Grundrechte der Europäischen Union, 7th edn. Nomos, Baden-Baden

Wolf S (2008) The regulation of foreign direct investment under selected WTO agreements: is there still a case for a multilateral agreement on investment? In: Tietje C (ed) International investment protection and arbitration: theoretical and practical perspectives. Berliner Wissenschafts-Verlag, Berlin, pp 71–105

Wolff J (2009) Ausländische Staatsfonds und staatliche Sonderrechte: Zum Phänomen 'Sovereign Wealth Funds' und zur Vereinbarkeit der Beschränkung von Unternehmensbeteiligungen mit Europarecht. Berliner Wissenschafts-Verlag, Berlin

Wolfrum R (2008) Art II. In: Wolfrum R, Stoll P-T, Feinäugle C (eds) WTO – trade in services. Martinus Njihoff, Leiden

Yanovich A (2011) WTO rules and the energy sector. In: Selivanova Y (ed) Regulation of energy in international trade law: WTO, NAFTA, and Energy Charter. Kluwer Law International, Alphen aan den Rijn, pp 1–47

Zazoff J (2011) Der Unionsgesetzgeber als Adressat der Grundfreiheiten. Nomos, Baden-Baden

Zdouc W (2004) WTO dispute settlement practice relating to the general agreement on trade in services. In: Ortino F, Petersmann E-U (eds) The WTO Dispute Settlement System 1995-2003. Kluwer Law International, The Hague, pp 382–420

Zwartkruis W, de Jong B (2020) The EU regulation on screening of foreign direct investment: a game changer? Eur Bus Law Rev 31:447–474

Chapter 5
Conclusion

FDI screening in the EU as a policy means to meet the EU and Member States concerns vis-à-vis foreign investors has significant shortcomings—whether *de lege lata* or *de lege ferenda*. Existing options for FDI Screening mechanisms, even those based on the recently adopted Screening Regulation, circle around rather narrow screening grounds of security and public order, at least when assessed in light of the concrete FDI scenarios of concern. Potential future options, on the other hand, face major legal limitations by EU primary law and International economic law. These conclusions reflect, as will be further outlined below, not only the EU-internal dissent with regards to the role of FDI screening in the EU generally and the Screening Regulation's scope more specifically. They also reveal a highly comprehensive and complex web of uni-, bi-, pluri-, and multilateral obligations of EU and Member States to grant FDI and foreign investors access to the internal market. As a result, for those actors in the EU and Member States who want to effectively meet their concerns vis-à-vis foreign investors, FDI Screening mechanisms do not provide the panacea some might have longed for. Rather, they must be complemented by other policy tools.

At its outset, this book analyzed the political rationale of FDI screening in the EU. It has been shown that this rationale is manifold and differs widely among the relevant actors, including the decision whether to screen FDI at all. Nevertheless, the discussions around the Screening Regulation allowed to identify four main concerns the EU and Member States generally have vis-à-vis foreign investors. They derive from a variety of major current policy challenges, such as a shift in international relations towards a multipolar geoeconomic world order, a crisis in multilateralism, and the Covid-19 pandemic. The first concern is that foreign investors may distort competition in the internal market, inter alia through state aid received from their home country governments. As a second concern, EU and Member States are increasingly reluctant to liberalize markets vis-à-vis foreign investors from home countries that do not reciprocate this treatment to EU investors. The third and probably most complex and controversial concern is about investors who pursue

© The Author(s), under exclusive license to Springer Nature Switzerland AG 2022
J. Velten, *Screening Foreign Direct Investment in the EU*, EYIEL Monographs - Studies in European and International Economic Law 26,
https://doi.org/10.1007/978-3-031-05603-1_5

interests that, if realized, harm important EU and Member States interests regarding defence, critical, or strategic assets. Last but not least, EU and Member States are concerned that foreign investors may undermine the protection of private information, in particular personal data of EU citizens.

To meet these concerns, the EU and Member States have identified FDI screening as a key policy means, which is why the EU adopted the Screening Regulation in 2019. The regulation inter alia creates a new, harmonized screening ground 'security or public order'. Yet, the decision of whether or not to adopt an FDI Screening mechanism remains the responsibility of the Member States—at the moment of writing nine Member States still have no FDI Screening mechanisms in place.[1] In addition, the Member States have two more legislative options: FDI Screening mechanisms on the grounds of 'public policy or public security' within the meaning of Art 65(1)(b) TFEU, and mechanisms on the grounds of 'essential security interests' pursuant to Art 346(1)(b) TFEU. As a result, the FDI screening landscape in the EU remains fragmented, while current legislative options for FDI Screening mechanisms are circling around screening grounds of security and public order, with the Screening Regulation's notion 'security or public order' as broadest available screening ground.

However, none of these screening grounds may significantly meet the EU and Member States concerns vis-à-vis foreign investors. This is even valid for the new screening ground, 'security or public order', which is to be interpreted in accordance with the grounds of exception 'essential security interests' and 'public order' in Arts XIV*bis* and XIV(a) GATS. Only in a few, high profile FDI cases may Member States meet the competition, harmful investor, and private information concerns. For instance, meeting the harmful investor concern is a realistic option for FDI targets in the narrow defence sector, but screening FDI in the dual-use sector is already subject to high hurdles. Another group of possible FDI screening targets holds monopolies or large parts of market shares in sensitive sectors. Still, Member States must establish a real possibility that the envisaged threat scenario will in fact materialize.

As a result, all current legislative options for FDI Screening mechanisms in the EU fail to considerably meet the EU and Member States concerns vis-à-vis foreign investors. The available screening grounds are too narrow.

In addition, the EU's flexibility to adopt FDI Screening mechanisms on broader grounds is also significantly limited. From an EU law perspective, the EU has only two legislative options, both with substantial shortcomings. The Member States, on the other hand, are not competent to adopt FDI Screening mechanisms on broader grounds than 'security or public order'.

As a first option, the EU may adopt FDI Screening mechanisms with an in two ways limited scope. Personally, the mechanism would need to apply only to foreign investors who fall *outside* the scope of the freedom of establishment. Substantially,

---

[1]Commission, 'First Annual Report on the screening of foreign direct investments into the Union' (Report) COM (2021) 714 final, p. 6.

the mechanism must only include FDI that falls *within* the scope of the freedom of establishment. To a so designed FDI Screening mechanism neither the freedom of establishment, nor the freedom of capital movement applies. The Fundamental freedoms would thus set no limits to the EU's flexibility to adopt a broader screening ground than 'security or public order'. Nonetheless, while this first option would cover all relevant groups of foreign investors, its substantial scope excludes significant parts of FDI. The threshold of investor influence required for an M&A to qualify as an establishment is significantly higher than the influence required to qualify as FDI.[2]

A second option meets this shortcoming, but comes with another. If the FDI Screening mechanism is only personally limited to investors who are controlled by a third-country resident, a broad ground of exception to the freedoms of capital movement and establishment applies: Art 64(2) and (3) TFEU, in conjunction with Art 49(1) TFEU. As the ground of exception provides no further substantial condition, the EU may adopt a broader screening ground than 'security or public order'. However, such an FDI Screening mechanism on broader grounds would, compared to the Screening Regulation, constitute a step backwards in the liberalization of capital movement within the meaning of Art 64(3) TFEU. This second option for an FDI Screening mechanism must therefore be adopted unanimously by the Council.

Given highly diverging positions on FDI screening in the EU, this seems to pose an insurmountable burden. Thus, the first option might be the only feasible legislative option for an EU FDI Screening mechanism on broader grounds than 'security or public order'.

International economic law—especially the GATS and FTAs—further limits the EU's flexibility to adopt FDI Screening mechanisms on broader grounds than 'security or public order'. Mainly three findings add limitations to the two options for FDI Screening mechanisms outlined above.[3]

First, to ensure GATS compliance, both EU law options must be narrowed to sector-specific FDI Screening mechanisms. General cross-sector FDI Screening mechanisms violate the EU's GATS commitments to NT (Art XVII GATS). Nevertheless, despite wide EU commitments, the EU may have more flexibility than one might expect. The test for specific commitments in case of FDI that this book submits showed that the EU may, for example, widely screen FDI in the electricity sector. Subject to a more comprehensive analysis of all relevant EU sector commitments, the FDI Screening mechanisms may thus at least cover a significant number of sectors that are at the centre of the concerns vis-à-vis foreign investors.

Second, FDI Screening mechanisms may exclude investors of FTA partner countries from their personal scope to avoid FTA violations. This applies at least to modern FTA partner countries—namely, to the parties of the FTAs

---

[2]The threshold of definite influence may be approximated by a rebuttable presumption in case the investor acquires 25% or more of the shares in the FDI target.

[3]The conclusions were not in detail analyzed under the less relevant Member States BITs, EU IPAs, and the OECD Code of Capital Movements.

examined here: Vietnam and Canada as well as the United Kingdom based on the EU-UK Trade and Cooperation Agreement. Such a limitation in personal scope would usually also be GATS-consistent, since modern EU FTAs typically eliminate substantially all NT discrimination within the meaning of Arts V(1) and XVII GATS. The future EU-China CAI, on the other hand, does not seem to require a limitation in the personal scope of FDI Screening mechanisms, since the EU's commitments appear not to considerably exceed the commitments already undertaken in WTO law, namely those under Art XVII GATS.[4]

Third, the MFN obligation of the GATS limits the EU's flexibility to differentiate between third countries, whether by design or application of the FDI Screening mechanism (Art II(1) GATS). FDI Screening mechanisms may, for instance, not differentiate based on lower levels of IP rights, private information, and competition protection in the investor's home countries. Differentiation in accordance with an allegedly higher level of government influence on business decisions is also prohibited.[5] This significantly limits the EU's flexibility to specifically address investors from third countries that are at the centre of concern—most importantly, China. It also underlines that the recent Commission proposal to screen FDI facilitated by foreign subsidies must undergo careful scrutiny to comply with WTO law.[6]

Consequently, both the current legislative options for FDI Screening mechanisms circling around the notions of security and public order as well as potential future FDI Screening mechanisms on broader grounds are subject to major legal limitations.

In light of these conclusions, one may finally be inclined to ask: Can this be? Have the EU and Member States really agreed to what appear to be major burdens to effectively screen FDI when adopting the Screening Regulation and entering into the different uni-, bi-, pluri-, and multilateral obligations in EU primary law and International economic law? The answer is: yes. While this answer relies on complex considerations that have been part of the analysis throughout this book, especially by interpreting the object and purpose of the relevant provisions, there are broad lines of argument that explain that these conclusions are not as unjustified and surprising as they may seem.

The Screening Regulation's shortcomings, namely its screening ground's rather narrow scope, are, at least to some extent, the result of diverging positions among EU and Member States. Its limited scope constitutes a compromise between the

---

[4]This conclusion is based on the negotiated EU-China CAI, published on 22 January 2021, and Commission, 'EU-China Comprehensive Agreement on Investment: The Agreement in Principle' (30 December 2020) <https://trade.ec.europa.eu/doclib/cfm/doclib_section.cfm?sec=120> accessed 2 February 2022, p. 2. If indeed the EU-China CAI did exceed the EU's GATS obligations, exempting China from the FDI Screening mechanism could not be justified by Art V(1) GATS. It only covers Mode three trade, and thus not all services supply modes pursuant to Art I(2) GATS.

[5]Depending on the concrete design and operation of the FDI Screening mechanism, the GATS may to some extent allow differentiation based on IP rights and private information protection.

[6]Commission, 'Proposal for a Regulation of the European Parliament and of the Council on foreign subsidies distorting the internal market' COM (2021) 223 final.

relevant stakeholders. As discussed, the political rationale of the Screening Regulation was not as clear cut as the identified EU and Member States concerns vis-à-vis foreign investors may let assume. While some emphasized the need for FDI, in particular for economic reasons, others stressed the concerns vis-à-vis foreign investors. As a result, the Screening Regulation adopted a deferential approach. On the one hand, the decision of whether to adopt an FDI Screening mechanism remains in the hands of the Member States. On the other hand, the screening ground 'security or public order' was defined by referencing the respective GATS notions ensuring a limited scope based on an agreement to which the EU and all Member States are parties and therefore all actors could agree on. In other words, the Screening Regulation's limited scope may also be interpreted as a deliberate political compromise. The EU could have gone further, provided a political consent had been reached.

With regards to EU primary law, it has been shown that it does in fact allow the EU to considerably regulate third-country capital movement. Though inherently oriented towards an open investment environment, expressed inter alia by the freedom of capital movement in Art 63(1) TFEU and its *erga omnes* effect, EU primary law also acknowledges the EU's and Member States' interest to align investment policies with other policies, such as its Foreign and security policy. Namely, Art 64(2) and (3) TFEU provide the EU with wide flexibility. Certainly, once the EU has introduced policies in a certain field of law, this policy becomes the *status quo* of capital movement liberalization in the EU compared to which any step backwards must be adopted unanimously by the Council. The Screening Regulation constitutes an illustrative example of this effect: By opting for a rather narrow screening ground, 'security or public order', the EU widely liberalized FDI inflows from the perspective of Art 64(2) and (3) TFEU. Accordingly, for political reasons the EU itself set a high bar to adopt broader FDI Screening mechanisms and other measures on FDI inflows in the future. Still, provided unanimity is reached, the EU preserves wide flexibility to regulate third-country capital movement. Put positively, this means that, if a certain regulatory objective is deemed important enough throughout the EU and unanimity in the Council is reached, the EU remains free to take the agreed regulatory steps. Art 64(3) TFEU thus sets a political not necessarily legal bar.

The legal limitations set by International economic law, on the other hand, have been committed to following other important rationales that remain paramount even against the backdrop of the EU and Member States concerns vis-à-vis foreign investors.

Regarding the limitations set by bi- and plurilateral agreements that widely liberalize the establishment of foreign investors through FDI, namely FTAs, one may assume that the EU and Member States only enter into such agreements with countries whose investors do not cause the same level of concern. Hence, FDI Screening mechanisms that allow to ban FDI only in a few, high-profile cases, such as those based on the Screening Regulation, may in fact be considered sufficient vis-à-vis investors from those countries. Further, even if this was not the case, the limited flexibility to screen FDI from FTA partner countries may be seen as an appropriate trade-off to gain other advantages; for example, enabling EU firms to participate in public tenders or promoting environmental and labour standards in such partner countries.

The legal limitations set by the multilateral obligations of WTO law, namely the GATS, on the other hand, may generally be considered to ensure that WTO members also, to a minimal extent, take into account other WTO members' interests when adopting political measures—an approach that should be welcome in the EU as an actor who by nature cherishes and promotes a rule-based multilateral world order.[7] Especially two rules are crucial in this context.

First, it is a common rule in WTO law to prohibit the regulation of international trade based on origin, whether regulating products, importers, or investors. Instead, governments have to come up with content-oriented, origin-neutral policies. Simply using the nationality of an investor as a proxy without consistently defining the (purportedly) origin-neutral policy goal is often prohibited, at least when differentiating between third countries and thereby violating the MFN obligation. For good reasons, this rule poses significant limits to considering foreign investors as agents of rivalling third-country governments. It seeks to counteract general mistrust against investors from other WTO members and among WTO members generally.

Second, WTO law commitments may not be frustrated by referring to open-ended national security exceptions. Instead, the protected 'essential security interests' are defined by an exhaustive list of narrower interests; mainly: nuclear materials, war, or provisioning military establishments. WTO members have the legal obligation to respect these limits, regardless of the debate around the justiciability of the WTO security exceptions. Accordingly, these security exceptions will not allow WTO members to justify their commitments based on broad strategic interests in the current geopolitical and geoeconomic shifts. This has—or should have—a paramount and imperative effect: geopolitical and geoeconomic interests are not to be securitized or militarized too hastily. This would risk to undermine the current order of international relations.[8]

Certainly, in times of a turn in policies—or at least political communication—towards long-forgotten notions such as trade war and systemic rivalry,[9] one may be inclined to leave such rules aside and seek solutions outside the WTO.[10] However,

---

[7] Art 21(1) subpara. 2, (2)(h) TEU.

[8] Weiß (2020), p. 830. From these two limits, some authors conclude that the former 'neoliberal order' of international trade and investment law is giving way to a 'geoeconomic order', in which economics and geopolitics may not be separated anymore, and narrow security exceptions become broader, more politicized security concepts, see Roberts et al. (2019), pp. 657–658, 665–666; see also Wigell (2016), pp. 145–146 (using the notion 'liberal institutionalist').

[9] Identifying China as a 'systemic rival' of the EU, Commission and High Representative of the Union for Foreign Affairs and Security Policy, 'EU-China - A Strategic outlook' (Joint Communication) JOIN (2015), pp. 1, 5, reaffirmed by European Council, 'Conclusions of European Council Meeting (1 and 2 October 2020)' EUCO 13/20, para. 26.

[10] A similar discussion circles around the question whether current challenges to WTO law may be met by reforming the WTO system or only outside the system. Generally in favour of a solution

such steps should remain the *ultima ratio*. More importantly, there is a considerable risk that such steps are in fact not taken due to newly arisen imminent urgency but for other political reasons—a development that these WTO rules precisely sought to forestall.

In sum, the legal limitations for FDI screening in the EU are thus well rooted in the rationales of the Screening Regulation, EU primary law, and International economic law. Due to the highly comprehensive and complex web of unilateral obligations in EU law as well as bi-, pluri-, and multilateral obligations in International economic law, any regulatory steps towards broader FDI screening must be taken with utmost care by clearly defining the pursued policy objectives and thoroughly identifying the applicable legal limitations. Whereas this does not prevent the EU from adopting broad FDI Screening mechanisms, they come with significant shortcomings as well as increased policy costs and political hurdles.

As a result, it is necessary to consider other available options that may complement FDI Screening mechanisms to more effectively meet the EU and Member States concerns vis-à-vis foreign investors. The GATS analysis has indicated important alternative policy means: Besides sector-specific FDI Screening mechanisms along the lines of the EU and Member States specific commitments to NT, more stringent and precise regulatory measures, such as FDI registration requirements, ongoing regulatory surveillance, and strict, effective sanctioning mechanisms seem valuable options. Indeed, ongoing surveillance by specialized regulatory authorities may detect risks even better and find alternative solutions to attenuate them appropriately. Another route are policies that are not targeted against FDI inflows, but instead support EU market incumbents. Such polices may include industrial policies that support key future technologies. Finally, the EU could strengthen the common capital market in order to boost intra-EU FDI so that EU market incumbents could tap additional intra-EU capital sources, and would need to rely less on third-country FDI. This strategy finds support in the economic analysis of FDI advantages to host countries that this book submits. FDI that is at the centre of the EU and Member States concerns serves first and foremost as a source of capital, not of technology and know-how. Intra-EU FDI is likely to have all of these positive effects.

Consequently, provided the EU and Member States want to effectively meet their concerns vis-à-vis foreign investors and defend their interests in light of the current major policy challenges, FDI screening may be one, but should not remain the only instrument in the EU's and Member States' policy toolkit.

---

within the WTO, e.g. Mavroidis and Sapir (2019); Mavroidis and Sapir (2021), pp. 175–176, 192, but also suggesting that plurilateral solutions within the WTO framework must be a start; favouring a mixed approach Howse (2020), p. 371; and sceptical Wu (2016), p. 261.

References

Howse R (2020) Making the WTO (not so) great again: the case against responding to the trump trade agenda through reform of WTO rules on subsidies and state enterprises. J Int Econ Law 23: 371–389. https://doi.org/10.1093/jiel/jgaa017

Mavroidis PC, Sapir A (2019) China and the world trade organisation: towards a better fit. Bruegel Working Papers 6. https://www.bruegel.org/2019/06/china-and-the-world-trade-organisation-towards-a-better-fit/. Accessed 2 Feb 2022

Mavroidis PC, Sapir A (2021) China and the WTO: why multilateralism still matters. Princeton University Press, Princeton

Roberts A, Choer Moraes H, Ferguson V (2019) Toward a geoeconomic order in international trade and investment. J Int Econ Law 22:655–676. https://doi.org/10.1093/jiel/jgz036

Weiß W (2020) Adjudicating security exceptions in WTO law: methodical and procedural preliminaries. J World Trade 54:829–852

Wigell M (2016) Conceptualizing regional powers' geoeconomic strategies: neo-imperialism, neo-mercantilism, hegemony, and liberal institutionalism. Asia Europe J 14:135–151. https://doi.org/10.1007/s10308-015-0442-x

Wu M (2016) The 'China, Inc.' challenge to global trade governance. Harv Int Law J 57:261–324

Tables of Cases

European Court of Justice: Judgments and Opinions of Advocates General

C-26/62 *Van Gend en Loos* [1963] EU:C:1963:1.
C-181/73 *Haegeman* [1974] EU:C:1974:41.
C-8/74 *Dassonville* [1974] EU:C:1974:82.
C-36/75 *Rutili v Ministre de l'intérieur* [1975] EU:C:1975:137.
C-35/76 *Simmenthal Spa v Ministero delle finanze* [1976] EU:C:1976:180.
C-5/77 *Tedeschi v Denkavit* [1977] EU:C:1977:144.
C-120/78 *Rewe v Bundesmonopolverwaltung für Branntwein* [1979] EU:C:1979:42 (*Cassis de Dijon*).
C-104/81 *Kupferberg* [1982] EU:C:1982:362.
C-286/82 and 26/83 *Luisi and Carbone v Ministero dello Tesoro* [1984] EU:C:1984:35.
C-72/83 *Campus Oil* [1984] EU:C:1984:256.
C-308/86 *Lambert* [1988] EU:C:1988:405.
C-221/89 *Factortame* [1991] EU:C:1991:320.
C-55/94 *Gebhard* [1995] EU:C:1995:411.
Opinion 1/94 *Accords annexés à l'accord OMC* [1994] EU:C:1994:384.
C-149/96 *Portugal v Council* [1999] EU:C:1999:574.
C-212/97 *Centros* [1999] EU:C:1999:126.
C-212/97 *Centros* [1998] Opinion of AG La Pergola, EU:C:1998:380.
C-302/97 *Konle* [1999] EU:C:1999:271.
C-7/98 *Krombach* [2000] EU:C:2000:164.
C-78/98 *Commission v Belgium* [2000] EU:C:2000:497.
C-251/98 *Baars* [2000] EU:C:2000:205.
C-367/98 *Commission v Portugal* [2002] EU:C:2002:326.

© The Author(s), under exclusive license to Springer Nature Switzerland AG 2022
J. Velten, *Screening Foreign Direct Investment in the EU*, EYIEL Monographs - Studies in European and International Economic Law 26,
https://doi.org/10.1007/978-3-031-05603-1

C-52 and 113/16 *SEGRO* [2018] EU:C:2018:157.

C-74/16 *Congregación de Escuelas Pías Provincia Betania* [2017] EU:C:2017:496.

C-106/16 *Polbud - Wykonawstwo* [2017] EU:C:2017:804.

C-382/16 *Hornbach-Baumarkt* [2018] EU:C:2018:366.

C-398 and 399/16 *X* [2018] EU:C:2018:110.

C-504 and 613/16 *Deister Holding* [2017] EU:C:2017:1009.

C-135/17 *X [Sociétés intermédiaires établies dans des pays tiers]* [2019] EU:
C:2019:136.

C-235/17 *Commission v Hungary* [2019] EU:C:2019:432.

C-563/17 *Associação Peço a Palavra and Others* [2019] EU:C:2019:144.

C-563/17 *Associação Peço a Palavra and Others* [2018] Opinion of AG Sánchez-
Bordona, EU:C:2018:937.

WTO Adjudicating Bodies: Reports and Related Documents

Argentina—Measures Affecting the Export of Bovine Hides and the Import of Finished Leather, Panel Report (19 December 2000) WT/DS155/R, WTO Online Database doc no 00-5282.

Argentina—Measures Affecting the Importation of Goods, Panel Report (22 August 2014) WT/DS438/R, WT/DS444/R, and WT/DS445/R, as modified by Appellate Body Report WT/DS438/AB/R, WT/DS444/AB/R, and WT/DS445/AB/R, WTO Online Database doc no 14-4794.

Argentina—Measures Relating to Trade in Goods and Services, Appellate Body Report (14 April 2016) WT/DS453/AB/R, WTO Online Database doc no 16-2077.

Argentina—Measures Relating to Trade in Goods and Services, Panel Report (30 September 2015) WT/DS453/R, as modified by Appellate Body Report WT/DS453/AB/R, WTO Online Database doc no 15-5027.

Brazil—Measures Affecting Imports of Retreaded Tyres, Appellate Body Report (3 December 2007) WT/DS332/AB/R, WTO Online Database doc no 07-5290.

Brazil—Certain Measures Concerning Taxation and Charges, Appellate Body Report (13 December 2018) WT/DS472/AB/R and WT/DS497/AB/R, WTO Online Database doc no 18-7793.

Brazil—Certain Measures Concerning Taxation and Charges, Panel Report (30 August 2017) WT/DS472/R and WT/DS497/R, as modified by Appellate Body Report WT/DS472/AB/R and WT/DS497/AB/R, WTO Online Database doc no 17-4582.

Canada—Administration of the Foreign Investment Review Act, GATT Panel Report (7 February 1984) BISD 30S/140.

Canada—Certain Measures Concerning Periodicals, Appellate Body Report (30 June 1997) WT/DS31/R/AB, WTO Online Database doc no 97-2653.

European Court of Human Rights

Islamic Republic of Iran Shipping Lines v Turkey, ECHR Judgment (13 December 2007) Case 40998/98, 2007-V ECHR 327.

National Courts

Atomausstieg, German Federal Constitutional Court (Bundesverfassungsgericht) Judgment (6 December 2016) 1 BvR 2821/11, BVerfGE 143, 246.

Tables of Legislation

EU Primary Law

Charter of Fundamental Rights of the European Union 2016, [2016] OJ C 202/391 ('CFR').
Treaty Establishing the European Community (consolidated version), [1992] OJ C 224/6 ('EEC').
Treaty Establishing the European Community (consolidated version), [2006] OJ C 321E/37 ('EC').
Treaty on European Union, [1992] OJ C 224/1 ('TEU 1992').
Treaty on European Union (consolidated version), [1997] OJ C 340/145 ('TEU 1997').
Treaty on European Union (consolidated version), [2016] OJ C 202/13 ('TEU').
Treaty on the Functioning of the European Union (consolidated version), [2016] OJ C 202/47 ('TFEU').
Protocol (No 27) on the Internal Market and Competition, [2016] OJ C 202/308.

EU Secondary Law

Commission Directive 2006/111/EC of 16 November 2006 on the transparency of financial relations between Member States and public undertakings as well as on financial transparency within certain undertakings [2006] OJ L 318/17.
Council Decision 2008/801/EC of 25 September 2008 on the conclusion, on behalf of the European Community, of the United Nations Convention against Corruption [2008] OJ L 287/1.

© The Author(s), under exclusive license to Springer Nature Switzerland AG 2022
J. Velten, *Screening Foreign Direct Investment in the EU*, EYIEL Monographs - Studies in European and International Economic Law 26,
https://doi.org/10.1007/978-3-031-05603-1

Council Directive 88/361/EEC of 24 June 1988 for the implementation of Article 67 of the Treaty [on the former European Communities Treaty] (Capital Movement Directive) [1988] OJ L 178/5.

Council Directive 2008/114/EC of 8 December 2008 on the identification and designation of European critical infrastructures and the assessment of the need to improve their protection (Critical Infrastructure Directive) [2008] OJ L 345/75.

Council Directive 2009/119/EC of 14 September 2009 imposing an obligation on Member States to maintain minimum stocks of crude oil and/or petroleum products [2009] OJ L 265/9.

Council Directive 2011/96/EU of 30 November 2011 on the common system of taxation applicable in the case of parent companies and subsidiaries of different Member States [2011] OJ L 345/8.

Council Regulation (EC) No 139/2004 of 20 January 2004 on the control of concentrations between undertakings (Merger Regulation) [2004] OJ L 24/1.

Council Regulation (EC) No 428/2009 of 5 May 2009 setting up a Community regime for the control of exports, transfer, brokering and transit of dual-use items (Dual-use Regulation) [2009] OJ L 134/1.

Directive 2009/72/EC of the European Parliament and of the Council of 13 July 2009 concerning common rules for the internal market in electricity and repealing Directive 2003/54/EC [2009] OJ L 211/55.

Directive 2009/73/EC of the European Parliament and of the Council of 13 July 2009 concerning common rules for the internal market in natural gas and repealing Directive 2003/55/EC [2009] OJ L 211/94.

Directive (EU) 2015/2436 of the European Parliament and of the Council of 16 December 2015 to approximate the laws of the Member States relating to trade marks [2015] OJ L 336/1.

Directive (EU) 2019/790 of the European Parliament and of the Council of 17 April 2019 on copyright and related rights in the Digital Single Market and amending Directives 96/9/EC and 2001/29/EC [2019] OJ L 130/92.

Directive (EU) 2019/944 of the European Parliament and of the Council of 5 June 2019 on common rules for the internal market for electricity and amending Directive 2012/27/EU [2019] OJ L 158/125.

General Programme for the abolition of restrictions on freedom of establishment [1962] OJ L 36/7.

Regulation (EC) No 1008/2008 of the European Parliament and of the Council of 24 September 2008 on common rules for the operation of air services in the Community (Recast) [2008] OJ L 293/3.

Regulation (EU) No 1219/2012 of the European Parliament and of the Council of 12 December 2012 establishing transitional arrangements for bilateral investment agreements between Member States and third countries (BIT Transition Regulation) [2012] OJ L 351/40.

Regulation (EU) No 596/2014 of the European Parliament and of the Council of 16 April 2014 on market abuse (Market Abuse Regulation) [2014] OJ L 173/1.

Regulation (EU) 2016/679 of the European Parliament and of the Council of 27 April 2016 on the protection of natural persons with regard to the processing of personal data and on the free movement of such data, and repealing Directive 95/46/EC (GDPR) [2016] OJ L 119/1.

Regulation (EU) 2016/1036 of the European Parliament and of the Council of 8 June 2016 on protection against dumped imports from countries not members of the European Union [2016] OJ L 176/21.

Regulation (EU) 2016/1037 of the European Parliament and of the Council of 8 June 2016 on protection against subsidised imports from countries not members of the European Union [2016] OJ L 176/55.

Regulation (EU) 2019/452 of the European Parliament and of the Council of 19 March 2019 establishing a framework for the screening of foreign direct investments into the Union (Screening Regulation) [2019] OJ L 79/I/1.

International Treaties

Comprehensive Economic and Trade Agreement (CETA) between Canada, of the one part, and the European Union and its Member States, of the other part, signed 30 October 2016, provisional application as from 21 September 2017 for most agreement parts, [2017] OJ L 11/23 ('CETA').

Convention concerning judicial competence and the execution of decisions in civil and commercial matters, 27 September 1968, 1262 UNTS 154 (1982) ('Brussels Convention').

Convention on the Organisation for Economic Co-operation and Development (with Supplementary Protocols Nos 1 and 2), 14 December 1960, 888 UNTS 179 (1973) ('OECD Convention').

EU-China Comprehensive Agreement on Investment (agreement in principle reached on 30 December 2020; still subject to legal and technical revision, as well as final conclusion by parties, namely adoption by Council and consent by Parliament; for parts of negotiated version, see <https://trade.ec.europa.eu/doclib/press/index.cfm?id=2237> accessed 2 February 2022) ('EU-China CAI').

Free Trade Agreement between the European Union and its Member States, of the one part, and the Republic of Korea, of the other part, 1 October 2015, [2011] OJ L 127/6 ('EU-South Korea FTA').

Free Trade Agreement between the European Union and the Republic of Singapore, 8 November 2019, [2019] OJ L 294/3 ('EU-Singapore FTA').

Free Trade Agreement between the European Union and the Socialist Republic of Viet Nam, 30 March 2020, [2020] OJ L 186/3 ('EU-Vietnam FTA').

The General Agreement on Tariffs and Trade, 30 October 1947, 55 UNTS 194 (1950) ('GATT 1947').

Investment Protection Agreement between the European Union and its Member States, of the one part, and the Republic of Singapore, of the other part, signed 19 October 2018 (not yet ratified by Member States, for a negotiated version, see

<http://trade.ec.europa.eu/doclib/press/index.cfm?id=961> accessed 2 February 2022) ('EU-Singapore IPA').

Trade and Cooperation Agreement between the European Union and the European Atomic Energy Community, of the one part, and the United Kingdom of Great Britain and Northern Ireland, of the other part, provisionally applied as of 1 January 2021, [2020] OJ L 444/31 ('EU-UK Trade and Cooperation Agreement')

Investment Protection Agreement between the European Union and its Member States, of the one part, and the Socialist Republic of Viet Nam, of the other part, signed on 30 June 2019 (not yet ratified by Member States, for a negotiated version, see <http://trade.ec.europa.eu/doclib/html/157391.htm> accessed 2 February 2022) ('EU-Vietnam IPA').

Vienna Convention on the Law of Treaties, 23 May 1969, 1155 UNTS 331 (1980) ('VCLT').

WTO, Marrakesh Agreement Establishing the World Trade Organization, 15 April 1994, 1867 UNTS 154 (1995) ('WTO Agreement').

——General Agreement on Tariffs and Trade 1994 (Annex 1A to the WTO Agreement), 15 April 1994, 1867 UNTS 190 (1995) ('GATT 1994').

——Agreement on Safeguards (Annex 1A to the WTO Agreement), 15 April 1994, 1869 UNTS 154 (1995) ('Agreement on Safeguards').

——Agreement on Technical Barriers to Trade (Annex 1A to the WTO Agreement), 15 April 1994, 1868 UNTS 120 (1995) ('TBT Agreement').

——Agreement on Trade-Related Aspects of Intellectual Property Rights (Annex 1C to the WTO Agreement, as amended on 23 January 2017), 15 April 1994, 1869 UNTS 299 (1995) ('TRIPS Agreement').

——Agreement on Trade-Related Investment Measures (Annex 1A to the WTO Agreement), 15 April 1994, 1868 UNTS 186 (1995) ('TRIMs Agreement').

——General Agreement on Trade in Services (Annex 1B to the WTO Agreement), 15 April 1994, 1869 UNTS 183 (1995) ('GATS').

——Understanding on Rules and Procedures Governing the Settlement of Disputes (Annex 2 to the WTO Agreement), 15 April 1994, 1869 UNTS 401 (1995) ('DSU').

——Revised Agreement on Government Procurement (Annex 4(b) to the WTO Agreement), 30 March 2012, 3009 UNTS (2014).

——Understanding on Commitments in Financial Services, 15 April 1994, 1867 UNTS 117 (1995) ('Understanding on Financial Services').

National Legislation

German Act on the German Federal Office for Information Security (Gesetz über das Bundesamt für Sicherheit in der Informationstechnik).

German Foreign Trade and Payments Act (Außenwirtschaftsgesetz).

German Foreign Trade and Payments Ordinance (Außenwirtschaftsverordnung).

German Securities Transaction Act (Wertpapierübertragungsgesetz).

German Stock Corporation Act (Aktiengesetz).

German Trade, Commerce and Industry Regulation Act (Gewerbeordnung).

Investment Canada Act (as amended) Revised Statutes of Canada 1985/c 28 (1st Supp).

Volkswagen Act (Gesetz über die Überführung der Anteilsrechte an der Volkswagenwerk Gesellschaft mit beschränkter Haftung in private Hand).

Tables of Official and Policy Documents

EU Documents

Commission, 'Towards a Comprehensive European International Investment Policy' (Communication) COM (2010) 343 final.
—— 'European Energy Security Strategy' (Communication) COM (2014) 330 final.
—— 'Reflection Paper on Harnessing Globalisation' COM (2017) 240 final.
—— 'Proposal for a Regulation of the European Parliament and of the Council establishing a framework for screening of foreign direct investments into the European Union' COM (2017) 487 final.
—— 'Welcoming Foreign Direct Investment while Protecting Essential Interests' (Communication) COM (2017) 494 final.
—— 'Foreign Direct Investment in the EU: Following up on the Commission Communication "Welcoming Foreign Direct Investment while Protecting Essential Interests" of 13 September 2017' (Commission Staff Working Document) SWD (2019) 108 final.
—— 'List of the Bilateral Investment Agreements referred to in Article 4(1) of Regulation (EU) No 1219/2012 of the European Parliament and of the Council establishing transitional arrangements for bilateral investment agreements between Member States and third countries: Notices of Member States' [2019] OJ C 198/1.
—— 'Report on Implementation of EU Free Trade Agreements: 1 January 2018 - 31 December 2018' COM (2019) 455 final.
—— 'A Union that Strives for More. My Agenda for Europe: Political Guidelines for the Next European Commission 2019-2024' (16 July 2019) <https://op.europa.eu/en/publication-detail/-/publication/43a17056-ebf1-11e9-9c4e-01aa75ed71a1> accessed 2 February 2022.
—— 'A European Strategy for Data' (Communication) COM (2020) 66 final.
—— 'A New Industrial Strategy for Europe' (Communication) COM (2020) 102 final.

—— 'Report on the Application of Regulation (EU) No 1219/2012 establishing transitional arrangements for bilateral investment agreements between Member States and third countries' COM (2020) 134 final.

—— 'White Paper on Levelling the Playing Field as regards Foreign Subsidies' COM (2020) 253 final.

—— 'Guidance to the Member States concerning Foreign Direct Investment and Free Movement of Capital from Third Countries, and the Protection of Europe's Strategic Assets, ahead of the Application of Regulation (EU) 2019/452 (FDI Screening Regulation)' (Communication) COM (2020) 1981 final.

—— 'EU-China Comprehensive Agreement on Investment: The Agreement in Principle' (30 December 2020) <https://trade.ec.europa.eu/doclib/cfm/doclib_section.cfm?sec=120> accessed 2 February 2022.

—— 'List of Screening Mechanisms Notified by Member States: (pursuant to Art 3(7) and (8) Screening Regulation, updated on an ongoing basis)' (14 January 2021) <https://trade.ec.europa.eu/doclib/docs/2019/june/tradoc_157946.pdf> accessed 2 February 2022.

—— 'Proposal for a Regulation of the European Parliament and of the Council on foreign subsidies distorting the internal market' COM (2021) 223 final (Foreign Subsidies Regulation Proposal).

—— 'First Annual Report on the screening of foreign direct investments into the Union' (Report) COM (2021) 714 final.

—— and High Representative of the Union for Foreign Affairs and Security Policy, 'EU-China - A Strategic outlook' (Joint Communication) JOIN (2015) 5.

Council, 'Council Conclusions on Security and Defence in the context of the EU Global Strategy' 9178/17.

—— 'EU Cyber Defence Policy Framework' 14413/18.

—— 'Council Conclusions on Security and Defence' 8910/20.

EU, 'EU Funding for Dual Use: A practical guide to accessing EU funds for European Regional Authorities and SMEs' (October 2014) <https://ec.europa.eu/docsroom/documents/12601/attachments/1/translations/en/renditions/pdf> accessed 2 February 2022.

—— 'Shared Vision, Common Action: A Stronger Europe: A Global Strategy for the EU's Foreign and Security Policy' (28 June 2016) <https://op.europa.eu/en/publication-detail/-/publication/3eaae2cf-9ac5-11e6-868c-01aa75ed71a1> accessed 2 February 2022.

European Council, 'Conclusions of European Council Meeting (22 and 23 June 2017)' EUCO 8/17.

—— 'Conclusions of European Council Meeting (1 and 2 October 2020)' EUCO 13/20.

Parliament, 'Report on the Proposal for a Regulation of the European Parliament and of the Council establishing a framework for screening of foreign direct investments into the European Union (COM (2017) 487)' A8-0198/2018.

—— 'Building an Ambitious EU Industrial Strategy as a Strategic Priority for Growth, Employment and Innovation in Europe' (Resolution) 2017/2732 (RSP).

WTO Documents

Canada, 'Mode 4 Commitments and Economic Needs Tests' (Communication from Canada to the Committee on Specific Commitments) S/CSC/W/47 (21 June 2005).

Committee on Technical Barriers to Trade, 'Decision on the Committee on Principles for the Development of International Standards, Guides and Recommendations with relation to Articles 2, 5 and Annex 3 of the Agreement' (Annex 4 to Second Triennal Review of the Operation and Implementation the Agreement on Technical Barriers to Trade) G/TBT/9 (13 November 2000).

Council for Trade in Services, 'Energy Services' (Background Note by the Secretariat) S/C/W/52 (9 September 1998).

—— 'Disciplines on Domestic Regulation in the Accountancy Sector' (Decision by the Council) S/L/64 (17 December 1998).

—— 'Guidelines for the Scheduling of Specific Commitments under the General Agreement on Trade in Services' S/L/92 (28 March 2001).

—— 'Economic Needs Test' (Note by the Secretariat) S/CSS/W/118 (30 November 2001).

—— 'Classification in the Telecom Sector under the WTO-GATS Framework' (Communication from the EC) S/CSC/W/44 (10 February 2005).

—— 'Energy Services' (Background Note by the Secretariat) S/C/W/311 (12 January 2010).

—— 'Mode 3 – Commercial Presence' (Background Note by the Secretariat) S/C/W/314 (7 April 2010).

—— 'Negotiations on Trade in Services' (Report by the Chairman to the Trade Negotiations Committee) TN/S/36 (21 April 2011).

Dispute Settlement Body, 'Russia—Traffic in Transit' (Adoption) WT/DS512/7 (29 April 2019).

GATT Council, 'Minutes of Meeting of 31 October 1975' C/M/109 (16 November 1975).

Group of Negotiations on Services, 'Services Sectoral Classification List' (Note by the Secretariat) MTN.GNS/W/120 (10 July 1991).

—— 'Definitions in the Draft General Agreement on Trade in Services' (Note by the Secretariat) MTN.GNS/W/139 (15 October 1991).

Ministerial Conference, 'Disciplines on Domestic Regulation' (Communication from certain WTO members) WT/MIN(17)/7/Rev.2, WT/GC/190/Rev.2 (13 December 2017).

Sweden, 'Import Restrictions on Certain Footwear' (Notification to the Council) L/4250 (17 November 1975).

Working Group on the Relationship between Trade and Investment, 'Modalities for Pre-establishment Commitments Based on GATS-type, Positive List Approach' (Note by the Secretariat) WT/WGTI/W/120 (19 June 2002).

Working Party on Border Tax Adjustment, 'GATT Working Party Report' BISD 18S/97 (2 December 1970).

Working Party on Domestic Regulation, 'Disciplines on Domestic Regulation pursuant to GATS Article VI:4' (Chairman's Progress Report) S/WPDR/W/45 (14 April 2011).

WTO, 'World Trade Report 2018: The Future of World Trade: How digital technologies are transforming global commerce' (Geneva, 2018) <https://www.wto.org/english/res_e/publications_e/wtr18_e.htm> accessed 2 February 2022.

—— 'Regional Trade Agreements: Database: "RTAs Currently in Force"' <https://rtais.wto.org/UI/charts.aspx> accessed 2 February 2022.

WTO members Afghanistan and others, 'Joint Ministerial Statement on Investment Facilitation for Development' WT/L/1072/Rev.1 (22 November 2019).

WTO members Albania and others, 'Joint Statement on Electronic Commerce' WT/L/1056 (25 January 2019).

WTO members Albania and others, 'Joint Statement on Services Domestic Regulation' WT/L/1059 (23 May 2019).

Documents of the UN and Related Organizations

IMF, 'Balance of Payments and International Investment Position Manual' (Washington, DC, 2009).

UNCTAD, 'World Investment Report 1998: Developments and Determinants' (New York, 1998).

—— 'World Investment Report 2000: Cross-border Mergers and Acquisitions and Development' (New York, 2000).

—— 'World Investment Report 2011: Non-equity Modes of International Production and Development' (New York, 2011).

—— 'World Investment Report 2013: Global Value Chains: Investment and Trade for Development' (New York, 2013).

—— 'World Investment Report 2016: Investor Nationality: Policy Challenges' (New York, 2016).

—— 'Development Status Groups and Composition' UNCTADSTAT <https://unctadstat.unctad.org/EN/Classifications/DimCountries_DevelopmentStatus_Hierarchy.pdf> accessed 2 February 2022.

UN General Assembly, 'Resolution No 68/262. Territorial Integrity of Ukraine' (27 March 2014) A/RES/68/262.

—— 'Resolution No 71/205. Situation of Human Rights in the Autonomous Republic of Crimea and the City of Sevastopol (Ukraine)' (19 December 2016) A/RES/71/205.

United Nations Statistics Division, 'Provisional Central Product Classification' (1990).

Documents of Other International Organizations

International Electrotechnical Commission, 'IEC Statutes and Rules of Procedure' (as amended, Geneva, 2001) <https://www.iec.ch/members_experts/refdocs/> accessed 2 February 2022.

International Organization for Standardization, 'ISO Statutes' (Geneva, 2018) <https://www.iso.org/publication/PUB100322.html> accessed 2 February 2022.

—— and International Electrotechnical Commission, 'ISO/IEC Guide 2:1991: General Terms and Their Definitions concerning Standardization and Related Activities' (Geneva, 1991) <https://www.iso.org/standard/19713.html> accessed 2 February 2022.

—— and International Electrotechnical Commission, 'ISO/IEC Guide 2:2004: Standardization and Related Activities—General Vocabulary' (as amended, Geneva, 2004) <https://www.iso.org/standard/39976.html> accessed 2 February 2022.

OECD, 'Decision of the Council Adopting the Code of Liberalisation of Capital Movements' (as amended, 12 December 1961), OECD Legal 0002 ('OECD Code of Capital Movements').

OECD, 'Benchmark Definition of Foreign Direct Investment' (Paris, 2008).

OECD, 'Balance of Payments BPM 6' (Paris) <https://stats.oecd.org/Index.aspx?DataSetCode=MEI_BOP6> accessed 2 February 2022.

Bibliography

Abu-Akeel AK, 'Definition of Trade in Services Under the GATS: Legal Implications' (1999) 32 The George Washington Journal of International Law and Economics 189.

Ackermann T and Köndgen J (eds), *Privat- und Wirtschaftsrecht in Europa: Festschrift für Wulf-Henning Roth zum 70. Geburtstag* (CH Beck 2015).

Adlung R, 'International Rules Governing Foreign Direct Investment in Services: Investment Treaties versus GATS' (2016) 17 Journal of World Investment & Trade 47.

—— 'WTO/GATS-Alien Framework Provisions in RTAs – A Closer Look' (2020) 19 World Trade Review 493.

—— and Mattoo A, 'The GATS' in Aaditya Mattoo, Robert M Stern, and Gianni Zanini (eds), *A Handbook of International Trade in Services* (Oxford University Press 2008) 48.

Aharoni Y, 'Reflections on Multinationals in a Globally Interdependent World Economy' in Karl P Sauvant, McAllister, Geraldine, and Wolfgang A Maschek (eds), *Foreign Direct Investments From Emerging Markets: The Challenges Ahead* (Palgrave Macmillan 2010) 37.

Akande D and Williams S, 'International Adjudication on National Security Issues: What Role for the WTO?' (2003) 43 Virginia Journal of International Law 365.

Alfaro L, 'Gains from Foreign Direct Investment: Macro and Micro Approaches: World Bank's ABCDE Conference' (2017) 30 (Suppl 1) The World Bank Economic Review S2–S15.

Alford RP, 'The Self-Judging WTO Security Exception' [2011] Utah Law Review 697.

Alschner W, 'Americanization of the BIT Universe: The Influence of Friendship, Commerce and Navigation (FCN) Treaties on Modern Investment Treaty Law' (2013) 5 Goettingen Journal of International Law 455.

Ambrus M, Rayfuse RG, and Werner W (eds), *Risk and the Regulation of Uncertainty in International Law* (Oxford University Press 2017).

Arnauld A v (ed), *Europäische Außenbeziehungen* (Nomos 2014).

Arnull A and others (eds), *A Constitutional Order of States?: Essays in EU law in honour of Alan Dashwood* (Hart 2011).

Ashiagbor D, 'Art 15 – Freedom to Choose an Occupation' in Steve Peers and others (eds), *The EU Charter of Fundamental Rights: A Commentary* (Hart 2014).

Ayres G and Mitchell AD, 'General and Security Exceptions under the GATT 1994 and the GATS' in Indira Carr, Jahid H Bhuiyan, and Shawkat Alam (eds), *International Trade Law and the WTO* (Federation Press 2013) 226.

Bacchus J and Lester S, 'The Rule of Precedent and the Role of the Appellate Body' (2020) 54 Journal of World Trade 183.

Bachlechner M, 'Liegenschaftserwerb und Kapitalverkehrsfreiheit' (1998) 1 ZEuS 519.

Badura P, 'Das öffentliche Unternehmen im europäischen Binnenmarkt' [1997] ZGR 291.

© The Author(s), under exclusive license to Springer Nature Switzerland AG 2022
J. Velten, *Screening Foreign Direct Investment in the EU*, EYIEL Monographs - Studies in European and International Economic Law 26,
https://doi.org/10.1007/978-3-031-05603-1

Bakker A, *The Liberalization of Capital Movements in Europe: The Monetary Committee and Financial Integration 1958 - 1994* (Kluwer Academic 1996).

Baldwin RE and Winters AL (eds), *Challenges to Globalization: Analyzing the Economics* (University of Chicago Press 2004).

Barba Navaretti G and Venables A, *Multinational firms in the world economy* (Princeton University Press 2004).

Barnard C and Scott J (eds), *The Law of the Single European Market: Unpacking the Premises* (Hart 2002).

Bartels L, 'The Chapeau of the General Exceptions in the WTO GATT and GATS Agreements: A Reconstruction' (2015) 109 American Journal of International Law 95.

Bast J, 'Art 5 EUV' in Eberhard Grabitz, Meinhard Hilf, and Martin Nettesheim (eds), *Das Recht der Europäischen Union: EUV/AEUV* (71st edn, CH Beck 2020).

Bauer H, Merten D, and Papier HJ (eds), *Handbuch der Grundrechte: Band V: Grundrechte in Deutschland - Einzelgrundrechte II* (CF Müller 2013).

Bayer W and Ohler C, 'Staatsfonds ante portas' [2008] ZG 12.

Becker U and others (eds), *EU-Kommentar* (4th edn, Nomos 2019).

Benyon FS, *Direct Investment, National Champions and EU Treaty Freedoms: From Maastricht to Lisbon* (Hart 2010).

Bermann GA (ed), *Trade and Human Health and Safety* (Cambridge University Press 2006).

Bhala R and Witmer E, 'Interpreting Interpretation: Textual, Contextual, and Pragmatic Interpretative Methods for International Trade Law' (2020) 35 Connecticut Journal of International Law 62.

Bings SL, *Neuordnung der Außenhandelskompetenzen der Europäischen Union durch den Reformvertrag von Lissabon* (Nomos 2014).

Bismuth R, 'Reading Between the Lines of the EU Regulation Establishing a Framework for Screening FDI into the Union' in Jacques H J Bourgeois (ed), *EU Framework for Foreign Direct Investment Control* (Kluwer Law International 2020) 103.

Blackwill RD and Harris JM, *War by Other Means: Geoeconomics and Statecraft* (Harvard University Press 2016).

Bogdandy A v and Windsor J, 'Understanding of Commitments on Financial Services' in Rüdiger Wolfrum, Peter-Tobias Stoll, and Clemens Feinäugle (eds), *WTO – Trade in Services* (Martinus Njihoff 2008).

—— and Bast J (eds), *Europäisches Verfassungsrecht: Theoretische und dogmatische Grundzüge* (2nd edn, Springer 2009).

Bognar Z, *Europäische Währungsintegration und Außenwirtschaftsbeziehungen: Eine Analyse des gemeinschafts- und völkerrechtlichen Rahmens der europäischen Außenwährungsbeziehungen* (Nomos 1997).

Böhmer A, 'The Struggle for a Multilateral Agreement on Investment; an Assessment of the Negotiation Process in the OECD' (1998) 41 German Yearbook of International Law 267.

Boklan D and Bahri A, 'The First WTO's Ruling on National Security Exception: Balancing Interests or Opening Pandora's Box?' (2020) 19 World Trade Review 123.

Bourgeois JHJ (ed), *EU Framework for Foreign Direct Investment Control* (Kluwer Law International 2020a).

—— and Malathouni E, 'The EU Regulation on Screening Foreign Direct Investment: Another Piece of the Puzzle' in Jacques H J Bourgeois (ed), *EU Framework for Foreign Direct Investment Control* (Kluwer Law International 2020b) 169.

Brakman S and Garretsen H (eds), *Foreign Direct Investment and the Multinational Enterprise* (MIT Press 2008a).

—— and Garretsen H, 'Foreign Direct Investment and the Multinational Enterprise: An Introduction' in Steven Brakman and Harry Garretsen (eds), *Foreign Direct Investment and the Multinational Enterprise* (MIT Press 2008b) 1.

Broadman HG, 'Multinational Enterprises from Emerging Markets: Implications for the North and the South' in Karl P Sauvant, McAllister, Geraldine, and Wolfgang A Maschek (eds), *Foreign*

Direct Investments From Emerging Markets: The Challenges Ahead (Palgrave Macmillan 2010) 325.

Bröhmer J, 'Art 64 AEUV' in Christian Calliess and Matthias Ruffert (eds), *EUV/AEUV: Das Verfassungsrecht der Europäischen Union mit Europäischer Grundrechtecharta* (2011) (4th edn, CH Beck 2011).

—— 'Art 63 AEUV' in Christian Calliess and Matthias Ruffert (eds), *EUV/AEUV: Das Verfassungsrecht der Europäischen Union mit Europäischer Grundrechtecharta* (5th edn, CH Beck 2016a).

—— 'Art 64 AEUV' in Christian Calliess and Matthias Ruffert (eds), *EUV/AEUV: Das Verfassungsrecht der Europäischen Union mit Europäischer Grundrechtecharta* (5th edn, CH Beck 2016b).

Bronckers MCEJ (ed), *New Directions in International Economic Law: Essays in honour of John H. Jackson* (Kluwer Law International 2000).

Buckley PJ and others, 'A Retrospective and Agenda for Future Research on Chinese Outward Foreign Direct Investment' (2018) 49 Journal of International Business Studies 4.

Bünning M, '"Im Anwendungsbereich der Niederlassungsfreiheit ist keine Berufung auf die Kapitalverkehrsfreiheit möglich": Anmerkung zu Bundesfinanzhof, Urteil vom 6 März 2013, I R 10/11' [2013] BB 1778.

Bungenberg M, 'The Division of Competences Between the EU and Its Member States in the Area of Investment Politics' in Marc Bungenberg, Jörn Griebel, and Steffen Hindelang (eds), *International Investment Law and EU Law* (Springer 2011a) 29.

—— Griebel J, and Hindelang S (eds), *Internationaler Investitionsschutz und Europarecht* (Nomos 2010).

—— Griebel J, and Hindelang S (eds), *International Investment Law and EU Law* (Springer 2011b).

Burgi M, 'Die öffentlichen Unternehmen im Gefüge des primären Gemeinschaftsrechts' [1997] EuR 261.

Burri M and Cottier T (eds), *Trade Governance in the Digital Age: World Trade Forum* (Cambridge University Press 2012).

Calliess C, 'Art 2 AEUV' in Christian Calliess and Matthias Ruffert (eds), *EUV/AEUV: Das Verfassungsrecht der Europäischen Union mit Europäischer Grundrechtecharta* (5th edn, CH Beck 2016a).

—— 'Art 3 AEUV' in Christian Calliess and Matthias Ruffert (eds), *EUV/AEUV: Das Verfassungsrecht der Europäischen Union mit Europäischer Grundrechtecharta* (5th edn, CH Beck 2016b).

—— and Ruffert M (eds), *EUV/AEUV: Das Verfassungsrecht der Europäischen Union mit Europäischer Grundrechtecharta* (2011) (4th edn, CH Beck 2011).

—— and Ruffert M (eds), *EUV/AEUV: Das Verfassungsrecht der Europäischen Union mit Europäischer Grundrechtecharta* (2016c) (5th edn, CH Beck 2016).

Cantwell J, 'The Relationship Between International Trade and International Production' in David Greenaway and L Alan Winters (eds), *Surveys in International Trade* (Wiley-Blackwell 1994) 303.

—— and Narula R (eds), *International Business and the Eclectic Paradigm: Developing the OLI Framework* (Routledge 2003).

Carr I, Bhuiyan JH, and Alam S (eds), *International Trade Law and the WTO* (Federation Press 2013).

Cavelty MD, 'Cyber-Security' in Alan Collins (ed), *Contemporary Security Studies* (5th edn, Oxford University Press 2019) 410.

Chaisse J, 'The Regulation of Trade-Distorting Restrictions in Foreign Investment Law: An Investigation of China's TRIMs Compliance' [2012] European Yearbook of International Economic Law 159.

—— and Matsushita M, 'China's "Belt And Road" Initiative: Mapping the World Trade Normative and Strategic Implications' (2018) 52 Journal of World Trade 163.

Chang P and others, 'GATS, the Modes of Supply and Statistics on Trade in Services' (1999) 33 Journal of World Trade 93.

Clostermeyer M, *Staatliche Übernahmeabwehr und die Kapitalverkehrsfreiheit zu Drittstaaten: Europarechtliche Beurteilung der §§ 7 Abs. 2 Nr. 6 AWG, 53 AWV* (Nomos 2011).

Collins A (ed), *Contemporary Security Studies* (5th edn, Oxford University Press 2019a).

—— 'Introduction: What is Security Studies?' in Alan Collins (ed), *Contemporary Security Studies* (5th edn, Oxford University Press 2019b) 1.

Collins D, *An Introduction to International Investment Law* (Cambridge University Press 2017).

Commission, 'The European Economy: 2003 Review' (2003) European Economy 6.

Copeland BJ, 'Artificial Intelligence' Encyclopedia Britannica <https://www.britannica.com/technology/artificial-intelligence> accessed 2 February 2022.

Cossy M, 'Some Thoughts on the Concept of "Likeness" in the GATS' in Marion Panizzon, Nicole Pohl, and Pierre Sauvé (eds), *GATS and the Regulation of International Trade in Services : World Trade Forum* (Cambridge University Press 2008) 327.

Cottier T (ed), *The Prospects of International Trade Regulation: From Fragmentation to Coherence* (Cambridge University Press 2011a).

—— and others, 'Energy in WTO Law and Policy' in Thomas Cottier (ed), *The Prospects of International Trade Regulation: From Fragmentation to Coherence* (Cambridge University Press 2011b) 211.

—— and Delimatsis P, 'Art XIV*bis* GATS' in Rüdiger Wolfrum, Peter-Tobias Stoll, and Clemens Feinäugle (eds), *WTO – Trade in Services* (Martinus Njihoff 2008a).

—— Delimatsis P, and Diebold NF, 'Art XIV GATS' in Rüdiger Wolfrum, Peter-Tobias Stoll, and Clemens Feinäugle (eds), *WTO – Trade in Services* (Martinus Njihoff 2008b).

—— and Molinuevo M, 'Art V GATS' in Rüdiger Wolfrum, Peter-Tobias Stoll, and Clemens Feinäugle (eds), *WTO – Trade in Services* (Martinus Njihoff 2008c).

—— and Schneller L, 'The Philosophy of Non-discrimination in International Trade Regulation' in Anselm Kamperman Sanders (ed), *The Principle of National Treatment in International Economic Law: Trade, Investment and Intellectual Property* (Elgar 2014) 3.

—— and Trinberg L, 'Art 206 AEUV' in Hans von der Groeben, Jürgen Schwarze, and Armin Hatje (eds), *Europäisches Unionsrecht: Vertrag über die Europäische Union - Vertrag über die Arbeitsweise der Europäischen Union - Charta der Grundrechte der Europäischen Union* (7th edn, Nomos 2015a).

—— and Trinberg L, 'Art 207 AEUV' in Hans von der Groeben, Jürgen Schwarze, and Armin Hatje (eds), *Europäisches Unionsrecht: Vertrag über die Europäische Union - Vertrag über die Arbeitsweise der Europäischen Union - Charta der Grundrechte der Europäischen Union* (7th edn, Nomos 2015b).

Cremer W, 'Die Grundfreiheiten des Europäischen Unionsrechts' [2015] JURA 39.

Cremona M, 'Regulating FDI in the EU Legal Framework' in Jacques H J Bourgeois (ed), *EU Framework for Foreign Direct Investment Control* (Kluwer Law International 2020) 31.

—— and Scott J (eds), *EU Law Beyond EU Borders: The Extraterritorial Reach of EU Law* (Oxford University Press 2019).

Crones L, *Grundrechtlicher Schutz von juristischen Personen im europäischen Gemeinschaftsrecht* (Nomos 2002).

Croome J, *Reshaping the World Trading System: A History of the Uruguay Round* (2nd edn, Kluwer Law International 1999).

Daerdorff AV, 'The Economics of Government Market Intervention, and Its International Dimension' in Marco C E J Bronckers (ed), *New Directions in International Economic Law: Essays in honour of John H. Jackson* (Kluwer Law International 2000) 70.

De Búrca G, 'Unpacking the Concept of Discrimination in EC and International Trade Law' in Catherine Barnard and Joanne Scott (eds), *The Law of the Single European Market: Unpacking the Premises* (Hart 2002) 181.

—— and Scott J (eds), *The EU and the WTO: Legal and constitutional issues* (Hart 2001).

Delimatsis P, *International Trade in Services and Domestic Regulations: Necessity, Transparency, and Regulatory Diversity* (Oxford University Press 2007).

—— 'Who's Afraid of Necessity? And Why It Matters?' in Aik H Lim and Bart de Meester (eds), *WTO Domestic Regulation and Services Trade: Putting Principles into Practice* (Cambridge University Press 2014) 95.

—— and Hoekman B, 'National Tax Regulation, Voluntary International Standards, and the GATS: Argentina–Financial Services' (2018) 17 World Trade Review 265.

—— and Molinuevo M, 'Art XVI GATS' in Rüdiger Wolfrum, Peter-Tobias Stoll, and Clemens Feinäugle (eds), *WTO – Trade in Services* (Martinus Njihoff 2008).

Dereje J, *Staatsnahe Unternehmen: die Zurechnungsproblematik im Internationalen Investitionsrecht und weiteren Bereichen des Völkerrechts* (Nomos 2015).

Descheemaeker S, 'Ubiquitous Uncertainty: The Overlap between Trade in Services and Foreign Investment in the GATS and EU RTAs' (2016) 43 Legal Issues of Economic Integration 265.

Diebold NF, 'The Morals and Order Exceptions in WTO Law: Balancing the Toothless Tiger and the Undermining Mole' (2008) 11 Journal of International Economic Law 43.

—— *Non-discrimination in International Trade in Services: "Likeness" in WTO/GATS* (Cambridge University Press 2010).

Dietz S and Streinz T, 'Das Marktzugangskriterium in der Dogmatik der Grundfreiheiten' [2015] EuR 50.

Dimopoulos A, *EU Foreign Investment Law* (Oxford University Press 2011).

Döhrn R and Heiduk G (eds), *Theorie und Empirie der Direktinvestitionen* (Duncker & Humblot 1999).

Dörr O, 'Art 31 VCLT' in Oliver Dörr and Kirsten Schmalenbach (eds), *Vienna Convention on the Law of Treaties: A Commentary* (2nd edn, Springer 2018a).

—— 'Art 32 VCLT' in Oliver Dörr and Kirsten Schmalenbach (eds), *Vienna Convention on the Law of Treaties: A Commentary* (2nd edn, Springer 2018b).

—— and Schmalenbach K (eds), *Vienna Convention on the Law of Treaties: A Commentary* (2nd edn, Springer 2018c).

Dunning JH, 'Trade, Location of Economic Activity and the MNE: A Search for an Eclectic Approach' in Bertil G Ohlin, Per-Ove Hesselborn, and Per M Wijkman (eds), *The International Allocation of Economic Activity: Proceedings of a Nobel Symposium held at Stockholm* (Macmillan 1977) 395.

—— and Lundan SM, *Multinational Enterprises and the Global Economy* (2nd edn, Elgar 2008).

Echandi R and Sauvé P (eds), *Prospects in International Investment Law and Policy: World Trade Forum* (Cambridge University Press 2013).

Eden L, 'A Critical Reflection and Some Conclusions on OLI' in John Cantwell and Rajneesh Narula (eds), *International Business and the Eclectic Paradigm: Developing the OLI Framework* (Routledge 2003) 277.

Eeckhout P, 'Constitutional Concepts for Free Trade in Services' in Gráinne De Búrca and Joanne Scott (eds), *The EU and the WTO: Legal and constitutional issues* (Hart 2001) 211.

Ego A, 'Europäische Niederlassungsfreiheit' in Wulf Goette, Mathias Habersack, and Susanne Kalss (eds), *Münchener Kommentar zum Aktiengesetz: Band 7* (4th edn, CH Beck 2017).

Ehlers D, '§ 7 Allgemeine Lehren' in Dirk Ehlers and Ulrich Becker (eds), *Europäische Grundrechte und Grundfreiheiten* (4th edn, De Gruyter 2014a).

—— and Becker U (eds), *Europäische Grundrechte und Grundfreiheiten* (4th edn, De Gruyter 2014b).

Ehring L, 'De Facto Discrimination in WTO Law: National and Most-favored-nation Treatment - or Equal Treatment?' (2002) 36 Journal of World Trade 921.

Elfring K, 'Art 3 TRIPS' in Peter-Tobias Stoll, Jan Busche, and Katrin Arend (eds), *WTO – Trade-Related Aspects of Intellectual Property Rights* (Martinus Njihoff 2009).

European Court of Justice (ed), *The Court of Justice and the Construction of Europe: Analyses and Perspectives on Sixty Years of Case-law: La Cour de Justice et la construction de l'Europe: Analyses et Perspectives de Soixante Ans de Jurisprudence* (TMC Asser 2013).

European Parliamentary Research Service, 'Digital Sovereignty for Europe' (2 July 2020) EPRS Ideas Paper <https://www.europarl.europa.eu/thinktank/en/document.html?reference=EPRS_BRI(2020)651992> accessed 2 February 2022.

Everson M and Gonçalves RC, 'Art 16 – Freedom to Conduct a Business' in Steve Peers and others (eds), *The EU Charter of Fundamental Rights: A Commentary* (Hart 2014).

Fassion J and Natens B, 'The EU Proposal for FDI Control: The WTO on the Sidelines?' in Jacques H J Bourgeois (ed), *EU Framework for Foreign Direct Investment Control* (Kluwer Law International 2020) 121.

Feinäugle C, 'Art XXVIII GATS' in Rüdiger Wolfrum, Peter-Tobias Stoll, and Clemens Feinäugle (eds), *WTO – Trade in Services* (Martinus Njihoff 2008).

Financial Times, 'What Are the Main Security Risks of Using Huawei for 5G' *Financial Times* (London, 25 April 2019) <https://www.ft.com/content/8b48f460-50af-11e9-9c76-bf4a0ce37d49> accessed 2 February 2022 (paywall).

Forsthoff U, 'Art 45 AEUV' in Eberhard Grabitz, Meinhard Hilf, and Martin Nettesheim (eds), *Das Recht der Europäischen Union: EUV/AEUV* (71st edn, CH Beck 2020a).

—— 'Art 49 AEUV' in Eberhard Grabitz, Meinhard Hilf, and Martin Nettesheim (eds), *Das Recht der Europäischen Union: EUV/AEUV* (71st edn, CH Beck 2020b).

—— 'Art 54 AEUV' in Eberhard Grabitz, Meinhard Hilf, and Martin Nettesheim (eds), *Das Recht der Europäischen Union: EUV/AEUV* (71st edn, CH Beck 2020c).

France, Germany, and Italy, 'Proposals for Ensuring an Improved Level Playing Field in Trade and Investment' (Paris, Berlin, Rome, February 2017a).

—— Germany, and Italy, 'European Investment Policy: A Common Approach to Investment Control' (Paris, Berlin, Rome, 28 July 2017b).

Frenz W, *Handbuch Europarecht: Band 1: Europäische Grundfreiheiten* (2nd edn, Springer 2012).

—— *Europarecht* (2nd edn, Springer 2016).

Fritzsche A, 'Discretion, Scope of Judicial Review and Institutional Balance in European Law' (2010) 47 Common Market Law Review 361.

Gaines S, 'The WTO's Reading of Article XX Chapeau: A Disguised Restriction on Environmental Measures' (2001) 22 University of Pennsylvania Journal of International Economic Law 739.

Gari G, 'Is the WTO's Approach to International Standards on Services Outdated?' (2016) 19 Journal of International Economic Law 589.

—— 'Recent Developments on Disciplines on Domestic Regulations Affecting Trade in Services: Convergence or Divergence?' in Rhea T Hoffmann and Markus Krajewski (eds), *Coherence and Divergence in Services Trade Law* (Springer 2020) 59.

Gaukrodger D and Gordon K, 'Foreign Government-controlled Investors and Host Country Investment Policies: OECD Perspectives' in Karl P Sauvant, Lisa E Sachs, and Wouter S Jongbloed (eds), *Sovereign Investment: Concerns and Policy Reactions* (Oxford University Press 2012) 496.

Geiger F, *Beschränkungen von Direktinvestitionen aus Drittstaaten* (Nomos 2013).

German Federal Government, 'Antwort der Bundesregierung auf Kleine Anfrage: Europarechtliche Beurteilung der geplanten Änderung des Außenwirtschaftsgesetzes' Drucksache 16/7668.

Globerman S and Shapiro DM, 'Modes of Entry by Chinese Firms in the United States: Economic and Political Issues' in Karl P Sauvant (ed), *Investing in the United States: Is the US ready for FDI from China?* (Elgar 2009) 22.

Gocke R (ed), *Körperschaftsteuer, internationales Steuerrecht, Doppelbesteuerung: Festschrift für Franz Wassermeyer zum 65. Geburtstag* (CH Beck 2005).

Goette W, Habersack M, and Kalss S (eds), *Münchener Kommentar zum Aktiengesetz: Band 7* (4th edn, CH Beck 2017).

Gosch D and Schönfeld J, 'Kapitalverkehrsfreiheit und Drittstaaten - Ein (vorläufiger) Zwischenstand' [2015] IStR 755.

Grabitz E, Hilf M, and Nettesheim M (eds), *Das Recht der Europäischen Union: EUV/AEUV* (71st edn, CH Beck 2020).

Gramlich L, 'Art 63 AEUV' in Matthias Pechstein, Carsten Nowak, and Ulrich Häde (eds), *Frankfurter Kommentar zu EUV, GRC und AEUV* (Mohr Siebeck 2017).

Greenaway D and Winters LA (eds), *Surveys in International Trade* (Wiley-Blackwell 1994).

Griller S (ed), *International Economic Governance and Non-economic Concerns: New Challenges for the International Legal Order* (Springer 2003).

Groeben H vd (ed), *Kommentar zum Vertrag über die Europäische Union und zur Gründung der Europäischen Gemeinschaft: Band 1* (6th edn, Nomos 2003).

—— Schwarze J, and Hatje A (eds), *Europäisches Unionsrecht: Vertrag über die Europäische Union - Vertrag über die Arbeitsweise der Europäischen Union - Charta der Grundrechte der Europäischen Union* (7th edn, Nomos 2015).

Grossman GM, Horn H, and Mavroidis PC, 'National Treatment' in Henrik Horn and Petros C Mavroidis (eds), *Legal and Economic Principles of World Trade Law: Economics of Trade Agreements, Border Instruments, and National Treasures* (Cambridge University Press 2013) 205.

Guastaferro B, 'Beyond the Exceptionalism of Constitutional Conflicts: The Ordinary Functions of the Identity Clause' (2012) 31 Yearbook of European Law 263.

Günther V, 'Der Vorschlag der Europäischen Kommission für eine Verordnung zur Schaffung eines Rahmens für die Überprüfung ausländischer Direktinvestitionen in der Europäischen Union: Investitionskontrolle in der Union vor dem Hintergrund kompetenzrechtlicher Fragen' (2018) 157 Beiträge zum Transnationalen Wirtschaftsrecht 1.

Habersack M, '§§ 95–116 AktG' in Wulf Goette, Mathias Habersack, and Susanne Kalss (eds), *Münchener Kommentar zum Aktiengesetz: Band 2* (5th edn, CH Beck 2019).

Habersack M and others (eds), *Festschrift für Peter Ulmer zum 70. Geburtstag am 2. Januar 2003* (De Gruyter 2003).

Hahn M, 'Vital Interests and the Law of GATT: An Analysis of GATT's Security Exception' (1991) 12 Michigan Journal of International Law 558.

—— 'Art 207 AEUV' in Christian Calliess and Matthias Ruffert (eds), *EUV/AEUV: Das Verfassungsrecht der Europäischen Union mit Europäischer Grundrechtecharta* (5th edn, CH Beck 2016).

Haraldsdóttir K, 'The Nature of Neutrality in EU Law: Article 345 TFEU' (2020) 45 European Law Review 3.

Heide D, 'Nach 50Hertz – Bundesregierung wehrt sich gegen weitere Übernahme aus China' *Handelsblatt* (Düsseldorf, 29 July 2018) <https://www.handelsblatt.com/politik/deutschland/sicherheitsbedenken-nach-50hertz-bundesregierung-wehrt-sich-gegen-weitere-uebernahme-aus-china/22858764.html?ticket=ST-1488581-LNjdVpvWA51nohcplElP-ap6> accessed 2 February 2022.

Heiduk G and Kerlen-Prinz J, 'Direktinvestitionen in der Außenwirtschaftstheorie' in Roland Döhrn and Günter Heiduk (eds), *Theorie und Empirie der Direktinvestitionen* (Duncker & Humblot 1999) 23.

Heinemann A, 'Government Control of Cross-Border M&A: Legitimate Regulation or Protectionism?' (2012) 15 Journal of International Economic Law 843.

Herrmann C, 'Die Zukunft der mitgliedstaatlichen Investitionspolitik nach dem Vertrag von Lissabon' [2010] EuZW 207.

—— 'Europarechtliche Fragen der deutschen Investitionskontrolle' (2019) 22 Zeitschrift für europarechtliche Studien 429.

—— and Streinz R, '§ 11 Die EU als Mitglied der WTO' in Andreas von Arnauld (ed), *Europäische Außenbeziehungen* (Nomos 2014).

Herz B, *Unternehmenstransaktionen zwischen Niederlassungs- und Kapitalverkehrsfreiheit: Grundlegung einer Abgrenzungslehre* (Nomos 2014).

Hilf M and Goettsche G, 'The Relation of Economic and Non-Economic Principles in International Law' in Stefan Griller (ed), *International Economic Governance and Non-economic Concerns: New Challenges for the International Legal Order* (Springer 2003) 5.

Hindelang S, *The Free Movement of Capital and Foreign Direct Investment: The Scope of Protection in EU Law* (Oxford University Press 2009).

—— 'Die steuerliche Behandlung drittstaatlicher Dividenden und die europäischen Grundfreiheiten: Die teilweise (Wieder-)Eröffnung des Schutzbereiches der Kapitalverkehrsfreiheit für Dividenden aus drittstaatlichen Direktinvestitionen – zugleich eine Besprechung des Urteils in der Rechtssache Test Claimants in the FII Group Litigation II' [2013] IStR 77.

—— and Hagemeyer TM, 'Enemy at the Gates?: Die aktuellen Änderungen der Investitionsprüfvorschriften in der Außenwirtschaftsverordnung im Lichte des Unionsrechts' [2017] EuZW 882.

—— and Maydell N, 'Die Gemeinsame Europäische Investitionspolitik – Alter Wein in neuen Schläuchen?' in Marc Bungenberg, Jörn Griebel, and Steffen Hindelang (eds), *Internationaler Investitionsschutz und Europarecht* (Nomos 2010) 11.

—— and Moberg A (eds), *YSEC Yearbook of Socio-Economic Constitutions 2020: A Common European Law on Investment Screening (CELIS)* (YSEC Yearbook of Socio-Economic Constitutions, Springer 2021).

Hoekman B, 'Assessing the General Agreement on Trade in Services' in Will Martin and L Alan Winters (eds), *The Uruguay Round and the Developing Economies* Report number WDP307 (World Bank 1995) 327.

Hoffmann RT and Krajewski M (eds), *Coherence and Divergence in Services Trade Law* (Springer 2020).

Hofmann P, *The Impact of International Trade and FDI on Economic Growth and Technological Change* (Springer 2013).

Hopt KJ and others (eds), *Handelsgesetzbuch: Mit GmbH & Co. Handelsklauseln, Bank- und Börsenrecht, Transportrecht (ohne Seerecht)* (38th edn, CH Beck 2018).

Horn H and Mavroidis PC (eds), *Legal and Economic Principles of World Trade Law: Economics of Trade Agreements, Border Instruments, and National Treasures* (Cambridge University Press 2013).

Howse R, 'The World Trade Organization 20 Years On: Global Governance by Judiciary' (2016) 27 European Journal of International Law 9.

—— 'Making the WTO (Not So) Great Again: The Case Against Responding to the Trump Trade Agenda Through Reform of WTO Rules on Subsidies and State Enterprises' (2020) 23 Journal of International Economic Law 371.

Hudec RE, 'GATT/WTO Constraints on National Regulation: Requiem for an "Aim and Effects" Test' (1998) 32 International Lawyer 619.

Immenga U and Mestmäcker EJ (eds), *Wettbewerbsrecht: EU-Wettbewerbsrecht* (5th edn, CH Beck 2012).

Irion K and Williams J, 'Prospective Policy Study on Artificial Intelligence and EU Trade Policy' (Amsterdam, 2019) <https://www.ivir.nl/projects/prospective-policy-study-on-artificial-intelligence-and-eu-trade-policy/> accessed 2 February 2022.

Jacobs FG, 'The Internal Legal Effects of the EU's International Agreements and the Protection of Individual Rights' in Anthony Arnull and others (eds), *A Constitutional Order of States?: Essays in EU law in honour of Alan Dashwood* (Hart 2011) 13.

Jaeckel L, 'Art 346 AEUV' in Eberhard Grabitz, Meinhard Hilf, and Martin Nettesheim (eds), *Das Recht der Europäischen Union: EUV/AEUV* (71st edn, CH Beck 2020).

Javorcik BS, 'Can Survey Evidence Shed Light on Spillovers from Foreign Direct Investment?' (2008) 23 The World Bank Research Observer 139.

Jung P, 'Art 54 AEUV' in Ulrich Becker and others (eds), *EU-Kommentar* (4th edn, Nomos 2019).

Kahl W, '§ 124 Die allgemeine Handlungsfreiheit' in Hartmut Bauer, Detlef Merten, and Hans-Jürgen Papier (eds), *Handbuch der Grundrechte: Band V: Grundrechte in Deutschland - Einzelgrundrechte II* (CF Müller 2013).

Kainer F, '§ 4 Die binnenmarktliche Niederlassungsfreiheit der Unternehmen' in Peter-Christian Müller-Graff (ed), *Europäisches Wirtschaftsordnungsrecht* (Nomos 2015).

Kalotay K and Hunya G, 'Privatization and FDI in Central and Eastern Europe' (2000) 9 Transnational Corporations 39.

Kamperman Sanders A (ed), *The Principle of National Treatment in International Economic Law: Trade, Investment and Intellectual Property* (Elgar 2014).

Kemmerer M, *Kapitalverkehrsfreiheit und Drittstaaten* (Nomos 2010).

Kern A and Andenæs MT (eds), *The World Trade Organization and Trade in Services* (Martinus Njihoff 2008).

Kerner A, 'What We Talk About When We Talk About Foreign Direct Investment' (2014) 58 International Studies Quarterly 804.

Kilapatrick C, 'Art 21 – Non-Discrimination' in Steve Peers and others (eds), *The EU Charter of Fundamental Rights: A Commentary* (Hart 2014).

Kindleberger CP, *American Business Abroad: Six Lectures on Direct Investment* (2nd edn, Yale University Press 1970).

Kindler P, 'Der reale Niederlassungsbegriff nach dem VALE-Urteil des EuGH' [2012] EuZW 888.

Kingreen T, 'Arts 34–36 AEUV' in Christian Calliess and Matthias Ruffert (eds), *EUV/AEUV: Das Verfassungsrecht der Europäischen Union mit Europäischer Grundrechtecharta* (5th edn, CH Beck 2016).

Klöpfer M, *Missbrauch im Europäischen Zivilverfahrensrecht* (Mohr Siebeck 2016).

Klotz R, 'Art 106 AEUV' in Hans von der Groeben, Jürgen Schwarze, and Armin Hatje (eds), *Europäisches Unionsrecht: Vertrag über die Europäische Union - Vertrag über die Arbeitsweise der Europäischen Union - Charta der Grundrechte der Europäischen Union* (7th edn, Nomos 2015).

Kluth W, 'Art 57 AEUV' in Christian Calliess and Matthias Ruffert (eds), *EUV/AEUV: Das Verfassungsrecht der Europäischen Union mit Europäischer Grundrechtecharta* (5th edn, CH Beck 2016).

Kok J de, 'Towards a European Framework for Foreign Investment Reviews' (2019) 44 European Law Review 24.

Körber T, 'Art 3 FKVO' in Ulrich Immenga and Ernst-Joachim Mestmäcker (eds), *Wettbewerbsrecht: EU-Wettbewerbsrecht* (5th edn, CH Beck 2012).

Korte S, 'Art 49 AEUV' in Christian Calliess and Matthias Ruffert (eds), *EUV/AEUV: Das Verfassungsrecht der Europäischen Union mit Europäischer Grundrechtecharta* (5th edn, CH Beck 2016a).

—— 'Art 54 AEUV' in Christian Calliess and Matthias Ruffert (eds), *EUV/AEUV: Das Verfassungsrecht der Europäischen Union mit Europäischer Grundrechtecharta* (5th edn, CH Beck 2016b).

—— 'Regelungsoptionen zum Schutz vor Fremdabhängigkeiten aufgrund von Investitionen in versorgungsrelevante Unternehmen' [2019] WiVerw (GewA) 79.

Kotthaus J, *Binnenmarktrecht und externe Kapitalverkehrsfreiheit* (Nomos 2012).

Krajewski M, *Verfassungsperspektiven und Legitimation des Rechts der Welthandelsorganisation (WTO)* (Duncker & Humblot 2001).

—— *National Regulation and Trade Liberalization in Services: The Legal Impact of the General Agreement on Trade in Services on National Regulatory Autonomy* (Kluwer Law International 2003).

—— 'Art VI' in Rüdiger Wolfrum, Peter-Tobias Stoll, and Clemens Feinäugle (eds), *WTO – Trade in Services* (Martinus Njihoff 2008).

Krolop K, 'Staatliche Einlasskontrolle bei Staatsfonds und anderen ausländischen Investoren im Gefüge von Kapitalmarktregulierung, nationalem und internationalem Wirtschaftsrecht: Anmerkungen zum Referentenentwurf eines 13. Gesetzes zur Änderung des Außenwirtschaftsgesetzes' [2008] Humboldt Forum Recht 1.

Krugman PR, Obstfeld M, and Melitz MJ, *International Economics: Theory & Policy* (Global edition, Pearson 2017).

Kumpan C, 'VO (EU) Nr 596/2014' in Klaus J Hopt and others (eds), *Handelsgesetzbuch: Mit GmbH & Co. Handelsklauseln, Bank- und Börsenrecht, Transportrecht (ohne Seerecht)* (38th edn, CH Beck 2018).

Kuner C, 'The Internet and the Global Reach of EU Law' in Marise Cremona and Joanne Scott (eds), *EU Law Beyond EU Borders: The Extraterritorial Reach of EU Law* (Oxford University Press 2019) 112.

La Feria R de and Vogenauer S (eds), *Prohibition of Abuse of Law: A New General Principle of EU Law?* (Hart 2011).

La Rochère JD de, 'L'effet direct des accords internationaux' in European Court of Justice (ed), *The Court of Justice and the Construction of Europe: Analyses and Perspectives on Sixty Years of Case-law: La Cour de Justice et la construction de l'Europe: Analyses et Perspectives de Soixante Ans de Jurisprudence* (TMC Asser 2013) 637.

Lackhoff K, *Die Niederlassungsfreiheit des EGV - nur ein Gleichheits- oder auch ein Freiheitsrecht?* (Duncker & Humblot 2000).

Lannon E and others (eds), *The European Union in the World: Essays in Honour of Professor Marc Maresceau* (Martinus Njihoff 2014).

Lecheler H and Germelmann CF, *Zugangsbeschränkungen für Investitionen aus Drittstaaten im deutschen und europäischen Energierecht* (Mohr Siebeck 2010).

Leible S and Streinz R, 'Art 36 AEUV' in Eberhard Grabitz, Meinhard Hilf, and Martin Nettesheim (eds), *Das Recht der Europäischen Union: EUV/AEUV* (71st edn, CH Beck 2020).

Lenaerts K, 'Exploring the Limits of the EU Charter of Fundamental Rights' (2012) 8 European Constitutional Law Review 375.

—— 'Direct Applicability and Direct Effect of International Law in the EU Legal Order' in Erwan Lannon and others (eds), *The European Union in the World: Essays in Honour of Professor Marc Maresceau* (Martinus Njihoff 2014) 45.

Lenz CO and Borchardt KD (eds), *EU-Verträge Kommentar: EUV – AEUV – GRCh* (6th edn, Bundesanzeiger Verlag 2013).

Lester S and Zhu H, 'A Proposal for "Rebalancing" to Deal with "National Security" Trade Restrictions' (2019) 42 Fordham International Law Journal 1451.

Lim AH and de Meester B (eds), *WTO Domestic Regulation and Services Trade: Putting Principles into Practice* (Cambridge University Press 2014).

Lippert B, Ondarza N von, and Perthes V, 'European Strategic Autonomy: Actors, Issues, Conflicts of Interests' (March 2019) SWP Research Paper 4 <https://www.swp-berlin.org/fileadmin/contents/products/research_papers/2019RP04_lpt_orz_prt_web.pdf> accessed 2 February 2022.

Lipsey RE, 'Home- and Host-Country Effects of Foreign Direct Investment' in Robert E Baldwin and L Alan Winters (eds), *Challenges to Globalization: Analyzing the Economics* (University of Chicago Press 2004) 333.

Lübke J, *Der Erwerb von Gesellschaftsanteilen zwischen Kapitalverkehrs- und Niederlassungsfreiheit* (Nomos 2006).

—— '§ 5 Die binnenmarktliche Kapital- und Zahlungsverkehrsfreiheit' in Peter-Christian Müller-Graff (ed), *Europäisches Wirtschaftsordnungsrecht* (Nomos 2015).

Lv P and Spigarelli F, 'The Integration of Chinese and European Renewable Energy Markets: The Role of Chinese Foreign Direct Investments' (2015) 81 Energy Policy 14.

Malbon J, Lawson C, and Davison MJ, *The WTO Agreement on Trade-Related Aspects of Intellectual Property Rights: A Commentary* (Elgar 2014).

Manthey NV, *Bindung und Schutz öffentlicher Unternehmen durch die Grundfreiheiten des europäischen Gemeinschaftsrechts* (Lang 2001).

Maresceau M, 'The Court of Justice and Bilateral Agreements' in European Court of Justice (ed), *The Court of Justice and the Construction of Europe: Analyses and Perspectives on Sixty Years of Case-law: La Cour de Justice et la construction de l'Europe: Analyses et Perspectives de Soixante Ans de Jurisprudence* (TMC Asser 2013) 693.

Martin W and Winters LA (eds), *The Uruguay Round and the Developing Economies* Report number WDP307 (World Bank 1995).

Martini M, 'Zu Gast bei Freunden?: Staatsfonds als Herausforderung an das europäische und internationale Recht' [2008] DÖV 314.

Martin-Prat M, 'The European Commission Proposal on FDI Screening' in Jacques H J Bourgeois (ed), *EU Framework for Foreign Direct Investment Control* (Kluwer Law International 2020) 95.

Matthes J, 'Unternehmensübernahmen durch chinesische Firmen in Deutschland und Europa: Unter welchen Bedingungen besteht Handlungsbedarf?' (6 October 2017) IW-Report 30/2016.

Mattoo A, 'National Treatment in the GATS: Corner-Stone or Pandora's Box?' (1997) 31 Journal of World Trade 107.

—— Stern RM, and Zanini G (eds), *A Handbook of International Trade in Services* (Oxford University Press 2008).

Mavroidis PC, *The General Agreement on Tariffs and Trade: A Commentary* (Oxford University Press 2005).

—— 'Highway XVI Re-visited: the Road from Non-discrimination to Market Access in GATS' (2007) 6 World Trade Review 1.

—— *The Regulation of International Trade* (MIT Press 2016).

—— *The Regulation of International Trade, Volume 3: The General Agreement on Trade in Services* (MIT Press 2020).

—— and Sapir A, 'China and the World Trade Organisation: Towards a Better Fit' (13 June 2019) Bruegel Working Papers 6 <https://www.bruegel.org/2019/06/china-and-the-world-trade-organisation-towards-a-better-fit/> accessed 2 February 2022.

—— and Sapir A, *China and the WTO: Why Multilateralism Still Matters* (Princeton University Press 2021).

—— and Wolfe R, 'Private Standards and the WTO: Reclusive No More' (2017) 16 World Trade Review 1.

Meester B de, 'Testing European Prudential Conditions for Banking Mergers in the Light of Most Favoured Nation in the GATS' (2008) 11 Journal of International Economic Law 609.

Melo ML de, 'Protection of Domestic Investors under the WTO and International Investment Regimes' (19) 2020 World Trade Review 589.

Mestmäcker EJ and Schweitzer H, 'Art 106 Abs 1 AEUV' in Ulrich Immenga and Ernst-Joachim Mestmäcker (eds), *Wettbewerbsrecht: EU-Wettbewerbsrecht* (5th edn, CH Beck 2012).

Meunier S and Nicolaidis K, 'The Geopoliticization of European Trade and Investment Policy' (2019) 57 Journal of Common Market Studies 103.

Miroudot S and Ragoussis A, 'Actors in the International Investment Scenario: Objectives, Performance and Advantages of Affiliates of State-owned Enterprises and Sovereign Wealth Funds' in Roberto Echandi and Pierre Sauvé (eds), *Prospects in International Investment Law and Policy: World Trade Forum* (Cambridge University Press 2013) 51.

Mishra N, 'Privacy, Cybersecurity, and GATS Article XIV: A New Frontier for Trade and Internet Regulation?' (2020a) 19 World Trade Review 341.

—— 'The Trade: (Cyber)Security Dilemma and Its Impact on Global Cybersecurity Governance' (2020b) 54 Journal of World Trade 567.

Moberg A and Hindelang S, 'The Art of Casting Political Dissent in Law: The EU's Framework for the Screening of Foreign Direct Investment' (2020) 57 Common Market Law Review 1427.

Moran TH, *Harnessing Foreign Direct Investment for Development: Policies for Developed and Developing Countries* (Center for Global Development 2006).

—— Graham EM, and Blomström M (eds), *Does Foreign Direct Investment Promote Development?* (Institute for International Economics 2005a).

—— Graham EM, and Blomström M, 'Introduction and Overview' in Theodore H Moran, Edward M Graham, and Magnus Blomström (eds), *Does Foreign Direct Investment Promote Development?* (Institute for International Economics 2005b) 1.

Mortelmans K, 'The Relationship Between the Treaty Rules and Community Measures for the Establishment and Functioning of the Internal Market – Towards a Concordance Rule' (2002) 39 Common Market Law Review 1303.

Mülbert P, 'Konzeption des europäischen Kapitalmarktrechts für Wertpapierdienstleistungen' [2001] WM 2085.

Müller-Graff P-C, 'Einflußregulierung in Gesellschaften zwischen Binnenmarktrecht und Eigentumsordnung' in Mathias Habersack and others (eds), *Festschrift für Peter Ulmer zum 70. Geburtstag am 2. Januar 2003* (De Gruyter 2003) 929.

—— 'Art 34 AEUV' in Hans von der Groeben, Jürgen Schwarze, and Armin Hatje (eds), *Europäisches Unionsrecht: Vertrag über die Europäische Union - Vertrag über die Arbeitsweise der Europäischen Union - Charta der Grundrechte der Europäischen Union* (7th edn, Nomos 2015a).

—— (ed), *Europäisches Wirtschaftsordnungsrecht* (Nomos 2015b).

—— 'Art 49 AEUV' in Rudolf Streinz (ed), *EUV/AEUV: Vertrag über die Europäische Union und Vertrag über die Arbeitsweise der Europäischen Union* (3rd edn, CH Beck 2018a).

—— 'Art 52 AEUV' in Rudolf Streinz (ed), *EUV/AEUV: Vertrag über die Europäische Union und Vertrag über die Arbeitsweise der Europäischen Union* (3rd edn, CH Beck 2018b).

—— 'Art 54 AEUV' in Rudolf Streinz (ed), *EUV/AEUV: Vertrag über die Europäische Union und Vertrag über die Arbeitsweise der Europäischen Union* (3rd edn, CH Beck 2018c).

Müller-Ibold T, 'Foreign Investment in Germany: Restrictions Based on Public Security Concerns and Their Compatibility with EU Law' [2010] European Yearbook of International Economic Law 103.

—— 'Vorb Art 206–208 AEUV' in Carl O Lenz and Klaus-Dieter Borchardt (eds), *EU-Verträge Kommentar: EUV – AEUV – GRCh* (6th edn, Bundesanzeiger Verlag 2013).

Muller G, 'Troubled Relationships under the GATS: Tensions between Market Access (Article XVI), National Treatment (Article XVII), and Domestic Regulation (Article VI)' (2017) 16 World Trade Review 449.

Munin N, *Legal Guide to GATS* (Kluwer Law International 2010).

Neergaard A, 'The Adoption of the Regulation Establishing a Framework for Screening of Foreign Direct Investments into the European Union' in Jacques H J Bourgeois (ed), *EU Framework for Foreign Direct Investment Control* (Kluwer Law International 2020) 151.

Nettesheim M, 'Unternehmensübernahmen durch Staatsfonds: Europarechtliche Vorgaben und Schranken' (2008) 172 ZHR 729.

—— 'Kompetenzen' in Armin von Bogdandy and Jürgen Bast (eds), *Europäisches Verfassungsrecht: Theoretische und dogmatische Grundzüge* (2nd edn, Springer 2009) 389.

—— 'Art 207 AEUV' in Rudolf Streinz (ed), *EUV/AEUV: Vertrag über die Europäische Union und Vertrag über die Arbeitsweise der Europäischen Union* (3rd edn, CH Beck 2018).

—— 'Art 2 AEUV' in Eberhard Grabitz, Meinhard Hilf, and Martin Nettesheim (eds), *Das Recht der Europäischen Union: EUV/AEUV* (71st edn, CH Beck 2020).

Ni V, 'EU parliament 'freezes' China trade deal over sanction', *The Guardian* (London, 20 May 2021) <https://www.theguardian.com/world/2021/may/20/eu-parliament-freezes-china-trade-deal-over-sanctions> accessed 2 February 2022.

Obwexer W, 'Art 4 EUV' in Hans von der Groeben, Jürgen Schwarze, and Armin Hatje (eds), *Europäisches Unionsrecht: Vertrag über die Europäische Union - Vertrag über die Arbeitsweise der Europäischen Union - Charta der Grundrechte der Europäischen Union* (7th edn, Nomos 2015a).

—— 'Art 4 AEUV' in Hans von der Groeben, Jürgen Schwarze, and Armin Hatje (eds), *Europäisches Unionsrecht: Vertrag über die Europäische Union - Vertrag über die Arbeitsweise der Europäischen Union - Charta der Grundrechte der Europäischen Union* (7th edn, Nomos 2015b).

OECD, 'Acquisition- and Ownership-related Policies to Safeguard Essential Security Interests: Current and Emerging Trends, Observed Designs, and Policy Practice in 62 Economies' (Research Note by the OECD Secretariat, Paris, May 2020a).

—— 'Investment Screening in Times of COVID-19 – and Beyond' (Paris, 7 July 2020b) Tackling Coronavirus (Covid-19): Contributing to a Global Effort.

Ohler C, 'Die Kapitalverkehrsfreiheit und ihre Schranken' [1997] WM 1801.

—— *Europäische Kapital- und Zahlungsverkehrsfreiheit: Kommentar zu den Artikeln 56 bis 60 EGV, der Geldwäscherichtlinie und Überweisungsrichtlinie* (Springer 2002).

—— 'Zulässige Versagung der Erlaubnis zur gewerbsmäßigen Kreditvergabe: Anmerkung zu EuGH, Urteil vom 3 Oktober 2006, Rs C-452/04 (Fidium Finanz)' [2006] EuZW 691.

Ohlin BG, Hesselborn PO, and Wijkman PM (eds), *The International Allocation of Economic Activity: Proceedings of a Nobel Symposium held at Stockholm* (Macmillan 1977).

O'Keeffe D (ed), *Judicial Review in European Union Law: Libor Amicorum in Honour of Lord Slynn of Hadley* Libor Amicorum Lord Slynn (Kluwer Law International 2000a).

—— and Bavasso A, 'Four Freedoms, One Market and National Competence: In Search of a Dividing Line' in David O'Keeffe (ed), *Judicial Review in European Union Law: Libor Amicorum in Honour of Lord Slynn of Hadley* Libor Amicorum Lord Slynn (Kluwer Law International 2000b) 541.

Olsen HP, Jemielniak J, and Nielsen L (eds), *Establishing Judicial Authority in International Economic Law* (Cambridge University Press 2016).

Ortino F, *Basic Legal Instruments for the Liberalisation of Trade: A comparative analysis of EC and WTO law* (Hart 2004a).

—— 'The Principle of Non-Discrimination and its Exceptions in GATS: Selected Legal Issues' in Alexander Kern and Mads T Andenæs (eds), *The World Trade Organization and Trade in Services* (Martinus Njihoff 2008) 173.

—— and Ernst-Ulrich Petersmann (eds), *The WTO Dispute Settlement System 1995-2003* (Kluwer Law International 2004b).

Pache E, '§ 10 Grundfreiheiten' in Reiner Schulze and others (eds), *Europarecht: Handbuch für die deutsche Rechtspraxis* (3rd edn, Nomos 2015).

Panizzon M, Pohl N, and Sauvé P (eds), *GATS and the Regulation of International Trade in Services : World Trade Forum* (Cambridge University Press 2008).

Patzner A and Nagler J, 'Regelung eines Mitgliedstaats zur Beseitigung der Doppelbesteuerung von Gewinnausschüttungen - Kronos International Inc./FA Leverkusen: Anmerkung zu EuGH, Urt. v. 11.9.2014, C-47/12, Kronos International Inc./FA Leverkusen' [2014] IStR 731.

Pauletto C, 'Comment: Digital Trade: Technology versus Legislators' in Marion Panizzon, Nicole Pohl, and Pierre Sauvé (eds), *GATS and the Regulation of International Trade in Services : World Trade Forum* (Cambridge University Press 2008) 530.

Pauwelyn J, 'Rien ne Va Plus? Distinguishing Domestic Regulation from Market Access in GATT and GATS' (2005) 4 World Trade Review 131.

—— 'Comment: The Unbearable Lightness of Likeness' in Marion Panizzon, Nicole Pohl, and Pierre Sauvé (eds), *GATS and the Regulation of International Trade in Services: World Trade Forum* (Cambridge University Press 2008) 358.

—— 'Rule-Based Trade 2.0? The Rise of Informal Rules and International Standards and How they May Outcompete WTO Treaties' (2014) 17 Journal of International Economic Law 739.

—— 'Minority Rules: Precedent and Participation Before the WTO Appellate Body' in Henrik P Olsen, Joanna Jemielniak, and Laura Nielsen (eds), *Establishing Judicial Authority in International Economic Law* (Cambridge University Press 2016) 141.

Pechstein M, Nowak C, and Häde U (eds), *Frankfurter Kommentar zu EUV, GRC und AEUV* (Mohr Siebeck 2017).

Peers S and others (eds), *The EU Charter of Fundamental Rights: A Commentary* (Hart 2014a).

—— and Prechal S, 'Article 52 – Scope and Interpretation of Rights and Principles' in Steve Peers and others (eds), *The EU Charter of Fundamental Rights: A Commentary* (Hart 2014b) 1498.

Perea JR and Stephenson M, 'Outward FDI from Developing Countries' in World Bank Group (ed), *Global Investment Competitiveness Report 2017/2018: Foreign Investor Perspectives and Policy Implications* (World Bank Group 2017) 101.

Perlmutter HV, 'The Tortuous Evolution of the Multinational Corporation' (1969) 4 Columbia Journal of World Business 9.

Peter S, *Public Interest and Common Good in International Law* (Helbing Lichtenhahn 2012).

Pinchis-Paulsen M, 'Trade Multilateralism and U.S. National Security: The Making of the GATT Security Exceptions' (2020) 41 Michigan Journal of International Law 109.

Pogoretskyy V and Talus K, 'The WTO Panel Report in EU–Energy Package and Its Implications for the EU's Gas Market and Energy Security' (2020) 19 World Trade Review 531.

Pohl J, 'Emergency, Security and Strategic Autonomy in EU Economic Regulation' (2020) 21 ERA Forum 143.

Prazeres TL, 'Trade and National Security: Rising Risks for the WTO' (2020) 19 World Trade Review 137.

Preisser MM, *Sovereign Wealth Funds: Entwicklung eines umfassenden Konzepts für die Regulierung von Staatsfonds* (Mohr Siebeck 2013).

Proelss A, 'Art 34 VCLT' in Oliver Dörr and Kirsten Schmalenbach (eds), *Vienna Convention on the Law of Treaties: A Commentary* (2nd edn, Springer 2018a).

—— 'Art 36 VCLT' in Oliver Dörr and Kirsten Schmalenbach (eds), *Vienna Convention on the Law of Treaties: A Commentary* (2nd edn, Springer 2018b).

Puig RV, 'The Scope of the New Exclusive Competence of the European Union with Regard to 'Foreign Direct Investment'' (2013) 40 Legal Issues of Economic Integration 133.

Puttler A, 'Art 4 EUV' in Christian Calliess and Matthias Ruffert (eds), *EUV/AEUV: Das Verfassungsrecht der Europäischen Union mit Europäischer Grundrechtecharta* (5th edn, CH Beck 2016).

Randelzhofer A and Forsthoff U, 'Art 56, Art 57 AEUV' in Eberhard Grabitz, Meinhard Hilf, and Martin Nettesheim (eds), *Das Recht der Europäischen Union: EUV/AEUV* (71st edn, CH Beck 2020).

Ranjan P, 'National Security Exception in the General Agreement on Tariffs and Trade (GATT) and India–Pakistan Trade' (2020) 54 Journal of World Trade 643.

Rauber J, *Zur Grundrechtsberechtigung fremdstaatlich beherrschter juristischer Personen: Art. 19 Abs. 3 GG unter dem Einfluss von EMRK, EU-GRCh und allgemeinem Völkerrecht* (Mohr Siebeck 2019).

Regan DH, 'Regulatory Purpose and "Like Products" in Article III:4 of the GATT (with Additional Remarks on Article III:2)' in George A Bermann (ed), *Trade and Human Health and Safety* (Cambridge University Press 2006) 190.

Ress G and Ukrow J, 'Art 63 AEUV' in Eberhard Grabitz, Meinhard Hilf, and Martin Nettesheim (eds), *Das Recht der Europäischen Union: EUV/AEUV* (71st edn, CH Beck 2020a).

—— 'Art 64 AEUV' in Eberhard Grabitz, Meinhard Hilf, and Martin Nettesheim (eds), *Das Recht der Europäischen Union: EUV/AEUV* (71st edn, CH Beck 2020b).

—— 'Art 65 AEUV' in Eberhard Grabitz, Meinhard Hilf, and Martin Nettesheim (eds), *Das Recht der Europäischen Union: EUV/AEUV* (71st edn, CH Beck 2020c).

Ringe W-G, 'Sparking Regulatory Competition in European Company Law: The Impact of the Centros Line of Case Law and its Concept of "Abuse of Law"' in Rita de La Feria and Stefan Vogenauer (eds), *Prohibition of Abuse of Law: A New General Principle of EU Law?* (Hart 2011) 107.

Roberts A, Choer Moraes H, and Ferguson V, 'Toward a Geoeconomic Order in International Trade and Investment' (2019) 22 Journal of International Economic Law 655.

Rodrik D, *The New Global Economy and Developing Countries: Making Openness Work* (Johns Hopkins University Press 1999).

Rosas A, 'The European Court of Justice and Public International Law' in Jan Wouters, André Nollkaemper, and Erika de Wet (eds), *The Europeanisation of International Law: The Status of International Law in the EU and its Member States* (TMC Asser 2008) 71.

Roth GH, 'Das Ende der Briefkastengründung? - Vale contra Centros' [2012] ZIP 1744.

Roth W-H, 'Investitionsbeschränkungen im deutschen Außenwirtschaftsrecht: Europa- und völkerrechtliche Probleme' (2009) 21 ZBB 257.

Rugman AM, 'The Theory and Regulation of Emerging Market Multinational Enterprises' in Karl P Sauvant, McAllister, Geraldine, and Wolfgang A Maschek (eds), *Foreign Direct Investments From Emerging Markets: The Challenges Ahead* (Palgrave Macmillan 2010) 75.

Rüthers B, Fischer C, and Birk A, *Rechtstheorie: Mit juristischer Methodenlehre* (10th edn, CH Beck 2018).

Ruthig J and Storr S, *Öffentliches Wirtschaftsrecht* (CF Müller 2015).

Sasse JP, *An Economic Analysis of Bilateral Investment Treaties* (Gabler Verlag 2011).

Sauvant KP (ed), *Investing in the United States: Is the US ready for FDI from China?* (Elgar 2009).

—— Maschek WA, and McAllister, Geraldine, 'Foreign Direct Investment by Emerging Market Multinational Enterprises, the Impact of the Financial Crisis and Recession, and Challenges Abroad' in Karl P Sauvant, McAllister, Geraldine, and Wolfgang A Maschek (eds), *Foreign Direct Investments From Emerging Markets: The Challenges Ahead* (Palgrave Macmillan 2010a) 3.

—— McAllister G, Maschek WA (eds), *Foreign Direct Investments From Emerging Markets: The Challenges Ahead* (Palgrave Macmillan 2010b).

—— Sachs LE, and Jongbloed WS (eds), *Sovereign Investment: Concerns and Policy Reactions* (Oxford University Press 2012).

Sauvé P, 'Multilateral Rules on Investment: Is Forward Movement Possible?' (2006) 9 Journal of International Economic Law 325.

Saydé A, 'Defining the Concept of Abuse of Union Law' (2014) 33 Yearbook of European Law 138.

Scharf D, 'Die Kapitalverkehrsfreiheit gegenüber Drittstaaten' (2008) 76 Beiträge zum Transnationalen Wirtschaftsrecht 1.

Schill SW, 'Der Schutz von Auslandsinvestitionen in Deutschland im Mehrebenensystem: deutsches, europäisches und internationales Recht' (2010) 135 AöR 498-540.

—— 'The European Union's Foreign Direct Investment Screening Paradox: Tightening Inward Investment Control to Further External Investment Liberalization' (2019) 46 Legal Issues of Economic Integration 105.

—— and Krenn C, 'Art 4 EUV' in Eberhard Grabitz, Meinhard Hilf, and Martin Nettesheim (eds), *Das Recht der Europäischen Union: EUV/AEUV* (71st edn, CH Beck 2020).

Schloemann H and Ohlhoff S, '"Constitutionalization" and Dispute Settlement in the WTO: National Security as an Issue of Competence' (1999) 93 American Journal of International Law 424.

Schmalenbach K, 'Art 26 VCLT' in Oliver Dörr and Kirsten Schmalenbach (eds), *Vienna Convention on the Law of Treaties: A Commentary* (2nd edn, Springer 2018).

Schmitt R, *Die Kompetenzen der Europäischen Union für ausländische Investitionen in und aus Drittstaaten* (Utz 2013).

Schnitger A, 'Die Kapitalverkehrsfreiheit im Verhältnis zu Drittstaaten: Vorabentscheidungsersuchen in den Rs. van Hilten, Fidium Finanz AG und Lasertec' [2005] IStR 493.

Schön W (ed), *Gedächtnisschrift für Brigitte Knobbe-Keuk* (Dr Otto Schmidt 1997a).

—— 'Europäische Kapitalverkehrsfreiheit und nationales Steuerrecht' in Wolfgang Schön (ed), *Gedächtnisschrift für Brigitte Knobbe-Keuk* (Dr Otto Schmidt 1997b) 743.

—— 'Das Bild des Gesellschafters im Europäischen Gesellschaftsrecht' (2000) 64 RabelsZ 1.

—— 'Der Kapitalverkehr mit Drittstaaten und das internationale Steuerrecht' in Rudolf Gocke (ed), *Körperschaftsteuer, internationales Steuerrecht, Doppelbesteuerung: Festschrift für Franz Wassermeyer zum 65. Geburtstag* (CH Beck 2005) 489.

—— 'Kapitalverkehrsfreiheit und Niederlassungsfreiheit' in Thomas Ackermann and Johannes Köndgen (eds), *Privat- und Wirtschaftsrecht in Europa: Festschrift für Wulf-Henning Roth zum 70. Geburtstag* (CH Beck 2015) 551.

—— 'Free Movement of Capital and Freedom of Establishment' (2016) 17 European Business Organization Law Review 229.

Schraufl M, 'Die Auswirkungen der Konkurrenz zwischen Niederlassung- und Kapitalverkehrsfreiheit auf Drittstaatensachverhalte im Steuerrecht' [2007] RIW 603.

Schröder M, 'Art 26 AEUV' in Rudolf Streinz (ed), *EUV/AEUV: Vertrag über die Europäische Union und Vertrag über die Arbeitsweise der Europäischen Union* (3rd edn, CH Beck 2018a).

Schröder W, 'Art 36 AEUV' in Rudolf Streinz (ed), *EUV/AEUV: Vertrag über die Europäische Union und Vertrag über die Arbeitsweise der Europäischen Union* (3rd edn, CH Beck 2018b).

Schröter H, Zurkinden P, and Lauterburg BC, 'Vorb zu Artt 101 bis 105' in Hans von der Groeben, Jürgen Schwarze, and Armin Hatje (eds), *Europäisches Unionsrecht: Vertrag über die Europäische Union - Vertrag über die Arbeitsweise der Europäischen Union - Charta der Grundrechte der Europäischen Union* (7th edn, Nomos 2015).

Schuelken T and Sichla B, 'Außenwirtschaftsrechtlicher Schutz vor drittstaatlichen Investitionen in Kritische Infrastrukturen: Notwendiger Schutz berechtigter Interessen oder Verstoß gegen das Europarecht?' [2019] NVwZ 1406.

Schulze R and others (eds), *Europarecht: Handbuch für die deutsche Rechtspraxis* (3rd edn, Nomos 2015).

Schweitzer H, 'Sovereign Wealth Funds: Market Investors or "Imperialist Capitalists"? The European Response to Direct Investment by Non-EU State-Controlled Entities' [2011] European Yearbook of International Economic Law 79.

Sedlaczek M and Züger M, 'Art 64 AEUV' in Rudolf Streinz (ed), *EUV/AEUV: Vertrag über die Europäische Union und Vertrag über die Arbeitsweise der Europäischen Union* (3rd edn, CH Beck 2018a).

—— 'Art 65 AEUV' in Rudolf Streinz (ed), *EUV/AEUV: Vertrag über die Europäische Union und Vertrag über die Arbeitsweise der Europäischen Union* (3rd edn, CH Beck 2018b).

Selivanova Y (ed), *Regulation of Energy in International Trade Law: WTO, NAFTA, and Energy Charter* (Kluwer Law International 2011).

Smit D, *EU Freedoms, Non-EU Countries and Company Taxation* (Kluwer Law International 2012).

Sørensen KE, 'Reconciling Secondary Legislation and the Treaty Rights of Free Movement' (2011) 36 European Law Review 339.

Sornarajah M, *The International Law on Foreign Investment* (4th edn, Cambridge University Press 2017).

Spies K, *Die Kapitalverkehrsfreiheit in Konkurrenz zu den anderen Grundfreiheiten* (LexisNexis 2015).

Spindler G, '§§ 76–94' in Wulf Goette, Mathias Habersack, and Susanne Kalss (eds), *Münchener Kommentar zum Aktiengesetz: Band 2* (5th edn, CH Beck 2019).

Stevenson A and Brown L, *Shorter Oxford English Dictionary on Historical Principles* (6th edn, Oxford University Press 2007).

Stoll PT, Busche J, and Arend K (eds), *WTO – Trade-Related Aspects of Intellectual Property Rights* (Martinus Njihoff 2009).

Storr S, *Der Staat als Unternehmer: Öffentliche Unternehmen in der Freiheits- und Gleichheitsdogmatik des nationalen Rechts und des Gemeinschaftsrechts* (Mohr Siebeck 2001).

Streinz R (ed), *EUV/AEUV: Vertrag über die Europäische Union und Vertrag über die Arbeitsweise der Europäischen Union* (3rd edn, CH Beck 2018a).

—— 'Art 5 EUV' in Rudolf Streinz (ed), *EUV/AEUV: Vertrag über die Europäische Union und Vertrag über die Arbeitsweise der Europäischen Union* (3rd edn, CH Beck 2018b).

Strik P, *Shaping the Single European Market in the Field of Foreign Direct Investment* (Hart 2014).

Svetlicinii A, *Chinese State Owned Enterprises and EU Merger Control* (Routledge 2021).

Sykes AO, 'Economic "Necessity" of International Law' (2015) 109 American Journal of International Law 296.

Syrpis P, 'The Relationship between Primary and Secondary Law in the EU' (2015) 52 Common Market Law Review 461.

Terhechte JP, 'Art 3 EUV' in Eberhard Grabitz, Meinhard Hilf, and Martin Nettesheim (eds), *Das Recht der Europäischen Union: EUV/AEUV* (71st edn, CH Beck 2020).

Thym D, 'Auswärtige Gewalt' in Armin von Bogdandy and Jürgen Bast (eds), *Europäisches Verfassungsrecht: Theoretische und dogmatische Grundzüge* (2nd edn, Springer 2009) 441.

Tiedje J, 'Vorb Artt 49–55' in Hans von der Groeben, Jürgen Schwarze, and Armin Hatje (eds), *Europäisches Unionsrecht: Vertrag über die Europäische Union - Vertrag über die Arbeitsweise der Europäischen Union - Charta der Grundrechte der Europäischen Union* (7th edn, Nomos 2015a).

—— 'Art 49 AEUV' in Hans von der Groeben, Jürgen Schwarze, and Armin Hatje (eds), *Europäisches Unionsrecht: Vertrag über die Europäische Union - Vertrag über die Arbeitsweise der Europäischen Union - Charta der Grundrechte der Europäischen Union* (7th edn, Nomos 2015b).

—— 'Art 54 AEUV' in Hans von der Groeben, Jürgen Schwarze, and Armin Hatje (eds), *Europäisches Unionsrecht: Vertrag über die Europäische Union - Vertrag über die Arbeitsweise der Europäischen Union - Charta der Grundrechte der Europäischen Union* (7th edn, Nomos 2015c).

—— and Troberg P, 'Art 43 EG' in Hans von der Groeben (ed), *Kommentar zum Vertrag über die Europäische Union und zur Gründung der Europäischen Gemeinschaft: Band 1* (6th edn, Nomos 2003).

Tietje C, 'Beschränkungen ausländischer Unternehmensbeteiligungen zum Schutz vor „Staatsfonds" – Rechtliche Grenzen eines neuen Investitionsprotektionismus' (2007) 26 Policy Papers on Transnational Economic Law 1.

—— (ed), *International Investment Protection and Arbitration: Theoretical and Practical Perspectives* (Berliner Wissenschafts-Verlag 2008).

—— 'Die Außenwirtschaftsverfassung der EU nach dem Vertrag von Lissabon' (2009) 83 Beiträge zum Transnationalen Wirtschaftsrecht 1.

—— '§ 10 Niederlassungsfreiheit' in Dirk Ehlers and Ulrich Becker (eds), *Europäische Grundrechte und Grundfreiheiten* (4th edn, De Gruyter 2014).

Titi C, 'The Evolution of Substantive Investment Protections in Recent Trade and Investment Treaties' (Geneva, November 2018) <https://ictsd.iisd.org/themes/global-economic-gover nance/research/the-evolution-of-substantive-investment-protections-in> accessed 2 February 2022.

Torremans P, 'Art 17 – Right to Property' in Steve Peers and others (eds), *The EU Charter of Fundamental Rights: A Commentary* (Hart 2014).

Tountopoulos V, 'Niederlassungsfreiheit: Genehmigungserfordernis für Beteiligung an Niederlassungsfreiheit: Genehmigungserfordernis für Beteiligung an "strategischen Aktiengesellschaften" – Nachträgliche Kontrolle der Beschlussfassung: Anmerkung zu EuGH, Urt. v. 8. 11. 2012 – C-244/11 (Kommission/Griechenland)' [2013] EuZW 32.

Trachtman JP, *The International Economic Law Revolution and the Right to Regulate* (Cameron May 2007).

Trebilcock MJ, *Advanced Introduction to International Trade Law* (Elgar 2015).

—— Howse R, and Eliason A, *The Regulation of International Trade* (4th edn, Routledge 2013).

Tridimas T, 'Abuse of Rights in EU Law: Some Reflections with Particular Reference to Financial Law' in Rita de La Feria and Stefan Vogenauer (eds), *Prohibition of Abuse of Law: A New General Principle of EU Law?* (Hart 2011) 169.

Tsagourias N, 'Risk and the Use of Force' in Mónika Ambrus, Rosemary G Rayfuse, and Wouter Werner (eds), *Risk and the Regulation of Uncertainty in International Law* (Oxford University Press 2017) 13.

Tuthill L and Roy M, 'GATS Classification Issues for Information and Communication Technology Services' in Mira Burri and Thomas Cottier (eds), *Trade Governance in the Digital Age: World Trade Forum* (Cambridge University Press 2012) 157.

UNCTAD, 'National Security-Related Screening Mechanisms for Foreign Investment: An Analysis of Recent Policy Development' (Geneva, December 2019) Investment Policy Monitor 22 <https://investmentpolicy.unctad.org/publications/1213/investment-policy-monitor-special-

issue%2D%2D-national-security-related-screening-mechanisms-for-foreign-investment-an-analysis-of-recent-policy-developments> accessed 2 February 2022.

Unger S, 'Anmerkung zu EuGH, Urt. v. 11.9.2014, C-47/12 (Kronos International Inc./Finanzamt Leverkusen)' [2015] EuZW 67.

Van Aaken A, 'Opportunities for and Limits to an Economic Analysis of International Law' (2011) 3 Transnational Corporations Review 27.

Van der Putten F-P and others, 'Europe and China's New Silk Roads: A Report by the European Think-tank Network on China (ETNC)' (Copenhagen, 2016) <https://merics.org/de/studie/europe-and-chinas-new-silk-roads> accessed 2 February 2022.

Velten J, 'FDI Screening Regulation and the Recent EU Guidance: What Options Do Member States Have?' (10 August 2020a) Columbia FDI Perspective 284 <http://ccsi.columbia.edu/publications/columbia-fdi-perspectives/> accessed 2 February 2022.

—— 'The Investment Screening Regulation and its Screening Ground "Security or Public Order"' (August 2020b) CTEI Working Paper Series <https://repository.graduateinstitute.ch/record/298429> accessed 2 February 2022.

Vidigal G, 'WTO Adjudication and the Security Exception: Something Old, Something New, Something Borrowed - Something Blue?' (2019) 46 Legal Issues of Economic Integration 203.

Voland T, 'Freitag, der Dreizehnte – Die Neuregelungen des Außenwirtschaftsrechts zur verschärften Kontrolle ausländischer Investitionen' [2009] EuZW 519.

Voon T, 'Can International Trade Law Recover? The Security Exception in WTO Law: Entering a New Era' (2019) 113 American Journal of International Law 45.

Wegener B, 'Art 19 EUV' in Christian Calliess and Matthias Ruffert (eds), *EUV/AEUV: Das Verfassungsrecht der Europäischen Union mit Europäischer Grundrechtecharta* (5th edn, CH Beck 2016a).

—— 'Art 346 AEUV' in Christian Calliess and Matthias Ruffert (eds), *EUV/AEUV: Das Verfassungsrecht der Europäischen Union mit Europäischer Grundrechtecharta* (5th edn, CH Beck 2016b).

Weiss M, *Goldene Aktien im Lichte der Rechtsprechung des EuGH: Unter besonderer Berücksichtigung des harmonisierten Übernahmerechts* (Nomos 2008).

Weiß W, 'Kompetenzverteilung bei gemischten Abkommen am Beispiel des TTIP' [2016] DÖV 537.

—— 'Adjudicating Security Exceptions in WTO Law: Methodical and Procedural Preliminaries' (2020a) 54 Journal of World Trade 829.

—— 'Art 207 AEUV' in Eberhard Grabitz, Meinhard Hilf, and Martin Nettesheim (eds), *Das Recht der Europäischen Union: EUV/AEUV* (71st edn, CH Beck 2020b).

Weller M-P, 'Ausländische Staatsfonds zwischen Fusionskontrolle, Außenwirtschaftsrecht und Grundfreiheiten' [2008] ZIP 857.

Wigell M, 'Conceptualizing Regional Powers' Geoeconomic Strategies: Neo-imperialism, Neo-mercantilism, Hegemony, and Liberal Institutionalism' (2016) 14 Asia Europe Journal 135.

Williamson J (ed), *Latin American Adjustment: How Much Has Happened?* (1990a)

—— 'What Washington Means by Policy Reform' in John Williamson (ed), *Latin American Adjustment: How Much Has Happened?* (1990b) 5.

—— 'The Strange History of the Washington Consensus' (2004-2005) 27 Journal of Post Keynesian Economics 195.

Wilmowsky P von, '§ 12 Freiheit des Kapital- und Zahlungsverkehrs' in Dirk Ehlers and Ulrich Becker (eds), *Europäische Grundrechte und Grundfreiheiten* (4th edn, De Gruyter 2014) 470.

Wojcik K-P, 'Art 63 AEUV' in Hans von der Groeben, Jürgen Schwarze, and Armin Hatje (eds), *Europäisches Unionsrecht: Vertrag über die Europäische Union - Vertrag über die Arbeitsweise der Europäischen Union - Charta der Grundrechte der Europäischen Union* (7th edn, Nomos 2015a).

—— 'Art 64 AEUV' in Hans von der Groeben, Jürgen Schwarze, and Armin Hatje (eds), *Europäisches Unionsrecht: Vertrag über die Europäische Union - Vertrag über die*

Arbeitsweise der Europäischen Union - Charta der Grundrechte der Europäischen Union (7th edn, Nomos 2015b).

—— 'Art 65 AEUV' in Hans von der Groeben, Jürgen Schwarze, and Armin Hatje (eds), *Europäisches Unionsrecht: Vertrag über die Europäische Union - Vertrag über die Arbeitsweise der Europäischen Union - Charta der Grundrechte der Europäischen Union* (7th edn, Nomos 2015c).

Wolf S, 'The Regulation of Foreign Direct Investment under Selected WTO Agreements: Is there still a Case for a Multilateral Agreement on Investment?' in Christian Tietje (ed), *International Investment Protection and Arbitration: Theoretical and Practical Perspectives* (Berliner Wissenschafts-Verlag 2008) 71.

Wolff J, *Ausländische Staatsfonds und staatliche Sonderrechte: Zum Phänomen 'Sovereign Wealth Funds' und zur Vereinbarkeit der Beschränkung von Unternehmensbeteiligungen mit Europarecht* (Berliner Wissenschafts-Verlag 2009).

Wolfrum R, 'Art II' in Rüdiger Wolfrum, Peter-Tobias Stoll, and Clemens Feinäugle (eds), *WTO – Trade in Services* (Martinus Njihoff 2008a).

—— Stoll PT, and Feinäugle C (eds), *WTO – Trade in Services* (Martinus Njihoff 2008b)

World Bank Group (ed), *Global Investment Competitiveness Report 2017/2018: Foreign Investor Perspectives and Policy Implications* (World Bank Group 2017).

Wouters J, Nollkaemper A, and Wet E (eds), *The Europeanisation of International Law: The Status of International Law in the EU and its Member States* (TMC Asser 2008).

Wu M, 'The "China, Inc." Challenge to Global Trade Governance' (2016) 57 Harvard International Law Journal 261.

Wübbeke J and others, 'Made in China 2025: The Making of a High-tech Superpower and the Consequences for Industrial Countries' (December 2016) MERICS Papers on China 2 <https://merics.org/de/studie/made-china-2025-0> accessed 2 February 2022.

Yanovich A, 'WTO Rules and the Energy Sector' in Yulia Selivanova (ed), *Regulation of Energy in International Trade Law: WTO, NAFTA, and Energy Charter* (Kluwer Law International 2011) 1.

Zazoff J, *Der Unionsgesetzgeber als Adressat der Grundfreiheiten* (Nomos 2011).

Zdouc W, 'WTO Dispute Settlement Practice Relating to the General Agreement on Trade in Services' in Federico Ortino and Ernst-Ulrich Petersmann (eds), *The WTO Dispute Settlement System 1995-2003* (Kluwer Law International 2004) 382.

Zwartkruis W and Jong B de, 'The EU Regulation on Screening of Foreign Direct Investment: A Game Changer?' (2020) 31 European Business Law Review 447.

Printed by Printforce, the Netherlands